ESSAYS IN HONOUR OF

# AMA ATA AIDOO
## at 70

A Reader in African Cultural Studies

D1569496

This book is dedicated to the memory of
Mme Elizabeth Aba Abasema Bosu, late mother of Ama Ata Aidoo
and
Mme Grace Njeri Githae, late mother of Micere Githae Mugo,

who both joined their respective ancestresses and ancestors in 2011,
in the final months of the completion of this book.

# ESSAYS IN HONOUR OF

# AMA ATA AIDOO

# at 70

## A Reader in African Cultural Studies

## Edited by ANNE V. ADAMS

**ayebia**

An Adinkra symbol meaning
*Ntesie matemasie*
A symbol of knowledge and wisdom

Copyright © 2012 Ayebia Clarke Publishing Limited
Copyright © 2012 *Introduction* by Anne V. Adams

All rights reserved

*Essays In Honour of Ama Ata Aidoo At 70: A Reader in African Cultural Studies*
Edited by Anne V. Adams

This Edition First published in 2012 by Ayebia Clarke Publishing Ltd
Ayebia Clarke Publishing Limited
7 Syringa Walk
Banbury
Oxfordshire
OX16 1FR
UK
www.ayebia.co.uk

ISBN 978-0-9569307-0-5

Distributed outside Africa, Europe and the United Kingdom
And exclusively in the USA by
Lynne Rienner Publishers, Inc
1800 30th Street, Suite 314
Boulder, CO 80301
USA
www.rienner.com

Distributed in Africa, Europe and the UK by TURNAROUND Publisher Services at
www.turnaround-uk.com

Co-published and distributed in Ghana with the Centre for Intellectual Renewal
56 Ringway Estate, Osu, Accra, Ghana.
www.cir.com

All rights reserved. No part of this publication may be reproduced in whole or in part,
except for the quotation of brief passages in reviews, without prior written permission from
Ayebia Clarke Publishing Limited.

British Library Cataloguing-in-Publication Data
Cover design by Amanda Carroll at Millipedia, UK.
Cover artwork by Getty Images.
Front cover photo © Nana Kofi Acquah.
Back cover and inside photos © Gilda L. Sheppard.
Typeset by FiSH Books, Enfield, Middlesex, UK.
Printed and bound by CPI Group (UK) Ltd, Croydon, CR0 4YY

Available from www.ayebia.co.uk or email info@ayebia.co.uk
Distributed in Africa, Europe, UK by TURNAROUND at www.turnaround-uk.com

Distributed in Southern Africa by Book Promotions (PTY) Cape Town
A subsidiary of Jonathan Ball Publishers in South Africa.
For orders contact: orders@bookpro.co.za

The Publisher wishes to acknowledge the support of Arts Council SE Funding

# Contents

To the reader *and* the critic, an apology, to the historian, a confession. The idea to commemorate, with an anthology, the milestone in Ama Ata Aidoo's life, of the attainment of seventy vital years, was based on the "fact" that her year of birth was 1942, this being the date published in the majority of literary-biographical sources. And, so, the 70th Birthday project took on its own life, heading toward 2012. However, "from knowledge gained since" through a few other sources – Ama Ata herself being not the least among them – 1940 had to be conceded as the birth year. Now, in the words of the Old Man (*Anowa*): "So, please/Let not posterity judge it too bitterly" that misinformation from the 'written tradition' has wrought this conundrum. Rather, we can just rationalise it as the explication of "Several years ago, when I was a bit older than I am now …"

# Libation for Ama Ata Aidoo

## Atukwei Okai

**Still Life: 70 White Roses.
77 Royal Staffs. Anowa.
Libation For An Outdooring:
Ama Ata Aidoo**

I

Agoo… ! Agoo… !

O Gracious Creator,
Our Lord Almighty !
AtaaNaa Nyungmo,
AtaaNaa Nyungmo,
Twedeampong Nyame,
Asaase Yaa, Odomankoma !

O heroic Elders of Cape Coast,
        Where are you ?
Maame Abasema. Nana Yaw Fama.
Oburmankoma, Adapagyan. Osun.

O beleaguered Elders of Africa,
        Are you there ?
Toussaint L'Ouverture. Queen
Dede Akaibi. Marcus Garvey.
Nkrumah. Fanon. Lumumba.

I offer you our generational
        kolanuts of veneration.

Before you kneels today
The soul of the child your
       concerns conceived
In the benevolent loins of
       the exasperated ages,
On behalf of our dearest dreams.

## II

I do not mention the name of one
and leave out the name of another-
I name you one by one,
I call you by your hallowed
       individual names.

Even though it was you who said,
You cannot shave a man's head
       in his absence,
I address you and address all of you–
(All protocol diligently observed.)

## III

She is casting her net wide
       across rivers and valleys,
       across deserts and forests.
She is flinging the flywhisk
       of her forebears
Till the tip touches the toes
       of the dream that dares,
Venturing into the vineyard
       of valiant visionaries.

She is twirling above the sacred
       *twinity* synagogue
Of antennae-hair crowning her
       Abeadzi Kyiakor head
The banner of the bold; she shall
       not be banished from
The fold where truth calls out
       to be told.

## IV
**Eta okpleng naa eeshɛle blema bɛlɛ !**

She sits atop the tip of a barrel
      of a gun,
Smoking an anointed seer's pipe !

## V
She is flinging questioning
      feathers
Onto the unshielded foreheads
Of the warrior winds unleashed
      from the still-smouldering
      shrines of our painful past.

She is sprinkling cowries collected
      from the armpits of the
      centuries
Over the flames of ancient wisdom
Interrogating the sentinels
      of our future.

## VI
**Eta okpleng naa eeshɛle blema bɛlɛ !**

She sits atop the tip of a barrel
      of a gun,
Smoking an anointed seer's pipe.

## VII
Do not
interrupt her incantations –
She has not
concluded her ministrations –

SHE IS STILL
DEEP IN CREATIVE MEDITATION ...
SHE IS STILL
DEEP IN CREATIVE MEDITATION ...

**Twa, twa, twa, ... ni omanye aba !**

# Introduction

# "Someone Should Lend Me a Tongue"[1]

## Anne V. Adams

On 17th October 2003, four writers were honoured at Accra's National Theatre as "Ghana's Literary Living Legends." For a US analogy, this award is Ghana's equivalent of the Kennedy Centre Honours for those who have influenced American culture through the arts. Along with her compatriots Kofi Awoonor (poet/novelist), Ayi Kwei Armah (*in absentia;* novelist), and Kwesi Brew (poet) – Ama Ata Aidoo (poet, novelist, dramatist, children's author, and critic) was fittingly feted for her contribution to Ghanaian cultural life. In other years Living Legends from other fields of the arts have been similarly honoured. The essence of the opening proclamation made by the Board Chairman of the National Theatre was that the ceremony was "not showcasing the talents of individual personalities but about mapping out a historical path ..." In other words, Ama Ata Aidoo was being recognised as a sort of topographer of Ghana's dynamic, constantly changing, creative terrain, in constant cultivation. Indeed, the litany of her contributions bespoke the measure of her impact on Ghana's cultural landscape.

It's true: Virtually every Ghanaian over forty, or at least those who finished secondary school, will have been required to read one of her plays, as attested to in this volume by more than one contributor. During the Ghana @ 50 cele-brations, throughout the year 2007, Ama Ata Aidoo's plays were a part of the programme of cultural events. Through the orality of her plays, her "codifica-tion" of some forms of spoken English in Ghana has contributed to the recognition of Ghana's unique brand of the language due to the influences from the Ghanaian oral heritage. And, her vocal feminism, through the creative writ-ings, the essays, speeches, support of women's writing and personal example – have earned her the reputation as one of the continent's leading feminist advo-cates and first among feminist African literary artists. Moreover, particularly, her influence on social issues has been transformative. Indeed, her depiction in *Changes* (1991) of marital rape was a catalyst for the public and parliamentary debate that would later be vindicated by the passage, in 2007, of Ghana's Domestic Violence Act. As researchers Fallon and Aunio stated in their 2006 report on the progress of the campaign for the bill, Ama Ata Aidoo, in projecting how Esi's presentation of the phenomenon of marital rape would be received by the social scientific community, "had the foresight to predict this exact same cultural struggle over marital rape that is currently being played out in Ghana."[2]

Given her beginnings, Ama Ata Aidoo's social and literary radicalism can be accounted for largely through her upbringing. In retrospect, her becoming a writer, her creative advocacy of Ghanaian and African cultural integrity and her feminism, are all logical outcomes of the experiences and nurturing by the people who shaped her. For the present discussion, a useful definition of "radical" is borrowed from the paper here by Biodun Jeyifo: "[T]o be radical is to be predisposed to considerable departure from what is usual or traditional; it is to desire or work for extreme or drastic changes in existing views, habits, conditions and institution." While Aidoo acknowledges her relatively privileged background, characterised by the wealth of her familial and "national" heritage (as she conceives of "national" in spite of the colonised space of her youth), she admits, in the "A Conversation with Micere Githae Mugo," published here, that she took for granted those milestones which others seem to admire as accomplishments. Growing up as the daughter of a Chief who rationally advocated equal education for girls and boys, her stated aspiration, as a female high school student in 1950s colonial Gold Coast, to become a writer was met with support and encouragement. Her curiosity, as a child, about Cape Coast's slave castles; her exposure, growing up in the Independence era, in the environment of Kwame Nkrumah's practice of Pan Africanism and his encouragement of scholarship and development of the arts from indigenous forms, created a "consciousness unusual for an undergraduate," as Mugo notes in the "Conversation." This was an undergraduate who wrote the play *Dilemma of a Ghost*, followed soon by *Anowa*. Aidoo comments matter-of-factly that spending her youth in the Nkrumah era "prepared (her) to be a nationalist." It goes without saying, that, for Aidoo "nationalism" embraces Africa more than the geographic space called Ghana. For the author of *Our Sister Killjoy*, Sissie's same concept of Africa is now being articulated three decades later, by one of a new generation of writers, Nigerian novelist Chimamanda Ngozi Adichie: "A nation is not about the geography of land but the geography of the mind. It is an idea, or a collection of ideas."[3] Thus can we appreciate the optimistic logic of Aidoo's choice of Zimbabwe for what would become a 16-year self-chosen exile: "Any African country that tries to do something, I am for ... until I'm disappointed again," she told journalist Jane Bryce, cited in her article in this volume.

Equally "logical" in Aidoo's trajectory is her candid feminism. As she tells Mugo in the "Conversation," her Akan matrilineal origins, the particular strengths of her mother and other women in her family, made independence and self-realisation among women – within their social and economic parameters – something taken for granted. With what she cites as her fortunate environment, that fostered a sense of zero limitations, where "they let a girl grow up as she pleases until she is married," as Sissie says,[4] Aidoo's naturally developed self-assuredness causes her to take in stride "accomplishments" such as being a first-generation-African-woman university lecturer, Government Minister and published writer. Her example has inspired and paved the way for many who have chosen similar paths, such as Adichie and our contributor filmmaker Yaba Badoe, who is preparing a documentary film on Aidoo, also to coincide with the 70th Birthday.

## After a half-century of publishing...

In spite of this good news of a life where she hasn't felt limited in her opportunities, the bad news remains the marginalised critical treatment that Ama Ata Aidoo's work and that of other women among African writers have received over the nearly half-century of published writing, recent momentum notwithstanding. Moreover, the critical attention that is accorded her work too often simplistically relegates her wholly to the marginal category of "women writers," i.e. writers who write about female characters or "domestic" or "personal" subjects rather than about male characters or "national" or "political" subjects. Such a bifurcation ignores the symbiosis between the "domestic" and the "national" and mutes the voices of one-half of the "nation." Moreover, it fails to see that the personal is necessarily political. And especially with regard to Aidoo's work, what could be more "national" and "political" than *Anowa* or *Our Sister Killjoy*, or "For Whom Things Did Not Change"? Recall: after Aidoo realised that the "more important things to write about" are not mutually exclusive from a story "about lovers in Accra," *Changes* (1991) would, ironically, subsequently add lighter fluid to the charcoals fuelling the *political* debate in the *national* Parliament on an issue called *Domestic Violence*, which is aimed at protecting *women* from their abusive *lovers*.

Without doubt, the most frequent – and chauvinistic – injustice perpetrated against Ama Ata Aidoo by critics is the mis-information that Aidoo owes her short-story title "No Sweetness Here" to Ayi Kwei Armah, in whose 1968 novel *The Beautyful Ones Are Not Yet Born* the phrase appears. In fact, Aidoo had won, in 1962, the All Africa Short Story Competition, given by Mbari Club, University of Ibadan, for that story, which was then published in the journal *Black Orpheus* the following year. She discusses her constant battle to claim ownership of this piece of intellectual property that is the title most frequently associated with her in the essay "To Be an African Woman Writer – an Overview and a Detail."[5] For most readers of this book it is not necessary to rehearse the matter of "African Women Writers Getting Dissed Out of History," (1998:32) as Aidoo titles the Epilogue of her essay "Literature, Feminism and the African Woman

Today."[6] However, an acknowledgment by Nobel Laureate Wole Soyinka, reported here from a 2005 conversation with Ivor Agyeman-Duah, concedes the entrenched marginalisation of women, in publishing as well as in other public spheres of endeavour.

As a "nationalist writer," in her own words and in the words of critics such as C.L. Innes, Aidoo places a high value on critical attention from colleagues in the community of African literature. Therefore, the cold shoulder she felt from her compatriots upon the publication of *Our Sister Killjoy* takes on heightened effect in the following encounter that I witnessed and have recounted elsewhere in print. A conference in Berlin, 1988, sponsored by the Berlin Artists Programme of the German Academic Exchange Service, had as its theme "Germany Seen from the Outside." "Outside" writers in attendance from Africa and the Diaspora included Chinua Achebe, Buchi Emecheta, Maryse Condé, Ngũgĩ wa Thiong'o, Ama Ata Aidoo, Miriam Tlali and Jean-Marie Adiaffi, all of whom gave lectures in the public sessions. In a closed dialogue between members of the German Writers Association and the invited writers, one question asked by the hosts was: "Has Germany figured in any of your writings? If so, how was it depicted?" The general response from the African and Caribbean writers in the room was "No; France or Britain, perhaps, but not Germany." End of that discussion. Sitting on the sidelines as an invited observer, I was appalled that no one mentioned *Our Sister Killjoy*, which had been published over a decade earlier (and had been turned down for translation into German).[7] When, at the end of the session, I asked the (otherwise outspoken) Ama Ata about her silence, her modest (or, in hindsight, perhaps disgusted) reply was that, if none of her fellow African writers present, nor any of the German host writers, was familiar with the work or dared to insert it into the discussion, it was not her place to do so. She told critic Femi Ojo-Ade, in a 1996 interview:

> I do know that people, Europeans, well, thank God that I didn't write it for them, but anyway I know Europeans found these books quite objectionable and I am speaking from knowledge and what people think and I have tried to deal with the objections and I agree with them that if you're European you should find this book objectionable because people do not think it's a kind of novel they expect from an African and definitely not an African woman and now I see what they mean, you know. How dare you talk about Nazi Germany! Blah, blah, blah, you know. That aspect of it is quite interesting.... Now when it comes to Africans I think that, initially, your male Africans – academic or literature person – didn't read it because they assumed that any book by an African woman would be kitchen literature ...[8]

The eloquent irony is that, in that dialogue with the German writers group, *Our Sister Killjoy* was the only one that could have enabled a conversation on this, the very theme of the conference.

That was 1988; the *West Africa* article that "Dissed"[9] African women writers by omission was from 1995; the acknowledgment by Soyinka was from 2005: all isolated incidents, of course, but involving pundits of African literary production and criticism. This, in spite of the fact that Margaret Busby's groundbreaking anthology *Daughters of Africa*[10] was published in 1992, having been preceded by the work of male critics Lloyd Brown and Eldred Jones in the 1980s.[11] And, like the Ghanaian Busby, other African women have been busy doing the work of anthologising and publishing critical studies of African women's writing, such as Abena Busia, Carole Boyce Davies, Micere Githae Mugo, Chikwenye Ogunyemi, Esi Sutherland-Addy, all contributors to the present book; as well as Tuzyline Jita Allan, Irène d'Almeida, Mildred Hill-Lubin, Adeola James, Penina Mlama, Helen Mugambi, Obioma Nnaemeka, 'Molara Ogundipe, Wangui wa Goro, among many still unnamed here. At the same time as Busby's book appeared, the monumental project, *Women Writing Africa*, headed by general editors Abena Busia, Tuzyline Allan and Florence Howe, was in process, having begun in 1991. The *Women* who are *Writing Africa*, by their very title, are laying their claim to the fields of literature and orature in which African women have been toiling all along. The four volumes, *Women Writing Africa: Volume 1: The Southern Region*,[12] *Women Writing Africa: Volume 2: West Africa and the Sahel*,[13] *Women Writing Africa: The Eastern Region* (v. 3),[14] *Women Writing Africa: The Northern Region* (v. 4)[15] – represent not only the *collected* voices of African women of verbal arts but also the *collective* sense, on the part of the editors of the individual volumes and their 250 contributors, of the righteous imperative of their task.

In addition to those publications of unequalled importance, it can be acknowledged by now that, in survey studies or critical anthologies of African literature appearing in recent years, where numerous writers are discussed,[16] Aidoo enjoys an increasing overall frequency and range of critical rubrics. Of crucial importance in the recognition of Aidoo's total oeuvre as the subject of critical study are the two books to date devoted to her work. Vincent Odamtten's full-length study *The Art of Ama Ata Aidoo: Polylectics and Reading Against Neocolonialism*[17] (1994), has received deserved praise for its nuanced integrated analysis of the corpus. Since his book was completed before the poetry volume *An Angry Letter in January* and short-story volume *The Girl Who Can & Other Stories* were published, Odamtten completed the job through an essay on those later works, in a second book devoted to Aidoo's work, the 1999 anthology *Emerging Perspectives on Ama Ata Aidoo*,[18] edited by Ada Uzoamaka Azodo and the late Gay Wilentz. (It would seem, though, that with more than a quarter-century, since 1972, of some degree of critical attention, the studies of Aidoo's work had evolved beyond the "emerging" stage.)

James Gibbs' meticulous Bibliography in this volume is an invaluable resource on Aidoo studies.

It is to be hoped that these publications, as well as other projects and events, such as academic colloquia honouring Aidoo, at Brown University (2010), and planned at the University of California at Santa Barbara (2012) and, equally importantly, in public spheres such as at the Schomburg Library as part of the Harlem Book Fair (2009) and, of course, the Ghana Literary Living Legends ceremony – can be seen to mark a turning-of-the-corner in academic and public appreciation of Aidoo's work and thereby extend the larger field of criticism on African women literary artists. This volume benefits from the enthusiastic participation from many of the most respected scholars who have published on Aidoo. And, at seventy, as forward-looking and energetic as ever, Ama Ata continues to produce, with her poetry gracing a just-published book, *Ghana: Where the Bead Speaks*, co-authored with Esi Sutherland-Addy and Kati Torda Dagadu, as well as a new collection of short stories, *Diplomatic Pounds & Other Stories* in-press with Ayebia Clarke Publishing Limited for 2012.

## The Present Volume: Festschrift cum Criticism

Interpreting the Literary Living Legends citation as the charge for a "cultural topographer," the present volume approaches the inventory of Ama Ata Aidoo's work from a cultural studies approach to literature. Useful for this purpose is the definition offered by H.K. Wright:[19] "Cultural studies ... is not merely a body of knowledge nor simply an inter/anti/post/disciplinary approach to the study of culture: *it is also, and more importantly, an intervention in institutional, sociopolitical and cultural arrangements, events and directions.*" (806 emphasis added). With Aidoo, the "institutional" intervention has been effected on several levels. As mentioned, her works have figured in the Ghana Ministry of Education's high school syllabus. Further, her women's writing project *Mbaasem* has developed into an institution that puts into practice her advocacy of nurturing women writers.

Recognising that the creative careers of most African writers are comple-mented by other roles that have contributed equally to their stature as writers, Wright cites some in the "pantheon:"

> African multi-role utilitarianism is the term I use to indicate that most African writers have eschewed singular identities and roles and have instead routinely taken on multiple and simultaneous roles (e.g. Nigeria's Wole Soyinka as poet, dramatist, literary critic and political activist; Ghana's Ama Ata Aidoo as dramatist, literary critic and politician and Kenya's Ngũgĩ wa Thiong'o as novelist, community activist, theatre developer, literary critic ...) (811).

The notion that they have consciously "eschewed" a singular identity as a writer is contestable. The activities of those three individuals have been the result of ideological commitment for which those various arenas are opportunities for more direct impact. In addition to those activities, we know that all of these writers, as well as numerous others, have held posts as university professors.

Although Wright has the continental African context in mind, his scope of the textual inventory in a cultural studies approach to literature is equally relevant for the present festschrift, in that it also reflects the contexts that produced the writers in question: A "cultural studies approach to literature studies in Africa...[recognises] the need to acknowledge and incorporate traditional African orature, new media and popular culture texts ..." (810)

Which brings us to the content of this volume. The presence here of scholarly papers on African orature (e.g. on proverbs, on Aidoo's children's stories and Ghanaian language influence in Aidoo's work); on new media (e.g. on "Nollywood", "Ghallywood" and TV's *Big Brother Africa*); on popular culture texts (e.g. on gender representation and contemporary urban forms in popular music) – their inclusion complements the literary-criticism core of the book. Our inventory extends the range of cultural-studies topics further, to questions of African national identity, race construction and gendered image, to relevant historical topics, e.g. on enslaved women in Ghana. For, the extra-literary theoretical and analytical insights from those discussions enhance our understanding of Aidoo's texts and contexts. For example, a discussion of Aidoo's re-telling of an internationally adapted story which originated with Ghana's revered educator from the early 20th century, Dr. Kwegyir Aggrey, demonstrates the connections between literature produced for African children and traditional wisdom valued by adults, as well as the universality of some African tales. As is revealed in the "Conversation" with Mugo, Aidoo's own life was crucially influenced by Dr. Aggrey, whose philosophy about educating girls persuaded Ama Ata's father to educate her. Or, the first-hand experience of the impact on Nigerian theatre from the video entertainment phenomenon helps us understand the declining audiences at Ghana's National Theatre for performances of Aidoo's plays and others. The studies on popular music and popular TV inform our reading of some of Aidoo's urban-setting short stories and even more directly, of stories in the 2006 collection by other women, which she edited, *African Love Stories*.[20] Two historical case studies of enslaved women inform our reading of *Anowa*, and indirectly, of *Changes*. And, beyond these full-length papers, other forms of cultural-studies contributions are contained in the "Tributes" from several associates, of whom two, for example, bear witness to Aidoo's community writers project for women, *Mbaasem*. As stated above, the cultural-studies articles complement the literary-criticism core. Of these the theoretical articles include discussions from postcolonial, feminist and Pan African perspectives. Specific studies of Aidoo's works range from detailed thematic or structural readings of individual texts to an analysis, using the whole oeuvre of Aidoo's practice of theorising through creative writing.

Hence, this somewhat eclectic collection draws on different sources for the essays. While the majority of the full-length essays were prepared and submitted specifically for this festschrift, a few are transcriptions of keynote or other invited lectures, some, even from a few years past, whose relevance to the vision for this collection makes them welcome inclusions. But, as this book is a form of word-celebration, it begins, appropriately, with the ritual Libation from the oral tradition, in the exquisite poetry of fellow writer Atukwei Okai, to invoke the blessings of the Creator and the Pan African Ancestors for the "celebration." Another form of greeting follows in the eloquent "Open Letter" from Margaret Busby, editor of *Daughters of Africa*, which appears here as a Foreword. Busby's letter reviews, through their personal relationship, not only Ama Ata's trajectory but also the difficult path of publishing for African writers, including the mentoring circle in which Ama Ata connected Becky Ayebia Clarke, starting her publishing company, to established publisher Margaret (of Allison & Busby), with the result that Ayebia Clarke would come to publish this present volume. How fitting it is, then, that Margaret and Nana Ayebia have both been recognised with the Order of the British Empire (OBE) and an Honorary Member of the British Empire (MBE) awards respectively by Her Majesty Queen Elizabeth II of England for their contributions in publishing.

"A Conversation" with poet/playwright/activist Micere Githae Mugo is an interview that presents insights unrecorded in other literary interviews with Aidoo. The resultant eclectic collection that constitutes this volume, in subject matter, academic discipline and in formal presentation, seems a fitting acknowledgment of Ama Ata Aidoo's innovations with subject matter, generic structure and style. Accordingly, working from the cultural studies approach to literature, the grouping of the papers into three major sections integrates the social sciences with literary analyses and literary theory. The heading for each section is an epigraph from Aidoo's work, effecting Ama Ata's presence in the "deliberations" – the *Bird by the Wayside*. In view of the diversity of the articles, all of the sections except the Tributes are preceded by their own introductions, in order to maximise the connections among the articles. Therefore, this general Introduction gives only an outline of the contents of each section.

## Section I – "That is the story I am telling you. I am taking you to bird town, so I can't understand why you insist on searching for eggs from the suburb!"

This epigraph, from the story "Something to Talk About on the Way to a Funeral," in *No Sweetness Here*, already "performs" the essence of the section's content. Two women friends are reviewing the history of a female pillar of their community. Through Aidoo's insertion of a conversation device adapted from Ghanaian language sources, the speaker expresses friendly exasperation at her listener's frequent interruptions with questions that will be answered in due course. The two pieces in this section consist of the reprint of the "grandma" of critical publications on African women writers, an article published fifty years ago by the Guadeloupean novelist and critic Maryse Condé and the "Conversation" with Micere Mugo. The two pieces "bracket" the history of literary criticism on African women thus far.

## Section II – "Because surely in our environment there are more important things to write about?"

This epigraph appears in Aidoo's "exercise in words-eating," at the beginning of *Changes*, reclaiming the legitimacy of writing a love story. The eight papers in this section are devoted to "important things" in the area of literary and cultural theory, including full discussions of specific Aidoo works. Some of the papers are transcriptions of invited lectures, some, keynote lectures – theoretical reflections from various humanistic disciplinary points of departure, including critiques of the disciplinary underpinnings of postcolonial literary studies and of historiography. In this section Aidoo's works are, rather, complementary, introduced in discussions e.g. from Historiography and Philosophy, in support of theoretical arguments. The second includes two full-length studies of Aidoo's texts.

## Section III – "Every woman and every man should be a feminist – especially if they believe that Africans should take charge of our land, its wealth, our lives, and the burden of our own development"

Aidoo's widely known feminist declaration from her essay mentioned above,[21] serves as the over-arching idea for the seven specifically gender-focused articles. Four discuss individual Aidoo texts, while three papers from other cultural studies perspectives on gender topics complement the literary papers. Those concern a theoretical consideration of (self) image construction among Black women; a study of gender attitudes in popular music and a historical study of self-determination among formerly enslaved women.

## Section IV – "[A] mixture of complete sweetness and smoky roughage. ...Oh, Africa. Crazy old continent ..."

This reflection, from *Our Sister Killjoy*, occupies Sissie's thoughts in the final section, "A Love Letter," as she is about to land back at home from her trip to Germany and to "her colonial home," the UK. It is a sentimental, poetic expression of Aidoo's nationalism, with its humour and pragmatic optimism. And, although the "love letter" is written to her former lover, who is not returning to Ghana, the fault line in their relationship is the fault line between their diverging views on the future of Africa. (In fact, this final section of the novel/prose-poem begins with a kind of prefatory vignette in which an African professor exasperatedly informs a Diaspora student of the long and epic history of Africa.) Thus, the twelve articles in this section present a panorama of topics that characterise this volume in honour of Ama Ata Aidoo as a "Reader for African Cultural Studies." Historically, the articles range from a narrative of a 19th century slave girl to the most contemporary TV and video activity; topically, they include papers on language, music and proverbs. And the eight articles are devoted specifically to Aidoo's work and address her drama, poetry, children's stories and short stories.

## Section V – "So as for this woman e be She-King"

At the end of the short story "She-Who-Would-Be-King," in the year 2026, when the Confederation of African States has elected a woman as president, a proper title for such a leader must be created in the people's language: "contri chief be President, all Africa chief no be President: e be King. So as for this woman, e be She-King." As this book is a celebration, it closes, as it opened, with expressions of tribute – Praise Songs in a variety of forms. They begin with a poem by Abena Busia, who constructs an eloquent praise-poem from the titles of Aidoo's works. The writer/filmmaker Yaba Badoe discusses the significance of the novel *Changes* for her generation of young African women. Ivor Agyeman-Duah's extended "visit" with Ama Ata Aidoo provides, among other subjects, one of the two testimonies to the work of the *Mbaasem* Centre. His is followed by Helen Yitah's narrative of one project that made a national contribution to literary development, for two years, through its weekly page in the largest circulated Ghanaian newspaper. Then comes a fond reminiscence by a fellow exile from Ghana during Aidoo's time in Zimbabwe and to whom Ama Ata dedicated one of her poems from that period. Chikwenye Ogunyemi's tribute combines the poetic with the political in its own form and in its characterisation of Aidoo, whom critic Ogunyemi has hosted and visited, taught and written about. The "Tributes" close with a praise song from fellow writer Ngũgĩ wa Thiong'o, whose friendship, as she speaks about it in the "Conversation," dates back to their 1960s meeting in Kenya. The "Tributes," presented on the occasion of her 70th birthday, are, collectively, the personal complement to the public celebration of the Literary Living Legends at the National Theatre on 17th October 2003.

On 14th May 2011 Ama Ata Ejinma Aidoo stood, bent over the casket, conversing in Fanti for a quarter of an hour with her mother, before the procession, in the rainy season's mighty send-off, departed to the cemetery in Abeadzi Kyiakor. One supposes that, among other things, the daughter was reassuring the mother that the stories would continue to be told.

# Foreword
# An Open Letter to Ama Ata Aidoo
## Margaret Busby

My Dear Sister Ama Ata,
Right to the brink of deadline, I have been thinking long and hard about what to say; it is not easy because so much is intangible, emotional. I am not an academic and will not here be attempting to examine or critique your works; there are others who are able to do that expertly.

In the end I simply want to say a few words from my heart to let you know something I have not said before, perhaps because I did not truly realise its import: that in a curious way you are responsible for my coming into being as a literary person.

The literary life for African women is not easy. Is there still need to say that to anyone reading this now? But how much harder things were in 1965, when you published your first play, *The Dilemma of a Ghost*. That was also the year my publishing company, Allison & Busby, was conceived, the year I graduated from London University, hardly out of my teens. So that was the fateful year the course of my working life was set.

The fact that you were already there and Auntie Efua Sutherland before you – strong women of my native land – buoyed me up, gave me the permission I did not even acknowledge needing to have the courage to follow my literary dreams.

The year I published my first titles at A&B in 1967, your story "The Message" appeared in Ezekiel Mphahlele's *African Writing Today*, one of the first anthologies devoted to literature in English from Africa – and how few women from the mother continent and her Diaspora were represented in any such collections at that time (or even in the next quarter-century leading up to 1992 when I was able to indulge myself by including over 200 in my anthology, *Daughters of Africa: An International Anthology of Words and Writings by Women of African Descent from the Ancient Egyptian to the Present*).

I can't remember when or where we first actually met in person, rather than on the page. However, I do remember chairing a conversation with you at the Institute of Contemporary Arts (ICA) in London, when your play *Anowa* was being performed at the Gate Theatre in Notting Hill. It was 1991, the same year you and Jayne Cortez announced the founding of the Organisation of Women Writers of Africa (OWWA) – "Formed for the purpose of establishing links between professional African women writers of different countries, OWWA's goals are to: Implement programmes and institute a newsletter for the exchange of ideas, experiences and in formation of common concern. Familiarize ourselves with each others' work, cultures, living conditions and viewpoints. Promote and foster greater popular interest in the literature and achievements of African women. Address the issues of translation, publishing, distribution, exclusion, inequality, cultural domination, censorship, new technology, democratisation and human progress. We invite you to join OWWA and add your voice toward improving communications and promoting the understanding and development of the literature of African women writers around the world." I was behind you all the way and the *Yari Yari Pamberi* International Literary Conferences were a wonderful chance for sister scribes to connect, first in 1997, then again in 2004 in New York and before too long, we hope, in Ghana.

Over the years, I applauded your talent for cross-cultural communication as well as for showcasing women's capabilities. I agreed when you uttered simple words of wisdom such as: "only an African knows what it is to be an African and only a woman knows what it is to be a woman and can give expression to the essence of being a woman," or explained what should have been obvious to everyone: "I write about people, about what strikes me and interests me. It seems the most natural thing in the world for women to write with women as central characters; making women the centre of my universe was spontaneous." I watched the publication of your books and marvelled that you could equally well create drama and fiction and poetry: *Anowa* and *No Sweetness Here* in 1970 (as Jacqueline Bardolph has said, your short fiction is still among the best produced in Africa), *Our Sister Killjoy or Reflections from a Black-Eyed Squint* in 1977, *Someone Talking to Sometime* in 1986, *Changes* in 1991 and *An Angry Letter in January* in 1992 – and what pride when *Changes* won the Commonwealth Writers' Prize! – *The Girl Who Can and Other Stories* in 1997. You shone the light for the African woman who was defiant against the odds and always showed solidarity with your sisters.

It was your story "Two Sisters" that I was proud to include in my anthology *Daughters of Africa*, unbelievably published twenty years ago now and your support was unconditional. In Cape Coast in December 1994, you warmly inscribed my personal copy: "Margaret, *Mbo, mbo na yɛ...*"

In recent years our too-few meetings stand out: having cake and white wine in your home ten years ago when you enthused to me about Mbaasem, your non-profit foundation to support African women writers and their work, committed especially to creating a congenial environment for women literary workers. (As you so aptly say: "Writing by its very nature is an individual activity that requires clearly defined time and space to pursue. African writers more than others and African women writers most of all, are dogged all their lives, by the problem of inadequate space and time to write. This is due to the peculiar environment in which we operate. There are no supporting structures for African writers outside their own resources and very few of us can say with any honesty, that we are the sole beneficiaries of even the meagre resources at our command. The reality is almost terrifying....) You invited me to a meal at the Shangri-La restaurant in Accra, where I remember your delight when I presented you with a copy of *Daughters of Africa* for the Mbaasem library – that would have been December 2001. Those hours we spent together were precious. A small regret is that all but one of the photographs we took then ("Hilarious!" you called them) were lost to me in some computer changeover.

In our email exchange later you wrote: "By the way, would you know Becky Clarke of Heinemann? She is a very bright, sensitive, young Ghanaian woman. (At least, a whole lot younger than yours truly!!!) I think that she could do with an informed and sensitive ear re: the stresses of her job. Somehow, I think you may understand her more completely than anyone in the world."

As it happens, Nana Ayebia, a.k.a. Becky, was already on my radar, but it was typical of your generosity that you suggested I counsel our fellow country-woman. When in 2003 she set up Ayebia Clarke Publishing Limited, it came naturally to me to try to help her succeed – passing on any tips I could muster about what to avoid in this minefield of a profession and sharing my experiences of decades in the trade, contributing whatever expertise she sought from me. This very volume with which we now honour you is testament to how far she has come.

In a similar way, it makes me proud to see the determination of our younger sister Bibi Bakare-Yusuf, who in 2005 established Cassava Republic in Nigeria. I am happy to hold her hand as she negotiates the unexpected hazards on the obstacle course of publishing and she knows that she can always count on me for moral and practical support whenever the pressures threaten to grind down the spirit of enterprise. Before us all there was the example of our dear departed Efua Sutherland as a pioneering African publisher and creative force.

I trust you believe that even across the too-many silences, when it may seem that I have been neglecting to communicate directly with you, you have been in my thoughts and I have sent you telepathically strength and support to keep on keeping on. From a remote distance I often followed your travels around the world – South Africa, Zimbabwe, Finland, Sweden and the USA. Sometimes when you passed through London you would phone to say "hello." The snatches of poetry with which you ended your emails kept me going, especially when the going was tough:

*Some days are longer*
*Than the neck of a giraffe.*
*Other days are shorter*
*Than the finger of a hand.*

*Some days are hard*
*Like stones in a stream.*
*Other days are soft,*
*Like a very pleasant dream.*

You were rightfully honoured in October 2003 at the National Theatre of Ghana as a "Living Legend," though you have truly not yet received all the rewards you deserve, your full due; but it must come. It will come. In the meantime we garland you here with a few birthday accolades.

*"There are days that are boastful*
*like champions before a fight;*
*but some days are very shy,*
*like our first morning at school.*

*There are strange days and busy,*
*very sour and hard to bite.*
*Yet, some days are easy,*
*full of sugar, fruit and spice."*

Here we are, in another century, a new phase of life, still with challenges still ahead. You have been an exemplar in so many ways – fiction writer, poet, playwright, lecturer, critic, consultant, politician, educator, professor, anthologist and cultural activist.

We are grateful for the lessons you have taught us and for your unfathomable contribution, to our enjoyment, to our knowledge, to our sense of self. You are a brave champion of women's words. Thank you for your writing, thank you for telling our stories, thank you for being you. You have done well; Sisi, *mbo, mbo na yɛ!*

With endless affection and respect,
Margaret
a.k.a. Nana Akua Ackon

# Section I.

## "That is the story I am telling you. I am taking you to bird town, so I can't understand why you insist on searching for eggs from the suburb!"[1]

Paying homage to the elders of literary criticism on African women, the book first acknowledges the earliest beginnings of such work, with a reprint of Maryse Condé's 1972 article, in *Présence Africaine*, "Three Female Writers in Modern Africa: Flora Nwapa, Ama Ata Aidoo and Grace Ogot." In asserting the phenomenon of a female African literary voice, Condé's assessments of writing activity by African women and of the texts of her three subject writers provide an engaging perspective – from 50 years ago – on topics that have received much treatment subsequently. Basing her evaluation of Aidoo at that time on only the two plays, Condé acknowledges, "Ama Ata Aidoo is a born writer," and observes, with respect to *Anowa*, that "she believes that a woman can and must act not only as an assistant but a guide for the man whose life she is going to share." Interesting is also Condé's opinion that *The Dilemma of a Ghost* "leaves us with the impression of a mere exercise in futility." The critic's dismissal of this play rests largely upon her critique of the figure of Eulalie, the Diasporan wife "confronted with 'Mother Africa'," an experience Condé herself had lived at roughly the same period, the mid-1960s, in Ghana, when the play was performed and published. In any case, Condé's conclusions, evincing reservations about Aidoo's (and the others') ability to assert a female literary presence for social and cultural change could still fuel productive critical debate today. While, admittedly, the presence here of Condé's article is largely symbolic, several papers might provide *respectful* back-talk to Condé, now with the perspective of fifty years. For example, Cheryl Toman discusses the feminist work of Senegalese Awa Thiam, to which Condé alludes in the context of lamenting the absence of creative writing by Francophone women (pre-Mariama Bâ, obviously). Also, Sue Houchins's treatment of *Anowa* here offers responses to Condé's reservations about the character's viability; and Kofi Anyidoho places Aidoo in the creative company of earlier, male, Ghanaian writers. Thus, Condé's initiative, re-printed here, finds worthy scholars talking back to her.

The second piece in this section is "A Conversation: Ama Ata Aidoo with Micere Mugo." Even though it has the form of an interview, this conversation is truly a *dialogue* between two sisters/age-mates/comrades/colleagues/fellow-writers/fellow-insurgents/fellow-mothers. Indeed, Ama Ata declares, in her first statement, that there is no one else she would rather do an interview with for such a publication than Micere. Hence, the quality of the interview reflects the quality of the relationship between them.

Micere Mugo is particularly well suited to this task, because the acquaintance has intellectual/professional as well as social underpinnings. Each has expressed her respect for the other in print. Aidoo, for example, in her widely read essay "To Be an African Woman Writer" describes Mugo the critic as "formidably uncompromising, both in terms of the aesthetic criteria and the political relevance against which she judges the achievement of the few African women writers whose works she has analysed" (159). Mugo, whose critical work has recently been collected in a volume, *Writing and Speaking from the Heart of My Mind*,[2] has similarly strong words to describe Aidoo as a critic and spokesperson for African women writers, citing her "characteristic articulateness" in exposing male chauvinism among critics, and "punctuating her extended argument with classic illustrations."

As the "Conversation" reveals, the acquaintance between Mugo and Aidoo dates back to the late 1960s in Kenya. But it would be in Zimbabwe, in the 1970s, with both as exiles with their daughters and as established writers and educators that the friendship would develop. Their engagement in educational development projects and in the encouragement of women's writing – the Ghanaian Aidoo, becoming the first president of the Zimbabwe Women Writers Organisation (!), and Mugo giving the keynote address "Women and Books"[3] at the 1985 Zimbabwe International Book Fair – and especially their mutual support as mothers – all combined as crucial sources and conduits for their shared ideological convictions.

In the course of the "Conversation," Aidoo comments on numerous topics that resonate in articles in the volume. Points from her upbringing in a matrilineal family appear in the paper of historian Akosua Perbi, who touches upon inheritance issues in matrilineal societies. The upbringing of girl-children is the subject of Naana Banyiwa Horne's paper on two of Aidoo's short stories and the special devastation over the death of an only daughter comes up in Sue Houchins's paper on *Anowa*. Other biographical references to *Anowa* from the "Conversation" include the possible origin of the Anowa figure from a story told by her mother. These issues are of interest in the papers by James Gibbs,

Omofolabo Ajayi-Soyinka, as well as Houchins. The "Conversation" also covers Aidoo's centre for women writers, Mbaasem, for which two of the "Tributes" provide testimony. Ivor Agyeman-Duah writes about the history, the support, the scope of the Centre; Helen Yitah reports on the Centre's project of a monthly writer's page in *The Ghanaian Daily Graphic*. And, at the very end of the "Conversation," Aidoo laments the total neglect of the oral tradition in the education system, expressing mild regret over her inability to effect such innovation during her time as Minister of Education – a subject discussed in Esi Sutherland-Addy's paper on orality in Aidoo's writings, in Section IV.

# Three Female Writers in Modern Africa: Flora Nwapa, Ama Ata Aidoo and Grace Ogot[1]

## Maryse Condé

From the very start, a question may be asked: why write about female African writers at all? Does this mean that one assumes that a female writer has, as a female, a particular message to deliver? That her universe and preoccupations differ from those of a male writer? Does it mean, in short, that one accepts the widely-spread belief that a woman is an altogether different being from a man whose place and part to play in the world have been defined by her very nature? Far from it! I simply believe that the personality and the inner reality of African women have been hidden under such a heap of myths, so-called ethological theories, rapid generalisations and patent untruths that it might be interesting to study what they have to say for themselves when they decide to speak. But the first evidence one has to face is that there are very few female African writers. Among those who have reached recognition outside Africa, Nigeria boasts of Flora Nwapa, Ghana of Efua Sutherland and Ama Ata Aidoo, Kenya of Grace Ogot while in Francophone Africa if there exists a number of researchers and writers of sociological studies, one is at a loss to find any lasting names in the literary field. What are the explanations for this dearth of talent? The educated woman is becoming such a common feature in Africa (university lecturers, doctors, members of Parliament, a function which does not necessarily accompany education though, and civil servants of all ranks) that it seems very superficial to attribute this female silence to the educational gap between girls and boys. When so many women can stand up and shout slogans for emancipation or deliver political addresses for the benefit of the ruling parties, what prevents them from taking a pen and writing about themselves? Should it then be attributed to a truly feminine "pudeur?" As if African women loathe disclosing their inner selves to the public? "Pudeur" does not seem a feature of the new generation that everybody complains, is characterised by such a greed for Western materialism that it will go to any lengths to get it. Isn't it rather the very complexity of her condition that forces the African woman to remain silent since she feels unable to come to terms with it?

African women stand at the very heart of the turmoil of their continent. Going back to colonialism, one is tempted to say that they were the first principal victims of the encounter with the West. The missionaries did not understand the position they held in their families and societies. They quickly labelled them "beasts of burden" and decided to liberate them through education. The education they provided them with, however, was just a fifth-rate imitation of what they were offering their own destitute girls in workhouses and "ouvroirs." They taught them how to sew, mend clothes, bake a few cakes and prepare European dishes. In exchange for such liberalities, their charges cultivated their land and grew their food. Mongo Beti, in Le Pauvre Christ de Bomba, gave an immortal description of what could happen in the sixties in the Cameroons. Everything relating to the status and condition of women in Africa, through lack of understanding and sympathy, was misrepresented. Polygamy became the shameful sign of African licentiousness and the bride price was a sign of callousness. Such misrepresentations could simply have been dismissed if a large number of African women had not fallen victim to them and come to regard their traditional past as an awful story "full of sound and fury."

What are we now to find in the work of the leading female writers? An echo of these misconceptions or a protest and a rebellion against them? A cold contempt for those Western judgments and a cool description of woman's experience? Or a disconcerting mixture of misconceptions, true descriptions and modernistic attitudes?

In 1966, Flora Nwapa wrote Efuru, the first novel to be published by a woman writer in Nigeria, followed shortly afterwards by Idu and more recently by a collection of short stories. The first novel is set in rural Iboland. Efuru is a beautiful, wealthy and respected woman who, however, cannot bear children successfully or be happy in marriage. Her only child dies in infancy while her first husband deserts her and she feels forced to leave her second one. The reason for this unhappiness is that she has been chosen by a river goddess to be her companion and, as far as earthly companions are concerned, she must remain alone. We are not going to compare the treatment Miss Nwapa gives to this story with the one Elechi Amadi gives to a similar theme in The Concubine. This is not our purpose. We are concerned with the picture that Flora Nwapa offers of a female character and her vision of the world. Speaking of the river goddess, Umahiri, Flora Nwapa writes at the end of her novel:

> She was as old as the lake itself. She was happy, she was wealthy,
> she was beautiful. She gave women beauty and wealth, but she
> had no child. She had never experienced the joy of motherhood.
> Why then did the women worship her?

These closing lines seem to give the clue to the whole book. No happiness can be achieved for a woman unless in childbearing. Throughout the story, this conviction is repeated over and over again. "We are not going to eat happy marriages. Marriage must be fruitful," say the village-women, watching Efuru and Eneberi swimming in a lake. "Of what use is it if your husband licks your body, worships you and buys everything in the market for you and you are not productive?"

Or later:

You don't pluck children from a tree, you know. You don't fight for them either. Money cannot buy them. Happiness cannot give you children.

From such lines, however, it should be wrong to conclude that Flora Nwapa herself simply adopts the belief that the African woman is merely there for breeding children. Efuru is portrayed as a very independent character. Unconcerned with her parents' opinions, she chooses her own husband, a young man who has not even enough money for her dowry and runs away to live with him. "Efuru and I have agreed to be husband and wife and that is all that matters." Having married the man of her choice, Efuru does not stop there and is no picture of meek obedience. She refuses to go to the farm and, instead, decides to trade. In contrast with her, Adizua, her husband, is almost a failure. He is so unsuccessful at farming that he joins his wife in trading but, once again, he is no good and Efuru is the brain behind the business. In every detail of her life, Efuru shows surprising determination and independence of character. She does not think twice about being seen everywhere with her husband: thus refusing the traditional pattern whereby the husband walks in front while the wife walks behind. In order to go trading, she decides to employ a maid to look after her baby daughter who is only eight months old. On all these occasions, Flora Nwapa is very careful to tell us the reaction of the other women of the village:

You want a maid to look after your only child? I advise you not to. You will regret it. What is money? Can a bag of money look after you in your old age? Can a bag of money mourn you when you are dead? A child is more valuable than money. So our fathers said.

With Eneberi, her second husband, Efuru acts as an adviser. When he contemplates building a house of his own, she refuses, explaining that a canoe would be better at that stage. Later, she is so broadminded that she accepts Eneberi's child from another woman under her roof and does not even blame him when she discovers that he has spent a few months in jail. It is not only in her marital relationship that Efuru shows surprising independence. She so believes in science and technique that she takes Nwosu, her maid's father, to a doctor friend to have an operation on his male organ. Here again, Flora Nwapa carefully describes Nwabata, Nwosu's traditional wife, all in tears, refusing to allow her husband to go to hospital where he will most certainly be poisoned by white witchcraft.

The complexity of Efuru lies in the fact that, although she shows such determination, she still remains strongly attached to tradition. She never questions polygamy ("only a bad woman would like to be married alone by her husband") and goes out of her way to find a second and a third wife for Eneberi. But is it really logical that she should be more upset by her husband's absence at her father's funeral (i.e. an offence against tradition) than by the discovery of the reason for his absence (his imprisonment on a charge of theft)? If she is so level-headed about taking a man to have an operation on his male organ, should she really be upset at having bad dreams that she runs to her father who in turn takes her to see a *dibia*? This contradiction can only be accepted as representative of the dichotomy in Efuru's (and Flora Nwapa's) mind. As far as the physical world is concerned, she can accept Western techniques and progress but, as for the spiritual one, she does not get rid of her traditional habits and beliefs. Flora Nwapa makes it very clear, however, that she does not fully accept these powers of the *dibias*, since one of them is obviously mistaken in pronouncing Efuru guilty of adultery that brings about the catastrophe and destroys her life. But the biggest contradiction is that Efuru, for all her qualities and gifts, considers her life as valueless since she fails to have a child. She can deliberately and willfully decide to leave her husband and therefore live by herself, but she cannot follow the logical consequences. She cannot find in herself enough resources to counterbalance her sterility and never thinks of devoting her energies to something else. To ask her to do so would be asking too much. If a woman rejects the view that the *"birth of a child is a crowning glory"*[2] is she still an African? Flora Nwapa categorically refuses the clichés of the weak and obedient female slave, a mere appendix to her husband's life, but she cannot go to the end of her analysis. The main objection, however, is that by making her heroine unique among her fellow-villagers and by reporting the unanimously hostile and adverse comments of the other women on every one of Efuru's decisions and actions, Flora Nwapa gives, in fact, a disturbing picture of narrow-mindedness, superstition, malevolence, greed and fear in traditional Africa and might go contrary to what she has thought to defend. In depicting her minor characters, she conveys a very poor impression of her society. Her men are weak, dissolute and irrational. Her women are a formidable gallery of malicious gossipers.

Ama Ata Aidoo's *The Dilemma of a Ghost* won a prize when it was first presented by the Students' Theatre at the Open Air Theatre, University of Ghana, Legon, in 1964. For her first play, Ama Ata chose to portray not a Ghanaian or an African but an Afro-American woman. I have no intention of blaming her for trying to depict the experiences of an alien. Quite the contrary. But I sincerely believe that she should have taken the trouble to study carefully her foreign model and give a true picture. The shock, bewilderment and despair that a person from African descent might feel when confronted with "Mother Africa" is often a tragic experience. Certainly, not a flimsy comedy in which the clash of cultures is summed up by the heroine's disgust at the sight of snails and her irrepressible love for strong drink. The over-simplification of Eulalie's character totally overshadows the otherwise worthwhile aspects of the play and in the end, *The Dilemma of a Ghost* leaves us with the impression of a mere exercise in futility.

*Anowa*, however, published in 1970, is certainly a very good play. Although the difference between Flora Nwapa and Ama Ata Aidoo is vast (Ama Ata is a born-writer), the world and vision of both writers bear strong resemblances. The action takes place in the Ghana of the late 19th century. Like Efuru, Anowa is a very beautiful, very intelligent girl with a personality of her own. She "has refused to marry any of the sturdy men who have asked for her hand in marriage" and insists on making her own choice. She decides upon Kofi Ako "a good-for-nothing-cassava-man" as her mother labels him. What is very interesting is the conception Anowa soon exposes of married life and of her role as a wife. As her parents heap insults and criticism on Kofi Ako's head, she simply replies:

> You will be surprised to know that I am going to help him do something with his life.

Very obviously, she believes that a woman can and must act not only as an assistant but a guide for the man whose life she is going to share. Unfortunately, like Efuru, her determination and faith in life are not to be rewarded. Shortly after marriage, Kofi Ako starts complaining of her strength of character:

> Ei, Anowa, you ought to have been born a man!

Although he loves her, a sort of fear very soon mingles with this sentiment. "Ah, my wife seems to be extraordinary in more things than one! (...) What were you in the spirit world?" Anowa shows a definite aversion for diviners and medicines although she does not dare reject them totally and, of course, she is barren. I deliberately say "of course" because, in these various female writings, the barrenness of the womb seems inseparable from the extreme fertility of the soul. In this play, anyway, it is not her sterility which brings about Anowa's despair and final destruction. It is the failure of her husband to prove himself to be a man. Anowa holds the sophisticated view that wealth and material riches do not amount to manhood. On the contrary, they destroy it:

> Money-making is like a god possessing a priest. He never will leave you until he has occupied you, wholly change the order of your being and seared you through up and down.

If she hints at her husband's impotence, it would be absurd to think that she gives sex an overwhelming importance and explains their failure as a couple to the absence of sexual relations. For her, the true meaning of life and success is to be found elsewhere. Where? Ama Ata Aidoo does not say. We are free to conclude that her heroine believes in a world in which spiritual and moral achievements are of the utmost importance and where a man is judged by the quality of his soul. I would not like to stretch the comparison too far. However, one remarks that the intellectually gifted and physically barren Anowa is, like Efuru, a much-wronged person and by the so-called diviners themselves:

> You did not want me to know? And the priest said it was my fault? That I ate your manhood up? Why did he say I did it? Out of envy? Did he not tell you that perhaps you had consumed it up yourself, acquiring wealth and slaves?

There again comes the belief that if not the spirits, then their mouthpieces in this world can err dangerously... Why should such a fate befall a girl gifted with so many qualities? Although it is not clearly stated, the supposition runs throughout the play that Anowa, although not actually chosen by a god, is no ordinary human being. She could have been a priestess but for her mother's refusal. She herself feels that she has not found her proper place:

> Mm, I am only a wayfarer with no belongings either here or there.

Her fellow villagers and her people, who are like an angry chorus in a tragedy, are always hostile to her since they strongly feel that she is different. In the end, they blindly hold her responsible for her husband's failure and death:

> But I say that all should be laid at Anowa's doorstep. What man prospers married to a woman like Anowa? Let the gods forgive me for speaking ill of the dead but Anowa ate Kofi Ako up.

Thus, like Flora Nwapa, Ama Ata Aidoo presents a very gloomy picture. She seems to have a deep distrust of the masculinity of African men. Her first hero, Ato Yawson, was a very weak young man torn between his family and his wife, his traditions and his love and quite unable to make up his mind. The second one, Kofi Ako, sells his manhood for money. Both writers convey the impression that a gifted woman simply has no place in African society. Not only because she cannot find a proper match, but because the price she has to pay for her unusual gifts is so high that she would be better born without them. There is something unnatural in a female being so perfect. It sometimes disturbs the order of the world and dark forces (either naïvely personified by Umahiri the Goddess in *Efuru* or unnamed in *Anowa*) are at work to destroy this dangerous female. In a word, intelligence, sensitivity and creativity are poisoned gifts. Happiness belongs to the mediocre, at least to the average.

It seems evident that in Efuru and Anowa are echoes of the inner conflicts and disillusionments of their female creators. In real life, they certainly had to fight to have their way: all in vain. Their victory only ends in solitude and death.

The first thing one must say concerning Grace Ogot is that she is a Christian. This does not mean that Flora Nwapa and Ama Ata Aidoo are not (they certainly are) but the ideals and code of values of this religion do not constantly appear in their writings. In fact, the works we have studied are set in traditional Africa where the people mostly revered their ancestors' gods. Nowhere is a religious clash hinted at. In Grace Ogot's *Land Without Thunder*, three short stories are centred around female characters: "The Old White Witch," "The White Veil" and "Elizabeth." In others, it is true, female characters appear, but no attempt is made to analyse their psychology, no interest given to their world and vision.

"The Old White Witch" opens with the story of a nurses' strike at Magwar Hospital. The reason for such a strike is the decision taken by the Matron Jack, commonly nicknamed the "old white witch," to force the African nurses to give bedpans to their patients. Such a practice cannot be tolerated according to indigenous tradition and if the nurses accept it, they won't be able to find any husbands. Although they are Christians, they remain strongly attached to their traditional customs. It is made obvious that the real issue behind the carrying of bedpans is a struggle between Christianity and indigenous traditions. For Matron Jack, "we must learn to serve our fellow-men whom we can see in order to love and serve God whom we cannot see."

The Reverend Odhuno, a black priest, sides with Matron:

> Listen carefully, my children. You are all grown-up women. The country put you here so that you may heal the sick and comfort the dying. Let not the devil mislead you – stay on and serve your master. Obey God's call – return to your rooms, change into your uniforms and continue to work in the Lord's Vineyard.

The leader of the strike is Monica Adhiambo, a bright and clever young nurse, very much liked by Europeans and Africans alike and Matron's favourite pupil. Upon her exhortation, the nurses boldly reply:

> If being a Christian means carrying faeces and urine, you can keep
> your Christianity too – we are returning to our homes.

From then on, every thing goes wrong in the short story. For after the nurses' departure, what is to become of the patients? Are they to die in their filth? Our sympathy remains with them and is held there by Grace Ogot's dreadful descriptions of their plight. After a few days, there is even greater danger of an epidemic. Grace Ogot, however, indulges in intellectual dissertations and forgets the human lives at stake. Instead of a decision being taken (either the nurses being called back and allowed to work on their terms or, the failure of the strike not due to the nurses' cowardice but their awareness of their patients' suffering), Matron Jack is portrayed discussing with her fellow-Europeans. Until one day a sick girl is carried into the hospital on a stretcher. To the staff's bewilderment, it is Monica Adhiambo. Although watched day and night by Matron Jack, Monica Adhiambo dies a few days after her admission.

What are we to understand from this? Should the death of Monica be seen as a punishment against Matron Jack who might feel that she had killed the girl herself? In such a case, this is certainly a double-edged punishment, like the one of an over-possessive and vicious lover who commits suicide to mortify the partner... Or is the punishment directed against Monica herself for having let her fellow-men die unattended and for having disobeyed her god's command-ments? We must not forget that the strike was described as a rebellion against God's will. There is, however, a very significant detail: Monica receives the Holy Sacrament on her death-bed from the hands of the Reverend Odhuno. If she dies then a Christian, her fate must be understood as a condemnation of her rebellion and the indigenous beliefs which animated it. In short, Christianity has the last word and so do the ways of the Whites...

The second short story that we have selected, "The White Veil," illustrates even more strikingly Grace Ogot's gift for badly-phrased questions and confused solutions. A girl called Achola is deserted by Owoli, her fiancé, because she refuses to give herself to him. To discourage any possible argument over the matter, Grace Ogot reminds us that indigenous traditions and Christianity coincide and recommend virginity in marriage. A few pages later, she contradicts herself by portraying a Christian English couple who do not hesitate to "misbehave" as Achola terms having sexual relations. Does that mean that Europeans can disregard their traditions while Africans should not? Eventually, Owoli becomes engaged to another girl and Achola, in despair, runs to a prophetess. Thanks to her trick, Achola reaches the church before Owoli's proposed wife and behind her veil is wedded in place of her rival.

> At the altar, Achola was sobbing before Father Hussen: 'He is mine. I have loved him all my life. He is mine.' And Father Hussen went down and tapped on Owoli's shoulder. 'My son, your wife is waiting for you.'

How far we are from Efuru's proud determination to walk out on a husband whom she still loves when she feels wronged! From Anowa whose courage and vitality were accused of eating Kofi Ako up! Must Christianity transform every African woman into a "female eunuch"[3] buying a man who does not want her through a shameful trap? Grace Ogot has so much admiration and respect for Christianity whose deep meaning, it seems, totally escapes her so that she does not realise that her characters are ludicrous. What is married life? A blessed ring, a few words from the Bible or, rather a prayer book?

The last short story, "Elizabeth," tells us of the ordeal of a young Christian girl who is expected to sell her body to her bosses for promotion and money. Her third employer, Mr Jimbo, rapes her on her office settee and in despair she runs away and takes up a job with the Church Army to care for destitute children. Alas, she soon discovers that she is pregnant and hangs herself in Mr Jimbo's laundry. Is that the solution that Grace Ogot offers to the problems of the growing number of young working women? Or should the alternative to death be found in the words of Mrs Karamani, the Labour Officer:

> Man has defied the laws of society; God alone will deal with him and it has to be soon!

What advice! Strongly reminiscent of what the priests and missionaries were giving to the slaves in the time of slavery.

What is then the conclusion?

It would be too easy to dismiss Grace Ogot and say she has no talent. On the contrary, Grace Ogot lacks neither style nor imagination. But her talents are totally wasted. She is so blinded by the European codes of behaviour, so confused as to the places of her traditional beliefs, that her female characters possess neither coherence nor credibility. Through badly digested Christianity and Western values, she sinks down to the level of cheap European literature for "midinettes" and other sub-products of the consumer society. She may believe that she is an emancipated woman "who reads books" but what she offers her fellow-countrywomen is a dangerous picture of alienation and enslavement. One feels tempted to advise her to join some Women's Lib. Movement to see how European females question the code of value and behaviour imposed upon them and to replace her Bible by Germaine Greer's book. In a word, Grace Ogot is a sub-product of the West and the solution of her problems will only be found when she comes to terms with them; when she no longer looks at the West as a child in awe of an adult, but as a critic and a judge.

Far more interesting and disquieting at the same time are Flora Nwapa and especially Ama Ata Aidoo. Here are two gifted women portraying gifted females like themselves, but ultimately destroying them. These murders are the expressions of a deeply-rooted conflict. Efuru and Anowa are not destroyed like Okonkwo in *Things Fall Apart* through the external forces of colonialism. They are destroyed from within. Flora's and Ama Ata's intelligence and sensitivity persuade them that the African woman has an important role to play in the future of Africa and that in the past it was the same. But for all this faith, there remains a doubt, a doubt on the value of their world nurtured by the daily sight of their complex and contradictory society torn between different ideals and poisoned by self-distrust. They do not bring this doubt into the open; they veil it under the disguise of Fate and Doom. And so their literature is, in fact, a literature of subtle protest, a protest against a world which does not allow "the beautyful ones to be born." If I paraphrase Ayi Kwei Armah, it is because, deep down, Ama Ata Aidoo is not very different. And it just lacks something for her protest to come out into the open.

# A Conversation: Ama Ata Aidoo and Micere Githae Mugo

## December 2010 at Brown University

## Part 1

**MGM**: Oh, at long last, Ama Ata Aidoo, this is really such a pleasure. And as I explained to you, first of all I want to congratulate you on your forthcoming 70th birthday. I really do believe that you are going to enlarge that circle of elders that we just want to commemorate for many, many reasons. And in this interview, I would like us to share with the world the many aspects of your contributions that we need to be commemorating. I will come to them later on. So, please don't be modest at all about telling us of the many glorious moments that we've witnessed – some of us – in your journey towards eldership.

**AAA**: I felt, if I was doing an interview for this project, then I would rather it was an interview with you. I feel honoured and flattered by your attention, my sister. It's great having you here at this time. And thank you for giving me the leeway, so that I can choose to answer the questions my way.

**MGM**: I want to begin with confirming your date of birth. For some reason, I read some place that mentioned 1941, and then on the Internet it said 1942. It then occurred to me that I'd never asked you when you were born.

**AAA**: Well actually, the truth of the matter is that I was born in 1940, which makes me already 70 years old. I think the date mix-up started a long time ago, when I was in the university or something. And frankly, I thought it was going to be elegant for me to reduce my age. I had put it in some sort of data, and I don't know how it found itself on the internet...but it stuck there. And although I've since then, on a number of occasions, given my correct birth date, it never really got corrected. So I don't think it's going to be any good what I tell you: what is on the internet is forever.

**MGM**: I hear you! Where exactly is Abeadzi Kyiakor in Ghana?

– 29 –

**AAA:** It's a village. I used to say it's a *small* village, but it's not a small village anymore. In fact, it's very much on its way to becoming a small town. But it's in the Central Region of Ghana. You've been to Ghana, and if you can picture a place that is exactly half-way between Accra and Cape Coast, or something like two-thirds of the way…it's there. It's a coastal place, not directly on the sea but we're not too far from the sea.

**MGM:** Okay. I'm really interested in family trees and how they unfold about who we are, where we're coming from, some of the experiences that have shaped us, our historical linkages and so on. So I wanted to know a little bit about yours because someone has written somewhere that you come from the royal family. What does that mean?

**AAA:** Well, I don't know where people get all these things from. And it's also the way they couch them. I don't want to be negative, but, as far as I'm concerned, as a colonised people, royalty comes kind of compromised. So, frankly I don't talk about it. But it is true that my father was the chief of Abeadzi Kyiakor and one of the kingmakers of Abeadzi District. My mother's father was also a chief, a big chief and that sort of thing. Yeah, but I am not into royalty.

**MGM:** To be fair to people who would emphasise that kind of connection in a family tree, within the indigenous set-up there were situations where such people played a critical role as representatives of their people rather than political opportunists or colonial collaborators.

**AAA:** But, Micere, you know me, and these royal things – that's not how I see myself. However, my father was a real chief and a good one, at that. Very, very good: very strong, very clear. My father was something else! There are stories about him. For instance, one of the things I could easily point to is that, when we were kids, the children from our village had to walk kilometres to the traditional capital to go to school. And then my father decided "No. No. No. This will not do." So, he literally worked on the District Education Management Office and insisted that we had to have our own school. And I was one of the pupils with whom my father opened our school. I've already said this in other interviews – but this whole thing to do with "If you educate a man, you educate an individual, and if you educate a woman, you educate a nation," I heard it first in our language, from my father the day he was opening our school. I remember it so clearly because at some point our father was looking at us, the new pupils and the audience, and he said something like: "I know some of you here might be wondering why we have girls also, but you see, girls must be educated." He read it clearly, quoting Dr. Aggrey.[1] He said something to the effect, "As the great man, Aggrey, said: 'If you educate a man you educate an individual…and if you educate a woman you educate a nation.' So, it's very good for us to start our school with girls also." He was that kind of person. And

– 30 –

I remember one of the stories that is often told about my father... Our village, in actual fact, is an island. During the rainy season, we were locked in. It's a big island. Now, for us to cross into town – and to Cape Coast and beyond – we had this river (we called it a river but probably other people would describe it as a stream). But when it was in flood, people couldn't cross it. So that was one of the reasons why my father started the school. And then during the First Republic, when the CPP[2] came to canvass help in the village, to help them win our district, he asked them clearly: "Well if we vote for you and we win, what are you going to do for us?" And the story goes, they said: "Chief, you tell us what we should do for you if we win." And my father was said to have told them, "You give us a bridge." And when they won, they gave us a bridge. Unfortunately, by the time the bridge was finished, my father was already dead. So he didn't see it, but it was definitely begun when he was alive. What I'm saying is that I don't like going around saying how I'm the Chief's daughter and so on – that's ridiculous. But I also know that as African Chiefs go, my father was one of the best.

**MGM:** Moving along, in *Sisterhood is Global* it comes out very clearly that your mother had a very strong "feminist consciousness" and was a very strong woman as well.

**AAA:** Well, I think it's not just my mother, but others too. I have always felt rather frustrated by the portrayal of African women as these weak, oppressed people. My point had always been that African women are no more marginalised and no more oppressed than women in other places, including the Americas, North and South, Europe... everywhere. Women have always been marginalised in every way – from the beginning of societies. I don't know what happened right at the beginning that turned things this way. I think, however, I also have to admit that the women among whom I grew up were really just kind of strong.

**MGM:** You are arguing, in essence, that in practice, notions of feminism are not a monopoly of any given culture...

**AAA:** No it is not. Within the parameters of their own existence, I generally think that I definitely grew up among women who can be described as strong in terms of an understanding of their own lives and what is expected of them, and how they should negotiate their own existence. That's what I mean. My mother, my aunt and so on and so forth...that's the kind of stuff they used to talk to me about, you see.

**MGM:** But, does it make a difference when you're born in a matrilineal society, as you are, in terms of how one conceives of oneself as a woman?

**AAA:** Again, having read and learned about other societies in other places, I think it does make a difference because…right from the beginning…you see, it's this whole thing with being wanted. You know, among the Akans, women at least are supposed to be the most wanted gender. That doesn't make anything better! You see, I have learned – or I've taught myself – that any kind of marginalisation, any indication to any child that she/he is not preferred is wrong. But given the preponderance of patriarchies and patrilineages around the world, I found the fact that I come from a matrilineal society certainly intriguing, interesting, and wonderful. Because as an Akan girl, people will refer to you again in very royal terms, such as: "You are a princess…you are this and you are that." And this kind of preference, which is very clearly stated among the women folk, is not shared by the men, who, in actual fact, seem to be resentful that they are not the preferred gender. I've overheard men be very nasty about women. The truth of the matter is that they know that whatever security they enjoy as men in Akan society is owed to who their grandmothers were, and not their grandfathers, you see? I once watched with amazement a woman who was the ambassador of the country (I think she had even gone to Oxford)…at any rate, somebody who was very highly educated (definitely among the country's intellectuals and political elite), lament the death of her only daughter in a way that indicated to me that, as far as she was concerned, with the death of this daughter – who was then in her late 20s – she had become *childless*. In the meantime, she had three living boys.

MGM: Wow! Moving on again, when did your interest in creative writing begin?

AAA: I became aware that I wanted to be a writer when I was fifteen. But I had been writing and had articulated it. When a teacher asked me what I wanted to do for a career, I just said: "Oh I want to be a poet" (laughs). Yeah, poetry…can you imagine?! Her response was: "Oh that's excellent, but you know, Christina… (Christina of course in those days) poetry doesn't feed anybody." And then she had proceeded to give me as a gift, what must have been some kind of an heirloom in her family: a silent Olivetti typewriter.

MGM: By the way when did you drop "Christina"?

AAA: After *The Dilemma of a Ghost* was published. I remember the first edition of *The Dilemma* had "Christina Ama Ata Aidoo." So it must have been after my graduation. However, I never took a legal step to get rid of "Christina," so in formal terms it is still my name.

MGM: I'm also really curious about your Pan Africanist vision, which I consider a very major contribution not just to African or Black writing, but to world conceptualisation of the historical connections of people of African origin. I'm specifically fascinated by the fact that this vision emerges in *Anowa* and *Dilemma*,

which were really early works. And I think this is something we need to celebrate on your 70th birthday, because I don't remember people that age at that
time coming up with such a clear vision of Pan Africanism. Did this have to do
with Nkrumahism, your growing up in Ghana or...?

AAA: I must confess that this probably had a lot to do with growing up in
Nkrumah's time, because his Pan Africanist vision was very clear and very
clearly articulated. And maybe it was also part of the environment I grew up in,
especially the village – because I didn't grow up in the city – and in the village,
frankly, we didn't have to even contend much with the British and colonialism.
Unlike East Africa and Southern Africa, these so-called British West African
places – thanks to the mosquito and other factors, such as the climate – were
rather hostile environments for the colonisers. They could not penetrate the
country and the countryside. They were forced to live their lives virtually along
the sea – like in the forts and in these special European areas along the coast.
They were certainly appointed as DCs (District Commissioners) and sent out
to the interiors of the country, but then, if you lived or grew up in a village that
was 20 miles from the nearest District Office, like I did, the colonisers or white
people or English were not in our world. You see? My point is that it was so easy
for someone like me to immediately understand where Kwame Nkrumah was
coming from and to absorb some of his message. Simply, if these white men are
sitting on us as the colonisers, then we don't need them. We don't need them.
Who are these people? I also think that my upbringing prepared me to maybe
become a nationalist.

MGM: Pursuing your Pan Africanist vision, the way you treat slavery in *Anowa*
is really a very thorough critique of what some have called internal "slave trading" involving our own people, which also helped European traders and the
ruling class...or rather those who made money trading with enslavers. So you
really connected very clearly that there was something internal going on and
that those who made money out of it profited by sending our people off with
empire enslavers. That consciousness for an undergraduate is unusual!

AAA: That's why I'm saying that maybe part of all of this was also the environment – my parents. Because, you see, although my father was a chief, he himself
was also rather critical of the system. And my mother was very articulate as
well, but again, she herself a Chief's daughter, had this kind of interrogative attitude towards the system she grew up in.

I probably should really pay attention – deal with this business of my parents,
who for all intents and purposes came from privilege (both of them in their own
way) and yet managed to retain this kind of interrogation of their societies. My
mother's father was not just a chief, but someone so rich that there was a song
the traditional priestesses used to dance to in this regard and I didn't know until

I was a university student (when I really heard the song properly) that they were singing about my grandfather. They were laughing, not to ridicule, but to express surprise as to how anybody could be as rich as this man. The song said he lived *upstairs* and that even his goats lived *upstairs* (laughs). However, going back to slavery, there had been internal slavery, but I think there was some kind of proscription against asking anybody about their origins. By the time I was growing up, it was against the laws – those so-called "Native Laws" – to call anybody a slave. And yet you were made aware, one way or another, that there had been internal slavery. But you don't talk about it and you shouldn't go calling anybody the child of a slave. Some nasty business and I think it bonded with me. And then, of course, you couldn't go to Cape Coast without passing the so-called "castles." I was something of a sickly child and so my poor mother was always carrying me to the big hospitals in Cape Coast, and you drove by the forts along the way. And no one talked about them – these forts, or these "castles," as we called them in Ghana. What were they for? Clearly, I was intrigued. So, when I learned from school – they didn't even teach us that much about the slave trade and slavery, but certainly there was some mention – and I realised what they were for, I think I was kind of traumatised and I couldn't get the story out of my mind. That people had actually been housed in these big houses, these forts, these "castles," and then been sent away. And then, of course, when Ghana became independent, these children of Africa – or the grandchildren of these Africans who had been carted away – started coming back ...There was a stream of African Americans, African Caribbeans coming and going, when Nkrumah was president (which itself is another long story): George Padmore, W.E.B. Du Bois...(I always feel like name-dropping when I say that I actually met him before he died). I met him and his wife. So, people like those, and there were others: Julian Mayfield, the Puerto Rican doctor, Ana Livia Cordero and of course I met Maya Angelou[3] in Accra when she was living in Ghana.

MGM: What a history! Ama, you and I first met in Kenya in the 60s. What I'd like us, again, to recognise and celebrate here is that, when you were working with Rebeka Njau and Elimo Njau at Paa ya Paa, the Paa ya Paa Gallery itself became a famous institution connecting writing and artistic creativity. And I remember you used to do dye work. You were a part of that heritage at that time in Kenya and so have left footprints there as a writer and as an artist. Can you say a little bit about that period of time?

AAA: It's a big part of my life. It's a long story, how I ended up in Kenya. But to put it as briefly as I can, I had met Primlar Lewis, an Indian woman who was married to an Englishman, while doing my own little wandering, starting from the US (long story), but to take you back in time, I had graduated in 64, and worked at the Institute of African Studies.[4] And, in fact, to put it as clearly as I can, the appointment to work at the Institute had come as a result of the production of *The Dilemma* at Legon, which had turned out to be some huge success. Then the Vice-Chancellor, who was no less a person than Connor Cruise O'Brien himself, literally orchestrated my appointment and I was recruited as a junior research fellow for the Institute of African Studies. And then two years later at Legon, I went with Efua Sutherland[5] transcribing stories and teaching English to the students who were doing Dance. This was the beginning of the School of Performing Arts, but at that time it hadn't been formally named the School of Performing Arts. And then I got an invitation as a representative to Harvard's international seminar – another big story. You wouldn't believe these stories, because some of the people I met at the time are such big names I don't even want to go into everybody, because it'll sound like name-dropping (laughs). Anyway, as a member of this summer thing at Harvard I met James Baldwin, Ralph Ellison and our group was even addressed by Henry Kissinger. After the seminar, I got a grant to stay in the US and write; so I did that and lived a bit in Cambridge, Massachusetts. And then I got invited to California[6] to the African Studies Department by John Povey. So I was wandering, bumming around getting to know a bit of the world. At some point I decided I would pass through England on my way back to Ghana. So I went to England, lived in Oxford and that's where I finished writing the first draft of *Anowa*. Before I left Ghana, there was a Sudanese professor at the Institute of African Studies and he had invited me to visit Sudan, so I said "Why not?" So I went to Khartoum, which was a story in itself. But before leaving England, I had met Primlar Lewis and in discussion she had said, "Come to Nairobi to visit us." So from Khartoum I flew to Nairobi.

**MGM:** So, please tell us about Nairobi, the Paa ya Paa Gallery and your visit there. What were you doing and what was going on in that space? What are your memories of Paa ya Paa?

**AAA:** Well, Paa ya Paa! As I said earlier, that one Nairobi experience became a big part of my life. What I don't remember too well is exactly how I met the Njaus (Rebeka and Elimo). They were friends of Primlar Lewis and so I met them (and Jonathan (Kariara), through Primlar and Charles Lewis. We became friends and took to one another immediately with both Mwalimu (Elimo) and Rebeka. That's how I got to know of Paa ya Paa. They would take me there. It was more than a place. It was like the base, the centre, of a whole lot of ferment in the arts. And I just became a very lucky recipient or participant, because I had not known when I came to Kenya that I would fall into anything like that. It was just wonderful for me, because, as you can remember, we would have readings there. And, of course, Paa ya Paa itself was an art gallery, so there was a lot of existing artistic inspiration there. Just being in the place, looking at those sculptured heads of Kimathi with the hair standing on end; images of the Mau Mau war of independence and others from the rest of

Africa. I just thought it was wonderful. And then, at some point – soon after I arrived, one of the things that happened to me – Elimo and Rebeka invited me to the University of Dar-es-Salaam. I got to know them at that interesting stage in their lives together, when Mwalimu (Elimo Njau) had just been appointed assistant lecturer at Dar-es-Salaam. So, during one of the trips back they invited me to go with them. We drove and the journey itself for me was very interesting. I spent some time on the campus in their home. And I remember getting invited to even speak to students at the Department of Drama because people knew of *The Dilemma of a Ghost*. We made an interesting trip to Morogoro one weekend and there was an incident in which the security people thought I was a Congolese woman who was involved in smuggling diamonds (laughs). Of course, it was very interesting for me. It was during that time that I met Babu (Abdulrahman Mohamed) and it's also when I first saw Mount Kilimanjaro close. It was a very rich experience. And then I returned to Nairobi and the whole business to do with meeting (Pasali) Likimani, who became Kinna's father – and then, of course, there was meeting you and meeting Ngũgĩ wa Thiong'o.

MGM: How long did you stay in Kenya for?

AAA: I think, all together, at least a year, because I stayed there and then returned to Ghana and then I came back, because, for some reason I decided at the time that I wanted to have Kinna born in Kenya. You may not remember this, but Pasali and I fell out – may he rest in peace. But he had been kind of jealous of my writing and told me that I shouldn't bother him because I had my writing. This hurt me very much, really, because writing is my writing…but you are you…and to ask me to literally "choose between me and your writing," I thought, was cruel, was unkind. And it was on that that we split. So, in the end, it was literally Jonathan Kariara, who took care of me, helping me rent my own place. I stayed for a while with the Lewises when I first came and then at some point I moved to the (YWCA) to be on my own and then later when Kinna was born we were for a while at Jonathan's and then I rented my own place. I then got an appointment at the Friends' World College, which is an American educational institution that is kind of worldwide. It's run by the Quakers. They had the African Centre of the Friends' World College in Kaptagat, near Eldoret. Kinna was about six-months old when we moved to Eldoret. So, the second phase of my stay was in Eldoret, teaching at the Friends' World College for nearly a year. I was fascinated when I heard years later that it had become the site of Moi University.

MGM: Was Friends' World College a teacher's college?

AAA: No. You see, I was like a literature consultant. The Friends' World College idea is some sort of an experiment in international education. The students are brought over, I think, basically from the US, with a few Kenyan students and the idea is that people will research and be immersed in their own line of study without really being in a classroom. So, I was like the literature person in connection with that.

MGM: What about your work in tie-and-dye? I remember associating you with tie-and-dye, as well as stimulating readings at Paa ya Paa. I thought to myself: this is such a young person who has become a writer at such an early age! You inspired us. In those days one was doing poetry here and there, but to imagine a whole published book was something else. *She* has done a book…and she is this young…it was inspirational…it really was.

AAA: Thank you. But it was Rebeka Njau who was doing tie-and-dye. I got to know that when they had me stay with them, especially when they took me to Dar-es-Salaam. Rebeka was doing the most incredible tie-and-dyes. So I learned it from Rebeka. And even when I returned to Nairobi, I was also doing tie-and-dye. I had this vision of me doing this thing for the rest of my life, because it's fun! And I continued when I was in Ghana doing tie-and-dye. But then, Rebeka, who had been my teacher, had moved on. Hers took off in a big way because, to begin with, she more or less graduated to real batik, which is a degree or a notch higher than plain tie-and-dye. And you may not remember this, but I remember very well that on a subsequent visit to Nairobi, Rebeka had changed the whole tie-and-dye thing into another form of art. I didn't graduate up into batik, but I still kept doing my tie-and-dye and then later on in Zimbabwe I tried to do it commercially.

MGM: Oh yes, I remember that…and Kinna as a young girl. By the way, when was Kinna born?

AAA: December 1969.

MGM: I want to observe that a lot of parents forget to celebrate, as either a part of their lives, or art, or achievements, their families – and their children in particular. But clearly, from your writing, and especially from your poetry, it is evident that Kinna is not just your daughter, but your friend, and in many ways a kind of intellectual mate. A number of your poems are dedicated to her. So, I really think your readers should hear a little bit of how having Kinna in your life has shaped you.

AAA: How having Kinna has shaped me. Kinna sometimes…well, not some-times…she literally believes or she tells me that even the writing I did before she was born was in anticipation of her birth (laughs). It's made my life. I don't know whether because she's been my only child or what, but you're right that we're kind of close. A bit more like friends, but sometimes she makes me feel like I'm the daughter. But so far we've been getting on quite well.

MGM: And what is it like having grandchildren?

AAA: Oh it's exceptional. I've always told myself that the wonder of having grandchildren – at least I've discovered – is in precisely having young people to love whom you didn't have to worry about. If things are working, if their parents are alive, then – touch wood – it is their responsibility that they're fed, that their critical comforts are taken care of. Basically, how they're trained is not your responsibility. You are there to love and be loved, and spoil them in ways that their parents wouldn't get to do.

# Part 2

MGM: Your experience teaching at Cape Coast: when was it? I remember, again, that historically that was also very important. You were a role model because there weren't many African women teaching at university level during those days, least of all in "English" departments. So I just want to get an idea of what kind of space that was.

AAA: It's interesting what you're asking. On one hand, I suspect that, like every-thing else, or like most things that I should have been aware of…and taking seriously…I took it for granted. I wasn't even clearly aware of how crucial or special it was, you see. Number one, because that's how really I've taken every-thing and it's terrible! There was also at the time in Cape Coast maybe about half a dozen of us women lecturers in different disciplines, maybe more – let's say ten. Now, of course when you do the ratio of ten women against maybe 150 men, we were still very special. So you see, all I know is that it was fun, on one level. But on another level, being a woman was brought home to me every now and then – the fact that I was a woman teaching there among the men. One incident, for instance, that I keep remembering was that one day after a lecture, I went straight to what we called the Senior Common Room. In there was somebody I had actually considered something of a friend (he himself was a mature student and his friends were of the faculty and he was very nice and was actually employed by the administration and was taking a degree as part-time). I remember, the moment I entered the Senior Common Room, him looking up at me really beaming. And he was sitting with a group of male faculty and he said, "Oh Ama, how are you?" And I said, "I'm fine." And then he said something to the effect: "I understand today your lecture was absolutely masculine" (laughs)!

You're talking about spaces. Now, every time I bring up this incident, people would annoy me by saying, "But of course he meant it as a compliment. It meant you were very good." And I would say, "Yeah, masculine!" So, that's one of the incidents that revealed to me how I was regarded.

**MGM:** I know you will chide me for this because you refuse to suffer from what I call "the-first-woman" syndrome, or the "first-and-only-one" syndrome. But really this is important and if it's a phase you'd rather not talk about, it's okay. Am I right to assume that you must have probably been the first woman to serve as a minister in any post-independence African government when you became Secretary for Education in Ghana?

**AAA:** Actually people say that, but I don't think I was. Maybe for Education, but there had been a woman member of the cabinet. She was the Minister of Social Welfare and Community Development during the Nkrumah era. So I don't think I was the first woman cabinet minister of Ghana; but I was pretty much the second or whatever.

You know how I am. I've taken everything kind of for granted. I was just busy being a minister. However, the fact that I am a woman was brought home to me literally during every cabinet meeting. For instance, when a male colleague was making a point about any issue everybody would be paying attention. After a while I noticed that when I was speaking on any issue – in those days people smoked a lot – that's when the smokers would look for their cigarettes and start smoking. Or they would be passing notes to one another. I'm sure they didn't mean to do this deliberately but that is how they made me feel, as long as I was the one doing the speaking, they would occupy themselves with some other activity until I had finished. It's like whatever I was saying wasn't important enough. *That* I noticed.

**MGM:** This is a familiar story, but it leads me to ask how you ended up in politics. Forgive me for saying this, but one thing I don't think you are is a good politician because you are too forthright. Why did you accept to serve as minister? What change did you see yourself bringing about?

**AAA:** For that one, I think the answer is fairly simple: I thought we were making the Revolution.

**MGM:** I hear you. The other milestone I really want us to commemorate on your 70th birthday within the contexts of Pan Africanist connectivity and location is your stay in Zimbabwe and what you contributed there imaginatively, intellectually and ideologically. Your presence in Zimbabwe was really quite significant and I'm delighted to say that our families got to bond while we all lived there. You talk of people who are not family biologically becoming relatives, but since Zimbabwe Kinna and you have been like a part of my extended family. In my view, that Zimbabwe experience was unique, especially what you contributed towards children's literature and writing. What comments would you like to make about your sojourn in Zimbabwe?

**AAA:** Well, I had been to Zimbabwe in 1982 as the minister of education for a conference. And, of course, as you recall, there was the whole ferment…the enthusiasm…the wonder…of Independence. So after I returned to Ghana from Zimbabwe and I left the Government – or I was sacked – the issue came up of what I was to do with myself as I didn't feel like returning to teach at Cape Coast. In the meantime, as a result of all that was happening to me in Government, Kinna had become ill. And at some point, family friends just said, "Why don't you just take Kinna out with you to give yourself some break from this environment." And of course, Micere, any normal person would have figured this thing out for themselves. But in my case, this is actually what happened. I sat down and literally did a whole lot of discussion with myself in terms of where to be and have my daughter with me. I had told myself that because of racism I wasn't so sure that I wanted Kinna, who was still very much in her early teens, to grow up outside Africa. I didn't want that complication in our lives, in her life, that early. I wasn't going to come to the US; I wasn't going to go to Europe or England. So I just decided, why not go to Zimbabwe? So it was a self-exile, I always have to emphasise. And at the time, I have to confess that I wasn't aware that they were chasing me out of Ghana. But I knew that I had to get out, so that's how I came to Zimbabwe. And what a lovely decision that turned out to be! Being in Zimbabwe and then having you there, it was such an incredible miracle – even today I can't kind of work around it, simply because, for me it's always been too big. I've tried not to understand it, simply because there's no way I can understand it; I can only accept it as a gift, you know what I mean? The fact that you were in Zimbabwe, I know that you had had to be in Zimbabwe literally as an exilee. I take it is a gift, and for me it was wonderful to have you and your girls there, and so many other people. I won't do a roll call. All that I'm saying is that those also became incredible for me in a whole lot of ways. As usual, I brought with me my naivety, lack of under-standing on some issues; and so it's not like there were no problems. As you know, there were problems, economically and so on. I tried to even earn money by doing tie-and-dye, then learned that the native community in Zimbabwe and Harare were very disapproving of the fact that I was a University lecturer and a writer and I had been a full-blown minister – and how dare I just do tie-and-dye?! (laughs). It was incredible. I kept asking myself, and the people who would bring the gossip to me: would they, rather, forgive me if they heard I was stealing to look after me and my child? Would it be preferable? All of these things were going on, but it was a nicely productive time. I think that overall in my life I could have published a lot more than I have, but at any rate, a novel like *Changes* was completely written in Zimbabwe. And my first collection of poems, *Someone Talking to Sometime*, was published in Harare. Even nearly half of the poems that became part of *An Angry Letter in January* were also written in Zimbabwe. Then, as you know, I did the children's stories and poems that were a part of the supplementary school readers' series and so on. So you are right:

it was, at least in terms of my own life, a very productive time. And my daughter went to school and graduated from high school in Zimbabwe.

MGM: What I describe as the historical coincidence of our contemporary presence in Zimbabwe was a most enriching time for us and our families. And let me congratulate you on having chosen not to go to the West or to the United States with Kinna. As you might remember, I relocated to Zimbabwe from America mainly to shelter Mumbi and Njeri from racism, because, for the first two initial years of exile from Kenya (1982–84), I was in the US and it was terrible. If you read the essay in Kofi Anyidoho's *The Word behind Bars and the Paradox of Exile*, you will realise what a very painful experience it was...

AAA: I knew that, as a "good neocolonial," sooner or later I was going to end up in the West some place. But I thought I should at least avoid having Kinna in those very formative years, like the teens.

MGM: Since then, my daughters have always regarded you as a mother: they speak of you as having been their second mother in Zimbabwe. So for us, you have always been a gift that we celebrate. You are also a gift to others in Zimbabwe. You are remembered as one of the writers that helped women's writing mushroom, right?

AAA: Thank you very much. I tell everybody that, all modesty aside (laughs), I was the first president of the Zimbabwe Women Writers.

MGM: And why not? Seriously, how do you manage to transcend the "Bigness" syndrome? Is it ideological?

AAA: I think it's a part of what I call my naivety (laughs). You've known me now for a very long time. I wish I were slightly more practical and therefore aware of issues that had to do with practical advantage. I don't want to talk about it, simply because the moment you start talking about how modest you are, then, of course, you are not being modest (laughs). The modesty itself goes out the window. However, it is also a world-view, isn't it? What I'm saying is it took me a very long time by the way, even after I'd published *The Dilemma...* for me to even tell myself that I was a writer. I remember that there was a time – I can't put a date to it – but I remember a time when I said "Oh, so I'm a writer!" But, otherwise, however I come across is how I was brought up, what I absorbed from the environment, like anyone else. We are creatures of our genetic makeup, the whole nature versus nurture thing. As I say, the way I was brought up, the people I have met across my life and so on. Not just my father or mother, but my cousin, who I called uncle, and his family, who took me on during my junior high school years. I think maybe I was just lucky to be some kind of a sponge and to have some healthy stuff to absorb. I was just lucky to have met people along the way who affirmed me; people who didn't laugh at me when I said I wanted to be a writer; people who encouraged me. I think all of that helps. What it does do is it makes for a very easy life, which has its own negatives. There was a certain kind of hardening up which I missed, you see?

**MGM:** What led to your decision to eventually return to Ghana after Zimbabwe, and what was your return like?

**AAA:** What took me out of Zimbabwe was an invitation from Vincent Odamtten to go and teach at Hamilton College. That is what started it. I was always going to return to Zimbabwe, but then the invitations kind of followed one another. It began with the University of Richmond, in Virginia: I had an invitation to go and spend a year there as a writer-in-residence. And then Vincent came with the invitation and so on, and before then I was a Fulbright Scholar to the Great Lakes. So there were these series of invitations to teach or to be a writer-in- residence in these American colleges and universities. And this continued for about eight years: from 1987–8 to 1996. It was like destiny was responding to my own restlessness, like I didn't want to be settled.

**MGM:** Tell me about your return to Ghana and specifically – because this is another milestone – about Mbaasem. We will not go into how difficult it is, financially, to found and run an organisation such as Mbaasem, but tell us: what does Mbaasem mean? What kind of vision inspired its founding and how is it doing?

**AAA:** Mbaasem actually literally means "Women's Affairs." *Ba* in Akan means 'a woman,' and *sem* means 'an affair/a word/a statement/a case.' I had always had this term literally swimming in my head as what I would want to call any small organisation that I had anything to do with in terms of its formation, as more or less describing the work of women writers. It refers to women's words, women's issues – their words, spoken and written. What inspired its formation? But, Micere, my sister, if I were to give you all of the sources of the inspiration, we would have to do another interview (laughs). It had to do with all the experiences, the negatives that I had encountered and suffered in my life as a woman writer. When you write as a woman, people come to your work as an afterthought. I thought the least I could do was to help put in place some small platform for dealing with some of these areas. We can never presume that Mbaasem is taking care of all the problems of African and Ghanaian women writers. Of course not, but just to address some of these issues.

**MGM:** What are some of the activities or events that have taken place in Mbaasem to address these gaps?

**AAA:** We have regular workshops. We had a writers' club, which used to meet monthly. Mbaasem Writers' Club has given birth to the current forum. It meets once a month to workshop in creative writing, mostly fiction, although every now and then we remind ourselves that fiction/prose is not the only form of writing. In fact, out of the forum's work, we are hoping that, by the end of 2011, we would have brought out an anthology of short stories. In the meantime, along the way, we also bought a page in *The Daily Graphic*, Ghana's oldest and most important newspaper. They gave us a page and we were publishing stories and so on. We realised there was a need for these spaces. Unfortunately, the *Graphic* literally took the page back without really discussing it with us. And I feel they've done it because we proved quite useful and now they don't need us. It's one of the unfinished businesses within Mbaasem, how to sort the whole thing out with *The Daily Graphic*. Although we are a women writers' organisation, the page was completely non-gendered. It published the work of older writers and younger writers: writers who were residents of the country and abroad. It was like an open forum on the page. It is my wish, one of my few hopes, that I will use your interview so that Mbaasem can raise its own funding so that we can pay for the page and the advertising.

**MGM:** Does Mbaasem have a writers' residential programme?

**AAA:** Yes, there is a residential aspect for it. We always hoped that women writers would come and stay from two weeks to twelve weeks and do some writing. As we speak, we have organised a short-story competition for teenage girls.

**MGM:** Now, I know that you will be leaving Brown where you have been for the last seven years. But really in just a minute or two, what have you been doing at Brown? What will you be taking with you and what do you feel bad, leaving behind?

**AAA:** It's been wonderful being at Brown. As you've been aware, they invited me and George Lamming, the great Barbadian/Caribbean novelist. They formulated this whole thing. The idea was that we would be teaching there – me from Africa, George from the Caribbean – for five years. After the first 5 years, they decided to extend the appointment for two more years and I think they've done wonderfully by us. I gave two full courses during the fall semester while I was at Brown. One was in literature and the other was in creative writing. I was invited to both the Africana Studies Department and the Literary Arts Department. But I think so far it's been a very active programme. For my literature classes, I offered contemporary African women's novels; that's what I did. Every now and then I would be tempted to remove the "women" bit and just do a course in the contemporary African novel. I resisted it successfully, because I told myself, "If you don't teach it, how many places in this world are people offering African women's novels?" So I persisted, and I'm glad I did. So that's what I offered in the Africana Studies Department. For the Literary Arts, I gave a writers' workshop every semester. This year I had the one-on-one, what we call independent study, with a graduate student working on novel writing. So for the Literary Arts, it's been work-shopping.

MGM: How do you deal with the situation that, clearly, it would be a mistake to exclude your own works, when you teach African women writers? If you teach your work, how do you teach it?

AAA: Well actually, I've been teaching *Changes*. It's been over seven years and it hasn't been easy. Even at Brown I knew that people were offering both *Killjoy* and *Changes* on their courses. So it occurred to me: "Look, why do I miss out on this?" What I'm saying is that, if it's a question of letting my students go away with some notion of where the African woman's novel is today and knowing that somebody else who was teaching the course was offering *Changes*, how could I – again, all modesty aside – not offer it? I never felt easy about it, but I thought that it would be a little more honest to offer the novel. It hasn't been an easy choice, as I say, and I've always felt funny. Perhaps what I should say is that teaching it is easy, but the decision to teach it isn't.

MGM: You are a rare craftsperson in combining various art forms to produce creative works: a playwright, a short story writer, a poet, a novelist, a children's writer, an essayist, a critic, a tie-and-dye designer. Working with all these media, would you be able to say which one you feel most passionate about, or is it an unfair question?

AAA: Well, no, it's a legitimate question for which I don't have a legitimate answer in the sense that, for instance, I had never seen myself as a novelist. But definitely I think about that crazy decision not to write a play unless I had a company to work with, which has turned out to be a really dreadful self-fulfilling prophecy. I made that decision after *Anowa* was published before I had seen the production. And somehow I found the whole issue so traumatising that I told myself: "No, I'm not going to write a play again unless I have a drama group to work with." This was silly because it means I haven't written another play. However, to give a very short answer to your question about what I am passionate about in terms of all these media, I think the honest answer is when I'm working in any of these genres I am passionate, because I have to be in order to produce. But I started by defining myself as a poet. Just in terms of execution time, poems are the easiest to produce, although they're probably the most complex.

MGM: Your return to Ghana: is it a comfort zone? There has to be something about home…

AAA: Well, yes, I think the very simple issue of home is critical. One, because, that's where I was born and apart from Zimbabwe I haven't really lived anywhere else. The longest I've spent in the US at any particular time was during an eighteen-month period. In England I lived there on and off for maybe two years. Now, why Ghana? My mother is alive and she is in her 90s and I think as her oldest daughter, I need to be by her. She's being looked after in my house. So I feel if I'm not teaching at Brown, I should be at home. But it is not a done deal that I will base myself back in Ghana – in fact I've decided I'm going to declare myself a creative writing refugee (laughs). Why are you laughing?

MGM: One other central issue is the use of orature in your work. Why are you so insistent on using this as a site of knowledge for your creative writing? It doesn't look like you can live without invoking orature in your stories (laughs). Is it your upbringing and is it a conscious act?

AAA: Well it started by not being conscious. It just came into my writing and well, that's because that's my source. This is where it all began for me. One of the earliest teachers we had in the village was interested in storytelling. Every afternoon in the class, to stop us from sleeping he would make us sit and tell stories. And then at the end of the school year, he used to take us around the surrounding villages doing skits and telling stories. And then there was my mother. She slept very early in the evening and woke up in the morning to tell me stories while I was sleeping. I find that whole thing so incredible – so warm. In fact, the story behind *Anowa* was that it was based on one of the stories she told me. And then I grew up in my father's house, where the most incredible, wondrous, ridiculous – just name it, happened there. I would come from school and find a wandering prophet. My father would be behaving like he had no other responsibilities in this whole world than to listen to the wandering prophet. That was going on and they would bring cases to handle and proverbs. I just had a really rich upbringing. So when I started writing, it just came through without much effort on my part. To a certain extent I feel that this kind of knowledge, information, art, should have been and should still be formalised into the education system. One of my regrets is that I hadn't fought hard enough to retain my position as Minister of Education because I feel that I could have impacted education in some of these ways, because unfortunately a number of our educated elite don't see that there's any point in handling orature.

MGM: My sister, all good things come to an end, as the saying goes and our time is up. I cannot thank you enough for this jewel of a sisterly conversation.

Thank you! Thank you!

# Section II.

## *"Because surely in our environment there are more important things to write about?"*[1]

If theoretical considerations of African cultural production provide the continuing stimulus for the search for meanings in the African imaginary, the eight essays in this section are compelling examples of *more* "important things" to write about. Although reference to Aidoo is made in seven of the essays, only the last two focus entirely on her writings and a third takes up an Aidoo text to substantiate a philosophical theory. However, the other essays in the section, which make tangential or no reference to Aidoo, are of equal importance because of their considerations of ways of thinking about phenomena that impinge on the universe of Aidoo's work. Historian Toyin Falola invokes the 19th-century mutiny on the slave-ship *Amistad* to suggest the imperative to decolonise historical memory and re-cast the narrative for Africans' inclusion in the narrative of the present – an objective to be realised, in part, through the academic discipline of Black Studies. In his argument, Falola points to the role of literature in defining African modernity, invoking, among other texts, *Our Sister Killjoy*. Thus, even the tangential appearance of this Aidoo title in the historian's theoretical argument augments our reading of the novel. Continuing with the matter of colonised spaces of academic inquiry, Biodun Jeyifo's elegant in-your-face exposure of the (post-) colonial politics operating in humanistic disciplines, particularly literary and related philosophical studies, makes a clear case for scrutinising, if not revising, the theoretical premises from which we critique texts from formerly colonised societies. For poet Kofi Anyidoho this is the imperative for a Pan African literary vision, in which he acknowledges Aidoo's part. Sweeping through Ghanaian literary history, from the 1912 wake-up call of J.E. Casely-Hayford's *Ethiopia Unbound* (1912) to Ama Ata Aidoo's 2026 vision of a female-headed Confederation of African States, in her short story "She Who Would Be King." That Confederation president is the offspring of an audacious girl-child who had, at age ten, declared her intention to become president of her country. Such a child would have been intellectually and culturally nourished on African/Diasporan texts that have shaped African peoples' narrative, in addition to texts from other peoples. Thus, the next essay on the obligations of the African writer in shaping the minds of Africa's children, by Naana Jane Opoku-Agyemang (Vice-Chancellor of the Ghanaian University that was established primarily to train educators) provides a philosophical framework that would not only produce such a female leader as Aidoo imagines but also support such a 21st century vision for Pan African literature as urged by Anyidoho – the reclamation urged by Falola.

As questions of liberating African cultural legacies are debated, others arise that go to the root of what it means to be African, especially in view of increasing geographic and psychological migration since political independence. The philosophical propositions posed by Helen Lauer serve as her basis for interrogating notions of "African" identity within the framework of the "politics of identity," and the social construction of race. Lauer scrutinises especially the cosmopolitan lives of increasing numbers of postcolonial Africans, as demonstrated in *Our Sister Killjoy* through Sissie's critique of her Britain-based "brothers." Lauer's argument could productively be extended to several characters in Aidoo's *The Girl Who Can & Other Stories*. Further on the issue of the social construction of race and its applicability to Aidoo's *Killjoy*, Susan Arndt reviews its history from ancient Greek classicism to 20th century German National Socialism. Arndt applies the theoretical concept of "the racial turn" to deconstruct "whiteness" for reading Sissie's experiences in Bavaria. And that Bavaria adventure, particularly, its very complicated relationship with Marija, is the subject of Nana Wilson-Tagoe's psychoanalytic reading of *Killjoy*. Through her analysis, Tagoe demonstrates Aidoo's practice of theorising through the creative work (also raised by Carole Boyce Davies in the next section) that, in turn, comes up as the subject of Ketu Katrak's essay, ending this section. In fact, Katrak, admitting this uncommon extension of the concept of theory, bases her assertions on her pedagogical experiences with Aidoo's oeuvre. As a result, Katrak's essay could be read as an extension of her pedagogically valuable Afterword to the Feminist Press edition of *No Sweetness Here*.

# The *Amistad*'s Legacy: Reflections on the Spaces of Colonisation

## Toyin Falola

I want to use as my starting point a great episode in the history of slave resistance, the 1839 mutiny now known as the *Amistad*. I wish to talk about how a moment transited into a permanent historical symbol and a template to understand race relations over time. The story is already well known and there is no need to present its essential details all over.[1] On board the *Amistad* slave ship on the high seas travelling toward the Northeast coast of America (from Havana to Guanaja), Joseph Cinque organised a bloody revolt against the Spanish crew. The hope of the temporarily liberated slaves was that the *Amistad* would be forced to sail back in the direction of Africa. The Africans had no detailed knowledge of ship steering and probably had to rely on one of the slave dealers, Montes, who bought them. Perhaps, Montes engaged in a deliberate trick: during the day he steered the ship toward the east and at night toward the United States. Or perhaps, the liberated Africans were unable to know how to steer back to Africa. Subsequently, the ship was intercepted by the US Navy who brought it to shore on Long Island, New York. The *Amistad* and the Africans were then taken to New London, Connecticut. A judicial hearing was announced in August 1839 while the Africans were put in a jail in New Haven. A trial ensued, with all kinds of drama, between nations and individuals in support of or against slavery. The legal issues were over the rights to the cargo – Spain or the United States? – and the status of the people – were they slaves or not? The *Amistad* episode energised the abolitionists who were able to enlist the services of a famous lawyer, John Quincy Adams, a former US president. A successful case of slave revolt galvanised the abolitionist movement, inserted itself into the American judicial system and ended in freedom for the slaves.

In September 1839, the initial case, described as criminal, was dismissed for lack of jurisdiction. In the following month, Professor Josiah Gibbs was able to locate an interpreter (James Covey) who was able to speak with the Africans, teach them English and introduce them to Christianity. Cinque and others turned the table, filing cases against Montes and his fellow slave dealer for false imprisonment and assault. The trial began in January 1840 and the District Court judge ruled that the Africans should be turned over to the President who should return them to Africa. An appeal followed in September 1840, but the Circuit Court upheld the decision of the lower court. The government took the case to the Supreme Court where John Quincy Adams and Roger Baldwin argued their cases. In March 1841, the Supreme Court ordered that the Africans should be freed immediately. Between March and November, the freed Africans learned more English and Christian education. In November 1841, they left for Africa as part of a missionary group. They arrived in Sierra Leone in January 1842 where they began evangelisation work. Some left the mission. In 1879, Cinque died and was buried in a cemetery dedicated to American missionaries.

My purpose is not to revisit the narrative, but to comment on what the episode represents to Africans and people of African descent. The *Amistad* episode provides us with the opportunity to examine issues around slavery, race and power, domination and memory, conquest and nationalism. I will limit my discussion to three broad interrelated themes:

i)   the manipulation of historical memory for politics and resistance by slaves to question or reinvent that memory;
ii)  the transition from the control of people to the conquest of land; and
iii) finally, the response by dominated people to reclaim their own past and struggle for inclusion.

The *Amistad* revolt, as well as the events before and after it, reveal the difficulties faced by black people to make their own histories in ways favourable to them. The conquest of Africa and the consequent Disapora created by Western forces was cultural, political and economic. This conquest, in its multi-faceted forms, is the colonisation of the spaces created by the African world. The interpretation of the conquest has equally entailed the colonisation of a people's memory.

## The Colonisation of Memory

In spite of the short narrative just presented, attempts have been made to erase the memory of the *Amistad* episode and related ones. For a long time, the standard narrative was that slaves accepted their conditions for four hundred years, and that many were even unhappy with the abolition and emancipation of the nineteenth century. Those who captured and used slaves were quick to write stories about slavery. In so doing, they sought to colonise the memory regarding slavery. There were three clever flanks, sometimes repackaged even today. The first is the fundamental attempt to justify slavery in religious, ideological and racial terms. Motives can be disguised, putting the economic circumstances under the carpet and so-called humanitarian ideas on the table. Second, there is the flawed thesis that in the long run conditions of slavery were better than conditions of underdevelopment. Indeed, not a few blacks have even expressed the self-hating opinion that they were better off having been shipped out of Africa. Third, and arguably the most persistent, a clever intellectual game to treat the slave trade as a blame game, presenting a balance sheet between those who demanded and those who supplied. In this balance sheet presentation, the Africans who stayed on their continent were forced to respond to a demand-side economy and were given an equal share of the blame. Those who have fallen to this balance sheet argument have been cleverly led to another problem: an attempt to divide blacks into antagonistic blocs, so that tensions can emerge between African Americans and continental Africans.

What also emerged from the colonisation of the African space after 1885 was the clever attempt to colonise the African minds. The image of Africans as docile, eager to take punishment and confident in bondage, since there was no better alternative for them, has deep roots. The presentation of Africans as passive and collaborators into the slave trade is also widespread in dominant circles, even up until today, simply to transfer the blame from the activities of the hegemonic elite to the victims of economic and political brutalities.

Western education, for a long time, became the tool of colonisation. Consciousness of race inferiority was accepted and internalised by many blacks. W. E. B. Du Bois spoke about double consciousness, defined as "this sense of always looking at one's self through the eyes of others, of measuring one's soul by the tape of the world that looks on in amused contempt and pity."[2] In his well-cited book, Carter Woodson spoke eloquently about what he called the "mis-education of the negro":

> ...the negro's mind has been brought under the control of his oppressor. The problem of holding the negro down, therefore, is easily solved. When you control a man's thinking, you do not have to worry about his actions. You do not have to tell him not to stand here or go yonder. He will find his "proper place" and will stay in it. You do not need to send him to the back door. He will go without being told. In fact, if there is no back door, he will cut one for his special benefit. His education makes it necessary.[3]

It took a while for new knowledge to replace decadent ones. Indeed, it was not until after the Second World War that the study of Africa received legitimacy in the majority of Western academic institutions.

The colonisation of memory is based on the assumption that knowledge about events such as the *Amistad*, slavery and imperialist domination can either be erased, where possible, or told from the point of view of the slave owners and conquerors. There is also the assumption that ignorance about the enslaved can be manufactured. The power of domination is turned into the power to construct memory. It is also the power to create silences when it was politically expedient to do so. The majority of Africans growing up in colonial Africa would never have been taught the history of slave resistance, talk less of hearing about the *Amistad*. Until the European power was about to end, there was no such academic project as the systematic study of Africa and its Diaspora. African students were told that they had no history, and they did not make any significant contributions to world civilisation.

The denial of a people's past is not that a past did not exist – there are no such peoples without a past – but a statement about power and the uses to which it has been put. When millions of people were enslaved and when their continent was forcefully conquered, it was a strategy both of justification and domination to deny the people a past, a memory. The maintenance of power also meant the creation of a new history to erase the previous history. The new history is of how domination has enabled the enslaved to benefit from their being in chains and how conquest has rewarded the colonised. Blacks were regarded as "the white man's burden" and to prevent their extinction, they needed to be saved. To be saved, they needed to be civilised. To be civilised, they needed to be enslaved and conquered.

The colonisation of memory is also based on the assumption that the coloniser was an effective teacher. The coloniser had become the ideal citizen, even in foreign lands. The colonised had been transformed into subjects, in their own spaces, and their land a big classroom. Did not a notable British geographer, James MacQueen, arrogantly proclaim, "If we really wish to do good in Africa, we must teach her savage sons that white men are their superiors"? He did. Policies followed that assumed the superiority of the slave masters and colonial officers, and the inferiority of blacks. Inferiors could not make claims to any credible knowledge. Their knowledge had to be colonised to teach them. The sources that sustained their epistemologies – orality, performances, arts, etc. – were delegitimised. They were told that to talk about the past, one needed written sources, not songs, not verbal slave narratives, not even the residues of their environments that yielded tremendous evidence. Egypt, Nubia and Ethiopia were grudgingly excluded, since they had written evidence of history, but the forces of change, the evidence of the past were connected to a meta-narrative that excluded black people as achievers and inventors. Even Hamites – a mythical horde of migrants from outside the continent – were invented as the creators of civilisations. Hamites were presented as caucasians who joined other light-skinned people to create African civilisation.

The colonisation of memory has been clever in assaulting worldviews and religions. Many Christian missionaries aligned their views with those of slavery and imperialism. Turning themselves into agents to spread civilisation, they were aggressive in their condemnation of indigenous worldviews, in despising indigenous religions, mislabeled as paganism. They ranged much wider in their criticisms, carefully primitivising indigenous creative endeavours in music, art, religions, languages and cuisines. Attires were redefined as costumes, nations converted into "tribes," and legitimate state-building wars into political anarchies. The violence of conquest was sanitised into legitimate wars of civilisation; the violence of resistance was presented as the activities of barbarians and cannibals.

The *Amistad* reveals notions of memory. Slaves were acquired from a position of power in terms of the technology to cross the sea, the manufacture of guns and gunpowder to generate the violence that produced the slaves, and the plantations where the slaves worked to produce sugar, tobacco, cotton and other products. The perception of slaves by their owners was framed in the context of unequal power relations. Similarly, the resistors were trying to overcome their powerlessness. Slave masters, in relations with their slaves, were using negative and limited knowledge about the uprooted men and women. Slaves were being looked upon not only as people in bondage but as the representatives of primitive people. Racism and evolutionism combined to generate stereotypes about black people in general. In the evolutionary tree, created by the Western idea of civilisation, the most superior culture was Western and white. Others might be able to progress toward the ideals of this superiority. The black race was considered to be at the lowest stage of evolution, basically children who needed time to become adults. Slaves were people with human anatomical features, but they were marked apart by race and evolution. Cultural evolutionism evolved partly out of slavery, and was reinforced by colonisation and perpetuated by stereotypes. In this colonisation of memory and experience, imagination ran wild, too wild. The most positive image of the African would be that of a "different person," but never superior to anyone, only better behaved or exhibiting greater intelligence than other blacks. Rural lifestyles and the simplicity of slaves were seen as reminders of how the world used to be before progress came to the West. Universalism was invented from a premise of arrogance that one group knows and understands the truth, the only truth, which others must accept. Blacks had to be invited to learn the truth, to move away from isolationism toward universalism. This is a form of control in which the claim of one truth becomes a strategy of domination, actually of total domination in the physical as well as epistemological sense.

The presentation of the *Amistad* resistors and of slaves in general has framed the meanings of Africa to Americans. They are meanings that show not the limitation of knowledge but the deliberate creation of false images, fake memories. If Africa does not denote "tribes" and natives, it can't mean the land of savages and cannibals. By extension, blacks are poor, ignorant, erotic and wild.

A stereotypical canvass is painted: an exotic set of people living in primitive huts in the company of wild animals in the jungle. Language comes out of imagination, feeding ideas that are perpetually negative, and supplying images of barbarism to entertain television audiences. Racism and exploitation have always coupled, very well accepted in the United States and elsewhere in the Western world. For many years, the United States established a successful slavery and segregation system. Slavery and racism were practiced in a combination that ensured exploitation. In the years after the abolition of slavery, racist views persisted in one way or another. Today, we find them in private discussions, exotic presentations, and the display of cultural arrogance. The common themes of Africa remain about animals, the jungle, and the primitive people who live there just to show that Africans are deprived and depraved.

The era of the *Amistad* saw the clearly reinforced invention of Western images of Africa. The slave trade era redefined racial and political relations. From the eighteenth century onward, race and culture were united in the Western construction of Africa. A monogenist view of a world created by Adam and Eve gave way to a polygenist one in which God created separate races and gave power to one to control others.

The *Amistad* enables us to question the colonisation of memory. The *Amistad* episode tells us about the fierceness of struggles for liberty and freedom. Moreover, we see hints and evidence of the value of heritage, the affirmation of culture, and the defence of humanity. Consider the importance of the slaves involved in the *Amistad* to formulate an identity of resistance in the Middle Passage. The struggles they produced led to a powerful representation beyond the symbolic – the representation of resistance as freedom and as politics, and of the culture of rebellion engrained in the experience of slavery itself.

Scholars have produced counter-narratives to demonstrate the misleading nature of the colonisation of memory. Today, we have a long list of works on resistance to slavery that document various episodes and tendencies. Such studies demonstrate the failure of the attempts to silence or kill the slave narratives of resistance. On the African side, limited documented evidence shows the examples of people who tried to prevent the slave trade, such as the activities of Queen Nzinga of the Matamba in Angola who, from 1630 to 1648, fought the Portuguese over taking African slaves. In Dahomey, King Agaja Trudo attempted to end slavery between 1724 and 1726. The pressure on the demand side made these attempts so feeble. Within Africa, the project of slave-making was a project of violence made possible with imported guns and gunpowder. In the brutal Middle Passage, slaves had to be overwhelmed and shackled to prevent their jumping into the sea and killing themselves. The routine of individual experiences in the Middle Passage is not necessarily captured in the historical records. The *Amistad* was a revolt on a slave ship, one that we know the best because of its prominence in the American legal historical records on slavery. But there were others as well. In 1730, ninety-six African slaves from the Guinea Coast staged a mutiny on board the *Little George*. They successfully confined the crew to the ship's cabinet, reversed the direction of the ship to the Sierra Leone River, abandoned the ship and jumped inland as free citizens. There was another case in 1740, in the same region, when a mutiny occurred on the *Jolly Bachelor* sailing on the Sierra Leone River. The *Jolly Bachelor* was attacked by free Africans who set the slaves free. Alexander Falconbridge, who had first-hand experience of the Middle Passage, recorded in his book that the spirit and aspirations that shaped the minds of the fighters in the *Amistad* was actually very common.

> As very few of the Negroes can so far brook the loss of their liberty and the hardships they endure, they are ever on the watch to take advantage of the least negligence in their oppressors. Insurrections are frequently the consequence; which are seldom expressed without much bloodshed. Sometimes these are success-ful and the whole ship's company is cut off. They are likewise always ready to seize every opportunity for committing some acts of desperation to free themselves from their miserable state and notwithstanding the restraints which are laid, they often succeed.[4]

Resistance in plantation economies was common. Those with the ability to read and write and with the opportunity to put their ideas in print, composed slave narratives which have survived until today. Slavery was not simply about domi-nation, as the narratives by slave owners tend to present it, but equally about resistance, as the activities of slaves do clearly show.

Slave owners attempted to control the memory of slavery. Many of their successors have equally attempted to appropriate the knowledge of slavery. In this appropriation, there is a deliberate attempt to minimise the evils of slavery by blaming Africans for selling their own citizens, by making the demand-side economy less significant than the bread-basket. The continuity of poverty, in repackaged slavery conditions, is blamed on the poor – alas! if only they can work harder! We have to reclaim the knowledge of slavery and of poverty in order to put events and actions in their proper context.

## The Colonisation of Spaces

The events that surrounded the *Amistad* were about the control of people. Around the same time, the control of space, manifested as colonisation and direct occupation, was about to commence. The Trans-Atlantic Slave Trade was moving to an end in the nineteenth century, but the forced movement of people from Africa was about to give way to a project of control of the entire continent and its people. Race was a key sponsor of colonisation. Racist theories of the nineteenth century constructed black people as inferior, a race that could be destined for extinction. A number of studies conducted by pseudo-scientists (e.g. John Burgess) provided a so-called conclusion on black inferiority. With its enormous ability to conquer others, Europe was confident about itself, its civilisation, its superiority. They celebrated the Industrial Revolution, the progress in science, the Enlightenment, and their ability to travel world-wide. They used their own evidence to construct an arrogance of culture that saw others, notably Africans, as far below them. This was not the time to talk about the equality of races or of humanity, but of racial domination. A combination of politicians and businessmen saw the wealth that could come from Africa. Their vision was one of domination and maximum expropriation, not collaboration, and their ideas began to spread. The colonisation of the black space was a global project, the domination of Africa by Western forces, technology and culture. The title of the famous poem by Rudyard Kipling, "The White Man's Burden," captures it all. The contents reveal a grandiose desire of greed:

> Take up the White Man's burden –
> Send forth the best ye breed –
> Go bind your sons to exile
> To serve your captives' need;
> To wait in heavy harness,
> On fluttered folk and wild –
> Your new-caught, sullen peoples,
> Half-devil and half-child.
>
> Take the White Man's burden –
> Ye dare not stoop to less –
> Nor call too loud on Freedom
> To cloak your weariness;
> By all ye cry or whisper,
> By all ye leave or do,
> The silent, sullen peoples
> Shall weigh your Gods and you.[5]

Kipling gave us the clues. God and whiteness were constructed by Kipling as allies to control others. These others were subordinate and child-like. The subordination required the colonisation of space indefinitely because the transformation of the "half-devil and half-child" was a never-ending job.

The creation of the European empire in Africa after 1885 was the colonisation of African space. Africa became an extension of Europe.[6] Colonial knowledge reflected this reality: the evidence of change, according to the colonisers, was produced by the colonisation of space. The colonisation of space, in combination with the Trans-Atlantic Slave Trade, led to the invention of Africa as the "dark continent" during the nineteenth century. It was during that century, all to justify the violent conquest of Africa, that the continent became presented as a place of strange customs: cannibalism, ritual murder and warfare. The propaganda in Europe, to support the military invasions of other lands, was that Europeans were dealing with people without civilisations: they presented to their own public stories of Africans still grappling to learn languages, arts and crafts. Nineteenth century science and philosophy were also propagating evidence of racial differences to explain human diversity. In 1859, Charles Darwin published his *The Origin of Species* which showed how different species evolved in relation to biology and environment, a conclusion which was racialised by various interpreters to mean that there was one race at the top of the hierarchy. Whites were on the top, followed by Asians, and then followed the inferior races – Africans, Native Americans, and Australian Aborigines.

The colonisation of Africa became so easy to justify in this circumstance. Conversion – the introduction of Western ideas to civilise Africans – became even a secondary point. Africans were said to be too far behind to be easily uplifted. Rather, what the "dark continent" needed was a trusteeship – as inferiors, characterised as the lowest form of humanity, they should be taken care of as babies. The colonisers did not see evidence of achievements, but of savagery and barbarism. Africans needed conquest, as a form of assistance. Scientific race theory now combined with imperialism to bring about the end of Africa's sovereignty from which it is yet to recover.

The colonisation of space, like the colonisation of memory, was based on lies – not ignorance, as many prefer to say, but absolute deliberate untruth. To start with, there was no foundation for their historical claims about the continent in relation to the European concept of progress and civilisation. Second, the conquerors described African nations as violent, but they conquered the place with violence. Their rule also unleashed violence that subsequently became part of a political culture. Africans were drawn into two World Wars whose objectives did not concern them. Third, in the conversion of Africans to Christianity, they used a rather strange concept of love – God appointed Europeans as prophets and saviours – which hid the cultural damage inflicted upon them. Christianity became a gift. Former slave-holders and plantation owners were now condemning Africans for slavery. The Trans-Atlantic Slave Trade lingered until the mid-nineteenth century, but the receivers of the slaves were now the ones to control the moral agenda.

The colonisation of space opened up the avenues for the exploitation of people. Irrespective of the system of colonial governance, be it a policy of indirect rule, assimilation, association, paternalism and various other categories of colonial relation, the objective was clearly the same: exploitation. A colonial dictatorship emerged, with white officers on top, protected by the army and police. Africans paid taxes to finance the administration, while they produced crops and minerals that were shipped abroad. Established precolonial nations and their political structures were swept aside. Changes occurred in all aspects of African life, producing anomie, confusion and fractured modernity, some of which has been captured in many literary and academic works.[7] The combination of slavery and colonialism laid the foundation of Africa's underdevelopment.[8]

## Counter-Colonisation Projects

Nationalism produced numerous forms of anti-colonial resistance, including violent ones. Indeed, the fall of the European empire in Africa was made possible by the ability of Africans to make the enterprise unworkable. Similarly in the Americas, the emancipation of slaves led to various demands for inclusion in political and democratic spaces. The demands unleashed various struggles into the twentieth century, most notably the Civil Rights Movement. Various forms of nationalist projects have survived until today.

Black people began to construct alternative forms of knowledge to counter the experience of domination.[9] Western-oriented universities emerged in different parts of Africa from the 1940s onward. A new generation of Africans acquired degrees and began to teach and hold positions of influence. In the United States, Black Studies programmes also emerged. As blacks contributed to scholarship, images of a lost past were recreated, narratives shifted from colonial condemnation to objective historical realities. New sources and methodologies produced new and rich histories. Non-written epistemologies emerged to describe the tragedies of the slave trade and the colonial encounters. When black people began to write, we see clearly the pain and anguish in the slave narratives. By the time we enter the twentieth century, academic writings developed as counter-discourses. In Africa, nationalist historiographies developed to present Africa-centred histories. Cheikh Anta Diop became famous, supplying ideas that led to the creation of the Afrocentric movement in the United States, popularised by Molefi Asante of Temple University.[10] Black Studies was created in the American academy against opposition, some even confronting violence in the 1960s. African nationalist historiography successfully provided rich evidence on the African past, pointing to established institutions and structures. The contributions of Africa to other cultures have equally been acknowledged, while debate continues as to what the Greeks owed to Africans.[11]

Activist scholarship created new approaches, some non-Western in their orientation and some adopting the methodologies of so-called mainstream departments. The agenda of Black Studies is anti-colonisation. Combining intellectual with practical projects, Black Studies concentrates on the investigation of and the methods to end the oppression and exploitation of black people. Race and racialisation should not just be seen as epiphenomenal, as many social sciences disciplines tend to emphasise. Conceived as a distinct discipline, Black Studies is not shy of action and rhetoric, and it's clear about its investigation of the past, present and future of black people to make various political and anti-colonial statements and demands.

The knowledge of counter-colonisation dismisses the so-called neutrality of Cartesian, Western models of knowing. Black Studies contested the claim to historical objectivity by those in power, while it maintains that race, class and gender must be at the centre of historical and cultural presentations. As Black Studies attain its maturation, its emphases attain greater clarity: at the centre of its epistemology is the promotion of an African ethos. Various writings fall on the structure of black communities and the language of liberation to address the omission of the black experience in the academy.

While the premise of Black Studies has been accepted in various quarters, its creation is a process of struggles against the colonisation of memory and the colonisation of spaces. In Africa, African Studies was born in the era of decolonisation in the 1940s and 1950s when scholarship was created by the political nationalism that saw the end of the European empire. In the United States, Black Studies struggled for inclusion in the universities as part of the Black Power and Civil Rights Movement. From the mid-1950s to the mid-1970s, it created its form and content. It presented itself as innovative, a challenge to racism, and a methodology to understand the people of African descent. Moreover, many argued that Black Studies would provide a space for black students on campuses to learn about their history and interact with people of their race and ethnicity.

The creation of Black Studies was part of the general package of knowledge connected with political emancipation. Various anti-hegemonic discourses grew in the non-academic setting as well. As far back as the nineteenth century, Frederick Douglas and other abolitionists had called for the creation of new knowledge that would refuse to accept the racist view that blacks were inferior to whites. Douglas was blessed with able successors, notables such as Du Bois, Alexander Crummell, Carter Woodson, who founded the *Journal of Negro History*, and Arthur Schomberg, all of whom supported the idea of reclaiming black history. In the 1920s and 1930s, Negro History Week and the Harlem Renaissance paid attention to black art, literature and culture. Scholarship was broadly defined around the conception of blackness, an all-encompassing umbrella for Africans and people of African descent.

During the twentieth century, many activists argued that black history would generate racial pride among the youth and promote racial harmony. A number of black students on campuses in Africa and the United States said that they were not Europeans and saw no reason to study Shakespeare, Mozart and Beethoven and that they preferred Langston Hughes. History became a relevant discipline to construct and defend nationalism, to repudiate the negatives about Africa, and to point to the achievements of black people world-wide. An intellectual patrimony of disciplines began to reinforce the ideas of cultural patrimony. Blending oral with written sources and placing Africa at the centre of discourse serves to prevent fragmented discourses on blackness, ones that would separate the history of slavery from European conquest or the history of the Civil Rights Movement in the United States from that of decolonisation in Africa.

The most sustained anti-colonisation project has been the use of culture – as an ideology, as a source of affirmation, as an agency of resistance. The ideas of Negritude and the Harlem Renaissance as cultural celebrations were emphatic in stressing the cultural difference of black people, and in calling for the use of culture for political purposes. More importantly, culture was promoted as a critical source of identity. The connections between culture and politics have been hugely successful. With words, eloquent, melodramatic and combative, many writers have reclaimed the lost glories of the past. Not only have they revealed stories of achievements, they also demolished the archives of Western domination. They redefined the notions and evidence of civilisation, adopting the definitions that elevate people of African descent. They intellectually centralised Africa, projecting it as the centre of the black world. Furthermore, the uses to which culture has been put have created a mode of struggle against oppression. Aimé Césairé, Léopold Senghor and others of the Negritude and Harlem schools opened up a new library of African tradition and philosophy.[12] They used culture to create unity among blacks, an ideology of cultural patrimony that sustained the politics of Pan Africanism. Blackness was turned into beauty, the construction of racial pride. To be black was to be proud, drawing no references to affirmation from whiteness.

The use of culture as a tool of resistance is arguably now the most dominant. In the United States, it has become less common to deploy violent rhetoric, in particular since the success of the civil rights struggles of the 1960s. The combative Black Power Movement of the 1960s has given way to a radicalised culturalist agenda of the Afrocentric movement. In Africa, violence is still a strategy to combat unjust power. Black-on-black violence reveals stresses and tensions among the marginalised. Various governments deliberately opted for the use of culture for political purposes, some to shore up authoritarian regimes and some genuinely motivated by the need to stop the erosion of African cultures. Festivals of old are repackaged and represented to newer audiences, in large measure to entertain them. Technologies of presentation, notably television and the internet, have made it much easier to popularise culture and to spread its non-political manifestations. The various governments, with the support of the United Nations and UNESCO, formulated ways to preserve culture, making it illegal to take works of antiquity out of Africa. Cultural patrimony is also regarded as the bedrock of identity and the "self-understanding of a people."[13]

By and large resorting to culture has been successful in a number of ways.[14] It provides the most effective politicising tool to create black political solidarity. Cultural patrimony provides the opportunity to network at the level of international organisations and to build a series of ties between and within continents. More importantly, it allows challenges to be mounted against mis-education, to reformulate damaged consciousness, and to assert mental autonomy as well as the independence of personality and the assertion of collective identities.

## Conclusion: The *Amistad*'s Legacy

An event as far back as 1839 continues to give us the opportunity to examine issues around history, race relations, and memory. The Trans-Atlantic Slave Trade is dead, the European empire in Africa has collapsed, and plantation slavery is no more. Yet, we still have the subordination of Africans and the people of African descent to Western global forces. What, then, is the relevance of the *Amistad* in today's circumstances?

First, we see the tensions between resistance and power. The connection is not hard to explain. What Africa lost to the Americas and the West is not just labour, but primarily power: the power to use its own labour and land for its own economies; the power to shape its future and define itself; and the power to relate to the rest of the world on its own terms. How blacks have responded represents the politics of resistance. Those with power have struggled to silence the past, the memory of resistance. A celebration of the *Amistad* and related episodes of resistance is necessary to prevent the colonisation of memory. If power wants to silence the past, it is our responsibility to keep the past alive, to bring back the ghosts to talk. This is our first major task, a rescue operation of the past. We have been successful in generating new knowledge and questioning many older assumptions. The so-called natives, as we can now tell, are not as dumb as the racialised images have presented them. They can see all the lies and present their own truths.

Second, in bringing back those ghosts, we have to continue to pay attention to the longer and larger legacy of the tradition of resistance and rebellion. We should not use our limited resources and fragmented intellectual power to celebrate the domination of our people by imperialists and empire builders whose main goal is the evil exploitation of our people. The enslavement that led to the *Amistad* and the colonisation of memory and the imperial conquest that led to the colonisation of spaces have been shown to be ephemeral. In resisting the colonisation of spaces, we have to pay attention to great moments and coura-geous leaders, patriots and nationalists who fought in defence of their own people. The *Amistad* is part of the tradition that must have a permanent stamp on our consciousness.

Third, the *Amistad* is a preface to the narrative of rebellion and civil rights, all informed by nationalism that questioned the Western model of suppression. Black intellectuals have challenged the racist idea of black inferiority. They have even moved further, as Du Bois did a long time ago in *The Souls of Black Folk*, to reject the construction of the world into two: the civilised and the uncivilised. Blacks cannot be at the margins of history.

Fourth, when moments of justice and fair play arise, even if it involves a few, they deserve the mobilisation of our full support. The *Amistad* trial shows the precedence in American law – gaining freedom through the courts. Law and the judiciary do favour the powerful elite, but they also provide opportunities for the poor and marginalised to express their grievances.

Fifth, the judiciary and other institutions of power are not enough for liber-ation. We see the limitations in the case of the *Amistad*. What is necessary is the acquisition of power, the distribution of key power to handle the negativity of the racial context. We have seen what happened to slaves without political power. And we can see what happens to free people without political power. The *Amistad* has shown us the consequences of powerlessness. With sufficient power, there would have been no lynching, dispossession and economic exploitation.

Sixth, the *Amistad* shows us the beginning of reparations and the Back-to-Africa Movement. The resistors demonstrated the illegality of slavery, and they wanted to seek compensation for their sufferings and also return to Africa. The two issues they raised continue to resonate today, and they assist us in framing the issues around reparations. Similarly, the *Amistad* also connects us to the events and analysis around the Middle Passage, which has been turned into a distinct sub-specialisation in Slavery Studies. We see the struggles on the high seas in the Middle Passage. The Middle Passage has been a connector, bringing Africans to the Americas and Americans to Africa. Where new identities have been formed and shaped has become the subject of controversy, especially since the publication by Paul Gilroy of *The Black Atlantic*,[15] which has been read as an attempt to erase Africa from the formation of African American identity. The desire by Cinque and his colleagues to return to Africa has been manifested by many others through permanent relocation to Sierra Leone and Liberia and until today by way of tourism by those of the African Diaspora.[16]

Seventh, we must insert the *Amistad* and all major forms of resistance into popular culture. There have been documentaries and films on the *Amistad*,[17] thus keeping the memory alive. This insertion into popular culture and the class-room is critical to keeping the memory of resistance alive. Popular culture must not be allowed to be part of the spaces of colonisation, but should instead occupy the spaces of resistance and nationalism. The academy must lend its full support to the creation of a just world where the ideology that created the *Amistad* will be crushed, and where the system that produced inequities will no longer exist.

Finally, blacks must be able to shape economic and political processes in order to assert themselves. Their ability to work turned them into slaves. The usefulness of their land and their ability to produce converted them from citizens into colonial subjects. Their ability to work and travel make them exploitable members in a globalised economy. It is not that blacks don't work, which they do; it is just the kind of work they do and who they work for that represent one source of trouble. While we should keep pointing to earlier, blatant racist discourses and formulations, we must also continue to specify the current neo-imperialist forms and representations against which we have to struggle. Discourses around aid, development, security, democracy and others present new challenges for resistance. We have to be alert to the dangers posed by seductive political propaganda that appeals to a sense of wanting to do good and imagining social justice while the actual intentions are disguised.

We have been successful in defining and using culture. However, the forces of global domination are getting stronger and they cannot be fully tamed by ideas drawn solely from culture. We have to create competitive technologies and economies. The *Amistad* shows the dimensions of cultures – in the longing to go back home, in the use of language, etc. – but what produced the result was action and resistance, that is the ability to mobilise culture in the service of politics. The gap between the West and Africa, between whites and blacks is not a gap about cultural difference or a gap structured by cultural peculiarities but by access to resources, inequalities in global economies, and the political domination of one race by the other. The African slaves who were part of the *Amistad* and the millions of others along with them were not forcibly converted into slaves only because of their skin colour but because there was an unequal economy in place. The colonisation of Africa was not made possible because one group was white and the other black, but because one had in abundance the Gatling and Maxim guns. Racism was justified on the grounds of political and economic interests, which is precisely how these interests were articulated to generate profit and maintain dominance. We have to close those crucial gaps in politics and economics. We have to construct power to remove blacks from the very margins of politics itself. Self-assertion must transcend the patrimony of culture to embrace the patrimony of entrepreneurship, clearly guided by the patrimony of power.

# Radical, Comparative Postcolonialism and the Contemporary Crisis of Disciplinary Identities: Outline of a Prolegomenon[1]

## (For Amilcar Cabral, Audre Lorde, Edward Said and Ama Ata Aidoo)

### Biodun Jeyifo

At the oral defence of a doctoral dissertation at Cornell sometime in the fall semester of the 2002/03 academic year, I inadvertently caused quite a stir by a casual remark that I made about the work of leading scholars and theorists of postcolonial studies in North America. It is important to state that the thesis that was being defended – which I had supervised – involved a study of three canonical works of contemporary fiction, Bessie Head's *A Question of Power*, Theresa Kyung Cha's *Dictée* and Thomas Pynchon's *Gravity's Rainbow*. In the dissertation, these three works were meticulously read within a conceptual framework of comparative explorations of the institutionalisation of, respectively, African, Asian American and American literary and cultural studies in the United States. Needless to say, this was a thesis as much informed by "theory" as by exegetically close reading of literary texts. Indeed, a hallmark of the thesis was an extended and original re-reading of one of the most challenging philosophical works of Jean-Paul Sartre, *Critique of Dialectical Reason*. My casual remark that caused the absolutely unintended and unanticipated commotion at this event came logically in the context of discussions on precisely the conceptual framework of the thesis being defended, these being the societal forces and the disciplinary trends that either combine or diverge to institutionalise single writers and bodies of texts as objects of academic study. What was my remark that generated this great excitement? It was an observation that the literary works of writers from the postcolonial, developing countries of the world do not feature at all, or feature very thinly, in the essays and books, indeed in the overall professional and intellectual interests of the most influential postcolonial theorists in North America, especially the three most visible scholars and theorists, Edward Said, Gayatri Spivak and Homi Bhabha. This remark caused total, if momentary, silence, to be followed by questions such as: "Are you saying that the most influential *postcolonial* theorists in North America don't actually write about the postcolonial writers of the developing world? Or: "Well, if they don't write about postcolonial literary works, *what* do they write about, what are the objects of their professional and intellectual interests?

Because my remark had been made with the reflexive, unthinking certitude that I was making an observation that was so widely known, so self-evidently a feature of the "postcoloniality" of Said, Spivak and Bhabha and many others in the North American academy that it would be received as an unremarkable piece of information about an important aspect of current North American intellectual and professional trends, I was in turn flabbergasted by the excited surprise which my remark generated. For good measure, I made another observation as a sort of "supplement" to my initial remark, uncertain whether or not it too would generate more startled reactions: "Well, I said, these influential postcolonial theorists actually not only do not write about *postcolonial* literary works, they do not write primarily on *literary* works." This, of course, only worked to heighten the question that had been previously asked: "Well, *what* do they write about"?

It is incontestable that the surprise generated by my remark at that thesis defence comes from two closely linked, unspoken but powerfully sedimented expectations about postcolonial studies. What are these expectations?

The first expectation is that the works of postcolonial theorists and scholars based in departments or programmes of literary and cultural studies *ought* to be about the postcolonial literatures of the world. Underlying this view is of course one of the most outstanding facts of the intellectual and cultural history of the last seven or eight decades, this being the emergence of postcolonial writers and literary traditions in South America, Africa, South Asia, the Caribbean, Australasia and the Pacific region and from the minority, immigrant communities in Europe and North America. These writers and traditions have produced some of the most significant, exciting and innovative trends in contemporary literature and literary-critical discourse.

The second expectation is more narrowly institutionally grounded, this being the expectation that scholars who are based in English or other departments of literary studies *ought* to write centrally about literary works, as single texts or as bodies and traditions of literary works. Of course for quite some time now and in many respects, this expectation is much more widely "observed" in its breach than its observance, for who does not know that in North America and the UK- as well as in many parts of the world – departments of English and

Comparative Literature have become a sort of institutional home-away-from-home for disciplines and fields as diverse and inclusive as philosophy, ethnography, area studies, gender and sexuality studies, disabilities studies and a host of many other emerging fields and programmes? But nonetheless, the expectation survives that English and Comparative Literature departments are primarily about the study of literary authors and texts.

I would argue that it is between these two expectations, or as I prefer to describe them, *acceptations*, that that the possibility of a meaningful response to that ringing question lies: if *postcolonial* theorists and scholars don't write primarily or even significantly about the postcolonial writings of the world, and if they are eminent faculty of departments and programmes of literary studies and don't write primarily about literary texts, what do they write about, what are the *objects* of their professional and intellectual interests?

"What do they write about?" This question is the point of departure for my lecture about postcolonial studies and what I am describing as contemporary crises of disciplinary identities. The question could be rephrased to say, "Is there a postcolonial text in this theory?" This reformulation of the question comes in the wake of other famous questions on this same subject of the interrogation of acceptations about the self-understanding of scholars in the field of literary and cultural studies. Two of such questions come to mind, one clearly an echo, a deconstruction of, or re-signification on the other: Stanley Fish's "Is There a Text in this Class?" (1980), and Mary Jacobus' "Is There A Woman in this Text?" (1982).

That question, "Is there a postcolonial text in this theory?" provides the point of departure for this lecture. For this reason, even though I can sense that you do want an answer to the question right away, I shall have to hold off for a while, a long while, on your expectation, leaving the question to hang for now. First, I wish to make a rather long detour through an exploration of what, in the title of my lecture I have designated radical, comparative postcolonialism before coming back to that burning question. I make bold to make this detour because I am presuming that I will not fail to sustain your curiosity, your desire to have my response to that hanging question, "Is there a postcolonial text in this theory? My certitude here rests on two reasons. The first of these is that the subject of my detour, radical, comparative postcolonialism – which Said in his magisterial book, *Culture and Imperialism* calls "post-imperial discourse" – has a tremendously fascinating intellectual interest in its own right. Secondly, it is my hope that I am not alone in thinking that delayed gratification in the public sphere is no less a valued experience than it is in that other well known sphere of the private and the erotic! And on that note, let me make one more observation before coming to the subject of radical, comparative postcolonialism.

You may have noticed that this lecture bears the subtitle, "Outline of a Prolegomenon." A prolegomenon is conventionally an initial, prefatory work written in the expectation that a longer, more substantial work is to come at some future date. Thus, to conceive this lecture as an outline of a prolegomenon is to indicate that what you will get in the lecture is a prolegomenon to a prolegomenon. Another way of expressing this is to say that I expect that this talk will generate far more questions than I can possibly answer at the present time. This is meant in all seriousness; but it is also said as a warning and a plea that any questions I am unable to entertain or engage adequately are to be perceived as questions directed at that prolegomenon I am yet to write, not at the *outline* of the prolegomenon which is what this essay is. As to questions which exceed both the outline and the prolegomenon, questions which hint at that substantial work of the future which will come after the prolegomenon, I encourage you not desist from raising such questions, because, though I may not be capable of responding to them substantially now, I hope to be able to do so in the future! On this note then, we may now move directly to the topic of radical, comparative postcolonialism, using as our frame of reference a symptomatic reading of the last years of the career of Raymond Williams.

Raymond Williams was without doubt the greatest British Marxist literary scholar, theorist and critic of the twentieth century. Williams was also Welsh. It was only near the end of his life that he expressed regret that imperialism, either in its colonial or postcolonial epochs and expression, had not featured much in his life's work. More specifically and portentously, Williams averred regretfully that his Welshness ought to have predisposed him to registering and exploring the deep, pervasive and enduring impact of imperialism on British life, politics and letters. This admission goes to the heart of the project of a radical, comparative postcolonialism, which, as I have remarked earlier, Edward Said designates "post-imperial discourse." Permit me to make a brief elaboration on this claim.

The word "radical" has two almost anti-thetical usages and meanings, but only one of these is in common or widespread use, while the other meaning is so little known that it almost has the status of a lost lexicon. This latter usage or meaning that is as forgotten or repressed as Raymond Williams' forgetting of his Welshness in matters of the impact of empire on British modern society is captured in the following synonyms that any good or standard dictionary will give for the first meaning of "radical:" root, original, foundational, fundamental. From these synonyms, we can see that being radical is going back to the root of things, to origins, to foundations. In the second, more widely known and used meaning of the word, to be radical is to be predisposed to considerable departure from what is usual or traditional; it is to desire or work for extreme or drastic changes in existing views, habits, conditions and institutions. In reflecting on how these two meanings and usages of the word "radical" relate to Raymond Williams' admission that he ought to have been attentive to imperialism in his life's work, let us note that the admission was made at the very end of his life. From this, let us ponder what the structure and contents of his life's work might have been if he had come to that realisation midway through his career, or if indeed he had lived for another decade or more and had set about making intellectual and ideological amends and "restitution." After all, Williams in this moment of Aristotelian *anagnorisis* – a term in dramatic theory indicating a moment of recognition which, like Hegel's "owl of Minerva," almost always comes too late – Williams in this moment was caught in a situation not too different from what many other scholars have experienced midway or even late in their career. This is the moment of recognition that being Native American or Chicana, being gay or transsexual, being disabled or eco-feminist, or being Muslim in a predominantly Christian, European or North American country is not a life experience that can be kept apart from one's professional life or, in the words of the title of this talk, one's *disciplinary* identity.

I would argue that what Williams would have done at that moment of anagnorisis if time were on his side would have been no different from what scholars such as these have done and that is to creatively integrate the irreducible or decisive aspects of their social identities with their professional, disciplinary identities. In other words, Williams would have had to refashion himself, never a simple, uncomplicated matter even for gifted scholars and theorists of the stature of Raymond Williams.

This huge problematic is what I had in mind in linking radical, comparative postcolonialism with contemporary crises of disciplinary identities in the title of this lecture: this project of radical, comparative postcolonialism calls for nothing short of or less than a reinvention of *scholarly* identities in line with social identities. And this is possible only on the condition that we come to a realisation that identity politics is as much present in academic disciplines, and often in as volatile a manner, as that other "identity politics" around the so-called new social movements (nsm) around race, ethnicity, gender, sexuality and disability that has been the subject of controversy in the last two decades.

On that last point, I cannot resist making the observation that, because Williams died in January 1988, when the debates over identity politics were gathering momentum, I cannot resist saying that identity politics did catch up with him, in the most positive and potentially empowering terms. It is my conjecture that if he had lived, if he had creatively refashioned himself, with his towering intellect, this in all probability would have led to a radical intervention in comparative postcolonialism of the last six or seven decades, in both senses of the word "radical." This is because, with his scholarly breadth and critical rigour, Williams would in all certainty have probed the epistemological and ideological significance of the historic fact that imperialism, in its colonial vocation, began in Europe centuries before it moved to the far-flung overseas colonies and dominions outside Europe. This needs to be stated more precisely: centuries before it achieved worldwide power and authority, colonialism had consolidated and perfected in the European heartland all the basic strategies, tactics and discourses of outright conquest and domination as well as the hegemonic ruses and manoeuvres that were later applied in the non-European worlds. This is without reference to the historic fact that in the second half of the twentieth century, as decolonisation outside Europe entered its last phase, colonialism, in the form of what has been aptly designated Soviet social imperialism, emerged and consolidated its hold over large parts of Central and Eastern Europe. These crucial, decisive facts of modern imperialistic colonialism are almost entirely buried under the present "universal" construction of colonialism as appertaining basically to the West and the non-West, the West being the coloniser or imperialiser and the non-West being the colonised or imperialised, with the colonisation of Ireland being generally conceived as an exceptionalism. Radical, comparative postcolonialism is the name of a thoroughgoing interrogation of this massive misrecognition of colonialism and imperialism.

The case of Raymond Williams is interesting or even "symptomatic" on many levels. The British Empire, at the height of its imperialistic world vocation, was the most extensive empire the world had ever known. In 1914, at the start of the first great inter-imperialist war of the twentieth century, known as the First World War, the group of small countries known as the British Isles which together are about the size of Uganda or the Federal Republic of Germany held dominion over more than three quarters of the world's territorial communities. It will perhaps forever remain a fascinating subject how this amalgamated group of isles on the northern tip of Western Europe the size of Uganda came to control such a vast expanse of the earth's surface and this point has indeed fired the imaginations of many historians and theorists of imperialism. But one aspect of this vast world-historical process has not received wide attention, and we need urgently to begin to address it and its many ramifications. Let me elaborate briefly on these issues.

More than any other European country, Britain had centuries of preparation at home in the British Isles itself for this vocation of empire building throughout the world; it had centuries-long preparation that derived from the ways in which, within the British Isles, the English established colonial dominion over the Irish, the Scots and the Welsh. It is indeed the great success of this prior preparation that serves, if not as an explanation, definitely as the historical coordinate of Raymond Williams' repression of the impact of colonial-imperial projects at home and overseas on British life, culture and society in the modern period in such great works of his as *The Long Revolution* and *Culture and Society*. In other words, once the colonial-imperial project had more or less been accomplished within the British Isles, once the all-important ideological and cultural links between capitalistic colonisation and progress or modernity had been secured at home in the British Isles, colonisation and imperialism would henceforth be constructed and endlessly reproduced as basically and exclusively something that happened between, on the one hand, Britain and, on the other hand, its overseas colonial dominions, this binarism being generalisable to the West and the non-West. What is truly astonishing in the British case about this binary construction of the West and the non-West is the fact that even though the *legalistic-constitutional* consolidation that incorporated England, Scotland and Wales into the amalgamated British state dates back to the Constitutional Settlement of 1688, the massive work of creating a British identity based on the hegemony of England and Englishness over Wales and Welshness and Scotland and Scottishness took at least another hundred years and, more importantly, dovetailed into and ran parallel to building and consolidating British imperial hegemony overseas.

From this brief profile, we can begin to provide a rough outline of radical, comparative postcolonialism that Edward Said designated "post-imperialist discourse." At the base of all formations and discourses of postcolonialism is the polarity of the West and the non-West, the one as the imperialiser and the other as the imperialised. All formations of postcolonialism of course accept that the range of experiences, histories and traditions extend far beyond this polarity, but virtually all are constructed on the almost unassailable conviction that the polarity of the West and the non-West constitutes the base of the formation of collective identities and subjectivities in nearly all regions of the world in the last two centuries, especially with regard to the deeply problematic connections and equations between colonialism, progress, rationality and modernity.

In both senses of the word "radical," radical comparative postcolonialism takes issue with this formulation, first by going back to the deep roots of modern colonial-imperial projects in the West itself, secondly by moving athwart most of the contemporary formations and discourses of postcolonialism, especially in their academic institutionalisation as curricular programmes and research and teaching agendas. Going back to the roots and at the same time moving in as yet mostly uncharted territory can only at the beginning be a provisional effort. With that cautionary observation in mind, in what follows I wish to focus on two particular areas of the intellectual explorations of colonialism and postcolonialism that are particularly susceptible to the fundamental redirection projected by radical, comparative postcolonialism. Since these domains are both distinct and closely interlinked, there is a need to give a careful outline of both their distinctiveness and their divergences.

One domain is the very broad, very capacious subject of discourses and practices around the "civilising mission" as by far the most serviceable and at the same time the most contradictory and utterly discredited justificatory ideology of Western colonialism outside the West, and the other is the much more focused topic of the composite range of academic disciplines which either emerged from, or achieved legitimacy within the intellectual cultures of the colonial-imperial projects of the West, in Europe, itself around what scholars have aptly designated the "civilising process." In other words, in Europe, in the West itself, the "civilising process;" but overseas in the colonies in the non-Western world, the "civilising mission." Now, my basic contention is that we cannot, we ought not to talk of one without the other. In other words, I would argue that it is time to move to the complex but profoundly significant articulation between the civilising process (cp) and the civilising mission (cm) as the enabling conditions, the intellectual and ideological condition of possibility for the emergence and consolidation of academic disciplines that were highly serviceable to the colonial-imperial projects both inside and outside Europe.

One of my greatest surprises in the research I have been conducting for this project of radical, comparative postcolonialism has been the failure, so far, to find serious, sustained attempts to explore connections between these two processes, "cp" and "cm." Where a link between the two is at all perceived, it is very tenuously made. My contention is that the "civilising process" in Europe and the "civilising mission" in the colonies are in fact fundamentally continuous and linked: one prepares the ground, the premises for the other.

Now, what is the "civilising process" in Europe? I must state here that my views on this topic are deeply influenced by the work of many cultural historians and philosophers, chief among whom are Norbert Elias and Michel Foucault. In fact, Elias' book on this subject is titled, precisely, *The Civilising Process*. Its English translation is published by Basil Blackwell; it is a monumental and seminal work. In my opinion, this is one of the most important books on the cultural projects of modernity; it is an absolute "must read" for anyone involved in cultural studies and cultural criticism at the present time. It meticulously describes and analyses the "civilising" of manners, conduct and personality which began in early modern Europe and extended into the period of the emergence of capitalism and the formation of the modern nation-state in Europe. As Elias describes and analyses it, this "civilising process" is a comprehensive project which pervades every facet of subjectivity and identity, from the minutest details of daily life and bodily experience such as the management of bodily effusions and the evacuation of waste, to large-scale macro-political processes like the formation of states and the monopolisation of power. What this gigantic project ultimately entailed is the formation of a certain type of personality which would be the ideal, prototypical "civilised" modern subject.

At every level, this ideal "civilised" modern subjectivity is constituted in opposition to instincts, dispositions and expressions that are considered wild, unsanitary, spontaneous and carnal. Seen from this angle, Elias' work is supplemented by the work of Michel Foucault in such books and monographs as *Madness and Civilisation*, *Discipline and Punish*, *The Birth of the Clinic* and *History of Sexuality*. In sum then, the "civilising process" entailed the separation of what is considered "civilised," rational and modern from what is deemed savage, irrational and unmodern. It dovetailed with the economic processes of class formation in Europe, as the transition from late feudalism to early capitalist modernity took place, providing the cultural sanctions for the separation of the lower social orders from the middle and upper classes. One has only to look at the discourses of the "civilising process" as it pertained to certain groups, certain nationalities, and even certain so-called "races" in Europe itself to see that nearly all of the stereotypes and phobic projections that were later applied to "natives" in the colonies in the course of the "civilising mission" – or "cm" as I shall henceforth refer to it – had been formulated and given their gestation in Europe's autotelic "civilising process" – henceforth "cp." Examples and instances of these are discourses about Gypsies, about Jews, about the Irish in connection with the colonisation of Ireland by the English, discourses about southern Europeans in relation to northern Europeans, and even discourses about the working poor in Europe. All of these discourses had inherent in them notions of who was "civilisable" or not, who was educable or not. Those who were not deemed educable or "civilisable" provided the stereotypes that were later applied to the "natives " in the colonies. Indeed, when I say "later applied," this has to be qualified because, at a certain historical moment, both projects – "cp" and "cm" – became parallel and directly continuous with each other. In fact, on the basis of this point, I argue that this is the missing element in Edward Said's seminal work, Orientalism, because Said ignores the fact that some of the stereotypes, some of the Orientalist constructions that were applied to the East were also applied to certain groups in Europe itself in connection with this gigantic project of the so-called "civilising process."

Because they are such gigantic, all-encompassing and contradictory processes, the scholarship, respectively, on "cp" and "cm" is vast. For instance, when I used the search engines of the World Wide Web to check on what is available on-line on both, I found 30, 000 hits for "cp" and 18,1000 for "cm." Of course, some of the individual items are no more than a sentence or an allusion in a book or article. But quite a substantial number are in the nature of substantial essays, monographhs and books. For me, for the project of radical, comparative postcolonialism, what is interesting is that virtually no link has been made between "cp" and cm," even though the connections are literally crying to be made. One connection that I find particularly engrossing is that of the in-built contradictions that marked the limits of "cp" in Europe and the "cm" in the colonies outside Europe. I would argue that in many ways the scholarly exploration of this connection between the contradictions of "cp" in Europe and those of the "cm" in the colonies outside Europe provides tremendous and exemplary oppositional resources for engaging imperialist politics everywhere in the world. Let me explain this carefully.

At the base of "cm" is the "civilising" of the colonised natives through education and instruction. But this is not merely or only through the formal educational institutions, although this was deemed a key element of "cm."

Educating the natives so as to "civilise" them was deemed to cover absolutely all spheres of life. In the panoptic view of the colonisers, it was to make "them," the "natives," the colonised, love "our" language, "our" religion, "our" philosophy, "our" arts, "our" ways of seeing the world, "our" mode of being, and above all, "our" way of seeing *them*. Make them accept that to *be* is to be like us, not in *their* chosen modes of being like us, but in our modes of being like ourselves. And precisely on that point, the project of "cm" ran into its phenomenological, not to say ideological limits, for how do you distinguish between *their* modes of being like *us* from our modes of being like ourselves, if we're not them and indeed refuse to be like them? And moreover, if all of them became like us, then we would have lost the rationale for ruling over them, not to mention the fact that this would take away our ability to exploit and dominate them and through that dominate the world. It was on the basis of the recognition of such limits that the project of "cm" almost everywhere in the colonial world was severely restricted to only sections of "native" populations. The thinking was: "civilise" just so many of them and not more, or else you are laying the foundations of your eventual defeat, especially in light of the fact that quite a number of them don't want to be "civlised" by us anyway, just as some of our own kin back home have been resistant to being refashioned into properly modern, civilised, bourgeois forms of subjectivity, as some of the books of Bataille and Foucault, among others, demonstrate.

I have invoked the names of Norbert Elias and Michel Foucault with regard to the vocation of "cp" within Europe. It is particularly interesting to compare similarities and parallels in their respective explorations of the violently coercive and repressive core of the touted humanising, lofty values of "cp." Again, this is a subject that, as far as I can tell from my investigations, has not received the attention of the vast scholarship on Foucault and Elias. And on this particular point, my Internet search registered 196,000 hits for Foucault and 114,000 for Elias. (Parenthetically, it is noteworthy that Foucault registered a far greater number than did Derrida and moreover, at 109,000 hits, Derrida registered fewer than Elias.)

As anyone who has read Elias' *The Civilising Mission* knows, our author meticulously tracks the "civilising" and "educating" of manners and conduct in Europe for nearly six centuries, going through a mountain of advice books and conduct manuals from the Middle Ages to nearly the present. Elias' objective is as crystaline as it is magisterial: to demonstrate the remarkable changes that occured in the content and modes of advice on manners, etiqette and attitudes, some of which would be deemed indecent and embarrassing to write or talk about today, except possibly by sassy, iconoclastic, counter-culture stand-up comics. Some of the changes registered by Elias over the centuries are startling in their similarities with Foucault's plottting of the maturation of the human sciences in their repressive, disciplinary effects. For instance, much in the manner in which

Foucault in *Madness and Civilisation* demonstrates that "madness" had its own voice and was free and unconfined before it became constructed as the Other of Reason, so does Elias demonstrate that between the 15th and 16th centuries, advice on courtesy, civility and personal comportment was a matter of public discourse and was remarkably frank and unfussily explicit. For instance, no less a figure than Erasmus wrote about as small, or by the standards of the age, as great a matter of how to blow one's nose into a handkerchief, adding that one should not examine the contents of the handkerchief afterwards, "as if looking for pearls." According to Elias, from such openness and frankness, a change began to occur in advice on manners, noticeably betwen the late 17th and early 18th century when, in the words of one commentator, "Open justifications are offered less and less; one is mannerly because it is the proper and polite thing to do and the implication is that "uncivilised" manners are both wrong and unspeakable, this marking the beginning of repression." By the end of the 18th century, according to Elias, the sequence of processes that would ultimately make for the massive repression of emotions in modern civilisation was more or less in place. It is remarkable that these are roughly the same datelines plotted by Foucault in several of his books with regard to the consolidation of the human sciences as disciplines that produced knowledges that rationalised and legitimated the large-scale surveillance, disciplining and administering of the persons and bodies of entire populations through initial test runs made on the bodies of targetted groups such as mad people, criminals, vagrants, the inmates of institutions like hospitals and asylums, homosexuals, racial minorites and foreigners, children and special categories of women such as "witches" and destitute, umarried, subaltern women.

It must be admitted that bringing Foucault and Elias together in the manner in which I am proceeding here is, intellectually speaking, going out on a limb. For one thing, the term "civilising process" is Elias's; it is not part of Foucault's conceptual or methodological armory at all. Equally important, Elias was a sociologist, whose influence has not really extended beyond the ranks of the social sciences, and even there, Elias's followers are not in the main the most theoretically daring and innovative of social scientists. Moreover, Foucault's mode of theorising is considerably more subversive of established social and intellectual hierarchies than Elias's. But once these and other important differences between the two have been acknowledged, I believe that Foucault can be critically but very productively assimilated into Elias's magisterial outline of the place of "cp" in the construction of European modernity on the basis of oppressions, reifications and alienations which derived from those constitutive polarities of savagery and civilisation, the life of the instincts and the pressures toward sublimation in all spheres of modern life, and above all else, the separation between the educable and civilisable as opposed to the uneducable and uncivilisable. In other words, Foucault in the conceptual universe of "cp" is a Foucault rendered more insightful for engaging the knowledge-power nexus in both "cp" and "cm" than Foucault on his own, especially the later Foucault. For instance, much has been written on late 18th, 19th and early 20th century disciplines and discourses that were based on data and "knowledge" observed and collected in the Third World under the aegis of colonialism: travelogues; the accounts of explorers and the diaries of mission-aries; anthropology, geography and cartography; ethno-linguistics as contrasted with comparative linguistics; and discourses of race in connection with phrenology. But it is hardly ever the case that discussion of these is brought into consideration with the rise of the human sciences as the foun-dation of reifying positivist social science in the service of domination and repression in Europe, as outlined by Foucault, or, which is an extension of the same point, with the combination of Foucault and Elias that I am urging in these observations.

This is an appropriate moment in this essay in which to return to the ques-tion which I formulated as "Is there a postcolonial text in this theory?" The question which provides the point of departure for the essay. In engaging this question, I wish for the last time in this to briefly invoke the case of another canonical figure of twentieth century Western high intellectualism as a counter or contrast with the example of Raymond Williams that I alluded to earlier. This is none other than Jurgen Habermas.

In an interview which was originally published in the *New Left Review* in 1985 and subsequently republished in a collection of major interviews with Habermas titled *Autonomy and Solidarity: Interviews with Jurgen Habermas*, this tower-ing figure of the European intellectual left, a scholar who is indisputably one of the foremost philosophers of the second half of the twentieth century, was asked the following question, which I am rendering in a paraphrase that is almost a verbatim reproduction: At the expense of any consideration of capi-talism as a global system, the Frankfurt School tradition as a whole concentrated its analyses upon the most advanced capitalist societies; in your view, do the anti-capitalist and anti-imperialist struggles of the Third World have any bearing on the tasks of democratic socialism in the West and conversely, does your own analysis of advanced capitalism have any bearing on the struggles in the Third World? Habermas' answer was "no" on both aspects of the question: "the struggles in the 'Third World' have no lessons for "us" in the advanced capitalist societies of the West and I don't think what I have to say about the struggles in the West has any bearing on "their" struggles out there." In fairness, let me say that Habermas did add that he was quite aware that this response was, in his own words, " a eurocentrically limited view," but nonetheless he stuck to the response anyway and added that he would rather pass on that particular question and move on to other questions.

It is important to emphasise that what Habermas is saying in this frank and stunning admission to being Eurocentric is not an example of what could be described as vulgar or garden-variety Western ethnocentrism. Furthermore, I would also distinguish it from the long and hallowed tradition of gratuitous and violent ethnocentrism of a shockingly great number of the most eminent of Western philosophers and intellectuals, about many of whom Said in *Culture and Imperialism* has some rather very interesting things to say. (Parenthetically, one of these is that the reason why the great figures of the Western intellectual and philosophical tradition were so totally un-selfconscious in being openly and blatantly racist and ethnocentric in ways that we find unbelievable today is because they were not only utterly convinced of Western superiority over all non-Western societies, they were also convinced of the durability, indeed the permanence of that superiority within the framework of the Western imperial domination of the world. On this account, adds Said, it was only when that sense of durability, of permanence began to be effectively challenged and began to crumble that Western ethnocentrism of the ideological, blatant, naturalised variety became self-conscious and went into decline.) Habermas belongs to neither the vulgar, garden variety of Western ethnocentrism nor the naturalised, ideological form that for a very long time was openly propagated by the biggest names in the Western intellectual tradition for nearly three centuries, from the 17th century to the beginning of the 20th century. What Habermas' position portends is both more limited and at the same time far more potent: he is saying that in the strictly *professional* aspects of the matter, his work as a philosopher does not require him to have any interest, any curiosity whatsoever in what happens in the Third World, just as he is utterly indifferent to the possibility that what he has to say as a professional philosopher would have any lessons for struggles in the Developing World. Here we find, I would argue, the fold-ing of a *social* ("racial") identity as a European, a Westerner into a *professional* identity as a philosopher. In other words, what we have here is identity politics of a very special – reified and reifying – kind.

At the very least, it takes one's breath away that a philosopher whose most recent book bears the title of *The Future of Human Nature* says quite openly and with absolute self-composure that he has no interest at all in a dialogue with the vast majority of the human community in the so-called 'Third World.' Indeed, in what is perhaps his *magnum opus*, *The Philosophical Discourse of Modernity*, Habermas staged a comprehensive critical review of the debates over the alleged exhaustion or end of modernity, in the process critically laying bare and rejecting tendencies in modern Western thought to make seamless metonymic substitutions between and among Occidentalism, civilisation, rationality, modernity and humanity, with the corresponding construction of the Other of Reason, the Other of modernity and the Other of civilisation as the non-West and the marginalised groups of Western society. What accounts for this abyss between the audacious scope of Habermas' reflections on the phenomenon of humanity and modernity and his professed disinterest in engaging in dialogue with the so-called non-West?

On the surface, the problems opened up by this question seem adequately covered by the interpretive value of the power and scope of exemplarity, of precisely an *exemplum*: if you write well and powerfully and deeply enough about any region of the world, what you write can be of great, perhaps even invaluable significance for other parts of the world, including the least likely places in the world. In the light of this view, whether or not Habermas has any professional interest in the Third World, whether or not he feels any intellectual curiosity about, not to say solidarity with, the billions of souls in the developing world, his book *The Future of Human Nature* could still be of great value to the writers and scholars of the Third World. In my concluding sections of this essay I will be arguing against this resolution of the Habermasian conundrum and I shall be doing so on the basis of what in the subtitle of this essay I have called the contemporary crisis of disciplinary identities. For now, all I wish to say on this topic is that Habermas' discipline, philosophy, is one of the last remaining disciplinary strongholds for the open and self-assured expression of, again to use Habermas' own words, a "eurocentrically limited view" even when an academic presumes to speak for, or with regard to the entirety of the human community. To this assertion, I would simply add that within the discipline of philosophy, that position is more and more being radically challenged and being rendered, if not entirely moribund, then defensively rearguard.

In case this last point seems extreme, I invite anyone who has read Habermas' *The Philosophical Discourse of Modernity* with as much profit as I have to re-read the vigorous, serial and extended critiques that Habermas makes in the book against the likes of Georges Bataille, Jacques Derrida and Michel Foucault on the precise question of the *disciplinarity* of philosophy. For Habermas: Bataille, Derrida and Foucault are the archenemies of Western, subject-centred rationality, especially with regard to the equation of rationality with modernity, civilisation and humanism. The ferocious assaults that Bataille, Derrida and Foucault wage against Reason in the name of a radically skeptical anti-modernity is, in Habermas' view, possible only because they went far outside philosophy qua philosophy to marshal their arguments which otherwise could not logically and convincingly be made within the protocols of philosophy. Whatever one thinks of the merits of this critique, what for me, at any rate, is crucial is that Habermas in these critiques makes no allowance whatsoever for inter-disciplinarity, for even tactical cross-disciplinarity as far as the critique of modernity via rationality is concerned. This is all the more surprising because Habermas demonstrates throughout the book not only his deep and extensive knowledge of aesthetic modernism, literary criticism and even mythology and mysticism, he in fact exudes considerable enthusiasm for these disciplines and discourses. In the face of the forcefulness of this anti-interdisciplinarity, this strict and rather rigid disciplinarity on the subject of the anti-modernity of Bataille, Derrida and Foucault, Habermas' expressed lack of interest in dialogue of any kind with the Third World seems indeed to derive from his conception of how far you can muddy the disciplinary waters of philosophy.

This profile of Habermas, which I admit is partial and in no way exhaustive of the entirety of his oeuvre, provides a useful backdrop for our hanging question of "Is there a postcolonial text in this theory?" For, at the core of the *professional* and intellectual interests of the most visible and perhaps influential postcolonial theorists in North America is an engagement of the two disavowals or refusals that we see in Habermas: the policing of the boundaries of philosophy on the vast subject of modernity and anti-modernity; and the exclusion of the non-West from the conversation. If I may express this self-positioning in terms of a slogan or a succinct manifesto which is not too reductive, it would go something like this: Like Bataille, Derrida and Foucault, we postcolonial theorists and critics will muddy the waters of philosophy, and whether or not you want to talk to us, we will talk about you and your Momma and your Daddy, and we will do so to your children, whom it is our obligation to teach! From this made-up slogan, I would argue that what we have in the postcolonial theorists in vogue in the Western academy are Third World Europeanists eloquently and powerfully against Eurocentrism but nonetheless deeply enamored of European philosophy and high intellectualism. In a precise formulation, I would name the bodies of the texts that endlessly engage their professional interests, texts and discourses that fuel their intellectual energy as the Western archives on the making of modern subjectivities, principally in the non-Western colonies but also in the metropolitan centres of the Western world. To the centrality of these Europeanist texts and discourses I would, of course, add the texts and discourses of the anti-colonialist nationalists of the high period of the decolonising movements: Gandhi, C.L.R. James, Fanon, Césaire, Mandela.

Both of these two bodies of texts and discourses are generally treated to devastating deconstructive readings by our postcolonial theorists, since the underlying view is that the two bodies of texts are mostly mirror images of one another. The view that Western textual archives – and not the Anglophone, Francophone, Hispanophone and Lusophone writings of the postcolonial countries – constitute core *postcolonial texts* is a profoundly counterintuitive response to the question, "Is there a postcolonial text in this theory?" especially where this view also conceives of nationalist texts as mostly or even merely derivative texts, products of the "colonial library," in Valentin Mudimbe's memorable phrase.

About this state of affairs two important things can be said. One is the fact that this view of what constitutes *core* postcolonial texts has served to considerably complicate and de-naturalise the view that the postcolonial writings of South Asia, the Caribbean, Africa, South America, Australasia and the Pacific region and minorities and Diasporic communities in North America and Europe ought, *naturally*, to constitute the primary or even exclusive canon of postcoloniality. Secondly however, as the significance and influence of many of these writings have become established aspects of the cultural and intellectual history of the present historical moment, revisions are being made on all sides as to the scope of what counts as *postcolonial* texts. Perhaps it is useful to give some significant examples here.

Two decades ago, Ngũgĩ wa Thiong'o loudly announced that henceforth he was no longer going to write in English but in Kiswahili and Kikuyu since, according to him, all Europhone African writings were not valid or authentic expressions of African literature. But in the last three years, Ngugi has substantially reviewed and fine-tuned that momentous decision. He has not exactly gone back to writing exclusively or primarily in English; what he has done is continue to write in Kikuyu while doing their translations into English himself. There is also the case of Gayatri Spivak and the ways in which she has considerably broadened the range of her textual repertoire and scholarly energy to include translations of significant writings from Bengali, together with critical commentaries on the translated texts. The case of Edward Said is particularly exemplary. This is perhaps best conveyed in the distance that Said traversed between *Orientalism* and *Culture and Imperialism* and the books in between the two. Where the magisterial account of the Western constructions of orientalism in the earlier book had pretty much left the "orientalised" with little or no agency before the discursive and interpellative power of the massive, monolithic monologue that is orientalism, *Culture and Imperialism* is a sustained and generous reading of texts from both sides, the "West" and the "Orient." The weight is still tilted to Western textual archives, but on almost every page of the book, Said demonstrates that he has, as it were, "gone back to school" and has been reading or re-reading postcolonial texts in fiction, social theory, cultural critique and feminist struggles from many regions of the developing world, all with a keen eye to powerful oppositional responses to imperialism. Is it pushing the logical premises of my arguments in this essay too far to see in these three examples instances of a refashioning of *disciplinary* and professional identities in the face of the great contestations and debates around social identities in our crises-ridden but ever-expansively multicultural world?

In bringing this to a conclusion, I would like to return very briefly to the idea with which I started, this being the notion that this is merely the outline of a prolegomenon to a big subject of research and writing; an outline of a prolegomenon, not even the prolegomenon itself. This is another way of frankly admitting that I realise all too well that I have barely scratched the surface of a huge subject in this essay. Rarely is the notion, the reality of identity in and of disciplinary and professional interpellations, ever encountered in contemporary discourses on identity politics and its achievements and discontents. This is hardly surprising given the hugely crucial fact that the notion itself of identities formed and structured through disciplinary and professional interests and investments is greatly under-theorised. And if this is the case, how could one hope for or demand that we pay vigilant and nuanced attention to the articulations between both vectors of identity, the local and specific space of the disciplinary and general and much contested spaces of the social? Is this not like putting the cart before the horse, the monograph before its prolegomenon?

But in postcolonial theory and postcolonial studies, there can be no question whatsoever that this question has been put over and over again, even if scant acknowledgment of this fact has been made. Raymond Williams famously put the question to himself at the very end of his professional life and close to the end of his biological existence. And as I hope to have demonstrated in my extensive review of the associated limits and contradictions of the civilising process in Europe ("cp") and the civilising mission in the colonies ("cm"), post-colonial studies implies a necessarily *comparative* dimension that greatly amplifies and expands these issues.

Radical, comparative postcolonialism, or if you wish, "rcp," is one site of this expanded scope of the postcolonial, with a precise location at the points where the rearticulations of the stereotypes, fictions and myths of "cp" and "cm" are coming back to haunt the contemporary world with a vengeance. A final word: if I may borrow from the comprehensive review of symptomatic articulations of *professional* and *social* identities that I have given in this lecture – Raymond Williams; Elias-Foucault; Ngugi; Spivak; Said – and couch my formulation in a quasi-mathematical equation, here's how I would describe radical, comparative postcolonialism: rcp = cm + cp raised to the power of zero and calibrated by an anti-capitalist, anti-imperialist ecofeminism!

# Literary Visions of a 21st Century Africa: A Note on the Pan African Ideal in Ghanaian Literature[1]

## Kofi Anyidoho

In her poem "Images of Africa at Century's End" Ghanaian writer Ama Ata Aidoo briefly reviews the history of Africa in its largely disastrous encounter with Europe and ends with a prospective view formulated into a very crucial question:

> when folks figure
> you are their slave
> your past belongs to them.
>
> And mind you, The Man will try
>            to grab our future too.
>
> Shall we let him?[2]

Earlier in the poem, Aidoo recalls the violence and distortion African civilisation has suffered, such as is symbolised in the "corrective surgery" said to have been ordered by Napoleon on the nose of the Sphinx "for not-at-all-looking like/his." The story does not end with Napoleon. We are warned of the likelihood of an even more complete appropriation, in the 21st century, of African civilisation and all its resources:

> But in the year 2020
> The New Sphinx would be unveiled
>
> full visage on view
> straight nose raised
> thin-lips tight
> and even, may be, blue-eyed:

a perfect image of the men
who vested so much interest
in his changing face.

The final question of Aidoo's poem is left unanswered, but there are important clues to be deduced from the fact that she dedicates the poem to Cheikh Anta Diop, John Henrik Clarke and Ivan van Sertima, among others. Quite clearly, these are pre-eminent pioneers in the building of solid intellectual foundations for a combative and self-determining Pan African agenda for the 20th century and beyond. It is significant to note that some of the earliest work towards the intellectual foundations of a Pan African agenda for the 20th century is to be found in Casely Hayford's 1911 classic *Ethiopia Unbound*.[3] Hayford's book was firmly dedicated to a Pan African ideal, to the liberation of African peoples worldwide from the incapacitating effects of slavery and colonialism. To achieve such liberation, Hayford seems to suggest, there was an urgent need for the re-education of African peoples.

We note also that when Kwame Nkrumah in his Pan African vision eventually urged the University of Ghana to establish an Institute of African Studies, he used the occasion of the formal inauguration of the Institute to restate many of the points earlier advanced by Hayford:

> One essential function of this Institute must surely be to study the history, culture and institutions, languages and arts of Ghana and of Africa in new African centred ways – in entire freedom from the propositions and pre-suppositions of the colonial epoch, and from the distortions of those professors and lecturers who continue to make European studies of Africa the basis of this new assessment. By the work of this Institute, we must re-assess and assert the glories and achievements of our African past and inspire our generation, and succeeding generations, with a vision of a better future.
>
> But you must not stop here. Your work must also include a study of the origins and culture of peoples of African descent in the Americas and the Caribbean, and you should seek to maintain close relations with their scholars so that there may be cross fertilisation between Africa and those who have their roots in the African past.[4]

It is a matter of considerable regret and of some embarrassment that despite such clearly articulated early agenda, universities in Ghana, and indeed all over the African continent, have not moved quickly enough to live up to the challenge of transforming themselves into major centres of intellectual and creative activity for the ultimate goal of a liberated and self-directed development of African societies and economies.

Fortunately, however, at least in the case of Ghana, we can isolate one group of people mostly associated with the university who have remained largely loyal to the Pan African vision laid out early in the last century by Hayford and later reformulated into a programme of action by Nkrumah. It is a remarkable fact that even during the era of independence in Africa, when many African political thinkers were understandably drawn to a narrow focus on mostly issues of national concern, several of the major Ghanaian creative writers gave serious consideration to Pan African concerns in their work. Ama Ata Aidoo in *The Dilemma of a Ghost* and in *Anowa*, raised an early voice on certain important implications of the slave trade and slavery for African peoples both at home and in the Diaspora. And in *Our Sister Killjoy*, she closely examined the new kind of enslavement and self-enslavement that has become a major and disturbing aspect of the neocolonial condition in Africa – the large numbers of Africa's migrant population mostly hustling their way into the former colonial metropolises only to find that life in these dream places so easily becomes a nightmare from which many have no energy to liberate themselves. Ayi Kwei Armah in *Why Are We So Blest?*, *Two Thousand Seasons* and *The Healers*, is unsparing in his diagnosis of the historical enslavement of African peoples and the mental bondage that has resulted from such enslavement.

As we move rapidly towards the close of the 20th century surrounded by an increasing deterioration in the material conditions of African people, we find something of a renewed vision in the works of this relatively older generation of Ghanaian writers. Kofi Awoonor in *Latin American & Caribbean Notebook* and in *Africa: The Marginalised Continent*, draws very closely on his duty tour as Ghana's Ambassador to Brazil, to Cuba, and to the United Nations, to reassess current and future prospects for African peoples in a New World Order that seems to give little, if any credit, to Africa's participation in the creation of the wealth of the nations of the world. In several of the poems in *Latin American & Caribbean Notebook*, we find a new kind of realism, often captured in a call for struggle towards a fuller participation in not only the planting of the fields but also in the harvest and the feast that must follow. These frequent calls for struggle take us beyond *Comes the Voyager at Last*, with its somewhat romantic and certainly mythical reunion of the Diaspora-born Brother Lumumba with the Mother continent from which his ancestors were torn away in a long trail of historical agonies across deserts and oceans into the jail houses of America as Babylon.

The poet Kwesi Brew in "Return of No Return," focuses his attention on an important aspect of Africa-Diaspora relations such as we find unfolding in Ghana of today. Almost as in the days of independence, an increasing number of Diaspora Africans are returning to Ghana, mostly to renew their contact with the "Motherland," occasionally to explore possibilities for a final return.

Significantly, the single most important stop on this voyage of return is inevitably the slave forts and castles at Cape Coast and Elmina. Kwesi Brew's title poem for the volume dwells at length on the paradoxes of Africa's furious history, symbolised in the slave fort or castle seen originally as the point or gate of no return, and now transforming, after many centuries, into a healing point of welcoming contact, though still filled with memories of pain and of death.

Of the new work by the relatively older generation of Ghanaian writers, Ama Ata Aidoo's short story "She Who Would Be King"[5] stands out for the vision of the future it presents for the African continent and for African peoples at large. The main action of the story is set in the year 2026, but the dramatic narrative opens with a flashback that takes us to half a century earlier, in 1977, at which time we find a "she-of-10-years-old" promising, indeed swearing, that she intended to become the president of her country. Those who thought then that the little girl Adjoa Moji was out of her mind, wake up fifty years later to find that although she does not exactly perform her miracle, she certainly has laid the foundation by becoming Professor and Dean of the Faculty of Law at the University. The real miracle is soon wrought by her thirty-three-year-old daughter Afi-Yaa, who is "elected as the first president of the newly-formed Confederation of African States, CAS or rather The CASE, for short." Perhaps, before we begin to applaud the delightful optimism of this short narrative, we must pause briefly to ponder the many trials African people must yet endure between the time of writing this story and the year 2010 which, according to Ama Ata Aidoo, finally ushers in the New Era of Hope:

> The entire continent went through hell in the last forty years of the 20th Century, and the first ten years of this century. She had been in hell of one kind or another for exactly five hundred years. But those fifty were something special. Man-made but accidental, man-made and deliberate, homegrown, imported, natural. Name it. If it was a calamity, Africa suffered it.
>
> At the height of the AIDS epidemic, the priests from different religions had had to set up camp in the cemeteries from 8 o'clock in the morning, and did not leave until late at night. To cheer themselves up, everybody joked that burials had become the hottest 9 to 5 job in town with no pay for overtime.
>
> Then there was The Drought. At its worst, those who were paranoid had said that white folks were fiddling with the planet – "They are fixing Africa to face the sun permanently..." "They are trying to fry us." "...part of the Great Plot to wipe us off the surface of the earth. So they will be free to take our continent completely. Instead of just holding on to it by devious and vicious means...."

The real tragedy was that in those days, you could find plenty of support for such fears. And very little to discount them with.[6]

Such delicate juxtaposition of despair and hope, of beautiful dream and negative reality, of elevating vision and cruel, relentless history, seems to be a recurring feature of much of this literature of a Pan African agenda for the 21st century. Perhaps it is all too tempting, and possibly fatal, to dwell too much on the glories of Africa's ancient civilisations or of a visionary, unified and viable Africa, without paying sufficient attention to the reality of Africa's current problems, without any reasonable suggestions as to how Africa lost her ancient glory and how best she may (re)gain that future glory. It is in this regard that we must salute Ama Ata Aidoo, especially in several of the poems in *An Angry Letter in January & Other Poems* and in some of the stories in *The Girl Who Can & Other Stories*, for taking on the difficult task of opening our minds to the possibility of an African renaissance, even as she details for us the gravity of many burdens that weigh heavy on Africa's past, present, and future. In so doing, Aidoo is very much at centre stage with other Ghanaian writers of her generation in writing a 21st century African future rescued from the despairs of 20th century Africa.

It is to such Future Africa that much of Ayi Kwei Armah's recent work is totally dedicated as foundational intellectual and creative work, such as we find in his last two novels, and in his 1996 Du Bois, Padmore, Nkrumah Memorial Lectures.[7] In *Osiris Rising*, we find a powerful demonstration of total dedication to painstaking intellectual labour in the cooperative efforts of the circle of creative minds to which the two principal characters – Ast [for Isis] and Asar [Osiris] – belong. In *KMT*, Armah insists on the need for common purpose, of companionship, in the life-long journey into knowledge of the self, knowledge of the craftsmanship of the soul:

> I will work with you to retrieve the fragments of our murdered memory. Let me be your companion on the forgotten paths of Maat....Let us work to turn forgotten paths into the remembered way. Let us mix the long memories of a people destroyed with new narratives of our own making, as we move into space of our own choosing, as we dream in images woven from our people's best desires, as we plan on designs drawn from our own reflection, then make again the universe that might have been but was not, here in this place, now in this time freed for our new creation.
>
> I will walk with you away from the superhighways of forgetfulness onto the paths of remembrance. Together we shall breathe energy into the faded memories of a people once destroyed. Let us walk together, invoking the future into now. (12–13)

In both novels, Armah's narrative warns us that this new vocation dedicated to Maat, the ancient kemetic principle of truth and justice, is no easy option, but fraught with unimaginable danger, as seen in the tragic end to the life and career of Asar in *Osiris Rising* and of Biko Lema in *KMT*, both of them cut down in their prime by ruthless forces opposed to a future of self-determination for African peoples. Indeed, the price tag on a prosperous Future Africa is indeed high, but every one of these writers, from Hayford to Awoonor, from Armah to Aidoo, reassures us that there is an ultimate victory worth fighting for, maybe even worth dying for.

# Writing for the Child in a Fractured World[1]

## Naana Jane Opoku-Agyemang

The topic has a deliberate contradiction. This opposition lies in an unusual correlation of the noun: "child" and the adjective: "fractured." The word "child" raises connotations of innocence, happiness, a time of assumed minimal consciousness of some of the pressures of the external world that can lead to its fracture. It is by no accident that children everywhere, regardless of race, class or other issues that might categorise them, behave in similar ways of being: playing, crying, laughing, creating and imitating adults. In particular, children like to be the same or appear to want to be the same. The sameness rests on the notion of an un-fractured world. A case in point is the school uniform that speaks to this psychology. On the one hand it is imposed, but in reality, it conforms to the ways, I think, in which children would like to see themselves and each other. Let me illustrate further. In countries where children in public schools do not wear school uniforms, it is interesting to observe them in their outfits for school. Nearly every child will wear jeans, running shoes, a jacket and a backpack. The differences would occur in the design and brand, betraying the economic standing of the child's parents or caregivers. I understand some knife each other for the jackets. Still on definition of our major terms, in contrast to the usual connotation of "child," the adjective "fractured" connotes something splintered, broken, cracked. The topic, then, makes a very bold attempt to recognise the hiatus that might occur in the world of the child and the ways in which the writer could identify and deal with this reality.

In other words, the world of the child may be so distorted that the smiles on parents' and adults' faces may stall, while some words such as "war" and "fight" and "soldier" and "gun" and "bullet" and "cutlass" and "kill" and "flee" and many others in this word category, may float around too often for any child's comprehension. The child's world may be plagued by disease, poverty, war, violent crimes such as robbery and rape. In what ways do we bring this reality to the world of the child? I suppose there are many, effective ways of achieving this. One way is to write directly about them, so that the child knows. Another may be, through the writing to empower the child to be able to deal with these. I choose to dilate on the latter. My thesis is very simple, I think: While focusing on the African child, both on the continent and in the Diaspora, I propose to lead the child to the recognition that the fracturing exists and, more importantly, that s/he can positively affect this anomaly. I do not intend to rehash the catalogue of woes that besiege us regardless of where we find ourselves, how rich the countries of our recent sojourn are supposed to be, whether potentially or in practice. The fact is that our world is fractured by many, many issues, too well known to be repeated here. To imagine a world without fracturing is not real; to prepare the child to understand and to recognise and deal with it is so. My words are directed at the writer for the African child: Please find ways of bestowing confidence in the child, because the fracturing must be confronted. There are also times when I will speak directly to the child: *Do believe that, yes, you can!*

The writing must demonstrate that we have not always been like this, singing for our food, our beautiful children gaining world fame through images with their fly-invaded faces, standing by their mothers, their faces tired from over-breeding... *Dear child, you have not always been so portrayed, your beloved fathers spending the best part of their lives sitting under trees drinking pito or palm wine, or perpetually abusive or having no idea how to plan and care for their families and/or absent, at best. You have not always gained fame by the statistics that tell that you are likely to die before age five, are very likely to be orphaned through your parents' dying from the HIV/AIDS pandemic, that you are malnourished, are street children, child labourers, have no access to quality education. You have not always gained fame only by your effectual smiles on the cover of advertisement for the perpetually needy. Maybe some of this is true, but the images never tell how you ended up this way and the historical and current roles of the governments of those better blessed... Child, you must always read between the lines and ask questions.*

We have not always been defined for, thought for, decided for, planned for. We have not always been told that the problem is that we are too many and have too little... The reverse is true: we feed the world! We have not always, as a result, been told which part of our bodies to cover when in intimacy with our loved ones, how many children we should have, how to treat our men and women and children, with anyone, just anyone who looks unlike us placing themselves above us... surely we have not always been like this. But this is also part of our fracturing. But how do you prove it? Really? That we have not always begged? Lived at the razor edge of life? That we have not always fought for no reason, killed each other for fun? Been ravaged by disease, have not been the worst off in education, poverty, famine, living conditions? Been happy to be insulted at embassies because the unpardonable rudeness of some of their employees may lead to a visa acquisition out of this hell-hole? Most arrive in our country with no idea of the physical locations of our embassies in their countries? That they can apply through the mail? And we cannot? Has it always been like this? Even if with a genuine visa you could still be refused entry into their country? That our world has not always been like this? That our markets have not always been the receiving ground for discarded face- and hand- and bath- towels, brassieres, handkerchiefs, socks, undershirts, underpants, boxer shorts? That we have not always worn others' cast away clothes, for which we pay more than the value of those items in former lives? Really, that we have not always been like this? That we had the intellectuals and thinkers and astrologers, the artists, scientists, the mathematicians, the agriculturalists, the healers...But, where did that knowledge go?

Writing for the African child in a fractured world could look at our past and tell the story properly. And so, the writer may wish to educate the self in the process. Write about us in ancient Egypt, laying the foundation of life. The history is important once upon some time ago, when the world was not idyllic. But then, it has not always been idyllic – never was – and has no plans of being so. But tell them what one of their fathers, Ayi Kwei Armah, has reminded us all in *Two Thousand Seasons,* that:

> We are not a people of yesterday. Do they ask how many single seasons have flowed from our beginnings till now? We shall point them to the proper beginning of their counting. On a clear night when the light of the moon has blighted the ancient woman and her seven children, on such a night count first the one, then the seven, and after the seven all the other stars visible to their eyes.
>
> After that beginning they will be ready for the sand. Let them seek the sealine. They will not have to ponder where to start. Have them count the sand. Let them count it grain from single grain.
>
> And after they have reached the end of that counting we shall not ask them to number the raindrops in the ocean. But with the wisdom of the aftermath have them ask us again how many seasons have flowed by since our people were unborn. (1)

Tell them not to believe the story that the people from faraway lands originally came to buy gold and ivory and that it was only later that they bought and sold Africans because the Africans themselves were doing it. So that, but for the Africans setting a bad precedent, they themselves would never have bought or sold anyone. That cannot be true. After all you will not go home and insult your parents because someone else does so. Tell them that the story of how it came about that Africans are scattered everywhere and caused fracturing that is not yet sealed is more complex than that. Let these children read Ama Ata Aidoo's *The Dilemma of a Ghost* to appreciate the anguish of those so taken away, as they scramble to rediscover themselves. Let them understand that a huge lode in this narration is that Africans in Africa fought to save their kith and kin, and that the fight was taken up on the Middle Passage, did not stop at the plantations. Tell them the story of *Anowa* of Aidoo's play of the same title, and encourage them to see Anowa's distancing from the spoils of enslavement as an example of fighting back an enterprise that she calls "evil" and which Armah calls "a disease" in *The Healers*.

Encourage the African child in Ghana to visit the slave castles and forts, to visit the caves of Sankana, the defensive walls of Gwollu, the waters of Nzulezo and find out why the "Slave River of Assin Manso is so named. At these locations they should ask questions of the elders who live there; their versions make good supplement to the tour guides. And tell them to interrogate the established notion of amnesia, depicted as the mindless forgetfulness of Africans." Armah explains it this way, also in *The Healers*: remembrance and forgetfulness are played against each other:

> The events that have shattered our people were not simply painful events. They were disasters. They were strange, unnatural catastrophes. Those who survived them could only survive in part because they found ways to forget the catastrophes. When you're still close to the past danger that threatened to wipe you out, even remembrance pains you. Our people forgot a lot of things in order to survive. We even went beyond forgetfulness. To forget thoroughly the shattering and the dispersal of a people that was once whole, we were gone so far as to pretend we have always been silly little fragments each calling itself nation."
> "Is forgetfulness natural?"
> "It is natural, but only for a while, not for all time. Forgetfulness helps the diseased cross over the time of greatest pain. It is a sort of sleep like sleep brought on by herbs to help a sick man rest when his disease has exhausted him. In that case forgetfulness works towards health. But when the period of forgetfulness is prolonged unnaturally, then it doesn't work towards health. It works toward death." (98–99)

My dear writer, when you write for children, couch the story in such a way that they will end up asking the elders of their families many, many questions. Let them begin with the meaning of their own names. I don't mean names such as Eugene, Suzette, Janice, Kimberly, Nhyira...*My dear young reader, I mean the name your family went into counsel when you were born and decided to give you, in honour of a life well lived and in the hope you would emulate the best parts of the same; the name given you as a way of regulating your social behaviour, that you would grow to become a respected member of the family, community and country and the world; the name that encapsulated all the best hopes for life. Find out what it means and why you have such a name and what kind of life is expected of you. When you have understood that, find out the names of all your grandparents as far as memory will go and of all your fathers and mothers and siblings; find out also the meaning of your hometown and the meaning of the clan to which you belong, the meaning of their symbol. After this find out if your hometown has a festival. Find out its origin and significance. Then, when you are done, find out the name of your ethnic group and its history. And the names of other ethnic groups you know and their histories also. Such would begin to make your world non-fractured.*

And while at it, remember to write stories that tell them to listen to all advice, even what appears to be nonsensical at first. But, the stories should enjoin them to think for themselves and arrive at conclusions after careful reflection only. Their conclusions should never be based only on those of their teacher' parents, friends, favourite siblings, counselors, advisors, Sunday school teachers, pastors, although these may also be legitimate. They should consider all these, but the conclusions should be theirs only. Such is one path towards living their dream life in good health and dignity in a whole world. Let the young readers know that they should not be afraid to make mistakes; they should be afraid not to try; be afraid not to learn from errors; be afraid not to think for themselves; be afraid not to take charge; be afraid not to think they cannot positively affect the world in which they live; be afraid of anyone who thinks s/he is so right that everyone else is wrong. *Make friends with those who create the context for learning to occur; you must do the learning. You are old enough to know what is right; do it. You are old enough to know when someone makes untoward sexual advances at you. Scream "No!" even if the person is your friend, your parent, uncle, aunt, teacher, pastor, anyone, I said. And never believe it; you will not die if you tell. You will, if you don't. And so, you will heal your world and leave a less fractured world for the next generation.* Let them know that great men and women have gone before them and that they can learn from their examples.

A proper place to begin is to look at the examples of Kwame Nkrumah. Let our children understand, in spite of what is said about Osagyefo and how it is rendered, our country would definitely not have achieved a fraction of what we only have the effrontery to complain about, without him. Tell of this man who was born a little over one hundred years ago and who never tired singing the song of the freedom for Africans on the continent and in the Diaspora. The song is found in some seventeen publications that he authored; the refrain is always "Africa Must Unite." He sang the song so persistently as to affect the liberation of Africans in many artificially created geographical spaces paraded as countries and who, prior to that, had been submerged under four hundred years of enslavement and more than a hundred years of colonialism following the centuries of enslavement. Nkrumah would not have oppression as a condition of any life. And if he is described as ambitious for wanting good drinking water, quality schools, rapid development, affordable housing, good health care and above all, a sense of control of one's own affairs for his people, then clearly more is betrayed of those who called him so and what they thought of the people than even of the great liberator, one of the best and finest gifts of nature to the world.

And closely following at his heels was Patrice Lumumba, who would not countenance praise for his oppressors on the day he celebrates his hard won independence from the same. He had the misfortune of being forced to make huge decisions when he had barely assumed office as Prime Minister. But Lumumba represents a strong sense of altruism. He was for a unitary Congo and against division of the country along ethnic or regional lines, while, like many other African leaders, he supported Pan Africanism and liberation for colonial territories. He proclaimed his regime one of "positive neutralism," defined as a return to African values and rejection of any imported ideology. Lumumba was a man of strong character, who pursued his policies regardless of opposing viewpoints. Encourage the young reader to find out the details of his life and passing and to determine why the image of Patrice Lumumba continues to serve as an inspiration in contemporary Congolese politics. Responses to the fracturing of our world have been costly, but necessary.

*Today he is decorated with so many well-deserved honours, the man who was before then seen as such a threat that he was locked up for some twenty–seven years. And then he had the heart to let go, in the name of the peace for which he had paid such a huge price, as to have his family grow away from him, his children die without his presence at their funeral, his world go by inside the walls of a prison on Robben Island. The world icon Nelson Mandela has received many South African, foreign and international honours, including the Nobel Peace Prize in 1993, the Order of Merit, and the Order of St. John from Queen Elizabeth II, and the Presidential Medal of Freedom from George W. Bush. In July 2004, the city of Johannesburg bestowed its highest honour on Mandela by granting him the Freedom of the City at a ceremony in Orlando, Soweto. Read all about Mandela. You may wish to be reminded that but for his former wife, Winnie Mandela keeping his memory alive, perhaps his fate could have been very different.*

Tell them of the likes of Yaa Asantewaa: don't believe those who deride the women who think for themselves with the accolade "Yaa Asantewaa," as if it were negative; such is the depth of our fracture. There is nothing negative about the name; that attitude is symptomatic of a fractured world that has lost sight of its heroines and, as a result, of itself.

Just listen to her voice:

> Now I see that some of you fear to go forward to fight for our king. If it were in the brave days of Osei Tutu, Okomfo Anokye and Opoku Ware, chiefs would not sit down to see their king to be taken away without firing a shot. No European could have dared speak to chiefs of Asante in the way the governor spoke to you this morning. Is it true that the bravery of Asante is no more?

I cannot believe it. It cannot be! I must say this: if you, the men of Asante, will not go forward, then we will. We, the women, will. I shall call upon my fellow women. We will fight the white men. We will fight till the last of us falls in the battlefields.

Yaa Asantewaa remains a much-loved figure in Asante history and the history of Ghana as a whole for the courage she showed in confronting injustice during the colonialism of the British. Beginning in March 1900, the rebellion laid siege to the fort at Kumasi where the British had sought refuge. The fort still stands today as the Kumasi Fort and Military Museum. Tell the children to tell their teachers, on such an expedition, while at it, they should also visit the statue raised in her honour and remember that the fact of the establishment of the Yaa Asantewaa Girls'_Secondary School at Kumasi in 1960 with funds from the Ghana Educational Trust speaks to national respect for this brave woman. *To highlight the importance of encouraging more female leaders in Ghanaian society, Yaa Asantewaa remains a much-loved figure in Asante history and the history of Ghana as a whole for the courage she showed in confronting injustice during the colonialism of the British. But, you know, child, this did not happen out of context. There were such brave women in her household and all around her. Yaa Asantewaa continued a tradition of women who behave like ordinary human beings with brains and hands and wills and a desire to live a dignified life. This is still true. And many need no lessons based on theories that grew without them in mind in the first place.* Write the story in such a way that the young reader would want to find more out about the Ama Nkrumahs, the Mable Dove Danquahs, Sophia Dokus of Ghana and such women from across the continent and in her Diaspora… *After the list of known names, find out the life and daily schedule of the woman who sells food in your school compound, koko and kose and waakye and kenkey and fish along the road, the one who works tirelessly on the farm and smokes fish along the shore.* These women whose names do not feature on any pension scheme and do not make the news…along with their male counterparts, such should make us bow our heads in shame if we do not try harder and work to improve the lives of their children.

All these women have a history that should form part of the writing. The history includes the history of the Amazones. Yes, let the young reader know that we know how to stand up for ourselves and that women have been part of the process, all the time.

Tell of the Mino of present day Republic of Benin.

*Once upon a time between 1645 and 1685, King Houegbadja ruled from Dahomey, and seeing the bravery of women, originally started the group which would become the Amazons as a corps of elephant hunters called the gbeto. They were also the royal bodyguards. Houegbadja's son King Agadja (ruling from 1708 to 1732) developed the female bodyguard into a militia and successfully used them in Dahomey's defeat of the neighbouring kingdom of Savi in 1727. European merchants recorded their presence, as well as similar female warriors recruited westwards along the coast, who gained the reputation as fearless warriors, acquitting themselves* well in battle. Indeed the males in the army did not see them as a threat; they called the female warriors mino, meaning "our mothers" in the Fon language. The mino were supposed to hone any aggressive character traits for the purpose of war; they trained with intense physical exercise. Discipline was emphasised. They were given uniforms, equipped, and their units were under female command. They consisted of between 4000 and 6000 women, about a third of the entire Dahomey army. They defeated the French army which had to run crying to the foreign army for reinforcement. We do not tell this story because it gives joy to read that they beheaded their captives, but to let them know that African women have become marginalised; they have not always been. If they watch the film titled *Dahomey Cobra Verde*, by German director Werner Herzog; or read the novel *Flash for Freedom!* by George MacDonald Fraser and the scholarly work by Edna Bay, especially *Wives of the Leopard*, they will find out more about these brave women.

Write for our children about Queen Amina Sukhera, of the royal house of Zazzau, who reigned for some thirty-four years, during which she introduced the cultivation of kola nuts into her area; tell of how she became involved in the military, earning much admiration for her bravery. Her military achievements brought her great wealth and power. She is credited as the architect of the earthen walls around the city of Zaria, for which the province is named.

And remember to write about their forebears who include Nzinga of Ndongo and Matamba of Angola, *who would not be disrespected nor have her people reduced to slavery; she resisted the Portuguese well into her sixties, personally leading troops into battle, who bravely fought the Portuguese, refusing to go along with oppression. In her old age, she devoted her efforts to resettling former slaves. Despite numerous efforts to dethrone her, Nzinga would die a peaceful death at age eighty on December 17, 1633. Only her death accelerated the Portuguese occupation of the interior of South West Africa, fuelled by the massive expansion of the Portuguese slave trade. Today, she is remembered in Angola for her political and diplomatic acumen, great wit and intelligence, as well as her brilliant military tactics. In time, Portugal and most of Europe would come to respect her. A major street in Luanda is named after her, and a statue of her was placed in Kinaxixi on an impressive square. Angolan women are often married near the statue, especially on Thursdays and Fridays.*

The framing of the content of writing for the child in a fractured world is for the young reader to know that images of African women as carrying a child on her back, a load heavier than herself on her head, ill-fed, followed by a stream of ill-spaced malnourished children, producing more without reason nor control, helpless, needing others to tell her that she is oppressed, is a very recent creation. Some of these are true, but our history tells us we have not all uniformly been like this. Let the readers look around them to women in the markets; indeed encourage them to spend one afternoon in the market observing the work women do here and draw their own conclusions, especially after they have observed them on the farms, as they smoke or salt fish, process gari, palm oil, palm kernel oil, coconut oil, shea nuts, make kenkey, pito…and have participated in these activities… Tell them that there was a man called Kwame Nkrumah who, in the wilderness, wrote some seventeen songs but sang one of them that summed them all up. The song was titled: *Africa Must Unite!* He sang this in Ghana. Then to Ghana, Guinea, Mali, he continued the song by supporting the struggle to self-determination all over the continent and beyond. *That may surprise you, but people had to die to make the point that they could move about freely in the land of their own birth and have a say in who ruled over them. Yes, Kwame Nkrumah sang that song throughout Africa and beyond, to embrace Africans who live away from the continent, and indeed his song was as well for all peoples who lived under oppression. To dedicate one's life to the service of the disadvantaged is also to do the will of God. The world will be whole when we eliminate oppression and fear and greed and ingratitude and selfishness.* Tell them by showing them that it is possible to live a full, satisfying life without these vices. Let them know that it was not easy for Nkrumah; indeed he was compelled to live away from his immediate family and his mother whose only child he was, and from those who loved and appreciated him.

Please make sure, dear writer, that you tell of the enslaved Harriet Tubman: *cook, nurse, army general, her experience of life of ill-health, pain and deprivation resulted in preventing the same to fellows. She would ensure that others fled enslavement. Tubman became the first woman to lead an armed assault during the US Civil War. In 1849, Tubman escaped to Philadelphia, then immediately returned to Maryland to rescue her family. Slowly, one group at a time, she brought relatives with her out of the state, and eventually guided dozens of other slaves to freedom. Travelling by night and in extreme secrecy, Tubman (or "Moses," as she was called) "never lost a passenger," as she later put it at women's suffrage meetings. Large rewards were offered for the capture and return of many of the people she helped escape, but no one ever knew it was Harriet Tubman who was helping them. When the far-reaching United States Fugitive Slave Law was passed in 1850, she helped guide fugitives farther north into Canada, and helped newly freed slaves find work.* Include the part of the narrative that says that when the American Civil War began, Tubman worked for the Union Army, first as a cook and nurse, and then as an armed scout and spy. *The first woman to lead an armed expedition in the war, she guided the raid on the Combahee River, which liberated more than seven hundred slaves. Her examples recall the heroic efforts of her forebears, Nzingha and Yaa Asantewaa. Incidentally, as a child, Tubman was told that she was of Asante lineage. Listen to Harriet Tubman when it was clear she would be sold: "liberty or death; if I could not have one, I would have the other." She travelled by night and in secrecy to ensure her own safety and that of others.* Let the child reader find out why Harriet Tubman was called Moses. *Danger did not stop her; ingenuity and subterfuge aided her.*

And tell them that there lived for forty years a man who, when he changed his name from Malcolm Little to Malcolm X and to El-Hajj Malik El-Shabazz (Arabic: الشباز مالك الحاج ), was not indulging in an idle pastime; it was an impassioned effort to find himself, trying desperately to find the true African family name that he never could know. Tell the young readers not to take for granted their heritage and that, as Africans, they have in excess. Some of their cousins who live outside of the continent have been compelled to abandon theirs and the results are not amusing. As for their cousins on the continent who are in a haste to hate themselves by fixing their gaze on the perceived negative aspects of their culture, they are even more to be pitied for going on a hunger strike in the midst of plenty. Anyway, let the young reader of the African world that is fractured know that El-Hajj Malik El-Shabazz, more popularly known as Malcolm X, is one of the greatest and most influential Africans in history. The fact that his father had died and his mother had been committed to a mental hospital by the time he was only thirteen-years-old, the fact that criminal activity that earned him years in prison did not stop him from developing himself to the extent of sharing his passion for the pride of place, of peoples, of African descent in the Diaspora. He wanted them to believe in themselves. *He knew this belief in the self was the spring of all actions that are beneficial. This lesson is useful today. It is not possible for everyone to believe in all the things he said or even how he said them, but we all need to believe in our abilities to make positive differences to our world.*

*Then, African child of a fractured world, go on to find out about Malcolm X's travels, how he died, why so many attended his funeral and who described him as "our shining black prince" and further lessons. Then, find out also who established the Committee of Concerned Mothers to raise funds to buy a house and pay educational expenses for Malcolm X's family. By so doing they behaved like Africans; you must always look out for each other.*

*And each time you sing the opening words of Ghana's anthem, Yen Ara Asase Ni, think of Ephraim Amu, who insisted on being himself and that was taken for blasphemy. Yes, our fracturing began a long time ago. You know, those days God could only listen to music coming from the piano and the violin and the cello. And if you want to go to church, you should wear suits, the heavier the wool, the better you stand a chance of God hearing you, and especially if, as a woman, you wore stockings (yes, the kind meant for spring); and the drums were the instruments of the devil. Such has been part of the nonsense that has led to our fracturing. You and I know better, thanks to persons such as Ephraim Amu.*

*Know child, that reading has not gone out of fashion; let no one tell you otherwise. The screen cannot replace the printed hard copy. Develop the joy of taking a book, moving to a corner where you can concentrate and enter the world of the book with little disturbance. Develop the joy of reading to yourself before you sleep, each night. Let books and reading be part of your daily activities; you will not regret this habit later on in life...And when you go to the library, look for and read the books by J. E. Casley-Hayford, Ama Ata Aidoo, Ayi Kwei Armah, Frantz Fanon, Walter Rodney, C. L. R. James, Richard Wright, Maya Angelou, Flora Nwapa, Bessie Head, Mariama Bâ, Cheikh Anta Diop, Ngũgĩ wa Thiong'o, Zora Neale Hurston, Wole Soyinka, Marcus Garvey, Robert Sobukwe, Chinua Achebe, Ken Saro-Wiwa, W. E. B. Du Bois, Che Guevara, Kwame Nkrumah, Martin Luther King Jr, Barack Obama...Be sure to include on the reading list Alex Haley's Autobiography of Malcolm X, and Abdul Alkalimat's Malcolm X for Beginners. A good place to begin is to read the speeches of these persons and their autobiographies also; that way you hear their unfiltered voices and may be less*

*impeded to make up your minds about them. Read about the empires called Ghana, Mali and
Songhai and many, many others.*

*And when you have access to the internet, look up information that speaks to your past, gives
you the true picture of your current circumstances. If the information cannot tell you why your
world is fractured and how you can fix it, then the information, no matter how trusted the
website, can only be of limited usefulness for you. Make sure that you eventually read books that
position you to add your own history, circumstances and possibilities to the website. Look out
for information on George Padmore, Rosa Parks, the Mau Mau, Sobukwe, ancient Egypt,
Ghana, Mali, Songhai, Mansa Musa, the rock hewn churches of Ethiopia, Benin bronze works,
stone work of Zimbabwe, the pyramids of Egypt, the knowledge of astronomy of the Dogons...
You can write your stories about these and many others.*

Do encourage the young reader to question the use of words such as: "uneducated," "illiterate," "informal," "non-formal"... and question why they are
nearly always invariably applied to people such as are around him/her. We all
know that within our traditional system education is for everybody—males and
females, even if there was division of labour and sometimes its associated
specialisation. In the sea fishing industry for example, males go onto the sea to
bring the fish. Who trains them? Are they reflected in our national budget on
education? Why? Why not? The women sort, transport, preserve and distribute
the fish. Who trains them? Are they reflected in our national budget on education? Why? Why not? These activities involve all the disciplines—mathematics,
chemistry, physics, biology the social sciences, the humanities and law.

When the reader looks around, away from the textbook and books in the
library and images on the internet, s/he will find African women who are highly
knowledgeable and who hold key positions in the business of healing (outside
of the government and privately funded hospitals and pharmacies); the priesthood (outside of the mosque and church); the building industry (outside of the
list of contractors, surveyors, architects, engineers, etc. who win huge
inter/national contracts); judiciary, (outside of the law courts); history (outside
of the faculty and departments of institutions of learning); food processing
(outside of the science laboratories and multinational industries); metal-
smithing (outside of the state funded metal processing units); resource
mobilisation (outside of the formal banking system); the creative arts (outside
of conventional authorships) – the list is endless. Indeed we find women in most
areas that require the use of the mind and skills.

So, if today we have few women in medicine, law, the science laboratories, the construction, food processing industries; if they are nearly absent
from the powerful financial centres, if some religious establishments are now
agonising whether women can become leaders as in occupying their highest
position, or we cannot find them in the boardrooms, houses of parliament,
senate – we need to do the most logical thing of all: lay these lapses where they
belong, which is certainly not entirely at the doorsteps of our culture. We need

to get out of the mode where others evaluate our cultures for us or, where we are taught to look at ourselves with fractured eyes.

## Conclusion

The education we have drifted away from, dear writer, lays emphasis on character building, respect for the self, family and community. It promotes social obligations including protection of the environment as well as the conservation of our natural resources. It is education of the mind as well as of the hand. The learner is encouraged to be economically independent, become a respected member of the community and be sensitive to the genuinely needy. The individual never has any doubt about who she/he is, because identity formation is always a crucial part of our education. Do find ways of bringing these missing pieces to the forecourt of the young reader's mind. *The point, young reader, is that this type of education is still available for our collective excavation.* These are invaluable lessons we should include in our march towards quality education by revising the form and content of reading material for young minds. We have borrowed from everywhere else but from our own existing systems; we should not be surprised that perfection within an alienating context is like lighting a match at the beach. It is not realistic to do the same thing and expect different results.

*Keep reading, keep asking questions, and position yourself to adding to the knowledge you receive. Know that some have come before you and many more will follow you. Part of your purpose here is to leave the world as whole as possible for other children.* And dear writer, do listen to the voices of children and believe them when they talk. Let that also play a central, healing role in the writing for children in a fractured world. Eventually, the child will be empowered to heal his/her world by reading material that builds confidence, justice, trust, respect for the self and others.

# Who is an African?

## Helen Lauer

## Introduction

On some interpretations, contemporary African identity seems to have grown irretrievably international. Correlatively, it has become fashionable to claim that our social and political identities are something we *choose* to *do*, not something we have been *given* and so have no choice but to *be*. These two themes – internationalism and self-determining agency – recur in the works of leading African poets, playwrights, fictive narrators and literary critics who have weighed in with Diasporan intellectual and artistic voices advocating a view of African identity as an individualistic pursuit. A nouveau politics of identity urges Africans to search beyond their national independence agendas, impelling a postcolonial quest that diffuses or even renounces the historic struggle against foreign hegemony.[1] Nowadays we are urged to embrace difference, to renew and re-invent ourselves without reference to any essentialist core or geographic boundaries. To be a cosmopolitan African is celebrated as meaning that one has chosen to define oneself without any limitations encoded by specific cultural heritages, spatial prosceniums or historical narratives.[2]

The cosmopolitan mandate borrows from recently popularised theories that treat social and political identities as complex social constructions. But as heuristic as it may seem, the idiom of "social construction" is less helpful than its varied usages in the politics of identity and critical social theory might suggest. For instance, the notion of a social construction does not accommodate the important albeit elusive differences between adopting an identity and really having one. This essay will examine critically two currently popular examples of the essentialist and structuralist genres of theorising about social and political identities. The two chosen models may be read as reinforcing the view of African identity as a trans-national social construction. One of these models was authored by the social philosopher Alex Honneth, whose psychoanalytic work is central to the foundation of current debates about the politics of recognition. The other model mentioned here comes from the influential political theorist Walker Connor, known for his advocacy work on stable nation-building. Both models can be interpreted as reinforcing views of "African identity" as a trans-national social construction – moreover, as a construct that can be improved upon by individual Africans seeking to expand beyond their nations' histories, or improved upon through social engineering schemes designed to enhance citizens' identities with a unifying supra-nationality and a group-transcendent vision and loyalty.[3]

But not everyone is comfortable with treating African identity as boundless and trans-national, nor as promethean and negotiable. Forty years after it was published, Ama Ata Aidoo's *Our Sister Killjoy or Reflections from a Black-Eyed Squint* (1977 *OSK*) remains potent and searing, in part because she spelled out the reasons for the revulsion experienced by a minority of "radical" African nationalists emigrating back and forth in the decade after independence, who objected to the efforts of other Africans at assimilation into foreign cultures. Through hindsight, the reader of *Our Sister Killjoy* today will find that in many respects the contorted, demeaning, and ultimately futile efforts at assimilation fifty years ago anticipated an unseemly underside of the current cosmopolitan euphoria.

In what follows, section I will consider reasons for objecting to the historic eagerness of African elites for "learning the ways of white people" (*Anowa* 1970, 115) and homogenising culturally in the global arena. Aidoo's very practical considerations suggest a more fundamental correction of what is wrong with relying conceptually upon a uniform theoretical model of self-hood: such a model misleadingly implies that the struggle for maximal social recognition is a universal human need. It will emerge that the compulsion to be securely niched in the dominant global culture is not actually an *a priori* given, lodged deep in every individual psyche, but rather is situation-dependent. The idiom of social construction will be critically examined, for it lends a sense of feasibility to the proposal that individuals enhance their chances of a successful and fulfilled life by re-inventing their own identities to suit the contemporary zeitgeist. Section II will challenge the assumption that a universalistic supra-national identity can emerge successfully within a population as a product of planned engineering. This expectation rests on a collection of mistaken or elemental inferences about social identity. For instance, it is assumed that, since group identities are in some way the effects of corporate or collective activity, then they can and should be improved through conscientious management under enlightened leadership.[4] Or, because people who understand each other must be speaking the same language, it follows that by encouraging homogeneity in language use a government will initiate greater understanding and lessen tension within conflict-ridden populations.

## Section I: Cosmopolitanism as Assimilation Redux

To this day Africans are obliged to stomach an offensive range of ambivalent reactions and confused receptions offered in North America, and Anglo-Europe, where Caucasians of many heritages and centuries have remained traumatised by their own alienating images and projected fantasies about Africans. Throughout her writing, published since the 1970s, Aidoo has explored a visceral and highly critical assessment of efforts at what was called assimilation back then, and what gets celebrated now as the cosmopolitan mutual embrace, revealing it as a pretence.[5] It is a pretence for Africans, because cultural reciprocity between nations of the homeland and a multiplicity of others in the global arena can rarely, if ever, be conducted between individuals recognised as political equals. A global imbalance in assuming the voice of authority in cross-cultural exchanges extends to discourse about moral obligation and international justice, wherein it is tacitly assumed that foreign experts are the appropriate interpreters of Africans' needs. With few exceptions, the mutual impact imposed and sustained between members of African cultures and European cultures is not initiated by the individuals involved so much as they are enforced by the coercive agendas of multinational corporate agencies. The vast majorities of African citizens continue to be linked only remotely, if at all, with citizens of other nations through programmes designed for expanding capital from the G8 centres of global business to their satellite peripheries, under the influence of forces functioning in principle today much as they did in the sixteenth century. In these arrangements there is hardly any reciprocity constructed or controlled by the individuals who are most affected. As one of the different kinds of examples, consider the identities of cotton farmers in Mali and Niger, affected through the distributive injustice sustained by the World Trade Organisation (WTO), which embroils and impacts quite differently the identities of other unwitting cotton producers in the USA and in Brazil.

Notwithstanding cynicism about cross-cultural dependencies developed and sustained for the benefit of multinational profiteers, cosmopolitanism has been advocated as a personal antidote to the varied injustices suffered by African nationals. Presumably if one has sufficient financial means, then in defining oneself as a cosmopolitan and refusing to collude with racist stereotyping and cultural branding, one can catapult straight over the economic and professional barriers sustained by social stereotypes. Kwame Appiah, for example, proposed the cosmopolitan option for Africans in a literary moment that he spearheaded two decades ago (*In My Father's House*, 1992).[6] He speaks from his own experience in regarding poly-cultural allegiance as a way of reclaiming his own agency. He interprets self-definition for contemporary Africans as a breaking away from the constraints of ancestral obligation, repressive convention, and inhibiting social tradition. Appiah displayed the profusion of foreign influences in his home town, Kumasi, twenty years ago as a sign that his Akan classmates and neighbours were maturing, as a sign that they were no longer being "done to" but that they were themselves up and doing at last, adopting modern ways of their own accord, and thereby reaffirming a deep ontological truth:

> Race and history and metaphysics do not enforce an identity. We
> can choose, within broad limits set by ecological, political and
> economic realities, what it will mean to be African in the coming
> years. (196)

But a central question remains unanswered by the elegant generosity expressed
in Appiah's normative forecast: Who is the "we" that will define African identity
in the future?

The question is not idle. Fuelled by an effort to reverse or at least offset the
brain drain effect and to comply with Millennium Development Goal number
eight,[7] the African Union toyed for some years with the scheme of issuing a
certified and legally authenticated African identity to anyone with a sufficiently
compelling portfolio to be welcome as an ideal development partner. In 2004,
the Ghana government followed the special passport initiative of the African
Union with the Ghana Joseph Project, offering business and development partnership citizenship opportunities to venture capitalists in the Diasporan
community. Expecting to encourage stronger ties with private entrepreneurs
through historic repatriation, the invitation included "collecting DNA samples
to establish the genetic link between our returnees/pilgrims and the homeland."
This is only one component of a programme supposed to "re-establish the
African nation as a nation of all its peoples..."[8]

This proposal begs for clarification. Even speaking metaphorically, in what
sense is it cogent to speak of Africa as a nation? Can African identity be
captured as if it were a uniform national character? Then again, metaphorically
speaking, who should be counted among the nationals of Africa? Is *anyone* and
*everyone* properly entitled as a matter of choice to adopt documentation that
identifies them as African? Can anyone opt out and adopt identification as a
supra- or meta-African? Legal eligibility and moral judgments aside, *can* African
identity be a matter of choice?[9] These questions are not so impertinent or disin-
genuous as they might seem. The genetic profile in every one of us eventually
traces back to Africa, where human-specific DNA emerged about 200,000 years
ago, with evidence of the first migrations around 100,000 years ago.[10]
Mitochondrial DNA varies less in human cells than in any other; genetically we
couldn't be more uniform as a species. So this indicates that racial divides are
indeed social constructions, ethnic rivalries even more so.

But the category of social construction is more suggestive than it is illuminating in that it gives the misleading impression that the identities we have are
readily subject to revision at will. Something which has been designed poorly
can and should be deconstructed and reconstructed – and would be, if only the
individual had the interest and strength of character. It is a truism that we can
all *choose* to accept or to reject many of the categories that others cast upon us,
insofar as we can choose with whom we move at school, for instance. But it is

not every child who can choose which groups to join at school for the simple fact that not every child can go to school. Choice used in the sense intended here provides a perfectly serviceable adage for teaching children how to cope with humiliating insults incurred on the playground from their peers or in the classroom from their teachers. But then again, even in the most privileged societies it is not every child who is comparably encouraged to disdain from tolerating demeaning treatment or abuse from peers and superiors; for example, women and men are socialised very differently in this respect. Discriminatory injustices aside, there are very many cases where assuming membership in a group *is* a matter of making one's own choice in the presence of clear alternatives. It is fatuous to point out that I cannot choose to join Facebook — less trivially, I cannot participate in democratic transformative politics through Facebook social networking — if I have no computer nor access to the internet. This and many other examples illustrate the vast inequities between individuals' economic capacity to formulate preferences and to act upon them. Recently Kwame Appiah (2006) stressed that the differentials in social privilege and entitlement existing worldwide cut across cultures and nationalities.[11]

A central theme of *Our Sister Killjoy* is Ama Ata Aidoo's caution against thinking that travel abroad and absorption in foreign societies under any condition is the way for Africans to cross this dividing line between having the economic wherewithal to determine one's lifestyle and having insufficient means to construct and pursue one's ideal of a quality life. Soon after independence many Africans made this fatal mistake of believing the myth that individual freedom and self-respect prevails overseas as a special socio-economic inheritance attached to a certain *type* of identity superior to their own. Aidoo narrates the mental suicide involving masquerade, self-deception and denial practiced by "been-tos" who remained adrift, ill-clothed and marginalised on the freezing sidewalks of foreign cities; and of those returning to Africa, who camouflage their hurt dismay with the received litany of lies about "the wonders of being overseas" (*OSK* 89–90). The same mistake is being made to this day by those constructing a hip, trans-national sense of belonging, when developmental economic relations amongst Africans, Europeans and North Americans are no closer to being an interplay among equals now than they were in colonial times. So, Aidoo warns her readers against the illusory option to engage in trans-national collaboration as a means of reinforcing African agency. Her cautionary reproof in *Our Sister Killjoy* remains relevant, admonishing Africans not to sacrifice their responsibilities and entitlements at home any more than necessary, since subjective agency[12] is not a matter of geographic location, nor is it accomplished through association with one cultural legacy rather than another. As she depicts through the distressing honesty of Sissie, the power of subjective agency is a function of self-possession and uncompromising, painful self-honesty. Aidoo interprets overseas assimilation as actually a self-defeating deferral to the imperial antagonist. Instead of building a self, free of past encumbrances like superstition and religious taboo, one relinquishes agency and integrity to a racist arena that sidelines and subjugates Africans wholesale. What is nowadays dubbed cosmopolitan freedom, Aidoo displays as subjugating oneself and surrendering one's responsibility – to react honestly and freely – to the indignities and humiliations, both huge and minute, which Africans undergo in transit (across the Atlantic, across Europe) over centuries of foreign imperialism (*OSK* 88–89).

Aidoo condemns as nauseating those Africans who display indiscriminate deference to foreigners' hypocritical overtures of hospitality. In the opening passages of *Our Sister Killjoy*, such obsequious collusion is personified in the character of the hapless Sammy, a diplomatic functionary, an African harlequin and factotum who is present at the scene of Sissie's introduction to her European sponsors. Sammy's assimilation and mastery of European cultural affectations are cloying and self-defeating in Sissie's eyes; ever after, the very sight of him involuntarily raises bile to her mouth ("Into a Bad Dream," *OSK* 1–16).

Alex Honneth, a widely read social philosopher, proposes a model of identity that appears to justify and normalise the behaviour of Sammy in pursuit of recognition and upward mobility. Honneth posits a primordial human need for recognition as the root cause of all struggles against social, economic and political injustice. He claims that to maintain self-respect throughout life we must constantly seek facsimiles of that primal acceptance upon which our survival and security depended in our infancy. He cites as primary evidence the direct injury that we all feel from degrading treatment or from public humiliation, from belittling verbal abuse or from outright physical assault. Indeed we all know first-hand that self-esteem can be damaged by receiving poor treatment. So, Honneth argues that the contra-positive equivalent must also be true. That is, since the absence of respect from others can trigger the experience of injury to our self-esteem and personal integrity, then it must also be the case that sustained self-esteem and personal integrity depend upon our sensing that other people recognise us as worthy of their respect. Thus, he regards the primal need for recognition as essential in all fights for social justice.

But Honneth's psychoanalytic template for the foundation of social morality seems to apply to only a narrow range of society. He overlooks the fact that individuals can harbour self-esteem and personal integrity even though from birth their subordinate status does not entitle them to expect that significant others will recognise or treat them as due certain deferential regard or as worthy of respect. Women generally occupy such a position in most societies. And both men and women in South Africa, who forged a new definition of citizenship through the second half of the 20th century, did so despite the annihilating, profoundly abusive conditions that prevailed throughout their lives and which had been legalised long before their birth.

Significant in this regard is the title chosen for the chronicle of an articulate ANC activist, Naboth Mokgatle (1971): *The Autobiography of an Unknown South African*.[13] Contrary to Honneth's theory, Mokgatle's self-respect and esteem that fuelled his fight for justice were strengthened precisely as he focussed his awareness on the abuse, insults and injuries perpetrated by significant authorities who actively deprived him of respectful recognition and intentionally disqualified his moral worth. Nor was this a one-off peculiarity unique to the psychology of one South African. The ANC ideology deliberately schooled activists in the anti-apartheid struggle to divorce themselves from interaction with liberal whites eager to offer them recognition and political reverence, precisely because such recognition and approval was seen as a weakening influence that threatened to undermine the uncompromising autonomy of the Black Consciousness Movement, an autonomous identity which was necessary to genuinely overturn (rather than to subtly perpetuate by colluding with) the white supremacist status quo.[14]

*Our Sister Killjoy* persists in its relevance because it presents global solidarity as a wholesale denial of what Euro-African relations have been like throughout history back to Roman times. A leitmotif of the book is the importance of building one's integrity by sustaining an identity that is immune to the allure of cheap overtures from the West, the importance of maintaining a sense of self-worth that is disgusted by the insolence of puerile objectification ("Into A Bad Dream" and "The Plums,"), and a self-possession unimpressed by education offered on terms that are invasive and self-abasing ("From Our Sister Killjoy," *OSK* 86–87). Aidoo's strongest characters counsel the reader to be uncompromising and honest about cross-cultural experience, not to lie about "the wonders of being overseas" (*OSK* 90), not to pursue the invitation to fit into the global arena at the cost of one's dignity, in penury and discomfort (*OSK* 88–89). In her sojourn abroad, Sissie is affronted everyday by the objectifying insults and insinuations she encounters on public buses and airplanes, in fine restaurants and institutions of higher learning, from even well-meaning European neighbours and strangers – all quite plainly these audacities and cruelties are not the handiwork of malicious hatred, they are the residual vestiges of that sordid history despite the best of individuals' intentions and convictions.[15]

One can read as another central teaching of the vignettes in *Our Sister Killjoy* Aidoo's caveat to avoid participating in the charade of presumptuous cosmopolitan solidarity extended to Africans who moved abroad in the 1960s and 1970s, finding themselves greeted with a fastidious yet crass enthusiasm by Europeans who were confused by their own clueless projections of the African experience (*OSK* 42–43). Aidoo portrays as unseemly and repugnant the cross-cultural forays by some Europeans into solidarity with the sons and daughters of newly independent Africa seeking the keys to the good life in their lands. Aidoo recounts the bewilderment and revulsion of Sissie, a young Ghanaian woman studying in Europe, who suffers an assortment of ambiguous assaults by unctuous Europeans experimenting with public shows of solidarity on public transport. Against a background hiss of racist slurs, Sissie sustains a particularly disturbing acquaintanceship with Marija, a lonely German who insinuates appallingly stilted overtures of uninvited intimacy and parodies of care which come off as a series of hopelessly awkward, hurtful gaffs – because they are conducted sporadically, furtively, and presumptuously, with so little genuine mutual understanding, belying an underlying suspect ambivalence on both sides ("The Plums," *OSK* 76–78).

The portrayal of what is called an *African* identity, in particular, has been notorious over centuries of international trade for its brutally effective results in marketing all sorts of commodities, including human beings. It serves the same function today, no less barbarically although perhaps less explicitly. For instance, irate university students and lecturers from Senegal to South Africa have been convinced, via "science" done by press release, that Africans have brought upon themselves the current environment of chronic contagion and escalating trends in premature mortality, primarily because their peculiar traditional identity as *Africans* encourages irrational sexual license as a cultural norm. This falsehood is staunchly sustained despite the overwhelming evidence of negative impacts accruing over the last twenty years from economic structural adjustment experiments. Although an informative exposure would require a summary of analyses too extensive to supply in this essay, the pretensions of HIV/AIDS science and drug marketing practiced upon Africans is one of many examples displaying variations on the theme of manipulating and promulgating beliefs about African identity to facilitate forces of coercive power.[16]

The considerations surveyed so far indicate that cosmopolitanism fails to fit the reality of African experience in two respects: it encourages African individuals to reach out and grasp for acceptance and success in a world which is historically antagonistic and economically annihilating. And facing in the other direction, cosmopolitanism invites individuals of former colonising cultures to presume that they may interpret African publics' needs, define African character, dismiss history and align with or identify themselves as Africans. In both ways, cosmopolitanism lies about what it means to be African.[17]

## Section II: African identity as a social engineering project

Perhaps more than any other regional heritage worldwide, the African's perspective has long been the focus of normative prescriptions, socio-economic revisionist programmes and development policies. Since the early twentieth-century period of colonialism before WWI, African identity has come to be regarded more and more as malleable – as subject to revision and improvement, by non-Africans especially. The politics of African identity have become increasingly more complicated as the African continent becomes more visible and accessible, as well as lucrative in its investment prospects, to the rest of the world.

Many noble things are said about being African. The core values most often attributed to Africans' belief and value systems include deference to one's immediate and distant family members and home community, protection of family reputation and honour, distributive justice among one's peers and cohort, lively commitment to one's ancestors and future generations, actively protectionist respect for the natural environment, interdependency of one's public life and personal affairs, exceeding care for one's spiritual relationship to the divine and high ethical standards.[18] These traits are lauded by an ever-widening range of people in geographic locations all around the Atlantic basin and beyond. Oddly, the problem of applying a uniform African identity to a widely diverse population across a huge continent is rarely taken as an obstacle by social scientists or Africanists generally – except sometimes by Africans themselves. On the contrary, theorists advocate reinforcing a centralised paradigm as uniquely African for a variety of reasons (Ama Mazama, 2003).

Apart from its economic utility, one popular reason for promulgating an univocal African identity is to serve as a means for alleviating ethnic conflict. Among those who regard social engineering as a feasible way of improving community relations, it is popular to suppose that group behaviour can be influenced (e.g. to dismantle sectarian or ethnic hostility) by reconstructing and expanding the identities of the combatants and the population at large. Walker Connor (1972) is a widely influential proponent of the view that identity reform will directly yield a safeguard against destabilising elements for a nation-state, even if adjustments of all the other superficial or "tangible" elements have failed – be they efforts to revise economic conditions, cultural prejudices, political affinities, or religious exclusions. Kwame Gyekye (1997) advocates a notion of "meta-nationality" as an elaboration of Connor's proposal to reinforce a nation-state's prospects for stability by ensuring that through language unification and other measures, the entire population comes to share a "single psychological focus" (Connor 353). Together with a mistaken view of the role that language plays in sustaining people's beliefs about themselves and the world, Connor's caveat inspired Gyekye to suggest that "good nation-building" entails a government's enforcing a uniform national language policy in order to build "a cohesive cultural identity" (Gyekye 92–95, 113).

Language by itself cannot cause a change in a person's world in the "tangible effects" of a transformed "view of self" (Connor 341). This is not to deny that what is said or insinuated about someone's identity within a particular language can indeed influence her self-perception. But it is not because the person speaks that particular language. It's rather the content of *what* is said in that language *about* or *to* that person which may incite her to violence. Comparably, the fact that someone has been forcefully deprived of her mother tongue and forced instead to speak a foreign language will impact adversely on her identity and her world-view. Ngũgĩ wa Thiong'o has been making this point repeatedly for decades.[19] But as he emphasises, it is the longterm effect of coercive imperialist enforcement, together with the humiliating denigration of a people's earliest and most intimate mode of self expression – not the very languages themselves existing as intangible structured entities – that does the damage.

Language *itself* is a poor indicator of identity anywhere you look. Speaking English in Accra does not identify you as an Englishman; and no one speaking French in Haiti or La Côte d'Ivoire now would thereby be presenting himself as a Frenchman. More poignantly still, speaking Arabic in Northern Sudan today does not flag you as an Arab. Arabic is a particularly interesting case with respect to using language as a theoretical vehicle for linking sectarian violence in some endemic way to ethnic identity. For Arabic, like English, further illustrates that the medium of language itself holds no monopoly over what people believe and feel. Arabic speakers contest their diverse and changing opinions about their own language and its uses as they participate in it. For instance, speaking Arabic used to attract prestige because it is the sacred language of Islam, spoken by the Prophet. But the version of Arabic that was once universally associated with high status is nowadays avoided by many Nubians in Northern Sudan as by many Algerians, Moroccans, Northern Egyptians and Tunisians, who wish to disassociate themselves from the vilification to which Sauds and others in the Middle East are subjected through the "axis of evil" rhetoric purveyed by satellite media. Propaganda about the Arab world and the Arab cause has virtually co-opted the term "Arab" to take the place of "Communist." For a week in November of 2006 the global media perpetually broadcast that the "violence escalating out of control" in South-eastern Chad was illustrated by a new raid on 20 villages "perpetrated by men who appear to be ethnically Arab."[20] The news feed begs the question: What does it mean to "appear ethnically Arab?" And to whom? Widely promulgated stereotypes of ethnic identity definitely can influence how people perceive themselves.[21] The ethnic categories featured in descriptions of the Darfur crisis from 2001 through 2005 would not have gained a referring capacity except for the profound influence of the global media saturating the way people of Darfur themselves began to describe their struggle to locally installed reporters, United Nations monitors, international NGOs (especially the American Washington-based Human Rights Watch, and the British-based International Migration Organisation). Other important organised mouthpieces are the leading regional rebel movements of the Sudan Liberation Army (SLA) and the Justice and Equality Movement (JEM), and the Sudanese government. Powerful vested interests (including the multinational oil conglomerates Exxon, Shell, and Elf, as well as the financing cooperative International Bank for Reconstruction and Development [IBRD] – also known as the World Bank) implement the policies of the International Monetary Fund (IMF) and control the global media. Corporately, these global agencies required that twenty-five years of escalating violence in Western Sudan be explained as if it emerged in 2001, at the completion of the World Bank's largest African development project in history, the Chad-Cameroon Oil Pipeline. And, so, explanations that entail reference to a group's propagandised identity as the cause of conflict can become habitual and thereby self-fulfilling.[22]

This crude sketch of the international media's impact upon local self-narratives suggests that people's identities are not limited to what they depict at the time and place they engage in decision making and interaction with the immediate environment. The limits of a group's identity are not discernible. Manifestly different identities seem, rather, to intersect with each other in countless unpredictable ways. So theoretical *talk* about identities – either as revisable social constructions or as hardwired components of an individual's personality – lends a misleading sense of clarity, concreteness and detectable locality to the sources and processes of individuals' decision-making in light of what they believe to be true and important.

African identity, perhaps more than any other collectively framed identity, cannot be defined, because it cannot be described – from outside or from within. Identity properly understood is not discursive. As Ama Ata Aidoo stresses in the struggle of several of her protagonists, what makes an identity African is essentially a matter of the way an individual makes her choices about how she will wear her hair, where she will look for employment, whom she will marry ("Everything Counts" 1970; *Changes: A Love Story* 1991). Cultural or social or political identity is properly expressed in the way it is lived, not how it is discussed. Thus, although we can and do evaluate the quality of a person's identity, we do not do so in terms of the truth or falsity of what she says. Instead we assess an individual's expression of one's identity in terms of one's authenticity – integrity, honesty, dignity – as we do judge other aspects of that individual by observing one's behaviour. And so the cosmopolitan's ideal of reconstruction is misleading, since, as an African, one's agency is not necessarily enriched by construing oneself a-historically nor as belonging everywhere and anywhere on the globe. Nor does it make sense to suggest that everyone, regardless of their birthplace, can claim to know what it means to be African. This being the case, it is unclear how to make group identity construction the subject of conscious and deliberate social programming except in ways that would leave African identity open to exploitation and abuse.[23]

## Conclusion

This essay has examined critically two normative proposals that are popularly linked: (i) that our identity can be taken up as our own construction, and (ii) that we should develop who we are by reaching beyond the spatial (geographical) and the temporal (historical) dimensions of our region of the world. Both of the structural accounts of the person in society that were reviewed here in Sections I and II support these joint principles of identity reconstruction as a feasible enterprise; so both can be interpreted as buttressing the attractions of a cosmopolitan identity for Africans as a revisionist programme: Honneth's definition of personhood appeared to explain the urge of some "been-tos" to demand for themselves a place of recognition – if only imagined – in the dominant global hegemony. And Connor's project for transforming group identity appeared to endorse that demand by institutionalising it. However, both of these theories are problematic, because they deflect attention away from the contingent facts of world history that established the grossly unequal interdependencies that actually have shaped our beliefs about who we ourselves and each other are, that is, our entitlements, feasible aspirations, rational options, rights and duties – the gamut. These beliefs have become fixed features of global discourse and the international landscape, without the knowledge, let alone the decision, of generations who are adversely affected.

So it is generally that universal or essentialist theories which propose to sketch the intrinsic structure of personhood, or that posit some *a priori* essential core of group solidarity, obscure the genesis of those group formations and interdependencies that already do exist – and which prevailing global authorities may be invested in maintaining. The main problem with theoretical talk that glibly lifts personhood and social identity away from the circumstantial facts that have shaped our lives is that it diffuses the likelihood of such awkward and usually quite ugly facts being discovered, and it mitigates their potential impact whenever they are exposed.

It is not facts about our identities or personhood as such, but historically specific facts about the conditions and political motivations behind the group formations and dynamics that have shaped our identities that must be highlighted through careful analysis. Remembering the history that transpired and the cultural particulars belonging to Kigali, Rwanda, in the 1990s, or in Ogoniland, Nigeria, in the same decade, is critical. It is critical to understanding African identity, because remembering is the only way to reveal how individuals may wind up recapitulating the very imbalances of entitlement and agency that their cosmopolitan efforts to abandon national allegiances and to erase cultural boundaries are intended to transform.

# The Longevity of *Whiteness* and Ama Ata Aidoo's *Our Sister Killjoy*

## Susan Arndt

Ama Ata Aidoo's *Our Sister Killjoy*,[1] published in 1977, is the first African novel set in Germany and with a focus on the continuity between colonialism, National Socialism and contemporary racism in Germany. It tells the story of the Ghanaian student Sissie who travels to Europe on scholarship – first Germany, then Great Britain. It is this encounter with Europe and the racist gaze which makes Sissie – in the sense of Simone de Beauvoir – a black woman. In the airplane she is confronted with racism, when she is seated with what *white* people call her 'friends' (meant two Nigerians she does not know) so that the *white* South Africans need not be bothered by a black woman. Having just arrived in Germany she is then greeted with the words: "Ja, das Schwartze Mädchen. (Aidoo 12)

> She was somewhat puzzled. Black girl? Black girl? So she looked around her, really well this time. And it hit her. That all the crowd of people going and coming in all sorts of directions had the colour of the pickled pig parts that used to come from foreign places to the markets at home ... And she wanted to vomit ... For the rest of her life, she was to regret this moment when she was made to notice differences in human colouring. (12–13)

Reduced to her blackness, Sissie adopts the socio-political identity of blackness and realises that the difference thus constructed serves to legitimate dubious hierarchies of power and is the foundation of racism: "... someone somewhere would always see in any kind of difference an excuse to be mean. A way to get land, land, more land/ ... Power to decide/ Who is to live, Who is to die/ Where/ When/How." (13–15)

By having evoked South Africa and Germany as locations, this power of racism of deciding who is to live where and how long is ascribed to National Socialism and Apartheid. Yet by situating her poetic novel in 1960s Germany

Aidoo simultaneously clarifies that Apartheid and National Socialism are only the tip of the iceberg of racism. Seen through the lense of her Ghanaian character Sissie, the reader enters the blunt racism of a Bavarian town, as embodied by two generations of men called Adolf. The narrative's focus is, however, directed at Sissie's encounter with a *white* woman who intends to overcome this racism yet, gets stuck with her structural and discursive involvement in racism, because she avoids reflecting upon her *whiteness*.

Thus, more than a decade before the analyses of writers such as Toni Morrison and bell hooks generated the academic field of Critical Whiteness Studies,[2] Ama Ata Aidoo's *Our Sister Killjoy* illustrates that racism is a matter of *whiteness*. Given this fact, I find that an appreciation of Aidoo's critical treatment of 'race' in her context of 1960s Germany, can be fruitfully informed by an analytical perspective of Critical Whiteness Studies. Sketching the history of *whiteness*, I read *race* in general and *whiteness* in particular as a colonial myth that can be traced back as far as antiquity and which gave rise to *whiteness* as a social position in the symbolic order of racism, thus necessitating the deployment of *whiteness* as a critical category of analysis. Thus framed, I elaborate on the concept of the 'racial turn.' To conclude, I will demonstrate the merits of *whiteness* as a critical category of literary analysis, by analysing Aidoo's negotiation of *whiteness* in *Our Sister Killjoy*.

## Concepts of 'Race' from Greek Antiquity through National Socialism and into the Present

We know that at least as early as the era of Greek Antiquity, human physical traits have been the basis for fabricating distinctions, which would eventually be employed to invent mental, social, cultural and religious differences and hierarchies, thus constituting political orders of power and discrimination. One of the best-known examples from Ancient Greece is that Greek imperialism under Alexander the Great, being in need of strategies to legitimate its acts of violence and exploitation, fabricated forms of demarcation which established a worldview pillared on a division between 'Greeks' and the 'rest,' who were generalised as 'Barbarians.' This division was grounded in a theory of 'pure descent' dependent on blood and/or geographical ties. Applying this paradigm, Aristotle elaborated the first and last formal and systematic theory of slavery. He argued that slavery was both natural and just, for in the same way that he saw the union of male and female as a natural drive resulting from the need to reproduce, he saw the pursuit of survival necessitating slavery. Additionally, he argued that nature defined who was born to be a slave and who a master: "[T]hat some should rule and others be ruled is a thing that is not only necessary, but also expedient; from the hour of their birth some," and he meant the 'Barbarians,' "are marked out for subjection" and "others," that is the Greeks, "for rule."[3] This allegedly naturally given order of master and slave would, as Aristotle continued to argue, manifest itself in physical attributes, which, in turn, would determine abilities. "Nature would like to distinguish between the bodies of freemen and slaves, making the one strong for servile labour, the other upright, and although useless for such services, useful for political life in the arts both of war and peace."[4] Besides bodily attributes such as 'physical stature,' the colour and texture of hair as well as 'skin colour' played an important role in Greek attempts to invent bodily differences as markers of differing abilities and mental dispositions as well as cultural hierarchies. In that vein, it was postulated that climate and other environmental factors influenced physical attributes. Just as much as Greek mappings positioned Greece in terms of geopolitics and climate as the centre of the world, the 'skin colour' of the Greeks was defined as being the centre and norm of all 'skin colours.' This is mirrored in the fact that the Greek term for 'skin colour,' *andreíkelon*, refers to what is considered to be the Greek complexion only. Insofar as it translated as 'human-like,' it seemed even to imply that all complexions different from *andreíkelon* existed outside the bounds of humanity.

*Andreíkelon* was contrasted with both the 'skin colour' of the Ethiopians, that is, all non-Egyptian African peoples, who had – as was etymologically implied – 'burnt faces' as well as with 'white skin.' Thus *andreíkelon* was situated as less dark or sun-exposed than black, yet darker than 'white skin.' The demarcation line between *andreíkelon* and 'white skin' was, however, drawn in a manner that was by no means clear or consistent – a fact which corresponded with the considerable polyvalence of 'white skin' in Greek society. There were two main connotations of 'white skin-colour': First, Greeks considered it a marker of Persians and people of Europe's 'extreme north' such as the Scythians, who were later replaced in discourse by the Gauls and Germanic peoples. In this context, 'white skin' (as opposed to the 'black skin' of the Ethiopians in the 'extreme South') implied cowardliness, harmlessness and effeminateness.[5] While in this respect *whiteness* was positioned as non-Greek, 'white skin' was, secondly, also the locus of an internal differentiation within Greek society along the lines of the structural categories of gender and class. Following from with the climate theory's postulate that 'white skin' was untainted (by the sun), bourgeois women, whose life was centred in the shadows of the house, were situated as white. In this case, *whiteness* carried implications not only of femininity (a connotation that resembles the interpretation of the *whiteness* of Persians), but also of beauty and grace. Moreover, in contemporary texts and pictures Greek philosophers are presented as pale or 'white-skinned' – a depiction often visually further heightened by their wearing of white clothing, which befits their prestigious social standing.[6] This characterisation of philosophers as 'white' can undoubtedly be interpreted as suggesting that they were distinguished not by physical, but rather mental work inside the house. Moreover, it implies that *whiteness* was accorded the potential for the qualities of wisdom, spirituality and a prestigious social standing and thus evaluated in a far more ambiguous and positive way than blackness.

The knowledge accumulated in Classical Antiquity that cultural differences manifested themselves physically and that physical differences conversely corresponded to mental and physical capabilities was further fostered in the ensuing centuries and enriched in discursive accordance with aspects of the Christian faith and the knowledge informed by it. In fact, emerging Christianity appropriated and abrogated the colour symbolism of Antiquity with colour symbolism informing a racialising politics of 'skin colour.'

Wolfram von Eschenbach's *Parzival* is a relevant cultural-historical document that demonstrates how 'skin colour' was conceptualised in the 12th and 13th centuries as a category of difference that was interwoven with religious difference and heavily influenced by Christian colour symbolism, thus demonstrating a presence of processes of racialisation and an awareness of the believed superiority of *whiteness*. Parzival's most essential trait is his Christian faith. Although he is not described explicitly as having 'white skin,' the importance of (his) *whiteness* comes to light in a reflexive fashion when other characters are introduced as being non-*white*: Belacane, who is positioned as a "dusky moorish Queen,"[7] and Feirefiz, her son.

Before Gahmuret meets Parzival's mother Herzeloyde, he falls in love with Belacane and sires Feirefiz with her. When leaving Belacane, he claims that he does not do so because of her "swerze"[8] [blackness], but rather because of her faith.[9] The mere fact, however, that he evokes blackness as a marker of difference (even though to declare it being non-relevant), suggests that in the binary opposite of Muslim/Christian a difference of 'skin colour' resonates, also.

The fact that von Eschenbach is well aware of the meaning of 'skin colour' is, indeed, manifested throughout the text, for example in the words with which the narrator depicts the love encounter between Gahmuret and Belacane: "The Queen disarmed him with her own dark hands. ... The Queen yielded to sweet and noble love with Gahmuret, her heart's own darling, little though their skins matched in colour."[10] Insofar as Gahmuret and Belacane's love is described as "sweet" and "noble," it seems to be unaffected by racialising notions; however, the very qualification evoked by the fact that their skin is described as "ungelîch," that is, "not alike," marks that there is knowledge about 'skin colour' being a relevant category of difference. Moreover, theorems of later 'race theories' are already anticipated in *Parzival* given that the child (Feirefiz) sired by their love is portrayed as divergent from the norm of human nature in that he is born with a skin that "was pied."[11] He was "both black and white ... His hair and all his skin were parti-coloured like a magpie."[12]

By comparing Feirefiz to a magpie, the rhetorical figure of 'colonial Othering' through the use of animal metaphors is applied. Moreover, by inventing him as a freckled human being (as is implied by his name Feirefiz translating as "pied son"), the racist thesis is employed that a cross-breeding of different 'races' will lead to abnormalities. Even if these are called "marvels," they position him as differing from the *white* norm. What is more, by making Belacane kiss the "white patches" of her son's skin, von Eschenbach has her even position *whiteness* above blackness,[13] thus devaluing (her own) blackness. In doing so, she is made to echo and affirm the epic's opening lines, where the magpie allegory is intro- duced.[14] Here, in the logic of Christian colour symbolism, the white (of the magpie) represents the colour of honour, loyal temper, courage, and Heaven, and is contrasted with the black (of the magpie) as the symbol of cowardice, shame, infidelity and Hell.

His white patches seem to enable Feirefiz, in contrast to his mother, who is fully black, to live in Europe and among Christians. Yet the fact that he has black patches makes Feirefiz Parzival's antithetical 'Other.' Analogously, in terms of religion, Feirefiz is in-between. While Belacane merely claims that she intends to get baptised, Feirefiz wholeheartedly takes this step. It is true that this allows him to see the Grail, marry its bearer, and thus enter Parzival's world. Because he was born a Muslim, however, Feirefiz is not allowed to belong to that world. While in other medieval works, such as the romance *King of Tars*, a person's converting to Christianity is accompanied by his becoming *white* (or his casting off of dreadful physical features), there is no indication here that Feirefiz's 'skin colour' or position in the symbolic order of 'skin colours' changes. On the contrary, ultimately, Parzival summons him to go back to where he belongs – namely to India, as the Orient is now geographically confined. This reveals that Feirefiz is to remain a 'foreigner' in Europe – and that the religion he was born into plays just as much a fundamental role therein as 'skin colour.' In actual fact, it is not Feirefiz who goes down in history as the first *white* Christian leader in the Orient, but rather his son, Prester John, born a Christian and to a *white* mother, who goes down in history as the first *white* Christian leader in the Orient. Ultimately, the characters of Belacane and Feirefiz do "not tell us that differences in skin colour were not important at that time, but rather that religious and cultural differences were already colour-coded ... The black/white dichotomy fuses with the one between Islam and Christianity."[15]

This fusion was performed particularly in the religiously motivated war for supremacy between the Spaniards and North African peoples in the Iberian Peninsula, which started in the early 8th century and was won in 1492 by the Spaniards. On the side of the Spanish, the war was accompanied by a rhetoric of anti-Islam racism that relied heavily on the aforementioned religious colour symbolism. A manifestation of this is the very fact that the apostle James, who became the Spaniards' patron called "matamoros" [moor-killer], was enveloped in *whiteness* – as is documented not least in 16th century paintings which surround him in light, dress him in white clothes and portray a desire for 'white

– 114 –

skin.' As for the other side of the coin, 'moor' would now become a generic term for any 'black person.'

This racialising hierarchy became intellectually, philosophically and socially buttressed during the Renaissance, when the European enslavement of millions of Africans was grounded on a claim of European superiority which was, in turn, pillared by both Christianity and the implementation of 'skin colour' as a naturally given category of difference. They were now fed into the construction of 'races.' Part and parcel of this invention of 'race' was that – in an obvious rebirth of Aristotle's theory of slavery and an exploitation of Christian colour symbolism – the 'white race' was deemed to be entitled to enslave and colonise those the *whites* claimed to be their racial 'Other.'

This excessive celebration of *whiteness*, as performed, for example, by Elizabethan cosmetics, found its aesthetic counterpart in a hyperbole of fairness that characterises English Renaissance literature. In Shakespeare's works, for example, where the word 'race' is used 18 times with reference to humans, 'fairness' is one of the 10 most commonly used words. Interestingly, besides the conventional appraisal of 'fairness' as a most cherished attribute of the female body, in his sonnets he also ascribes 'fairness' to a *white* aristocratic man. This seems to correspond to the economic and political need of early colonialism to constitute *whiteness* as a new marker of power, which then, of course, could not remain a realm of women, but needed to become a domain of English/European masculinity. Yet by thus praising homoerotic love, he simultaneously challenges contemporary notions of 'fairness.' This becomes even more striking to the degree that – in the so-called "dark lady"-corpus of his sonnets – Shakespeare opposes the beauty ideal as propagated and embodied by Queen Elizabeth I in particular and the Elizabethans in general. His lyrical "I" ascribes 'fairness' not to a brunette *white* "dark lady" – as is commonly claimed, irrespective of the fact that the woman is clothed in blackness and associated with slavery yet never called a lady and associated with "darkness" only once – but to a black female slave who has been forced into prostitution. This, for example, is manifested when, in sonnet 130, he declares: "My mistress' eyes are nothing like the sun ... If snow be white, why then her breasts are dun/If hairs be wires, black wires grow on her head; I have seen roses damask'd, red and white, But no such roses see I in her cheeks."[16] In his challenge of Elizabethan notions of fairness and beauty, the lyrical "I" even goes as far as resituating blackness as the embodiment of beauty: "In the old age black was not counted fair/Or if it were, it bore not beauty's name; But now is black beauty's successive heir; And beauty slandered with a bastard shame."[17]

It is the author of these lines who has also invented characters like Othello and Caliban. Postcolonial Studies has argued that these characters represent racist images of the colonialist 'Other.' I agree and yet do not hold that Shakespeare conforms to the rhetoric of early colonialism and racism. On the contrary, as I argue elsewhere, he manipulates it in order to subvert both the racism and the colonialist gaze on non-European 'Others' of his time.[18] While *Othello* aestheticises the presence of black slaves and ex-slaves in Europe and the racism which they are exposed to, *The Tempest* addresses the colonial fantasy that the people in the colonies are inferior to *white* people and hence born to be most willingly enslaved and exploited by them.

In *Othello* we witness how Othello cannot but fail because Venetian society pretends to integrate him yet denies him equality and keeps him imprisoned in *white* colonial fantasies from the outset. Iago's infamous "I hate the Moor" (I.iii.404–6) soliloquy signals that racism triggers his intrigues, which do not leave Othello any other option than to fail and die socially and physically. Insofar as Iago phonetically alludes to Santiago and therewith evokes the name of Santiago Matamoros, the very patron saint of Spain who became known as "Moorkiller,"[19] Othello's quest for revenge, murderous deed and tragic end are presented as just as 'man-made' and produced by racism as the demonising *white* fantasies it apparently confirms. Yet ultimately, Iago is just the tip of the iceberg. Thus, for example, the Venetians address Othello by name whenever he is present, yet are quick to speak of him as 'the Moor' or use other derogatory terms as soon as he is absent. Even Desdemona and the Duke, who seem to be most willing to integrate Othello, remain discursively entangled in the colonialist rhetoric of exoticism and "silence and evasion" in "matters of race" (Morrison, 1992: 9) Moreover, by holding a central role in his play the character of Othello opposes the Elizabethan and Jacobean tendencies of staging blacks as monstrous villains who are incapable of employing language. Caliban, however, is repeatedly marked by topoi such as monstrosity, cannibalism, beastliness and viciousness,[20] which are to imply that he lacked humanity, in effect, and speech. Ultimately, however, we have to be aware that we see what we are told to see by the white gaze, which, in fact sees different things. Caliban cannot be a monster, a fish, a tortoise and a devil at the same time. Thus, isn't their gaze to be mistrusted? Trinculo's first encounter with Caliban seems to confirm this. As he gapes at Caliban, he verbalises his impressions as follows:

> What have we here, a man or a fish? [...] A fish, he smells like fish [...] a strange fish: were I in England now [...] and had this fish painted; [...] when they will not give a doit to relieve a lame beggar, they will lay out ten to see a dead Indian [...] I do now let loose my opinion; hold it no longer; this is no fish, but an islander, that hath lately suffered by a thunderbolt. (2.2.24–37)

Ultimately, we are told that Trinculo sees what his scheme to financially exploit the European thirst for exotic 'Otherness' and his drunken state want him to see.

In point of fact, we do not see Caliban, but Trinculo's gaze on him. Analogously, all the other labels may be read as colonialist fantasies rather than naturally given traits of Caliban. The character of Caliban, then, does not represent the colonial 'Other,' but rather the colonialist mainstream rhetoric that was, among other things, becoming popular through travel writers such as Sir Martin Frobisher, Richard Hakluyt and Sir Walter Raleigh. In the final analysis, in the character of Caliban Shakespeare personifies the *white* gaze and its colonialist "spectacle of strangeness" (Newmann, 1987: 154) in order to subvert it. After all, Caliban is not unable to communicate, but rather knows how to use his intelligence and language (even in blank verse) as a powerful means of resistance, thus duping[21] and endangering *white* people.[22]

Shakespeare may have invented a resistant Caliban in order to encourage and empower the colonised, to revolt like Caliban; yet he may also have invented him in order to warn Europe not to underestimate the colonised people and their willingness to defend their land and their lives.

Shakespeare was right after all. Resistance accompanied Europe's violent endeavours right from the beginning and Caliban (emancipated from traits of the racist gaze) became a central topos of anti-colonial literature of resistance. Racism, however, did not stop. On the contrary, the 18th century witnessed the scientific grounding of the ideology of 'race' in the Pan European project of Enlightenment, as represented by Kant, Voltaire and Rousseau – and Hegel, as well. Thus entrenched, racism survived the abolition of slavery. When colonialism rushed into imperialism, racism seconded a rhetoric that disguised colonial violence as the 'white man's burden to civilise the world. And while colonialism was still terrorizing people of colour, National Socialism emerged. Thus racism has become the common discriminatory basis for Colonialism, National Socialism and Racial Cleansing and Racism in modern time.

Even when National Socialism in Germany was crushed – which served in no small measure as a catalyst – and Europe's colonial world had been destroyed by revolutionary processes of liberation, the *white* Western world did not unlearn racism. What it did learn, however, was to taboo it. As Toni Morrison puts it, the "habit of ignoring race" is widely considered "a graceful, even generous, liberal gesture (9–10). This is particularly true for Germany. The 'race' frenzy committed by National Socialism in the name of 'race' gave birth to a historical sense of shame in Germany, which, paradoxically enough, in turn, has resulted in a longing to silence 'race'/*race* and racism. Just as much as Germany's endeavours of remembrance with respect to National Socialism would necessarily remain insufficient, *white* European and US-American societies cherish forgetting or ignoring the legacies of slavery and colonialism.

Where the past is, however, not reassessed, it manages to rule the present. This is to say that Europe's failure to face its history of slavery, colonialism and National Socialism appropriately causes its ideology of racism and the related myths survive largely unchallenged. Racism continues to exist structurally and discursively. It has invaded the *white* Western archives of knowledge as performed in media, language and education. As a consequence, there is a symbolic order of *race* which, up until today, assigns people social positions in a politically powerful way.

Here we have reached another essential factor in the matter of *race*: The "silence about 'race'"[23] was not accompanied by an overcoming of the racist rhetoric of 'Othering'; in fact, it simply performs as a silence about (discussing and being aware of) *whiteness*[24] – just like Aidoo's Marija. And it is Marija, the *white* Bavarian woman in *Our Sister Killjoy*, who teaches us that racialising hegemonies, differences and positions that are anchored structurally and mentally cannot be overcome by simply claiming that 'races' do not exist, that *whiteness* does not matter or that we are "all alike."

## The 'Racial Turn': *Race* and *Whiteness* as Critical Categories of Analysis

A theoretical concept which, in the manner of Shankar Raman, I have labelled the 'racial turn,'[25] offers a methodological framework to negate the notion of human 'races' and yet to speak about what this myth has done with and to the world, and how racism has infected Europe discursively and structurally. To say it in the words of Colette Guillaumin's famous quotation: "Race does not exist. But it does kill people."[26] In a double movement of thought the racial turn leads away from 'race' (written in inverted commas) as a biological construct and simultaneously towards *race* (written in italics) as a social position and analytical category of knowledge and criticism.

Furthermore, in my definition the racial turn is concerned with surpassing conventional notions of 'race' as a matter of blackness and overcoming contemporary visions that conceive *white* as 'unraced,' 'neutral' and 'universal.' The 'racial turn' posits *whiteness* as the 'unmarked marker' and 'invisible normality' of processes of racialisation, thus resituating 'race' in its given relationality.[27] Thus framed, the 'racial turn' deconstructs *whiteness* as the subject, norm and engine of the history of 'race.'[28] In this vein, *whiteness* is not to be misunderstood as a naturally given entity based on pigmentation or other bodily attributes. Rather, *whiteness* is to be read as having been fabricated by history. Not natural visibility, but practiced, constructed and interpreted visibility is significant. The focus is not 'skin colour,' but rather its ideological construction. Moreover, the racial turn identifies that *whiteness* is a "currency of power,"[29] guarantees privileges and evokes collective patterns of perception, knowledge and action that have a discursive and structural impact on societal processes. What is important in this respect is that *whiteness* is at work even if masked *by white* people's unawareness. *Whiteness* is not, as George Yancy convincingly argues, an individual choice, but a systemic position which is a form of inheritance whose longevity needs to be acknowledged and faced.[30] Yet, insofar as *whiteness* interweaves with other structural categories – for instance sex, gender, nationality, education, religion, mobility or health – ruptures, qualifications and amplifications of power and privilege connected to *whiteness* occur. Caused by this networking of hegemonies and symbolic orders, *whiteness* manifests itself (though within the systemic boundaries of *whiteness*) in a dynamic and complex way. This does not allow, however, negotiations that would stipulate individual *whites* as off-*white*.

In the endeavour to revisit the history of *whiteness*, *whiteness* needs to be employed as a critical category of analysis. The fruitfulness of this approach is to be exemplified by analysing the negotiation of *whiteness* in Ama Ata Aidoo's poetic novel *Our Sister Killjoy*.

## African–European Encounters between Racism and Lesbian Love: Ama Ata Aidoo's *Our Sister Killjoy*

The novel's poetic description of Sissie's stay in Germany in the 1970s centres upon her relationship with Marija. Being entrapped by the above mentioned "sense of shame" about National Socialism, the German woman considers Sissie as her great chance to prove that she is 'the good *white* person.' The *white* Bavarian housewife asks the Ghanaian student to become her friend, taking this as a proof that she has nothing to do with the racism of her hometown in general and her husband Adolf in particular. To intensify her ambition, she asks permission to call her Sissie – "a beautiful way," as is explained in the novel, "they call 'sister' by people who like you very much" (28). While the Ghanaian woman agrees to this request, the author has, by means of applying various narrative devices, long since made it clear that an alliance of this kind cannot be realised. This is symbolised in another dialogue about 'self-naming.' When Marija tells Sissie that her own name means Mary in English, Sissie replies that she was called Mary in school, too. Just like Parzival, Othello and Caliban, Sissie is put off balance in the belief of being considered equal by a *white* character only to be taught that *white* privilege and *whites'* habit of defining people of colour will spoil the party. After all, the *white* woman rejects the notion of sisterhood thus evoked by Sissie. Claiming an ownership of names Marija stresses that Maria is a German name – (24) and that she does not consider it appropriate or even possible that this could be the name of an African woman. Her ignorant seizure of something that does not belong to her and her attempt to privilege herself in this questionable fashion symbolises her imbeddedness in the racist and Eurocentric discourse of her society. Her discursive rootedness in the rhetoric of colonialism also comes to light when she, for example, employs the rhetoric of the "white man's burden," saying that Christian missionaries had to go to Africa to save the 'heathens,' or thinks that Ghana is near Canada, after

– owing to a gaze that homogenises the colonial 'Other' – first taking Sissie for an Indian. Through passages like this Aidoo makes it clear that racism frames the encounter of Marija and Sissie, positioning it in the same long history that contextualised encounters such as those of Parzival and Feirefiz, Desdemona and Othello, Prospero and Caliban.

Another illustration of how the power of racism structures the encounter of the two women, Aidoo calls both Marija's husband and son Adolf and has the narrator emphasise that "a daughter of mankind's self-appointed most royal line, The House of Aryan" and "a little black sister" who would no longer exist if everything had gone according to the Führer's plan (48) simply cannot become friends. When reminding her readers that thousands of people of colour died in medical experiments, concentration camps and other internment camps, Aidoo neither attempts to equate African and Jewish victims of National Socialism nor intends to order a hierarchy of victimhood. Rather she recalls the fact that there are structural and discursive continuities between colonialism and National Socialism as well as manifold entanglements between racism against black people and Anti-Semitism. Moreover, we are told that National Socialism did not mean the end of racism and that present-day forms of racism cannot be understood without tracing their roots and re-visiting their routes.

It is, however, neither Germany's history of racism nor Marija's embeddedness in its structure and archive of knowledge (of von Eschenbach's *Parzival*, for example) which dooms the sisterhood of the two women to failure. Rather, it is Marija's willing ignorance and her belief in what bell hooks has called the "myth of sameness" (119) that lies at the gist of the matter challenged by Aidoo's novel. Toni Morrison outlines how the process of "evasion," as she calls the *white* ignorance of the fact that *whiteness* matters, has in fact made *white* people believe it to be a liberal gesture to ignore 'race'/*race* (9–10). The problem does not, however, lie in the naming of racism and its ideology of difference, but in *not* naming it. "To notice is to recognise an already discredited difference. To enforce its invisibility through silence is to allow the black body a shadowless participation in the dominant cultural body – and Feirefiz function to put Parzival on a pedestal comes to mind here. According to this logic, every well-bred instinct argues *against noticing* and forecloses adult discourse" (9–10), and what Morrison calls a responsible culture of remembering.

Analogously, Aidoo's poetic novel shows that Sissie does not have the choice of ignoring her blackness, while Marija is neither aware of this nor reflecting upon her *whiteness*, including her personal responsibility for historical and contemporary performances of racism. Rather, she believes that it is enough to quietly befriend an African to be a good *white*.

Sissie's belief in sisterhood that evades any reflection upon the power of difference informing the two women's relationship recalls the attitude of *white* Western feminists to speak of women, yet meaning *white* women only. Thus framed, they claim the existence of a universal womanhood employing it as a grounding pillar for global sisterhood. Ultimately, they end up speaking on behalf of women of colour without entering a dialogue on equal terms, yet attempting to appropriate their problems and voices. Aidoo's narrator picks up on the notion of a universally valid womanness, so gladly belaboured by *white* feminists, only to dismiss it again immediately:

> In Asia/Europe/Anywhere: For/Here under the sun/Being a woman/Has not/Is not/Cannot/Never will be a /Child's game [...] Now Marija was saying that she was, oh so very sorry, that she had no hope of ever visiting Sissie in Africa; but she prayed that one day, Little Adolf would go there, maybe. And there is always/SOUTH AFRICA and RHODESIA, you see. (51)

Just as Marija refuses to explore Africa, leaving the task to her son 'Adolf' and identifying mainly with the *white* settler colonies, the feminist world alliance founders upon *white* feminists' incapacity to look to Africa and overcome the racist history of feminism in Europe. Rather than shouldering their responsibilities, *white* women prefer women's solidarity based on amnesia.

The pitfalls of this strategy come to light metonymically, when Marija attempts to appropriate Sissie's body. She tries to seduce Sissie – first with plums, then with a concrete proposition: "Sissie felt Marija's cold fingers on her breast. The fingers of Marija's hand touched the skin of Sissie's breasts..." (64) When Marija's lips touch her, Sissie breaks free – escaping both the seizing of her body and the history of *white* appropriation of black bodies. She leaves Germany the next day.

This flight is an option which distinguishes Sissie from those people of colour and Jews who were enslaved, tortured and killed by Germans in the era of colonialism and National Socialism – as well as those Africans who have been murdered in racist attacks ever since 1945. But what about Marija: Will she have learned her lesson? Will she understand that racism continues to exist in Germany? Will she be able to acknowledge that racism is not to be overcome by black people loving (and forgiving) *whites*, but only by *white* people giving attention to their *whiteness* and revisiting its histories and narratives, thus being able to face their responsibility for unlearning racism?

# Psychoanalysis, Gender and Narratives of Women's Friendships in Ama Ata Aidoo's Writing

## Nana Wilson-Tagoe

Critical and theoretical engagements with women's friendships are rare in the criticism of African literature. Within the broader field of contemporary feminist scholarship, such friendships, when explored in critical writing, are often over-shadowed by questions of sexuality and a theoretical focus on lesbianism as a distinct sexual identity. In African cultural and social contexts, however, such friendships often denote more than romantic attachments. Often interwoven with kinship affiliations, age-group associations, and class-based friendships, they mirror the wider social and cultural life and present contexts for a variety of intimacies and expressions that are crucial for the construction of women's identities. Because the intimacies and mutual self-disclosures that support such friendships can aid or hinder women's identity formation, the trope is frequently used in literature as a strategy for doubling characters and representing the complex and multiple identifications of women. Women's friendships become, then, a means of mutual recognition and interpretation as each friend acquires self-knowledge through the mirror provided by the other's eyes.

Bakhtin theorises this phenomenon of identification as a fundamental conception of human existence, where the *other* plays a decisive role:

> In life, we do this at every moment: we appraise ourselves from the point of view of others, we attempt to understand the trans-gredient moments of our very consciousness and to take them into account through the other...constantly and intensely, we oversee and apprehend the reflections of our life in the plane of consciousness of other men (quoted in Todorov, 94).

In his evaluation of Bakhtin's work, Todorov derives a general principle out of Bakhtin's statement: "We can never see ourselves as a whole, the other is necessary to accomplish, even if temporally, a perception of the self" (95). African women writers have enlarged the metaphorical possibilities of this phenomenon in narratives that interrogate notions of femininity, dramatise splits in women's identities, and negotiate cultural, social and sexual anxieties of African women. In focusing on narratives of women's friendships in the writing of Ama Ata Aidoo, I aim to tease out a range of theoretical possibilities in the use of such friendships as literary tropes. The psychoanalytical and gender perspectives that frame my discussion will, hopefully, move my analyses beyond the surface content of women's friendships and illustrate their cognitive, social and psychic ramifications in Aidoo's writing.

I approach a psychoanalytical critical perspective with both caution and expectation, because on one hand, the particular emphasis that psychoanalysis places on the unconscious may appear to set it in opposition to the objective social systems of economics, politics and history, through which African literature has traditionally explored gender and identity. Yet, on the other hand, a psychoanalytical perspective need not be apolitical and can be made to coexist with various other determinants in the exploration of gender and identity. What is, after all, original and universally applicable in psychoanalysis is not just the discovery of the unconscious but the accompanying recognition that it is inseparable from the conscious realm and capable of disrupting its meanings. By exploring how memories, perceptions and sensations of the unconscious impinge on our conscious thoughts and actions, psychoanalysis can reveal how ideologies and norms of gender are internalised and lived by men and women. It can open up a territory of meanings beyond those rooted in sociology and biology, the normal categories through which we examine political, social and gender issues. Such complex relations between conscious and unconscious states vary over time and across cultures, and what an African literary praxis needs is a psychoanalytical model that not only rethinks the assumed opposition between conscious and unconscious realms but frees psychoanalysis itself from an excessive emphasis on Western family structures and notions of individuality.

I explore such a model by reading narratives of women's friendships in Aidoo's works both as thematic strategies and as forms of theorising about politics and gender. My aim is to tap the critical potential of psychoanalysis for unravelling unconscious motives and desires and help illuminate the internal dynamics and multiple meanings of Aidoo's texts. Freud believed that such hidden desires only manifested themselves in dreams, obsessions and neurotic symptoms. But in a later evaluation of Freud's work, Lacan elaborates a wider reading of the unconscious, explores it as a language and demonstrates how it can speak through consciousness and expose ambiguities, gaps and silences in conscious speech. For the literary critic seeking to decipher the relations between the conscious discourses of texts and their unconscious ones, such an approach offers an illuminating strategy for reading frequently overlooked struggles between the avowed politics of texts and their disruptive rhetoric. Such struggles, I believe, are what hold the key to the wider ramifications and multiple meanings of women's friendships as tropes in African women's writing.

We can trace a trajectory of such narratives from the early texts of Flora Nwapa and Mariama Bâ to later and newer texts like Dangaremgba's *Nervous Conditions* and Yvonne Vera's *Stone Virgins*. Within this continuum, however, Ama Ata Aidoo's 1977 novel, *Our Sister Killjoy*, presents unique instances of the psychological and cultural uses of such friendships in literature. The novel's narrative of a friendship across the boundaries of race, culture and sexual orientation presents a context within and against which Aidoo's earlier play, *Anowa*, and her later novel, *Changes: A Love Story*, may be fruitfully explored. In the friendship between Aidoo's protagonist, Sissie, and Marija, the German woman who befriends her, we have a drama of self and other that illuminates the multiple and complicated identities of the two women. Most commentators on *Killjoy* note its powerful and dominant nationalist and Pan Africanist discourse. Few however, grapple with the extra layer of space and meaning that disturbs the coherence of the dominant nationalist themes. Yet the tensions between the public collective ideology and the private personal narrative of desire and yearning are crucial for a fuller grasp of this complex novel.

The declared bias in the title of Aidoo's novel-*Our Sister Killjoy or Reflections from a Black-eyed Squint*-may appear to pre-empt a didactic and pedagogical reading, but *Killjoy* is a performative novel of intersecting narratives, conflated temporalities and multiple layers, all of which require equal attention. Its four sections work in different ways through narrations, observation, recollections, and "knowledge gained since," to make meaning of the protagonist's journeys through Europe. Sissie's journeys are themselves contexts for a much larger enquiry into the impact of European modernity and African counter-strategies for confronting it. In spite of the implied narrator's confident assertion at the beginning of the narrative that "things are working out/towards their dazzling conclusions," Sissie's journeys crystallise the doom that has befallen African people in the wake of a European modernity that "chokes all life and even eliminates whole races of people in its path of growth" (112). This recognition comes with an even more insistent and urgent warning: "An enemy has thrown a huge boulder across our path. We have been scattered. We wander too far. We are in danger of getting completely lost" (118). Commentators on *Killjoy* tend to view all its sections from this "dialectic of negativity" and from Sissie's counter-offensive against it. For instance, Korang's excellent essay on the novel is framed around Aidoo's political, nationalist and Pan Africanist agenda and shares some of the most incisive insights about the novel's public discourse:

> For Sissie to leave home is to amplify her perspectives; it is for her
> to know that a Western-sponsored modernity is implicated in an

unequal distribution of economic, social and psychic resources that perpetuates the dependency complex of so-called 'Third World' people. It is to know that she lives in a neo-colonial global formation in which the march of capitalism increasingly foreshortens a truly catholic, human perspective (54).

For Sissie to succumb to Marija's sexual advances is to excessively forget herself, it is for herself to be annihilated. Her resistance to Marija's sexual advances figures what Aidoo sees as the need to actively cultivate an African self-presence to counter the subtleties that seek our consent to the decadent forms of the West (58).

These are all perfectly valid and persuasive readings and Korang is right in pointing to ideological links among all four sections of Aidoo's novel. It is true that seduction as a subtle instrument of the new universalism, comes in multiple forms in the narrative, and a recurring metaphor of food as eroticism, seduction and containment links the narrative of Sissie's camp and Marija's home to all the associations of the German castle. In all these thematic and ideological linkages, it is Sissie's alert and discerning eye that proclaims and insists on the connections. She is in this sense a figuration of Aidoo's protagonist in *Anowa* who takes on the burden of telling her society truths about itself.

Yet, in spite of these dominant layers of meaning, Korang's readings would not represent the totality of the *Killjoy* narrative, if we also consider its gaps, silences and unconscious undercurrents. If we see "all of reality as made up of only what can be seen, smelt, touched and explained" (*Killjoy*, 46), then Sissie, the young, confident, self-possessed "African Miss," is the mirror opposite of Marija, the German housewife who befriends her. We may see the two women, then, as separated by race, culture, class, sexual orientation and education and read the narrative of their friendship as reinforcing the boundaries that separate them. But this pivotal section of the novel which Aidoo entitles, "The Plums," is in fact, a recollection and restructuring of Sissie's remembrance of the encounter and is presented by an implied narrator who is slightly distanced from both Sissie and Aidoo. Such a structuring of narrative not only leaves Sissie herself open to irony and critique, but also provides a context for unravelling tensions between words and silences, between enactments and gaps and between reality and the unconscious. We should read this section of *Killjoy*, then, with these dualities in mind, since the narrative itself repeatedly distinguishes between those "for whom things are only what they seem to be and those who look beyond the surfaces of things."

A dominant layer of the narrative of "The Plums" enacts a drama of difference in which histories and borders continually intrude on communication and personal relations, as if to complicate easy notions of sisterhood across race and history. It is a significant aspect of the novel's structuring that, before her meeting with Marija, Sissie has been made aware of skin colour as a means of differentiation and has recognised her difference not from a defensive position as an "other" of the white world, but by seeing whiteness as different and strange. More crucially, she has understood how ideas of difference and otherness can be used to justify all forms of plunder and subjugation. It is this emerging sense of difference (made possible by another's eye) that dictates Sissie relationship with Marija. "The image I see in the mirror," Todorov observes, "is necessarily incomplete...only someone else's gaze can give me the feeling that I form a totality" (95). It is through Marija's gaze that Sissie reinforces a sense of difference shaped by race and history. Marija's mis-recognition of Sissie, her ignorance of the painful historical forces that have produced Sissie and other migrants as postcolonial subjects, provokes Sissie to continually interrogate past history as it impinges on her present location. Indeed, both Sissie and Marija, for different reasons, define each other according to their individual experience and knowledge. This is why, in spite of being the most sustained and intimate narrative of *Killjoy*, it is also the most choppy and the most punctuated by interior monologues (mostly Sissie's) that frequently break the flow of the narrative.

The two women talk from different locations and different levels of self-understanding, and at a glance, their friendship appears to be the most unlikely and awkward of relationships. Sissie makes an instant connection between the German castle and Marija's class and gender location in German history. Yet Marija herself seems unaware of these connections and would make an "other" of Sissie, the African woman who should have no right to a European name:

> 'Mary, Mary...and you an African?'
> 'Yes.'
> 'But that is a German name!' said Marija (24).

Marija's innocence and ignorance are what force Sissie to make even wider historical connections between the German castle, her own presence at the youth camp, and the meaning of their friendship. The relationship between them thus survives in the narrative as a pull between its potential and its possible doom. At a number of times during their several meetings in Marija's house, they would sit, each with her own thoughts, connecting only at an emotional level when their eyes met and they would each smile. These conflicting pulls are encountered even in the working out of the symbolism of Mairja's garden and her fruit trees. Sissie prefers Marija's plums (loaded with symbolic associations of her own youth and sensuality) to her tomato which, in Marija's garden, appears not like the vegetable she knows back home but "strange, exotic, lush, crimson, perfected" (37) The meaning and possibilities of this friendship, then, are continually interrogated. The succulent plums are balanced against the artificially produced tomatoes and further qualified by the suggestion that the relationship itself would be short-lived. Marija's plums "were of a sheen and succulence she had not encountered anywhere else in those foreign lands. *And which unknown to her then, she would not be encountering again*" (40, my emphasis).

The pivotal and defining moment in these conflicting pulls, however, comes during Sissie's last walk to Marija's house and on an occasion when she feels truly excluded by the German language. In an environment where Sissie as a black female has become something of an exotic ("As for the African Miss, Ah …h…look at her costume. How charming. And they gaped at her, pointing at her smile. Her nose. Her lips…" [43]), her meeting with the old German couple, their repeated gestures and references to their skins and hers, and Marija's reluctance to translate their words, are enough to disrupt any sense of security Sissie has been tempted to feel in the friendship. The narrative is deliberately built to enact both possibility and failure:

> A cool breeze was blowing. The river was a dark grey in the somewhat twilight and lapping quietly against the stone and concrete embankment. It was one of these moments in time when one feels secure, as though all of reality is made up of what can be seen, smelt, touched and explained…[Sissie and Marija] walked on. Happy then, just to be alive (46–47).

After the encounter, Sissie and Marija still walk on. "Along the main thoroughfare of the town. Now their inner joys gone, too aware of the sad ways of man" (48). It is at this point that Sissie defines herself categorically against Marija, lumping her with Germany's sordid history, no longer recognising her gendered and class location within this history:

> Who was Marija Sommer?
>     A daughter of mankind's
>     Self-appointed most royal line
>     The House of Aryan-
>     An heiress to some
>     Legacy that would make you
>     Bow /Down/Your head in/ Shame and Cry (48).

Thus, by the time Marija makes her sexual advance and embraces Sissie, Sissie has already crystallised an image of her as inseparable from her country's history. It is in this light that the narrative presents this drama in Marija's bedroom. Sissie's references to sin, crime and sodomy are, in this case, not in tune with the narrative's thematic thrust, which is both historical and cultural.

For, while the encounter in the bedroom is sexual in nature, Sissie's immediate thoughts are thoughts of home and of the protectiveness of another and different kind of woman's embrace – her mother's cloth wrapped completely around her. In Sissie's eyes the two women are no longer just Marija and Sissie who have derived solace from the warmth of each other's company, shared stories, enjoyed the pleasures of Marija's garden, and, in the case of Sissie, gorged on Marija's succulent plums; they are now simply entities, representing their different races, histories and sexual orientations. Marija's loneliness is, in this sense, symptomatic of the imperial greed, and her single tear shed for the collective loss of human bonds that is directly linked to capitalist greed.

This delineation of the friendship of Sissie and Marija reflects the dominant racial and nationalist layer of the narrative that presents Sissie as "bearing the burden of political vision and affirming an Africanist self through a poetics of a will-to power, a strong survivalist ethic" (Korang, 52). But there is another layer of narrative – a subtle, nuanced and enigmatic layer that haunts the public story of difference but dwells in the margins and gaps of the narrative. For *Killjoy* is also a love story and a narrative of desire. The notion of desire as I use it here connotes more than just sexual longing, and I use it here to describe all those yearnings and longings that are either conscious (apparent in the textual surface of a narrative) or unconscious (buried somewhere in a text and revealed in gaps, silences or symbolic language).

There are two sections of *Killjoy* in which the public and political discourse exist in tension with the subjective narrative of desire. In the final section, entitled, "The Love Letter," this tension is visible in the text. Sissie begins an imaginary dialogue with her lover, pleading for a terrain of equal sharing of language, history, politics and fantasy. She abandons the attempt almost immediately, and the rest of the letter then centres on her own thoughts, becoming a kind of internal monologue in which she debates her choices, examines the positions she has taken, and reconciles herself to abandonment by her lover and the prospect of emotional anguish and loneliness. The debates in this section centre on a collective politics of re-affirmation and empowerment that demands both a creative and emotional energy and a rethinking of received notions of gender and femaleness. Should a woman's thoughts and voice be prominent in this dialogue? Has she the right to point a direction for the collective good? Should she have opinions and convictions about the political agenda? Debating her choices and arguing her positions as she writes her letter, Sissie is caught in a double bind, maintaining her political convictions while also (for the first time in her journeys), confessing publicly her desperate need for her lover. "If there is anyone I may have sinned against, it is me. That desiring you as I do, needing you as I do, I still let you go" (117). Sissie's choices, however, leave us with a set of questions: Why should love be incompatible with public politics? Why can't the subjective co-exist with the collective? This is the dilemma that Sissie grapples with in the final sections of her narrative and which she attempts to resolve by envisioning a new language of communication and refashioning in which men and women can share fears, fantasies, histories and anxieties. Sissie conceives of this almost utopian concept of language symbolically, not as language per se, but as a medium for refashioning a world, for transforming relations between men and women as a basis for transformation. But Sissie's dialectical engagement with the material and the psychic remains only a vision and a longing since she abandons the dialogue with her lover and refuses to send the letter. Yet the vision remains in this final section of the narrative as a longing and a desire, and it points a way to how we should read the silences and gaps not only in the narrative of "The Plums" but also in Aidoo's play, *Anowa*.

I make the above connections because it seems that this tension between the public/political and the subjective/psychic is a dialectic that all of Aidoo's politicised female protagonists must confront and negotiate. In *Anowa*, the protagonist's inability to recognise or negotiate this tension leads to her disorientation and hysteria as well as to some confusion in the reader's or audience's mind about the purposes of Anowa's actions in the final moments of the play. For whereas we recognise tensions between Anowa's ideological vision and her maternal longing, we are not always sure whether her disorientation is the result of revulsion at her husband's new capitalist ideology or her disappointment at his emotional and sexual rejection of her. Anowa bears an almost super-human burden of vision that makes her wiser than the wise ones. Yet, in spite of her priestly nature, she is also a woman with human desires and yearnings. How does a character manage or negotiate these ideological and psychic realms? I make this argument in order to emphasise the significance of Sissie's awakening to her psychic, emotional and sensual being in the narrative of "The Plums," and to suggest that Anowa neither had a "double" to project her dual nature nor a space in which to touch both the ideological and sensual sides of her being

How, then, do we read desire in a text that continuously foregrounds the political and collective narrative of the group? Such discourses of desire, Claudia Tate observes, "are unconscious discourses or implicit narrative fragments that fulfill latent wishes, much like dreams" (12). What our reading must seek to unravel is how such discourses are located in relation to the dominant meanings of the text and how they mediate those meanings. In *Killjoy*, the greatest irony of the friendship between Sissie and Marija resides in the double mirrors the women offer each other. Sissie comes to see Marija as different and "other." Yet in an environment where Sissie herself is frequently in danger of being seen in one-dimensional ways as "das Schwartze Madchen," the "African Miss," "the idealistic one" or simply, "our sister," it is her friendship with Marija that provides a space for a view of her inner private self as a woman and as a sexual being.

In *Killjoy*, the narrative of "The Plums," though pivotal and crucial for Sissie's self-development, is slightly removed from the more politically charged meetings between Sissie and the brothers in London. It is, therefore, a private space where Sissie can talk to a willing audience about Africa, re-live her memories of her travels and encounter her emerging self. Here the impersonal and collective name, "Sissie," adopted by the brothers "who treated me like their sister" (28), acquires a personal dimension and a different ring (as Sissie remembers) when Marija pronounces it in that special way "[as] though she was consciously making an effort to get the music in it not to die too soon but rather carry on into far distances" (46). Chris Dunton points to an important dimension of the friendship when he distinguishes the different meanings that Sissie and Marija attach to Marija's gift of plums:

> For Marija, the plums are a way of reaching Sissie, of touching her sensibility, and in their physical appearance, they are a homage. For Sissie, the gift represents what the friendship gives more generally, a validation of female qualities in which she can find comfort and self-substantiation (432).

Indeed, it is within the space Marija provides that Sissie can admit to her anxieties and share the ambiguous burdens of the feminine condition. Here, away from the brothers, she can voice disquiet about their hypocrisy in matters relating to the female body. Worried that Marija's cake would pile more weight on her, Sissie's conscious mind immediately connects with buried thoughts and anxieties about womanhood even within her political community:

> Who does not know that/Plumpness and/Ugliness are the/same Besides, my sister/If you want to believe the/Brothers/Telling/ You/How Fat they/Like their/Women/Think of the/Shapes of the ones they/Marry (47).

In relation to Sissie's own emotional and sensual development during this trip, the plums have more symbolic inferences than we have grasped in our critical commentaries. Dunton asks, "on what precise grounds is Sissie able to empathise with Marija?"(432). But the significance of the plums also has a lot to do with Sissie herself, even though they are given by Marija as a way of connecting with her. James Ivory sees them as gluttonous temptations: "Aidoo introduces the plums as a source of personal and gluttonous temptation for Sissie... a temptation that Sissie must overcome herself not to become a willing 'victim' of self-colonisation" (263). Renu Samantrai has another equally valid perspective on the symbolism:

> The plums link Sissie and Marija; through them Aidoo asks the

reader to consider the factors which unite and divide her charcters. They reinforce the lessons learnt from the intersections and mutual constructions of categories of identity formation: that no category is fundamental, unmediated by other factors, and that all identification is both strategic and split (154–155).

These differing and equally valid interpretations of Marija's plums point not only to the complexity of the symbolism but also to the multi-dimensional layers within a text that on the surface (and through its title) appears to invite a one-dimensional reading. Ranu Samantrai's point about multiple identifications demonstrates the significance of the Sissie/Marija section in the overall narrative of *Killjoy*. Sissie cannot be a nationalist focused on race alone. Her categorisations of Marija as heiress to a sordid German past and of herself as the little black girl would hold only partial truths when seen in relation to the second section of *Killjoy*. Samantrai's insight leads me to the point I want to make about Marija's plums and their relation to Sissie's other forms of identification. At another equally important level, the significance of the plums relates to Sissie herself, even though they are given by Marija as a way of connecting with her. They reflect Sissie's colour, desirable youthfulness, attractiveness, freedom, and even her exotic quality at the material time, and they awaken her to her own sensual and sexual being. "So she sat. Our Sister, her tongue caressing the plump berries with skin colour almost like her own" (40) For someone known to always carry Africa's problems on her shoulders, and who would later confess to not being womanly enough, this moment of awakening is significant and should add another layer of identification to Sissie's personality and character.

Yet such an awakening by itself adds very little knowledge to Sissie's understanding, especially her understanding of the kinds of manipulations and the crude forms of power that sexuality itself may generate. Our insights about the symbolism of the plums must therefore be linked to Sissie's fantasies about having a delicious love affair with Marija as a man. While these fantasies may be inspired by Marija's space and Sissie's own heightened sensuality, the narrative is orchestrated to reveal the unconscious cravings and dangerous traps of such fantasies. Sissie believes that only her gender separates her from the pleasures of such sexual liaisons, but her fantasising gives her an insight into the crude pleasures and the debasing impact of the masculine power she craves. Indeed, Sissie often finds herself embracing and relinquishing this seemingly exclusive masculine power and recognising that it is, after all, not a natural given and therefore susceptible to change. For Sissie this insight alone provides a major grounding not just for interrogating notions of masculinity and dominance, but also for challenging the basis of so many other rigid definitions including those she has herself adhered to. Such blurring of distinctions between categories and definitions is reflected in *Killjoy*'s structuring of narrative, and, to some extent, they disrupt the unitary discourse of the black-eyed squint.

*Killjoy* presents different ways of blurring distinctions between categories even within what may appear to be a unitary discourse. For instance, a significant irony in the friendship of Sissie and Marija is that, while it presents a context for self-revelation and the multiple identifications of women, it remains fraught, because its boundaries of race, history and sexuality seem untranscendable. Commentators on the novel interpret this situation in different ways. For Kofi Owusu, the boundaries suggest that "things are not connected in a vacuum; that indeed, the contexts of gender, race and history are inextricably linked to a person's – any person's – identity" (359). Aidoo, however, probes these boundaries throughout *Killjoy* not as an immutable given but as part of a human yearning for a different future for mankind. A narrative of desire and yearning allows Aidoo to characterise or represent boundaries and at the same time put forward the possibility of transcendence as a recurring yearning throughout the narrative. Thus, Sissie is categorical in her rejection of Marija and has no doubt about the gulf that separates them in terms of race and history. Yet the language of Sissie's leave-taking encodes conflicting pulls of departure and longing that keep attention focused on the moment of encounter rather than on departure:

> Perhaps
> There are certain Meetings
> Must not happen?
> Babies not born
> Who come with nothing to enrich us
> Too brief their time here –
>
> They leave us with
> Only
> The pains and the aches for
> What–could-have-been – but-
> Was-not (73)

The contrasting moods of the two stanzas speak for themselves. If the meeting of Sissie and Marija is imaged in the repeated aborted births of an *Abiku* the pains and aches of leave-taking deepen our loss for what might have been. Sissie herself takes her leave of Marija but is fated to revisit her encounter over and over again because of the insights she gains which will always inform her life – insights about loneliness, about the value of laughter and about anguish and yet the necessity of leave-taking. In representing this narrative of friendship, Aidoo's craft moves beyond the notion of character per se, towards the act of representation itself and the duality that is inherent in all things. Sissie repeatedly sees Marija in terms of this duality. Yet Sissie herself, for all her burden of vision, is also represented in terms of this duality. Sissie herself appears to grasp this duality when in "The Love Letter" she recalls a particularly tender moment with her lover but also hints that it was the last close and loving moment before the break-up. When Sissie's lover says to her, "I know everyone calls you Sissie, but what is your name?" (131), we do not get to hear Sissie's answer, but we can surmise that he too wanted to decipher the other Sissie behind the public political figure.

Because the friendship of Sissie and Marija is mediated by borders and boundaries, it would be a useful exercise to explore a contrasting narrative of women's friendship in the different contexts of Aidoo's later novel, *Changes: A Love Story*. Published in 1991, fourteen years after *Killjoy*, *Changes* is contextualised in a different terrain and therefore yields a different narrative and throws up different characters. *Killjoy* was preoccupied with the aftermath of European imperial expansion and its impact on African and non-Western worlds. *Changes*, on the other hand, focuses on the changing Ghanaian and West African world in the 1970s and 1980s. Aidoo characterises the world of *Changes* as a confused neocolonial African world that is only nominally independent, barely able to feed itself and without any real consensus about its values. Because the novel examines how social and cultural changes are managed, its narrative evokes both the present and the immediate past simultaneously, so that the processes of change unravel before us. *Changes* focuses primarily on three contrasting marriages that are linked to each other and to other marriages in the past. All three marriages intersect with each other for a particular dialectical effect that holds possibilities for rethinking the meaning of modernisation from the perspectives of women's lives within cultures. For, while they range across different time periods (traditional, colonial, modern) and geographical spaces in West Africa, the fundamental issues of gender and power, of female desire and aspiration and their constant collision with male power and prerogative, link the narratives to suggest how little things have changed in the area of gender relations.

What kinds of protagonist does such a context throw up and what would it mean to examine the trope of friendship within a framework of psychoanalysis and gender? The friendship between Esi and Opokuya, which functions as the principal trope of exploration in *Changes*, is crucial for thematic development and narrative strategies. But as contrasting characters, the two friends also function as doubles who represent women's multiple identities. How we grasp all these functions really depends on how we read the novel. If we read *Changes* (as it is commonly and, to some extent, rightly read) as a narrative of the dilemmas and choices of educated women in a changing society, then the friendship of Esi and Opokuya may be seen as a narrative of the different ways in which women respond to gender identification in changing social and political contexts. On one hand, their ability to exercise choice as women would "give significance to their existence," while, on the other hand, their individual choices would represent their different aspirations.

If, on the other hand, we read *Changes* as an attempt to rethink social reality itself from the vantage position of women's lives, then the trope of friendship becomes a much more radical instrument that moves beyond mutual support, validation and self-disclosure into a deeper psychoanalytical probing. In such a reading, Opokuya, good, wise, and self-sacrificing as she is, will not only be the double of Sissie but would also be implicated in Esi's "adventure" and experimentation. For as self-centred and opinionated as Esi is, she is the only character able to put her emotions, desires, fears and anxieties out in the open, the only character willing to envision alternatives. It is, therefore, through her friendship with Esi that we can unravel the equally potent desires, aspirations and anxieties that lie buried in Opokuya's unconscious and surface in her consciousness as received wisdom and "truth."

The friendship of Esi and Opokuya functions in other ways in Aidoo's novel. Unlike the emotionally charged and anxiety-riddled relationship of Sissie and Marija, forged through mutual loneliness and calculation on Marija's part, the friendship of Esi and Opokuya is a freely chosen relationship, very much like the old kinship and age-grade affiliations that defined and still define women's friendships in most communities. Because it is also class-based, and the two friends make so few demands on each other, it has a surface ease that differentiates it from the stresses of borders and boundaries in Sissie's relationship with Marija. Aidoo presents the friendship most beautifully. She allows the two friends to know themselves from the mirror held by the other and yet manages to make the relationship the most constant and "intimate" relationship in the novel. Even at a most vulnerable moment when Esi appears blinded by desolation and the temptation to have her physical needs satisfied even by a friend's husband, she is able to come back from the brink by remembering that there is something called friendship:

> And hadn't her friendship with Opokuya been, so far, the most constant thing in her life? And that whereas mothers, fathers, grandmothers and other relations are like extra limbs we grow, a friend symbolises a choice? And to maintain a friendship is a choice?... In any case wasn't the need to maintain that friendship greater on her part? (104)

I want to argue that it is because of the surface ease of this friendship that Aidoo chooses to rely on gaps, silences and symbols to critique and problematise it, moving it from a strategy of doubling as mirroring and copying to doubling as critique and challenge.

In the narrative both Esi and Opokuya represent the new middle class, cushioned by their education, mobility, allowances and huge bungalows from the harsh lives of the ordinary folk who hover around the margins of the city and the narrative. Aidoo's thematic interest is not solely in the lives of these professionals, even though the narrative focus on them may appear to suggest otherwise. Her interest is on how women's lives and relationships may illuminate social and political realities of the larger society, and how far the society can move to transform its gender regulations and therefore its social fabric. It is in this project of transformation that the two friends may hold crucial mirrors against each other through the unsaid, the nearly said and the silences.

If the narrative casts the two friends as opposites (Esi, the selfish one, and Opokuya, the good woman), it is only to qualify these definitions later on in the novel. For Esi's experimentations with different forms of relations with men and different ways of being alone may appear like her own personal and eccentric quests. But such explorations, even her wild attempts to tease out the implications of marital rape in an African context, are interrogations aimed at rethinking marriage, sexuality, careers, and women's mobility within a changing modern society. Indeed, the narrative itself appears to support Esi's explorations since it presents a divided and unequal neocolonial society on the verge of collapse and riddled with dangerous confusions. Esi's discussion with Opokuya about the need for some personal space, time and freedom in marriage draws only a set of clichés and assumptions from Opokuya in response:

> "My sister, if a man loves a woman he would want to have her around as much as possible."
>
> "To the extent that he would want me to change my job because he thought it took me away from him?"
>
> "Yes," said Opokuya, wondering where she had acquired such ideas from, and the confidence to express them so forcefully. "To the extent that he would want you to change your job."
>
> "But when we first met, Oko told me that what had attracted him most about me was my air of independence!"
>
> Opokuya had began to giggle, and then discovered she could not stop. "You see, it happens to all of us. Esi, listen, men are not really interested in a woman's independence or her intelligence. The few who claim they like intelligent and active women are also interested in having such women permanently in their beds and in their kitchens" (45).

> "No matter what anybody says we can't have it all. Not if you are a woman. Not yet."

"Our society doesn't allow it."
"Esi, no society on this earth allows that" (49).

Opokuya speaks as if with the confidence of someone else's voice. Yet, as we are soon to discover, her outward conformity masks anxieties that are not different from those voiced and put out in the open by Sissie. Her daily conflict with her husband over the use of the car is presented as the only non-serious bone of contention in the Darkwa household. But the car symbolises desire and a host of other freedoms and possibilities, and her lack of access to it on most days speaks more to her confinement and containment than she is willing to admit. Indeed, her confused and nervous reaction upon seeing Sissie's new car reveals how much of an object of desire a car and all its associations have come to symbolise for her:

> Opokuya opened her mouth. No sound came out. She shut it again. For some time she kept doing that: opening and shutting her mouth. Then it was Esi's turn to be surprised. In all the years of their friendship, she had never ever seen any piece of information, or indeed anything kick and crush her friend in this way (153).

Does Opokuya's outward cheerfulness mask hidden anxieties and suppressed desires? Whose words, then, does she repeat so confidently as she talks of women and what they can and cannot do in their societies? Opokuya is known as a 'good woman' and is often the yardstick by which Esi's husband, Oko, measures Esi's qualities as a wife. Yet a closer look at Opokuya's life shows her as a woman who allows her family to exploit her status as a wife and mother, and is equally exploited and underpaid in a state institution in spite of her odd and inconvenient schedules. Unlike Esi who would put her fears, anxieties and yearnings out there in the open, Opokuya is often evasive about the real state of her marriage and would suppress even the thought that her husband might be having an affair. Aidoo's use of the two friends to dramatise different relations to gender norms works effectively to reveal the complex and often contradictory ways in which women process and internalise gender roles and the social codes built around them. Opokuya's evasions and suppressed selfhood makes any kind of penetrating self-scrutiny and alternative visions almost impossible, and it is not a surprise that she frequently legitimises assumptions and clichés that Aidoo feels should be posed as problems and continually challenged.

One of the major ironies in *Changes* is that, in the final analysis, the novel's radical vision is not articulated by any of the educated women whose lives, marriages, disappointments and suffering preoccupy the novel's action. Rather, this vision is given to the old grandmother, who makes a fundamental connection between all forms of domination, diminishment and inequity, wherever they occur in the society. It is Nana's encompassing vision that eventually retrieves the political issues hovering around the margins and unites them with the centred narratives of marriage and gender. She is not just the character who poses the larger problem; she is also the only one who envisions the solution:

> Life on this earth need not always be some humans being gods and others being sacrificial animals. That can be changed. But it would take so much. No, not time...What it would take is a lot of thinking and a great deal of doing. But one wonders whether we are prepared to give our minds and our bodies that much (111).

Ironically, Nana's statements encompass the drama that has gone on within the three marriages, just as Opokuya and Fusena are implicated in Esi's experimentation with alternative forms of man-woman relationships. Crucially, the unmasking of Opokuya's suppressed "desire" renders her as dissatisfied a wife and woman as Esi has been, and she could conceivably be included in Esi's final hope that "...maybe, someday, her bone-blood –flesh self, not her unseen soul, would get answers to some of the big questions she was asking of life" (166).

In employing a psychoanalytical framework in this interpretive project, I have merely sought to push for the multiple and subtle underpinnings of Aidoo's writing and probe the nuanced co-existence of larger political issues and inner stirrings and yearnings in her writing. In a broad sense, this duality is what our critical endeavours strive daily to illuminate. But for reasons more related to the historical emergence of modern African literature as an object of study, the political and social issues easily deciphered in the conscious discourses of texts preoccupy us first and foremost. A framework of psychoanalysis, applied in a general sense, provides a strategy for reading how unconscious stirrings speak through the ambiguities, gaps, and silences of conscious speech. This strategy is what I have applied in reading Ama Ata Aidoo's two novels, *Our Sister Killjoy* and *Changes*. Particularly in relation to *Killjoy*, the framework has helped to push analysis beyond a valid narrative of difference to an engagement with complex strategies at work in the encounter between Sissie and Marija. It has opened up those subtle and multiple complexities of women's subjectivity that would be obscured if we read Aidoo's text solely in terms of a national allegory in which the libidinal is subsumed in the political and the allegorical.

# Teaching Aidoo:
# Theorising via Creative Writing

## Ketu H. Katrak

> We cannot assume that all literature should be written. One does-
> n't have to be so patronising about oral literature . . . the art of the
> speaking voice can be brought back so easily . . . We don't have
> to write for readers, we can write for listeners.
>
> Ama Ata Aidoo[1]

> When people ask me rather bluntly every now and then whether
> I am a feminist, I not only answer yes, but I go on to insist that
> every woman and every man should be a feminist – especially if
> they believe that Africans should take charge of our land, its
> wealth, our lives and the burden of our own development. Because
> it is not possible to advocate independence for our continent
> without also believing that African women must have the best
> that the environment can offer. For some of us this is the crucial
> element of our feminism.
>
> Ama Ata Aidoo[2]

Ama Ata Aidoo's multi-genre creative writing in English – drama, novel, poetry,
satirical narrative and essays – is rooted in her indigenous Akan story-telling
traditions, as well as in her strong feminist commitment to work towards a just
and equitable society for women and men in postcolonial Ghana as well as other
parts of the African continent and the black Diaspora. Indeed, her vision encapsulates local concerns of ordinary Ghanaian people in her creative writing, even
as she includes a global perspective in overlapping struggles for full autonomy
and liberation for black people. The two epigraphs above demonstrate in Aidoo's
own words her dedication, for the past nearly fifty years since the publication of
her first drama, *The Dilemma of a Ghost* (1965), to drawing on the rich traditions of
orality such as the "dilemma tale" and its fascinating recreations in her drama or
short story. Indeed her mastery of the craft of a short story or drama, blurring

strict divisions between the genres of narrative and dramatic, serves her deep commitment to expose gender inequities and indeed, to assert the African roots of feminism.[3] As Tuzyline Jita Allan asserts, Aidoo's essay, "To Be a Woman" "qualifies as a manifesto of African feminism" where Aidoo "links female subordination with the marginalisation of the woman writer in Africa."[4]

In this essay, I explore Aidoo's creative gifts via what I call a unique kind of "literary theorising" that provides provocative critical reading practices for teachers and scholars of Aidoo's work as well as that of other writers from the so-called "third world" who are dedicated to social justice in their decolonising societies. Literary theorising enables me to derive theoretical insights from within Aidoo's short stories, novel, essays, political satire and other writings. I explore a continuum from her creative voice that evokes socio-cultural issues and gender prejudices to Aidoo's theorising on issues of culture, gender and language, similar to that of other prominent African writers such as Ngũgĩ wa Thiong'o and Wole Soyinka.[5] In giving full critical attention to Aidoo's theoretical explorations (in her creative and critical writing), I attempt to extend what is accepted usually as "theory" in Western academia and include the writer's own analyses in essays, interviews and other occasional publications.

In pedagogical and scholarly literary activity, I regard theory as a tool, even as what Barbara Harlow calls "strategy" that assists in critical reading practices.[6] The uses of theoretical concepts, in general, can enhance the interpretation of creative work when the scholar and teacher selects theory that is relevant in illuminating the creative work and its world-view rather than opting for a critically fashionable or academically acceptable theorist or theoretical model. At times, the use of mainstream theory (that may have been radical at a different historical point in its own social context) may not serve to illuminate creative writing set in a different cultural milieu and world-view or the theory may overshadow the creative work. Further, the use of theoretical jargon may render the analysis incomprehensible to the author her/himself and to her/his constituency. As a socially responsible scholar and teacher, I strive to keep the creative writing primary and not subservient to the theoretical agenda. And I select theorists and theoretical paradigms that heighten an understanding of the creative text and not engage with theory for its own sake.

I articulate three (and there can certainly be others) broad types of literary theorising that are useful in teaching Aidoo. First, I propose that theoretical insights be derived from the creative text itself such as from the imaginative representation of character, socio-cultural and political issues. In this critical reading practice that I have used in my book *Politics of the Female Body: Postcolonial Women Writers*, the short story or drama gets primary voice.[7] Theoretical insights about postcolonial society can be derived from Aidoo's excellent short stories that provide a creative entry into the lives of ordinary people in postcolonial Ghana – stories of young and old, the arrogant educated ones and the non-

English-educated, the pain of mothering in the title story, "No Sweetness Here," and losing her only son, the beautiful Kwesi to his father in a divorce battle and then losing him entirely in death by snake-bite. Other stories portray old women reminiscing on how their own men have exploited them and continue to do so with younger women, some of whom participate in such sexual exploitation for material benefits.[8]

This strategy of literary theorising unravels the notions of love and marriage (monogamous and polygamous), the search for self-fulfillment by the highly educated female protagonist, and her rocky path to autonomy and liberation in Aidoo's novel, *Changes: A Love Story*. In an early interview, Aidoo had expressed that, given the many urgent needs of postcolonial society, writers did not have the time or leisure to "write about lovers." She had to "eat" those words, as she herself admitted, when she published *Changes* in which the many-faceted representation of the emotion of love is deeply political. However, as Tuzyline Jita Allan comments in her insightful Afterword to *Changes*, Aidoo's early work had also portrayed romantic love leading to troubled marriages as in the Ghanaian Ato and his African American wife, Eulalie in the drama *Dilemma of a Ghost*, and in Anowa's choosing her husband, Kofi Ako, against the protests of her mother and community in the drama *Anowa* (1970). In *Changes*, "the three major women characters," notes Allan, "resist victimisation" (Allan, 180). The protagonist Esi's financial independence (enabled by her MA in Statistics) gives her the confidence to get a divorce from Oko, who has committed "marital rape" on Esi's body. Although Esi's decision is not supported by her mother and grandmother, she is not socially ostracised as Anowa was, even though this modern woman is still in search of a space where she can be fully fulfilled as a woman who loves her career and who also desires fulfillment in her personal life – a challenging juggling act in the context of her society.

Esi enjoys her body quite openly – a rare depiction in African fiction. Her search for love is theorised via her body itself that is caught in the dilemmas between tradition and modernity and that remains unfulfilled in different relationships – as Oko's wife, and then as the second wife to womaniser Ali. Theoretical concepts from postcolonial feminism are played out via the narrative and the remarkable dramatic segments (inspired by Akan oral tradition) where Esi's mother and her grandmother Nana discuss Esi's predicament. "Love is dangerous," says Nana, addressing her granddaughter lovingly as "my Lady Silk." Useful critical thinkers who engage with concepts such as the personal as political, the female search for autonomy, gender as situated within the socio-economic realities of postcolonial societies include Carole Boyce Davies' Introduction to *Ngambika: Studies of Women in African Literature* and Ada Uzoamaka Azodo and Gay Wilentz's edited volume, *Emerging Perspectives on Ama Ata Aidoo*, as well as postcolonial feminist theorising by other women of colour theorists such as Chandra Mohanty, Hazel Carby and Lucille Mathurin Mair.[9]

In the Introduction to her important edited volume *Third World Women and the Politics of Feminism*, Mohanty outlines the commonality and differences among women of colour struggling against different forms of domination: "What seems to constitute 'women of colour' or 'third world women' as a viable oppositional alliance is a *common context of struggle* rather than colour or racial identifications. Similarly, it is third world women's oppositional *political* relation to sexist, racist, and imperialist structures that constitutes our potential commonality" (original emphasis).[10] Mohanty is also attentive to how feminism is defined differently in various societies, how white middle-class feminist concerns differ from those of black women who are themselves to be carefully distinguished in terms of their particular histories and geographical locations whether as black British, black African, African American or Caribbean. At the same time, I would add a cautionary note against a knee-jerk rejection of feminist theorising that is not undertaken by native constituents themselves. I would rather advocate that as scholars we engage with concepts as and when useful rather than with the proponent of such concepts whether they be Caucasian, Asian or African. In light of this argument, Dorothy Smith's articulation of "relations of ruling" (quoted by Mohanty) and its connection to power, capitalism and patriarchy remain useful:

> "'Relations of ruling' is a concept that grasps power, organisation, direction, and regulation as more pervasively structured than can be expressed in traditional concepts provided by the discourses of power. I have come to see a specific interrelation between the dynamic advance of the distinctive forms of organising and ruling contemporary capitalist society and the patriarchal forms of our contemporary experience" (quoted in Mohanty, 13).

Mohanty's 2003 work *Feminism Without Borders*, taking her earlier analysis further, is illuminating in analysing Aidoo's novel, short stories and drama: "I firmly believe that an anti-racist feminist framework" remarks Mohanty, "anchored in de-colonisation and committed to an anti-capitalist critique, is necessary at this time . . . I outline a notion of feminist solidarity, as opposed to vague assumptions of sisterhood or images of complete identification with the other. For me, such solidarity is a political as well as an ethical goal" (3).

My second proposal of literary theorising places Aidoo's creative work and theoretical material (such as on colonisation and its impacts on language, gender, political systems) side-by-side for exploration. In this approach, theory must serve to heighten the reader's grasp of the creative representation. One must be vigilant not to fall into a hierarchy (even subconsciously) where theory takes primacy over the novel or poem being analysed and worse, where the theoretical voice renders the creative work invisible.

I have used this critical reading practice where theory and the creative work are studied concurrently in graduate seminars in the fields of Postcolonial Literature, Third World Women Writers and African Women Writers. I begin these seminars with assigning two of Aidoo's short stories, "Everything Counts" and "For Whom Things Did Not Change," from her collection *No Sweetness Here*, along with selections from Frantz Fanon's *The Wretched of the Earth* (written in about six weeks prior to his premature death at the age of 37) dealing with issues of the violence of colonisation, nation-building, national culture, the native elite that often sells out its own people after independence.[11] Theory as expounded by Fanon is brought into sharp relief via Aidoo's skilful creative writing. My goal is to draw my students into complex socio-cultural, gender and political issues faced by postcolonial societies such as Ghana via both the theorist's and the creative artist's representations – Fanon's exploration of colonial domination, the role of the writer in nation-building, de-colonising struggles after independence and Aidoo's vivid story-telling with characters such as the educated Kobina being served by the disillusioned Zirigu whose reasonable request for electric lights or a flushing toilet are not fulfilled by the new "black skin white masks" leaders. Zirigu's poignant question at the end of "For Whom Things Did Not Change:" "What does 'Independence' mean?" brings to life Fanon's critical analysis of the exploitative class whose newly acquired power is totally self-serving and dismissive of the needs of ordinary folk like Zirigu. In this post-independence era and "the mourning after" as Neil Lazarus put it, the poor like Zirigu continue to be deprived of social amenities; the non-English-educated are left behind in the march to "progress;" "big men" freely exploit young women; racial, gender injustice and western notions of female beauty horrify the 'been-to' Sissie in the opening story "Everything Counts," in *No Sweetness Here* who is aghast at seeing all her female students wearing huge and luxuriant wigs and where a beauty contest is won by a mixed-race girl with naturally long hair and light-coloured skin.[12]

My third method of literary theorising proposes that a reader work out a dialectical connection between the theoretical concepts drawn from the creative text with ideas taken from theories external to the creative work. Theory, derived from the creative text, may be in dialogue or contestation with an external theory. Several examples illustrate this dialectical approach, for instance, the notion of violence as derived from Aidoo's representations of the disillusionment of ordinary people in postcolonial society (*No Sweetness Here*), continuing unequal power relations between the global North and South as revealed scathingly in Aidoo's satiric work, *Our Sister Killjoy*, the persistent patriarchal order and women's inferior status (*Anowa, Changes*), and the theorising of gender in African and black Diaspora societies such as by Patricia Hill Collins, Cheryl Johnson-Odim, Karen Sacks and Ella Shohat among others.[13]

Even prior to Diaspora Studies, one needs to engage critically with the foundational reality of the slave trade through works such as Walter Rodney's *How Europe Underdeveloped Africa*, and Angela Davis' *Women, Race and Class*.[14] In *No Sweetness Here*, Aidoo draws a skilful arc between Africa and the New World – the opening story portrays Sissie returning home to Ghana after her studies in Europe and the final story, "Other Versions" depicts an African American woman whom the narrator-protagonist sees on a subway in the US, and whose eyes and demeanour remind him of his own mother. Aidoo links Africa to African America and to the black Diaspora. It is as if Aidoo wants to leave the reader with one foot in each continent of Africa and North America, linked through the violent history of the slave trade and ongoing economic disparities, racial and gender prejudices.

Aidoo's drama, *The Dilemma of a Ghost* also spans the continents of Africa and North America – the African American Eulalie marries the Ghanaian Ato in the 1960s zeal for discovering roots and returning "home" to Africa. Even this early play demonstrates Aidoo's ambition in depicting cultural values and gender politics as they unfold in a traditional Ghanaian setting where the community is worried about Eulalie's "infertility" (the usual assumption when the couple has no children) whereas she and her US-returned husband have decided to practice birth control – a concept foreign to the traditional family and one that was not explained by the irresponsible Ato to his mother and family. The play ends with a poignant gesture of Eulalie being led gently and physically by Esi, her mother-in-law, into the family home and communal fold. Ato, ironically, who is alienated from his culture, is lost on the crossroads of making choices between his acquired American values and his native Ghanaian ones.

The dialectic connection between Africa and the black Diaspora is evoked in Aidoo's complex play, *Anowa*, where the spectre of slavery practiced by blacks themselves stealing and supplying their own people to the European enslavers is raised. Anowa is an exceptional woman who defies tradition by marrying the man of her choice, Kofi Ako, judged to be a "weak, cassava man." Anowa is rendered an outsider by her own family, hence she leaves her native Yebi vowing never to return and indeed she does not, only her corpse is brought back for burial. Anowa enables Kofi to be a strong and prosperous man, working alongside him as an equal. However, when Kofi is enamoured with wealth and starts acquiring slaves, Anowa rejects this on fundamental moral grounds. Even though this system of slavery was very different from the one practiced in the New World where the slaves were considered chattel property, nonetheless, Anowa refuses to participate in such ill-gotten wealth. As Kofi "expands" (as noted in Aidoo's stage directions) with rich clothing and wealthy accoutrements, Anowa dresses like a beggar. As with the issue of fertility in *The Dilemma of a Ghost*, here too there is a twist to the story and the usual blaming of the female is demystified when Anowa realises that Kofi is infertile. He has always refused to take another wife and finally, she publicly declares that he has lost his birthing seeds in his zeal for wealth: "My husband is a woman. He is a corpse. He is dead wood. But less than dead wood because at least that sometimes grows mushrooms" (122). This humiliation drives Kofi to shoot himself with a gun (an acquisition that came with Western influences) and Anowa drowns herself, choosing to die in a natural world. Perhaps in death, it is implied that Anowa's spirit will be accepted in ways that she was not in her human life. The Old Man, one of the choral figures along with the Old Woman, has the last lines of the play: "She (Anowa) was true to herself. She refused to come back here to Yebi, to our gossiping and our judgments . . . Ow, if there is life after death, Anowa's spirit will certainly have something to say about that!"

Although *Anowa* ends tragically, Aidoo brings in a hopeful note in imagining that Anowa's spirit will have the power and authority that she was denied in life. Anowa was an exceptional woman, ahead of her time, who could not survive in a traditional society where a woman was supposed to be as her mother Badua puts it, "without a brain and a mouth." Among the choral figures, named symbolically as "the mouth-that-eats-salt-and pepper" the Old Man is more sympathetic to Anowa than the Old Woman. He lays the blame on society for Anowa's unfortunate end: "Who knows if Anowa would have been a better woman, a better person if we had not been what we are?" However, the Old Woman is unrelenting in her criticism of Anowa: "What man prospers, married to a woman like Anowa . . . that witch? . . . Anowa ate Kofi Ako up!" However, even as the Old Man is gentler towards Anowa than the Old Woman he does not blame Kofi Ako at all for the sad fate that befalls his wife. "Kofi was, is, and shall always be/ One of us" (Prologue). Another illustration of the dialectic connection between theory and practice is found in Aidoo's use of orality in her written work, which when placed next to theorists of orality such as Walter Ong and others on oral literature in Africa, demonstrate Aidoo's unique style that brings back what she calls, "all the art of the speaking voice" in her written work.[15] In short stories like, "The Message," and in the dramatic-dialogue sections of *Changes*, Aidoo gives new life to orality by putting multiple heard voices into print. She is also leaning on the Akan tradition of a *heard* "dilemma tale" where a social problem is probed by a community from different points of view, by taking many opinions, analyses, even gossip and other indigenous ways of knowing into consideration. This is evident in the story, "In the Cutting of a Drink," where the narrator talks to his village community, reporting on his mission and often asking for a drink to wet his throat. He recreates the story of the lost child, Mansa, who left the village and ended up as a prostitute with a mouth like "clotted blood" in the city.

A dialectic connection is probed between *Changes* and postcolonial feminist theory that probes the dilemmas of tradition and modernity in postcolonial societies, and where men call upon tradition or modernity to suit their own needs. Women are often left with a double-edged sword holding the blade and not the handle, unable to control the movement of their lives even when educated and financially independent. Education itself is a double-edged sword for women in societies that are still transitioning toward equality of the sexes, and educated women often have a heavy task in balancing family and their personal needs for fulfillment. An educated woman like Esi (or Maiguru in *Nervous Conditions*, the novel by Zimbabwean Tsitsi Dangarembga) carries a huge burden in postcolonial societies that are at different stages of modernising, especially in terms of changing patriarchal notions of women's place in the family and their child-bearing responsibility (as if womanhood and mother-hood are elided so that without a child a woman is considered a failure). Maiguru, like Esi, equipped with an MA, decides "to efface" herself so that her husband, the family patriarch, Babamukuru, and his ego may not be threatened. Her income goes to him and his family. Only once in the novel does she speak her mind about the unfair treatment of educated African women and leaves the family, only to return. Postcolonial feminist theorising on motherhood and children and Aidoo's short stories and novel explore the ties that bind women and keep them in relationships even when they become violent or unfulfilling in different ways.

Feminist theorising on female friendship is portrayed in *Changes* when Esi rejects the unconscionable sexual advances made on her by Kubi, the husband of her best friend, Opokuya. Esi realises that her loyalty to her female friend is far more important than a sexual liaison with Kubi. In her refusal, she asserts a sense of female solidarity; however, Aidoo also deromanticises this notion since women do exploit other women. Esi herself has had an affair with a married man that deeply hurts Ali's first wife, Fusena. In a classic scene the community of elder women persuade, i.e. force, Fusena to accept her husband's decision to marry a second wife. Here, Aidoo boldly depicts the reality of the elder women themselves sadly perpetuating patriarchal domination and upholding tradition even when this is not acceptable to Fusena. There is no single, straightforward, or easy road to liberation. Aidoo's representations skill-fully draw out the many compromises and self-abnegations that women have to make and at other times, as with Esi, who seems to abandon her only daugh-ter who is taken care of by Oko's family after the divorce. Aidoo de-romanticises mothering as m/othering for Esi. It is simple to criticise Esi for leaving her daughter; nonetheless, Aidoo's purpose here is to probe the options that a woman may have or not have, as she tries to have self-autonomy and fulfillment on her own terms without having to prove her womanhood in the sole role of motherhood. A similar though differently articulated reality is found in the African American Zora Neale Hurston's classic novel, *Their Eyes Were Watching God* where the vibrant female protagonist does not have chil-dren. One reason might be that Hurston wants to focus on the protagonist's own psychological development through three marriages and different situations of female domination.

In conclusion, Aidoo's rich creative texts speak to us across time and space. She takes on the role of the griot in African oral tradition as one who remembers her community's history, who narrates it in story form, or as a poem or a dramatic scenario. Her many representations of the lives of ordinary women and men, their struggles of survival with dignity often in difficult situations, makes remarkable contributions to world literature in English. Aidoo's voice is unique and profoundly significant for twenty-first century students, scholars, and yes, also policy makers and development experts who can learn from her incisive questions and complex representations of the many dilemmas facing contemporary postcolonial societies in our present time.

# Section III.

*"Every woman and every man should be a feminist – especially if they believe that Africans should take charge of our land, its wealth, our lives, and the burden of our own development"*[1]

Substantiating Aidoo's concept of feminism among Africans, the articles in this section come from a broad range of perspectives. They include a historical study of 19th-century Ghanaian women's self-definition; reflections on black women's (self-)image, or popular perceptions – physical, spiritual, social – at various life stages; and the beginnings of what constitutes an African feminist conversation between Anglophone and Francophone writers. The first two papers focus on the novel *Changes*, with the new social and economic challenges of 1980s urban middle-class life. From different perspectives Mary Jane Androne and Ram Prasansak analyse the effects of gender and class on self-definition of both men and women, and of the function of economic power also on both genders. In their treatment of the social historical factors that impact these issues, both of these papers draw upon relevant work by historian Emmanuel Akyeampong, whose paper later in this section examines relevant considerations from an earlier historical era. Following the two discussions of *Changes* as a pathbreaking African feminist text is Cheryl Toman's paper on Aidoo's two essays, one of which, published first in *Sisterhood Is Global*, she refers to in the "Conversation." These are the platforms where she first articulated the notion of feminism for Africa and indeed, voiced the credo that forms the heading for this section. But Toman amplifies the influence of Aidoo's essays by bringing them into conversation with the writings of Francophone African feminists, namely Senegalese sociologist Awa Thiam (alluded to by Maryse Condé), whose *La parole aux négresses* (*Speak Out Black Sisters*) had been published as early as the 1970s and the Ivorian poet/novelist Tanella Boni, who has recently published a monograph on the psycho-sociological status of African women. The early socialising of girl-children, which obviously plays a major role in their self-perception and functioning in the larger society as women, is the topic of Naana Banyiwa Horne's article discussing two of Aidoo's short stories, one from each of the two collections.

Although the remaining three papers in this section on Aidoo and femininsm do not focus on her works, her persona unmistakenly figures in two of those. Carole Boyce Davies reflects on aging among black women and the image – physical, social, political – they project, especially in exemplars such as Morrison and Aidoo and offers a celebration grounded in theoretical underpinnings and embracing a pantheon of visible black women from Amy Jacques Garvey to Chimamanda Ngozi Adichie. But, as the next article reminds us, in spite of all such physical, social, political representations of black female strength – and they particularly pay homage to Ama Ata Aidoo – there remain sexist, if not misogynistic, characters that pervade African and Diaspora popular culture, from American hip-hop to Ghanaian hip-life. A study conducted by theatre scholar Awo Asiedu and sociologist Akosua Adomako Ampofo reveals recent positive efforts to bring about change in this area of Ghanaian cultural life. The paper that closes this section, by historian Emmanuel Akyeampong, completes a kind of circle for this section. In presenting cases of enslaved women in post-abolition 19th-century Ghana, who made difficult choices regarding their domestic status, it anticipates the spirit of self-direction such as Aidoo would later develop in *Changes*, as discussed in the opening two papers of the section.

# Nervous Masculinities: Male Characters in Ama Ata Aidoo's *Changes*

## Mary Jane Androne

"To be a man is hard"[1]

In her Afterword to the Feminist Press edition of Ama Ata Aidoo's *Changes*, Tuzyline Jita Allan argues that the novel "is as much about stasis as it is about change" (Allan, 179). She goes on to offer a nuanced analysis of the ironies that accompany the progress women appear to be making in Accra in the 1980s and argues that the hegemony of embedded patriarchal privileges compromises women's emotional relationships with husbands and lovers. I would argue that Aidoo's novel also depicts the profound masculine anxieties that surface even while male characters seem to be benefiting from "the patchwork of patri-archies" (quoted in Lindsey and Miescher, 3) that circumscribe love and marriage in contemporary Ghana. In representing a range of modern Ghanaian men – Ali Kondey, a Muslim, son of the world and owner of a successful travel agency, Oko Sekyi, headmaster of a new secondary school, and Kubi Dakwa, a senior civil servant – Aidoo highlights the growing pains that accompany gender-role changes and reconfigured marriage and familial structures. Each of these male characters embodies the particular anxieties urban life imposes on a professional man with one foot in traditional culture and another in an emerg-ing society where women wield greater economic and social power. While Ali Kondey attempts to be a modified version of the African "big man," whom Karin Barber describes as a man with a large family in charge of a number of people and who uses his wealth to support his enclave and contribute to the community, I would argue that Ali ultimately exemplifies Homi Bhabha's "mimic man," since he more closely resembles a European capitalist and really internalises colonial values, even while he tries to retain some aspects of tradi-tional African patriarchal culture (Barber, 736). While not as rich as Ali Kondey, Kubi Dakwa and Oko Sekyi use their bureaucratic power to announce their importance. At every point, however, Aidoo reveals their "nervous conditions" or their confused sense of their roles as husbands, fathers and lovers, and it is this aspect of *Changes* that I would argue is overlooked by critics who read the novel as an ironic commentary on the limits of women's social progress. Embedded in Aidoo's dramatisation of the tense dance enacted by professional urban women with men hanging on to male privilege is a profound sense that the men are just as anxious and rattled as the women who always seem to settle for less.

In *Making Men in Ghana*, historian Stephan Miescher discusses the evolution of the "big man" role in Africa. He suggests that while the "big man status and Akan ideas of adult masculinity . . . proved to be resilient," they were reshaped to embrace "the British model of capitalist accumulation" (Miescher, 199). In considering the leadership of the big man as Karin Barber has defined him, Miescher and Lindsay suggest that the changing economic and political circumstances dramatically altered the big man's relation to community. They describe the big man as a leader "who attracted dependents by his ability to provide for and protect them; in turn, they supported his claim to be 'big' by contributing labour or productive resources, serving him personally, or enhancing his reputation for generosity" (Lindsay and Miescher, 141). Miescher suggests that the ideals of big man status, however, have endured despite the changes "monetised economies" brought, since generosity, the commitment to share wealth and "communal responsibility" have "deep roots" in Asante culture (Miescher, 168). But, he argues, along with the "British model of individual capitalist accumulation" (168) the idea of "entrepreneurial individualism" (175) further removed the big man from the communal values at the heart of Asante culture. What is important for Aidoo's portrayal of the male characters in *Changes* is her recognition of how colonial rulers imported ideas that dramatically altered the economy, hence gender roles and the behaviour and practices that went with them. In his study of Aidoo's fiction, Vincent Odamtten comments on how "the consolidation of colonialism and its preference for a male-dominated elite, led to disruptions and escalating tensions in a socio-economic system . . . that had privileged women" and which "kept the society from becoming overtly anti-female" (Odamtten, 8). His analysis of Aidoo's fiction foregrounds her recognition of how the "perks and privileges . . . British colonialism afforded the average African male" resulted in "the erosion of pre-existing social arrangements" where men and women had complementary but equal roles (Odamtten, 8). In lamenting the changes that the colonial presence brought to Ghana, Aidoo comments that what is "most frightening about the colonial experience" is "what happened to our minds" (quoted in Odamtten, 17). Aidoo's sense of the "colonised mind" runs through much of her fiction, and her analysis of this phenomenon in *Changes* centres on how damaged women are when men adopt colonial ideas of gender.

In his study of the evolution of urban life in Ghana's history, which produced gender tensions in the 1930s, historian Emmanuel Akyeampong writes that;

"urban men accused urban women of an individualism that perverted the ideal of social fusion of male and female in marriage" (Akyeampong, 228). He cites two popular songs from this era – "You Like Cloth but You Don't Want Children" and "Give Me the Bush Girl," which suggest the same conflicts Aidoo's men and women are experiencing in 1980s Accra. His analysis of this earlier era centres on the related facts of money, sexuality and female autonomy, which, he argues, underlay the gender tensions of the 1930s. Akyeampong refers to the "elaboration of romantic love" as "an important male response to alleged female materialism," and this imported convention also emerges in *Changes* (Akyeampong, 229).

The opening chapters – which first describe Esi Sekyi's meeting with Ali Kondey, who becomes her lover and eventually her next husband and, second, her quarrel with her husband, Oko, which ends in marital rape – clearly announce the themes Aidoo addresses in *Changes* centring on marriage and gender roles. In reflecting on Oko's attack, Esi ironically realises "there is not, and never was, any word or phrase in the society's indigenous language which describes that idea or item" (*Changes*, 12). The episode, however, is a defining moment for Esi, who recognises that the marriage is over since "[h]er husband wanted too much of her and her time" (*Changes*, 38). Oko's anxieties centre on his friends' opinion that he is "not behaving like a man," since his wife travels all over the world and has only produced one daughter. Of the three male characters Aidoo focuses on, Oko is the man who least understands the changes attendant on marriage to a woman who is a successful government statistician making more money than he does and whose job provides him with a comfortable house. The pressures from his friends and his female relatives who completely disapprove of Esi and urge him to get "a proper wife," intensify Oko's frustrations and his determination to change Esi's behaviour. In many respects Oko's ideas about women and marriage emerge from Western ideas of romance and do not reflect traditional African attitudes toward women and work. Odamtten cites the work of sociologist Merun Nasser, who comments on the historical importance of African women's economic autonomy, which, she claims, "limits the relationship of dominance and subservience between the sexes" (quoted in Odamtten, 16). In light of this, Odamtten goes on to make the related point that "for a Ghanaian woman to be wholly dependent economically speaking, on her husband . . . would mean that a woman was not a woman" (Odamtten, 9). Oko, however, has internalised the imported notion of marriage, that his status and possessions should define his wife and determine her happiness, and he assumes his rank and money will insure her respect and admiration for him. When he gets a promotion and is appointed superintendant of a new school outside Accra, he is "baffled" that Esi is not impressed with his new office and spacious bungalow, which would be, according to British practice, "a house in the country" for her and their daughter Ogyaanawa. The anxiety Oko experiences in his marriage to Esi, though, does not completely disappear even after their separation when his "mother came and deposited a breathing parcel on his doorstep, in the form of a very beautiful and very young girl" (*Changes*, 71). Oko easily accepts her because "she looked so soft and easy" but finds himself "struggling not to think of her as too stupid to take Esi's place" (*Changes*, 71). In comparing the two women to beverages, Oko decides that "being with Esi was forever being drunk" (*Changes*, 71), but he forgoes the intoxication of Esi's intelligence and stature and resigns himself to the tamer "fruit juice" of a girl.

Aidoo's narration of Oko's fate and his choice is unsettling, however, because the reader understands that Oko is attracted to Esi's independence and success, but he is unable to accept the loss of stature it imposes on him. While he speculates that "it was always possible that some alternative existed which would have been acceptable to Esi," he ends up feeling "genuinely baffled" – "tired and bitter" – as he reflects that having "to fight with your woman's career for her attention is not only new in the history of the world, but completely humiliating" (*Changes*, 69–70). One sign that Aidoo views Oko as limited, if not weak, is the way he is influenced by his female relatives, who see Esi as a "gangling witch" and by his boarding school friends who reflect colonial notions of women's dependence which do not define either a traditional African woman or a successful professional woman like Esi. Miriam Gyimah's observation that the language Aidoo gives Oko as he is lusting after Esi reinstates the hierarchical gender order since he imagines himself the "headmaster" and his wife as the desirable "schoolgirl" (Gyimah, 390).

Esi's meeting with Ali Kondey, in the first chapter, introduces a more complicated African man, but one who is ultimately beset by his own anxieties, which result from his attempt to replicate the "big man" status of his grandfather and father at the same time that, as a "been-to" African he mimics the behaviour of a European businessman. It is in Aidoo's characterisation of Ali Kondey that the prototype of the African "big man" merges, then, with Homi Bhabha's "mimic man." Emmanuel Akyeampong comments that "the image of the aristocratic 'big man' was characterised by generosity, the use of imported drinks, rich cloths, gold ornaments, and a large number of wives, children and dependents" (Akyeampong, 222–223). And this does describe Ali's grandfather, who had been "quite rich." "He had owned an impressive number of sons, cattle, horses, sheep, goats, wives and daughters. All definitely in that order of value" (*Changes*, 24). Ali's father travelled and traded throughout West Africa with wives "in each of his favourite stops on his trade routes" (*Changes*, 23). Ali Kondey has a clear sense of his family's history and the roles his male ancestors played, and in his own modern way he tries to replicate their successful lives and honour his northern Muslim heritage. His grandfather's house "had stood on the exact spot where Burkina Faso, Ghana and Togo met, he had assumed the nationalities of

Ghana, Benin, Cote d'Ivoire, Burkina Faso, Niger, Mali, Nigeria and Togo" . . . and his "father had lived, travelled and traded through them all" (*Changes*, 23–24). And as the narrator observes, "Ali loved his father completely, and was very proud of the part of himself that met his father's approval, as well as that part of himself which he knew, secretly, resembled his father" (*Changes*, 24). While Ali matches his grandfather's and father's success as traders with his international business – Linga Hideaway Travel and Tourist Agency with offices in many countries and headquarters in Accra – he is unable to distribute gifts in the same spirit or function in a polygamous marriage as they did and it is this failure that Aidoo delineates most clearly. In *Making Men in Ghana*, Stephan Miescher observes that although "expectations of elders and big men have changed . . . [b]ig men were expected to share their wealth and act like the precolonial leaders" (Miescher, 153). First, Ali fails in "sharing wealth" as pre-colonial leaders did and, more importantly, as a contemporary urban husband, he is plagued by guilt in attempting to marry and maintain a second wife. Ali gives gifts to Esi's family to soothe their indignation that he did not follow traditional practice in approaching them with relatives rather than employees when he comes to arrange his marriage to their daughter. And he is also guilty when he finally takes Esi north to meet his family in Bamako "armed with plenty of real and symbolic kolas to say he was sorry" (*Changes*, 133). Ali, however, can only use gifts as bribes, and he is unable to manage two wives, let alone the large, polygamous families both his father and grandfather supported.[2]

Ali violates the traditions of his religion and culture in regard to second wives at every turn. All the arrangements of this union are designed to serve his desire to own Esi as if she were his mistress and not his wife. He not only never consults his wife, Fusena, when he decides to take Esi as a second wife, but he cannot bring himself to tell her when he actually marries Esi or when he goes to see her. The two women never meet and Ali finds himself struggling with his own guilt as he runs to see Esi for "wild and desperate lovemaking" before rushing home to Fusena. Miriam Gyimah points out that his desire to appropriate Esi emerges from a colonial impulse since "his behaviour is representative of the phallocentric and colonialist attitude, which holds that a woman, like vacant land without a history, can be freely claimed, occupied and appropriated" (Gyimah, 392).

Tuzyline Jita Allan argues that the "romantic love peril" and "its penchant for controlling women" as it emerges in *Changes* "offers a parable of the incompatibility of female autonomy and romance" (Allan, 183). When Ali tells Esi he wants her to become his second wife, he gives her a gold engagement ring, which she questions; "But the ring, this ring, it's not exactly a part of our way of doing the two or more wives business is it?" (*Changes*, 90) The extent to which Ali has imbibed the ideology of western romance comes through when he insists that it is "a damned useful custom" as he demands, "you've agreed to be my wife, Esi, you start wearing my ring" (*Changes*, 90). That she becomes "occupied territory" in accepting his ring is clear to Esi, and this is confirmed when, after arguing over it, Ali bluntly explains that she must wear the ring "to let the rest of the male world know that she is bespoke" (*Changes*, 91). Ali's insistence on his ownership of Esi as symbolised by the ring, then, predicts the failure of this polygamous marriage in a contemporary setting, since Esi will be unable to function freely and, despite his intentions to have two wives, Ali will not be able "to look after them properly," as he had claimed he could. To be both "owned" and neglected within a marriage is not a situation either Fusena or Esi can find acceptable as modern Ghanaian women.

The romance and marriage between Ali and Fusena which precedes the action of the novel, bears no resemblance to the multiple marriages of his male forebears who acquired women at various destinations on their travels, fathered their children, supported them, but only visited them occasionally. Ali's marriage to Fusena came after a long friendship during their university years and is based on equality, mutual interests and their shared Muslim faith. Fusena sacrifices her teaching career to care for their children, endures years in London reduced to a domestic role while Ali pursues an advanced degree, and she redirects her considerable talents to operating a successful kiosk when they return to Dakar. She tolerates Ali's affairs but is futilely enraged when he announces his imminent marriage to Esi: "She had allowed Ali to talk her out of teaching, hadn't she? And now the monster she had secretly feared since London had arrived. Her husband had brought into their marriage a woman who had more education than she did" (*Changes*, 100). Aidoo records the painful acclimation Fusena must endure in "accepting" this arrangement. She travels to Bamako to consult Ali's relatives who "are surprised that a scholar of his standing and a modern young man would want to have a second wife" (*Changes*, 105). Fusena leaves, though, "quick to realise that if the men had asked the women to talk to her, then, of course, they were not going to get Ali to give up the idea of marrying his graduate woman. She really could not believe that the beautiful journey that had begun on the teacher training campus was ending where it was threatening to" (*Changes*, 107). That Ali is unable to divulge the fact of his second marriage to Esi or even inform her of his visits to his second wife, reveals the strength of Fusena's hold on him as well as his sense that he has deeply violated his relationship with his "real" wife.

Ali goes through with the marriage to Esi because he has the power and the legal right to do this, but unlike his father and grandfather the guilt that his modern consciousness inevitably produces reminds him of his real "home" and his more enduring bond with Fusena. Aidoo foregrounds the way Ali's plans are disrupted through her use of *nutinyawo*, or prose-poetry interludes, and the Bird of the Wayside narrator. Vincent Odamtten defines the latter, a narrative device

Aidoo employs throughout much of her fiction, as an extra-communal voice who is "ignorant of the community's laws and customs" and who "inadvertently offends in the telling of the tale" (Odamtten, 24). He also suggests that the Bird of the Wayside is a "protean/transhistorical" voice, which reinforces its outsider status and allows it to transcend the immediate dramatic situation and offer more distanced commentary. Present throughout *Changes*, the Bird offers some of the cold but honest commentaries on the action and, as Odamtten observes, these narrative interruptions force the reader to become an eavesdropper who perceives "the clear and clouded motivations behind the actions of the characters . . . and knows their private thoughts, the hopes and fears that haunt them, as they race and blunder toward their individual and collective fates" (Odamtten, 162). These narrative interruptions deliberately control the reader's understanding of characters and events, and the variety of tones that emerge from the voices of the Bird of the Wayside, the *nutinyawo* and dialogues is a distinctive feature of *Changes*. In addition, Aidoo includes the voice of Esi's grandmother, Nana, whose commentaries are another facet of the mosaic of views that emerge in the telling of the tale. In this sense Aidoo creates a hybrid genre which, in its variety of perspectives, qualifies the central love plot centred on Esi and Ali. At critical moments the Bird of the Wayside enters into the consciousness of both Esi and Ali and reveals their second thoughts, and this has the effect of undercutting the prospect of the union and questions the wisdom of such a marriage. The Bird exposes Ali's self-delusion, when the narrator says, "Like all 'modern Western-educated Africans,' Ali couldn't help it if he regularly bruised traditions and hurt people. But at least he knew he was one of the more sensitive ones" (*Changes*, 133). When Ali asks Esi to become his second wife, she asks, "And your wife? . . . What does she feel about it? Or have you discussed your plans for me with her? 'I have' said Ali, too quickly, too loudly. He was clearly nervous, since he knew he was not speaking the truth" (*Changes*, 86). And after the marriage is finalised with Esi's people, the narrator comments: "All the spirits should have been appeased: ancient coastal and Christian, ancient Northern and Islamic, the ghost of the coloniser" (*Changes*, 115). Here the skepticism works to diminish the prospect of a happy union; the very evening of the marriage Esi finds herself alone while Ali is at "home with his wife and children," and she is reminded that "they had told her to be careful. That being one of any number of wives had its rules" (*Changes*, 115–116).

The poetic interlude at the beginning of Part II, which records the dialogue between two women, Aba and Ama, offers a detached, cynical view of men leaving women "for other women" (*Changes*, 101), as these contemporary Ghanaian women exchange comments on the evolution of gender roles. Their conversation rehearses the historical changes of men, money and power in relation to women and marriage and concludes with the observations:

Aba:   We must not forget that these days it could be the woman
        herself who would have such power. . . .
Ama:   Nor should we forget high education, a degree or two.
Aba:   A government job with side benefits.
Ama:   One of the topmost posts.
Aba:   One of the largest pay packets. (*Changes*, 102)

This dialogue precedes Ali's negotiations for his marriage to Esi and reminds
readers not only of the traditional sources of money and power that men have
always had, but also that "these days it could be the woman herself who would
have such power" (*Changes*, 102). Aidoo's irony here notes the subtle shift from
owning "sheep and goats" and "kola pits" to the conspicuous materialism – "cars
that race for money, horses with jockeys, aeroplanes" – of the wealthy players
in contemporary Ghana. It suggests, of course, that not much has changed.
However, in concluding this interlude with a reference to women's altered roles,
the capitalist values of powerful men and the fast-paced world where marriages
are negotiated, Aidoo hints at the complicated pressures African men face in
wielding power in this new environment.

   In reflecting on his marriage and home after he takes Esi as his second wife,
Ali celebrates the intimacy and comfort he shared with Fusena as he recalls how
they usually spent the New Year's holiday:

> Depending on how they felt, they talked or sat in a relaxed
> friendly silence. In recent years, he would sometimes select a film
> he knew both he and Fusena would enjoy, and show it on video.
> When the New Year actually arrived, he would open a bottle of
> champagne, and they would both have a glass . . . Then they
> would wish one another a happy New Year, then go to bed, make
> love and sleep. On New Year's Day they had an open house.
> (*Changes*, 119)

Clearly Ali was more comfortable, less rattled and less guilty, when he lived
monogamously with one wife and family. His own conscience will not allow
him to embrace a polygamous existence as he imagined he could. Again Aidoo
inserts another *nutinyawo* to emphasise Ali's unease:

> Guilty in spite of the fact that by all the precepts of his upbring-
> ing Esi was indeed his wife, and yet by 'home' he meant only one
> place, which was where Fusena and his children were. Hopelessly
> guilty because he knew that there was not the slightest possibility
> of him ever being able to establish any rituals in the relationship
> with Esi. (*Changes*, 119)

Sadly, though, Ali's guilt pangs and his worries about Fusena do not lead him to change his behaviour or to confront his situation honestly. Instead he allows himself an easier way out. He continues to embark on casual, covert affairs, which diminish him and dishonour both Fusena and Esi. In essence, he becomes an exploitative, modern capitalist who "takes" whatever sexual opportunities come his way.

Shortly after marrying Esi, Ali begins to feel the strain of the role he is supposed to be playing; Aidoo's poetic interlude allows the reader to hear Ali's confusion:

> How did our fathers manage? ... He knew the answer. They, our fathers, lived in a world which was ordered to make such arrangements work. For instance, no man in the old days would be caught in his present predicament: that is wondering which woman he would be making love to on a New Year's Eve. (*Changes*, 119–120)

And his guilt over his betrayal of Fusena is not the only conflict Ali has to contend with. During one of his hurried visits to sleep with Esi, he is interrupted by an enraged Oko who demands to know where "my wife" is and who ends up in a physical struggle with Ali. After retreating to his office "to calm his nerves," Ali calls Fusena, who is frantic with worry over his absence and begs him to return home for a family dinner. Nervously, he then phones Esi, "He had virtually crooned to her, apologising for his contribution to the embarrassment she had suffered" and admitting to "feeling bad" (*Changes*, 131). One thing Ali discovers early on in his marriage to Esi is that his world is not "ordered to make such arrangements work" (*Changes*, 120). He ends, then, frazzled, rushed, conflicted and aware that he can never become the "big man" who oversees and provides for numerous dependants, shares his wealth with his community and who feels pride rather than guilt as he moves from one wife to another. At this point Oko finally "gives up" his already divorced wife, declaring to himself, "Why make the bitch think she was the only woman in the world? He was going to leave her and get on with his life" (*Changes*, 131). Like Ali he, too, is "tired."

The marriage to Esi lasts less than a year. Ali compulsively phones Esi to give excuses – "to announce his imminent departures," "he phoned from the different cities and towns inside and outside the country." He sends gifts:

> And what gifts! He brought her gold bangles from the Gulf States and succulent dates from Algeria...He brought her huge slabs of chocolates from Switzerland and gleaming copper things from Zambia and Zimbabwe. He brought her shimmering silk from the People's Republic of China, the Koreas, Thailand. (*Changes*, 157)

Ali's most telling gift is a handsome, expensive maroon car which he delivers on New Year's Day and which Esi understands is a "bribe," "like all the other things he had been giving her. They were meant to be substitutes for his presence" (*Changes*, 147). Outside, Aidoo's Bird of the Wayside narrator alternately describes Ali as "visibly shaken," "worn out," "nervous," "feeling bad," as well as "guilty." Finally, Ali admits to himself that "He really could not keep it up" (*Changes*, 157). When Vincent Odamtten observes that the personal choices that emerge in the midst of all the gender tensions within this city are a result of "the confrontation between traditional Africa and imperial Europe" (Odamtten, 165), he identifies the real source of Ali's anxieties as a man in contemporary Accra. Caught in the interstices of two roles, the "big man" with multiple wives who comes and goes as he pleases bearing gifts to ease his way, and the successful African "been-to" capitalist who uses his power and privilege to indulge in adulterous affairs, Ali jets from place to place in the process of amassing wealth. While he may appear to fit this second stereotype, Esi hears of his womanising and is aware of his subservient, young and pretty new secretary; he shows signs of weariness and is "nervous" in attempting to mimic this prototype, too.

The cars and houses that are central tropes throughout *Changes* convey the extent to which property and individual acquisition are contemporary measures of masculine success in Accra. Here Aidoo's text reflects Homi Bhabha's concept of the way in which the "mimic men" are "authorised versions of otherness" (Bhabha, 88). "The ghost of the colonisers" Aidoo refers to is no where more present than in the houses owned by Kubi Dakwa, Oko Seyki and Ali Kondey. Kubi's house, Sweet Breezes Hill, in the colonial residential area, was the bungalow built for an English surveyor "sent to these deadly mosquito-infested regions to administer the territories on behalf of their royal majesties, and generally civilise the natives" (*Changes*, 16). As a later version of his English predecessor, Kubi Dakwa insists on parking his government-issued car "in the place in the car-park marked out for the surveyor's car. He was convinced that the car should be parked there all day" (*Changes*, 17). When Bhabha suggests that the mimic man is "the effect of a flawed mimesis, in which to be Anglicised is emphatically not to be English" (Bhabha, 87), he points out the discrepancy between the English civil servant who had occupied Sweet Breezes Hill and worked as a surveyor in colonial Ghana and Kubi Dakwa who is "almost the same, but not quite" (Bhabha, 89). Kubi's self-conscious compulsion to announce his status betrays his awareness that without the house and the car visibly present in the allotted space, the world will not know who he is. The metonymy of the car for the man actually illustrates the mimicry Bhabha identifies as "partial representation" (Bhabha, 89), which is the inevitable reminder of the "coloniser's presence" (Bhabha, 88). Kubi's chronic and repeated struggles with his wife, Opokuya, over who will drive the car every morning only highlights his anxieties, as he reflexively demands the status and the freedom the car confers, knowing that he complicates his wife's need to fulfill her professional and familial responsibilities. He too is "guilty" and makes "concessions" to Opokuya since, like Ali, he has affairs and flaunts the perks of his job because he has the power to do this.

As a northern Muslim living in southern Ghana, Ali insists on residing in the *zongo* at the entrance to Nima, whose buzz of activity reassures him that he has not completely abandoned the traditions of his culture. Unlike his father's and grandfather's, Ali's house, though, is the residence of a successful capitalist and is restricted to his wife Fusena and their children. The wall Ali builds to surround it never encloses a large, polygamous family with multiple wives, servants, dependants and supporters, and he never spreads his wealth beyond his family except to secure lovers or appease offended relatives. In becoming a man, Ali internalises the most oppressive patriarchal attitudes from his traditional Northern roots as well as those from neocolonial Ghana. As Odamtten comments, "Mansa Musa's general attitude, his socialisation affects his son," and Ali also adopts the Western notion of the "role of man as the head of the household" (Odamtten, 167). In this sense, Ali takes the worst of all possible choices from both worlds and discards the enlightened ideas of gender roles that favour the equality of men and women. What gets lost, then, are positive notions of the importance of women's work and autonomy that would have characterised Ghanaian women in the past as well as professional, educated Ghanaian women in the present.

Simon Gikandi, in his Afterword to Mugambi and Allan's *African Masculinities*, asserts that the crisis of masculinity has been a central trope throughout the history of African literature. He suggests that "deep anxieties about the meaning of gender" have been dominant emotions in male characters from Sundiata and Shaka to Okonkwo and comments ironically that, "Masculinity is often more important to the African cultural text when it is apprehended in crisis or failure as part of a negative dialectic of identity" (Gikandi, 296). To view Oko, Kubi and Ali in this context is to see their anxieties and their quests to establish themselves as men in both their professional and their private lives as a part of the constantly shifting culture that requires intricate adjustments that often are impossible to make.

The strategies Oko, Ali and Kubi employ, then, in the Accra of the 1980s, to ease their masculine anxieties over their changing positions in society and their status with women echo the same tensions Akyeampong records from the pre-World War II era in Ghana. In attempting to solidify their status by becoming revised African "big men," Ali, Kubi and Oko actually become "mimic men" who revert to European symbols of wealth and power, conspicuous cars and houses and hidden mistresses.

Aidoo leaves the problems of both men and women unresolved at the end of

*Changes*. In this sense, her novel, like many of her other works, is a "dilemma tale" or a narrative which raises questions and states problems in an effort to provoke thought on serious political or social issues (Odamtten, 19). That Esi must resign herself to being a mistress more than a wife or that Ali moves about under layers of guilt and anxiety, suggests that no one wins in this struggle and that the social conditions which create this unease are still to be addressed. But the novel does not conclude simply with dissatisfied women and rattled men. For, in spite of Esi's bitter consciousness of her mistake in marrying Ali, she, along with Fusena and Opokuya, hear her grandmother Nana's words that it is women who can upset the balance and, as Sally McWilliams puts it, "see and act beyond the joke that marries male domination to neocolonial relations" (McWilliams, 352). In the end, Fusena's radiating anger keeps Ali coming home, Esi staves off Kubi's attempted seduction and Opokuya gains a new sense of autonomy with Esi's refurbished car. When Nana insists that, "It can be changed. It can be better," and instructs Esi that it will "take a lot of thinking and a great deal of doing," she predicts the way women will force men to move for real "changes" to occur (*Changes*, 111).

# Gendering Commodity Relations in Ama Ata Aidoo's *Changes: A Love Story*[1]

Ram Prasansak

Many literary critics of Ama Ata Aidoo's *Changes* have paid special attention to sexual and gender politics in the realm of everyday life.[2] Though persuasive, their readings neglect, however, a broader historical and economic context of the novel, uncritical of the heroine's privileged class position as a government worker and her proto-western feminist consciousness. Putting the novel in its historically specific context of the 1970s and 1980s, I argue that Aidoo makes a double critique of neocolonial capitalism and western feminism through her nuanced representations of commodity relations peculiar to Ghana's political economy.

In these decades of extreme material scarcity, certain commodities under the state-classified category "essential commodity" disappeared from the market, causing grief to the majority of Ghanaians. Imported alcohol was one of those rare commodities whose presence in the novel serves a significant ideological function for Aidoo. She sustains the critique of neocolonial capitalism through exposing Esi's abundant possession of imported spirits. In so doing, she aligns the heroine to the group of the powerful "big men," locally known as *abirempon*, who have historically enjoyed the privilege of consuming luxurious commodities.

Aidoo simultaneously articulates this exposure with a critique of liberal feminism that not only cautions against a premature celebration of female autonomy but also calls for foregrounding the structure of class relations in the production of female subjectivity. She develops this by a subtle dialectical comparison between Esi as an emerging bourgeois subject and other urban working-class women such as market traders, fishwives, and street hawkers who appear only briefly in the novel.[3]

# Historicising *Changes*

Although the novel was first published by the UK Women's Press in 1991 and reprinted by the US Feminist Press in 1993, David Wehrs suggests that the story takes place in either the 1970s or mid-1980s.[4] Building on Wehrs's observation, I scale down the probable range to the period between 1975 and 1985. One crucial indicator is the novel's reference to informal spare parts business run by "Kokompe" engineers (155) Jonathan Dawson states that this type of small-scale vehicle repair business gradually emerged as a significant informal sector in the early 1970s and provided jobs for local entrepreneurs. Its fortune, however, began to change when the imported vehicle business resurged in the mid-1980s: "1985 is most commonly cited as the year when business began to decline."[5] My reading of *Changes* takes into account the scarcity of imported consumer goods and the politics of the informal sector.

In the novel, Aidoo makes so few references to the colonial past that it is difficult to discern how the old forms of colonial economic domination have persisted in the postcolonial present. However, if pulled together, the sporadic and fragmentary descriptions of economic activities and banal situations provide a coherent picture of Ghana's political economy. I suggest that Aidoo's depiction of imported alcohol as a commodity form sheds light on not only Ghana's subordinate position in the global economy but also its internal class and gender relations.

Aidoo's subtle engagement with the economic history of Ghana is perhaps best captured in the scene where the narrator describes Kubi's and Opokuya's bungalow. Built in the 1930s, the house was the property of a British colonial surveyor. Having described the bungalow as a vestige of colonialism, the narrator mentions the influx of British colonisers in the Gold Coast:

> In time, quite a sizeable group of Englishmen had come bringing their women with them. They had lived close to one another so that they would be well-placed to fight those natives with guns, the mosquitoes with alcohol, and general boredom with women. Of course, they always could and they often did import both alcohol and women from 'home.' But then, there had also been more than adequate local supplies of both. So in the end they banned the local liquor to force the natives to buy expensive English gin and Scottish whisky, and then proceeded to take over the local women. (16)

This passage brings into sharp focus the economic domination of the British Empire. The references to the importation of Western alcohol and the prohibition of the local spirits are indicative of a form of trading monopoly. While the one-way traffic of this commodity generated wealth for the British colonial state, it insidiously moulded the Gold Coast as a perfect model of the import economy. This colonial capitalism, however, was met with a form of native resistance.

According to Emmanuel Akyeampong, by the early twentieth century, liquor revenue was the leading contributor to the overall revenue of the colonial state. However, international organisations for the regulation on liquor traffic, the temperance movement in Britain and Gold Coast chiefs pressured the state to ban the importation of liquor. In 1930, restrictive liquor laws were passed. The prohibition of gin and genever (Dutch gin) imports, combined with the depression of the 1930s, caused the decline of colonial revenue. While attempting to revise these laws to resuscitate finance, the colonial state discovered that the natives had all along distilled local gin known as *akpeteshie*.

Since the local gin was regarded as a threat to the colonial revenue, the state intervened by prohibiting its distillation and consumption, but to no avail. The illicit production of this spirit was rising in the 1930s partly due to the demand of migrant wage labourers. This gin, which was produced in the rural areas, had to be smuggled in to urban retailers. While it eluded the eye of the state, it created job opportunities for working class natives, facilitating the rural and urban economies. Because of its illicit mode of operation, we can understand the trading of the local gin as part of the informal economy. Though branded illicit, this cheap local gin carried a subversive political function: *"Akpeteshie* became an important symbol in the struggle of the working classes against the snobbish upper classes, traditional authorities and the colonial state."[6]

Aidoo's brief account of the prohibition of the local gin is by no means random. I argue that it demonstrates her understanding of the ways in which the state produces class and gender subjects. In addressing the broad circuit of the trading relation between the British metropole and the Gold Coast colony, she draws attention to the intertwining issue of the regulation of wealth by the state and the illicit mode of wealth creation by the sub-proletariat. She complicates it by bringing into play gender relations at a local level.

Aidoo provides no direct connection between the prohibition of the local gin by the colonial state and the increase in prostitution with the advent of the British colonisers. Nevertheless, we can infer that she is crafting a broader context of urbanisation where alcohol consumption was associated with prostitution. As Akyeampong argues, *akpeteshie* comes to represent a new urban culture that created jobs for musicians, actors, liquor retailers and prostitutes.[7] The way Aidoo refers to the Gold Coast women as one of the "local supplies" suggests that she is referring to prostitutes. Like the local gin, the local women were a commodity for Englishmen.

These historical accounts reveal that alcohol contains multiple meanings. On the one hand, it served as an illicit commodity subject to the sumptuary law of the state for the revenue purpose. On the other hand, it carried a gendered meaning as it was associated with female prostitution in a new urban setting with a heavy concentration of male migrant workers and foreigners. In this scenario, a drinking woman can be associated with prostitution. This association is a recurring issue in Aidoo's works, most prominently in "In the Cutting of a Drink" in *No Sweetness Here*.[8] This short story is told by a male villager who is on a mission to find his lost sister in Accra. In utter shock, he finds out that one of the prostitutes, the "bad women of the city," he dances with in a bar is his lost sister Mansa (36). Through the eye of this villager-narrator, Aidoo portrays prostitution as a new form of urban work that radically disrupts the traditional definition of work and morality. As the narrator ends the story in disbelief, "My brother, cut me another drink. Any form of work is work...is work...is work!" (37).

Similarly, the gendered and economic meanings of alcohol reverberate in the postcolonial world of *Changes*, most prominently in the Twentieth Century Hotel scene. Waiting for her friend, Esi is deciding whether she should have some drink. Embodying her consciousness, the narrator tells us, "She could go and sit down to have a beer. But she knew this was not really done. A woman alone in a hotel lobby drinking *alcohol*? It would definitely be misunderstood" (32: emphasis original). Esi is acutely aware of the cultural association of women and alcohol. It surely is a sign of prostitution. However, I argue that Aidoo places more emphasis on Esi as a consumer who has a privileged access to luxurious commodities than as a prostitute who is a commodity-object. I locate Aidoo's subject-object subversion in her description of the hotel.

> In the lobby other voices bubbled as though in a boiling cauldron,
> mixing with the clinking of glasses, the steps of men and women
> coming in and going out, some popular music that intruded subtly
> from one of the hotel's bars: high life, Afro, rock, Afro beat...funk,
> whatever. In the distance and from a neocolonial African city that
> had barely managed to drag itself through one more weekday, the
> tired traffic hummed and crawled itself home for the barest of
> evening meals and a humid tropical night. (33)

By labelling Accra as "neocolonial," Aidoo emphasises the burden of colonial history that immobilises postcolonial Ghanaians. It is worth noting how the narrator leads us away from the luxurious lobby to the static streets where common people labouriously struggle to make ends meet on a daily basis. Notwithstanding a fear of being misunderstood, Esi decides to have the beer anyway. Though this decision signals a sense of liberation from gender and sexual constraints, the description of what lay outside the property of the hotel makes it inconvenient to celebrate with Esi. For people around her cannot afford what she can.

In context of 1970s material shortages, which the above passage accurately describes, alcohol was classified as an "essential commodity." It was rarely available in the market and fiercely subject to price-control decrees. Aidoo uses this commodity relation to criticise Esi's privileged class position. This critique is most conspicuous in the scene at her bungalow. After she has made love with her second husband Ali, Esi offers him a drink to choose from: "I've got just about everything, everything. Beer; wine: white, red, pink; rum: white and dark; proper scotch and all; vodka; cognac ..." (77). This passage exposes the abundant possession of imported alcohol, critically underscoring Esi's bourgeois subject-position. This exposure not only recalls Aidoo's previous reference to the colonial importation of Western alcohol and prohibition of *akpeteshie* but also shapes her critique of neocolonial capitalism.

In the colonial context, the possession and consumption of alcohol indicated class differentiation between the big men *"abirempon"* and the commoners.[9] Aidoo obviously aligns Esi to the first group. The class division between these two groups is even wider if we consider that most – if not all – of the spirits in her possession are not locals but imports. The type of alcohol one consumes is suggestive of one's class status: "[i]mported drinks were seen as symbols of social status among the upwardly mobile in the Gold Coast" whereas "[f]rom its origins, distillers, retailers and consumers of *akpeteshie* were regarded as "low-class" and "filthy" people by *akrakyefo* (educated gentlemen) and *awurabafo* ("ladies")."[10] In the postcolonial period of the 1970s and 1980s, the fact that essential commodities such as beer and imported drinks were available only to the educated class is telling of the continuous unequal redistribution of wealth. Reading the consumption scene back into the colonial world, it appears that Aidoo is rewriting a gendered relation where a female subject by means of education and employment gains more access to resources that were previously dominated by men.

## Gendering Informal Economy

Aidoo develops a double critique of neocolonial capitalism and western feminism not only through a representation of Esi's conspicuous consumption but also a dialectical comparison between the bourgeois heroine and other urban working-class women such as street hawkers, market traders and fishwives. She incorporates these "minor" characters through the literary devices of poetic fragment and analogy. Building on the work of Fredric Jameson, I term them "the political unconscious" as the force that does not appear obvious in the narrative thrust. Jameson writes:

> The literary structure, far from being completely realised on any one of its levels tilts powerfully into the underside or *impensé* or

*non-dit*, in short, into the very political unconscious, of the text, such that the latter's dispersed semes – when reconstructed according to this model of ideological closure – themselves then insistently direct us to the informing power of forces or contra-dictions which the text seeks in vain wholly to control or master.[11]

I argue that the peculiar ways in which the sub-proletariat figures surface into the novel are suggestive of their clandestine mode of wealth accumulation that Esi as a government data analyst cannot comprehend and yet desires to regu-late. I view the disciplines of statistics and sociology as producing normative knowledge about urban populations. In a Foucauldian sense, their knowledge production can be seen as a tactic of governmentality where urban subjects become the target of regulation.[12] At the historical juncture of economic stag-nation, this tactic was inexplicably linked to the discourse of economic formalisation that Ghanaian governments upheld as a solution to the crisis-management of capital.

The "political unconscious" comes into presence in the first chapter. In their first encounter, Ali offers Esi a ride home after they have finished the business. Having turned it down, Esi finds it uncomfortable to deal with the silence. The narrator describes the situation:

> Therefore, since she knew silences sometimes have a way of screaming strange messages, she spoke, to fill the air with words.
>     They know that art well
>     who trade in food –
>     pad up
>     where resources are scarce, or
>     just for cool profit:
>     grains for sausages
>     some worms for burgers
>     more leaves for *kenkey*! (3: emphasis original)

The passage is peculiar in many ways. First, aesthetically, this is the first frag-ment that does not fit well with the preceding mode of realism. As Waleska Saltori Simpson points out, "this brief poem interrupts the linear narrative and allows the reader a glimpse of Esi's inner thoughts, while at the same time repre-senting the attitudes of an omniscient narrator or the dilemma tale storyteller... who understands the overall action of the narrative and is thus able to embel-lish his or her account with informative details without overtly intervening to offer a solution."[13] While Simpson also underlines a multiplicity of female voices made possible by this narrative technique, her argument stops short at explain-ing the implication of the analogy being drawn in the above passage. This leads to the second point. Thematically, there is no obvious logical connection between Esi's interaction with Ali and the concurrent description of food traders. How do we understand the analogy between the art of discoursing (filling up the silence with words) and the art of trading (cutting down the cost by using cheaper materials) especially in the situation where Esi is the thinking subject and the hawkers the object of her thought?

To state the most obvious aspect of this analogous relation, what Esi in this particular scene shares with the petty traders is a struggle to bargain in a hostile environment. For Esi, put in the framework of giving, to turn down an offer from Ali is to deny an indebtedness to and dependence on the giver. Having done so, she feels a sense of independence: "Esi became aware that something quite new and interesting was trying to make itself felt in that room that early evening, late in the month of June" (3). While this passage registers her romantic attraction to Ali, it also marks her emerging feminist consciousness. Throughout the novel Esi tries to assert her autonomy. It is noteworthy that in the first pages Aidoo carefully constructs Esi's character as a professional working woman with authority. She grants her heroine a formal direct speech when she introduces herself to Ali: "I'm from the Department of Urban Statistics" (1). For Esi, to accept a man's offer is to reinforce the inferior status quo of "the feminine" whereas to decline it is to reassert her political power granted by the state.

As for the hawkers, the message from the poetic fragment is ambiguous. On the one hand, it demonstrates their struggle to eke out a living in the time of material shortages. On the other hand, it disapprovingly describes their economic survival strategy as profiteering "just for cool profit." The ambiguity raises the question of what kind of attitude Esi has toward them. To tease out this implication requires an understanding of the role they play in the Ghanaian economy.

Despite the strange manner of their entry into the discourse of the novel, the street hawkers or petty traders are banal actors in the street scenes of Accra. Their products – prepared foodstuffs and especially kenkey – are the staple foods of Ghanaians. The novel's glossary describes kenkey as "[a] coastal Ghanaian staple of cooked corn meal and one of the solid foundations of a vast national food industry" (167). It underscores the significance of this seemingly marginal trade to the national economy as a whole. These small traders provide goods and services to the large section of the urban labour force. However, what the glossary and the poetic interlude do not provide is the gender specificity of the traders. In her study of trading, especially among the coastal Ga in Accra in the 1970s, Claire C. Robertson points out that the trade in prepared foods was dominated by Ga women.[14] It can be thus inferred from this description, combined with the common fact of the domination of market women in Accra and Ghana in general, that Esi is creating some sort of alliance with these women traders based on gender identification. Indeed, we can very well read

Esi's unconscious reference to the market women in her encounter with the predatory Ali as a sign of her envy of their ability to speak up to master a difficult situation. Aidoo represents the discursive skill and psychological strength of female traders very well in "Payments" in *The Girl Who Can & Other Stories*. This short story is a long monologue of a fishwife who spits on an arrogant middle-class nurse in the fish market. It sympathetically reveals the hard-working life of a market woman who struggles to fulfil family obligations as a wife to an unemployed husband and a mother to a sick child and to make a decent living out of the tough fish business. It is this fishwife's ability to make a masterful speech that Esi of *Changes* envies.

We should, however, question the unmediated immediacy of the relationship between Esi and the market traders. As much as Esi wants to assert her female autonomy by drawing on the strength of the market women, their social positions are different. We can establish their relationship in a self-other dialectic. As part of the urban population, the market women are the "other" that the data analyst Esi processes and produces as a category of knowledge. We can even put this dialectic in the dualistic conceptual categories of formal and informal economies. While the heroine works in the formal sector as a government salariat, the other women operate in the non-wage zone of the economy. The formal and informal sectors should not be conceptualised as two distinct economic spheres because they are interdependent. Kwame Ninsin even argues that their relation is asymmetrical: "the informal sector is an indispensable product of the formal sector of the periphery capitalist economy: it is in fact functional to its survival…the informal sector is assigned the role, in the national division of labour, of producing inexpensive goods and services for the consumption of this majority of the population that cannot afford the expensive consumers goods and services produced by the formal sector."[15]

Esi's ambiguous attitude toward the kenkey traders reinforces their different social formations. While she is apparently aware of the conditions of resource scarcity under which these women traders operate, she nonetheless speculates that they do it "just for cool profit." This speculation casts doubt on Esi's own understanding of Ghana's socio-economic situation and the plight of these traders.[16] If the narrator in this passage grants us access to Esi's inner thoughts about the traders, s/he does the same in the passage where Esi encounters another group of the urban population: the fishermen. This time her attitudes become less ambiguous as the narrator is more explicit about her lack of such an understanding.

As Esi is driving towards the Hotel Twentieth Century to meet her friend, she is overwhelmed by the beauty of the beach area surrounding the hotel. Looking for a parking lot, she is wondering "how people who had such scenes at their backyards felt on a daily basis. Then, ashamed of herself for automatically applying a research approach, she told the sociologist in her to shut up"

(31). While she is carried away with the beauty and the possibility of a research topic, the narrator gives us a sort of counter-description to the scene:

> The beach was only a couple of kilometres to the right of the hotel, and the fishermen who were busy packing up their boats down there might have been amused if they had heard her thoughts. For at that time, what they were wondering was whether the government would fulfil its promise to help them get motorised boats and better nets, and when the Minister of Power would stop increasing the price of kerosene; and that night out at sea, would it be warm? For definitely, a chillier wind than they were used to was blowing through their lives. (31)

Throughout the novel, little do we know what kind of statistics work she does for the Department of Urban Statistics. While the ironic distance of the passage is aimed at ridiculing Esi's political naivety, it addresses the superficiality of her research that has more to do with the leisure activities of the fishermen than the harsh economic situations they are facing. The description of the scene outside the hotel only recalls that inside the hotel that I previously discussed. If the sound pleasure from all kinds of music – "high life, Afro, rock, Afro beat...funk" (33)– is juxtaposed with the humming of the traffic outside the hotel, the visual aesthetic pleasure Esi derives from the neighbourhood – "the vision of so much gold, golden red and red filtering through the branches of the coconut palms" (31)– is put into sharp contrast with the image of the fishermen shivering in the cold dark nights. More importantly, the description emphasises the soaring price of one of the consumer goods: kerosene. Aidoo deliberately juxtaposes the fishermen's lack of this fuel with the abundance of fuel consumption that the character Kubi as the senior civil servant enjoys: "the government paid for its [his car] fuel consumption and general maintenance" (17). In meticulously mapping the uneven urban development of Accra, Aidoo sheds light on the unequal access to the allocation of scarce national resources between the civil servants and the sub-proletariat.

In constantly drawing our attention to Esi's political insensitivity to the economic conditions of the urban population and in describing, albeit ambiguously, the economic practice of the prepared food traders as profiteering, Aidoo appears to create the character Esi as a normative subject whose rationality is determined by a larger politico-economic mechanism of price control that the Ghanaian state deploys to manage the crisis of capital accumulation. In other words, pricing is not only a technique of economic domination but also an index of moral economy. The phrase "cool profit" is highly suggestive of a large profit margin that the hawkers gain from their trade and of the consequent social disapproval. In Ghanaian popular discourse, those who sell their produce higher than the regulated price are considered evil. In the public imagination, they are portrayed as witches, thieves and vampires.[17]

I argue that the peculiar way in which these traders appear in the text *out of nowhere* and their economic practices are condemned, while the narrative is focused on the heroine, implies a collective and objective perception of their social class as an economic malaise that needs to be cured. Put another way, the large profit margin of petty trading on which Esi speculates is created neither out of one single transaction nor from a whim on the side of the traders. Rather, profiteering has been historically regarded as an economic malpractice peculiar to the petty traders. A formal attempt to cure this illness can be traced back to the colonial period. Brodie Cruickshank, the first Collector-General of the Colony, describes his amazement with "the peculiar partiality of the natives of the Gold Coast...for pedling."[18] He describes this economic activity as a social malaise: "Men, women and children are indiscriminately infected with this passion, which absolutely assumes, from its inveteracy, the character of a confirmed malady."[19] Cruickshank diagnoses the Gold Coast nation's illness with a clear political and economic interest. He laments the un-organised labour and credit system that these trading activities induce. Put in the conceptual framework of formal and informal economy, the colonial government attempts to organise labour production in industrial and agricultural sectors as well as regulate petty trading in the informal sector.

Reading the profiteering of the *kenkey* traders (through Esi's eyes) "objectively," I argue, trivial as it makes itself in the novelistic space, it represents one of the most distinctive economic malpractices in Ghana in the 1970s and 1980s. Mike Oquaye describes the late 1970s as the era of *kalabule*.[20] Probably derivative of a Hausa expression *"kere kabure"* – keep it quiet –, kalabule includes a range of corrupt practices from hoarding, profiteering, black marketeering, and smuggling. The marketplace dominated by women was the sphere where these malpractices were said to be prominent. It became a site where the government made an intervention by implementing price-control decrees of "essential commodities" ranging from milk, flour, rice, sugar, fish, meat, beers, and spirits in the midst of high inflation and extreme material scarcity. As it became common for the general consumer to complain against the high prices by the kalabule sellers, the latter became the usual suspect and target of public frustration. Esi's attitude toward them fits within this fold.

Although the umbrella term "kalabule" lends a coherent understanding of the economic culture of Ghana, it is important to differentiate the economic capabilities of different groups of traders. This means taking into account the intensity of capital involved and their position within the system of commodity distribution. Esi's attitude toward the profiteering of the street hawkers has to be considered in the real historical context that the novel does not provide. In the case of the *kenkey* traders who add more leaves (presumably banana leaves or corn husks as wrapper) into dough balls, Robertson gives a more inclusive picture of their position within the distributive system of commodity. During the time of high commodity prices, when corn was expensive, the women traders strategised their art of trading for economic survival by making the size of the ball smaller rather than raising the price. As *kenkey* was and still is vital for the national consumption on a daily life basis, the traders received a great deal of complaints. Robertson compares these female traders to the cornsellers with whom they shared an interdependent but unequal trading relation. While the price of corn was high, that of *kenkey* that used corn as its quintessential material was controlled by the government. During the time of shortages, the price of *kenkey* did not rise up as fast as those of other commodities. And if the sellers raised it, they had to deal with public discontent. Comparing the *kenkey* trade to the black market in terms of their performance during the economic crisis, Robertson remarks, "there is no black market in kenkey in time of government control. This may be the reason why so many women complained about the lack of profit in *kenkey*. Inflation hit them worse than anyone else. In spite of price controls on corn, the black market flourishes."[21]

In the corpus of the feminist criticism that examines, to use Nada Elia's words, "levels of feminist consciousness,"[22] there is a consensus that Fusena, Ali's first wife, is the most marginalised female character. Juliana Makuchi Nfah-Abbenyi, for example, states that "Fusena...is represented as the most stifled of these three modern African women [Esi, Opokuya, and Fusena]. She is stifled and silenced at varying and multiple levels," which include her subordination to Ali, his patriarchs in Nima and their wives and sisters.[23] Reading against the grain, however, I argue that Fusena is not quite marginalised if we ground her within the historically specific context of material scarcity. On the contrary, she occupies a relatively secure economic position in Accra. In the novel, we are told:

> He [Ali] bought her a massive kiosk at a strategic site in Accra. They said of it that what Fusena's kiosk did not sell was not available anywhere in the country. And when she heard they were saying that she made more money from the kiosk than the largest supermarket in town, she only smiled to herself. (67)

The intensive scale of her trade and the vast variety of commodities she owns easily render her one of the "commodity queens." Ernest Dumor points out that the business of these market elites "operates approximate monopolies because of their ability to exercise control over a substantial part of supply of particular products critical to the domestic market and their relative power to restrict competition in the distributive sector."[24] Similarly, calling for a more careful classification of women and their profits, Robinson states, "In order to classify women according to their profits, one must consider three aspects of their businesses: commodity, location and function."[25] Following Dumor and Robertson's points, we need to distinguish the street hawkers like the *kenkey* traders from the market mammies like Fusena, since they occupy different positions within the system of commodity distribution. The first group is located at the end of the chain, buying the commodities from the wholesalers or the producers in the prices that are already above the ceiling of the state-controlled price (as Robertson shows in the tension between the corn producers and the *kenkey* sellers). The market mammies in the wholesale business are involved in corruption. As Emmanuel Hansen points out, "[t]his class of women, through a system of carefully worked out alliances with the managerial class, erected a complex network of relations which enabled them to receive goods directly from either the state shops or from the factories and released them at very high prices either on the local market or preferably on the market of the neighbouring countries..."[26] Although Fusena may not fit this category neatly as in Hansen's account, it is possible to say that she has a monopoly over certain types of out-of-market commodities through Ali's plausible connection with the government. It remains dubious as to how Ali gets such a "strategic site" for his wife because the acquisition of the kiosks and market stalls is very competitive.[27] In my conjecture, Ali may have bribed one of the kiosk distribution officers.[28]

## Speaking for the Other (Women)

By way of concluding this article, I explore the political message Aidoo conveys to the reader on the problematic of representing women's voices. I have thus far brought to attention the different class formations among the category "woman." The presumed gender homogeneity is radically disrupted if we situate the female characters within the specific systems of commodity distribution and price control in Ghana. I suggest that Aidoo's sporadic depictions of the uncanny sub-proletariat female subjects are aimed at undermining the growing feminist consciousness of the heroine that is rather individualist. Aidoo develops this critique through the literary technique of analogy.

As the "kenkey" episode shows, Aidoo has an idiosyncratic way of presenting the sub-proletariat characters. In the second chapter, she introduces the reader to another group of the urban working-class population: the fishwives. This chapter centres on the failing conjugal relationship between Esi and her husband Oko that begins to get worse after what Esi terms "marital rape" (11). Concerned with gender and sexual politics, this chapter sets up the dominant themes of love and marriage for the rest of the novel. It also generates some debates whether "marital rape" is one of "imported feminist ideas" or actually exists in Akan or other indigenous African cultures (11). It is noteworthy that this is the first time the word "feminist" appears in the novel. However, as this issue has been well debated, I draw attention to the peculiar way in which the narrator describes Esi's agony after the "marital rape" scene. It is a description that eerily features the fishwives:

> She sucked her teeth, or made the noise which is normally described, inadequately, in English as a sucking of the teeth. It was thin, but loud, and very long. In a contest with any of the fish-wives about ten kilometres down the road from the Hotel Twentieth Century, she would have won. (10)

Like the prepared-food traders, the fishwives are drawn in an unlikely analogy with Esi. Because they are short-lived in the course of the novel and overshad-owed by the life-story of the protagonist, the peculiar presence of the fishwives is likely to either go unnoticed or be regarded as an excessive component of the text. However, I argue that this aesthetic idiosyncrasy is ideologically consis-tent rather than random. The sub-proletariat figures are carefully put into a dialectical relation with the central character. Their class position as the polit-ical unconscious that returns to interrupt the master narrative of the text is hinted by Aidoo herself. In addressing the creative and censorship process of her writing, she says:

> I didn't make references to fishermen, it is just that it came in from her own [Esi's] immediate mind and universe. Of course, you always have a choice of cutting them out but I have always known that I had better not do that because that would be terrifying. It would be like acting as the chief censor on my own imagination. If I am scared of censorship applied from outside, how much more for auto-censorship. That is even more dangerous for a writer.[29]

Comical as the teeth-sucking contest may sound, the scene conveys a serious political meaning. This analogy is made to reconcile the incommensurable voices of two female subjects positioned within two distinct socio-economic formations: the middle-class and the working-class. In attempting to tune in their voices, the narrator has highlighted yet again, as in the "kenkey" episode, an instance of women's suffering and struggling in their everyday-life situation. A gender homology is attempted through a presumption that sucking teeth is a natural gesture of women or a "lower-class" behaviour that Esi somehow shares. We can read Aidoo's deployment of it as underscoring shared gendered experi-ences and behaviours between Esi and the fishwives while simultaneously marking the class differences between them. In fact, as a close examination of the passage shows, this is not a simple analogy where two voices are equally balanced, because one is the dominant. If the contest ever happened, Esi would have been the winner. Therefore, analogy is not simply a comparison between two subjects but also a disruption between them, a disruption that creates some space for a contestation for representation. Theoretically put, as the fish market functions as an anti-thetical to the Hotel Twentieth century, the working-class fishwives are constitutive of, but also simultaneously extraneous to, Esi's subjectivity. They are the 'other' whose subjection cannot be subsumed within the parameter of Esi's experiences.

The incommensurability of the female voices is transposed into the urban spatial arrangement that would further reveal a class division between Esi and the fishwives. The above passage not only makes a reference to the fishwives but also shifts focus from Esi's bungalow to the fish market located near the hotel. It suggests that Aidoo has consistently paid attention to the unevenness of urban spatialisation. She reminds her reader that while the hotel is the centre of the business for the neocolonialists like Esi, it is also, surrounded by working-class subjects.

She underscores this by staging the unequal electricity consumption between the hotel and the fishing village surrounding it:

> The Hotel Twentieth Century was blazing with light, consuming enough electricity to light up the whole of the nearby fishing district. But the fishing villages did not have electricity. In fact, all that the fishing community knew of that facility were the huge pylons that stood in their vegetable patches, and the massive cables passing over the roofs of their homes as these bore the electricity to the more deserving members of society. Like users of hotel lobbies. Like Mrs Esi Sekyi and her friend, Mrs Opokuya Dakwa. (43)

While this passage self-evidently underwrites the class differences between urban subjects, Aidoo further undermines the growing feminist consciousness of Esi by utilising Esi's close friend Opokuya to remind Esi of the heterogeneous categories of women. She devotes a great deal of textual space to the dialogue between Esi and Opokuya at the hotel. It serves not only as an expression of feminist bonding, but also as a reminder that gendered meanings of the text should not be extracted from Esi's experiences alone but also from the other women around her.

The political question of speaking for the other (women) which implies an appropriation of the other voices culminates in this hotel scene. At one point in the conversation Esi mentions to Opokuya that life is so hard on "the professional African woman" (50) and "life is just hard on women" (51), she seems to homogenise the experiences of all (African) women. The slippage of her liberal individualism that does not take into account the other women around her is fiercely counteracted by Opokuya's more politically sensible observation: "'Esi, isn't life even harder for the poor rural and urban African woman?" (51). Opokuya adds, "But remember it is always harder for some other women somewhere else" (51). As I have shown, Esi does see these "other women" but does not comprehend them because of her differing class status. Significantly, Opokuya's sharp remark delays a feminist calling for sisterhood politics that elides a class division between heterogeneous groups of women. In fact, the difficulty of speaking for the other was hinted earlier when the narrator describes that Esi's expression – sucking the teeth – is "inadequately" translated into English. Her agony does not translate well into the lives of other women, the political unconscious, who toil at the margins of her universe.

# African Women and Power:
# Ama Ata Aidoo's Essays "To Be a Woman"
# and "The African Woman Today"

## Cheryl Toman

[S]ome [ …] shouted that I was not fit to speak about public
matters – that I should leave politics to those best qualified to
handle it, and concentrate on doing what I do best, which is writing plays and fiction.

Ama Ata Aidoo[1]

Ama Ata Aidoo's landmark essays, "To Be a Woman" (1982) and "The African
Woman Today" (1992) brought out African women's voices in published form,
essentially "introducing" African women to the non-African world. Aidoo was
one of the first authors to formulate a truly Afro-centric definition of African
feminism and power without having to resort to merely defending the African
woman against racist stereotypes pervasive in American and European feminist
discourses. Prior to Aidoo's works, outsiders knew African women essentially
through anthropological texts which did not allow women of the continent to
speak for themselves. Although Aidoo admittedly is recognised more for her
creative writing in the form of novels, plays and poems, these two aforementioned short essays – for which, ironically, she received some criticism initially
– unequivocally shaped African feminisms and paved the way for the Afro-
centric writings and research of Aidoo's contemporaries and successors such as
Buchi Emecheta, Ifi Amadiume, Amina Mama, Oyèrónké Oyěwùmí, and
Tanella Boni, among others. The impact of Aidoo's socio-political writings in
particular was far-reaching, as she was able to transcend borders established
since colonial times with a power to engage African women from Anglophone
and Francophone worlds in a common conversation about their past, present
and future. Aidoo and authors whom she inspired expressed in no uncertain
terms what the African woman herself has contributed to feminism all along,
shifting scholarship and research from an initial focus that had attempted to

demonstrate how the African woman "needed" Western-defined feminism to improve her condition in society. As Oyèrónké Oyĕwùmí pointed out, early feminist scholarship had "created its very own African woman" (27) and the cross-cultural research leading to such writings had been "primarily a narcissistic undertaking" (30). Oyĕwùmí reiterated what had been stated some years before by Chandra Mohanty who declared, "Without the overdetermined discourse that creates the third world, there would be no (singular and privileged) first world" (353).

Aidoo's 1982 essay, "To Be a Woman," clearly set two milestones: it not only positioned Aidoo as one of the first African contributors to feminist scholarship but it also argued that African women historically were living feminism long before women of other cultures. Aidoo echoed what Filomina Steady had claimed one year prior to the publication of "To Be a Woman." That is, that the black woman would be seen as the "original feminist" (Steady, 36) if Afro-centric constructs of motherhood and sisterhood were to be incorporated and accepted into an overarching definition of 'feminism.' The concepts behind African motherhood and sisterhood potentially empower all women regardless of social class or level of formal education. This awareness was especially evident among African women writers and activists, eventually leading them to articulate conceptions of global feminisms.

Aidoo's earliest essay marked a period in Anglophone African women's writing which paralleled similar consciousness movements across West Africa. Approximately two years before Aidoo introduced "To Be a Woman" as a talk for a United Nations Institute on Teaching and Research (UNITAR) seminar held in Oslo, Norway, in July 1980, Senegalese sociologist, Awa Thiam, had published La parole aux Négresses [Speak Out, Black Sisters], a monograph that received a good deal of international attention.[2] Hence, by the end of the 1970s, Aidoo was already recognised internationally as one of Africa's first women writers, and her participation in UNITAR gave her additional exposure to Africans and non-Africans alike who were working both inside and outside the academy. Aidoo's talk was then published as an essay in the volume entitled, Creative Women in Changing Societies: A Quest for Alternatives (Nicol, 1982). In African feminist scholarship, the contributions of Thiam and Aidoo most certainly paved the way for others like themselves by creating a niche for those who wished to further the interdisciplinary study of African women. For example, we can cite Nigerian scholar Ifi Amadiume's work in social anthropology that argued the relevance of social history and political economy in formulating more insightful perspectives on gender and matriarchy within African feminism (Amadiume, 2011). Amadiume came to challenge not only Western scholars of matriarchal theory such as Johann Bachofen, Lewis Henry Morgan and Friedrich Engels, but she also questioned one of the earliest known Afro-centric scholarly texts addressing the status of women, Cheikh Anta Diop's L'Unité *culturelle de l'Afrique noire* [*The Cultural Unity of Black Africa*] (1959). Although Diop recognised the power of individual African women in his book, Amadiume later criticised him in both *Afrikan Matriarchal Foundations* (1987) and *Reinventing Africa* (1997) for having failed to discuss actual "systems which institutionally and structurally guaranteed women power" in Africa (1987, 83). Amadiume's studies were thus the first critically acclaimed works on African matriarchy[3] thanks to other pioneers such as Ama Ata Aidoo who first sought to challenge the notion of not only a European-invented Africa, but even of an Africa perceived from the eyes of the African male alone.

Awa Thiam and Ama Ata Aidoo are just two of the many African women who have recounted their own history, and yet they were among the first to have told this story to outsiders who up until that time had created their own versions of the past. Each one a rebellious thinker in her own way, Thiam and Aidoo discussed highly related social issues in a complementary and innovative manner. Having written *Speak Out, Black Sisters* from the standpoint of an African social scientist, Thiam produced a work that was undoubtedly ground-breaking for the 1970s. As a creative writer and public intellectual, Aidoo directly challenged a Western-influenced feminism which considered the African woman to be powerless and submissive.

Each with her respective yet complementary style, Thiam and Aidoo had many ideas in common and both encouraged the African woman to speak out – to shout even – until she was no longer ignored. Thiam wrote, "Time to take the floor in revolt and say 'No!' To give to speech the power of action" (Thiam, 13), while Aidoo urged women to express themselves in no uncertain terms and with defiance: "Clarity therefore became the only reliable companion and weapon for a fighting woman" (1982, 264). Both Thiam and Aidoo were critical of white feminists of their generation who spoke of a Western-invented notion of "sisterhood" with which they supposedly reached out to African women without even attempting to recognise, let alone understand, the African model based on solidarity and the African construct of motherhood with its inherent power in co-mothering society's children, biological or not. That is, according to Oyèrónké Oyěwùmí, motherhood as it is conceived in its own right, and not merely one constructed in relation to or in opposition to fatherhood (13). As Amadiume would emphasise some time later in *Reinventing Africa*: "The Western 'sisterhood' of the 1960s and 1970s was a false and baseless fabrication, with neither a material nor historical basis. African women do not understand sisterhood individualistically, as do European women" (198).

Thiam and Aidoo did not back down from confronting some of the most recognised figures in feminism of the time and often they took on the entire movement itself. Thiam blasted Kate Millet for the following analogy which Millet made in a speech in Paris in 1976: "Rape is to women what lynching is to blacks." Thiam responded in *Speak Out, Black Sisters*:

We must make it clear that [Millet] is referring to white women, which she does not do. [...] European feminists do not seem to know: they continue to satisfy themselves with the false comparison between the situation of blacks and that of women – by which we must understand white women, even if they don't say so explicitly. [...] You would think that black women did not exist. In fact, they find themselves denied, in this way, by the very women who claim to be fighting for the liberation of all women. (114)

Aidoo in turn defended the African American woman for her ambivalence towards the early Women's Liberation Movement in the United States: "Who can blame her? Knowing as she does that during slavery 'Miz Ann' (your average white wife of the plantation owner) often actively collaborated in the degradation and brutalisation of the black female" (1982, 263). Through these important writings by Thiam and Aidoo, the notion of a global sisterhood without qualification had now been officially challenged, paving the way for entire volumes on the subject to be written later, such as Obioma Nnaemeka's *Sisterhood, Feminisms and Power* (1998)[4] and Oyèrónké Oyěwùmí's *African Women and Feminism: Reflecting on the Politics of Sisterhood* (2003).

In an attempt, however, to provide a fair account of the African woman's status within her society, Thiam's bold approach sometimes worked against her as white feminists allowed themselves to concoct negative and unfounded stereotypes based on both their misuse of Thiam's interviews with African women and their misinterpretation of her social scientific findings. Although Thiam's essay also presented many contradictions to Western perceptions, those who already held pre-conceived ideas of a battered and broken African woman all too conveniently focused on certain elements of Thiam's text that seemed to support their conclusions. Thiam stated in her book, for example, that with the exception of "a few intellectuals," "the black African woman, be she town-dweller or villager, married, divorced, or single, has a deplorable life" (114). To make matters worse, Thiam also conveyed to self-admiring white feminists exactly what they had thought all along – that traditional African societies held no promise of empowering women. Thiam wrote:

First of all, we must get rid of the myth that African societies are matriarchal. If people think that having a say in deciding on who the children should marry, organising the domestic chores, and looking after the household is the same as having power, they are seriously mistaken. [...] A woman's sole right is to have no rights. (15)

Clearly, it was never Thiam's intent to support Western feminism's racist conclusions concerning the African woman but rather to show that the women whom she cited in her research indeed had voices of their own. As Thiam most powerfully reminded her readers: "Anyone who is expecting feminist diatribes should not read on. Black women from Africa are talking here" (15).

Of course, there are many parts of Thiam's essay not to be overlooked which allude to how colonialism destroyed positive aspects of African traditions in regards to women. "The women of black Africa have suffered enough from these colonial and neocolonial attitudes" (80) Unfortunately, Thiam's ideas that were critical of the more unprogressive facets of traditional society coupled with similar ideas reiterated by other African feminist social scientists were too often the only side presented in Western feminist discourse. This was most apparent perhaps in debates concerning female circumcision in Africa as Thiam's work was one of the earliest written on that subject. As Cheryl Johnson-Odim stated, "There are a number of African women who are leading the battle against female circumcision, but many resent what they feel to be sensationalistic nature of the campaign by many First World feminists" (Okonjo-Ogunyemi 231).[5]

Ama Ata Aidoo's creative works faced similar skewed interpretations by Western-oriented critiques which may be one reason why Aidoo was led to address important social issues in her essays. In a 1987 article by Katherine Frank that was included in the *African Literature Today* issue entitled, *Women in African Literature Today*, Frank claimed that Ama Ata Aidoo's *Our Sister Killjoy* espoused a "world without men" as the only solution for patriarchal oppression (15). Thus, Frank reduced African sisterhood to merely a "world [African women] create apart from men" (20) and she later concluded that since "men held all the power in African society," African women could therefore only get what they want "by consorting with the enemy in a kind of psycho-sexual guerilla warfare" (24). Unfortunately, Frank wasn't the only scholar to misinterpret African customs and social practices as "evidence of culturally sanctioned and institutionalised forms of lesbianism" (Oyěwùmí 14). What scholars such as Frank missed entirely was the reality that African societies are often organised into dual-sex systems of power with each sex managing its own affairs (Okonjo, 45). Although it is true that Western women exhibited little willingness and desire to grasp such a concept, it did not help matters that they simply had no reference point to facilitate such understanding, since the only recognisable structure of power in the West was the patriarchal model whereby major economic and political roles are held by men to an overwhelming extent. Western women accompanying their husbands to Africa during the colonial period or even those who worked there as missionaries or teachers had little or no opportunity to interact with African women firsthand since any dealings between the coloniser and the indigenous people were almost exclusively conducted by men alone. Although the situation has been improving somewhat over the years, women's institutions of power in Africa still tend to be ignored, as we continue to see global charitable organisations, transnational corporations, and most national governments headed by men (French, 351) and thus so-called development programmes in Africa continue to favour assistance to men over women.

In terms of a response to thoughts which continued to be expressed by non-Africans, powerful voices such as Aidoo and Buchi Emecheta were incensed enough to write additional essays addressing such misconceptions. Emecheta's brilliant essay "Feminism with a Small 'f'" (1988) continued in the spirit of Aidoo's "To Be a Woman" by being one of the first to refer to an African brand of feminism. Emecheta's essay was initially presented as a lecture at the Second African Writers' Conference in 1986 in Stockholm in the presence of Ama Ata Aidoo who was also a participant. Many of the tenets of African feminism that Emecheta introduced had always been supported by Aidoo – for example, the idea that the African child belongs to many mothers (Emecheta, 173) and that true rewards of African sisterhood are experienced, to cite just two examples, by women "who cultivated sisters either through marriage or through the village age-group" (Emecheta, 177). In addition to her articulation of sisterhood, Emecheta dared to say that African women sometimes made polygamy work for them and proved it[6] (176) – making all too evident the bias of Western feminism in its debates on polygamy which tended to compare only the best scenarios of monogamous marriage in the West with the worst possible situations of polygamous marriage found in Africa. Not so ironically, Aidoo herself addressed similar issues of managing love and career goals with all the obstacles presented by the social, political and economic realities of contemporary Ghanian society in her novel, *Changes: A Love Story* (1991). Aidoo's protagonist, Esi, leaves a troubled monogamous marriage for a polygamous one, for she believes it will allow her greater flexibility and more independence. The originality of *Changes* is that it profiles a modern, well-educated and professional woman who considers polygamy as a possible option for a freer existence. Further, as Juliana Makuchi Nfah-Abbenyi points out, the novel also makes "a specific point about women working together and putting collective action to their benefit against oppression" (58). In her own matter-of-fact style reminiscent of Aidoo's, Emecheta directly addressed from an Afro-centric perspective all of these interrelated subjects such as love, marriage, culture and solidarity, concluding that African feminism "tends to be much more pragmatic" in comparison to its Western counterpart (177).

The remarks which followed Emecheta's presentation in Stockholm were also published along with her essay, and in the transcript of this discussion, Ama Ata Aidoo applauded Emecheta's vision of feminism by adding:

[...] we hear that feminism is something that has been imported into Africa to ruin nice relationships between African women and African men. To try to remind ourselves and our brothers and lovers and husbands and colleagues that we also exist should not be taken as something foreign, as something bad. African women struggling both on behalf of themselves and on behalf of the wider community is very much a part of our heritage. It is not new and I really refuse to be told I am learning feminism from abroad. [...] So when we say that, we are refusing to be overlooked, we are only acting today as daughters and grand-daughters of women who always refused to keep quiet. We haven't learned this from anybody abroad. (183)[7]

In 1992, four years after this exchange between Aidoo and Emecheta, the journal *Dissent* published yet another of Aidoo's essays, "The African Woman Today." Here, Aidoo continued her struggle to dispel myths about the African woman that the Western world – and its media in particular – had created. "The African Woman Today" had been inspired in part by persistent images of the African woman and child depicted in a state of constant poverty, hunger and helplessness which were diffused to promote Live Aid, a series of mega-concerts in Western nations meant to bring famine relief to Ethiopia.[8] The project's founder, singer/songwriter Bob Geldof, was hailed as an international hero for his efforts, having been knighted by the Queen of England (Aidoo, 325) and later emerging as a nominee for the Nobel Peace Prize. Aidoo was less impressed with Geldof, however, after taking into account his promotional materials and accompanying photo-journalism for the benefit concerts which all had fixated on a most damaging image of the African woman – "she is breeding too many children she cannot take care of, [...] is old beyond her years, she is half-naked: her drooped and withered breasts are well exposed: there are flies buzzing around the faces of her children, and she has a permanent begging bowl in her hand" (Aidoo, 319). Aidoo blasted this particular depiction of the African woman as a mere "media creation" (320) but qualified her statement nonetheless by noting: "But if she does exist, she is a result of the traumas of the last five hundred years' encounter with the West, the last one hundred years of colonial repression, the current neocolonial disillusionment, and of a natural environment that is now behaving like an implacable enemy" (320).

Indeed, Aidoo's purpose in writing "The African Woman Today" was clearly to challenge what is meant by "development" and to demand an explanation on how we arrive at its definition. Many African writers and activists soon echoed these same sentiments expressed by Aidoo, such as the Malian scholar and author Aminata Traore who declared in 2000, "Africa is not poor; it has been impoverished" (453). Since political and economic institutions of power are traditionally led by men, women's power and potential are virtually ignored in so-called development projects. Thus, Aidoo's essay is one of the first attempts by a public intellectual, at least, to view development issues from an Afro-centric perspective.

In "The African Woman Today," Aidoo reminds us: "In most countries of Africa, whole sectors of the economy, such as internal trade, agriculture, agro-business and health care are in the hands of women" (319e). To this day, almost two decades later, statistics still confirm Aidoo's assertion. For example, African women grow 80% of the food that feeds the continent (Seager, 24). In fact, the rallying cries of Western feminist movements demanding the "right to work" have always perplexed African feminists since, as Aidoo states, "In West Africa, virtually no family tolerates a woman who doesn't work" (1992, 382) – an idea, she claims, which has been "drummed into us since infancy" (1992, 382). If anything, as Amina Mama pointed out in her book, *Beyond the Masks*: "Black women were suffering from chronic overwork" (11). Yet, despite this awareness about African women and work, Aidoo reveals that; "Africa's women farmers may get the rawest deal of all." She explains:

> Although it may now be fashionable to admit that women have been the backbone of the continent's agriculture, that is a very recent trend. Earlier on, their existence was not even acknowl-edged. Governments never mentioned women in agricultural policies. So the burden of constant poverty, of working on the farm from sunup to sundown and then coming home to take on dozens of other roles, was added to the deprivation of being invis-ible to policy-makers. (1992, 323)

Despite the realities that Aidoo reveals, this is not to say that the African woman fits the mould of the negative media images so commonly displayed in the West. Indeed, one of the most powerful and thought-provoking concepts expressed in "The African Woman Today" shows how Aidoo puts such conflict-ing images into perspective:

> A way to appreciate some of the contradictions in the position of African women today is to adopt a bifocal mode of looking at them. This would reveal that in relation to their men, they were just as badly off as women everywhere. But viewed from outside, internationally, the picture changes somewhat. Vis-à-vis the rest of the world, the position of the African woman has not only *not* been that bad, but in some of the societies, she has been far better off than others. And this should include the self-congratulatory West. (324)

Very much in the spirit of Ama Ata Aidoo's "The African Woman Today" is the recently published monograph entitled, *Que vivent les femmes d'Afrique?* [What Is the Life of African Women?] (2008), by the Ivorian writer, Tanella Boni. Like Aidoo, Boni is known primarily for her creative works of fiction, but this book promises to be one of the most significant contributions to African feminism to appear since Aidoo's essays. Boni's study of the African woman cites specific examples from all over the continent and from every colonial heritage, creating an even more extensive cross-cultural conversation that Thiam and Aidoo had initiated through the simultaneous expression of similar ideas three decades earlier. In her work, Boni provides sufficient historical background that serves to situate the African woman in various social, political and economic contexts, but the main purpose of Boni's essay – much like Aidoo's motivation in writing "The African Woman Today" – is to speak of the here and now and to do so in a way that places the African woman in the proper perspective. That is, Boni depicts African women as powerful without diminishing the hardships they face on a daily basis, and furthermore Boni tackles realities that perhaps Aidoo could not have even envisioned at the time she wrote her own essays. For example, one topic of discussion that Boni undertakes is the African woman's essential and complex role as entrepreneur, as observed in markets in particular all over the continent. In "The African Woman Today," Aidoo described the African woman's relationship to the market as both a "business arena and a home away from home" (324). However, this image lies in stark contrast to the difficult and even hostile environment of the market that the Writer-Turned-Teacher-Turned-Trader encounters in Aidoo's more recent short story, "Choosing" included in *The Girl Who Can & Other Stories* (2002). As Aidoo's short story shows, the effects of globalisation cannot be ignored and are profoundly felt on many levels by the average African market woman today, but as Boni points out[9]:

> Through real-life situations, they are learning the new codes and they know that the global networks by which all sorts of merchandise transit are not easy to penetrate. Customs officers, freight agents and border police are not meaningless words to them. They are familiarising themselves with a new vocabulary and with new ways of managing their enterprises. (47–48)[10]

Thus, since the so-called global economy impacts the African market today in a most dramatic way, the workplace of the African woman is bound to change as well. Boni reminds us that, "the streets and the markets make up the African woman's territory" (Boni, 49),[11] to what a non-African may perceive initially, such spaces have always been much more than a simple location to buy and sell goods. The market thus should be considered "a place where there is an exchange of information and acquaintances, but it is also a space of survival where women are allowed to breathe" (Boni, 48)[12]. Such exchanges and networking bring countless advantages to African women, and afford them new opportunities. Evolving with the times, the African market is reflecting and responding to changes in the sphere of commerce. Already in 1992, Aidoo reminded us that the African woman's workplace now ranges from "highly sophisticated modern office complexes to the pavements of the cities where their kiosks stand" (322–323).

Boni's *Que Vivent les Femmes d'Afrique?* clearly presents some disturbing factors that have altered the world that Aidoo had described in 1992. One change involves the sheer numbers of African women impacted by war and conflict on the continent, subject to atrocities such as mass rapes and the recruiting of female child soldiers. While Aidoo might not have addressed these issues directly in her own essays, she had already alluded to the underlying causes explaining the violence that touches the African woman today, especially since the dawn of the 21st century.

In several recent conflicts in Africa – in Rwanda, Congo, Sudan and Côte d'Ivoire, to name a few – rape in warfare has become a military strategy in itself whereby raping one or several women who are perceived as representing the side of the enemy amounts to a conquering of foreign territory of sorts. Boni posits that when girls at a vulnerable age are subjected to rape and other forms of violence during war, they sometimes have no choice but to cling to the perpetrators for survival and are thus more easily programmed to become child soldiers themselves (97) whereby any defiance thereafter is punishable with further violations of the girl's body.

Pervasive throughout human history, rape both within the context of war and outside of it is of particular interest to feminist scholars of all races, ethnicities and cultures. However, traditional culture is not the primary factor responsible according to Aidoo, and even Boni concurs that tradition, at times, can even look favourably upon women in certain respects (66). Firstly, Aidoo claims that "much of the putting down of women that educated African men indulge in and claim is 'African culture' is a warmed-up leftover from colonisation" (1992, 324). In spite of Thiam's initial claim in *Speak Out, Black Sisters* that matriarchal societies in Africa held no vestiges of power for the contemporary African women, she too acknowledges that this had not always been the case: "In former times, African women did have a say when decisions of great importance were made" (Thiam, 11). Two examples of exceptional women whom Thiam cites are Zingha who led the resistance against Portuguese colonisation in Angola in the 17th century and Abla Poku, Queen of the Baulé of Côte d'Ivoire, who settled her people along the Camoë River in the 18th century in order to prevent their massacre by the Asante (Thiam, 11). One might also add the 19th century Ashanti Queen Mother Yaa Asantewaa, who led Ashanti troops against the British forces in 1900, in the last of the Anglo-Ashanti wars. Aidoo cites matrilineages enduring to this day in coastal West Africa and among the Akan in Ghana in particular as evidence of societies where women are not-so-ironically the least oppressed in Sub-Saharan Africa. Aidoo faults rather the influence of Islam and Christianity – and not traditional African culture – for women's loss of power (1992, 321) which men had not only respected in the past but had even come to fear.[13]

In "The African Woman Today," Aidoo presents the riddle which characterised the African woman as she had observed her in 1992:

> [W]hether formally educated or not, "traditional" or "modern," [African women] do not fit the accepted notion of them as mute beasts of burden. And they are definitely not as free as African men (especially some formally educated ones) would have us believe. In fact, they fall somewhere between those two concepts (321–322).

The beginning of Aidoo's essay adds that the African woman certainly did not match the downtrodden image assigned to her by the Western media either. Some years later, Tanella Boni's study would support Aidoo's assertion and provide us with an Afro-centric counter-image of the African woman's body which is much more empowering: "The body of the African woman is never nude, but rather dressed and adorned in cultures from head to toe. Thus, a body is never simply clothed, but it is dressed in symbols. African women are well aware of this" (23–24).[14] Reminding us that the modern African woman "lives at the crossroads of several cultures" (23), Boni defies the image transmitted to us through the likes of "travel brochures, photos and postcards" – not to mention through Bob Geldof – all claiming to depict an "authentic" Africa (23).[15]

Reiterating the call for the African woman to stand up for herself just as she had expressed in her first essay, Aidoo states in "The African Woman Today:" "It is high time African women moved onto centre stage, with or without anyone's encouragement" (325). Furthermore, Aidoo believes that every man and woman should be a feminist (323), since true independence, she explains: cannot be achieved if women are not offered the best environment in which to thrive (323). Aidoo identifies this concept as a "crucial element in our feminism" (323) – in other words, in a brand of feminism defined by all Africans, women and men alike.

In the conclusion of *Que Vivent les Femmes d'Afrique?* Tanella Boni seems to echo the same sentiments expressed by Thiam and Aidoo, refuting the notion that African women were absent from history and challenging the submissive images projected onto them by the West (Boni, 200). Alongside examples of exceptional African women – from warriors of the kingdom of Dahomey (123) to contemporary political figures such as Liberia's president Ellen Johnson-Sirleaf elected in 2005 (127) – Boni also includes an assessment on how the average African woman currently lives:

> Today, many African women, educated or not, are no longer happy with giving advice to men behind the scenes or in bed; they have granted themselves the right to think for themselves, to conceive of ideas, to imagine solutions, to take initiatives and to act – such is the case even among those who are illiterate (201).[16]

With the 1965 publication of the play, *The Dilemma of a Ghost*, Ama Ata Aidoo became one of the first African women to publish her creative writing, but her key role in defining African feminism through her essays should not be under-estimated, as many scholars of African Studies have supported throughout the years. Tuzyline Jita Allan praised "To Be a Woman" as "an essay that qualifies easily as a manifesto of African feminism" and she credits Aidoo for bearing the "prodigious responsibility of holding in check the structures of gender and cultural domination" (171). Esi Sutherland-Addy and Aminata Diaw included "The African Woman Today" in the critically-acclaimed *Women Writing Africa* project precisely because – as Sutherland-Addy sums up – the essay "spans centuries and geographical space to (re) place African women in an historical narrative while simultaneously marking the ironies and obstacles affecting their lives" (376). Ada Uzoamaka Azodo and Gay Wilentz describe Aidoo as a "fore-runner" who emphasised "that an acceptance of a Western feminism born from the patriarchal societies of Europe and the US may not be what feminism set up to be for all peoples at all times" (xv-xvi). Obioma Nnaemeka stated that Aidoo was a leader in asserting that "feminism is indigenous to the continent" (10) to which Aidoo's essay "To Be a Woman" surely attests.

Both "To Be a Woman" and "The African Woman Today" were original and bold contributions that changed the direction of African Studies and Feminist Studies at critical times in history. These essays are powerful because they reflect a culmination of Aidoo's analysis of gender issues in African society, based on a lifetime of interactions with women across the continent and beyond. Furthermore, they evidence the various levels of mentoring and support Aidoo provided not only to her peers but especially to young African writers and scholars who follow in her path and who, in turn, explore their own ideas of African feminism which complement those first presented by Aidoo. But perhaps one of the most notable qualities of Aidoo's essays concerns their ability to reach every reader. Thus, "To Be a Woman" and "The African Woman Today" will always be remembered for a number of reasons: they serve as a declaration and affirmation of African feminism and they possess the undeni-able power to teach those living outside the global south about the realities concerning the African woman.

# She-Kings in the Trinity of Being:
# The Budding Girl-Child in
# Ama Ata Aidoo's Short Stories
## Naana Banyiwa Horne

"The good child who willingly goes on errands eats the food of
peace."

Ama Ata Aidoo, "The Late Bud"

"[T]he child that will not do anything is better than sheep."

Ama Ata Aidoo, "The Late Bud"

"[C]ontri chief be President, all Africa chief no be President: e be
King. So as for this woman, e be She-King."

Ama Ata Aidoo, "She-Who-Would-Be-King"

Ama Ata Aidoo epitomises women writers who, given their own subject positions, maintain a keen awareness of "their task as producers of images that
participate in the dominant representations of their culture and simultaneously
undermine and subvert those images by offering a re-vision of familiar scripts"
(Lionnet, 132). Operating in consciousness of literature's role as a mediating
force that structures our sense of the world, Aidoo does not merely perpetuate
cultural myths but creates new mythologies that position both writer and reader
"to engage in a constructive re-writing of their social contexts" (Lionnet, 132).
Unlike many texts generated by African women writers with pulsating accounts
of the gross oppressions inflicted upon women to keep them downtrodden and
the detrimental outcomes of such oppressions,[1] Aidoo, in her discursive practice, leans toward insinuating rather than rendering centre-stage the full force
of the numerous challenges that compromise women's self-actualisation. She
positions female characters – otherwise marginalised and socially silenced
through institutionalised collaborations between indigenous and Western patri-
archies and colonial and neocolonial oppressions – at the centre of textual

representations. Her unassailable reputation for consistently taking readers into the intricacies that complicate women's journeys into self-actualisation is realised because of the depth of understanding she has acquired of the interface between self-envisioning and the dominant representations of any culture.

Scholars have acknowledged Aidoo's august contributions to rendering centre-stage the multidimensionality of female subject positions. Consistently, she establishes an integral link between the quest for selfhood and female body space. She juxtaposes the contending demands of their desire for autonomy with the deeply entrenched need to maintain integrity to communities that ensure their centredness.[2] Nowhere is this dynamic more strongly inscribed than in her textual representations of the girl-child. She has published at least three memorable short stories, in each of which the focal lens zeroes in on the girl-child, rendering her a central character in her own right.[3] Yet, despite the international feminist attention her works have attracted, there is still a dearth of scholarship on her formidable textual representations of the girl-child.

This essay addresses this omission by exploring Aidoo's construction of the girl-child and female body space in three short stories, "The Late Bud," "The Girl Who Can," and "She-Who-Would-Be-King."[4] Her positioning of girl-child protagonists at the centre of textual representations is mapped out in consonance with a conscious exploration of specific socialisation processes and ideals. This process enables the redefinition of female autonomy within multiple subjectivities that are simultaneously inscribed within global, African and female-centred spaces. By insinuating rather than focusing on the numerous challenges that compromise female self-actualisation, she redirects her energies towards the location of the dynamism inherent in female body space and the conscious cultivation of selfhood at centre-stage.

In these three short stories, Aidoo affirms that female selfhood is best cultivated within a womanist epistemology constructed in a woman-centred world of ancestors/grandmothers, mothers/aunties/other mothers, and daughters/girl-children/age-mates. This environment locates the individual girl-child meaningfully in a cultural milieu that fosters female emancipation. "She-Kings," the term in the title, is inspired both by the author's coinage of a term that defines her lifetime commitment to the advancement of female selfhood through creativity, scholarship, and activism as well as the designation of the futuristic first female head of the Confederation of African States in "She-Who-Would-Be-King." And the term "trinity of being" is double-voiced to encompass the vitality of the tripartite female-centred world and the multi-directed process of becoming for the girl-child. The dynamic process of socialising the girl-child to balance the self's drive for autonomy with the communal ethos through active engagement with her community locally and beyond produces she-kings. Each girl-child protagonist, by learning to connect meaningfully to her multi-generational world, emerges as "She-King," one whose sense of personhood becomes grounded in her growing knowledge of the self as an elemental cog in the wheel of being. Her efficacy emanates from fashioning effective ways of connecting the generational past fundamentally to the present, to pave the way for a viable future. It is little wonder that all three girl-child protagonists become distinguished by their ability, despite their youth, to make bold choices backed by conviction to bring about transformation in themselves and their worlds.

A dialogic reading of "The Late Bud," published in the 1970 collection of short stories, *No Sweetness Here*, illuminates it as the Aidoo short story that poignantly explores the processes whereby mothers consciously "grow" girl-children at whose core they entrench the essential ideals that inoculate the world against the excesses of patriarchy. Attributes such as empathy, tenacity, generosity of spirit, and mindfulness of children as the vested future of the group are deemed essential to womanist socialising projects. Through Yaaba's life journey, Aidoo plots the womanist epistemology undergirding the conscious growing of "she-kings" – the prescribed process mothers engage to ultimately transform the girl-child not only into a "good daughter," but a she-king. The she-king's moment of epiphany culminates in the keen awareness of her need to be in constant dialogue with the communal ethos that is committed to engendering female agency.

"The Late Bud" is the perennial story of "woman-being," with mothers, other-mothers, good children, and bad children as the primary players. The good child/bad child dichotomy that drives the plot resonates with many females, young and old. Yaaba, the tomboyish girl-child protagonist constantly butts heads with a mother whose determination to raise a resourceful child is indomitable. The propelling force of this narrative is situated at the confluence of the tension between Yaaba's determination to liberate herself from what she conceives of as the oppressiveness of being female and Maami, Yaaba's mother, who calculates to inculcate in her daughter the discerning ability to own the sum of her self-definition. This sum totals a holistic sense of self that emanates from the recognition that true autonomy stems from resourcefulness. Yaaba's life journey culminates in her awareness that a she-king is not an island but a trajectory that feeds integrally into her wider community as an agent for its transformation.

Aidoo's own process as a Ghanaian woman writer places her firmly within the dialogic tradition Mae Gwendolyn Henderson explores in black women's writing:

> What is at once characteristic and suggestive about black women's writing is its interlocutory, or dialogic, character, reflecting not only a relationship with the 'other(s),' but an internal dialogue with the plural aspects of self that constitute the matrix of black female subjectivity" (118).

In "The Late Bud," the interlocutory or dialogic process that epitomises the journey of most she-kings is specifically brought to light in the turbulent mother-daughter relationship that develops between Maami and her daughter Yaaba.

Given the inter-generational matrix of girl-children, mothers/other-mothers and grandmothers/ancestors, the she-king's striving for autonomy antedates her maturation into a full-fledged individual who effectively strikes a balance between the self and the community. Maturation brings with it the awareness of not only becoming resourceful but owning one's resourcefulness. Yaaba, the late-blooming girl-child protagonist whose life experience is captured by the title, epitomises the classic "bad" female child. Her preferred space is the outdoors and best mode of being is playing. She chooses to be the daughter "[e]very mother might call . . . a bad girl" since she "never stayed at home to go on an errands. Even when . . . around, she never would fetch water to save a dying soul" (104). Guarding her personal freedom with a single-mindedness that ends up being counter-productive, Yaaba's deviance is accentuated by her sister Adwoa's enthusiastic embrace of the "good daughter" ideal. She trenchantly resists giving up her "bad-child" ways to earn the designation of the "good" girl-child because being "good" seems to be in contestation with her desire for autonomy. In her immaturity, her understanding of autonomy is fused with being absolutely uncompromising:

> She [Yaaba] enjoyed playing by the Big Trunk, for instance. Since to be a good girl, one had to stay by the hearth and not by the Big Trunk throwing pebbles, but with one's hands folded quietly on one's lap, waiting to be sent everywhere by all the mothers, Yaaba let people like Adwoa who wanted to be called 'good' be good. Thank you, she was not interested. (104)

Yaaba's cognitive process manifests excesses typical of young minds. Notwithstanding her immaturity, what distinguishes this specific girl-child is the interlocutory process that characterises her life choices. She challenges the proverbial patriarchal assumption that males think but females feel rather than think. Her acceptance of the "bad girl" identity conferred on her derives both from her knowledge of and interrogation of the mothers in her world who "do not say anything interesting to themselves. It is their usual complaints about how difficult life is. If it is not the price of cloth or fish, then it is the scarcity of water" (106). Finding the positioning of her elders "all very uninteresting" (106), her rejection of the "good child" designation becomes her way of contravening the convention of the domestication of females. Privileging the outdoors over the hearth becomes Yaaba's symbolic tool for breaking free of the gender constraints placed on girl-children. She revokes the female burden of submissiveness and dutifulness with its concomitant anxieties about everyone else's well-being that is often attained by sacrificing the female's comfort and pleasure. She even projects herself into the future by vowing to make adult choices that will set her apart from the female elders of her world: "I will always play with my children when they grow up. I will not grumble about anything. . . ." (106). However, through interrogating the processes engaged to acclimatise the girl child to living constructively, Yaaba ultimately grows to recognise that any meaningful self will have to evolve in relation to the communal ethos; a genuine sense of self emanates from the recognition that true autonomy stems from resourcefulness.

In one of the few cursory references to "The Late Bud," Naana Opoku-Agyemang acknowledges this story as the only one in Aidoo's *No Sweetness Here* collection "to deal with the conflict that can result from the process that turns the young person child (Yaaba), into a woman" (138), noting also "that the socialisation factor is at the base of women's unhappiness" (138). The brevity of her attention to this story does not allow an exploration of the socialisation process that can render mothers effective in raising "good daughters." Nonetheless, she seems to insinuate that Yaaba's mother merely desires good daughters without working meaningfully towards inculcating in her daughters those attributes that become definitive of "good daughters." This possible misperception mandates a scrutiny of the womanist epistemology at the centre of "The Late Bud."

The essence of the mothers' process is an enthralling woman-centred space in which mothers seductively do motherwork to instill the ethos of community, the ethic of hard work and generosity of spirit in their daughters. The concept of seduction is specifically chosen in recognition of the deliberateness with which the means employed for teaching by the mothers is matched to targeted objectives in support of a world-view in which "service," meaningfully rendered, fosters nurturance and well-being to counter the culture of privilege and violence engineered by masculinist ideals. The distinctive aspect of this womanist epistemology is women reclaiming the significance of what they are about by redefining themselves outside exploitative, patriarchal norms that reduce women's resourcefulness by gendering their productivity as less significant than male productivity. The opening quotation of this essay, "The good child who willingly goes on errands eats the food of peace" (103), is affirmed as "a favourite saying in the house" (103). It is the mantra in this mother-centred world which "Maami, Aunt Efua, Aunt Araba" (103), and all the women/mothers say regularly in a manner that makes it definitive of woman-being.

In addition to affirming the ethic of hard work that is central to being a resourceful person and the empathetic spirit that fosters peace, the mantra defines woman's position as custodian of her world, a mode of being that transcends biology to assert the female's centrality in safeguarding and promoting the collective social and cultural values.[5] Naana Opoku-Agyemang, in delineating Maame's relationship with Yaaba, indicates:

> Yaaba wants to express herself outside the modes deemed appropriate for a growing young person. For example, she wants to climb trees and play outside the hearth, much to the consternation of her mother, the major socialising agent in her young life. Her mother discourages her through all manner of ways including withholding food, teasing her and concealing her affection for her. The problem is that the older woman equates her daughter's love for the outdoors with lack of concern. She commends the virtue of showing affection, as amply displayed by her other daughter, Adwoa, who conforms to her vision of an ideal daughter – one who constantly squats by the hearth. (39)

This perspective undermines the womanist epistemology undergirding the effective socialisation of girl-children that Aidoo delineates primarily through Maami and Yaaba. In fact, counterpoised to the "good-child" mantra is "the child that will not do anything is better than a sheep" (113). This saying creates space for the Yaabas of their world and also hints at their potential for redemption. What Maami withholds from her difficult child are not regular meals. "Oh, if it was a formal meal, like in the morning or evening, that was a different matter. Of that, even Yaaba got her lawful share. . . . But not this sweet-sweet porridge" (104). Mothers specifically employ such titbits as a seductive tool in their promotion of the ethic of hard work and resourcefulness; it is a reward system that sweetens mothers' relationships with deserving children. While all mothers appreciate empathetic children, the crucial problem does not seem to be "that the older woman equates her daughter's love for the outdoors with lack of concern" (Opoku-Agyemang 39). Yaaba's choice to blatantly shirk participation in the daily rigours necessary for sustaining life bespeaks, to her mother, indolence and a lack of responsibility that should generate concern in any mother.

Granted, the cult of domesticity embodies oppressiveness because of its tendency to render the female a beast of burden; yet even Yaaba recognises the value in what constitutes women's work and its enhancement of life universally. In spite of the young girl's unyielding love of play, her own elemental needs compel a secret acknowledgment of the limitation in her position; neither does her choice not to run errands quell the sense of dejection she experiences from being excluded from the pleasures generated from engaging meaningfully with the female-centred world. That Yaaba herself is a beneficiary of the hard work women invest in elevating the quality of life for their children constitutes an unvoiced acknowledgment, not only of the ethic of hard work that is central to the womanist epistemology, but also its effectiveness in governing the cultiva-tion of self-hood. These mothers, having been girl-children in their time, are aware of the constraints of being female in a world that saddles females with the primary business of sustaining human communities. Conversely, they place the ideals of femininity in contexts that render them primary to the cultivation of life-sustaining womanist cultures that attest to female ingenuity. Thus female-mandated activities such as cooking and maintaining the home that are typically tagged tedious or lackluster in global gender politics are redefined to acquire a new appeal.[6]

Notably, the mothers, in instilling the mantra of the good child, not only frame it around service and culturedness but also model these ideals themselves by showing off their feminine skills. They prepare for the deserving – those who have earned the privilege of eating the food of peace because they will-ingly go on errands – "something delicious like cocoyam porridge and seasoned beef" (103). The mode of presentation of these titbits for the deserving is play-fully inflected with seduction. The food itself seems to have been co-opted by the mothers into seducing with its enticing aroma:

> First, as they stirred it with the ladle, its scent rose from the pot and became a little cloud hanging over the hearth. Gradually, it spread through the courtyard and entered the inner and outer rooms of the women's apartments. . . .The aroma did not stay. It rolled into the next house and the next, until it filled the whole neighbourhood. (103)

The gushing aromas of this feminine paradise that greets the reader entering the female-centred world of "The Late Bud" dialogically juxtaposes the contending demands of Yaaba's overdetermined desire for autonomy against the community ethos of hard work and connectedness embodied by the mothers.

The effectiveness of the mother's seduction process is bourne out by the fact that, habitually, Yaaba will leave off playing and run home as soon as she sniffs the aroma of the "sweet-sweet porridge" of cocoyam and seasoned beef, in the hope that she will be invited to "eat the food of peace" that the mother has prepared to reward her children who willingly go on errands. Even more signif-icant is Yaaba's ardent yearning to be included in the communion of connectedness defining the communal ethos that the sharing of the "titbit" represents:

> 'Nsia, Antobam, Naabanyin, Adwoa, come for some porridge.'
> The other children trooped in with their plates and bowls. But not [Yaaba,] the figure by the wall. They chattered as they came and the mother teased as she dished out their tidbits.

'Is yours alright? ... But my child, this is only a titbit for us, the deserving. Other people,' and she would squint at Yaaba, 'who have not worked will not get the tiniest bit.' (104)

Yaaba even suffers the mother's wicked teasing and sometimes outright chastisement for her waywardness in order not to get completely excluded from this affirmation of maternal love, because even the self-proclaimed "bad girl" seems to value the generosity of spirit – the heart that drives effective mothering.

Pertinently, the "bad child" is not completely cut off but contained in a dialogic mode that renders her an insider-outsider. As a girl-child, Yaaba is biologically an insider in the woman-centred world of the story. However, the choices she makes – shunning housework to play *soso-mba* by the Big Trunk but quick to run home as soon as she sniffs food – dialogically locates her outsiderness. Yaaba's choices are inflected masculine: they are aligned with male privilege and are exploitative. She exploits maternal tenderness – "inevitably, a mother's womb would cry out for a lonely figure by the wall and she would be given some porridge" – the same way patriarchy exploits women's generosity of spirit. Neither is she beyond using force to get what she wants by "ambush[ing] some child to rob him of the greater part of his share" (104) of the food that is specially prepared by Maami to reward deserving children and to reinforce the value system upholding the womanist agenda.

A critical reading of Yaaba reveals the complexity of her situatedness as one whose "interlocutory character . . . is . . . not only a consequence of a dialogic relationship with an imaginary or 'generalised other,' but a dialogue with the aspects of 'otherness' within the self" (Henderson, 118). Given her intelligence, she cannot be totally oblivious to the negating influence of the self-serving and unproductive nature of her pursuits that, rather than seal her autonomy, entrench her dependence on and exploitation of the beneficence of others. Her embrace of the "bad girl" identity is not as solid as she makes believe, because, deep-down, she yearns for her mother's validation. Her craving for maternal acknowledgment is especially painful and diminishing:

> "[T]here was something which disturbed Yaaba. No one knew it, but it did. She used to wonder why, every time Maami called Adwoa, she called her 'My child Adwoa', while she was always merely called 'Yaaba'.
>
> 'My child Adwoa, pick me the drinking can. . . . My child you have done well. . . .'
>
> Oh, it is so always. Am I not my mother's child? (104)

The depth of the dejection Yaaba experiences on account of Maami's refusal to acknowledge their special kinship as mother and daughter come to mirror for

Yaaba the implications of her choice of the "bad girl" identity and the chagrin she causes her mother. After all, do not good mothers deserve good daughters? And if Yaaba is truly Maami's daughter, then should she not possess similar attributes as her mother? Further, if she is a legitimate member of the woman-centred world of "The Late Bud," then the tenacity of the mothers in cultivating good daughters cannot be lost on her. Hers is, at one and the same time, "a relationship of difference and identification with the 'other(s)'" (Henderson, 118). Revoking the identity of docility and submissiveness asserts her difference from other girl-children like Adwoa, who seem overly eager to please; at the same time, her pain as a daughter who is not claimed as her mother's daughter, mirrors that of the mother whose daughter opts to grow into a "bad girl."

The interlocutory character of Yaaba, even as it fans her rebelliousness, ultimately pushes her to confront her own positionality and its true ramifications, to finally reposition herself to work towards her attainment of true autonomy. Her moment of epiphany arrives on "the afternoon of the Saturday before Christmas Sunday" (105). It is a busy day for mothers and their children, preparing for the festivities of Christmas day, but a typical day of play for Yaaba, until a fish bone stubbornly lodges itself in her throat from rushing through her afternoon meal of *kenkey* and stewed fish. The bone's stubbornness, mirroring Yaaba's intransigence, most possibly jolts her into realisation. Needing more help than is immediately available to her forces a dialogic exploration of her positionality as a girl-child in a female-centred space to which she is not integrally connected. Even though she is having no success dislodging the fishbone from her throat:

> She did not want to tell Maami about it. She knew she would get
> a scolding or even a knock on the head. It was while she was in
> the outer room looking for a bit of kenkey to push down the trou-
> blesome bone that she heard Maami talking in the inner room.
> 'Ah, and what shall I do now? But I thought there was a whole
> big lump left. . . . O . . . O! Things like this irritate me so. How
> can I spend Christmas without varnishing my floor?' (105)

The overwhelming situation Maami finds herself in echoes Yaaba's own dialogic situatedness of simultaneously identifying with Maami's predicament in spite of her difference, her otherness, as a girl-child who chooses play over the burdens of femininity.

It is this identification that finally brings about a change of heart and conscious effort on Yaaba's part to *become* Maami's daughter. At the crucial moment when she finds relief from the threat of choking to death by pouncing upon left over *kenkey* acquired through Maami's resourcefulness in enhancing the life of her family, Yaaba overhears Maami's lament: "If only *my child Adwoa* was here. I am sure she could have run to the red-earth pit and fetched me a hoeful. Then I could varnish the floor before the church bells ring tomorrow" (106, Italics added). Yaaba is shocked into the realisation that being a daughter is not merely biology but a dialogic relationship that is social, political, historical as well as spiritual. For a daughter to earn the public acclamation "My child" from a mother mandates that the girl-child work on relating to the mother in a manner that socially inscribe that nomenclature. Mothers work conscientiously on raising their children and, their efforts are rewarded by children responding positively to the hard work invested in them by their mothers. Yaaba, nonetheless belatedly, comes to understand how essential reciprocity is to the communal ethos: mothers tenaciously working to "grow" good daughters who, in their turn, will maintain the efficacy of their worlds through their agency. Yaaba grows to realise that refusing to reflect the benefit of her mother's care is counter-productive and that Adwoa's empathetic relationship with Maami is what has earned her sister the coveted designation "My child Adwoa" from her mother.

It takes Yaaba confronting her own vulnerability from almost choking to death, by gobbling her food "more quickly than a hen would have swallowed corn" (108), to render her more empathetic to the demanding task of Maami's ensuring everyone's well-being. This insight marks the beginning of her transformation, leading to her decision to accompany her playing friends to the pit to get her mother the red-earth needed to varnish the floor to keep the hearth homey on Christmas day. Notably, the entire community wakes up to witness Yaaba's traumatic coming of age and to assist at her rebirth into a she-king. Naana Opoku-Agyemang rightly notes:

> Through this drama that wakes up the entire neighbourhood, the point is made that the demonstration of consideration and understanding on the one hand, and the love for natural self-expression on the other, are not mutually exclusive. In other words, the young woman can express herself outside the confines of society's ideas of girlhood and still retain her fundamental humanity of caring. The fact that the whole community bears witness to Yaaba's efforts is important in making a public statement about the need to revise set ways of evaluating behaviour. (139)

Opoku-Agyemang's articulation captures the complex situatedness of the mother-daughter relationship only minimally, as it overlooks the problematic of excessiveness that Yaaba displays in her self-expression.[7]

Yaaba's awakening has all the trappings of the melodramatic mapping of the proverbial wonder-child/late-bud syndrome, with a significant peppering of situational irony, as her one empathetic gesture to gain recognition from her

– 197 –

mother turns detrimental. At the clock's strike of one in the morning, she decides to begin preparations for her expedition with the twins to the pit to dig and carry the red-earth for Maami, so she will not have to celebrate Christmas on a "hardened, whitened floor" (106). Since Yaaba does not have the basic tools that resourceful young girls possess, she is forced to grope in the dark for her sister Adwoa's "*apampa* and a hoe" (110). She is knocked unconscious from tripping over the family water supply, spilling the tray full of water on the freshly varnished floor Maami had swallowed her shame to borrow a chunk of red-earth from a neighbour to complete. Suddenly awakened by the commotion, Maami, in the hope of scaring the presumed intruder away, starts screaming, "Thief! Thief! Thief!" (110). But once she secures a light, what she finds, instead, is "Yaaba, sprawled like a freshly-killed overgrown cock on the tray" (110). The scream the mother utters on witnessing the limp body of her daughter wakes up her entire community, who rush to her aid.

The lifeless body of Yaaba symbolically images the death of the "bad girl," leaving room for the emergence of the nascent she-king. The "complex situatedness" (Henderson, 118) of this enigmatic child is captured in the various speculations about what she may have been up to. "Some said Yaaba was trying to catch a thief, others that she was running from her mother's beating" (111). Her epiphany arrives in the entire community's collective effort to figure out the cause of the disruption, revive the unconscious child, console the distraught mother and, at the same time, caution restraint in the handling of difficult children while expressing wonderment at the transformation wrought in the proverbial "bad girl." Yaaba's epiphanic moment grounds her firmly in the communal ethos, especially the integrity of empathy to the womanist agenda in nurturing she-kings. The mere intimation of her desire to alleviate the distress of her overwhelmed mother is all it takes to earn Yaaba her deepest wish, Maami's acknowledgment of her as her child. Once she is revived by the medicine-man and everyone finally retires, Maami "knelt by the sleeping Yaaba and put her left hand on her bound chest. 'My child, I say thank you. You were getting ready to go and fetch me red earth? Is that why you were holding the hoe? My child, my child, thank you'" (113). And even in her dazed state, the long-awaited affirmation from Maami is not lost on Yaaba. It firms her resolve to work on earning Maami's undying affection.

"The Late Bud" is a testimonial to the tenacity and generosity of spirit that sustains effective mothering. Through the discursive exploration of the multiple subject positions of her female characters, Ama Ata Aidoo renders vibrant the dialogic process that contextualises the cultivation of girl-children not only into good daughters but she-kings who learn to live courageously, fashioning their personhood in consciousness of their personal well-being and that of their wider community, locally and globally. In the end, Yaaba does confirm the age-old saying by the mothers that "the child that will not do anything is better than a sheep" (113). Ironically, these words are usually uttered in acknowledgment of a child who willingly undertakes the performance of a task before being asked. In the manner of a true she-king, she acts out of conviction, once she works her way through the relevant value system and meaningfully connects it to action rather than succumbing to coercion or following blindly.

The 1970 publication date of "The Late Bud" places it in the first wing of feminist writings by contemporary African women that speak back not only to patriarchy but to Western feminists who positioned their class-oriented issues as monolithic feminist causes without attention to culture, race, or class. In addition to drawing attention to those typical patriarchal oppressions that complicate African women's lives, Aidoo also seems to caution against blind rejection, by young females like Yaaba, of cultural attributes that are conventionally gendered female in their pursuit of selfhood. Yaaba, in her misguided pursuit of autonomy rejects both female gender roles and values that her world recognises as central to the sustenance of humanity that the womanist epistemology reinforces through its teachings. However, in fairness to her, it is important to acknowledge the dearth of opportunities for the advancement of females her world presents which, in turn, fuels her desire to buck the conventions of her gender. More importantly, her conscious engagement with the processes of enculturation distinguishes her from the run-of-the-mill "good girl" who passively internalises the norms that engender submissiveness. Notwithstanding the limitations of her rural environment, Yaaba, by the end of the story, shows promise in maturing into one who will be capable of devising effective ways of drawing on the wisdom of her elders to connect meaningfully to her world, in order to pave the way for a viable future. She possesses the personal hunger for autonomy that best fuels innovativeness and productivity.

The two stories, "The Girl Who Can" and "She-Who-Would-be-King," in Aidoo's 1997 collection, first appeared in MS Magazine (March 1985), and A Rising Public Voice: Women in Politics Worldwide (The Feminist Press, 1995), respectively. They connect historically by setting and content to "The Late Bud" in defining the cumulative gains, over time, in the feminist movement and the enhanced opportunities for female autonomy. Unlike the earlier story in which the strenuousness of motherwork and the growing pains of the girl-child as she strives to overcome the burdens of her gendered identity take up most of the narrative, exposing the vulnerabilities plaguing mothers and daughters equally, in these later stories, the clarity of vision manifested by the young female protagonists in confronting life-choices is what compels attention.

Both setting and comportment position Yaaba as a precursor of the new generation of girl-child protagonists. "The Girl Who Can," like "The Late Bud," is set in a rural area, a big village in the Central Region of Ghana, named Hasodzi, in a tripartite female-centred environment. The Mfantsi name of the place bespeaks its sedentary life. But it is also evident that conventional gender barriers have become blurred enough to encourage a more effective integration of girl-children into their societies. This story, among the three, is the one authentic girl-child narrative in which a young girl gives voice to her own experiences and perspectives. Narrated by a schoolgirl, a star athlete, the story is structured by Adjoa's growing awareness of the complexity of her situatedness as character and narrator. Her youthful perspective on life is privileged while she simultaneously controls how the reader comes to view the adult characters in her world along with the issues that structure or threaten life in her female-centred world. The narrative perspective of "The Girl Who Can" diverges from the other two narrated by ubiquitous narrators who morph into the all-seeing eye embodying the community itself.

In narrating the events of the story Adjoa employs a mode of telling that gives ample indication of her naiveté through the use of devices such as "They say," in order to authenticate the information she is reporting and qualifiers such as "Maybe" and "As far as I could see" (10). In stark contrast is Nana's authoritative stance, which becomes evident in the very first words she utters: "You, Adjoa, you don't know what life is about . . . you don't know what problems there are in life" (27). Nana's words inscribe Adjoa's naiveté and the positionality of the girl-child as the lowest on this age-defined totem pole that makes Adjoa the targeted butt of elders' jokes. However, one of the main advantages of the girl-child being the narrator is the openness with which she exposes the internal dynamics of the three-generational female-centred household while, at the same time, managing to maintain her youthful integrity. This efficacy is attained through the conscious structuring of the story to capitalise on the situational ironies inherent in the intergenerational matrix of the familial relationships. Ironically, our young girl narrator's naiveté is what privileges her perspective, because it accentuates her earnestness and forces critical attention to the idiosyncrasies of those at the helm of the female-centred tripartite as well as the latent aspects of the situations depicted. In effect, considerable humour is generated by the juxtaposition of the overt authoritativeness of Nana, the oldest member of the trinity, against the hesitance and naiveté of Adjoa, the youngest. However, the humour is tempered by the narrative potential of the dilemma tale[8] that is tapped in exploring the problematics inherent in this generationally inscribed world. "Essentially, the dilemma tale is a narrative whose primary function is to stimulate serious, deep-probing discussion of social, political and moral issues that confront human beings in their everyday lives" (Odamtten, 1994: 11). While the humour masks the gravity of the intergenerational problematics, the dilemma tale conventions re-inscribe the dialogic dynamics that drive the narrative.

For someone described by Nana as ignorant of the myriad problems in life, the first actual move Adjoa makes as narrator is to put at the discursive centre the problematic of intergenerational communication itself. "[T]hey say I am seven years old. And my problem is that at this seven years of age, there are things I can think in my head, but which, maybe, I do not have the proper language to speak them out with. And that, I think, is a very serious problem" (27). Adjoa redirects attention away from what "Nana considered as 'problems', or what Maami thinks of as 'the problem'" (27); she zeroes in on a matter that affects especially the young. In a world in which elders occupy the prestigious position of owning knowledge by virtue of experience, they would much rather poke fun at youngsters like Adjoa than take on the responsibility of communicating meaningfully with them. Scrutiny of her narrative stance indicates that her naiveté is more imagined than actual, Nana being, after all, the main person who draws undue attention to it. This girl-child serves as the critical lens through which the issues informing this woman-centred intergenerational narrative are filtered. She voices the perplexity she experiences in deciding "whether to keep quiet and not say any of the things that come into my head, or say them and get laughed at" given how difficult it is to get "any grown-up to listen to you even when you decide to take the risk and say something serious to them" (27). Adjoa challenges the perennial human angst of failed communication and intergenerational discontent that emanates from the age-old dismissive behaviour of elders towards younger generations, designated "elderism:"

> I find something quite confusing in all this. That is, no one ever explains to me, why sometimes I shouldn't repeat some things I say; while at other times, some other things I say would not only be all right, but would be considered so funny, they would be repeated so many times for so many people's enjoyment. You see how neither way of hearing me out can encourage me to express my thoughts too often? (28)

Vincent Odamtten addresses this issue in his article "The Bird of the Wayside: From *An Angry Letter . . .* to *The Girl Who Can:*"

> [A]lthough reliant on the world and discourse of adults from whom she gets knowledge, [Adjoa] is not fully persuaded that they really have all the answers to her young life's problems. Indeed, Adjoa is quick to realise that even though her grandmother, Nana and her mother, Maami, may talk of 'problems' or 'the problem,' there is a fundamental one neither of the adults are prepared to engage. (247)

By making the girl-child the narrative voice in this story, Aidoo makes the reclaiming of voice for girl-children a universal imperative.

As the narrative unfolds, the intergenerational implications undergirding what Nana considers as "problems" or what Maami thinks of as "the problem" are explored. Nana's myriad "problems" are defined by the gender constraints of her era: a combination of limited access to formal education and other resources conducive to the enhancement of female quality of life. Compounding these constraints are stringent reproductive expectations with which women of Nana's generation were confronted. Her generational anxieties culminate into what becomes for Maami *the overwhelming problem* to which the following exchange attests:

> Nana:    'Ah, ah, you know, Kaya, I thank my God that your very first child is a female. But Kaya, I am not sure about her legs. Hm . . . hm . . . hm . . .' And Nana would shake her head.
>
> Maami:  'Mother, why are you always complaining about Adjoa's legs? If you ask me . . .'
>
> Nana:    They are too thin. And I am not asking you!' (29)

In this contentious situation, the inherent dialogism in the dilemma tale is brought into play as Adjoa positions herself simultaneously inside the female-centred trinity of being, chronologically and outside it, ideologically.

As daughter and granddaughter to Maami and Nana, respectively, Adjoa's dialogic placement makes her cognizant of the framing of either woman's problematic both by her generational position and by her familial relationship to the girl-child. The prerogative to voice one's ideas is recognised by Adjoa as both a marker of authority and an instrument of oppression. In this age-inscribed trinity, "Nana has many voices. There is a special one she uses to shut everyone up" (29). Conversely, Maami, Adjoa's mother and Nana's daughter, is the ultimate voiceless individual in the story. Constantly berated by Nana for the imagined defects in her daughter's anatomy and her bad taste in men, Maami can, at best, only muster up "small courage" (29). Most of the speech acts between Nana and Maami typically leave Maami weeping quietly inside, though Nana "never heard such inside weeping" (29). Ironically, in a world in which barrenness is considered the worst possible state a woman can find herself in, and motherhood is revered, it is not patriarchy that defaces women but ageism (older women *lording* it over younger women) that generates the oppression. Interestingly, Adjoa's placement as the youngest generationally, makes her the beneficiary of cumulative change, over time, giving her more voice than her mother. Even as Adjoa is affected, to an extent, by "all this business to do with my legs" (28), she never loses sight of the fact that she, as a person, is the one who has ultimate control of her body. "After all, they [the legs in question] were mine" (28), she states unequivocally, adding, "I have always wanted to tell them not to worry" (28) about her legs.

Adjoa's precocity is reflected in her ability to reason that, genetically, there should be no problem with her anatomy, since "Nana gave birth to my mother and my mother gave birth to me," and the two women possess "two pairs of legs which must surely belong to the approved kind" (30). Her ideological positioning as the "other" of the others generationally enables her to free herself of the gender constraints that dominate the lives of earlier generations. Consequently, she is able to maintain her place in the trinity generationally without allowing herself to be trapped within the period or gender confines that plague her grandmother and mother.

Having drawn attention to elderism, it would be remiss not to recognise the colonial implications of this problematic. In a world where indigenous wisdom is undermined by Western ways of knowing, the legitimacy of indigenous knowledge systems over which elders preside is eroded. This is the real problematic that undergirds elderism. Elders' lack of cognizance of the Eurocentric-derived knowledge system causes them to be patronising towards the young or to consign the smartness of the young to the domain of cuteness. Odamtten's remarks regarding "The Late Bud" more fittingly sum up Nana's dilemma as "the limitations of a gerontocracy that inhibits the honest exchange of information between adult and child" (1994, 107–108). That Nana is a victim of this phenomenon is underscored in the narrative as the issue of formal education crops up. Affirming the benefits of formal education is the one subject that gives Maami voice. While Nana suspects it is a waste of time, it is the one subject on which Maami speaks with authority and Nana listens. Adjoa informs:

> My mother . . . kept telling Nana that she, that is, my mother, felt she was locked into some kind of darkness because she didn't go to school. So that if I, her daughter, could learn to write and read my own name and a little besides – perhaps be able to calculate some things on paper – that would be good. (31

Formal education is also the one issue that ultimately confirms the trinity's agency in empowering females. Maami's sounding off on school and its benefits provide the one occasion on which we see the most rapport between her and her own mother. Listening to Maami expatiating on the virtues of education, "Nana would just laugh" (31) and acquiesce jokingly: "Ah, maybe with legs like hers, she [Adjoa] might as well go to school" (31). Ironically, what Nana expresses possibly in good humour proves prophetic. It is as a student athlete that Adjoa triumphantly consolidates the woman-centred tripartite housing, the intergenerational trinity and lays to rest, once and for all, the gendered chasm that has been the source of rupture in her world.

When news arrives that Adjoa has been selected to represent her school as a runner on the district level, Nana finally makes her peace with her granddaughter's spindly legs. Incredulous initially, she becomes Adjoa's most dedicated fan, once she goes to "ask into it properly" (31). Upon getting confirmation that Adjoa has been selected to represent her school in athletics, Nana assumes the responsibility of washing Adjoa's school uniform and even borrows a "charcoal pressing iron . . . and ironed and ironed and ironed the uniform" (31) the entire week of the games. In addition, she dresses up every afternoon of the district games week and accompanies the school children to watch the games. Nana's enthusiastic support of her granddaughter's athletic prowess is unmatched. When Adjoa wins the trophy for her school:

> Nana said that she didn't care if such things are not done. She would do it. You know what she did? She carried the gleaming cup on her back. Like they do with babies, and other very precious things. And this time, not taking the trouble to walk by herself.
>
> When we arrived in the village, she entered our compound to show the cup to my mother before going to give it back to the Headmaster. (32)

The manner in which Adjoa narrates the impact of her athletic prowess on Nana reveals the depth to the older woman that is usually hidden under her brash exterior. Having witnessed her granddaughter's athletic prowess, Nana becomes overwhelmed by the recognition that "thin legs can also be useful . . . That 'even though some legs don't have much meat on them, to carry hips . . . they can run'" (32–33).

Lifted up by her granddaughter's accomplishment, Nana can look towards the future with optimism and also free herself of the outmoded ideas that make her so cantankerous. She finds herself acknowledging that if "'[t]hin legs can run . . . then who knows . . . ?'" Nana's muttering is full of hope. She acknowledges the future's potential to usher in a world of possibilities for the girl-child. "The Girl Who Can," in addition to highlighting the benefit of female-centred spaces in fostering intergenerational connectedness, reveals that advancements in the lives of the young to serve as visible reminders of the positive changes wrought by time in the lives of females. Additionally, improvements in the lives of girl-children exponentially impact the lives of all, male and female, young and old, in the community at large. That the young can make vital contributions to influencing change is strongly affirmed by Adjoa's example in "The Girl Who Can." The gender gap seems to be closing with time and the domain of athletics is the key area that this story highlights as bridging that gap.

The grain of hope on which "The Girl Who Can" ends carries over overtly into "She-Who-Would-Be-King," a story that encompasses the lives of three generations of females. Education is tagged as a definite marker in the advancement in the women's lives. It is not clear whether all three women or only daughter and granddaughter are the beneficiaries of higher education; however, it can be surmised that the grandmother, dubbed the Old Queen by her family, has enough education to impact her life positively. "Her life has been very difficult, and full of surprises that were not always pleasant. She could never plan her life. So time had often taken her into some awkward places" (56). But unlike the grandmothers and mothers in the stories discussed earlier, she possibly worked at the University Guest House where the story starts. It is in the kitchen of the University Guest House that Adjoa Moji, her ten-year-old daughter "(whose story this should have been)" (56), responds with aplomb, to the twenty-five year old male's query of what she aspires to be in the future, that she will be president of the nation. To his skeptical response that the men of the country are not ready for a woman president, she retorts, "No? We shall see" (55). Adjoa Moji grows to be a lawyer and the Dean of the Law School, an advancement that is impressive in its own right. It is, however, Afi-Yaa, the Old Queen's granddaughter, who grows to become the "First President of Africa" (61). In the end, even the Old Queen is forced to acknowledge "that she really is quite comfortable" even though "if anybody had ever told her that a day would come when she would feel this much at peace with herself and the world, she would have laughed in her face" (56).

The title of this story affirms the focus of this analysis by accentuating the process whereby she-kings are created as well as the intergenerational effort that is essential in bringing the cultivation of she-kings to fruition. The trinity of woman-being, constituting ancestors/ grandmothers, mothers, and girl-children is located at the centre of this story that assembles "at least, four generations of the family . . . as well as representatives of several different branches of it" (56) under the same roof in celebration.[9] The narrative diverges from the rural setting of the first two stories, to the urban. Though it is presented chronologically, beginning half a century earlier, the climax of the story, the election of Afi-Yaa as "the first President of the newly formed Confederation of African States" (57), is narrated so compellingly that the opening sounds somewhat like a flashback, needed to put the climax in perspective. In a way, the opening stands in relation to the climax of the story in a manner similar to the way in which Adjoa Moji's ten-year-old encounter in the guest house kitchen is rendered prophetic to Afi-Yaa's election. The opening and the closing, therefore, appear in the manner of addenda to the climactic futuristic event that takes place in 2026, at the beginning of the second quarter of the twenty-first century. This perception is reinforced by the replicated anecdotal format in the narration of the opening and the closing. The narrative opens with: "An encounter that took place in the kitchen of a university guest house. Half a century earlier, in 1977" (55). The closing segment repeats the opening format: "An encounter that took place in another part of town, the evening of this same day of 25th May, 2026" (59).

All aspects of life seem to be impacted by the electronic age and globalisation is evident in the lives of all, especially the girl-child. While the sketchy nature of the story mimics the zooming pace of modernity and its dizzying progress with limited interpersonal communication, that women-centred spaces are integral to the geometric advancements in the lives of girl-children finds support in Afi-Yaa's being the beneficiary of three generations of female achievers. Upward mobility is visible in the lives of the women in this story, Afi-Yaa becoming not the President of a nation but of the Confederation of African States. Though the Old Queen's life has been undoubtedly the hardest, to her credit, her daughter aspired to be the first female president of her nation and actually became a lawyer and Dean of the Law School. Significantly, the educated males sound sour and daunted while the women are basking in the closing of the gender gap. The masses, however, seem to take things in their stride. The workers of the seventy-four year old manufacturer who, at twenty-five, had been convinced the men of the "country will [n]ever let a woman be their President" (55), devise the term "She-King" for Afi-Yaa, the "all Africa chief" (62). They proclaim that if "contri chief be President, [. . . then], all Africa chief no be President: e be King. So as for this woman, e be She-King" (62).

In the three stories analysed in this essay, girl children clearly thrive in women-centred spaces where different generations of females can assemble together and draw inspiration from each other. Clearly, female body space plays an essential part in the cultivation of girl-children into she-kings. Though life is not easy for most females, the sense of community and camaraderie that thrives in female-centred spaces proves instrumental in fostering the ethic of hard work and love of work in younger women, especially since they themselves become beneficiaries of the life-sustaining impact of women's work. Younger females tend to respond positively to the nurturing influence of the older women in their worlds and, in turn, are inspired to aim at becoming resourceful in their own right. The culmination of the inspiring manner in which women raise girl-children is the generation of she-kings who are graced with courage, innovativeness and productivity.

# Black Women of a Certain Age, Power and Presence: Ama Ata Aidoo's and Toni Morrison's[1]

## Carole Boyce Davies

## Between Generations

Chimamanda Ngozi Adiche in an interview on "African Voices,"[2] which I heard, interestingly, in Algeria while attending the 40th anniversary of the Pan African Cultural Festival of Algiers, spoke casually of key themes that preoccupy her in her most recent collection of short stories, *The Thing Around Your Neck*.[3] In this particular discussion, she claimed Chinua Achebe's influence, as she should, even down to living in a house that Achebe had once inhabited at Nsukka (The University of Nigeria, Nsukka) in Eastern Nigeria. Chimamanda, in this way, identifies herself as coming out of the house of Achebe, for reasons of literary history, but also ethnicity, and a certain descent as an African writer.

But clearly there is another house out of which Chimamanda comes, that is the house of African women's writing, in which Ama Ata Aidoo is indeed a literary foremother. For writers like Ama Ata Aidoo had pioneered in articulating a spectrum of issues that Adichie and her generation of African women writers now assume. This is how Chimamanda describes two of her current preoccupations in that interview:

- the idea that marriage is not set up for the benefit of women and indeed can be dangerous for women but that women are conditioned to behave "as though marriage is a prize."
- the hypocrisy of denying that same sex relationships existed/exists in Africa

One can easily recall the novel *Changes*[4] by Ama Ata Aidoo as an entire meditation on the first of these concerns – the perils of marriage. *Changes*, set in contemporary urban Ghana, has as its protagonist a young woman, Esi, who names marital rape and rejects an unsatisfactory marriage, but, as she opts out of her marriage, is seduced into becominng the second wife in a polygamous marriage, which also is not a satisfying option. The entire text can be read as that critique of marriage which Adichie identifies, but without the losses being assigned to the woman this time. These are women living as professionals in a contemporary world in which mobility is critical. Motherhood is not an essential, defining identity, even though she is a mother. Instead, there is a lusty enjoyment of her sexuality and Esi comes in the end to claim herself under these conditions as she continues to find answers to difficult questions:

> So the marriage stayed, but radically changed. All questions and their answers disappeared ... She had had to teach herself not to expect him at all ... Esi believed Ali when he insisted that he loved her very much. She knew it was true: that he loved her in his own fashion. What she became certain of was that his fashion of loving had proved quite inadequate for her ... she comforted herself that maybe her bone-blood-flesh self, not her unseen soul, would get answers to some of the big questions she was asking of life (165–6).

Thus, it is my contention, though, that in the field of African women writers, Ama Ata Aidoo has to be also identified as setting some of the early themes and discussions of modern African literature. Writers in Adichie's generation are able now to put those and other related issues casually on the table because writers like Ama Ata had already done daily battle and so claimed a place for African women's writing. Ama Ata herself describes some of her encounters in "Ghana: To Be a Woman:"[5]

> As a writer, I not only cope with aloneness; I have to actively seek it in order to produce. Yet as an academic, can I maintain a vibrant intellect, condemned as I am to ostracism because I refuse to consider marriage the only way to live? (259).
> And when someone you consider a friend refuses to talk to you because of a book you've written, he is trying to drive you insane with speculation. For: 1) Is he angry with you for daring to write a book? Or, 2) Is he ashamed of you because you wrote that book? Or, 3) Is he jealous because he wished he had written that book? (262–263).

These kinds of questioned speculations are less relevant to the second generation of African women writers, since a writer like Aidoo had already taken on some of these challenges directly. In April 2010, I had the fortune of a lunch meeting with Ama Ata Aidoo in Accra, Ghana (in the company of Anne Adams and 'Molara Ogundipe) a few days after attending the funeral celebrations for Mama Naa Morkor Busia. In what was more a conversational setting than a formal discussion or interview, Ama Ata asserted in response to a related question that Chimamanda maintains positive relations with the generation of African women writers who preceded her and particularly Aidoo herself. Not surprisingly then, during a more recent visit to India, Chimamanda was quoted as saying:

> "Being a Sub Saharan African writer, you're supposed to be like Chinua Achebe, who is called the father of modern African literature. But you're probably compared to him because people don't know any other writers from Africa," she said. "Then I always want to know who the mother of African literature is. And also, why does African literature need a father and a mother at all?" (*The Times of India*, 1/25/11)

The field of African women's writing and its criticism is now a rich one, with many of its historical contours being filled in with works like *Women Writing Africa*.[6] Indeed *Women Writing Africa* identifies at least five generations of African women writers. So, after the earlier work on *Women in African Literature*[7], which was meant only to clear the ground, a casual search reveals contributors to that collection like Naana Banyiwa Horne,[8] Marie Umeh,[9] and Irene d'Almeida have gone on to produce a variety of critical studies on various writers, or published anthologies like *A Rain of Words*,[10] or their own individual poetry collections. Individual works are now actually titled *Feminism and African literatures*, and indeed the field of African feminisms can be identified as itself a rich and vibrant area. The work of Ife Amadiume,[11] Obioma Nnaemeka,[12] Oyèrónké Oyĕwùmí, [13] and journals like *Feminist Africa* and *Jenda Journal*, the conferences and various collections of individual scholarly work, papers at African Studies Association, African Literature Association, and so on, broaden the discussions on African women.

One of the cleverest stories in *The Thing Around Your Neck* is Chimamanda Ngozi Adichie's "The Headstrong Historian." I read this as writing back to Achebe by reworking some of the same turf that he had covered, but by this time, making the person affected by colonialism a grandmother, the resisting subject able to take the fight forward via the female line – the granddaughter, who becomes a thinker and a scholar of African history, who wants to recapture her grandmother's innate resistance and unfulfilled quest for justice.

Interestingly, like Sissie in Ama Ata Aidoo's *Our Sister Killjoy*,[14] Chimamanda has several stories and a variety of her characters encounter the contemporary experience of living abroad, this time in the United States and then return home to Africa or, as in the American Embassy story, decide not to even bother to accept the humiliation.

Meanwhile, the scholarly appraisal of the work of Ama Ata Aidoo have progressed steadily, from individual theses and essays by scholars like Naana Banyiwa Horne to the book by Vincent Odamtten *The Art of Ama Ata Aidoo, Polylectics and Reading against Neocolonialism* [15] (1994) to the critical edition *Emerging Perspectives on Ama Ata Aidoo* (1999).[16] The work of Nana Banyiwa Horne[17] has aided my own thinking as I developed a chapter to Aidoo's *Anowa* in *Migrations of the Subject*[18] (1994). A wonderful overview by Tuzyline Jita Allan to the Feminist Press issue of the novel *Changes: A Love Story* (1993) provides more than a commentary on the novel but is itself a wonderfully detailed study of Aidoo's entire oeuvre.

## "Being a Woman" – African Feminist Positioning

Perhaps we can identify a conscious women's rights positioning in Ama Ata's early affirmative critique of issues which were of concern to African women as they appeared in the feminist anthology, *Sisterhood Is Global.* [19] In many ways this essay became one of the first articulations of some of the realities of African women in the early "postcolonial" period and this is worth reiterating. The fact that this short reflective essay, "To Be a Woman," followed the statistical information on the Republic of Ghana itself as it related to the condition of women in key areas like marriage policy, divorce, herstory, rape, sexual harassment and used some of the writer's own experience, provides an operational context for what followed and became usable information for those wanting to embark on some form of women's rights analysis.

Particularly striking was her assertion that she came of age with the recognition that it was taken for granted that a woman fulfilled a catalogue of service roles but stressed that this condition was no "less ridiculous than anywhere else" (259). From there she went on to enumerate the challenges of being a writer when societal expectations instead demanded one's service. One of her conclusions was that "the criteria for judging human accomplishments, if they are exclusively masculine," (261) renders women outside of the prevailing definitions of what constitutes a full and functioning human being.

And it is here that she offers one of her first associations about marriage that becomes a pretext for the Adiche preoccupation in *The Thing Around Your Neck*, with which I began. In Ama Ata's words:

> marriage has proved singularly effective as an instrument of suppression. It has put half (or often more than half) of humanity through mutations that are thoroughly humiliating and at best ridiculous. (263)

I follow this logic of "half the world" as proposed by Claudia Jones[20] with a chapter titled exactly that, which asserts, among other things, women's right to at least half of the world's resources. But, Ama Ata also offers another important and allied conclusion which Claudia has repeatedly targeted in a variety of essays: "the fact that a colleague understands the finer points of Marxism or is the most fearless fighter in the bush does not automatically mean that he has the haziest notions of woman's capabilities." Her final cautionary statement, which has indeed proved reality in several locations – as the outcome of women's participation in revolutionary struggles: "And don't be shocked if – when victory is won – they return you to the veil as part of the process of consolidating the gains of the revolution."

This was of course written in the early days of the second wave (1980s) feminist movement, a point at which Aidoo identifies the issues of organisation and social transformation and above all "visualising a world in which the position of women has been revolutionised" (263). In a subsequent essay which can be read as a follow-up to her earlier work, titled "The African Woman Today," [21] Aidoo broadens the field and begins by critiquing the dominant media representations of African women as perpetually begging for aid while flies cover their children. She also provides a listing of African women who transcended expected limitations. She further makes the point that one should re-assess indigenous African societal patterns, the conquest of the continent by Europe and be clear about the apparent lack of vision or courage in the leadership of the postcolonial period. Here is where she makes her famous assertion:

> When people ask me rather bluntly every now and then whether I am a feminist I not only answer 'yes,' but I go on to insist that every woman and every man should be a feminist – especially if they believe that Africans should take charge of our land, its wealth, our lives and the burden of our own development. Because it is not possible to advocate independence for our continent without also believing that African women must have the best that the environment can offer. For some of us this is the crucial element in our feminism. (323)

This is a position on women that some of the most progressive developers of Africa had come to articulate and she cites Dr. Kwegyir Aggrey on this ("If you educate a man, you educate an individual. If you educate a woman, you educate a nation" ["To Be a Woman," 259]) though it is often attributed to Nkrumah (arguably, Aggrey's most famous mentee). But also, the late Thomas Sankara of Burkina Faso is credited with that position as well. For Aidoo, the contemporary and recent gender reactionary positions of African men owe some of their origins to the European Victorian notions of women's place which were imported with colonialism. She makes this point in a bit more detail in her essay, "That Capacious Topic: Gender Politics," which appeared in the book edited by Philomena Mariani, entitled *Critical Fictions: The Politics of Imaginative Writing* (1991).[22]

Aidoo, like other continental African feminists, sees the emancipation of women as the "last possible hope for ourselves and for everyone else on the continent." (1992:324) And we do know that the African Union's Protocol on the Rights of Women in Africa (2005) (ratified by 23 countries as of this date) has enshrined many of these points that African feminists have been battling for over the years on women's rights as human rights. Article 6 of the Protocol, for example, deals with marriage, with ten items pertaining to women's rights in marriage – from rights to property to fair treatment and relations to children. Article 5 discusses the elimination of harmful practices, defining these as "all behaviour, attitudes and/or practices that negatively affect the fundamental rights of women and girls, such as their right to life, health, dignity, education and physical integrity."[23] Article 7 deals with separation, divorce and annulments of marriage; Article 12, on the right to education and the removal of barriers which discriminate against women in educational settings; and in the definitions category, violence against women is defined as:

> ...all acts perpetrated against women which cause or could cause them physical, sexual, psychological, and economic harm, including the threat to take such acts; or to undertake the imposition of arbitrary restrictions on or deprivation of fundamental freedoms in private or public life in peace time and during situations of armed conflicts or of war.

What are now fundamental rights in an international law instrument are issues that a writer/activist like Aidoo, as we have shown, had already challenged as limiting the full possibilities of African women.

## Aidoo's Creative/Theoretical Intervention: Reclaiming The African Diaspora

The creative/theoretical intervention is a framework I have been using to indicate that there are writers who do their theorising within the creative work itself. Aidoo is definitely one of that small and illustrious group of thinkers and writers for whom creative expression has its own life but for whom, as well, the creative work is allowed to carry theoretical and political positions. And she has done so in her articulation of a Pan Africanist/feminist positionality.

For Aidoo, then, these positions as articulated in her work and in her writing have always been a double or triple play of sorts:

- Between nationalism and feminism and articulating both of these as she does in *Our Sister Killjoy* which itself was caught in the possibilities of Africa immediately after independence
- Between western feminist positions and their limitations and a recognition of African women's legacy of advancements before European women's self- assertions
- An assertion of an African feminist politics that sees gender as allied to other streams of analysis and representations such as class, the politics of de-colonisation, etc.

Thus, a work like *Anowa*, I have argued in *Migrations of the Subject*, can be read as one of the most important theorisings of Diaspora and middle passage textualities within the body of the play itself. Aidoo remains one of a small group of African writers to actually engage some of the historical, personal and ideological issues on the African side which helped shape the African Diaspora. But within that framework, she skillfully embeds the talented, creative and ambitious woman as not at all complicit as her character Anowa navigates outside of traditional inequities and is on the road to independence and full partnership but along the way is stymied by male dominance which is also read as male impotence.

We can, therefore, explore a variety of creative texts by Aidoo which pursue a systematic reclaiming of the black female self as well as the African Diaspora subject. In her play *The Dilemma of a Ghost*, for example, she provides the African return story suggested via the "I will take you home" narrative of the first generation of African male students, which existed as subtext in Hansberry's *A Raisin in the Sun* via Assageai. Here, she presents us with a Eulalie who moves with her Ghanaian husband to Ghana to a conflicted and ill-prepared set of social/familial relations. Eulalie, for her part, begins by violating some fundamental relationships, bringing with her a set of assumptions from her African American experience. Aidoo nonetheless presents the husband, whom some read as the ghost with an inability to navigate appropriately his family's expectations and cultural demands with his wife. Still these, in the end, only get resolved via the women of the family who decide that there is a possibility of a certain redemption and reconciliation in spite of cultural differences and the separation which diasporisation had created.

The play *Anowa*, as we indicated, has a major Middle Passage text at its core, mediated through the myth of Anowa re-told by Aidoo. This Anowa is caught like Janie of Zora Neale Hurston's *Their Eyes Were Watching God* (1938) who becomes the mayor's wife in the Big House but, like Janie, also rejects it, preferring to remain outside of the trappings of a new, oppressive colonial power which enriches itself in the beginnings of the economic globalisation via the slave trade, a then new capitalism, using one's own people as commodity and thereby at the expense of one's sense of self. Here she also has her male protagonist, Kofi Ako, operating thereby with a certain impotence which could be read as well as his own attempt to claim a flawed masculinity when this is not his initial inclination at all.

*Our Sister Killjoy or Reflections from a Black Eyed Squint* deals with the African woman's appearance in the West, sexualised and racialised. As Chimamanda confronts this in the contemporary, we see an early and tentative attempt to deal with the issues of same-sex sexuality which appear as a kind of minor subtext at the level of desire of the German woman for the African woman's sensuality. The larger narrative structure, experimental in its form, engages the African student abroad and what we begin to see as the development of the second level African Diaspora,[24] being described now, which was identified then as the absence of a commitment to a return, even as Sissie idealistically returns, having navigated Europe and with a surprised recognition of the inherent limitations of those who had colonised others.

Through it all, Aidoo has revealed that ongoing skill in developing short stories which confront myriad realities of African women, from her first collection, *No Sweetness Here*[25] to the more recent, *The Girl Who Can & Other Stories*.[26] Still, she also reveals a desire to maintain the value of love and affection in her edited collection of *African Love Stories*.[27]

## Toni Morrison's Locks: The Power and Presence of the Black Woman Writer

As we celebrate Ama Ata Aidoo at 70, we also see a Toni Morrison at 80, both examples of what it meant to be a black woman writing at the critical conjunctions of de-colonisation in Africa and Civil Rights/Black Power periods in the United States. In both cases there is a challenge to entrenched notions about creativity, women's voice, and above all the ability to challenge power relationships in Africa and the African Diaspora. I have been exploring the meaning and visuality of women of a certain age, prompted, in part, by ongoing work on Claudia Jones, even though she died at what seems now, on reflection, as the early age of forty. But spending the last ten years or so on that project, I have had the opportunity of examining her image from a variety of subject and object positions – youth and age, her representations in the US and UK; as she travelled in Russia, China, Japan. The other, of course, is also confronting myself and my colleagues of similar age, as we, too, are becoming women of a certain age, power and presence. I also think of my mother and how she navigated her own body, self and location in the world.[28]

This consideration still also comes from an intellectual place, as well, from teaching and thinking about the intersections of Pan Africanism and feminism, in which Aidoo has to be also located. The absence of a conjunction between those two twentieth-century political movements means that a number of women get erased if we are not able to bring these fields into conversation. Examining the African Diaspora as well and the various versions that emanate from African American, African and Caribbean women allows us also to examine how the women of those movements were often erased but were still obviously continuously battling distorted representations as they also provided their own self-re-presentations as they claimed their own full selves…at any age.

Conscious, still, of the implications of *Black Looks*,[29] as bell hooks would call them, and the sense that throughout history black subjects of photographic representations, even from black photographers, have looked back, glared, side-eyed, stared back, refused photographing, but also enjoyed the pleasure of selecting their own self-representations, as they challenged or confronted the dominant culture's predominantly negative representations (Willis, xix).

Thus Amy Ashwood Garvey is photographed in her later years always in *kente*, but before that talks back to Marcus Garvey, re-claiming her own sexuality in the following terms: "Garvey knew nothing about sex life. He might have been the greatest propagandist in the world, he might have been the King of Africa and even won my heart, but he lacked the ability to hold my love."[30] Later on, the second Mrs. Garvey, Amy Jacques Garvey writes a letter to W.E.B. Du Bois in which she begins by saying: "I am bottled up here in this small island with two small boys to support, etc," but goes on to advise the great Du Bois not to use the word "negro" in his writings and to provide a variety of references to offences of the word and instead identified the preference for the use of the word "African" as preferable, ending her letter with: "No, don't use it. Except where an organisation bears the name." (210) ("Letter to W.E.B. Du Bois on Pan Africanism").[31]

Toni Morrison's ability to render visual images in literary form but also as she is rendered, gives us some of these enduring representations. From *Sula* (1974) to *Beloved* (1987), *The Bluest Eye* (1970) and *A Mercy* (2008), "vivid visual images abound as key signposts in complex plot sequences and memorable narratives."[32] Morrison's iconic/iconoclastic self-presentation as a black woman and artist is perhaps the best explicator of her own intellectual and aesthetic projects.

But how one views the writer, before she was the iconic Toni Morrison, is perhaps best captured through the eyes of one of her more illustrious students – Kwame Ture, viewing her as a young man viewing a young professor:

> My freshman English teacher I've never forgotten. She was an
> instructor and a challenging teacher who was really down with
> black literature and our people's culture. But this teacher was
> unusual in one other respect; she was young, stylish and really
> fine. Her name was Toni Morrison. She and her tall walking

partner, another young, equally fine and elegant sister named Eleanor Traylor, would turn heads as they walked across the quadrangle.[33] (*Ready for Revolution*, 129)

On her teaching and later writing and editing this is what he says:

So naturally, their sections were always overenrolled with ardent young Howard men. Who arrived in class to discover with some dismay that the young women were also smart and very serious teachers. A combination of assets that made for interesting classes indeed. About eight years later my teacher and I met again when she would be my editor at Random House for both *Black Power* and *Stokely Speaks*.

Again, on Toni Morrison at a different age, here are his words:

So it was with considerable pride some years ago that I received the news in Conakry that my instructor/editor was now a Nobel Laureate in literature. I was proud, because even though that prize remains a relic of northern European pretensions to cultural hegemony, they will occasionally stumble upon a worthy African writer (like Mahfouz, the Egyptian) who is grounded in their people's culture, struggle and experience. Ms. Toni Morrison was clearly one of the Committee's more inspired choices. (130)

How one visualises the writer herself – i.e. the embodied writer and the visualising of her work over the years is well represented in these versions, from the gaze of one who was at once student, later activist and adult Pan Africanist reflecting on his life. How we visualise her is also significantly identified here as well. Thus in Paris as she was honoured, a young hip-hop artist who works in the public art/mural tradition reinterpreted her using the publicly circulated photograph, brilliantly dominating the work, but with a tree in the background with lynched figures hanging as the "strange fruit."

Deborah Willis, in her introduction to *Posing Beauty: African Images from the 1890s to the Present*,[34] uses a concept that I like, called "participatory self-representation," which she links to "the important aesthetic and ideological issues engaged within the photographic image" (xvii). She identifies the title, *Posing Beauty*, then, as "being derived from the concept of posing – both positioning the subject and questioning the trappings of beauty" i.e. "how beauty is posed and realised" (xvii). One of her more helpful questions for me, as applied to Toni Morrison's representation: "Can women be both strong and beautiful?" My reading of the Toni Morrison locked images reveals a definite "yes." The graying locks convey not weakness in age but a certain power in continuance and transcendence to higher levels each time. The "re-semanticising of blackness" that Wynter[35] identifies as central to Rastafari with their locks as visible signifier is relatedly another entry point. One of the fundamental principles of Ras-Tafari around issues of "itality"[36] is re-captured, re-affirmed and then re-presented in a mature Toni Morrison via a definite glamour that never separates the locks from the person but provides a holistic representation of a black woman of power at an age when "no respectable black woman ever tells anybody how old she is" – a quote I learned is part of the Toni Morrison lexicon.

For my own approach to this subject I also interviewed people in two different sites – the first: The Callaloo Conference in Addis Ababa, Ethiopia, June 2010, having just visited Shashamane, the home of the Rastafari community where they practiced a particular set of enactments and actualisations of the Rastafari principle of return to Africa but as well a modern African diasporic version of navigating African communities in the spirit of Pan Africanism. Those responses, from writers/literary scholars largely had to do with: majesty, strength, power, force, a creativity and self-presentation to be emulated. The second set of responses came from students and faculty at Cornell University's Africana Centre during Fall, 2010 to the open-ended question, "What do you think of Toni Morrison's locks?" which seemed more practical and provided responses from wanting to know who did her hair to not wanting to separate the hair from the meaning of the writer, to suggesting that the locks images that have to do with roots, or fishtails, or colour but also self-determination and power. One returned questionnaire wanted to ask its own question: "Are African Diaspora self-presentations in 2010 still political as we think I assume they are?" And an answer, "I would suggest no such split between aesthetics and politics." Another: "When I think about the locks of Toni Morrison, I think about the beauty of Africans. Another: "untamed black beauty – natural, untampered-with and raw. You cannot look at her locks without thinking of what her hair is "supposed" to be – i.e. relaxed, proper etc. And of course, given her age, comes the surprise – as in the "Wow" she is rocking locks; she has not given into the societal standards. At the same time, I have to say they are absolutely beautiful...sexy, even."

The narrative aspects of the photograph tell their own stories, as do the narratives themselves. Thus, "Toni Morrison's Locks" becomes a visible signifier for the engagement with the continued politics of "redefining beauty" which began with the Black Arts/Black Power Movements and beyond. A continuing politics of representation allows us to *Visualise Toni Morrison at 80, and Ama Ata Aidoo at 70*. The fact that Aidoo is always publicly dressed in African attire with a headtie gives us another visual counterpart. Thus, we are given wonderful examples of thinking, writing women to emulate, women of clarity and presence, who never stopped their challenges to women's subordination as it related to a set of intersecting oppressions, like Nawal El Saadawi, who at 80, lived to see and participate in the fruit of her rebellion against a range of oppressions, articulated and realised in the youth-generated revolution which removed a thirty-year dictator through holding down Tahir (Liberation) Square, Cairo, Egypt, on February 11, 2011.

Ama Ata Aidoo has to be identified in a line of thinking and writing African women ranging from Amy Ashwood Garvey to Toni Morrison, Mabel Dove Danquah to Nawal El Saadawi who demonstrated an assumption across Africa and the African Diaspora of a full and prominent Pan Africanist/feminist sensibility which had at its core the full liberation of all African peoples and a willingness to articulate these at multiple levels.

# Towards Alternative Representations of Women in African Cultural Products[1]

Awo Mana Asiedu and Akosua Adomako Ampofo

## Introduction

Cultural products, such as popular music, theatre, literature and film, reflect society and its values and at the same time influence societal values. This double reflexivity implies that the images or messages presented in/by these products cannot be taken for granted, as they potentially have the power to shape the consciousness of society. It is for this reason that the ways in which women are portrayed in African cultural products, from the elite literary genres to the ubiquitous popular genres of music and film, are of concern to us. Ama Ata Aidoo, to whom this volume is dedicated, has consistently presented sympathetic, realistic and empowering images of women in her work and is an example of how an artist may positively influence society.

This essay, an outcome of our research into the representation of women in Ghanaian popular music, discusses the possibilities of alternative representations of women in African cultural products, particularly music and literature. Although our research demonstrates that not all male artists are culpable in misrepresenting women,[2] we maintain that there is a real danger that a male-dominated production will continue to replicate gender stereotypes and misrepresentations in cultural products. We argue, therefore, that, although male artists may be educated and encouraged to show greater responsibility in their representations of women, greater female participation in the creation of these products would go a long way to provide alternative representations of women.

In this regard, we examine the ways in which Ama Ata Aidoo's example may be applicable in the arena of popular music. We analyse songs by two contemporary, popular Ghanaian female musicians to show how they, as women, represent women/womanhood in their music. We ask if the fact of their being women has necessarily impacted their representations of gender in any particular way. We compare and contrast this with Aidoo's work, which, we posit, has always been consciously aware of gendered images and the need to represent women in a positive and empowering manner (Danysh, 2000; Adams, 2011).

The essay first establishes the important role played by African artists and their products in society. We then go on to highlight the stereotypical and negative ways in which women are often represented in the arts. In the third section of the essay we discuss aspects of our own research on the representations of women in Ghanaian popular music. We examine Aidoo's example and the songs of two Ghanaian female musicians to draw some conclusions on women in popular music and advocate how such stereotypical and negative representations could be reduced and more positive representations expressed.

## The Role of Artists and the Place of Cultural Products

Artists, creators of cultural products, have tremendous influence on their societies. The role of the artist in the African context has always been entertainer, as well as educator. Taking traditional storytellers as an example, these were expected not only to entertain their listeners but also to impart valuable life-sustaining lessons, especially to younger members of the society. This dual role as entertainers *cum* educators is taken very seriously, not only by the artists themselves but also by the consumers of their products (Osofisan, 2001; Barber, 2000; and Asiedu, 2003).

Popular music can also be a potent form of cultural identity; it can become a powerful vehicle for cultural and political expression through which images, sounds and attitudes are circulated throughout the culture and body politic. In Zimbabwe, for example, the tradition of song as a form of social commentary has been well established (Vambe, 2001). Popular music is therefore a powerful medium for (re) enforcing and dictating what is in vogue or acceptable to society. The values and life perspectives of young people worldwide are indisputably influenced by popular culture images and narratives (Frederiksen, 2000). The way young people dress and speak is often traceable to the images popular artists present to them. This happens on a subconscious level and is reinforced by peer expectations and pressure. The recent practice of young Ghanaian men plaiting their hair and wearing earrings is one example of such influence traceable to a style that is common among popular musicians, especially of the more contemporary genres such as *Reggae, Hip-life* and *Hip-Hop*. As Gecau suggests, popular songs, and thus popular musicians, provide alternative conceptions of the world and life in contrast to the norms of "official society" (1995: 559), thus appealing to the youth, who are constantly searching for new identities outside of their parents' and the older generation's prescriptions.

In the April 2008 edition of *The New Legon Observer*, a special issue dedicated to Highlife music, the editors make an important observation:

The story of the bringing together of our various peoples into the colonial state…Ghana, has been ably recorded for us by historians, political scientists, constitutional and countless other experts. Our various great expectations as well as our record of blunders have been itemised and analysed…by generations of economists, statisticians and various other development experts. But for our complete treasury of our collective human story in all its full complexity, we must also turn to the singers of our countless songs: our songs of joy…our songs of boundless love. Indeed our singers have created songs for all that we have experienced as a people who are forever hoping against hope, a people always striving against countless difficulties towards a higher level of development, individually, collectively. (1–2)

The editorial thus assigns popular Ghanaian music a role equal to, if not above, that of historians and other experts responsible for documenting the life of the people. In the lead article in this special issue John Collins, renowned musicologist, recounts the important role popular musicians played in the independence struggle and later in Nkrumah's Ghana, where the premier found it expedient to employ the services of popular musicians and theatre artists to push his political and ideological agendas. Other historical examples such as the use of protest music, poetry, theatre and dance to garner international support for the struggle against apartheid are worthy of note here (Gilbert, 2007). Fugard, Ntshona and Kani's collaborations resulting in internationally acclaimed anti-apartheid plays such as *Sizwe Bansi Is Dead* and *The Island* are but a few examples.

The forgoing discussion points to the power and influence of artistic cultural products, suggesting that the images they present should not be taken lightly. How are women represented in these products and how do these representations influence the ways in which society views women? The next section discusses the ways in which women are represented in cultural products.

## Representations of Women in African Cultural Products

Cole (2007: 270) opens her discussion of gender theory and Ghanaian popular culture with the startling statement: "Sexism in African Popular Theatre is so ubiquitous that 'it goes without saying.'" She demonstrates in her article how the negative portrayal of women in Ghanaian popular theatre is taken as normal, how female characters are presented in unfavourable terms and how the treatment meted out to them borders on the misogynistic. This misrepresentation of women is not limited to West African theatre. Mercy Mirembe Ntangaare, in her article "Portraits of Women in Ugandan Theatre" also notes that:

...on the stage women are commonly stereotypes used to rein-force usually negative ideas which support conservative patriarchy and male sexual titillation. They are very seldom rounded or remotely realistic characters, being rather idealised dreams or demonic visions of femininity. (2002: 64)

Dina Amin, writing about the Egyptian experience, observes that "male drama-tists have perpetually portrayed women as mindless, irrational, jealous, hysterical, materialistic and, at times, downright ridiculous" (2002: 15).[3] The case of popular music is perhaps even more worrisome, considering the ubiquity of music as against theatre. The lyrics of contemporary Ghanaian *highlife* focus almost solely on romantic love and sometimes provide sexual innuendo; in the case of *hip-life* there is a definite macho flavour to the lyrics; the majority of the local rap singers are men and to a large extent there is a tendency to objectify women in the songs and videos of the genre (Collins, 2000). Beyond this, we found from the analysis of the over two hundred songs we collected that women are portrayed as exploitative, unfaithful, unreliable, enchantresses, witches, jeal-ous, competitive (typically with other women over men), and materialistic.[4]

There are, of course, popular songs (and literature) which present positive images of women. Our survey of songs reveals that women are frequently praised as mothers and lovers in non-objectifying ways. The problem, however, is the apparently disproportionate number of songs which *does* objectify and infantilise women. It may be argued that, in a society where male domination is so rife, the negative portrayals of women may not even be evident to musicians and consumers. Even male musicians and other artists who may consider themselves as pro-women may inadvertently project negative images of women in their work without consciously meaning to do so.[5] In the arena of literature, both popular and so called literary,[6] women are depicted by male authors less favourably than men and are often presented within the limited domestic sphere as wife and mother, as mere sex objects for the pleasure of men, or as peripheral to male characters (Newell, 2000; Danysh, 2000; Ntangaare, 2002; Amin, 2002). That people may take cues from these art forms and be guided thereby is beyond doubt. Research has shown how African audiences actively seek to learn lessons from theatre performances which they may apply to their lives (see Barber, 2000; Asiedu, 2003). The need for articulating the problem of negative representations of women in these art forms and pushing for change cannot be overemphasised.

## Our Research: Changing Representations of Women in Popular Music

Our research project on Changing Representations of Women in Popular Culture, with a focus on Ghanaian popular music, was part of a larger international research consortium titled "Pathways of Women's Empowerment." The project was funded by the UK Department for International Development (DFID) with other partners, including the Centre for Gender Studies and Advocacy (CEGENSA)[7] at the University of Ghana, the Department for Interdisciplinary Women's Studies (NEIM) at the Federal University of Bahia, Brazil; BRAC University, Bangladesh; the Social Research Centre (SRC) at the American University in Cairo, Egypt; and the Institute of Development Studies (IDS) in the United Kingdom, which coordinated the project.

In our particular project, we explored the gendered stereotypes of women in popular music, and sought to contribute to reflection on, and creation of, alternative (empowering) narratives about women through song. The methods in this scholarly-activist project included the collection of over 250 songs; analyses of song texts; workshops with diverse persons from the music industry; discussions with consumers of music (taxi drivers and students); a song competition; a launch of the winning songs; and discussions and reflections in the print and electronic media.

In one of the workshops with popular musicians and other people in the music industry, it emerged that the situation was due partly to the fact that the popular music industry in Ghana is largely a male domain – for the most part men write song lyrics, men produce the music and men perform. There was a suggestion by some participants that an increased participation of women in the industry might minimise or at least counter the overwhelming negativity and stereotypical images presented. The danger that a male dominated production of culture will continue to replicate gender stereotypes and mis-representations is very real. We found Cole's (2007) work to be particularly relevant for our study in this regard. She presents "the changing discourse on gender over a 55 year period" (270) through the analysis of three archetypal female characters in Ghanaian concert party from the 1930s through to the 1980s. Cole demonstrates clearly how, in the earlier years, when there was no female participation in the production of Concert Parties, there were more negative representations of women. It was not until after women began to participate in the creation of concert party plays that stronger and better representation of women was possible:

> Ghana's concert party narratives and character types became more hospitable to women over time, and shows portrayal of female characters in an increasingly sympathetic light. The presence of actual women in the creation and production of plays was central to making this cultural form more inclusive of a range of female gender roles. (2007: 280)

Evidently, this suggests that female participation in cultural production may help in more positive representations of women. Writing/singing about oneself presents an opportunity to project one's own perspectives and priorities. It goes back to the idea of history narrated from the point of view of the oppressed as opposed to history narrated from the point of view of the oppressor. Variations between the two accounts are bound to reflect the particular viewpoint of the authors. Newell's study of Ghanaian popular fiction supports this view, as she notes that "Ghanaian women's writing seems to manifest a 'feminine positionality' which transforms, embellishes and amplifies the plots and character types to be found in popular, male-authored narratives" (2000: 155). Aidoo as a writer, without a doubt, upholds this viewpoint.

## Ama Ata Aidoo: The Epitome of Empowering Representations of Women

A cursory look at Aidoo's oeuvre of short stories, plays, poems and novels immediately reveals that women are at the centre of her work. A more careful study of her work further reveals a realistic, sympathetic and sophisticated portrayal of women. Her representation of women, however, resists a simplistic label of feminism, as her work is not solely defined by gender politics. Adams (2011) clearly articulates this when she notes; "In Aidoo's works ... contested issues from all spheres of society are imbricated and of equivalent valence; for her, gender is but one of several roots of conflict" (203–4). Thus Aidoo's women protagonists are from all walks of life, modern and traditional, educated and uneducated; they range from fish mongers, prostitutes, and hairdressers, to housewives, university professors and other professional women – these are believable characters, far from being stereotypes.

One fascinating strategy Aidoo adopts in her work is intergenerational comparisons of women within the same family. An interesting example is found in her short story "She-Who-Would-Be-King." The story starts with an exchange between a ten-year-old girl and a man of about twenty-five years. The young girl declares her intention to become the president of the country, to which the man replies "I don't think the men of this country will ever let a woman be their president." Rather than accept such an assertion as true, the girl throws him the challenge: "No? We shall see." In the story, fifty years after this exchange, in the year 2026, a 36-year-old woman has just been sworn into office as the first president of the Confederation of African States. This woman is the daughter of the precocious ten-year-old in the earlier exchange. Though the ten-year-old had not attained her dream of becoming president, her daughter had achieved that dream; while she herself had become a university Professor and Dean of the Faculty of Law. A third woman presented in this futuristic short story, is the Professor's 86-year-old mother, referred to as "The Old Queen." She is a woman who has had a hard but satisfying life and in her sunset years is surrounded by her doting and proud family: a dignified matriarch. Thus, Aidoo traces in a very interesting way the lives of three women over three generations, presenting very affirmative and inspiring possibilities for women.

Aidoo transforms popular notions and images about women and turns them on their head. Newell notes how she adopts the figure of the "good-time girl," from "popular, male-authored narratives," instilling them with "new, politicised messages for readers" (2000: 160). Aidoo also does something similar with traditional wisdom and folklore. In *Anowa*, her powerful play about the slave trade, she transforms the folktale about the girl who refused all the suitors her parents found for her, marrying her own choice of a man against her parents' wishes and in the end regretting this, into a fascinating tragic tale of a strong woman with a mind of her own, who chooses her own path, obstinately refusing to conform to societal norms and pressure and is willing to live with the consequences. Aidoo's writings are replete with examples of young girls and women resisting the status quo, breaking barriers and going beyond the stereotypical aspirations and prescriptions of society. As Adams notes; "The refusal to accept conformist delineations of normative behaviour or spheres of activity is a central theme in every one of Aidoo's stories that feature girls" (2011: 11).

## The Example of Two Ghanaian Female Musicians: Akosua Agyepong and Mzbel

The discussion thus far suggests female participation in the production of cultural products affects the ways in which women are represented. The question then is, will more women singing about themselves necessarily introduce new and more positive images in popular music? Schultz (2002) has noted that Malian female popular musicians address women in many songs and disapprove of their "difficulties" in the urban centres where relationships with relatives and friends are so often ruled with envy, and any sense of moral obligation is so often undermined by "money" (802). They denounce the evils of polygamous marriage, such as back-biting co-wives and husbands who fail to treat their co-wives with impartiality; they acclaim women for their accomplishments as mothers and spouses and encourage them to feel "proud" of their elegance and accomplishments. There is characteristically a mixing of "women's problems" with an appeal to "feel good" about being a woman, despite the difficulties she has to put up with, and many songs represent procreation and motherhood as a central source of women's dignity (802). How empowering are these representations by these Malian female pop stars Schultz discuses? Though the songs foreground women's issues, are they necessarily non-stereotypical? We examine these more closely with examples of two Ghanaian female popular musicians.

Akosua Agyepong, a female musical icon of the early 1990s, came to the public's attention because, not only was she attractive, as many women musicians are, but she presented a rather Afro-centric image and had a fairly good education, having recently graduated from one of the more prestigious all-girls high schools in Ghana. She also went on to marry one of the "bad boys" of music, Amandziba. Her popular song, *Me ye Obaa*[8] released in 1990, is in one sense a celebration of womanhood. The chorus proclaims proudly, "I am a woman, God made me a woman. He created me very well (He did it well)." She affirms womanhood and proclaims there is every reason to be proud of being a woman, for the creator created us well. Here is a picture of someone comfortable with her gender identity. The next stanza affirms a fellowship of women: "We are women, God created us as women, He created us well." She claims kinship with all women and affirms that we were all created "well" as women. There is a sense of pride in these proclamations. The song, however, progresses into a passionate moralising narrative of how women should relate to men. She first of all implores women, especially young women like herself, to listen to their parents and be obedient to them. While there is nothing wrong with what she advises, it immediately places her narrative onto a trajectory of traditional norms and values which younger people are, in her song, being exhorted to adhere to. She, predictably, goes on to present some desirable qualities of a dignified, respectable woman:

- She does not give in to just any man
- She places high value on herself
- She dresses with decorum and not in a provocative manner
- She does not jump from man to man nor have multiple lovers
- She introduces her lover/anyone who shows an interest in her to her parents; if the man really loves her, he would willingly go and see her parents
- Once she has found her true love, she must remain faithful to him, no matter what, for this will earn her the man's trust and proper care.

A promiscuous life, she sings, would only end in the woman's getting pregnant with no one claiming responsibility for the child. This is the height of disgrace, as no man would then be interested in marrying such a woman, and the child would have a miserable life without a father. As though to emphasise this, she reminds us that there are several young girls without fathers. Abortion, though an option, could lead to death, if one is not fortunate, she concludes.

Akosua Agyepong's image of acceptable behaviour for women in relation to men thus fits very neatly into traditional expectations of women, the prescribed stereotyped status quo. The reason women must fit into this mould, however, she suggests, is to win the respect of men and find a man of their own to marry. Here is a woman singing about women. She does not objectify women nor present them as sex objects, but she does place them in a somewhat dependent position. They are to derive their value from their relationship with men. In order to do so, they must be careful not to go outside the norms of society's dictates for a decent woman. Though she presents women as having the power of choice, they really cannot choose to go outside society's norms. They can only choose that which society has sanctioned. A single mother is likely not to be able to look after her child and give her/him a decent life without a father. Thus she represents stereotypical images and expectations of women, namely their dependence on men. Marriage is the aim and women must be careful to get the right man and then all would be well. This female icon has accepted the norms of society for the conduct of women in relation to men and is willing, not only to accept these, but also to celebrate them as good.

Another contemporary female music icon, Mzbel, presents a more radical feminine persona in her song *16 Years*, generating quite some controversy, especially when her lyrics are taken together with her own sexy personality and the music video which accompanies the song. The words of the chorus of the song are as follows:

> I be 16 years,
> I go dey be like this o
> If you touch my thing o I go tell Mummy o
> I be 16 years,
> I go dey be like this o
> If you touch my thing o I go tell Poppy o

The rest of the song (mostly in Twi) and the music video suggest that a 16-year-old girl is sexually harassed by an older man and she stands up for herself by insisting she will tell her parents should the man persist. Mzbel thus describes a common dilemma young women face, and presents a stance which they may adopt in defending themselves. Young women, she suggests, must not allow themselves to be victims of unscrupulous men. The images in the music video along with the lyrics present an attractive young woman, who by her appearance may be inviting male attention, but as she sings:

> I no dey cheap, so make you try back off
> You dey hear me, oga boys, go back off
> Gidigidi, mempene, I be innocent
> Mehwe me jeans ne me skirt, free style, I am aware[9]
> Brother hwe me back, ne me chest
> Wei ye TV, but you for know say
>
> I be 16 years,
> I go dey be like this o

In other words, she seems to insist, "I have the right to be who I am and to dress the way I want in jeans and skirts which may reveal my body and sexuality, but it does not mean I am cheap and I am not a television for you to keep watching; just take your gaze off me. My attractiveness does not give you the right to take advantage of me." Her song further warns that if a man insists on harassing innocent sixteen-year-olds, it could result in his arrest by the police and he would have to face the wrath of the then Women and Juvenile's Unit (WAJU)[10]

> Oh, police go catch you
> Catch you pe, straight to the WAJU
> WAJU nso ho no ara na wobeyi wo

Mzbel thus points to the fact that there are laws in Ghana on the side of women which can protect them from sexual harassment. In the music video, the offending man is indeed dragged to court where he is convicted and faces disgrace.

Mzbel is advocating a certain level of personal freedom for women, where they may be who they wish to be without falling victim to self-serving men. This song generated quite a debate in our focus group discussion with taxi drivers. While some felt the song was a positive warning to men not to take advantage of young women, and thus was empowering for women, others felt it was a dangerous song, which encouraged young girls to dress provocatively to tease men. Indeed, Mzbel is perceived by some sections of society as promoting promiscuity, the sort Akosua Agyepong warns women against in her song *Me ye Obaa*. This perception was underscored on one occasion where she sang this song to an audience of university students who had themselves invited her to a social function. At the end of her song, Mzbel was:

> ...stripped naked of her tiny performance attire, which eye-witnesses branded as very seductive and suggestive and (sic) torn into pieces. Her nudity was (sic) in the process exposed to the public for ridicule and contempt. Eyewitnesses said but for the timely intervention of the university's private security personnel at the scene, she would have been raped or (sic) the worst would have happened to the hip-hop star. According to the reports, in the ensuing drama some of the students who had joined her to dance fondled her breasts.... (Mirror, Wednesday, 2 November 2005)

Interestingly, this same song recently won Mzbel international attention as she was invited by the Minnesota African Women's Association (MAWA) to participate in an African Women in the Diaspora conference and to speak on the theme "Addressing the Cultural Rights and Practices that Harm African Women and Girls – the Role of African Men, Women and Youth." She was also to share her experiences "on how to deal with some of society's abusive cultural practices, by speaking up and fighting back." Commenting on how she became a part of the US programme, she said "apparently, MAWA had been browsing my website and listening to some of my music. They later got in touch with my manager in London and that was how it all started. They will be using my song, '16 Years' to promote the event." (*Graphic Showbiz*, Thursday, May 1st, 2008). Thus this pretty sexy music icon and her song about young girls and their sexuality is seen as empowered and empowering by this American women's association.

Evidently, by steering away from the usual stereotypical images of women within the African context, Mzbel has waded into controversy. She has remained unfazed, however, and continues to perform her brand of music. In spite of the controversy surrounding 16 *Years*, there is no denying that Mzbel presents a strong case against violence against women. Nothing can be an excuse for rape or child defilement. She also empowers women with the knowledge that the law is on their side and they need not suffer sexual harassment in silence.

## Conclusion

The two songs by the female musicians presented above affirm the fact that it is possible for women to sing about themselves and issues that concern them. The fact that they are women, however, does not guarantee that they will necessarily present empowering and non-stereotypical images of themselves. As we argued in the beginning of this paper, cultural products reflect society and its values and also influence society. As artists are products of their societies, it is only to be expected that they would in their creations embody the values, both negative and positive, of their societies. Happily, however, many artists are willing and able to go against the grain of their societies thus contributing to influencing them for change. Not all male artists misrepresent or objectify women in their work, and clearly not all female artists may be willing to go against the grain of society in presenting "controversial" or unusually empowering images of women. As part of our research, we organised a music competition to encourage empowering lyrics about women. Out of the 27 entries we received, only two were from women and out of these two, one was disqualified because her entry was a gospel song which had nothing to do with women. All three top winners were men.

We contend, nevertheless, that the idea of encouraging an increasing number of female artists in the production of popular music should be seen as part of the solution. This is because males not only dominate within hip-life and high-life popular music genres, but also have a tendency to project sexist, objectifying, and/or misogynist messages through their songs and/or the images of video. The idea of increased representation parallels the political project of equality within development discourse, namely the tendency of development's gender analysis framework to stress the need for more women to be involved in political representations, whether as policy analysts and employees in development organisations or as holders of "decision-making" positions in politics, economics, or the judiciary. The point, however, remains that empowering representations cannot be achieved solely by increasing the number of women within the field of popular music, be they musicians or media personnel. Such an ahistorical position decontextualises and depoliticises the power dynamics that demarcate gender relations within the music industry in particular, and within Ghanaian society in general. Increased representation will neither always nor automatically translate into more positive portrayals of women or more meaningful messages – it is a necessary but not a sufficient condition. Thus, combating the entrenchment of hyper-masculinity within popular music will undoubtedly require more ammunition. Achieving gender equality is as much about men and masculinities as women and feminism. Too many development initiatives continue to focus on women in isolation, hence the fact that the participants in the workshops we organised, our focus group discussants and the participants in our music competition were mainly men was particularly useful. The issue of "gender fatigue," where men, or society, are weary of the seemingly endless whining of feminists for more of one thing and better conditions in another, may be relevant to the question of whether women's empowering messages will have greater impact if sung by male or female musicians or promoted by male or female media persons. It can be speculated that if a man were to promote such notions – given that many men are the harbingers of patriarchal practices, and many male musicians are promoters of disempowering messages within popular culture – which would be a deviation from the norm, he might attract more attention, or perhaps lend greater legitimacy to the message. While such a scenario may be critical for pragmatic reasons, we would still insist that girls need to hear the right messages from other women – they should not look only to men as their saviors – they need female role models too. Ama Ata Aidoo, the celebrated Ghanaian writer, points the way for other women artists. She has always written from a perspective uniquely her own, a perspective which has produced empowered/empowering and realistic images of women; and thus can be held up as a model for other female artists, be they writers, dramatists or musicians.

# Ties that Bound: Slave Concubines/ Wives and the End of Slavery in the Gold Coast, c.1874–1900

## Emmanuel Akyeampong

## Introduction

Strong young women that made life choices often in conflict with societal norms or expectations have been an important theme in Ama Ata Aidoo's plays and novels.[1] In this essay I examine similar choices made by strong women in the last quarter of the 19th century with the abolition of slavery or emancipation in the Gold Coast. I use court cases in Anlo in southeastern Gold Coast between 1874 and 1900 to discuss slave wives and concubines who, despite British reluctance to interfere in slave marriages and local intimidation in what were small communities, opted for freedom or to redefine their place and identity in Anlo society. It has been established historically that the majority of slaves in Africa were women, valued for production and reproduction.[2] Claude Meillassoux has cautioned us not to privilege sexuality and reproduction as the basis of the African preference for female slaves, and that theoretically slaves were "sexless" and female slaves in Africa were valued above all else as labourers.[3] That notwithstanding, it is also important to remember that not all slaves were acquired for productive purposes, and social and political reasons for acquiring slaves were equally important in pre-colonial Africa, where wealth was considered in people. Female slaves were acquired strategically as wives and concubines to expand the ranks of patrilineages and matrilineages in precolonial Africa. Kinless outsiders, their offspring belonged to the lineage of the owner.[4]

The 19th century witnessed a phenomenal expansion in plantation slavery in Africa or the commercial production of cash crops based on slave labour. In this century, even adult males, previously unwanted and thus exported through the Atlantic Slave Trade, became valuable as labourers. Agricultural slave villages proliferated with slave families, as slave owners considered that slave marriages and children gave slaves a vested interest in the community and reduced the incentive for flight. Case studies of slave plantations in West Africa exist for northern Nigeria and southwest Mali, among other places.[5] It is ironic that this expansion in plantation slavery within Africa had been promoted in part by the European abolition of the export slave trade at the beginning of the 19th century and the introduction of trade in cash crops ("legitimate trade") as a substitute, which had generated a need for agricultural labour and for porters to carry produce to coastal traders.

In Anlo, the case study for this essay, the export slave trade persisted until the 1860s, encouraged by the scarcity of land, especially fertile land. The lagoons and creeks that stretched inland across Anlo country provided excellent facilities for smuggling. Export slave trade in Anlo facilitated an increase in internal slavery. The Anlo exhibited a preference for young women and children as slaves. Slave women were often married to men in the owner's lineage, and slave children – and slave offspring – grew up as junior "kinsmen."[6] A master controlled his slave wife or concubine and offspring to a degree not possible in a marriage to a free Anlo woman. Trading families used slaves in the processing of fish and salt, which were sent into the interior with European goods. These slaves also served as porters, carrying goods to trade marts.[7] Slaves were also used individually or in small numbers on farms, and absent was the pattern of large numbers of slaves toiling on land belonging to "big men" or chiefs west of the Volta River. Anlo lands were owned by clans and wealthy individuals and there were no stool lands, making chiefs dependent on court fines and gifts from resident traders. Effective British presence after the transfer of Danish spheres of influence, including Anlo and Ada, in 1850, finally curtailed the export slave trade in Anlo. By the mid-1860s, many Anlo traders had switched to trade in palm oil, as Krobo producers, the centre of palm oil production then, directed their produce to the Anlo coast.

The timing of British emancipation in 1874–5 was particularly painful for the Anlo, not only because slaves as elsewhere in the Gold Coast constituted the most important form of moveable wealth, but also because of an onset of global economic depression in the later quarter of the 19th century and a glut in the global market for fats and oils. Indebtedness and social insecurity was rife in Anlo, encouraging pawnship and the outright sale of people, especially women. It was in this context that some slave concubines and wives in Anlo made difficult decisions to oppose their masters/husbands and their adopted lineages, to opt out of forced "marriages," to claim their children, and to form new unions of their choice. They faced the opposition, often violent, of their masters, and the indifference of the colonial administration, which sought to minimise the potential social disruption that could result from emancipation. Though historical evidence has substantiated that most slaves on emancipation chose to remain with their masters and renegotiate their relations, the court cases cited in this paper provide a different window on emancipation, unearthing the voices and perspectives of a few brave women who dared to imagine a different social reality for themselves.[8]

## The Abolition of Slavery in Colonial Gold Coast

British defeat of Asante in 1874 paved the way for the declaration of a Gold Coast Colony south of Asante. Anlo's alliance with Akwamu and Asante had been demonstrated in Anlo's support for Asante and Akwamu in the Krepi War of 1869, when Asante invaded the northern Ewe. To prevent Anlo from joining Asante in the 1874 war, a British military force invaded and subjugated Anlo before the main British army advanced against Asante. Thus Anlo became a part of the British colony in 1874. To galvanise domestic support for imperialism, official rhetoric in Britain advocated how the imposition of colonial rule would end slave trade and slavery in British colonies in Africa. But as British officers in the colonies in Africa testified to the pervasiveness of slavery and how slaves constituted a vital part of the wealth and social capital of chiefs, the British government became reluctant to move against domestic slavery in Africa.

The British Aborigines Protection Society drew public attention to the persistence of slave dealing even within the proximity of British forts in the Gold Coast, compelling an embarrassed British government to act.[9] Unwilling to stir chiefly opposition or pay compensation for the emancipation of slaves, Britain opted for the "Indian model" of abolition. It abolished the "legal status" of slavery, though it did not outlaw slavery. As Miers explains: "Theoretically, those slaves who wished to do so could remain with their masters, but those who left could not be legally forced to return or to work for their owners."[10] Slave trading was outlawed with the assumption that, deprived of new recruits, slavery would die a natural death. There was, however, an important departure from the Indian model in the Gold Coast: all children born in or entering the protectorate after January 1, 1875 were to be considered free. Both the British and the French colonial governments in Africa, pressed by similar considerations, abolished the legal status of slavery but chose not to publicise this fact. On Maraka plantations in the French Soudan in 1905–6, thousands of slaves left the slave agricultural villages when word reached them that the French had abolished the legal status of slavery since 1902. As most of these slaves had been recently captured in the wars and raids of Samory Touré, Tieba of Sikasso and others, they knew where home was, and the imposition of French colonial peace in that larger region encouraged the exodus of 1905–6. It is estimated that, by the end of the exodus in 1908, about 200,000–500,000 had abandoned their masters.[11] Nothing this sensational took place in the Gold Coast or in Anlo, where the records suggest that the majority of ex-slaves chose to remain with their former masters.[12]

The smuggling of women and children in the Gold Coast would continue into the 20th century. Dumett and Johnson point to a considerable trade in slaves down the Volta River in the 1880s and 1890s.[13] In terms of emancipation, the greatest obstacles were faced by women. Miers again highlights how colonial rulers tended to see female slaves as women and wives, placing their conflicts with their masters in the domestic domain and not in the sphere of slaves versus masters. The patriarchal attitude of colonial officials and the men who usually dominated native and Muslim courts often meant that the rights of females were ignored.[14] Unless a slave lodged a complaint for cruel treatment with a district commissioner or a magistrate or sought legal assistance to be liberated, colonial officials were warned to refrain from interfering in existing relations between masters and slaves. Thus, the climate was not particularly supportive for slave wives and concubines in Anlo who sought to revise their status.

## Breaking Bonds: Contesting Slave Marriage and Family in Anlo

Masters in Anlo either incorporated their female slaves into their lineage through marriage or found them slave husbands to root them in the community. Female slaves had to succumb to such arrangements, and some would choose the early years of emancipation to insist on their choice of partners and to revoke the earlier arrangements of their slave masters. In 1889, Buafo [Boafo], an Akan slave from either the northern part of Eweland, with its history of Akan immigrants, or Akanland west of the Volta, sued Quaccoe [Kwaku] Duah for seducing his wife. Seduction of a wife in Anlo attracted an adultery fee of about £1–16 for commoners. Beyond the monetary compensation, pacification in adultery underscored a man's exclusive rights to the sexuality of his wife – that he had customarily married his wife – and the community's endorsement of that monopoly. Buafo explained the situation to the court:

> My wife Arkuah [Akua] and I were slaves to a certain man, long since dead. The defendant about eight years ago came to Jella Coffee [Dzelukope] where we live and seduced my wife. I sent a man named Patchow to defendant and he admitted having had connection with her. I claimed the amount of £1-16-0 but plaintiff soon after left the district. Lately I saw the defendant but as it was so long since the former offence I said nothing. About seven days ago my wife, who had been living with me continuously, suddenly left me and claimed protection in the court from slavery. I heard that defendant had taken her and was hiding her in the house of a countryman in Housa [Hausa] camp. Sergeant Awudu Kaba told me this.[15]

Since adultery was considered a case between men, a point on which patriarchal British and Gold Coast societies seemed to agree, Arkuah's testimony was not solicited by district commissioner (DC) Francis Lamb of Kwitta [Keta]. Quaccoe Duah claimed not to know her whereabouts, and it does not appear the court tried to find Arkuah. In his defence, Quaccoe Duah argued that:

> I have met the plaintiff's wife about nine years ago, but have not met her to speak to since. I do not know where the woman is now. When I met her nine years ago, I had connection with her, and she told me that she had no *real husband*, but a man who was a slave with her *was called such* [emphasis mine].

What can be inferred from Duah's defence, if he was being truthful, is that Arkuah had no emotional ties to the slave compatriot her master had married her to, and for her the marriage was not "real," in spite the endorsement of the slaveholder's community. The district commissioner dismissed the case.

Miers points out the complexity of "freedom" in African contexts, and how colonial officials were puzzled that the slaves they proclaimed free and issued freedom certificates to did not see themselves as free nor consider themselves free in the eyes of their former masters and the communities they lived in. These slaves would insist on paying the ransom amount for their liberation, for it was such an act that emancipated them in their eyes and those of the host community. Likewise slave wives did not consider themselves free or their marriages legitimate despite colonial endorsement, cognizant that as slave wives no bride wealth had been paid to them for their union.[16] For Arkuah in our Anlo case, colonial emancipation provided the opportunity to reject her former marriage to her slave husband and to seek a union of her choice. For Buafo, the aggrieved slave husband, a successful suit and the payment of the adultery fee would have elevated him to the status of a free man, whose marriage was attended by the sanctions prescribed for free born marriages. As a slave couple, it is very unlikely that any bride wealth had been exchanged, as both were the property of their master. It was the payment of bride wealth that legitimated a marriage and necessitated the payment of the adultery fee if the sanctity of the marriage was breached.

Indeed, the passage of colonial laws ending slave dealing witnessed a last spurt in the sale of women and children, and many were brought from northern markets down the Volta River to Ada, and from there eastwards to Anlo. On the frontier of Gold Coast colony, many Anlo acted as if they were beyond colonial jurisdiction. Slave owners avoided Keta, the district headquarters of the colonial administration, and relocated their slaves to outlying regions. They continued to acquire slaves, creating slave families through marriages with the intent of expanding their network of dependents, a strategy that was particularly important to chiefs throughout the Gold Coast. Chief Amagashie of Aferingba (Afiadenyigba) and Quitta (Keta) fell foul of the colonial government in this regard. He was brought to court for slave dealing in 1886 over a Mossi slave he had originally purchased in 1880, long after the declaration of the Gold Coast colony. In his defence, he argued that colonial presence was ephemeral in Anlo in 1880, and that many owned slaves. It is clear from his evidence that he quit Keta in order to avoid freeing his slaves.

> The law abolishing slavery is hardly yet in force on the other side of the lagoon many people there still hold slaves. When I was [at] Quitta and the abolition took place any slaves I held were free to go or stay. When I moved to Afianba, I often saw slaves brought along from the interior and out of pity for some I redeemed some of them and gave some of them wives. They did little odd jobs about the farm or house. With reference to Kwasi Moshi, I bought him at Afiangba about six years ago. The English law was hardly then in force there and many were brought down. There seem to be many in Moshi and the interior people buy them for salt and bring them down. Many Ada people did this. The boy Moshie I treated well. I gave him a wife and a gun. He went on badly at last and contracted many debts. He asked some of his companions to pay his debts but they would not and in the end they took him away and sold him to pay his debts. I did not know he was taken away at the time. .... .... I heard the two men Kwasi and Daku were employed by the creditors to sell prosecutor K. Moshi.[17]

In spite of Chief Amagashi's claim that he knew nothing of the sale of Kwasi Moshi for debt, the judge, C. Dudley, agreed with the complainant Moshi that a slave cannot be sold without the consent of the owner. Chief Amagashi was fined £20 for slave dealing. In the process of transforming his slaves into social dependents that he could still retain under colonial rule, Chief Amagashi "gave some of them wives." But the threat of sale remained as a sanction for slaves, as slavery and slave trade co-exist in a necessary and complementary relationship. Even in slave systems where violence was minimal, the market and the possibility of sale acted as a veiled glove that kept slaves and people of servile origins quiescent. Even in the face-to-face communities of Anlo, the presence of a market in slaves was a daily reality for servile peoples.

Slave wives or concubines were not mistaken in their position that their unions were lowly esteemed compared to that between free born. Lacking protective kinsmen, as slaves are outsiders, they suffered abuse in relationships, and their children were sometimes not even secure from their slave masters/fathers. And the colonial government persisted in its position that these were domestic matters it could not intervene in. Gbedashi's case against Yabua [Yeboah] of Accra, from 1886, illustrates this predicament:[18]

> I am a native of Agbosomeh town. My family sold me to the prisoner about twenty years ago and I lived with him until 1877 and bore him a daughter the first year he bought me. In 1877 he sold me to a man named Toffa living at Kedje [Kedzi] and the year after he took my daughter named Odofoley away and sold her to a man named Kpo of Akeyfey about 18 miles from Addafia. I lost sight of the girl until two years ago when she sent a message to me that she had been sold by her father the prisoner, and that was how I knew. I sent to try and get her back, but the buyer wanted 32 bags of cowries which he said he had paid for her. I could not get so much money and so a few days ago I sent for the prisoner and told him what I had heard, he got up in a rage and said that it was his own daughter and if he sold her, he sold her. So I applied for a warrant against him.

District commissioner R. E. Firminger adjourned the case for a day, and on the following day Yabua presented his defence:

> About 20 years ago I bought the prosecutrix from her family. She was my slave and concubine. No English Government was here at that time. It was when the English and Accras came here and fought the Awwoonahs [Anlos, probably in 1874] that I took my daughter away and gave her in pawn to a man named Kpo for money I lost during the war and which I had borrowed from him. It is true what the prosecutrix says that I sold her the year before I pawned my daughter both the events were before the British Government came here and there was no law then against my doing so

The case was adjourned for another two days to enable Toffah, who had bought Gbedashi from Yabua, to give testimony. Toffah confirmed that:

> I bought the woman Gbedashi from her husband the prisoner long before the English came here it was about 1864. After she lived with me three days she went off and I have never seen her since.

DC Firminger dismissed the case, obviously seeing this as a domestic matter and following the government's directive not to intervene in such situations.

This is in sharp contrast to the case cited above between Kwasi Moshi and Chief Amagashi, a matter involving two men, which the colonial officer viewed as a straightforward case of slave dealing. This was despite the accused admitting to both the sale of his wife and to pawning his daughter, even though the law that abolished slave dealing had also outlawed pawnage.

The abolition of slavery occasioned a rise in pawning, especially of women. Dumett and Johnson comment that:

> The antislavery ordinances of 1874–1875 had no diminishing effect whatsoever on the transfer of individuals from one household to another as security for debts. On the contrary, the laws appear to have sparked a trend in the opposite direction, as well-to-do merchants, heads of farming families, and kings and chiefs turned to pawnage as a way of continuing to add domestic servants and dependents to their households as a substitute for "slavery."[19]

For Asante, Gareth Austin has noted the feminisation of pawnship between 1800 and 1950, a trend that was paralleled in the Gold Coast colony.[20] It is striking how Yabua and Toffa sought to predate their ownership of slaves and pawns before the commencement of British rule, contending that their actions could not be made illegal retroactively. Gbedashi, on the contrary, dated her sale and that of her daughter to 1877 and 1878, well after the commencement of British colonialism in 1874, and hence illegal. Gbedashi's interpretation of her slave marriage to her owner as lacking emotional ties and security are borne out by Yabua's testimony, framed in the language of property rights and not kinship. He owned his slave concubine and the offspring of that relationship; both women constituted wealth to Yabua.[21] It is likely that Gbedashi's date for her resale to Toffa (1877) is accurate, and probably aware that colonial rule had made illegal the status of slavery, she boldly walked out of her second slave marriage to Toffah after only three days. Toffa, perhaps also aware of the tenuousness of the marriage, did not pursue Gbedashi. Almost a decade later, Gbedashi would use the colonial courts to try and reunite with her daughter, the only affective relationship that held meaning for her.

It is unfortunate that even after colonial rule had commenced in the Gold Coast, husbands could use the threat of sale to keep even their free wives in line. Adedie was married to Fiato as a young girl. In her own words, "I was compelled to marry him." It is not clear whether there was a debt involved, and Adedie was given in marriage as part of the arrangements between her family and Fiato. That Adedie did not love Fiato is clear: they quarreled often and Adedie refused to live with him. For three years between 1883 and 1886, Fiato insisted on the return of Adedie to their marital home or her payment of £12, which could have been bride wealth or a debt Fiato paid on behalf of Adedie's family. Adedie's position was not negotiable: "I refused to live with him and he threatened to catch me and sell me."[22]

Even slave wives who were treated with consideration by their masters/husbands could not set aside the fact that their marriages were irregular and involuntary. In January 1892, Husunuyor, a farmer at Echi, brought Begyie to the DC's court in Keta for seizing his niece Agagey and selling her. One Milebah bought the niece from Begyie and she became his slave wife. Husunuyor also sued Milebah for slave dealing for having bought his niece. It seems the sale, from both the accounts of Agagey and Milebah, took place between 1880 and 1884. Agagey's testimony ends our discussion of slave marriages and families, and it is instructive on how the women involved in even secure relations considered their involuntary unions:

> I think it was 12 years ago since I was seized by Begyie. Begyie was no relation of mine he stole me and sold me to the accused. I do not know how much he got. I have lived with the accused all the time. He treated me well. I live with him as a slave wife. As I am a slave to him, I wish to go to my family, then perhaps if the prisoner likes I will join him again and be his wife.[23]

Agagey found comfort and emotional security in her forced marriage. The marriage had produced children. She wanted the marriage to be consensual, and to have the dignity of her husband approaching her family for her hand. DC A. M. Kirkham, in the circumstances, decided to be lenient with Milebah, and sentenced Milebah to one month in prison with hard labour. It is likely that Milebah and Agagey were reunited on terms Agagey found affirming.

## Concluding Remarks

In patriarchal precolonial societies where marriages were treated as mechanisms for reproducing kin groups and strategies for cementing social alliances, the emotional needs of young women and their expectations in marriages often tended to be discounted. Since young women were usually married to men much older than them, they tended to be widowed while still of childbearing age, and were pressured by family to remarry. Jean Allman and Victoria Tahsjian point out how menopause was welcomed by Asante women for it freed them from the burden of remarriages when widowed, enabling women to focus on trade, accumulation and building female social networks.[24] For pre-colonial Asante, Thomas McCaskie tells the life story of the Oyoko royal of Kumasi, Amma Sewaa, sister of Asantehene Osei Kwame (1777–1803). After an early marriage to Apaw Panin, a son of Asantehene Kusi Obodom (1750–64), which produced six children, Amma Sewaa was widowed in her twenties. She decided on a love marriage for her second relationship, marrying Nkwantananhene Boakye Yam Kuma, someone whose ancestry "was impeccably sound rather than exalted or even especially distinguished," sometime in the late 1780s or early 1790s. From the perspective of her royal lineage, she had married beneath her station and this was an unorthodox marriage.[25] For Amma Sewaa, this was an emotionally satisfying marriage.

Women in the Gold Coast and Asante have historically sought to define marriage and family on terms that met their emotional needs. Moving from parental and lineage control to that of husbands' and the kinsmen of husbands, women's pursuit of independence and accumulation have been in the context of their relationships with men. While marriage has always been valued culturally in the Gold Coast and Asante, women found marriage as defined by men emotionally limiting. So in the 1920s and 1930s, when colonial trade and cocoa farming opened up independent means for accumulating wealth and thus becoming financially independent for women in the Gold Coast Colony and Asante, many opted not to marry. In Sefwi Wiawso and parts of Asante, this was perceived by men as a moral crisis. In both places, spinsters were rounded up by chiefs, who ordered them to choose a husband and marry within the shortest possible time.[26] From the onset of colonial rule, the establishment of a dual legal system with native or customary courts and British common law courts would also provide women with opportunities to approach colonial courts for redress in domestic disputes, the maintenance of children and alimony.[27] This essay has examined how slave wives and concubines in the early decades of colonial rule availed themselves of colonial courts and the abolition of slavery to sever involuntary marriages, to renegotiate the terms of marriage, and to reunite with children begotten in slavery and separated by masters. Using case studies from Anlo, the essay underscores the major obstacles women had to overcome – small face-to-face Anlo communities, without the support of kinsmen, and often with the direct opposition of colonial officials–to gain their freedom. The essay sheds light on the meaning of freedom, marriage and family for dependent women at the end of the 19th century.

# Section IV.

## *"[A] mixture of complete sweetness and smoky roughage. ... home with its unavoidable warmth and even after these thousands of years, its uncertainties ... Oh, Africa. Crazy old continent..."*[1]

Following upon the historical study of self-emancipating 19th-century women that concludes the previous section, this section opens with another case study, by historian Akosua Perbi, of an enslaved girl whose descendants in the 21st century personify one of Ghana's conundrums of tradition: chieftaincy succession. At the root of the matter in this case is the issue of kinship lineages established through marriages of enslaved women to masters of royal lineage. Perbi's essay as well as that of Sue Houchins, which follows, illustrates the critical role of matrilineage in determining kinship lines among the Akan. It is an issue that arises in Aidoo's story "No Sweetness Here." In a search for cultural origins and narrative documentation of an Anowa figure, Houchins posits a radical theoretical framework that yields possible explanations from Ghanaian and wider West African lore, including those of "earth mother," "mami wata," "lineage source," "priestess," and others. The "priestess" story in *Anowa* is taken up also in James Gibbs' paper, as an interpretation of traditional cosmology among the Akan. Further discussions of Ghanaian and continental traditions underlying cultural practices are presented in the two following papers. Kofi Asare Opoku's inventory of statements of proverbial wisdom from around the continent on the subject of peace-making clearly resonates with Aidoo's childhood acquaintance, from her father's court, with proverbs in the service of conflict resolution. As a result, her skill with proverbs is one element that underlies the famously oral character of her wriring. Just as Asare Opoku elucidates the proverbs' didactic function for children and their civil-law function for adults, Vincent Odamtten's analysis of Aidoo's children's stories exposes, in her packaging of the juvenile narratives, their wisdom, like that of the proverbs, which addresses all ages and generations.

Following the essay on the children's stories are three essays that focus on other shorter works and other literary qualities of Aidoo's oeuvre. Jane Bryce's recounting of the 1985 Zimbabwe International Book Fair, followed by an analysis of Aidoo's first poetry collection, places the pieces within the context of her life and pre-occupations during her Zimbabwe sojourn. The two articles that follow treat aspects of Aidoo's work in comparison with that of other writers. My own essay posits affinities between Aidoo and the Senegalese writer Sembène Ousmane, exploring through their short-story collections their similar radical treatments of their respective socio-historical subjects. Then Esi Sutherland-Addy'sessay illuminates Mfantse linguistic features that characterise the oral quality that is a hallmark of the writings of Aidoo and of one of her Ghanaian literary forerunners, Kobina Sekyi.

The four essays that close this section are concerned with performance and the evolution of cultural sites of performance. Omofolabo Ajayi-Soyinka's first-person chronicle of a production of *Anowa*, a quarter of a century ago, for a celebratory occasion at Obafemi Awolowu University at Ife is itself a historic document in theatre studies. Conflicting intra-mural political interersts (influenced by the extra-mural climate in mid-1980s Nigeria) affecting the production, not to mention a *revision* of the script itself, result in a production that concludes with a *happy ending* in which *Anowa and Kofi Ako become the proud parents of a bouncing baby*. But, that imbroglio notwithstanding, at least, it happened in an era when live theatre was thriving in Nigeria. Ajayi-Soyinka's fellow playwright Femi Osofisan brings a sobering analysis of the threat to Nigeria's – and, by extension, Africa's – live theatre enterprise posed by the explosion of the home video industry *Nollywood* and its like, around the continent. Further in the popular-culture sphere of entertainment TV are the mushrooming Reality TV shows, of which *Big Brother Africa* is a continent-wide phenomen among the young urban middle class (such as implicitly populate Aidoo's *Changes* and some of the short stories of the collection *The Girl Who Can*). Sociologist Mansah Prah presents the results of her study of fans and participants, offering an entertainingly revealing picture of a growing sector of contemporary popular culture in (globalised) Africa. The concluding essay in this section is a eulogy to an icon of Ghanaian contemporary music. Kwesi Yankah celebrates the life of the late Mac Tontoh, star trumpeter, whose name and sound were synonymous with the ensemble *Osibisa*. Yankah brings his expertise in cultural anthropology to bear on his stirring biographical reminiscence of this creative performer's contribution to the development of progressive popular music forms, from the grafting of international influences onto Ghanaian musical roots, in ways much like Aidoo's projects, influencing adult performers and mentoring talented youth, and establishing a trademark contemporary Ghanaian sound.

# A Historical Case Study of a
# Slave Girl in Asante Mampong[1]

## Akosua Perbi

## Introduction

Among the various kinds of historical sources available to scholars in African
Studies, oral tradition occupies a special place, not only because it is basically
oral testimonies about the past, transmitted in a community from one person to
another, but also because of the manner in which it is transmitted, the sentiments it recalls in passing and the attitudes it reveals. Its particular focus on
noted individuals – such as kings, chiefs, queens, captains of warrior organisations who in the past performed heroic deeds, lineage ancestors as well as
ancestesses and significant historical events, etc. – holds particular fascination
for me, especially when those oral sources challenge, corroborate, or provide
supplementary data, etc. Such testimonies are embedded not only in speeches
and narratives but also in songs, poetry, proverbs, music and artifacts.
Accordingly, they have turned out to be of academic value as sources of data for
historians and other scholars in the Social Sciences and Humanities as well as
creative writers and other artists whose artistic imagination enables them to
make the past alive, relevant and inspiring to their contemporaries.

It seemed to me as I thought about this Festschrift that what I can share with
Professor Ama Ata Aidoo and colleagues is the episode of a dilemma I noted in
1990, in the course of my fieldwork on indigenous slavery in Ghana, concerning a slave girl from Northern Ghana, who became part of a royal household in
Asante in the 19th century. The episode took a new turn at the close of the 20th
century, not only because the slave girl whose status changed in the particular
location in Asante was dead and gone, but because the change did not super-
sede related customary codes. This story is a historical case study typical of the
experiences that many women went through in Ghana during the period of
slavery in pre-colonial times. The case has repercussions in the dilemma at the
heart of the incessant chieftaincy disputes that currently plague Ghana.
Namely, the distinction between lines of descent in the same family according

to those who are of "the real, proper, or true blood" and those who are of "adopted blood" and therefore members of the family by default because their ancestor or ancestress did not have "the proper blood," a distinction long overdue for abolition.

## Relocation of a Girl in Slavery

Her name was Niana. She represents one of many women who experienced enslavement during the pre-colonial period of Ghana's history. Her story came out in the 1990s during a chieftaincy dispute in Asante Mampong, a town 36 miles north of Kumasi, the Asante capital (See Map, Appendix 1), which happens to be my hometown. I have gleaned her story from oral tradition, court records that also rely heavily on traditional oral history and secondary sources.[2]

Niana is described in oral tradition and court records as a *Grunshie* slave who was bought at the Salaga market in the 1800s and taken to an Asante town called Kokofu.[3] A royal couple in Asante Mampong purchased her in Kokofu and took her to Asante Mampong, where she lived and remained until her death. Her descendants still live in Asante Mampong. Niana's story will be looked at from her ethnic background, her process of enslavement, her experience at Salaga market, her migration from Northern Ghana to Southern Ghana, her transit at Kokofu and her final residence at Asante Mampong.

## Ethnic Background

Niana was a *Grunshie* woman. *Grunshie* was the name used in pre-colonial times to describe the ethnic groups located beyond Walewale in Northern Ghana. Most of them inhabited the present Upper East Administrative Region of Ghana and part of modern Burkina Faso (See Map, Appendix 1). Unlike ethnic groups like the Dagomba, Mamprussi and Gonja, who were in centralised states, the Grunshie were a non-centralised group, who lived in small units under clan heads bound together by kinship ties. In the 1930s a British anthropologist in Ghana described the Grunshie as Nankese people and the most numerous of the ethnic groups in northern Ghana. The name was given to them by the Kasena, whom they in turn called Yulse. "This name in most cases was objected to by other tribes as having a disparaging and derogatory significance."[4]

In the 1970s the famous Ghanaian historian Professor Albert Adu Boahen remarked "Grusi is a general term used to describe a large congeries of closely related peoples who live in the Upper Volta and Northern Ghana. Among them are the Mo, the Sisala, the Kasena, the Vagala and the Tampolense."[5]

In the Upper East Region there were two important traditional offices, "Chiefship" (*Naam*) and "Earthpriestship" (*Tendana*). In the past the holders of these two offices were the most important and influential persons in the community.[6] The office of the Earthpriest *Tendana* was essentially a ritual one. He was expected to know the wishes of the gods of the land and to carry them out. He was also called upon, like a chief, to settle disputes, particularly those that dealt with land matters.[7]

## Process of Enslavement

Niana was one of the many victims of slave raiding and kidnapping that took place in pre-colonial Ghana. Oral narratives indicate that all the modern administrative regions of Ghana were involved in slave raiding and kidnapping, which reached their height in the 1880s and 1890s in Northern Ghana. This was especially rampant in the non-centralised states that did not have chiefs and armies to protect and defend them.

In the 1920s the British District Commissioner in Northern Ghana reported that the regions that currently constitute the Upper East, Upper West and Northern regions of Ghana were permanent reservoirs for slave hunting and slave raiding expeditions. He noted with dismay what he called "islands of anarchy" in the Mossi and Dagomba states. He related that the Dagbon people raided the Dagarti, Grunshie, Kanjarga, Frafra, Kusasi and Lobi peoples.[8] Under Asante domination, the Northern peoples made sacrifices by going to war to obtain slaves to pay to the Asante representatives. It was common sight to see the Kpembe contingent in Grushie country hunting for slaves to give to their Asante masters. "The Grushies suffered a lot from raids and kidnapping."[9]

Incessant slave raiding and kidnapping in Northern Ghana caused the people of Gwollu in the modern Upper West Region and the people of Nalerigu in the modern Northern Region to build defence walls around their towns. Sankana, a town near Wa, the current regional capital of the Upper West Region, had huge caves for people to run into for protection against slave raiders. According to oral narratives, the raiders mostly came on horseback and at daytime when there was a lot of activity going on. They came with such speed, holding whips with which they gathered people in a swoop along the way. It was a horrifying experience to be caught. People would cry and scream and try unsuccessfully to resist being forcibly carried away. Niana was one of such people.[10]

Oral narratives recall four Zabarima slave raiders, namely Alfahan Dan Tadano, Alfa Gezaro Dan Mahama, Babatu or Mahama Dan Issa and Isaka Karaga Dan Alzima. Of these four slave raiders the one whose name is mentioned the most in Northern Ghana is Babatu. The Sissala Buwala Clan remembers another slave raider called Ali Giwa, who was one of Babatu's captains. Ali Giwa raided the towns between Banda and Tumu and created so much distress among the Debi towns that when the British offered them colonial protection they accepted it wholeheartedly and composed a song, *Ali Giwa bra tulo ko na naraa tsugagbaga* (meaning, "Ali Giwa, return and see whether people are still slave trading").

Oral narratives in both Northern and Southern Ghana recall the activities of the great Mandinka warrior Samory Toure. He operated in the Northern and the Brong Ahafo Regions of modern Ghana during the 1880s and 1890s. Niana's time of being bought, according to Asante Mampong oral narratives, was in the 1800s, the period when slave raiding and kidnapping was at its peak in Ghana.

The victims of slave raiding and kidnapping were sent to slave markets scattered across the length and breadth of northern Ghana. In the case of Niana, oral radition specifically mentions Salaga market as the place where she was bought, meaning she had been sent there.

## Experience at Salaga Market

Niana found herself in a very important town in Northern Ghana. Salaga was in the Gonja Kingdom, which was founded in the 16th century by Mande horsemen (See Map, Appendix 1). Some travellers and traders who visited Salaga during the closing decades of the 19th century attributed Salaga's importance as a market to its strategic position. It had a great advantage over all the slave markets in pre-colonial Ghana because of its position near the source of the rivers of the big Volta stream. Three natural waterways met in Salaga: the Black Volta from the West, the White Volta from the North, and the Red Volta from the South. Salaga was also linked to the western and central branches of the trans-Saharan trade routes and therefore connected to two of the four main routes that linked West Africa to the Sahara and North Africa.

Niana witnessed the hustle and bustle associated with the immense activities in markets. She saw traders from Ghana and outside Ghana flock to the market. She saw Mossi traders from modern Burkina Faso bring slaves, livestock, cotton, shea butter and mats to Salaga. She also saw Hausa traders from modern Nigeria bring slaves, livestock, cowrie shells, woolens, carpets, silks, leather ware, silver ware, iron pots, copper and brass ware. She witnessed the arrival of traders from Gyaman in modern Côte d'Ivoire bring woven and sewn cloths, while traders from Timbuktu supplied shawls and tobacco. She also witnessed the presence of traders from Kano in modern Nigeria and several other towns of the Niger River region as well as traders from North Africa.

Niana saw traders of virtually every ethnic group and state from Ghana visit the market. The principal traders were the Akan of Asante, Brong, Kwahu and Akyem. This was because one of the major items of trade highly demanded in Salaga was kola nuts which grew only in the forest areas inhabited by these Akan people. The nuts were in great demand in West Africa and North Africa. In addition to kola nuts Ghanaian traders from the South brought to Salaga market ivory, rubber, gold dust, salt, tobacco, calico, dried fish and European goods such as liquor and cloth from the coast. It is not surprising that Niana was purchased at the market by an Asante trader and taken to an Asante town.

The period of trading in Salaga was during the dry season that lasted from December to April. Salaga market was divided into two sections: one, for food-stuffs such as yams, rice, maize, livestock; clothing materials, leather ware, silver-ware, brass-ware etc; the other, for "human-ware." There were also two principal sessions in the market. The first was often a morning market, conducted under shades and stalls. The second session was the market held in the open air. It was often in this session that slaves could be found, and Niana was in this session.

Traders' memoirs and travellers' accounts of the conditions of the slaves in the market are very gruesome. The slaves were chained together in groups of ten to fifteen by the neck and waist of one to another, and they waited in the open air, exposed the whole day for purchasers from morning to evening in the piercing sun, hungry, thirsty, naked and ailing. Other slaves were fastened to a long rope with iron shackles on their legs. This was done to make sure that the slaves did not run away. The plight of mothers and little children is described as follows "[M]others show their empty breasts and their small hungry chil-dren."[11] Niana went through the same experience of being chained and waiting in the burning sun. The slaves were kept in houses and camps and brought to the market everyday until they were purchased.

From the accounts given in oral tradition and the court records, Niana was a young girl when she was bought. She must have been a teenager because she had her first child when she came to live in Asante Mampong. Prices of slaves varied according to supply and demand, but the price of female slaves, especially the younger ones, was often higher than that of male slaves. Since she was bought from an Asante trader, she would have been exchanged for kola nuts, cowries or gold dust. In 1889, a German traveller called Blinger visited the Salaga market and observed that a male slave was sold for 300 cowries and a female slave was sold for 400 cowries.[12] In 1929, Rattray was informed that a female slave cost two shillings while a male slave cost one shilling and six pence and that in the past a male slave cost nine thousand kola nuts while a female slave was worth fourteen thousand nuts.[13] There was a higher premium on female slaves because of their sexuality and reproductive roles. What happened in Ghana is confirmed by global literature that indicates that, although the slave population of Africa consisted of men and women, boys and girls, the preference, so far as indigenous slavery and trade were concerned, was for women and girls, whilst in the Atlantic trade the preference was more for male slaves than female slaves. The males were needed in the Americas to perform "back-breaking tasks." In the Muslim world the demand was more for female slaves than male slaves.[14]

## Migration from Northern Ghana to Southern Ghana

Niana hailed from the modern Upper East Region of Ghana. She was forcibly moved through slave raiding and kidnapping to Salaga in the modern Northern Region of Ghana. From Salaga she was bought and taken to Kokofu and then to Asante Mampong, both located in the modern Asante Region of Ghana (See Map, Appendix 1). She travelled a distance of about 300 miles.

In pre-colonial times this kind of journey was done on foot. People usually moved in large groups and often with armed guards. When night fell they slept along the way. Some towns provided sleeping places where people could sleep after payment of a fee. Other towns did not have such places while others could not afford the luxury of such places and so slept in the open air. There were also refreshment stations along the way, where people could buy food and water. Others carried food and water that they would need during the journey. The slaves carried these items as well as the trade goods. It was a long and tiring journey. Some died on the way either from fatigue or ill health.

## Transit in Kokofu

Niana found herself in Kokofu because the Asante trader who bought her was either from that town or did his business in that town (See Map, Appendix 1). Kokofu belongs to the Oyoko clan, which migrated from Asantemanso to Kwaaman. There were no known slave markets in the Asante Region during pre-colonial times, but a number of individual transactions took place. The motive of this trader is not clearly given in the records. Whether he brought Niana to be part of the servants in his household or whether his intention was to sell her is not clearly stated. Interesting, though, is the fact that the court records relate that the man who bought her in Kokofu was himself from Kokofu though resident in Asante Mampong. It was his wife who was from Asante Mampong. We do not know whether the two men were related but there must have been some communication between them for this kind of deal to have been made possible. We are also not told what was exchanged for Niana, but it was most likely kola nuts, cowries, gold dust or foodstuffs.

Agriculture was the basic occupation in Kokofu, where the important soft cocoyam called "kooko" was cultivated. Oral tradition relates that the town earned its name from this food crop "kooko fuo" (Kooko farm). Kokofu was part of the Asante Confederacy, which formed the core of the Asante Empire. The Oyoko group of states that formed part of the Asante Confederacy were Kumasi, Juaben, Kokofu, Bekwai and Nsuta. The Non-Oyoko group of states were Asante Mampong, Ofinso, Adanse, Ejisu, Essumegya, Kumawu and Denyaase. The founders of the Oyoko group of states were all related to one another. Those of Kumasi, Juaben and Bekwai were regarded as brothers with

Kumasi as the senior, while the founder of Kokofu was regarded as the maternal uncle of those three.[15]

## Residence in Asante Mampong

Niana found herself in a new residence at Asante Mampong, which was very much like Kokofu in terms of vegetation, mainly forest, and in terms of agriculture, predominantly farming. Asante Mampong was, in addition, on the route to Northern Ghana and it was for many years the most important Asante town on the trade route to the North. Between Asante Mampong and Kumasi was the Mampong Scarp which formed a natural barrier between Asante Mampong and Kumasi. Asante Mampong had common boundaries with Nsuta and Agona.

Like Kokofu, Asante Mampong was part of the Asante Confederacy. It was one of the "Amantuo," the earliest territorial units of the Asante state. The importance of Asante Mampong in the Asante political set-up has its origins in the formation of the Asante Union by Asantehene Osei Tutu, supported by his able adviser Okomfo Anokye. Asante Mampong was given a Silver Stool and made the second in command of the Asante Nation, while the whole Asante Nation received the Golden Stool as its symbol of office. The Golden Stool was believed to contain the spirits and souls of every Asante. The Asantehene "held the head of the Asante Nation and the Asante Mamponghene held the feet."[16] This important town was where Niana came to live.

Niana was brought to the home of a woman called Nyarkoa Akosua, a member of not only the Bretuo royal family but also of the Baabriw royal house. There were four royal houses in Asante Mampong, namely Baabriw, Wiredu, Botase and Kodiokrom. The Baabriw royal house had three sub-families, Santeni, Sarfo Kantanka and Kweku Abereka. Nyarkoa Akosua's husband, an Oyoko royal from Kokofu, was called Nana Mpianin. The records do not tell us why Nana Mpianin resided in Asante Mampong with his wife instead of in Kokofu. It is, however, likely that, as a royal, he was attached to the Palace of the Asante Mamponghene to study court etiquette and palace administration. This was a common practice among Asante royals in the past. Asantehene Osei Tutu, for example, served in the Akwamuhene's court and returned to Kumasi when his uncle the Asantehene died, after which he returned to be enstooled as chief. He went to Kumasi with his loyal friend he had met in Akwamu, Okomfo Anokye. Nana Mpianin became Kokofuhene, with the stool name of Nana Kwame Appia Agyei and ruled from 1830 to 1842, during the reign of Asantehene Kwaku Dua I. Interestingly, Niana's name is used throughout the court records with an occasional reference to "alias Okra." This appears to be very significant. The word *Okra* in the Akan/Asante language means 'soul.' In pre-colonial times slave owners in Ghana had various options with respect to naming of their slaves. Some owners gave their slaves their family name or the name of a relation. Other owners gave their slaves names that commemorated a situation they had gone through. Sometimes the slaves were given proverbial names. Others were given answer or response names. For example, when the owner called the slave he/she expected a specific response. Sometimes slaves were given day names like Akosua, Akua, Kwabena, Kwame, as a reflection of the day the slave entered the household. Slaves who won the hearts of their owners earned names of commendation. Other owners kept the slaves' "alien" names.[17] The latter is what the royal couple opted to do. But they also sometimes called Niana "Okra."

*Okra* had another connotation among the Akan/Asante. He/she could be the king's, chief's, or queen's "Soul Bearer." Akan/Asante traditional belief required the king, chief, and queen to appoint a boy or girl who personified his/her soul. The child was chosen from among the royal princes and princesses. They were required to be aged between four and fourteen years old. When the king, chief, or queen rode in a palanquin the *Okra* sat in front of him/her, holding a sword and wearing a hat made from the feathers of an eagle. He/she was considered very sacred, and was required to observe all the taboos imposed on the king, chief, or queen he/she served. When the *Okra* attained the age of puberty he/she was discharged. The king or chief presented the male *Okra* with a gun and a wife.[18]

The Akan/Asante believed that a person consisted of two parts: a physical part, the flesh, and a spiritual part, the soul. The soul *Okra* directed all the deeds of a human being. Successes and failures depended on the condition of the *Okra*, who could communicate with the gods and even with the Supreme God. When a person died, the *Okra* became a spirit *Saman*.[19] If Niana was named *Okra*, it meant that she was a very important part of the life of the royal couple. She filled a void which they appreciated. She must have won the heart of her owners to receive such an additional important name whose meaning had deep spiritual significance.

According to oral tradition and the court records, Nana Mpianin presented Niana to his wife as a domestic servant. This meant that Niana's job description involved household chores such as cooking, washing, fetching water and firewood, sweeping, cleaning and running errands. It is likely that, with her Northern background Niana cooked some delicious Northern foods such as *tuo zafi, omo tuo, waakye*, added to the culinary etiquette of the royal household. She would surely have known some herbs that would be of medicinal value to heal and to make strong. She would have sung some of her ethnic songs as she worked non-stop in the house. In fact, according to oral tradition slaves were expected to work very hard, leading to the Akan expression *odonko adwuma* ('slave work'). They were also expected to do all the menial work in the house, as reflected in[20] the Akan proverb *atantanie nti na ye to odonko* ('we buy a slave because of filthy work'). Nevertheless, as a young girl she would have also had some time for rest and play. An elderly woman from a royal family in Kumasi opined that games such as *ampe* and *aso* played by young girls were introduced into Asante by the female slaves from Northern Ghana.[21]

The court records relate that "during the course of her stay with Nyarkoa Akosua this domestic servant was impregnated by Nana Kwame Appia Agyei and gave birth to a daughter Obiyaa Akosua, whilst Nyarkoa Akosua gave birth to Nkwantanan Akosua."[22] Niana must have been a pretty girl to have attracted such attention and affection from her master/owner. It was a common phenomenon in pre-colonial Ghana for female slaves to be married by kings, chiefs, traditional political office holders, traditional priests, men of varied professions, men of royalty, ordinary free men as well as male slaves. Oral tradition states that beautiful and neat female slaves found themselves as wives of kings, chiefs, nobles and members of royalty, while others served as concubines. In the case of Niana the wording in the court records reflects a situation not of actual marriage but probably of concubinage. The idea of a domestic servant turned concubine living in the same house with her mistress: What a complication in the royal household! Incredible! One wonders about the new relationship between the mistress/owner. However, Niana was not sent away by her mistress; otherwise her story would have been different. Nyarkoa Akosua graciously kept her all the same.

Niana's story becomes more fascinating: First of all, once she was part of the royal couple's household, she became a member of their family, particularly that of her mistress, because Asante was a matrilineal society. If Nana Mpianin had formally married Niana, he would have adopted her into his family, lineage, and clan, according to Akan/Asante customary law. But as he did not do this, the alternative was for the mistress to adopt her into her family, lineage, and clan. The kinship system was the core of Ghana's pre-colonial social structure. Kinship ties were derived from consanguinity, marriage or adoption. The ethnic groups in pre-colonial Ghana integrated slaves into the kin of their owners. Through adoption, Niana became a member of the family – no ordinary family, it was a royal family. The family was of great sociological significance in pre-colonial Ghana. It went beyond that of the nuclear family to include members of the extended family, servants, and slaves. By customary law in pre-colonial Ghana, the stranger was a member of the family of the person with whom he/she lodged, or of the family of his/her landlord/landlady, or of the family to which he/she voluntarily attached himself/herself upon giving drink to the head and the elders of the family. If he/she was not attached to any particular family, he/she belonged to the family into which he/she married. It was by reason of this customary law that slaves became members of their owners' families. One process of integration of the slave into the family was through adoption. Another process was through marriage. Slaves, servants, and strangers, therefore, became members of families either through adoption or marriage. In Niana's case she became a member of her mistress' family through adoption, because her master/owner did not formally marry her.[23]

Second, Niana was impregnated by her own master/owner and had a child with him. From the language of the court records she was not officially recognised as a second wife, although pre-colonial Ghanaian society was a polygamous one. But this act by the master/owner created another form of bonding for Niana. She was not driven out of the royal house but she continued to perform her domestic duties and enjoy the rights and privileges slaves had in pre-colonial Ghanaian society. For example, the slaves had the right to be fed, clothed and housed and taken care of. They had the right to be well treated and to also enjoy legal protection.[24]

Third, the child Niana bore became a free woman. According to Akan/Asante customary law a child conceived between a slave and his/her owner or between a slave and a relative of the owner was recognised as a free man or woman. If the child had been conceived by a slave and a free man or woman other than the master or mistress, the child became half free and was called *Okanifa* ('half-Akan'), considered property of the owner of the slave. From the records it is clear that Niana had only one child by her master/owner. She did not bear any more children by any other man.

Fourth, in a matrilineal society the child/children a slave woman had with a royal, free man or a commoner became the bona fide property of the man. Oral tradition attests to the fact that this issue made many men desire to have children with slave women. If the man formally married the slave woman, she became part of her husband's family, or *abusua* and enjoyed all the privileges thereof. So, while the child of Nyarkoa Akosua and Nana Mpianin became part of her mother's *abusua*, by Akan/Asante customary law the child of Niana and Nana Mpianin became part of her father's family, because the slave woman had no family in her new home. In Akan society the *abusua* (family) was the basic social unit. Nkansa-Kyeremateng avers that the matrilineal arrangement among the Akan/Asante made the female the maintainer of the family. At any time there was no woman to keep it going, the family became extinct. The arrangement made the husband only a facilitator, as expressed in the Akan proverb *Abofra se ose nanso owo abusua"* ('the child resembles the father but he/she belongs to the family').[25]

Fifth, since Niana had a child, she began a line of descent, while her mistress continued her line of descent, since she already had an ancestress. Niana became the ancestress of her lineage. Among the ethnic groups in Ghana that were matrilineal, every woman who had a child originated a family. The Akan believed that a child consisted of two parts: the mother's blood and the father's spirit. Niana's child Obiyaa Akosua received her mother Niana's blood and her father Nana Mpianin's spirit. Nyarkoa Akosua's child Nkwantanan Akosua received her mother Nyarkoa's blood and her father Nana Mpianin's spirit. The impression one gets from the court records is that Nyarkoa Akosua's family recognised the two lines of descent and regarded Nyarkoa Akosua's line as being of "real, proper or true blood," whilst that of Niana was described as being of "adopted blood." This means that Nyarkoa Akosua's family accepted Niana and her descendants as part of the *abusua* and clan but not as part of the lineage, as Akan/Asante customary law proposed. Otherwise, the chieftaincy dispute would not have occurred in the 1990s for a distinction to be drawn between being members of one family but not of the same lineage.

On 28th July 1992 the Tribunal of the National House of Chiefs, in its twenty-page judgment, reiterated, on page 15, that the two lines were different: It "became two separate lines and even though the two regarded themselves as members of the same family, they were not united by blood since they flowed from different ancestresses not united by blood."[26] Nyarkoa Akosua's ancestress was traced by the Baabriw Bretuo Royal House to:

> Afi who gave birth to Nana Akuamoa Boateng and three daughters namely Nana Takyiwa Pinaman, Abena Saka and Apaa Korkor. Abena Saka gave birth to Sarfo Kantanka 1 and Abena Adoma, whilst Apaa Korkor gave birth to Afua Gyapomaa and Abena Dwamena Onipaba who got married to Nana Opoku Ware 1 and begat Nyarkoa Akosua. Nyarkoa Akosua whom Niana served as a domestic servant was a child of Asantehene Opoku Ware 1 and a Mampong royal woman. Nyarkoa Akosua got married to Nana Mpianin who later became Kokofuhene under the stool name of Nana Kwame Appia Agyei.

The Report of the Judicial Committee of the Ashanti Regional House of Chiefs noted the following in July 1991:

> Nyarkoa Akosua got married to Nana Mpianin who later became Kokofuhene under the stool name of Nana Kwame Appia Agyei. … Nana Appia Agyei went to Kokofu and purchased a Grunshie woman named Niana alias Okra, and presented her to his wife Nyarkoa Akosua as a domestic servant. Nyarkoa Akosua and Nana Appia Agyei gave birth to a daughter Obiyaa Akosua, while Nyarkoa Akosua gave birth to Nkwatanan Akosua. Nkwatanan Akosua had two issues, Oduro Frikyi (at one time the Mamponghene) and Nana Kobi his sister who begat Nana Adwetewa (also on one occasion Mamponghene), Akyaa Afreh, Nana Marboa and Akua Kyem.[27]

Sixth, a long-term effect of Niana's residence in Asante Mampong is that she has created a genealogy which cannot be erased, a genealogy which is traced from the 1800s, that is, from the early 19th century to the 21st century. If Nana Appia Agyei ruled Kokofu from 1830 to 1842 and had a child with Niana before he was enstooled, then Kokofu Stool history agrees with Asante Mampong Stool history when it refers to Niana's stay in Asante as being in the 1800s, most likely the early 1800s.[28] Niana's genealogy began when she became a member of her mistress' family and became resident permanently in Asante Mampong. If she had remained in her hometown, her story would have been different. In Northern Ghana descent was traced through the male line, and, so, the genealogy of her family would not have been traced through her. As the story turned out, Niana and her descendants did not return to their original homeland in the Upper East Region. They became adopted members of the family of her mistress, as they narrated during the proceedings of the Baabriw Bretuo royal family chieftaincy dispute in which they were involved.

As was a common Akan and Ghanaian practice, Niana must have passed her oral history down to her daughter Obiyaa Akosua. Niana would surely have told the child about her hometown in the Upper East region, her ethnic group, and life in her original homeland. She would have told Obiyaa Akosua how she was enslaved, what she experienced at Salaga market, her travel to Kokofu and her final destination in Asante Mampong. Obiyaa Akosua would in turn have passed the oral history on to her daughter called Kriguruwa/Krubuwa. Kriguruwa/Krubuwa would also have passed the oral history on to her children, and her children would have passed the oral history on to their children until it reached the children of the 21st century. This oral history would contain not only oral narratives but some songs, poems and other forms of oral tradition. This is because women in Ghanaian society have been recognised from time immemorial as custodians of culture, repertoires of knowledge and transmitters of oral tradition.

Seventh, following the Akan/Asante belief that a child consisted of two parts, his/her mother's blood (*Mogya/Bogya*) and the father's spirit (*Ntoro*), inheritance and succession to property were traced through the blood. This was the foundation of the Akan/Asante matrilineal system of inheritance and succession. The blood was perpetuated through the clan. It was the spirit which determined the make-up of a person, his/her character, personality, power and soul (*Okra*). It was believed that the soul (*Okra*) of a person was a special deity in the human being that could cause the death of the body, should the *Okra* be offended. The *Okra* of a father could cause the death of a child, if the father's *Okra* was offended and was not appeased. The *Okra* could cause the death of his own children, if the mother committed adultery.[29]

# Conclusion

Niana's story is a wonderful case study. It is pitched against the background of the acquisition and roles played by female slaves in pre-colonial Ghana. This is indeed "history made alive and real." It is an incredible story spanning 200 years and narrated in Court proceedings so clearly and in oral tradition so authoritatively as if it happened only a couple of years ago. It is not too difficult to find out and to know about the traditional history that deals with the ways in which female slaves were acquired and the roles they performed in pre-colonial Ghanaian society. It is, however, not common to find specific names of people, names of places, and dates, as we find in Niana's case.

Her story is that of enslavement through slave raiding and kidnapping in the modern Upper East Region of Ghana. Her experience as a slave for sale in the Salaga market is heartrending. Her migration from Northern Ghana to Southern Ghana and her final stay in Asante Mampong, where she not only became an adopted member of a royal couple's family but had a child with her master/owner, is an amazing one. Finally, Niana began a line of descent that has remained in the palace records and in oral tradition up to the present. The memory of this breathtaking story will live on.

# Appendix 1

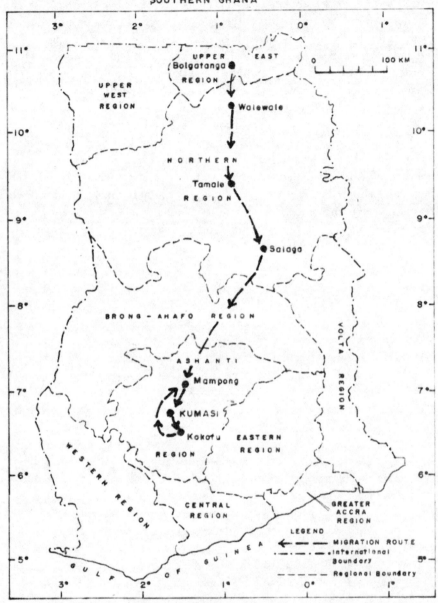

MAP SHOWING NIANA'S MIGRATION FROM NORTHERN TO SOUTHERN GHANA

# *Anowa,* Paradoxical Queenmother of the Diaspora[1]

## Sue Houchins

In *The Art of Ama Ata Aidoo,* critic Vincent O. Odamtten observes that the play *Anowa*[2] is "overdetermined,"[3] a term derived from Freudian and Marxist literary theory. It describes narrative plots that move along trajectories in what appears to be a logical arc toward a single conclusion; however, the effect is the consequence of several competing causes – some ideological or historical, others aesthetic or formal. Commonly critics resolve this seeming conflict by either prioritising "one of the manifest causes" or by advancing another reason that is "less evident" at first reading but becomes more compelling upon further consideration;[4] that is, they may choose either an ideological rationale for the conclusion or a formal one. However, by classifying *Anowa* as a riddling tale, a kind of fefewo,[5] Odamtten draws attention to the ambiguity that defines the genre and that may allow for *both* the historical-political forces and the formalistic dictates to work together to shape the outcome – if, in fact, there is a single definitive ending to this very complex work – for the enigma of this play may lie as much in the multiple causes for the final actions of the characters as in those actions themselves.

This essay will posit an additional reading of this now canonical play that will respect and extend the convincing historical-political narrative offered by Odamtten and take further advantage of the open-endedness of the dilemma story by keeping in play the ideological force and the aesthetic determinants. While only gesturing toward the temporal setting of the drama, this study will analyse the institution of indigenous slavery as a technology of gender transformation, disrupter of kinship systems, and a re-former of lineages. Slavery provides more than the context for the play's action. The constitution of the ranks of slaves, the system for increasing their number, and their function in the economic system of the Gold Coast as well as the protagonist's empathy for bondspeople and her resistance to the institution that subjugates them – all these socio-political factors collectively impact the narrative structure, the trajectory of the plot. This article will also explore the formal effect of folkloric motifs and the intertextual relationships between the protagonist of *Anowa* and the epic heroines of the same or similar name in Ayi Kwei Armah's novel *Two Thousand Seasons*. After a short comparative study of the trope of "barren women"[6] as founders of new communities, this essay will read Anowa's walk into the sea as an example of a narrative writing itself beyond its ending through the suggestion of a new representation of the rebellious daughter/wife as a Mami Wata and a founder of a Black Atlantic (Diasporic) community.

The temporal structure of *Anowa* not only forms an arc – in a variation on the classic marriage (romance) plot[7] – from a foreshortened narrative trajectory in a courtship that is only suggested, through marriage and childlessness, to "death" – but it also represents the history of Ghana as concentric ripples or multiple eras radiating from causal eruptions – some suggested through allusion (for example, in a historical libation to the relocated ancestors in the Prologue or the singing of the African American slave spiritual "Swing Low Sweet Chariot" in Phase Three) – which, when read together, cast light on each other to reveal a coherence of modes by which race, gender/sex, and sexuality are imbricated across time. The action of the drama takes place when the British begin to consolidate their colonial hold on the Gold Coast and through missionaries, teachers, and administrators, to influence a transformation of gender relations in the indigenous culture and to circulate European ideologies of racial and ethnic differences. This is the ideal era from which to scrutinise these changes in Akan societies. *Anowa* is literally located *in medias res*, in the middle of things. By focusing on domestic slavery that evolved into a major commodity that promoted West Africa's entrance into and participation in international markets, Aidoo reflects back to fifteenth-century encounters between European merchant-seamen/brokers and African traders and then their later commerce with slavers headed for the Americas; and she portends the neocolonial bondage of newly independent African states to European and American influence and aid. Further, she remembers and depicts the position of Akan women – Fante and Asante – in traditional matrilineal societies that were inflected by patriarchy, examines the decline of their status as European notions of gender inequality permeate and influence the growing class of wealthy indigenous merchants of nineteenth-century Gold Coast societies, and, finally, forecasts their struggle to establish gender parity now, in the drama's future.

If, at first, one focuses on the issue of slavery, which is a point of contention in the marriage between Anowa and her husband Kofi Ako, the matter of sex/gender must necessarily emerge collaterally, not simply because the posses- sion of bondspeople precipitates disputes within the couple, which arguments Kofi Ako tries to resolve by asserting his dominant status as male. But, also, Anowa paradoxically proposes what might be a form of slave concubinage – marrying Kofi Ako to an Oguaa woman – as a remedy for the couple's childlessness. Thus, the play provokes the informed audience to recall that "[m]ost slaves in Sub Saharan Africa were women,"[8] those same slaves who were the object of the third in a series of half-hearted decrees of emancipation promulgated by the British in the year (1874) of the final action of the play.

A slave is, by definition, a *stranger*, asserts Saidya Hartman in *Lose Your Mother*: "Torn from kin and community, exiled from one's country, dishonoured and violated, the slave defines the position of outsider. She is the perpetual outcast, the coerced migrant, the foreigner, the shamefaced child in the lineage."[9] That is, drastic separation – social and/or geographical – made one vulnerable to, and was the consequence of, slavery kinlessness occasioned by war, widowhood, debt, ostracism, estrangement, banishment, and orphanhood became synonymous with slave status, and so, too, was an extraordinary form of living death: On very rare occasions, a member of the aristocracy was enslaved rather than sacrificed.

For example, after an *oba panyin*, Awura, a queenmother, had faithfully followed the promptings of her *obosom*, a personal god "envisaged as a daughter of the Moon Mother-goddess," and had successfully led her people to a place of safety "where water was more plentiful, or the soil more fertile," she solidified her claim to the foundation of a new clan through the traditional planting of a fig-tree[10] and the sacrifice of one of her own children, "preferably a daughter at the age of puberty. . . But the sacrifice had to be voluntary, for only if the sacrificial victim wholeheartedly agreed to die, could the blessings be achieved." Listed by the informants to Eva Meyerowitz, art curator and anthropologist, as modes of or substitution for this sacrifice are the following: "[I]n general the prince or princess was strangled and the body buried in the middle of a sacred stream; or the body was pounded in a mortar and the bloody remains buried in the fields. Sometimes a pregnant princess was beheaded; or *the victim was given to a stranger to be taken away to another country*."[11] She was, thus, disowned by her family and declared without relations.

Thus, slavery, understood as expulsion/exile from the living communal body, constituted radical social marginality. In a sense, the slave, as an instance of abjection, was a social corpse; slavery was, to echo Orlando Patterson, *social death*.[12] So those who no longer had ties to family in a society where lineage defined belonging; those who could, in the words of Anowa's father Osam, "never find their ways back . . . [who got] lost . . . [and did] not know the names of the founders of their houses . . . [who did] not know what to tell you if you asked them for just the names of their clans" (31–2), were "wayfarers," "wanderers," "foreigners" – all terms synonymous with the slave – were so cut off as to be effectively dead, consigned to oblivion, *sacrificed* like the queenmother's daughter (Robertson and Klein 3, 7).[13] In this play, these wanderers are not simply the focus of Anowa's intense empathy; they are also a site of paradoxical convergence, where the figures of a noble lady and the abject slave intersect and where binaries of social location are deconstructed.

The journey, the very act of wandering toward the place of purchase, became a locus of social liminality,[14] where the slave underwent a process of total objectification, when "[h]e or she became a thing."[15] Edward Alpers[16] and Claude Meillassoux (55, 58) maintain that, during this period of abjection/marginality, men and women alike became *"asexual agents of work"* valued only for the load they could carry with speed over great distances. Thus, the gender ambiguities – "You ought to have been born a man" (*Anowa*, 24) – remarked by Kofi Ako, during a respite in an early trading expedition when he and Anowa still carried equal loads, connoted, in part, Anowa's trop(e)ic relation to slaves as wanderers, as porters, and as marginal to society. And in equal part, it also will become a divination of causes or, more severely, an assignment of blame for her barrenness as punishment for her antipathy toward the social institution of slavery; an indictment of her outspokenness on the issue; and, indeed, even retribution for her monstrous, freakish ability, as a woman, to think rationally and independently. But this scene also gestures toward a growing gender ambiguity in both members of the couple. The sheer multiplicity of readings attributable to this single observation by Kofi Ako in the context of the gendered transformations wrought by slavery and colonialism is typical of the problematising function of the genre of the play, the traditional oral dilemma (riddle) tale.

Kofi Ako's comment on sexual indeterminance reflects not only the degendering function of the trek in the process of inducting the individual into a new status as slave but also the transformation of Akan notions of gender differentiation through contact with the British and their Victorian definitions of femininity and masculinity. Thus, the husband's admonishing his wife for her unseemly assertiveness on this and subsequent expeditions may signify his adoption of European notions of gender difference, at least, as they pertain to Anowa. Therefore, it is also an assertion of his newly acquired sense of class difference, which means that indigenous/traditional definitions of gender, what he wants Anowa to eschew, paradoxically still obtain for his slaves and porters. Thus, Anowa's refusal to dress in a style befitting her new class, her love of the road, and her inability to adapt to the more restrictive codes of gender-differentiated behaviour, is a betrayal of her class, which further emphasises her solidarity and identification with slaves, as well as a form of marital infidelity. Her statuslessness emphasises her own social abjection. This refusal of class privilege makes her neither mistress nor slave, but somewhat more a slave, given her insistence on wandering/travelling and working.

If *Anowa* were to conform to the dictates of the marriage plot, which ends in reproduction and the replication of modes of production, then the appropriate resolution of the narrative would be the extension of the couple's lineage through offspring, the reproduction both of the ideology of the trader class Kofi Ako represents and of the modes of economic production emblematic of that socio-economic group. However, in this dilemma tale there are no *biological* progeny, and the demise of their household signals Kofi Ako's failure to expand the economic and social systems as well as the ideologies of the developing merchant class to which they belong.

The Gold Coast depicted by Aidoo is illustrative of an early capitalist community capable of producing surplus goods for trade with internal and external markets – either across Africa or with Europe and the Americas. Women slaves in these indigenous societies were occupied in both *productive* and *reproductive* modes of production. The former type of labour yields surplus value – more than is needed to subsist – that can be turned into capital for re-investment. The latter mode consists of two categories: first, daily or physical reproduction "which includes the domestic tasks necessary to sustain a household on a daily or periodic basis;" and, second, "the reproduction of the relations of production" which comprises both "the generation and the transmission of the ideology that [supports] the slave/free, male/female hierarchies, and the provision of services which attest to the high social status of the free-born members of the household."[17]

However, Anowa's attempts to re-form the politics of gender might constitute a subversion of several of the aspects of reproductive labour. For instance, her insistence on a status of equality analogous to one of Kofi Ako's sisters in their matrilineal society – not to a wife either in the traditional or the new European sense – her refusal of the perquisites of mistress in a slaveholding society, and the barrenness of her marriage constitute but a few of the matters that identify her as discursively liminal – that is, occupying the margins between master or mistress and slave, between man and woman and thus deconstructing these hierarchies; thus, her *narrative* labour is, in fact, both counterproductive and counterreproductive – maybe even discursively "queer."

'Common sense' would tempt one to assume that the reproductive labour which refers to the biological function of women – "the bearing and rearing of children to increase the number of slaves or freeborn children" (Strobel, 119) – is what increased women's value as slaves. But such was not often the case; for the rate of birth among slaves in both Africa and the Americas was not equal to one child per slave. Slavewomen were "subfecund." Therefore, "slave reproduction [in Africa] took place mostly through purchase or capture," a method which ensured that the workforce replicated itself and augmented its numbers according to its specific needs (Robertson and Klein, 9; Meillassoux, 51–54; Strobel, 119–120).

Paradoxically, some slaveholders experienced the same precipitous decline in fertility, as did their slaves. In such cases, masters occasionally purchased slaves expressly for concubinage in their households. The status of such women and the children they produced with masters among matrilineal peoples like the Akan had particular complexities. On one hand, assimilation was sometimes more difficult because the lack of continuity, kinlessness, in the maternal line marked the offspring as a "stranger." Despite Kofi Ako's contention that slaves who were talented and intelligent on occasion became "patriarchs of houses where they used only to serve," Anowa counters that these fortunate circumstances are conditional on there being "no freeborn people around" (37).

The power these "outsiders-on-the-inside" wielded gave rise to the belief articulated by the Old Man of the chorus in *Anowa* that the presence of slaves in a household weakened and obscured the rightful inheritors of the lineage. Folk wisdom held that the acquisitiveness and conspicuous consumption exhibited by greedy aristocrats and wealthy merchants like Kofi Ako made the master of many slaves vulnerable to a particularly virulent mania – "[M]oneymaking [which] is like a god possessing a priest:" a malady which ultimately robbed these men of their virility: "[E]very house is ruined where they have slaves.... One or two homes in Abura already show this/They are spilling over with gold and silver. . . But where are the people? (*Anowa*, 39–40; Meillassoux, 54).

However, the stigma of barrenness was most often laid upon the freeborn wife who, when all other remedies failed, sought, in consonance with the traditions of her society, another wife for her husband. It is a cruel irony, however, that in *Anowa* a whiff of slave concubinage permeates this common recourse. Several times during the play Anowa suggests to Kofi Ako that she will solve the couple's childlessness by finding "them" another wife: "One of these plump Oguaa mulatto women [women from Cape Coast]. With skin as smooth as shea butter and fresh palm-oil on yam" (35). In societies that practice polygyny, it is both right and proper for a first wife/a "mother-wife" (35) to initiate the discussion of and the subsequent negotiations for her husband's other consorts. But in the light of studies that assert the mixed-race women of Cape Coast were often not only the offspring of slave concubines but were themselves also renowned concubines,[18] Anowa's offers to procure an Oguaa woman implicate her in the very slave system she decries; furthermore she is proposing a remedy that would produce a child of dubious lineage for the couple. Thus, this plan involves her to some degree in what Robert J. C. Young describes as the "transgressive, interracial sex, hybridity and miscegenation" of colonial desire (xii, 9, 180). That she is aware of at least a minimal linkage between subjugation, slavery and the type of marital arrangement she proposes – or is it marriage, in general? – is apparent by the lines of dialogue that precede her proposal: Anowa has been arguing against Kofi Ako's purchase of slaves as porters for his trade goods. In fact, she is despondent at the prospect of being left home to "rest" with Kofi Ako while an overseer acts as their agent. Her husband suggests she can "look after the house;" and it is then that Anowa retorts that she "is going to marry [Kofi Ako] to a woman who shall do that" (34–39 – thus making her position interchangeable both with that of wayfarers and with the co-wife, thereby equating their statuses and, by extension, likening all wives to slaves.

Further, Anowa is exemplifying women's paradoxical roles both in the reproduction of ideology and as potential agents of its change. For the Oguaa woman, as part of a coastal population, a society which assimilated the culture and customs of invaders and traders and which exchanged its slavewomen – a combination of kinless indigenous women, some Fante, and others captured from other ethnic groups – for trade goods, is a site of racial and cultural hybridity. So the introduction into the household of the woman with "skin like a buttered yam" would reproduce and enforce the prevailing ideologies of male and class dominance, as well as heterosexual reproduction; but her hybridity would produce the following change: "[S]uch women are more civilised . . . have learned the ways of the white people" (Anowa, 54).

But Kofi Ako refuses to participate in this concubinage – even as he involves himself in the same commerce that produces his potential bride's body as property – and rejects the offer of the Oguaa woman as a solution to their barrenness. It might be because he knows the futility of such a venture, his having actually "sold his birth seeds" through witchcraft to obtain wealth. And/or maybe "the doctor"/"the priest" has divined other causes (55): perhaps (1) Anowa's unfulfilled election by a jealous god, an obosom, and/or (2) Kofi Ako's impotence, his lack of (hetero-)sexual desire – Anowa has "not seen [his] bed in years . . .; now that [she thinks] back on it, [he] has never been interested in any other woman" (61) either. The play leaves the causes ambiguous, unresolved. Worst yet, Anowa's indictment: "[He] is always with [his] men" (34) could encode the most profound challenge of sexual liminality. And/or maybe his failed but very real commitment to forming the new, modern African couple, to reforming marriage into a union of equals, to being "the new husband and [Anowa] the new wife" – like sister and brother in this matrilineal society (26–7), like friends – keeps him monogamous despite the sanction and frequency of polygyny within his ethnic group.

The Oguaa woman, whom the two never acquire but who haunts the discourse on slavery and barrenness, becomes an object of ever-receding desire for Anowa, if not for Kofi. The text describes the woman with such intense gustatory sensuality that both reader-audience and Anowa can almost taste her succulent corpulence, can almost feast their minds' eyes on her voluptuousness. This concubine is a present-absence, an absent-presence in an implied triangle of desire, the other half of the female-female bond which, if completed, might have more drastically diverted the narrative trajectory. As it is, the play stops with a double death which may connote its ideological recuperation into the dominant social and political value system through an acknowledgment of the main characters' failure to succeed to re-produce biologically and ideologically – that is, either to re-form or to replicate, to produce anew gender and class relations. But since Anowa is a child of many reincarnations (Anowa, 7); hers may not be a death at all.[19] The latter possibility leaves the text open-ended.

Mercy Oduyoye adopts Anowa as the organising trope in her black feminist/
womanist theological treatise, as the metaphorical matriarch of contemporary
African women, as the "personification of Africa as a woman." In her book
*Daughters of Anowa*, she lauds Ama Ata Aidoo's depiction of the legendary
wanderer as heroic in her resistance to slavery, and "[h]er insistence on chosen
toil as self-realisation," but she laments Anowa's *suicide* as "a final capitulation to
the dictates of society."[20] Certainly a traditional feminist first-reading of the play
would support this interpretation. But despite the efforts at anthropological
contextualisation in Oduyoye's text, this audience-reader/I suggest/s – no doubt
with hubris – that additional folkloric contextualisation of this "mythical . . .
prophet and priest . . . ancestress" (Oduyoye, 6) of African and African
Diasporic women, could yield a more complex and, therefore, a richer interpretation of the final actions of the play. Also, this critic contends that further
inquiry into the identity of Anowa and her folkloric sisters in orature, literature,
and history, might produce a supplemental – perhaps unrecuperated or, if recuperative, differently inflected – but still black/Africana feminist, reading.

The back of the battered edition of the play that serves as a source for quotations in this essay explains that "*Anowa* is based upon a version of a Ghanaian
legend . . . [about] a beautiful girl who refuses the suitors of whom her parents
approve and marries the man of her choice; but finds over the years no joy." In
an interview with Adeola, James Aidoo explains the origins and the transformation of that tale, "My mother 'talks stories' and sings songs. *Anowa*, for
instance, directly grows out of a story she told me; though as the play has come
out, she cannot even recognise the story she told."[21] Added to these vague references to Anowa's origins in oral tales are three important pieces to the puzzle
of identity contributed by Oduyoye. In a footnote she traces the derivation of
the name *Anowa* to the Fante of the Mankessim and Saltpond areas of Ghana;
and she connects the Aidoo version of the story to its retelling three years after
the play in Ayi Kwei Armah's epic *Two Thousand Seasons* (6). A few pages later she
relates the story of a Fante queenmother, Eku, who leads a migration of Akan
people south "toward the savannah and the Atlantic" (8) not as the source of the
tale but as an example of Anowa's courageous female kinswomen, her "daughters." But beyond the familiar story of the recalcitrant daughter and these
meagre clues, there is little else. In fact, a search through indices and anthologies of folktales in several major collections yields nothing; and inquiries of
Ghanaian historians and folklorists provide no clues to a single foundational
tale from which she sprang.

The elusory provenance of Anowa suggests she is just what Aidoo represents
her to be, a composite of several historical personages, cultural icons, folkloric
figures and motifs. In this case, perhaps close textual analysis threaded through
a warp comprised of Armah's epic novel *Two Thousand Seasons*, the histories and
the myths of Akan progenitrices and African women revolutionaries might

provide a glimpse of Anowa somewhere in the interstices of conflated oratures and, thus, might facilitate speculation about who she thinks she is and what she thinks she is doing.

In such folkloric speculation, the motif of Anowa's wandering, which permeates the drama and which intensifies and metaphorises the issue of slavery – both indigenous and trans-Atlantic – accrues to itself additional, more complex and profound interpretations when read against both Oduyoye's Fante tale of Queenmother Eko-Aso and Armah's Anoa. (Both are examples of *Oba Panyin Awura* discussed above.) Called by her personal god, *obosom*, to lead an incipient clan's migration toward a more abundant source of water, or a safer, more fertile homeland, matriarchs among the Akan – i.e.. the Fante and the Asante – were, like Anowa/Anoa, priestesses and seers. According to Armah's epic history of the Akan, *Two Thousand Seasons*, this people – who act as metonyms for all blacks – were always wanderers, who "journeyed . . . looking not for escape but for greater space in an open land."[22] These first "migrations were but an echo to the alternation of drought and rain" (9). In addition, he includes among these early sojourners other travelers: "[m]overs in the mind" (7, emphasis added), migrants through time, historians who remembered the past and prophets who foresaw the future.

For example, Armah records a period of patriarchal rule which devolved into a struggle for power among clans, and he observes that it was always "women's voices" (15) which counseled peace and spoke of the future, but often to no avail. Anoa/Anowa is one of a series of such women who are timeless in their panoptic gifts for seeing both what lay behind and what lies ahead as a means better to elucidate the present. Thus, Aidoo's play, set in the middle of Ghanaian history, *in medias res*, reflecting on the community's past and the nation's prospects, is an analogy for its eponymous vatic heroine, is an objective correlative of her mythic timelessness. And Armah, by counting time in relation to a central figure of Anoa, the third in a line of major women seers, the prefiguration of two more to come, places her and her prophecy of "two thousand seasons of destruction" at the core of a people's story of subjugation, submission, resistance. This central figure "was not the first to bear that name" (Armah, 21).

The Akan can barely remember the fragments of a tale about the first "priestess Anoa, . . . *who brought the wrath of patriarchs on her head*" (Armah, 21, emphasis added) during an era of violence which preceded the "rule of women . . . fertile time . . . creation's time" (18). That first Anoa "was possessed by a spirit hating all servitude . . . that same spirit possessed all women" (21) who, in consonance with the later Anoa-of-the-two-thousand-seasons prophecy, tried to re-instill an ethic from a former Edenic period, when the Akan lived *"the way of reciprocity,"* the way of mutual respect, "the giving, the receiving, the living alternation" (26, italics added). Astoundingly graceful and beautiful, the second and central

Anoa had many suitors, but she "knew her soul was shaped for other things. It was not that she was scornful of the wife's, of the mother's life; instead, her ears heard other voices, other thoughts visited her spirit" (24) and counseled celibacy. Thus inspired, she harangued her community in two distinct, "twin," registers: one, a *killjoy*,[23] which shrieked predictions of doom; the other that calmly urged a return to the way of reciprocity – both voices forecasting two thousand seasons of slavery, Anowa/Anoa-of-the-two-thousand-seasons was but one in a lineage of prophetesses, each arising when the community was *in extremis*. Armah chronicles the ceaseless efforts of this succession of visionary maroons, guerrillas of resistance to wrest the land of Anoa and the spirits of her descendants from the hands of "predators," "destroyers," and "zombies" – indigenous and foreign opponents to the way of reciprocity. And he predicts Anoas will continue to rise up, to *reincarnate* themselves until the ethic of mutuality is established.

Juxtaposed to each other, the works of Aidoo and Armah reveal the archeology and trop(e)ic complexity of the folkloric Anowa/Anoa,[24] the conflation of several oral narratives. The accretion to the standard tale of the girl who chooses her own husband (the cover of the first Longman paperback edition, 7, 15; Odamtten, 48) of other folktales – i.e. i.e.the legend fragment of Anowa's opposition to slavery; her possible election by an *obosom* as priestess/wandering queenmother, servant-leader to her people; and her strong association with water – produces a tangle of motifs, each with its attendant customary plot trajectory which complicates the narrative, forestalls simple resolutions to the dilemma, and which, through the ambiguity this aggregate elicits and intensifies, the play's interrogation of dominant ideologies. Though a felicitous reconciliation of these seemingly disparate folk identities – if such coordination were even possible – would not resolve the textual indeterminacy, it might elucidate a heretofore unexamined corner of the work; however, it might augment other readings of the play.

This article, then, tries to re-identify Anowa through a critical alchemy which amalgamates elements from the Anowa folk cycle – that is, discreet tales attributed to a single character and collected as one loosely related national myth – to an appropriate socio-cultural or historic context and then compounds those distinct materials to give a new dimension to the dramatic heroine.

Wandering explored as emblematic of slavery is a nexus of several motifs. First, as a trope of separation in a society which defines itself through kinship ties, "wayfaring" connotes a state of profound alienation from the people who, the place where, and the gods that animate the vagrant subject; for "distance is the hatred of those who love," observes Armah of an eloping couple (*Seasons*, 8). Anowa's father, Osam, worries about his daughter's failure to return; and, comparing her to others who marry and move away but do come home "to attend funerals, pay death debts, return for the feeding of family stools," he laments, "The children of women like Anowa and their children-after-them never find their ways back. They get lost. For they often do not know the names of the founders of their houses. . . No, they do not know what to tell you if you ask them the names of their clans" (31–32).

But wandering has another valence. The founding of a new clan by a matriarch is the result of her questing, *wandering* at the bidding of her personal god in search of another habitation, a new homeland. The conflation of the figures of slave and queenmother seems a paradoxical one, but in the person of Anowa, it works to destabilise the hierarchy between mistress and slave. Though the trek itself deconstructs gender so that male and female slave are (mis)treated the same, and though that same journey seeks to construct instead the unequal binary relationship of mistress/master and slave, Anowa refuses all these categories in favour of pursuing the "way of reciprocity."

It is only in pursuing her compulsion to wander and to labour that Anowa is content; for she is diminished by the lack of work, by leisure, disoriented by confinement in the luxurious house built from the profits of her husband's trade, and devastated by Kofi Ako's threat to send her back home to Yebi. He reports that the traditional practitioner he has consulted about her barrenness and unconventional behaviour diagnoses her as "too restless . . . always looking for things" (28). Finally, as she accepts her marginality, she brands herself a "wayfarer. . . a traveler . . . someone . . . [who] does not belong . . . has no home, no family, no village, no stool . . . no state, no territory" (36–7). Thus, her refusal of the trappings of power and wealth that Kofi Ako proffers allies her, identifies her "with the common pain" (38) of slaves, signifies her sensitivity to "the general wrong," and qualifies her as an empathetic leader who governs with the compassion of a mother. Also, in her rootlessness, she is reminiscent of a queenmother's daughter sacrificed/traded into bondage as collateral insuring the prosperity and fecundity of the community/nation. Queenmother and daughter are one.

Encoded, as well, in the queenmother figure are a number of other Anowa-related motifs besides wayfaring: first, this figure is a prophetess-priestess; second, the homeland is often closely associated with a body of water; and third, the founder of a clan is timeless, capable of reincarnation.

Not all priestesses are queenmothers, founders of houses; but queenmothers share with priestesses their close communion with the supernatural and their profound intersubjectivity. This deep empathy with others causes Anowa's mother, Badua, to observe: "[A] priestess lives too much in her own and other people's minds" (13). Early in the play, Osam and Badua allude to a time when they considered apprenticing their daughter to a priestess; and later Anowa recalls a vision, a nightmare she had in childhood which prompted that discussion of her vatic calling. When she was young, she cajoled her grandmother into explaining the Atlantic trade in slaves. Anowa was so traumatised by the betrayal her people wrought on each other that she had a dream in which she envisioned herself as a big woman from whose

> insides were huge holes out of which poured men, women and children. And the sea was boiling hot and steaming. And as it boiled, it threw out many, many giant lobsters, each of whom as it fell turned to a man or woman, but keeping its lobster head and claws. And they rushed to where [she] sat and seized the men and women as they poured out of [her], and they tore them apart, and dashed them to the ground and stamped upon them. [S]ince then, any time there is a mention of a slave, I see a woman who is me and a bursting as a ripe tomato or a swollen pod. (46)

This vision is not prophetic in the sense of forecasting the future; for, by the time of this incarnation of Anowa, the trans-Atlantic trade had almost run its course, though the even more ancient indigenous trade continued into the next century. But it is prophetic in the depth of its insight into the political and moral consequences of acts and in the intense identification Anowa feels with her newly discovered constituency, slaves.

A priestess-prophet may perform various functions for her community. Chief among these is her role as medium, "one who speaks in place of or on behalf of the god"[25] – in fact, she may "become too much like the gods [she] interprets" (*Anowa*, 12). In the introductory chapter of *Revealing Prophets: Prophecy in Eastern African History*, Johnson and Anderson analyse the significantly different forms that prophetic-priesthood has assumed over history and across geographic locations. Extrapolating from African anthropological, classical and biblical literatures, they arrive at this very simple definition that is flexible enough to adapt to more specific socio-historical contexts: the prophet is an inspired – inspirited or enthused – person who is "concerned with the wider moral community at a social or political level"that is, a community which may inhabit a territory which spans political boundaries and which may not have a common language or ethnicity nor be related through kinship, but "whose members have reciprocal moral obligations to each other" (17–18). The source in many African communities of the moral inspiration, of the message that speaks to issues immediately confronting the particular group, is often a god or gods who work by instilling dreams or by possessing the votary through trance (Johnson and Anderson, 1–25).

Clearly, those in Anowa's childhood community who knew of her dream were aware of its moral and political mandates, hence the consideration of her apprenticeship. Her continued proclamations against the institution of slavery evoke nasty quips from Badua – "And who does she think she is? A goddess" (33) – and Kofi Ako – "[W]hat is wrong with you? If you want to go and get possessed by a god, I beg you, go. So that at least I will know that a supernatural being speaks with your lips" (37). Each retort implies that the community is aware of the real possibility that she is "one born to dance for the gods" (20) but has rejected her inspired message. If, indeed, Anowa was destined to be one of the god-elected prophets, the consequences of not heeding the call are dire; for, according to Osam, "[A] prophet with a locked mouth is neither a prophet nor a [hu]man. Besides the yam that will burn, shall burn, boiled or roasted" (13).

There are dire ramifications for the individual who does not consciously embrace her vocation and for the community which thwarts or rejects her. For example, "the gods will surely punish Abena Badua for refusing to let a born priestess dance" (9), predicts the Old Woman of the chorus – in an unusual moment of insight – for the loss of an only daughter in a matriliny is punishment indeed. But this is too narrow a vision of the consequences. For instance, when one reads this redaction of the Anowa myth against Armah's Anoas, one discovers that celibacy and/or barrenness seem(s) a condition of the visionary office. Or, if one looks at the portrayal of some other god-chosen women in contemporary African literatures (i.e. the protagonists of *Efuru*, *The Concubine* by Elechi Amadi, and *Ripples in the Pool* by Rebeka Njau) – albeit from other ethnic groups – barrenness appears to be a folkloric motif associated with election, especially to a deity or spirit associated with water. While the indeterminacy which enriches the play occludes a reading which attributes the couple's childlessness and their violent deaths solely to fate – to ignoring the mandates of a god or to not accomplishing what one's *obosom* has ordained – it seems a likely contributing factor.

If the unusually long period – six years – which elapses between Anowa's puberty and her betrothal has any significance, it may lie in her vague intuition of her chosenness, her uniqueness. It is not just her extraordinary, her astounding beauty which singles her out as someone to be "feared" (31), as abjected, but also her indefinable strangeness which makes all who encounter her uneasy. For instance, her father remembers that "[s]he was never even a child in the way a child must be a child" (31). She has wisdom beyond her years. As one who "listens to her own tales/Laughs at her own jokes and/Follows her own advice" (7f), she has kept to herself the reasons for selecting Kofi Ako, whom her mother describes as "a watery male of all watery males" (15). Certainly by foreshortening the traditional plot trajectory only to suggest the period of courtship through pantomime at the play's start, by implying that Anowa and Kofi Ako have seized the pretext of her habitual evening chore, drawing water, for an assignation, the audience-reader never hears her explain her attraction to Kofi Ako. However, much beyond Anowa's volition may be the impulse to marry a man whose virility has been in question from the onset of the betrothal, it may indeed be fated. At least, this is the ironic and inadvertent wisdom of the

Old Woman, never Anowa's champion and ever the guardian of tradition: "Who heard the Creator tell Anowa what she was coming to do with her life here? And is that why, after all her 'I don't like this' and 'I don't like that,' she has gone and married Kofi Ako?" (20). On the one hand, Armah's Anoa of-the-two-thou-sand-seasons knows her mission from the onset, and so this huntress, an African Diana of sorts, forswears marriage and physical motherhood. On the other hand, Aidoo's Anowa might be an unknowing conscript of her god who preor-dains and coerces her fated barrenness.

Ironically, then, despite the community's disapproval of her choosing her own spouse, Anowa may have had less say in the decision than it appears. Though it is presumptuous to speculate about the intentions, the workings of gods – even fictional ones – this critic will risk the consequences. Logically barrenness should disqualify Anowa from the role of a queenmother, particularly in a society that calculates maturity and belonging by the responsibilities one accepts and accomplishes in marriage and that judges success by what one produces and re-produces. But it is also a matrilineal society, one which reck-ons kinship, connection, relationship through its women – mothers and sisters – through a genealogical reckoning that is horizontal as well as vertical. Perhaps in this sense Anowa is not really barren.

Matriliny is encoded throughout the play, in Armah's novel, as well as in the title and text of Aidoo's first novel *Our Sister Killjoy*. For example, in the name of the dictates of this kinship system calculated through women, Osam accord-ingly assumes no responsibility for counseling his daughter to her uncle, Badua's brother. In addition, Kofi Ako muses that people have commented on Anowa's enthusiasm for and support of his trade, likening it to the loyalty and love of a sister, which is so unlike a wife in this community that requires that a woman split her allegiances between her natal and her conjugal families. Armah recounts in *Two Thousand Seasons* a story of women's bonding through a symbolic sisterly kinship. When a true "daughter of Anowa," a reincarnation of her prophetic spirit called Abena, is captured and enslaved in one of the coastal fortresses, she looks in the eyes of another woman captive, a near "zombie" saved from export to work in the slave-fort dungeons, and asks her name. "Call me your sister," is the reply (182). Much later, when Abena returns from marronage as a member of a liberating guerrilla army and a released woman prisoner greets her, "Ei, my sister!" (261), the reader is encouraged to infer that this is a reunion of social/political kin.

One might view *Anowa* as a rethinking of the political structure of the nation aborning, as an "imagining of community" beyond biological kinship (perhaps even beyond geographical borders), and as advocating a matrilineal ethos, a "way of reciprocity." In this sense, the trope of mothering, even in the face of barrenness/childlessness, operates within the grammar of national and familial re-mythologising. In contrast to other West African slaveholding, patrilineal, societies (e.g. Dahomey), the matrilineal Akan had "always a strongly egalitarian ideology," which ideally manifested itself in affording "a common civil status" to all residents of Fanteland. Also, "[g]enerational, and especially, gender hierarchy" among these peoples was less obviously restrictive before British cultural intervention which encouraged "conformity with European ideas of marital authority."[26] So, in the height of colonial incursions, Anowa laments and, in the aftermath of the British transmogrifying onslaught, Sissie and Oduyoye reiterate that "in other lands a woman is nothing. And they let her know this from birth. But here, O my spirit mother, they let a girl grow up as she pleases until she is married. And then she is like a woman anywhere: in order for her man to be a man, she must not think, she must not talk. O – o why didn't someone teach me how to grow up to be a woman?" (*Anowa*, 52; Oduyoye, 6–8; Killjoy, 11).

The presence of latent or secondary patrilineal organisation (the authority residing in a senior uncle, for example) among the matrilineal Akan facilitates the adoption of European gender norms; but the seam suturing the two kinship systems and their different approaches to civic, social, and religious empowerment is still perceivable (Jay, 147–8). A place of social tension, it constitutes a discursive snag, a knot in the weave of the text, where Anowa plies her transformative craft. This is a locus of both *scriptible* and *lisible* diversion which stops the process of re-mythologising, a site marked by the eruption of barrenness which calls a halt to, which stops or breaks, the narrative of patriarchal – marital/heterosexual and colonial – dominance.

The drama posits several determinants for the couple's childlessness: either Kofi Ako's congenital impotence; his bartered virility exchanged for wealth; the sterilising effects of dependence upon slaves; or Anowa's vocation as abjected priestess that Badua says robs her of her humanness; her restlessness metaphorised as wandering – physically and mentally – perpetually on a de-gendering trek. Furthermore, barrenness is a controlling trope for gender/sexual ambiguity in Aidoo's re-mythologising. It not only represents an instance of deconstruction of gender hierarchies, but this destabilisation of sexual binaries also threatens all constructs of unequal difference in power – i.e. i.e.master/slave; European/African. However, though barrenness menaces the ideological foundations of narrative, it cannot signal a revolutionary halt in plot, one that predicts lasting social change; the narrative trajectory does not and cannot really end at the conclusion of the drama. Thus, that the story is helpless to avoid recuperation is signaled by Kofi Ako's suicide, but *not* by Anowa's death by drowning. Barrenness, then, doubly tropes, intensifies ambiguity: discursive deconstruction and narrative bifurcation – i.e. i.e.Kofi Ako's recuperative sterile suicide alongside Anowa's possibly fertile resurrection. Thus, childlessness merely stalls the plot, and then it permits the story to *write itself beyond its ending*.[27]

Her nightmare among the sea creatures implies that Anowa's motherhood transcends biology, "blood" kinship, and posits some other kind of social bond like that forged by the Anoas-of-the-two-thousand–seasons or by barren mothers with whom the Western reader may be most familiar – i.e. the biblical Sarah, Anna, Elizabeth, and Mary – all of whom by their inability to reproduce, by their perversion (inadvertent or willed) of the mandate "to be fruitful and multiply," in the words of Patricia Berry, "stop [the story]. This stopping feels disruptive, since it cripples the narrative force."[28] The damming agent, the putative barrenness – has the mythic function of turning reproduction in on itself, restricting/binding/tying the family in the story and the story, itself, "in a tight internal knot, . . .[in] its own thickness" (151). But narrative blockage is but half of Berry's subject of enquiry; for, like this study, she is equally concerned with what re-animates plot movement.

The barren women and/or the "virgins" of the biblical texts become through supernatural intervention progenitrices of new nations, of new peoples bound by a fictive kinship (and not necessarily through biological ties) *and/or* by allegiances to a new way of behaving in society. They are queenmothers. The stopping place they mark in the mythic narrative is a crossroad, a site of transformative possibility. In other words, the apparently autochthonous generative powers of the barren mother, her ability to reproduce parthenogenetically and to embody an oxymoronic fecund barrenness, "fertilises something back on itself" (Berry, 151), thereby, conferring an illusory mythic purity or imagined homogeneity in a renascent/resurrected line, giving the paradoxical impression of both continuity with old traditions and the establishment of a new more authentic order, and emphasising the uniqueness and singularity of the collective entity which results. In this sense Anowa is the mother of the African Diaspora/the black Atlantic.

Anowa's barrenness and her transcendent queenmotherhood of those who issue from her visionary body, those broken by slavery and crushed by colonialism, place her among a tradition of mythic mothers of imagined communities. In addition, the setting of her dream-vision within the sea, within the black Atlantic, suggests that her domain is water and thus makes her kin/sister to both those queenmothers who seek out deep streams in times of drought, who bury their beloved sacrificed daughters in these homestreams, and to the Mami Watas – patronesses of barren women – who abound on the African continent and throughout the entire dispersion of African peoples.[29]

Among the many functions of Mami Wata(s) is the succor of women who, are ostracised because they are childless. Devotional association and mystical unification with her/them provide a niche for these women in a society that defines biological reproduction as normative. Thus, her importation into and syncretisation with various African cultures is a gesture which is both affirming and subversive of the host culture. Because the rituals connected to her worship share much with ceremonies already practiced among the ethnic groups which accept her, and because her votaries do not seek to displace but rather strive to co-exist with followers of indigenous deities, a Mami Wata's presence complements the culture in which she settles. Yet in the latitude she gives women, in particular, to seek autonomy and either to forego or to participate in the "joys of motherhood," even when they are childless, she is subversive.

As a denizen of rivers, Mami Wata, in Igbo lore, fuels her homefire with fish. (Nwapa, 183) That is to say, she burns sperm for heat, light, and cooking.[30] In Morrison, Beloved emerges from the stream wearing little silver fish – sperm – as ornaments in her seaweed dreadlocks.[31] And among the Akan, for whom water is a trope for semen (Oduyoye, 114, Meyerowitz, 99),[32] sperm is the environment in which she lives, which supports her life, the very medium she breathes. That this barren female spirit is so closely associated with male seed emphasises her fluid sexuality (so to speak), her sexual indeterminacy, and accentuates her liminality, her abjection, her function as an agent of the deconstruction of gender/sex, thus, her resistance to the regulation of heterosexuality.

Anowa's return to the sea, her "drowning," is, among many things, a critique of the institution of marriage, which thwarted Kofi Ako's and her attempts at its transformation and impeded their own metanoia into the new man/husband and the new woman/wife. But, no matter how it looks, her entrance into a watery domain is not a complete capitulation to marriage's/heterosexuality's prescriptive power; for, as the Old Man observes in the very last speech of the play, if there is reincarnation – and the Akan believe there is (Meyerowitz, 96–7), especially for queenmothers (Meyerowitz, 27) – Anowa will have the last say (*Anowa*, 64). For as the barren yet prolific queenmother of the black Atlantic, Anowa is not the progenetrix of a single or homogeneous community, not a literal *blood*/lineage, but a people seeking and claiming "the way of reciprocity," sharing an ideology. Paradoxically she is a founding mother without a stool, a seat of power – so to speak – of a clan of wandering stoolless people. Her imagined community, her race-(trans)nation, consists of those searchers for "the way" who are dispersed across the continent, in the lands bordering the Atlantic, and among the living-timeless[33] – the ancestors, who inhabit the sea.

A reading of the first chapter, "The Way" in *Two Thousand Seasons*, reinforces this interpretation of Anowa/Anoa as a figure/a technology of the Racial Symbolic, a term this article coins after Lauren Berlant's description of the National Symbolic. Both are "discursive practices" that provide a communal consciousness which functions to produce, through the mobilisation of technologies of nation (or, in this case race) – that is, through the evocation of "icons, metaphors, hero[in]es . . . and narratives" – the same intensity of allegiances (i.e. a sense of identity or identification) as that impelled by birth-lineage and which thus transforms individuals into "subjects of a collectively-held history."[34] Early Armah espoused a kind of Pan-Africanism, and he defines Anoa's community, the collectivity for which she is an icon, in essential-ist terms: Anoa's "people are scattered even in the desert, across the sea, over and away from this land, and [they] have forgotten how to recognise [them]selves . . . That [they] the [b]lack people are one people [they] know" (2, 4). His novel reiterates through its narrative structure and tropes that Anoa, the prophet-priestess, mother (a Mami Wata), seeker-foundress of a new site of generation – a waterfall, pool, and spring – is located like Aidoo's Anowa at the centre of the whirlpool of racial time/history which marks with each concentric circle radiat-ing out from the moment of her first augury, with each cycle/*season* of reincarnation, an era of the socio-historical formation of race: i.e. the slave trade, then colonialism, then neo-/post-colonialism. Thus, Anowa/Anoa as a trope for blackness/Africanity itself is a technology of race, a mechanism for constructing and maintaining a racial-(trans)national culture – a Racial Symbolic.

So Anowa's wandering into the sea – her "drowning" – understood in the context of her many incarnations, becomes a sojourn among not only the socially dead but also the ancestors, those lost in the Middle Passage.[35] In a discussion of the "African Roots of Black Seafaring," W. Jeffrey Bolster summarises the creation of a "[b]lack Atlantic maritime tradition . . . that reflected [West] Africans' fusion of the sacred and the secular." For example, he describes Faro, a sexually ambiguous water spirit who "maintained an individ-ual's soul or vital life force after death. Refreshed and purified under water, the soul would appear in the next-born member of the family." Citing the research of Howard MacGaffey, Bolster reports that the Atlantic Ocean constitutes for the Kongo peoples one of the world's watery Kalunga lines which separate "the living from the spirit world." This "'ideal barrier'" is the threshold to the domain of "those departed who had been exceptionally wise and strong" and who can traverse this boundary at will in order to return to their communities as prophets.[36] And, of course, there is Mami Wata, whose ubiquity in the waters of the African world is undoubtedly in part the result of both the slave trade and the great number of African and African-descended mariners in the navies of Europe from the late sixteenth through the nineteenth centuries.

During 1993, a particularly affecting painting by Joseph Turner began to haunt the imaginations and the texts of two scholars of the black Atlantic: Paul Gilroy,[37] cultural theorist and Michelle Cliff,[38] art historian and author of fiction and poetry. The picture *Slave Ship: Slavers Throwing Overboard the Dead and the Dying, Typhoon Coming On* (1840) became an emblem for them and for this researcher, who went on pilgrimage to Boston to reverence it, of the horrors of the Middle Passage and the scattering/fragmenting of the community, living and living-timeless in exile or in transit. It is the illustrated version of Anowa's nightmare. This painting of the ship *Zong*, whose captain notoriously threw a portion of his cargo – slaves living and dead – overboard to collect insurance payments on his loss, is significant for Gilroy because it represents, in part, the important role of the sea and ships in the creation of the black Atlantic world – its politics, its poetics, its religious vision. For Cliff and more recently for Fred D'Aguiar,[39] literary critic and novelist, and M. NourBese Philip, the author of the poetry cycle *The, Zong!*, [40] the painting is as much or more about the population in the sea, who are signified on the canvas by one beautiful and terrifying woman's leg extended above the surface of the waves – an Anowa/Anoa's leg?

Aidoo writes about Anowa's/Anoa's Pan African political kin – mother-daughter-sister fighters in the resistance – in an essay published in 1996 entitled "Literature, Feminism and the African Woman Today."[41] In seeking to redress the image of African women in the West, she sings a litany of African women guerrillas who span generations of black Atlantic history: i.e. Nzingha, Zumbi, Yaa Asantewaa, and Nehanda. Embedded in this census of revolutionaries is the "folkloric," "fictional" Anowa. Given the noble sisterhood, matrilineage, in which Aidoo inserts/includes Anowa and acknowledging the reincarnation of, the kinship of her spirit with other mythologised women resisters, it would be a mistake to call her disappearance into the sea a suicidal defeat, a complete narrative recuperation into the dominant ideology, as does Oduyoye. (Because the audience hears – "witnesses," in a sense – the report of the gunshot which signals Kofi Ako's suicide, but, in contrast, they hear indirectly of Anowa's demise through the Old Woman's prattle, the protagonist's watery *ending* seems unreal because it is at a remove.) Further, African Americans might be tempted, in the spirit of Aidoo's litany of courageous ancestors, to append at least two folkloric women to her catalogue: Nanny, Anowa's Akan mother-sister, a sorceress-warrior who led the Windward Maroons against the British; and the unnamed woman of Igbo Landing whose legend re-lives intertextually in *Praisesong for the Widow* by novelist Paule Marshall[42] and in *Daughters of the Dust* by filmmaker Julie Dash.[43]

There are two versions of the latter folktale which are analogous to the two opposing interpretations of Anowa's death. Marshall and Dash tell of a shipload of slaves who, intuiting the nature of the life they would live on American plantations, simply walked on the water back to the Bight of Biafra. But in the libational introduction to *Spirits of the Passage*, Rosemarie Robotham tells the story this way:

> When a slave ship from Nigeria puts into its first American port, the captives emerge with a young woman at the lead. This mystic moves forward silently, the others behind her . . . [Her] feet turn and enter the creek that leads to the sea. The waters swirl around her ankles, splash up her legs, close over her waist, cloak her shoulders. The other Africans follow her without a word [until] . . . their sculpted black heads disappear below the horizon and the surface of the Atlantic stitches together in their wake as if they never were there. (11)[44]

If one considers that the way a narrative plot finishes – but not necessarily ends – constitutes an interpretive act, then the disparity between these two versions of the Igbo Landing story is analogous to the distinction between Oduyoye's reading which laments Anowa's defeat and the one espoused in this essay which takes solace in the promise of her return. Each route is an encounter with death; each has its own measure of triumph – that is, each is an act of resistance to domination. Paul Gilroy and Eric Lott assert that both (1) the historical incidents of radical black Diasporic women who embrace "the positive preference of death" over subjugation, as well as (2) the depictions of these profound acts of resistance by black feminist writers exemplify a "revolutionary eschatology" which, when transformed by/in cultural productions of the black dispersion, create "arts of darkness," in the many valences of race and of death that phrase evokes (*Black Atlantic*, 57–68).[45] To connect Anowa's drowning with this discourse of liberating death as part of the racial symbolic of the Diaspora undoubtedly says as much about this critic's (my) positionality (African American and female) as it does about the intertextual, interfolkloric relationship between *Anowa* and the legends of African female heroism that this essay catalogues as part of its hermeneutical process. It is as if the plot of the Igbo Landing story comes to a fork in its trajectory: the unnamed priestess can walk over or under the Atlantic surface to return home. Each route is a response to the threat of death – social and/or biological – each has its own measure of triumph – that is, each is an act of rebellion. It is the echo of this resounding "no," the reverberation of this refusal even unto death that haunts the living and impels their small acts of resistance; that reverberates through the generations which re-live and thus rein-carnate its defiant spirit; that spreads in ever-widening concentric circles through time and through a people from the centre which marks the moments of Anowa's and the young Igbo mystic's entrance into the waters of the beyond.

In addition, the trope of reincarnation which this article reiterates is reflected in the genre of the play. *Anowa* is a typical dilemma tale, open-ended and writerly. Thus, it offers for its audience-readers' reflection not only questions about the causes and significance of her death but also a series of other related conundra: (1) the connection between seemingly discreet social constructions of difference and unequal power relations – i.e. *economic*: master/slave, coloniser/colonised (Europe/Africa) and *social*: husband/wife (male/female), master/slave, white/black (Europe/Africa), sacred/secular; (2) the relative fixity of these relations and of the connections between them; (3) the strategies for displacing, deconstructing, or destroying them; and (4) the efficacy of such strategies. Since these issues represent ideologies that are so profoundly entrenched in discourse that they cannot be dislodged; they are interrogated but are left unresolved at the play's finish.

# The Call to the Priesthood and Other Stories in Ama Ata Aidoo's *Anowa*

## James Gibbs

A three-line dedication at the front of Ama Ata Aidoo's *Anowa* reads:

> For my mother
> "AUNT ABESEMA"
> who told a story and sang a song

As with much in the play, the dedication prompts a double-take, a question. In this instance, the question is "Why does the playwright address her mother as 'aunt'?" Several possibilities suggest themselves. For example, it may be that "mother" is being used with an extended meaning to indicate "one of my mothers" or "one of those I called 'mother'." Or it may be that so many of her contemporaries in the family addressed her (birth) mother as "aunt" that young Ama Ata picked up the usage. Aidoo expects "us," her readers and the members of her audiences, to make considerable effort in grappling with issues prompted by the tasks of translation she has been involved in. She also wants "us" to think about what is involved in moving from one family system (and society) to another. She does not find it either desirable or necessary to explain all the "translation" work she is involved with: she is a master of effective transliteration. The challenge she throws down extends from the language to the structure of her play and prompts the reader (or member of her audience) to ponder what is happening to Anowa in *Anowa*. This makes it a "dilemma play." Also, since I suggest several narratives are interwoven, it ensures that we are never quite sure what story and what song "Aunt Abesema" might have passed on.

*Anowa* is full of stories and of references to stories. The eponymous protagonist is at the centre of several tales, and lurking within the text are "shadows" of other narratives. For example, reference is made to the familiar tale of the "Headstrong Daughter," the self-willed girl who rejects approved suitors and leaves home to marry the man she has chosen. This story exists in many variations along the Guinea Coast and in most, but not all, the man selected is a superficially attractive stranger who turns out to be a monster. Aidoo has spoken of another narrative source for her play, a local anecdote, possibly her aunt's tale, which caught her imagination. It concerned a domestic quarrel that led to public knowledge of a couple's circumstances and from there brought about the breakdown of their marriage. (Aidoo, 1987: 24.)[1]

The play also incorporates "narratives" of a more general sort. Abena Badua, Anowa's mother, wants to be able to tell a happy "tale of motherhood" (153). She wants her daughter to follow the approved and accepted path through life – and she claims she has a right to insist on this partly because Anowa is her only daughter. To flesh out this tale or "life story:" Abena Badua wants Anowa to get married, become a mother and, in the fullness of time, enjoy an honoured position in the community. This, however, is not to be. It seems that Anowa has shown signs of being different, of having another, a different "life story." She was "restless" as a child and, when the play opens, she has gone six years beyond puberty without getting married. She is referred to as a "wanderer" and becomes a "wayfarer" – a word given a special, negative weight in the play, suggesting vulnerability, insecurity and, most importantly, rootlessness. Anowa goes her own way, partly because she is headstrong, and partly because she may be living in a different story.

Again and again, the audience of the play is made aware that Anowa may be the protagonist in this other story that I will title "The Calling to the Priesthood," the tale of the girl who should have become a priestess but rejected the call. For the outsider like me it is not easy to appreciate just how a vocation might manifest itself and just what the effects of resisting the vocation might be. However, the clues in the text and a "research note"[2] by Bridgid M. Sackey, based on information gathered in a relevant part of Ghana, provide helpful background. Sackey's essay is entitled "The Call to Traditional Priesthood among the Akan of Ghana and the Consequences of Its Renunciation" and my extensive debt to it in this essay will become obvious.

Drawing on continuing investigations in what she describes as "three Fante-Akan towns located in the Central Region," Sackey writes about belief in the possibility of a call to the priesthood being manifest through a person being possessed by a deity, and of the call being confirmed before the world through the strange behaviour exhibited by the youthful candidate. Those who reject such a vocation may, according to Sackey's article, do so because it "does not help with human capacity development." Sackey observes that if they demur and reject their destiny they incur the wrath of the deity. Among the punishments regarded as possible, Sackey includes "infertility, mental diseases, successive and inexplicable deaths in the family and even the death of the person." I suggest that selective use of Sackey's findings is useful in understanding Anowa, particularly in becoming aware of the several stories that meet in the central character. These stories contribute to making Anowa a complex and disturbing presence. She grows in stature to raise issues related to gender, history, morality and "human capacity development." She is a nineteenth-century figure whose experience is relevant for women and men in the twentieth and twenty-first centuries.

From the exchange between the Old Man and the Old Woman that forms the Prologue to the play, the audience learns that Anowa is "unfortunate," exceptional, self-sufficient. The Old Man speaks of her as follows:

> A child of several incarnations,
> She listens to her own tales,
> Laughs at her own jokes and
> Follows her own advice. (143)[3] Harvard and footnote here

Her mother, Abena Badua, is criticised for "[spoiling] her shamefully," but Abena Badua defends herself by going onto the offensive and attacking those who have repeatedly gossiped about Anowa. By talking this dubious position she encourages the audience o cultivate a critical attitude to the information she is providing from the stage. The final lines of the Prologue are strongly empha-sised, indeed they resonate with significance, and take us to the centre of our interest here. The Old Woman's exit line is: "And the gods will surely punish Abena Badua for refusing to let a born priestess dance!" This assertion does not come with unchallenged authority, but it is an idea that is planted in the mind of the audience and "watered" by being mentioned again. It demands to be taken seriously and it establishes Anowa as the central figure in the tale of the nimble-footed girl, a "born priestess," who did not respond to a sacred summons.

The detailed account of what I take to be Anowa's call comes much later on in the play, but is conveniently considered here. In the third and final phase of the drama, Anowa recalls that when she was young she questioned her grand-mother with a persistence that irritated the old woman (184–6). The grandmother told the little girl about a visit she had paid to the coast, about seeing the sea and the "houses," or castles, built by the "pale men." She gave an account of the foreigners, who looked "As if you or I/Were peeled of our skins/Like a lobster that is boiled or roasted," and she talked of the trade in human beings in which they were involved. The night after hearing all this, Anowa has a vivid nightmare composed of apocalyptic distortions of what she had been told. She falls ill, and the experience prompted talk about "apprentic-ing [her] to a priestess." Anowa says she doesn't know what came of this "talk," but the weight of evidence from the play suggests, as we shall see, that her mother must have successfully opposed the suggestion that the dream followed by the illness constituted "a call" or confirmation of a call. Anowa recovers her health, but the nightmare leaves a legacy that she describes in the following words: "... since then, any time there is mention of a slave, I see a woman who is me and a bursting ripe tomato or swollen pod" (186). Anowa's moral scruples about trading in and owning human beings lie at the centre of the play. They come between her and her husband, and eloquently raise the issue of the how the humane individual is treated by a society that dwells in darkness. The image of the "woman who is me" and the "bursting ripe tomato" indicates how personally and intensely she feels about slavery.

Aidoo does not follow point for point the example of the "Call to the Priesthood" that Sackey's article presents, but I think we can assume, because she directs attention to "the talk of apprenticing," that Aidoo means us to take this dimension seriously. The word "nightmare" used above to describe the terrifying dream is, incidentally, one that carries within it, even in English, a sense close to possession. The definition of "nightmare" in the *Concise Oxford Dictionary* begins: "female, monster sitting upon and seeming to suffocate a sleeper, incubus..." We should also notice that linking the nightmare with an account of slavery enables Aidoo to provide an element of psychological consistency, an "explanation" for Anowa's intense unhappiness when her husband, Kofi Ako, starts buying human beings.

In view of the "denial of call" theme, it is significant that both Abena Badua and Anowa are punished. Anowa disappoints her mother by rejecting the role her mother wants her to play in the "Tale of Motherhood": she moves away from her home, and, after an arduous, childless existence in which she amasses wealth but does not find happiness, she ages prematurely, begins to show signs of insanity and commits suicide. These "punishments" closely follow those listed by Sackey. The list, it will be recalled, includes: "infertility, mental diseases, successive and inexplicable deaths in the family and even the death of the person."source & page number?

The responsibility for "spoiling" Anowa, by refusing to countenance employment as a priestess is laid firmly on the shoulders of Abena Badua. Osam, her father, is able to remind his wife of his position in the following terms: "I have always asked you to apprentice her to a priestess to quieten her down." Badua acknowledges she has resisted this, insisting, somewhat intemperately, that she "[is not going] to turn [her] only daughter into a dancer priestess" (147). Pushed to explain her attitude, Abena Badua says "... in the end [priestesses] are not people. They become too much like the gods they interpret." We are informed that *"her voice grows hysterical and her face terror-stricken"* as she *"enumerates the attributes of priesthood."* The suspicions triggered by this bizarre delivery are strengthened by her enumeration of what priestesses do. Her list includes "[counselling] with spirits, reading "other men's souls," swallowing dogs' eyes, jumping fires, and drinking goat's milk and sheep's blood. She concludes her catalogue: "They do not feel/As you or I/ They have no shame" (148). Predictably, Abena Badua insists that she wants Anowa to "be a human woman." By this she means successful in the terms regarded as "normal" in Yebi, where normality means marriage, motherhood, and, in due course, a place at clan meetings. Abena Badua makes respectability and responsibility concrete by saying: "a captainship in the army/Should not be beyond her/ When the time is ripe!" (148).

Osam is aware that child guidance is not an area where his wife is open to persuasion and he knows that his position (since theirs is a matrilineal society) is marginal in this matter. As a result, he resigns himself to the inevitable, offering only the following, fatalistic prediction: "the yam that will burn, shall burn, boiled or roasted" (149). This represents a pusillanimous reluctance to challenge his wife's intense and unbalanced outburst. An outburst which, I suggest, is undermined not only by the hysterical delivery but also by Abena Badua's scorn for "dancing" and the banality of the aspirations that emerge.

A moment after Osam has delivered his assessment, Anowa is heard calling from the street. This is a violation of proper behaviour in itself but only a minor infringement compared to the outrageous conduct she is about to exhibit. She runs on stage and announces that she has met the man, Kofi Ako, she wants to marry (151). At this point, Abena Badua brings into the open parallels between her daughter and the protagonist in the familiar, clearly inscribed "Headstrong Daughter" narrative by saying "you want to behave like the girl in the folk-tale" (151). But even while that element is being emphasised, the spiritual dimension is also borne in mind. For example, in justifying his reluctance to become involved in the crisis, Osam refers back to a tangled occasion when he was targeted by his wife's relatives over the issue of vocation. Speaking of the matri-clan, he interjects: "Did they not say in the end that it was I who had prevented [Anowa] from going into apprenticeship with a priestess?" (153) Clearly Osam can never do the right thing as far as some of his in-laws are concerned, and the oral tradition distorts his position. As on a previous occasion, a lighting cue gives a line resonance, and the movement of the play allows the audience time to think about what has been said. The suggestion behind the line is that his wife's "people" had been among those who felt that Anowa might be failing to heed a call to the priesthood. The audience recognises that Abena Badua must have fought tenaciously on several fronts, perhaps alone, to keep Anowa out of the sacred grove. Incidentally, I am convinced that we are right to detect in the mother's restricted vision an acute, contemporary awareness of the way girl children are sometimes held back from self-development by the conservatism of older women.

The "second round" of the family conflict begins, when the lights come up again, with Anowa accusing her mother of being a "witch" (). Without conceding for a moment that she is a member of a coven, Abena Badua throws at her daughter the accusation that she has claimed to have spiritual insight: she says Anowa has "divined her out" – thereby acknowledging, even though sarcasm, the special dimension she has sought so hard to deny (155). Anowa's spiritual connections, and the possibility that she is herself a "witch," will be raised again later in the play. No reconciliation between mother and daughter is possible but, once again, a significant spiritual dimension to Anowa as an exceptional woman has been suggested. A moment later Anowa is slipping back from potential witch into a role in the "Headstrong Daughter" story: she leaves her parents expressing her shocking determination to remaining in self-imposed exile (156). This is an astonishing position to adopt, and one that encapsulates her willfulness.

In the choric exchange between the Old Man and the Old Woman that follows, attention is once again drawn to the notion that "Anowa should have been a priestess." The Old Man reminds the audience of his reference to a "born priestess" who dances when he says:

> Abena Badua should have known that Anowa wanted to be some-
> thing that she herself had not been… They say from a very small
> age, she had the hot eyes and nimble feet of one born to dance
> for the gods. (157).

The "nimble feet" seem to proclaim, to those that have eyes to see, that Anowa has a gift that should be used in the service of the deities. However, the Old Woman steers attention away from certainty towards the ambiguity on which drama thrives by referring to the mystery that surrounds an individual's destiny. She is given a "Hmm" that provides the actor with plenty of scope for "non-verbal communication," and then says: "Our ears are breaking with that one," meaning: "We have heard about the vocation too many times." The Old Woman then sows seeds of uncertainty by asking: "Who heard the Creator tell Anowa what she was coming to do with her life here?" This question, which expects the answer "No one," takes us into territory opened up earlier on by Osam's fatalistic observation about the "yam that will burn." It takes us into theological territory and reminds us that Aidoo is also offering us an Anowa for whom fate has prepared a fire.

The Old Woman continues: "And is that why, after all her 'I don't like this' and 'I don't like that,' she has gone and married Kofi Ako?" (157) This takes us back to the "Headstrong Daughter" narrative. However, since Kofi Ako comes from a family that is well known to the "headstrong daughter," there is a move away from the "familiar narrative" at this point: a stranger has not been selected. Aidoo shifts even further away from her source by presenting a husband, Kofi Ako, who is in no sense a "Complete Gentleman," to use the term memorably employed by Amos Tutuola in describing the husband in his version of the story. The "picky" Anowa selects a husband who is by no means dashing or outstanding. Abena Badua calls Kofi Ako a "good-for-nothing, cassava man," and he certainly has easily recognised shortcomings. A director might cast an actor with legs like cassava sticks in the role to illustrate the truth of the angry woman's observation. Kofi Ako is also vain and self-regarding, vulnerable and morally myopic, and the actor playing him has to suggest these qualities.

Near the end of the play, a version of the anecdote I mentioned earlier as having been passed on to Aidoo about the Couple who Quarrelled in Public comes to the fore. Anowa, unaware that there are eavesdroppers, speaks openly about her husband's impotence, and Kofi Ako walks off and shoots himself. In the course of the play, Aidoo has provided a variety of hints about the causes for the couple's childless state. For instance, early on we learn that the "doctor" consulted by Kofi Ako is reported to have said "there is nothing wrong with (Anowa's) womb" but her "soul is too restless" (166). Later the credulous Abena Badua shares with the audience a persistent rumour "that (Anowa) and her husband sold their birth-seeds to acquire their wealth." (170). Osam, as usual more pragmatic than his wife, modifies this by interjecting an "unsuperstitious" and more plausible, psychological explanation for childlessness when he says: "it certainly looks as if she and her husband are too busy making money and have no time to find out and cure what is wrong with her womb" (171). Kofi Ako's reluctance to countenance the second wife that Anowa offers to secure for him should be read as the result of his impotence, rather than as a commitment to monogamy. He doesn't want to risk more people finding out about his condition.

Sackey's suggestion that childlessness follows, or, more precisely, was believed by her informants to follow, rejection of a vocation should also be borne in mind at this point. As should the possibility that there is a moral and psychological dimension to the drama. Aidoo would be within her rights to allow an element of poetic justice to operate: she could have simply told a story of a wicked man, a trafficker in human beings, who is punished by childlessness, impotence, and public humiliation. There are certainly suggestions that Kofi Ako's decision to buy and sell human beings makes domestic happiness impossible. This reflects a sense of justice that frequently finds expression in Ghanaian discourse: those who do evil will be punished on this earth. The playwright is in a position to show that this happens in the world of the theatre.

When the scene shifts to Anowa and Kofi Ako, Aidoo continues to "break our ears" with talk of the vocation to the priesthood. Bewildered by Anowa's energy, drive and commitment, Kofi Ako asks: "Anowa, is it true that you should have been a priestess?" She replies, with an affirmative to which Aidoo adds a curious question mark so that the text reads "O yes?" (176). This formula creates difficulties of interpretation and performance. Should the actor try to communicate the affirmative or the interrogative? This problem is followed by others. Anowa's lines are: "But how would I know. And where did you hear that from?" This time the absence of a question mark (after "know") requires consideration and so does the fact that the vital question, for so I take it to be, is not answered. To further complicate the issue, the stage directions ask for a dimension that no performance could convey entirely. (The actress playing) Anowa has to say these lines *Looking genuinely lost*. This is as close as we get in the play to finding out what the playwright wants to suggest is at the root of Anowa's state of mind. It seems Anowa really is sincerely flummoxed by the question: she is unsure how one recognises a vocation to the priesthood. I must say that by this point, I think Anowa is being less than totally honest with Kofi Ako about her analysis of her own experiences. The third part of this fractured speech, "Where did you hear that from?" can be taken to represent an enquiry which the audience, having heard the conversations between her parents and between the Old Man and the Old Women, could answer very easily. "We" know that Anowa's vocation has been the talk of the community and of her extended family. It has been "breaking our ears." The query should also be taken in the context of a tradition of dialectical exchanges in which aggressive questioning is an essential part of debate, discussion and argument.

A little later Kofi Ako asks: "Who were you in the spirit world?" (178) This brings together many questions, and predictably, in view of the ambiguities in the play, it is not answered. In fact, to the outsider it opens up lines of enquiry for which there is no space in this paper.

In Phase Three, Anowa is introduced as behaving very strangely. She is described as "flitting about like a ghost" (188), and is accused, for a second time, of witchcraft, a very sensitive issue. Specifically, she is said to have "stared so hard at Takoa's baby" that the infant started having convulsions. It is being rumoured that she "is swallowing the baby because she is a witch" (188). She talks to herself, saying, "O my husband, what have I done, what have I done?," which suggests that she is bewildered, consumed by regret or remorse. When she takes control of the stage, she expresses the anger she feels at her husband for having children fan his empty chair, and then ruminates on pregnancy and motherhood. She greets a picture of Queen Victoria (unamused) with "hei sister" and shares her sense of dislocation with the Empress of India, by asking "Do you sometimes feel like I feel, that you should not have been born. This recalls a line that was given great prominence in the angst-ridden twentieth century "never to have been born is much the best." Although philosophical influences from Aidoo's experience of mid-twentieth century European thought may be at work, I think that Anowa's cry relates specifically to her position as a woman who has not been able to find fulfilment in the society into which she has been born. Anowa moves on to bewail to "her spirit mother" the frustrations that enclose a woman in her society at marriage. She says "… here, O my spirit mother, they let a girl grow up as she pleases until she is married." Through a prayer placed within a traditional context, Anowa reveals that she has become more acutely aware of gender prejudices and the limitations on women's "capacity development" in Ghanaian society. These are themes that Aidoo has returned to again and again in her writing, and reference to her novels and short stories is very illuminating.

When Kofi Ako enters we see what sort of a "monster" he has become, and what Anowa has come to resent. He is richly dressed, endlessly self-regarding, callous, suspicious of the community, frightened of women. After a lull during which Anowa compulsively rearranges plates on the sideboard and digs her toes into the skins covering the carpets on the floor, she launches into an enquiry about what the "priest" had said on his last visit. Reconstructing statements from Kofi Ako's comments and questions, it becomes clear that the visit has reintroduced the issue of Anowa's vocation. Eventually, Kofi Ako says: "Why don't you wash your mouth so you can be a priestess at last." Although constructed like a question there is no question mark. This may simply continue the inconsistency in punctuation or indicate a rhetorical style already noted. In this instance it seems the man does not expect an answer. However, these are just the opening exchanges in a scene that shows Anowa at her most tenacious, and at her most lucid. Indeed she does "divine him out," she "smells" his weakness through insight and analysis that some might term "witchcraft." Though she has long been a stranger to his bed (where his impotence would have been revealed) (203), she "sniffs" her way to the conclusion that Kofi Ako no longer exists, to translate the Akan idiom: "he is not there." She asks, in a way that effectively "translates" her question for the non-Akan speaker: "Kofi, are you dead? (pause) Kofi, is your manhood gone?" She then provides her own diagnosis for his behaviour with a question followed by a "question-answer:" "... tell me, is that why I must leave you? That you have exhausted your masculinity acquiring slaves and wealth?" (203).

Kofi's attempts to silence Anowa as she asks, now in the hearing of many witnesses, whether the priest had offered the same diagnosis suggests the accuracy of her words. Her conviction is memorably expressed through giggles – a powerful weapon to turn against the male. She says, and her "translation is no longer necessary:" "He is a corpse. He is dead wood. But less than dead wood because at least that sometimes grows mushrooms ..." Her torrent of words, and the fact that they are heard by the eavesdroppers, drives Kofi Ako from the palace to kill himself. The couple have finally become characters in the anecdote about the Overheard Domestic Quarrel. By this time, Anowa has drifted into madness and from there it is a short step to her own death by drowning. As Sackey has put it, the final punishment for rejecting the vocation to the priesthood may be "the death of the person."

## Conclusion

The exploration of narrative has been a preoccupation of Ghanaian dramatists such as Efua Sutherland, Martin Owusu, Asiedu Yirenkyi, Mohammed Ben-Abdallah and Yaw Asare. Ama Ata Aidoo's Anowa is a particularly subtle contribution to the tradition in that it incorporates a series of stories that are laid on top of one another as part of a complex design. Elements of gender and history, ideas about destiny and morality, notions of conformity and individuality, of vocation and opportunity, flow from one story, tale or anecdote to another. In reading or watching the play, one is acutely aware that one is in the presence of a formidable and alert intelligence, acutely aware of debates about the position of women that flourished from the 1970s.

The foregoing essay has left unanswered some of the many questions Aidoo raises about destiny and the spirit world, about witchcraft and outside influences that the foreign critic is ill-equipped to comment on. However, thanks to Sackey's essay, it is possible to throw some light on at least one aspect of a complex and rewarding drama that is deeply rooted in a particular community.

# Yesterday's Quarrels and Today's Playmates: Peacemaking and the Proverbial Wisdom of Africa

## Kofi Asare Opoku

If we do not forget yesterday's quarrels, we will not have anybody to play with tomorrow

(A Yoruba proverb)

Although the continent of Africa is currently plagued by seemingly unending conflicts and devastating turmoil, these are not congenital but solvable; for, Africa is home to profound wisdom traditions with respect to peace that kept African societies together in the past and continue to do so today. During colonial times, however, these wisdom traditions were overlooked or even despised; but many thoughtful people today acknowledge the indispensability of these wisdom traditions to the solution of many of Africa's problems, as well as problems elsewhere in the world.

In the proverbial wisdom of Africa, one finds a wealth of ideas, principles and values that guided past generations of Africans to settle, as harmoniously as possible, the disputes that marred human relationships. It is these ideas, principles and values embedded in African proverbial wisdom that this essay sets out to unravel for consideration in our search for solutions to the problems of peace-making and conflict resolution.

## Conflict Is Normal

Conflicts and misunderstandings are a normal part of human existence in any community. They arise in the course of interactions and relations between humans in community and also because of human individuality which brings about differences in tastes and preferences. As a profound reflection on this normal human experience, the Akan of Ghana say: *When trees are close together, they rub against each other.* A Zambian proverb reflects the same insight: *Trees that are together, brush against each other* (Sumbwa, 1993: 16). If the trees stood far apart from each other, they would not rub or brush against each other, and they don't; and so conflict is an altogether normal human experience. The possibility of misunderstanding in human relations is recognised in the proverbial wisdom of Africa, as the Yoruba say: *In being friendly, one should give allowance for the possibility of misunderstanding* (Areje, 1985: 54), and the Baganda of Uganda, recognising conflict or misunderstanding as normal, add: *People who live together cannot fail to have quarrels* (Lule, 2006: 40). Conflict, however, is not altogether bad, for through it humans learn to understand each other.

But even though quarrels and misunderstandings are inevitable, African wisdom sagaciously suggests that they can and must be resolved, and that accepting each other later, or reconciling after a quarrel, are all normal and undoubtedly expedient. *There is nothing like friends who never quarrel and enemies who never reconcile* (Adekunle, 2008: 37), says a Yoruba proverb, while the Swahili assert: *Those who quarrel are those who make up* (Ibekwe: 155). The soft tongue and the sharp teeth provide ample insights into peaceful and harmonious living in human society, as a Yoruba epithet puts it: *The tongue and the teeth often come into conflict; to quarrel and get reconciled is a mark of responsibility* (Albert, et al., 1995: 6), and *No sojourner on earth is immune against dispute; no disputants remain enemies forever* (Albert, et. al, 1995: 6).

The right to annoyance is justified in African wisdom, but when forgiveness is sought, it is inglorious to be stubborn in that annoyance, hence the Yoruba proverb: *It is only a bastard that would be offended and would not get annoyed; and it is only a bastard that would be begged or appealed to that would demonstrate his stubbornness* (Adekunle, 2008: 35). And another Yoruba proverb in the same vein is: *Only a bastard will not be vexed, only a bastard will not yield to a plea for peace* (Olaoba, 1999). The Oromo of Ethiopia, maintaining the principle of reconciliation, and suggesting that in the end there is more wickedness in refusing to reconcile than in fighting, say: *The one who does not fight is an ass; the one who fought and will not be reconciled is a devilish person* (Cotter, 1996: 85).

## Revenge Is Counterproductive

The emphasis on reconciliation is based on the intuitive and penetrating insight that revenge is counterproductive, and that returning evil for evil brings one to the level of those who perpetrate it. The Senegambian proverb: *He who kicks a donkey in return is no better than the donkey* (Khan & Khan, 2004: 21), reflects the value of non-retaliation, while the same idea is given expression in the Yoruba saying: *If one sees the corpse of a wicked person on the ground and one kicks it, there are then two wicked people* (Owomoyela, 2005: 257). To warn people vividly about the consequences of taking revenge, a South African proverb wisely cautions: *Before you go out to revenge, make plans for two funerals.*

Indeed, African proverbial wisdom points out that how one treats others reflects more on oneself than on the others and the evil that one inflicts on others reflects on oneself: *The blemish of the yam is the blemish of the knife; whoever besmirches other people's name besmirches his or her own* (Owomoyela, 2005: 258). And, similarly: *Whoever defames others defames himself or herself – the evil that one does to others reflects on oneself* (Owomoyela, 2005: 258). In order to avoid situations that cause conflicts and tensions, people are encouraged not respond to the sayings, actions and temptations of their adversaries. In this regard, the Akan proverb that encourages people not to behave like those who tempt them: *If you are taking your bath and a mad person comes to take your cloth away, put on another cloth before you chase him/her out on the street, otherwise, everybody will say that both of you are mad* (Opoku, 1997: 68) suggests that peace will prevail if provocative actions and sayings are not responded to. The same desire for peace through the avoidance of, and non-response to, provocative situations, finds eloquent expression in the Yoruba proverb: *The dove pronounces incantations and believes the pigeon does not understand, not knowing that the pigeon, for the sake of peace and maturity, does not take offence* (Adekunle, 2008: 68

## The Golden Rule

Behaving towards people the way one would like to be treated, or treating others as one would like to be treated, is the foundational principle of peace and harmonious living in society. The Akan of Ghana express the principle of justice and fairness in their proverb: *What you don't like, don't do it to your neighbour* (Ibekwe, 1998: 138). And the visual adinkra symbol 🐾 , the Akan version of the Golden Rule, *Bi Nka Bi* – One must not bite another, or bite not one another, is an exhortation to respect each other, and protect each other from harm. And, urging people not to do to others what they do not want done to them, the Oromo say: *Thrust it upon yourself and see* (Cotter, 1996: 198). This reciprocity also extends to plant and animal life: *When cutting off a tree in the forest, one should make a comparison with oneself* (Areje, 1985: 110ditto), and the Igbo of Eastern Nigeria maintain: *A person trying to kill a snake should remember that the snake also wants to live* (Ibekwe, 1998: 137). The tendency to put others down in order to make one's own position become preeminent is wisely countered by the Swahili proverb: *It is not necessary to blow out the other person's lantern to let yours shine* (Ibekwe, 1998: 138); and since people would like others to treat them with decorum, the Yoruba assert: *Behave with decorum toward me, and I will behave with decorum towards you: only those who approach one with decorum earn decorum in return* (Owomoyela, 2005: 320). Besides, even one's enemy may possess something which can help him/her, and this is what the Maasai mean when they say: *There is no man without gum plant in his hand* (Massek & Sidai, 1974: 30).

## Peace Must Be Deliberately Sought

Making or searching for peace is not a sign of palpable cowardice: *Abstaining from fighting is no timidity* (Chakanza, 2000: 145), the Chinyanga of Malawi say, while the Igbo affirm: *If a person loves peace, it does not make him/her a coward* (Ibekwe, 1998: 141). Peace is achieved when people interact with each other and communicate with each other, and it is more desirable when people are connected, not separated from each other, hence the Swahili proverb: *It is better to build bridges than walls* (Ibekwe, 1998: 141). To avoid conflict, an effort must be made to take into account the interests and preferences of all, and to make an effort to bring about peace, as the Malagasy proverb puts it: *One does not like heat and the other does not like cold: make it tepid and still remain friends* (Ibekwe, 1998: 142). Harmonious living in society is so important that it is considered indubitably wise to let go of personal grievances in the interest of future peace, and this the Yoruba affirm by saying: *If we do not forget yesterday's quarrels, we will not have anybody to play with tomorrow.* At the personal level, the proverb suggests that holding on rather tenaciously to a grievance prevents us from passing over an offence or injury, thereby imprisoning ourselves in our own little box; thus rendering us incapable of realising our own sense of interior freedom that can move us towards joy and contentment. But, if we are able to do this, then we open ourselves to something larger and demonstrate that we are indeed free persons who are larger than any story of hurt in the past. In short, to dwell on the past does not change anything, it only makes us prisoners to situations or persons we do not forgive.

## Forgiving and Forgetting

The wisdom of letting go brings about peace and the Oromo underscore this in their proverb: *By saying 'let it be,' people remain together in peace* (Cotter, 1996: 85). The Swahili provide further insights in their proverbs: *To forget a wrong is the best revenge* (Ibekwe, 1998: 164), and *To forgive a wrong is the best revenge* (Korem & Abissath, 2004: 90). The Zulu see the act of forgiving as winning the victory and say: *He/she that forgives gains victory* (Ibekwe, 1998: 73). The Yoruba understand forgiveness as putting an end to a quarrel: *One who forgives ends the quarrel* (Ibekwe, 1998: 73); while to the Akan, not forgetting a crime causes a person to commit a crime: *If you do not forget a crime, you commit a crime* (Ibekwe, 1998: 73). And seeing beyond the immediate offence and looking into the future, the Chala of Northern Ghana proffer the advice: *If someone offends you, forgive him, because you do not know what will happen tomorrow* (Kleinewillinghofer, 2007: 130), while to the Yoruba: *He who forgives us puts litigation to shame* (Adekunle, 2008: 82).

## Accepting Different Tastes and Preferences

African wisdom also recognises that individual tastes and preferences differ from person to person, and the Akan proverb: *Obi apede ne odompo nsono* – someone's favourite meat is the intestines of the wild dog (Opoku, 1997: 95) – underscores the importance of the acceptance of the fact of differences in individual tastes and preferences. The Hausa of Northern Nigeria affirm this idea in their proverb: *One bird flees from water, the duck seeks the very middle of it* (Whitting, 1940: 37); besides, one is free to do one's thing as one pleases, hence the Yoruba proverb: *The monkey somersaulted and failed to land erect, and the gorilla, resting among the roots of a large tree exclaimed, 'Ha!' The monkey responded, 'Nobody has the right to fault one over how one performs one's signature stunt'* (Owomoyela, 2005: 426). Individual preferences and tastes do not exclude religious preferences, and the acceptance of this fact explains the inherent tendency towards pluralism in African societies and the fact that people of different religious persuasions belong to the same families and live in the same localities in many parts of Africa.

There are other African proverbs that can be used to buttress tolerance, openness and peaceful coexistence, such as: *One must come out of one's house to begin learning; If you have not been outside of your home, you do not say that your mother's soup is the best; Truth is like a baobab tree, and one person's arms cannot embrace it; However big one eye may be, two are better;* and *Hunt in every forest, for there is wisdom and good hunting in all of them.* The absorbing ideas enshrined in these proverbs, when taken seriously, can provide a basis for much-needed flexibility in pluralistic situations and lead to the avoidance of costly conflicts. They also provide a basis for holding multiple perspectives and a healthy coexistence, not only of ideas, but also of people of differing persuasions.

With respect to the realisation of inter-religious harmony and peace, the proverbs cited above provide a useful basis for reflection. They espouse the kind of openness, found in the Yoruba proverb: *It is not one road only that leads to the market* (Owomoyela, 2005: 426), which helps to create tolerance for different beliefs and values and avoids costly and unyielding dogmatism. Furthermore, only openness can bring about inter-religious harmony and such openness distinguishes wisdom from folly, as the Shona proverb puts it: *The wise person does not say that what he/she says is the final word, but the fool insists* (Hamutyinei & Plangger, 1987: 363).

From the African insights, tolerance becomes too weak a word with respect to what brings about peace in religiously pluralistic situations. Tolerating someone's religious orientation, preference or practice, simply means putting up with it. For, ideally, on the basis of one's own persuasion, one would want to convert the other, forcibly or persuasively, or wipe it out altogether. But since one cannot, one merely puts up with it, out of powerlessness or resignation. What brings about genuine peace in religiously pluralistic situations is *mutual acceptance*, in which the birds that avoid water, accept the duck which chooses the middle of water.

## Peaceful Means of Resolving Conflicts

Peaceful means of resolving conflicts unhesitatingly recommend themselves with beneficial results, and to urge moderation in resolving conflicts and problems, the Maasai recommend: *Don't use a spear to separate cattle* (Massek & Sidai, 1974: 36); and a West African proverb says: *Fire will not be quenched by adding more fuel* (Gleason, 1992: 51). And, insisting that subtlety is better than force, the Kikuyu say: *Fire is not put out by another fire* (Njururi, 1969: 95). African wisdom recommends dialogue as a peaceful way to resolve conflicts, and thus communication becomes an effective tool in the process of making peace. The Kikuyu say in this regard, *Talking is making friends, keeping silent is making enemies* (Njururi, 1969: 65), and underscore the value of communication in the proverb: *A matter is resolved by talking it over* (Wanjohi, 2001: 102). Urging that every dispute be settled by patient negotiation, the Shona add, *A case cannot be settled by fighting* (Hamutyinei & Plangger, 1987: 307), for according to the Shona ancestors, to use violence in order to bring about a settlement is tantamount to admitting defeat (Hamutyinei & Plangger, 1987: 307). And, putting diplomacy far above military operations, the Shona also say: *The greatest war is the war of the mouth* (Plaatje, 1916: 77), an idea expressed by the Akan proverb: *Conflicts are resolved best with the tongue, and not with an axe*, while the Malawians say: *When two mouths meet, conflict is averted*, expressing a preference for peaceful negotiation over violence.

## The Importance of Communication

Basic to desirable human interaction is communication, and living together means talking to each other, and in this regard the Yoruba provide two useful proverbs: *We cannot dwell in a house together without speaking to one another* (Korem & Abisssath, 2004: 155), and *One does not qualify to live with a person without also qualifying to talk to the person* (Owomoyela, 2005: 312). Thus communicating with each other is the hoe with which peaceful relationships are cultivated, and the person who does not talk or communicate with others exposes himself/herself as an unkind person, as the Maasai say: *It has been said, 'unkind is the one who does not speak'* (Massek & Sidai, 1974: 24).

Arch-enemies can even sometimes be brought together and Swahili councillors, in trying to reunite rival parties, often remind them that if they are not able to forget their differences completely, they could at least create room for tolerance. A frequently used expression in such circumstances is:

*Mbwene shumndwa na mbuzi, wachandamana pamoya*
*Na mwana kuku na kozi, wana wao wachileya*
*Na mtu msi maozi, akionya watu ndiya*
*Hayano sikuambiwa, niwene kwa mato yangu.*

I have seen a wolf and a goat going together
And a hawk and a hen feeding their chicks in common
And a blind person showing people the right way
This I've not been told, I've seen with my naked eyes.

(Madumulla, 2005: 69).

## Oneness of Humankind

An Akan proverb that solemnly affirms the unquestionable oneness of humankind says: *Nnipa nyinaa ye Onyame mma, obi nye asase ba* – All human beings are the children of God, none is a child of the earth (Opoku, 1997: 11). The Ewe also express the same idea in their proverb: *Ahloe be kae yedzi, kae yefo tso ati nu?* – The antelope says, which of my children did I bring forth and which one did I get from the bark of a tree? (Dzobo, 2006: 55). These proverbs express the idea of oneness of humanity which, if embraced and practiced, would make enduring peace on our planet a possibility. None of the antelope's children was plucked from the bark of a tree; all were given birth to by the mother antelope, as the Ewe proverb clearly puts it. Humankind, therefore, constitutes one universal family and each person is part of the body of the Creator, just as a wave is part of the ocean. And when we come to accept the fact that each person is an expression of the Creator, including those people we love and respect, as well as those we may choose to disrespect, revile or even avoid, for whatever reason, then undiminished kindness, deep compassion and courteous service would not be far-fetched ideas and peace in our troubled planet could be achieved.

## Egalitarianism

The acknowledgement of the fact that all people have equal social, economic and political rights, a fundamental principle that leads to peace in human societies, finds expression in the Akan proverb: *When the parrot eats, the toucan also eats* (some of the food) (Opoku, 1997: 103). Achebe also writes about this basic sense of egalitarianism in Igbo society, in *Things Fall Apart*: "We shall all live. We pray for life, children, a good harvest and happiness. You will have what is good for you and I will have what is good for me. Let the kite perch and let the eagle perch too. If one says no to the other, let his wing break (1994:19). Peace and justice are inseparable, indeed justice creates peace, for its absence leads to an irreconcilable breach of peace; and the person who wants peace must not trample on another's property or rights, as the Akan proverb puts it: *If you trample on another person's property in looking for your own, you will never find your own* (Opoku, 1997: 26).

## Words and the Search for Peace

In the search for peace in community, African wisdom amply acknowledged the role of language in the achievement of peace as well as in the perpetuation of violence, and came up with a number of proverbs expressive of this insight. To acknowledge the power of the tongue to hurt, the Oromo say: *The tongue does not have a bone but breaks the bones of people* (Cotter, 1996: 51), and to further accentuate this fact, the Oromo go on to say: *Wounds from spears will heal, but wounds from tongues will not heal* (Cotter, 1996: 86). The fact that the tongue cannot only hurt but inflict hurt that is even deeper than that of a knife, caused the Akan to say: *The wound inflicted by the tongue is more painful than the wound inflicted by a knife* (Opoku, 1997: 18), an idea reflected in the Kikuyu proverb: *Cutting by tongue is not the same as cutting by knife* (Njururi, 1969: 24). The Swahili also recognise the power of the tongue to inflict deep and permanent damage in their proverb: *A cruel word is a wound of the heart, it does not heal; and even if it heals, the scar never departs* (Ibekwe, 1998: 203). These proverbs draw attention to the power of the tongue and caution people to watch their tongues which are harder than sticks, as the Ovambo proverb puts it: *The tongue is harder than a stick* (Kuusi, 1970: 39).

## Conclusion

The vast array of ideas, principles and values reflected in the proverbs discussed above all come out of the African experience in dealing with conflicts, disputes and misunderstandings. The proverbs suggest various approaches to living in peace in community and provide a source of knowledge about peace and how to achieve it. The existence of this body of knowledge, however, has not prevented violence from occurring in the past and in the present, nevertheless this body of knowledge has helped to achieve peace under many circumstances and it continues to be a resource, not only for Africans, but also for other people who search for solutions to the problem of peace-making in our world today.

# Not Just for Children Anymore: Aidoo's *The Eagle and the Chickens* and Questions of Identity

## Vincent O. Odamtten

The fact that Ama Ata Aidoo's works for children have hardly been given any critical attention may be due, in part, to the fact that the stories in her only collection for children may be seen as "folk tales," variants of the well known Ananse tales. As such their only value may be seen as a folklorist curio or an attempt to recapture a precolonial "age of innocence." Perhaps it is the awkwardness of addressing a writer whose oeuvre seems fiercely and exclusively directed at an adult audience. Nevertheless, these short stories are as important to understanding the focus of Aidoo's concerns as her more critically acclaimed adult oriented works, from *The Dilemma of a Ghost* to *Changes*, which were ostensibly written for a more mature audience. This essay examines her short-story collection *The Eagle and the Chickens and Other Stories*, which was published in 1987 while she was in Harare, Zimbabwe. Afram Publications (Ghana) Ltd. republished the collection in 1989. The four stories that are the subjects of this inquiry are "The Eagle and the Chickens," a tale first told by Dr. Kwegyir Aggrey, the noted Ghanaian educationist and nationalist; the next tale, "Rain," seems to raise an ecological concern before that subject entered our consciousness; the next is "Daylight and Darkness" which intimates a critique of capitalism's excesses; and the last is "Winds that Blow," which is perhaps an allegory of these times. After a brief comment on the titular story, my examination will proceed serially and then return to "The Eagle and the Chickens" before I conclude.

Aidoo prefaces her collection with a "Dedication" to "All the Children of Ogya Adze... and their Age-Mates In Ghana, Nigeria, Zimbabwe and throughout the Whole of Africa. With Hopes That They May Grow Up and Help to Build a Better World Than The One They Were Born Into." Such a declaration signals not only the author's understanding of the ideological function of such literature, but underscores the task of the reader/audience as witnesses to these narrative performances. "The Eagle and the Chickens" opens with an acknowledgment that:

> [t]his story was first told by Dr Aggrey who was born at Anomabu in Ghana in 1875 and died in 1927. Dr Aggrey was one of the Africans who looked upon formal education as a means to fight for freedom. This tale is an allegory. The eagle represented the oppressed people of Africa. The lesson of the story is that no one likes colonisation, good or bad. As soon as a colonised people get the chance, they will fight for their freedom and fly away from oppression, like the eagle. (1)

Thus, it is clear from such foregrounding that this narrative (and I would suggest the others in this collection), carry a particular ideological inflection and are politically purposeful.

In Aidoo's retelling of Dr. Kwegyir Aggrey's allegory, she places it within a historicised context. The human actors – the farmers, their wives and children – live within a recognizably modern world in which commerce is essential yet in this tale, as in the others, there is an underscoring of a reverence for, a utilitarian relationship to, the *"ancient forest... full of wild animals, wild birds and all sorts of strange wild fruits"* (emphasis added, 1). The farmer enters the forest to hunt and "to look for wood and rope to repair his granary" (1). It is on such a visit that the farmer finds the wounded eaglet that had fallen from its nest high up in the trees and takes it back to his home, perhaps from curiosity or to nurse it back to health. Over the objections and concern voiced by his wife, "Today it is only a baby, but it will grow. And when it becomes a fully grown eagle, it will eat the chickens and the goats and maybe even the children!" (4). Perhaps, because of its iconic nature, or more particularly as a result of its oral flavour, most people will be familiar with the narrative and its outcome. However, before we turn to look at the next tale, we need to make sure that we have all heard the same story. The eaglet recovers its health and the farmer keeps it with the wife's chickens. As the eagle grows in the company of chickens, it acquires the mannerisms of chickens, "wherever the chickens went, it followed them... pecked at the same food... drank water from the same trough as the chickens" (5). Yet, there was no denying that this was an eagle and not a chicken, as the farmer's wife reminded him, "You must now send away the eagle. It is getting too big" (5). The farmer is reluctant to let the eagle go, since it does not appear to want to express its essential *"eagle-ness,"* it seems tame, a testament to man's power over nature, his ability to change the ontology of other species, the master of domestication and hybridisation. After a number of tries to get the eagle to fly, "the eagle flapped its wings and lifted itself off the farmer's arm... Just like a plane. It flew over the forest towards the east where the sun was shining very brightly" (10–11). The farmer finally acknowledges, "An eagle is an eagle. You cannot make a chicken out of an eagle, just by feeding it corn!" (11).

The lessons to be drawn from this are complex and I shall return to them in a while.

In the next story, "Rain" we have the coming together of multiple concerns, all of which are thematically addressed in a variety of situations and relationships depicted and examined in Aidoo's plays, poems, short stories, novels and critical writings. This tale concerns the lessons learned by a ten-year-old girl, Aba, after she comes back with her brother, Kofi, from her parents' farm and meets their great-grandmother, "whom everyone called 'Nana'" (12). As the two children try to sneak past their great-grandmother to fetch a cool drink of water from the large earthenware pot in her room, Nana tells them that there is no water left in the house. Aba looks in all the water containers in the house, finally finding some warm water to drink from the metal drum. In the meantime, her brother "Kofi had quietly disappeared… Somehow, grown-ups never seemed to get angry when her brother played about during the day. Yet they were always telling her how she must stay around the house doing this or that, just like now" (14). This narratological observation about male privilege is as much a reflection of Aba's thoughts as it is the storyteller's deliberate address to her audience, a strategy that those familiar with Aidoo's use of orature in her written works will recognise. The story is as much focused on the inequality between the genders, as it is concerned with the wisdom of our elders and maintaining the resources of a good household/nation. After washing the dirty dishes, Aba is instructed to go to the stream to fetch water in the company of some of her friends. Although she weakly protests, telling Nana that on their way from the farm, Kofi and she saw rain clouds, her great-grandmother admonishes her, "Always remember, my child, that you should never say you have got water, unless it is already in your water pot. The water that hangs in a raincloud belongs to no one…" (16–17). As much as this is a variation on counting one's chickens before they are hatched, Aidoo's elaboration of this cautionary proverb also suggests that the vital resources of the village/nation, in this case, "water… belong[s] to no one."

Aba and her friends set off to the stream where, after fetching water in their buckets, they are drenched by a rainstorm as they start their return to the village. Thinking that it must have also rained in their village, the young girls reason that it would be ludicrous to carry buckets full of water to a village that has been inundated by a rainstorm. Due to peer-pressure, they all decide to empty their heavy buckets and run back to the village. By the time they reach the outskirts of the village they realise that the rain that beat them did not fall in the village. Aba, crestfallen, returns to tell Nana of the fool's errand that they had undertaken and how their impulsive behaviour led to the empty buckets. The story ends with the promise of hope as Nana and Aba see the rain clouds moving over the village and they hear thunderclaps and her great-grandmother cautions, "Remember my child, that this thunder we have just heard also promises rain. But it hasn't fallen into our waterpots yet!" (26).

"Daylight and Darkness" seems to be most removed from our present, yet as an allegory it most clearly speaks to our day and age. As with all good tales, this one begins:

> Once upon a time, long, long ago, a man and his wife lived in a cave deep in the forest. In those days, the sky was very near to the earth and people could talk to God. So they could ask God to do anything they wanted and God did things for them very quickly. (28f)

This tale of prelapsarian harmony, if not domestic bliss, is soon to be disrupted by the seemingly endless tasks and chores that need to be done on any given day. Tellingly it is the man who "complained that cleaning the skins and beating the bark took so much of his time that he was always behind with his work" (28). He soon wishes that the night would never come so that he could finally complete all his tasks. In response to his wife's astute observation that, "the kind of sleep we enjoy in the day is not enough to give us the proper rest we need to begin the life of every new day" (29), the husband's simplistic retort is "if there are no nights, there will be no need to begin living each day. Life will just go on. We will do what we like, when we like, for as long as we like. Then, when we are tired, we can also sleep for as long as we like" (29). Unfortunately for this couple, God overheard them and decided to intervene and because the husband had called God, although the wife had not agreed to her spouse's plan, God granted the man's desire.

It soon became apparent to the pair that a twenty-four cycle of work, with little or no sleep was not good for the human being:

> From that time, life was strange for the man and the woman. They continued sleeping badly. Often when they tired, they could not sleep at all.... They got angry with one another quickly and started quarrelling.... Then they caught fever. Very weakly, they went to fetch herbs to make medicine. But because they were not eating properly, every time they drank the medicine, their stomach ached and they felt even more ill. (32–34)

Ultimately, the woman cries "Oh God" (34). To their surprise God immediately shows up and asks what they want. To their excited pleas for a return of the night God jokingly asks, "Shall I take away the day and bring back the night all the time?" The pair answer, with a resounding "No!" (35). The couple wish "everything the way it was before" (35); but this desire is not a nostalgic return to the past, since it is tempered by the harshness of experience and the knowledge that there are real, often traumatic, unintended consequences in the implementation of extreme solutions to life's problems. As much as this story situates the characters and problems in a mythic world, the lessons are perhaps even more appropriate in our modern postcolonial world. The idea of an endless workday may be the capitalist's dream; however, the dystopian consequences of a radical disruption of our circadian rhythms so clearly articulated in Aidoo's cautionary tale leave us in no doubt about the toll on the human and natural environment that such a relentless exploitation of resources would entail.

It is fitting that the final story of the quartet, "Winds That Blow" takes place in the modern era and the young child at the centre of the narrative, Tendai, asks his uncle, Sekuru John, who works in the city, about the nature of the "wind." The uncle's return to the village becomes the pretext for increasingly complex explanations about the wind. Along with Tendai we learn that sometimes the wind is soft and slow and as it pushes the air, it can carry away a balloon (38). Other times the wind blows more strongly and is able to knock ripe fruit, like mangoes, from tree limbs onto the ground (39). Soon after this incident Sekuru John goes back to the city and promises to return for the Christmas period.

Tendai's uncle's return is greeted with joy and the family celebrates the season with eating and conversation. On one such carefree afternoon, a sudden wind begins to blow and it gets stronger and stronger. A storm was in the offing and as the rain begins to fall, all run for shelter in their houses. "After some time, Mai-Tendai, Tendai's mother, said 'Where is Tendai?' Then everybody saw that Tendai was not in the room" (42). Near panic ensues; however, Sekuru John takes charge and diligently searches for the missing child, whom he uncovers beneath a blanket on the corner of a bed. The sobbing child reveals that he is afraid because of the loudness of the wind and how the storm is shaking the tree branches and the house itself (43). Uncle Sekuru John assures his nephew that all will be fine, since their house has been well built. The narrative ends with Tendai musing over how nature produces breezes, winds and storms: "He thought how strange the world is, as a storm continued to blow and shake the house they were sitting in" (44footnote). This ending roots the stories very much in the present and the "storm" assumes a metaphorical, even mythic dimension, as we consider how Africa and other developing countries are buffeted by the winds of greed, exploitation and even ineptitude, our populations huddle in the nation-states we have built hoping that they are strong enough to give us shelter.

The titular narrative of the collection, *The Eagle and the Chickens and Other Stories*, first told by Dr. Kwegyir Aggrey, the noted Ghanaian educationist and nationalist, like the oral literary flavour it embodies, has been retold and used for various purposes around the globe. Significantly, its retelling or appropriation in the West has most often been deployed as a narrative for the promotion of a "rugged individualistic" ideology, above all else. What is noteworthy about Aidoo's *original* treatment is not only its grounding in an African soil, but, as with the other stories in the collection, it addresses the complex issues of both individual and collective identity, hybridity, location and the environment in ways that underscore the often conflicted relationships between human activities, the natural world and its processes. What is ultimately striking about this collection is the accessibility and faithfulness to the ideological struggles that support the political, economic and cultural struggles that beset the African continent, its Diaspora and the world at large. In short, Aidoo's children's stories, while they apparently educate and entertain the next generation of readers, their use value is best articulated in what they say to adults about the world *they* have inherited and made, unmindful of the best practices of *sankofa*, critical inquiry and action.

# Someone Talking to Sometime:
# A Dialogue across Time and Space

## Jane Bryce

In this tribute to Sissie Ama, I look back to a particular time and place: the time was 1985, the place Harare, she had just published her collection of poems, *Someone Talking to Sometime*, with a Zimbabwean publisher. At that time I was a full-time graduate student at the University of Ife, Nigeria and a part-time free-lance journalist, eking out a dwindling scholarship by writing for the Nigerian and British press. Thanks to a commission from the Lagos *Guardian*, I was able to travel to Harare to report on the Third Annual Zimbabwe International Book Fair (ZIBF)– whose theme that year was "Women and Books" – and extend my research on African women's writing. Ama Ata, who had by then been living in Harare for two years and was a distinctive presence at the Book Fair: humourous, vocal and conspicuous in her West African wax prints and head-ties, often found encircled by enthralled schoolchildren on the grass, signing copies of her new book at the College Press table or moving haltingly (from a knee injury suffered in a recent car accident) towards the platform at the writers' workshop to make another of her outspoken contributions.[1]

I didn't know it then – nobody did – but that celebratory moment in 1985 may have marked the high point of Zimbabwe's immediate post-independence experience. Five years after the end of the liberation war and the Lancaster House agreement which had installed Robert Mugabe as President, the country appeared to have everything to look forward to. Arriving from the cheerful din and chaos of Lagos, I was struck by the orderliness of Harare – its world-class hotels, efficient transport system on well-maintained roads, good communications, its trimmed hedges and working traffic lights – the effective infrastructure of a still thriving settler culture. Beyond that, the public commitment of its socialist government to education and literacy, the presence of government officials like Comrade Nathan Shamuyarira, Information Minister, who opened the Fair and Comrade Teurai Nhongo, Minister for Community Development and Women's Affairs, who opened the workshop on "Women and Books," suggested that ZIBF was set to become *the* major meeting place for publishers and writers on the continent. Only time would disclose the hidden irony of Shamuyarira's declaration: "The book is an essential tool in the struggle for liberation. Governments should provide a tolerant political framework for writers to express their views on alternative ways of organising society. We should be able and willing to learn from progressive writers." (Quoted in Bryce, *New African*, October 1985: 53). In 1985 Ama Ata was one of those progressive writers, ready to lend her support to the on-going liberation struggle and especially Comrade Nhongo's call to "break through the elitist circles of publishing to make books available to all women...to be involved in development and literacy projects, to enable women to write and read their own books."

In Ghana, Ama Ata Aidoo had been Minister of Education from 1982 for eighteen months under President Jerry John Rawlings. Her attainment of this position arose directly from the birth of independent Ghana out of the colonial Gold Coast in 1957 and President Nkrumah's insistence on education for all. Having benefitted from his policy, Ama Ata was committed to the ideals Nkrumah espoused, especially education as a basic right and Pan Africanism. Though Nkrumah's political reign ended in disillusionment, Ama Ata's Pan Africanism carried her to Zimbabwe, where she enthused about what she had been able to accomplish in a short time. Living in Zimbabwe, she told me, "is enormously awakening and enriching." The proximity of apartheid South Africa meant "there's always a hot air blowing on your neck," and as a writer she found,"the very fact of being here widens my awareness of Africa and the people of this continent. The very notion that the government can encourage debate on something like socialism is *something*. I don't know that just by crowing socialism anyone is going to eat, but it definitely indicates a willingness to consider alternatives and I can identify with that" (Interview, 1985). The acute financial distress in which she found herself after leaving her post in Ghana galvanised her, since "because of just the need to survive, I've had to do other things which I wasn't doing before in order to earn money." She was "very, very broke," and a friend suggested she write a radio play. When she sat down to think about it, she realised a subject had been "bugging her" for some time. "Aha! polygamy. It's always portrayed, especially by Westerners, as something terrible for African women and I said, maybe in an environment where everything is right for it, polygamy works in its own way." So the play's heroine, "a young, petit-bourgeois type," becomes a second wife in the belief that "you have much more time to yourself, because half the time the man's somewhere else." Aidoo's readers will recognise this as the germ of *Changes*, the novel she published in 1991. But then, "a radio play was something I'd never done before, never thought of doing and never thought I'd be able to do." In Zimbabwe, she did it. It was the same thing with children's stories. "I have all my life wanted to write for children and I hadn't the talent or even the courage to begin. But when I had to because I needed the money, I produced stories I didn't even know were in my head" (Interview). What gave her the impetus was a request from the Curriculum Development Unit of the Ministry of Education for supplementary readers for schools, the effect of which could be judged from the enthralled response of the children in the reading circle on the grass at the Book Fair.

But the story that seemed to be emerging, of opportunity and self-realisation in the context of social development, was almost immediately contradicted by other details that came into view. Ama Ata was strongly critical, for example, about women's position in Zimbabwe. "Really, Zimbabwean women are not to be compared with women in West Africa. I mean, one is talking about traders, farmers, judges ... I am just overwhelmed by the energy and strength of West African women," compared with women elsewhere. She cited the recent passing of the Age of Majority Act, by which a girl officially became a woman at eighteen, saying such a thing would never have been necessary in Ghana, where women had never been formally discriminated against. On the other hand, she commended "the sheer commitment of the government to the development of women and the struggles which are coming up to support this" (Interview). You only had to flip through the pages of the liberal monthly magazine, *Moto*, to be made aware of the issues facing women: rural poverty, lack of land rights, illiteracy, bride price, baby-dumping by women unable to cope. Yet these problems were to an extent common across Africa and the public commitment to solving them had indeed created a climate of optimism in Zimbabwe. At the Women and Books workshop, jointly organised by the Zimbabwe Writers' Union and Zimbabwe Publishing House, the presence of numbers of women of all social classes was a testimony to their belief in the possibility of change. The emphasis on the necessity for women and men to work together for socialist transformation, however, inevitably repressed the more questioning voices. One of these belonged to the writer Dambudzo Marechera, who challenged socialist piety by asking whether men should be there at all and what about lesbianism? As always, Marechera was playing the dual role of philosopher-agitator; he had precisely identified the limitations of socialist openness by his reference to same-sex love, participants in which Mugabe would later notoriously describe as "worse than pigs and dogs." Again, Marechera opposed Kenyan writer-in-exile, Micere Mugo, who called for the demystification of literature through socialism, by drawing attention to "the brutal self-censorship" of writers afraid to publish anything "unpatriotic" (Bryce, *Guardian* 18/08/85, 9).

To speak of this today is to recall a time when public debate was still possible in Zimbabwe, even at the expense of harassment and marginalisation. Marechera was speaking from the position of a subversive modernism whose time had not yet come in his home country, though his extensive influence and reputation among young Zimbabweans today testifies to its enduring relevance. The emphasis on a suitable femininity for socialism ironically obscured the degree to which Marechera's concerns chimed with those of ordinary women attending the Book Fair, who expressed fear of censure and retribution for trying to write while running a family. One woman's story of how her husband destroyed her manuscript and extinguished the lights at night to stop her writing was not so far from Marechera's experience of being locked up the previous year to keep him from "disrupting" the Book Fair. With hindsight, the meshing of personal and political repression is glaringly obvious. Contradictions, gaps and silences such as these notwithstanding, Ama Ata Aidoo was to play a key developmental role for a decade or so in Zimbabwe, not least as chair, by 1991, of Zimbabwe Women Writers, a women's organisation with branches all over the country. She was a figurehead in a society emerging from colonial rule and civil war and in the construction of a new, socialist African state.

All the more intriguing, then, to witness the apparent contradiction between her effervescent joy at the publication of her poetry collection, *Someone Talking to Sometime*, and her blunt statement that "Africa is in a mess" (Interview); her untiring commitment to education, literature and women's rights and her pain at the failure of both personal relationships and political systems on the continent. Of the joy, she explained: "When I got the usual author's six copies, I was dancing around here like it was the first time I was going into print. I think it was because I haven't really published a book since *Our Sister Killjoy* and then, I've been literally suppressing my poetry and now I realise I shouldn't have and I feel especially happy that they're out." The car accident responsible for the limp had brought home to her, she said, the possibility that she might die with the poems unpublished and made her confront her misgivings about writing poetry at all, especially in English, in a more pragmatic light. "Who cares? I do these things to myself, suffering about language and so on. Nobody really just cares."

Written over a period of fifteen years dating back to 1966 (the year of the overthrow of Nkrumah), these were the poems "that literally got themselves written in spite of that self-imposed ban." The root of this self-suppression – her anxiety about relevance – was common to many writers in the aftermath of Independence. The book is emblematic of two key moments in African writing: the ferment of idealism and optimism of the immediate post-independence years, when writers saw their role as one of uplifting the nation; and the onset of disillusion that followed the dissipation of that dream in West Africa in a welter of coups and economic hardship. Both moments supported the idea of the writer as spokesperson, whether as praisesinger or critic; an essentially social, committed role encapsulated in the title of Chinua Achebe's 1964 essay, "The Novelist as Teacher" (Achebe, 1975). A more contentious idea that was to bedevil writers and critics alike for two decades was the so-called "language question," the dilemma in which they were caught between acceptance of "The African Writer and the English Language" (Achebe, 1965), and the necessity, through the use of African languages, of *Decolonising the Mind* (Ngũgĩ wa Thiong'o, 1986).

Aidoo's investment in this debate is evident from her comments. To write poetry in Africa in a colonial language, she said, was to produce "a further departure, further gaps, more mileage between you and the community around you" (Interview). As a novelist and a dramatist, even using English, she could make her language accessible; as a poet she was tormented by the mystifications endemic in the form. But there is something other than language and form that may have preyed on her mind. Poetry, said Ama Ata, "is so painful it has a way of bringing out the inner layer of any writer" (Interview). This emotional rawness, combined with the poems' overwhelming focus on intimate relationships, may have created a further barrier in a context where, as Aidoo said of love in her novel, *Changes*, "surely there are more important things to write about?" (epigraph, unnumbered page). The poems, then, offer themselves as markers of a particular kind of rebellion that today has come to be a given in African writing, but then was something like a guilty secret. Now that African women are writing in numbers, we recognise an *aesthetic of the personal* as intrinsic to the way African women have figured themselves into the narrative of national identity. Ama Ata's struggle brings home to us the real price of being a forerunner, of setting out on a journey where the horizon has been set by male writers and politicians whose concerns define the field.

As a result, perhaps, of a perceived need to withhold too great an unmediated access to her inner life, *Someone Talking to Sometime* is remarkable for the ways it evades categorisation and straightforward interpretation. The book itself as a material object contributes to this indeterminacy, from its unattributed cover design of two faces close together but looking away from each other towards the reader; its inclusion of unnumbered pages and poems not listed in the contents; the absence of several pages (32–40 and 57–64) and the repetition of other pages (49–56); to the inclusion of end notes (as in the end of the book) without any indication in the text, so the reader first discovers them belatedly and then has to work to match them to their point of reference. Uncertain whether it was only my copy that was defective I went online to see if another, correct edition had been issued. I found the only edition, the College Press one of 1985, was selling on Amazon for US $121: in other words, it has rarity value but has been read by relatively few people. All of this may be unintentional on the part of the writer, but the cumulative effect of ellipsis, of words left unspoken and meanings left undefined, is enhanced by these errors of presentation. The title *Someone Talking to Sometime* is deliberately ambiguous, and in 1985 I asked Ama Ata about it. I notice that, in my 1985 review in the journal *New African*, I reproduced her response without making anything of it. When I listen now to the interview, I see that she was handing me the key to understanding the collection. "I have a thing about time," she said, "that I can't even begin to explain…All I can say is I've always seen time as a dynamic, concrete principle, with whom it's possible to communicate" (Interview).

Perhaps I needed to grow up and communicate with time myself, before I could appreciate the profundity of these words. When I asked, "And the Someone is you?" she responded, "I imagine. I suppose it's me since I'm doing the talking. Or am I doing the talking? But it's not just me, or me now. It was me then. It's like a story I wrote but now it's finished." What is that story? In the absence of a linear pathway, the reader has to rely on certain recurring features of the collection to provide a map. Time is a constant, as is place (New Orleans, Accra, London, the Rift Valley, Boston, Sahara, Lagos, Louisiana, "between Africa, the West Indies and the US South" (44); the speaking voice is paramount, nearly every poem being addressed to a named individual; the predominant tone is irony, with a range from gently fun-poking to savagely satiric; thematically, the poems deal with loss, death, disillusionment, loneliness, isolation, longing, love, political activism, friendship, change, history, colonialism and independence.

But it is perhaps the formal aspect which conceals and reveals the most. Poetic elements are a feature of Aidoo's prose works, to the extent that (as I noted in a previous article) "her narrative mode has been described in Ewe…by Victor Odamtten…as a *fefewo aloo nutinyawo kple eme nyakpakpawo*: a collection of prose-poetry narrative performances and a meditation for the reader's contemplation" (Odamtten, 160). She herself has likened her technique to the use of "interspersed song" within an oral epic recitation (Bryce, 1999). The poems, in a free-form verse of varying line-lengths and groupings of lines, give a similar impression of "interspersed song" within a larger dialogue and take the form of conversation, lyric, riddle and lament. While being firmly grounded in a specific material reality, they are marked by indeterminacy, obliqueness, gaps and absences, refrain and repetition, doubling, paradox and ellipsis, all devices which shadow and privilege the human voice. They approximate, in other words, as nearly as possible the allusiveness and immediacy of orality. The use of Akan, though limited to a few phrases or an occasional couple of lines, alerts us to the imaginary which underpins the poetry and takes on a special significance within the collection.

The dedication (on an unnumbered page), "For some of the ancestors," exemplifies this. Four ancestors are invoked in English: her father, maternal and paternal grandfathers and grandmother, after which a poetic invocation in Akan calls on them "…for life/for strength/for peace of mind and/the courage with which /to fight/to redeem, keep and maintain/our land and her/people." This dedication/invocation pays obeisance to traditional performance, but is more than an honouring of forebears: it solicits their help with a specific task, that of "redeeming, keeping and maintaining." Although no indication is given of the reason underlying it, the subsequent poems make clear that the greatest need is for redemption. The dedication is metonymic of the work that will follow, which reiterates the importance of connection and history in the face of loss and displacement. It initiates a conversation, the dialogue of *Someone Talking to Sometime*, and gives us a clue as to how the materiality of the past may be accessed through certain ritual uses of language. Lisa McNee sheds further light on this phenomenon in her discussion of Cameroonian writer Werewere Liking's dedication to *Love-across-a-hundred-lives*, "to her 'grandmother-daughter, my double,' her 'grandfather-son-husband/This swatch of our entrails/This endless journey of twists and turns/Only to meet again always/Always Siamese and twins/Mirrors and reflections of love'" (McNee, 2009: 113). Liking, like Aidoo, is both a dramatist and a novelist whose work explores how to convey an oral aesthetic in a literary form. McNee borrows the idea of "a translation without an original" (109) to denote the act of "intersemiotic translation or transmutation" (114) undertaken, not only by her, but, she argues, by all African writers whose imaginary involves a cultural world which they must somehow access in a foreign or second language. We can see Aidoo's poetry, then, as a response to "a loss of bridges to the past, a loss of conversations with ancestors," a way of remembering and reconnecting with both (115).

The emphasis in Liking's dedication to the double and the twin is striking in the light of a poem more-or-less halfway through Aidoo's collection: "Wondering about him who said no to the glare of the open day" (*STTS*, 68), and dedicated to her still-born twin brother. Twins, or a twin-like relationship, are a predominant trope in much past and recent African writing, such as novels by Nigerians Sefi Atta, Helon Habila and Chimamanda Ngozi Adichie.[2] A similar trope figuring in Nigerian writing from Soyinka, Okigbo and Clark to Okri is the negative one of *abiku*, the child who comes and goes between the human and the spirit world. In Yoruba culture, the need to placate a dead twin so as to free the living one is met by the use of *ibeji*, twin statues. For the Igbo, *abiku* or *ogbanje* "refers to the mystical, unsettled condition of simultaneously existing in several spheres" (Ogunyemi, 62). It can be individualised and internalised, as in the case of Dambudzo Marechera, who claims for himself the role of the "doppelganger" who terrorises African literature with his difference (Marechera, 3). In all these cases, the spirit double is a familiar one who may play a negative or a positive role in society or the life of the individual. For Aidoo, the dead twin is a potent personal symbol of the synchronicity of death and life; through him, she is in permanent contact with the spirit world and talks directly to it:

> My Brother
> since it's
> me is doing
> the seeing,

I shall tell you of
the glorious things
up here...(70)

Her report to her dead brother includes such items as "cedis that fly," dreams that disappear and:

... friendships that last
Forever and
Divorces whispering in the wind. (71)

The ironic tone of the poem is compounded by the paradoxical play that deliberately confuses positive and negative, past and present, life and death, as in:

They still
Marry us in our
Shrouds, and
Bury us in the fineries
Of the wedding day. (71)

Other lines express anguish and intense emotion which give the lie to ironic distance. At the start of her meditation on her brother's death, Aidoo reflects on her mother's resignation in the face of loss and asks, "so who am I to scream?" Yet, she goes on: "...I/Do rant and rave/howl at hell and heaven too" for the fact that once a woman had to bear four to keep two, and now "they/order and/plan/you/for only/one or/none" (69). As the poem progresses, the list of items becomes more and more sombre – "cold hearts/envying minds/ugly tongues/and cruel hands.../Aching groins," concluding:

...where they say
Lie
All other
Million tales
For the telling of
Which even
That eternity
Shall not give me
Time enough.

No,
Not time enough. (72)

This poem can stand as an exemplar of Aidoo's poetic technique throughout the collection: the persona is that of tale-teller, the one who enshrines experience in language; an individual is either directly addressed ("Sissie," 18; "Omafumi," 9; "My dear," 51) or implied through the dedication ("For Kinna," 19; "for Steve Hymer," 28; "for Kojo," 31; "for Violet," 44; "an apology to Patricia," 41); strong, at times shocking, feelings are expressed, but the emotional tone is held in check by irony, and this in turn unsettles the reader by creating ambivalence about the correct way of reading, the appropriate response.

The first section, "Of Love and Commitment," opens with "Crisis," an unlisted poem on an unnumbered page (facing 9), which is so allusive and ambiguous as to be almost impossible to decode. The poem is structured around a series of questions, three in all, which begin by asking whether faith — "Counting cowries/clutching crosses" – can afford any comfort for "private sorrows and/public despair?" The second question is framed as an interrogative answer: the only solace seems to be to "hug my grief for warmth," wishing that some remembered happiness could "last through a lean/season or two?" But memory brings only "the sound of tragedy knocking." Faith and memory having failed, she asks finally:

> Shall I know
> Joy,
> When it comes again
> The next time around?

The lines speak clearly of emotional exhaustion and emptiness, but give no clue as to the cause, except perhaps the line "a solitary sleeper's pillow." As the tone-setting poem for a section on love and commitment, "Crisis," warns us of betrayal, disillusion and heart-sickness. Ama Ata told me in 1985 of a young woman in the audience at some of her readings, who came to her to ask why she never read this poem aloud. She said she couldn't read it: it had been written eight years earlier but was still too painful (Interview). Eight years earlier would have been 1977, a date which is explicitly mentioned three times in a collection in which, being centrally concerned with time, dates can be assumed to be of some importance. In "Greetings from London," for example, the persona asks:

> Sissie
>
> Do you remember when
> Grandfather severed a.leg in
> 1867
> Climbing palm trees so

The machines in
Manchester
Would not die for lack of
Oil? (18)

Meanwhile, these lines from "For Steve Hymer – a propos 1966" (28) may
denote a lament for a dead comrade:

...if we still grieve
For you and Roger and
Us – the so-called living –
It's only because
Death visits us in more ways
Than one
Stephen. (30)

Or, given that February 24, 1966 was the date Nkrumah was overthrown, it may
denote the death of a dream for Ghana and the continent to which she (aged
twenty-four in 1966) and many others subscribed. In "Greetings from London,"
she describes herself (is it she? Since she's doing the talking?):

Meanwhile
I hold a sherry in my hand
Eating shit for a shilling
Which is not there. (19)

Between 1867 and 1966, nothing much appears to have changed as far as the
situation of the ordinary Ghanaian is concerned (as Aidoo notes in the title of
her short story, "For Whom Things Did Not Change"). So, then, 1977? The
year began on January 13 with a wave of popular resistance to political corruption in Ghana, which was met with violent suppression by the then military
ruler General Ignatius Kutu Acheampong, of which there are many echoes in
these pages. The final section, titled "Someone Really Talking to Sometime
This Time" (so they weren't before?), begins with a poem titled simply "1977."
It begins with an epigraph in Akan, translated in a note as:

Don't you know
this
is the way of the world?
Someone cried
that year
you
laughed.

Nor shall
we stay
where
we are today.

That
wont be
life. (120)

Interestingly, these lines, attributed to Aba Abasema, refer to "Someone," an anonymous interlocutor whose role is similar to that adopted by Aidoo in the collection. Aba Abasema is, in fact, the name of her mother – the same mother who refused to weep at her twin baby's death in the earlier poem. Akan, therefore, as in the dedication to the ancestors, acts as a sign of a particular world-view: that of the oral culture in which Ama Ata grew up and of which the outspoken grandmother in *Changes* is a representative. We hear this admonitory voice continually in Aidoo's work, offering wisdom which Ama Ata herself, educated and westernised, can no longer live by, as expressed by the ironically impatient retort:

Please Nana,
Don't ask
Me
What the world is coming to. (103)

The mother and grandmother inhabit a universe whose horizon is known and their wisdom is appropriate to it; Aidoo's meanwhile is characterised by the painful condition of change and flux. Aba Abasema's words earlier remind the daughter that life itself is change; yet the change brought about in late twentieth-century Africa by rapid urbanisation, political instability and new expectations based on Western education was hitherto unsuspected, for which Aidoo's generation had to devise their own rules of behaviour. In the novels, *Our Sister Killjoy* and *Changes*, Ama Ata dramatises the effects of change in the lives of her female characters, Sissie and Esi. In the poems, we are given access – though mediated and partial – to its effects on herself.

Of 1977, the poet declares, "You must be my/Year of the Dragon!" (97); it is also "the/blasted mouth/of a/bloody time" (99). The poem that follows, Of 'Maami Aba Okese:' born 1977, died 1977' (99footnote), reinforces the theme of death-in-life that pervades the collection and recalls the still-born twin. We do not know whether the poem is personal, in the sense that the lost child might be her own; what we know is that it provides another occasion for her to "rant and rave/Howl at hell and heaven too" (69). Again, faith fails to comfort:

> Saints complain and
> Martyrs whine
> As
> Minutes drop like the
> Bullets of a million
> Iron
> Molecules on
> My mind.

Here, time is a physical manifestation with the power to wound, as though time itself were the cause of the grief she feels:

> These are times to seal in
> Vaults –
> To be opened a
> Billion years after
> The last of
> My seed are
> Dead and
> Gone. (100)

The poem above is close to the end of the collection. Yet the poem which gives its title to the opening section, "Of Love and Commitment," dedicated "for Omafumi," is similarly preoccupied with time. Ostensibly a love poem, it is both the story of a relationship and a meditation on the loss of love, a lament for a time of hope filled with activism, meetings and protests and a personal lament for the way love was obliterated by those very activities. The title can be taken as gesturing towards both intimate and public or social, meanings of its terms – love and commitment. It begins with the trademark question: "How did I know?" and proceeds, with a characteristic mixture of self-deprecating irony and fierce emotion, to detail the beginning, middle and end of the affair:

> I knew because all of a sudden, I started doing
> Things I had never done before,
> Things I never knew I could do,
> Things I always knew I should never do. (9)

The persona, fully aware of the unequal gender politics of the revolutionary time – of which the names Malcolm and Stokely are signs – nonetheless sees herself performing the feminine role in relation to this man, and celebrating it:

The room was unlived-in,
The tap had not run for months,
The saucepans uncooked-in,
The guitar – unplayed.
And I
Who had never
Been able to look after
Myself,
Knew
I could
Look after
You. (10–11)

All too soon – in a way, simultaneously – the relationship comes to an end. The three end-stopped lines... :

The packing took a long time.
Or the talking did.
The night was long and very short. (12)

...occur twice, heightening the sense of time foreshortening towards its end, even while it stretches to infinity. In a now-familiar paradox, she tells us:

It was so long
We wrote
A poem
A short story
Three long plays
A novel
Finished our formal studies
Saw the kids through school
Solved
Other personal problems
Frustrated
Neo-colonial scholarship
And made the revolution. (13)

Simultaneously:

There was not time
Enough
To see
What was in one another's eyes. (13)

Now the poem, which has hitherto been conversational and open-ended, relying on the cumulative story-telling effect of the short broken-up lines, takes another turn. As if stepping across an invisible line – between different kinds of discourse, perhaps, or from the everyday world of events to the ritual world of heightened symbolic meaning – the last three stanzas abruptly immerse us in an impassioned lyrical invocation freighted with love and longing. The sound of thunder, the flash of lightning, prompt the anxious enquiry:

> Is my love's window open?
> Is my love's door ajar?
> Perhaps the rain gets into his room?
> Perhaps the wind blows out his clothes? (13)

The concatenated questions, whose anxiety is reminiscent of the line: "What are you thinking of? What thinking? What?" in Eliot's *The Wasteland*, denote a departure which has already taken place, leaving the room empty and uncared for. Abruptly, she leaves her hair unbraided to...

> Hurry to my loves room
> I must hurry to shut his window
> I must hurry to my true-loves room
> Before the rain gets in, sister,
> Before the rain gets in. (13)

A similarly estranged moment occurs a page or so earlier, when, in an apparently unconnected reference, we are told "Kwame Atta should not have died" (12). Kwame Atta being the male-name counterpart of Ama Ata, designating in each case a child born on a Saturday, may well signify the lost twin, as suggested by the following revelatory utterance:

> For where shall I carry
> A double soul
> Doubly restless
> And an incestuous desire for
> My brothers? (12)

These lines unsettle the love-story, returning us to the lament for her brother, the lost double. "Incestuous desire" refers, perhaps ironically, to the revolutionary "brotherhood," and its occluded sexual relationships, the absence of a space for femininity within it except as the weaker adjunct, "sister." Yet it may also be read as desire for the real brother, and for a male alter-ego. Either way, it viscerally expresses the conundrum of the human desire for completion in another and the way it can never be fulfilled.

Yet, said Ama Ata in 1985, "I can't despair. Not to be hopeful of tomorrow is a luxury I can't afford." Then she immediately qualified this: "Maybe I'm not such an optimist as I would want people to believe and as I take such great pains to let other people believe" (Interview). Certainly, one looks in vain in this collection for any unambiguous affirmation, even in the concluding poem, "Tomorrow's Song," with its potentially joyful title. The title of the penultimate poem, "Woaeenn 1" (109), is glossed in the notes as meaning "clear, crystal clear or wide-eyed clarity" (120), and this succinctly expresses the perspective adopted in the poems. The tone in the closing pages is no less clear-eyed, and there is no softening in the view of a society populated by figures such as "torturer on a monthly salary" and "the ardent revolutionary-fascist" (113). There ensues a three-way conversation between "she," "he" and "the Child," in which the Child exonerates the father of blame for his absence from her life with the words:

> In the end
> You would only have given the best you had
> Or
> Thought you had:
> A few rags from the past
> Some solid present pain...(116)

The only vision offered by the Child's voice, the voice of the future, is that, "We have to/nurse our flickering hopes/through this damp night" (117). Then, just as we think nothing more is to be expected, comes another of Aidoo's unexpected turns. In words scattered almost at random around the page, syntax broken, dissolving finally into ellipsis, "Who knows," she asks:

> ...but in some thicket where time has counted itself out
> some unsane souls are searching for the
> roots
>                    which
> shall drag
> out
> the sneeze
>
> that... (117)

To paraphrase this elusive musing: somewhere at the end of time, or at least the hostile present time, in some liminal space (thicket), someone, against all rational expectation, may yet be seeking a cure (root) to the sickness (sneeze) afflicting us. The outcome, predictably, is left unarticulated: "that..." trails away into unspokenness, as though even to think the possibility of an alternative were too heavy for utterance. Yet this passage, like the occasional lines in Akan, may be read through the tropes of tradition which punctuate the poetry as traces of a former time. The recurring trope of death-in-life is closely related to the ancestors and to the spirits of those who have passed over. It reminds us, however bleakly, that though death is always present, through the ancestors we are perpetually connected to the world beyond the material present and that there is always the possibility of another reality than the one we inhabit. The Akan words and passages are signs of that other world, in which living and dead permanently co-exist. The lines…:

> Na merepaa wo
> Na maye den? (25)

…are glossed as "What shall I do if I cursed you, since my fate is intertwined with yours?" (118). And so there she was in Zimbabwe because, "Any African country that tries to do something, I am for." And then she added, "Until I'm disappointed again" (Interview).

In focusing on the significance of time and illustrating it by examples from a handful of poems, I have inevitably left out other aesthetic and political concerns with which the collection engages. The density and contradictory impulses of these poems suggest complex meanings which demand close atten-tion, while the intricate mesh of image and form of which they are woven means that they act as signposts to the rest of the collection. What I have tried to convey is the extraordinarily detailed, yet deliberately ambiguous way its author, a major literary voice best-known for her plays and novels, uses poetry as the outlet for thoughts and feelings she could express in no other way at this particular period in her life. Seeking the autobiographical in literature is both unfashionable and of questionable value. I have attempted rather to provide a context that enables us to decipher the personal story too often submerged by the political metanarrative. This personal story allows us to take the measure of the human price of postcolonial political upheaval in Africa. The writing of African lives has to date been mostly a fictional process; *Someone Talking to Sometime* offers us, in coded form, a writer's inner self. If you haven't had a chance to read it, it's a bargain at $121 on Amazon.

# "Tribal Scars" on the Body of "The Girl Who Can:" The Imperative of African Social and Cultural Self-Redemption in the Short Stories of Aidoo and Sembène[1]

## Anne V. Adams

It is obvious why both Ama Ata Aidoo and Ousmane Sembène are legitimately labelled as feminist artists. They both, in nearly equal measure, feature women as protagonists or otherwise crucial figures in their works. And, in their treatment of gender matters both invest the female characters with the same compelling subjectivity and agency as their males. Similarly, Sembène and Aidoo are both recognised as radical writers, uncompromisingly challenging traditions and inherited attitudes by exposing them to public scrutiny, for the purpose of reforming some, abolishing others. Indeed, their names are not infrequently associated together in critical discussions of constructively irreverent African writers on social and cultural issues. Yet, at the end of the day, one of these two is generically categorised – and praised – as a radical artist, "...a virulent critic of colonialism and especially, postcolonialism, and of some entrenched traditional attitudes and behaviour of [African] culture,"[2] while the other, to the writer's critical disadvantage, is generically categorised – and praised – as a writer about "women's issues."

However, self-acknowledged feminist and generally acknowledged standard-bearer of African feminist writing that she is, Ama Ata Aidoo insists that the reader (or critic) misses the point in construing her work as being circumscribed by gender:

> Whatever gender, whatever nationality we belong to, we must also resist any attempts at being persuaded to think that the woman question has to be superseded by the struggle against any

local exploitative system, the nationalist struggle, or the struggle against imperialism and global monopoly capital. For what is becoming clear is that in the long run, none of these fronts is either of greater relevance than the rest or even separate from them. (quoted in Odamtten, 81)

Regardless of how they are perceived, Aidoo and Sembène are best known for their larger works: Aidoo for her novels and plays; Sembène for his novels and films. To be sure, those works have been and continue to be the subjects of comparative studies with many others in those genres by other writers, African and non-African. However, as this essay will demonstrate, it is the genre of the short story that provides the best terrain for reading Aidoo and Sembène in tandem, enhancing, through the engagement, the appreciation of each of them as radical exponents of African writing. As representative products of the short story genre, Aidoo's and Sembène's short stories are exemplars of the genre:

It does not claim to shape the whole of social reality, nor even to depict that whole as it appears from the vantage point of a funda-mental and topical problem. Its truth rests on the fact that an individual situation – usually an extreme one – [that] is possible in a certain society at a certain level of development, and, just because it is possible, is characteristic of this society and this level. (Lucas quoted in Balogun: 6)

Ousmane Sembène's collection *Voltaïque* (1962; translated as *Tribal Scars* 1974) and Ama Ata Aidoo's two collections, *No Sweetness Here* (1972) and *The Girl Who Can and Other Stories* (2002), focus precisely on everyday-life situations in which some force or another will inevitably push a character to the extremity of choices. Through their respective treatment of "the struggle against any local exploitative system, the nationalist struggle" and "the woman question" both writers exercise "virulent criti[que] of colonialism and, especially, postcolonialism, and of some entrenched traditional attitudes and behaviour of Senegalese [or Ghanaian] culture."

As the scant mention in F. Odun Balogun's *Tradition and Modernity in the African Short Story: An Introduction to a Literature in Search of Critics* (1991) attests, Ousmane Sembène's short stories have received virtually no critical attention in English (and little that I could find in French). As an integral work the volume *Tribal Scars* is virtually invisible in critical studies of Sembène's fiction. Occasionally, one of the stories appears in an anthology, or an individual story is mentioned in the context of a particular topic in African fiction. Even Balogun's compre-hensive inventory of published volumes and individual short stories by African writers makes only the briefest reference to "The False Prophet." Nevertheless, he does list Sembène among the "great masters" of the genre (a list which also includes the likes of Tolstoy, Achebe, Hemingway and La Guma). By contrast, Aidoo is not ranked by Balogun among the "great masters,"[3] but her stories are cited, curiously enough, with the highest frequency of any writers in his study (with the exception of the two writers whose work he treats in-depth, Achebe and Taban lo Liyong). More importantly, Aidoo's short stories, at least those from No Sweetness Here, have received substantial critical attention from the field.

The focus of this essay is the common quality in the short stories of Aidoo and Sembène that justifies reading them together as radical authors, i.e. their "virulent criti[que] of … entrenched traditional attitudes and behaviour of Senegalese [or Ghanaian] culture," which often are the object of "the struggle against … local exploitative system[s] and which, for these two writers, have particular valence for 'the woman question'." A productive matrix for a comparison is provided in Sembène's allegorical title story "Tribal Scars." A group of fraternising Dakar buddies has been engaging, for several weeks, in intense discussions of the mystery behind the origin of scarification among some African ethnic groups. The explanation that is finally uncovered is presented, by one of their members respected as the most knowledgeable, as a piece of national mythology. He recounts a tale from the era of the slave trade, pointing out that a premium was placed on unblemished captive bodies. A boatload of captives, due for immediate deportation, was set free by the African slave hunter, who not only killed off the European ship's crew but also re-captured the liberated captives, to sell them himself to the next team of Europeans to come. One proud and resourceful captive, Amoo, escaped with his nine-year-old daughter Iome and fled back to their village. But in due time the slave hunters reached this village, causing the few remaining desperate villagers to flee. Amoo, who had already killed his beautiful wife to keep her from being enslaved, took his knife and inflicted multiple cuts on the wailing Iome, saying to her: "This is going to hurt, but you'll never be a slave," then left the child to the care of his old, crippled mother-in-law, shortly before he himself was captured. The story ends as follows:

> The news spread for leagues around. People came from the remotest villages to consult the grandmother. And over the years and the centuries a diversity of scars appeared on the bodies of our ancestors.
>     And that is how our ancestors came to have tribal scars. They refused to be slaves. (TS, 116)

Because of its putative mythological origin, the story "Tribal Scars," the last one in Sembène's collection and from which the volume takes its title, is unique in the collection, which consists otherwise of narratives of contemporary realism (including one animal allegory of colonial relations). However, as S.K. Boafo suggests, a thread that is woven into all of the stories is the essential fabric of this myth: "[I]t is the critique of African society, a critique in which *the author assigns to Africans themselves a major part of the responsibility for their fate*, for the vices and faults to be found in Africa. And this is what gives the last story its representative value" (12, emphasis added).[4] The myth demonstrates that, even after throwing off the yoke of European enslavers, a handful of treacherous Africans have exploited the situation to re-enslave their own people. The slave hunter, Momutu, trying to recruit Amoo to his team, explains calculatingly:

> "This is our work," Momutu went on. "We scout the grasslands, take prisoners and sell them to the whites. Some captains know me, but I entice others to this bay and some of my men lure the crew off the ship. Then we loot the ship and get the prisoners back again. We kill any whites left on board. It's easy work and we win all round." (*TS*, 107)

The narrator tells us, however, that Amoo, who was familiar with and repulsed by the likes of the treacherous Momutu, "was not made in their evil mould" (*TS*, 108).

Sembène's critique that places the responsibility for their own fate on the shoulders of Africans – the imperative for them to redeem their own integrity – characterises precisely a high proportion of Ama Ata Aidoo's stories, as well. As is the case in Sembène's other stories, the enslaving "Momutus" of contemporary Senegal or Ghana come in diverse forms: individuals, institutions, or beliefs, attitudes, and practices. Thus, Aidoo stories like "The Girl Who Can" illuminate such "entrenched traditional attitudes and behaviour," which have the effect of a form of social or cultural oppression, if not enslavement. Seven-year-old Adjoa, the first-person narrator of "The Girl Who Can," is a bright child with sharp insights, who, however, is demoralized by never being taken seriously by adults. Adjoa has, from her earliest conscious memory, internalized the "problem," harped upon by her beloved grandmother, that the little girl's physique fails to meet the standard for a woman's body. And what is Adjoa's near-deformity that the grandmother constantly evokes? It is her long, thin legs that are supposedly not fit to support hips to carry babies, as a woman must do. (Ironically, though, this "deficiency" works to gain Nana's agreement that the girl might as well continue with her schooling, since, with such a body so ill-equipped for maternity, she's not much good for marriage.) However, pupil Adjoa excels at track and field, ultimately convincing Nana that, "'saa'[5], thin legs can also be useful ... thin legs can also be useful ... That 'even though some legs don't have much meat on them, to carry hips ... they can run. Thin legs can run ... then who knows? ..."(*GWC* 32–33). The concluding question in Nana's expression of amazed enlightenment, "then who knows? ..." makes clear that a moment of socio-cultural revelation/revolution of a sort has happened as a result of this "problem" with her grandchild. But, to seven-year-old Adjoa: [T]hat's how I was feeling and thinking all along. That surely, one should be able to do other things with legs as well as have them because they can support hips that make babies. Except that I was afraid of saying that sort of thing aloud. ...It's much better this way. To have acted it out to show them, although I could not have planned it." (GWC, 33). What Adjoa has been thinking and feeling all along, and what is dawning on her grandmother when she wonders "Who knows...?" is, Who knows what other possibilities there are for girls' bodies (and, by extension, for girls' whole selves) if the bindings of gender-role determinism were to be removed? Aidoo is laying the responsibility for undoing such entrenched cultural attitudes on the shoulders of the Nanas and her generation, inspired by the achievements of the Adjoas, who otherwise have no voice.[6]

To be sure, the spindly-legs issue is a relatively inconsequential instance of entrenched gender-role determinism, with its concomitant physical valuation standards; nor is it really presented as a matter of major socio-cultural import (after all, spindly-legged women do carry pregnancies). But this story is one which serves Aidoo's purpose of exposing entrenched attitudes as forms of culturally inflicted limitations that must be eliminated through confronting the harmful attitude or practice followed by the necessary action to uproot it.

Sembène inscribes, with "tribal scars" on little Iome, the imperative of painful, radical action necessary to rescue her from enslavement. Such "tribal scars," in less violent but no less urgent presentation, can be figuratively transferred to the body of little Adjoa, Aidoo's "girl who can," in her anguish from the psychological fetters of being denied a voice and the constant jabs from her grandmother about her physical "inadequacy." Adjoa's "act[ing] it out to show them" the retrogressive effects of the restrictive attitudes about a girl's body results in a form of liberation experience for Nana and for herself, potentially yielding new gender conceptions.

But if Adjoa's tribulations and small triumph are just a mild form of "tribal scars" in Aidoo's work, other stories present stronger cases. In fact, the futuristic tale "She-Who-Would-Be-King," from The Girl Who Can collection, can be posited as a fitting partner-complement to Sembene's historical legend "Tribal Scars." The title, "She-Who-Would-Be-King" suggests, appropriately, a girl-child, of approximately the same age as Iome and Adjoa, who ignores the normal parameters of aspirations for a girl, breaking barriers where necessary. The protagonist ("whose story this should have been" [GWC, 56] ) of this futuristic tale, which spans the half-century between the mid-1970s and the 2020s, declares, at age ten, that she wants to be president of her country. Responding to the expected reaction, "I don't think the men of this country will ever let a woman be their President," she retorts, "No? We shall see" (GWC, 55foot).

Aidoo deploys this futuristic mode to rehearse every imaginable crisis for the continent in the time-span covered: "Man-made but accidental, man-made and deliberate, home-grown, imported, natural... Name it. If it was a calamity, Africa suffered it" (*GWC*, 58). Those calamities included an AIDS epidemic, "The Drought," the "Great Plot to wipe us off the surface of the earth," and rains that caused all the major rivers – Nile, Niger, Congo, Zambezi – to overflow their banks. "[T]hose fifty [years] were something special" (*GWC*, 58f). Now, in 2026 the ambitious little girl is Professor Adjoa Moji, Professor and Dean of the Law Faculty of the university in the capital city of what is now the Confederation of African States, which has united the individual countries.[7] But she, "whose story this should have been" (*GWC*, 56), is not president. Rather it is her 36-year-old daughter Afi Yaa, who, on 25th May, 2026, has been elected First President of Africa. So, even though it took an additional generation for the little girl's aspiration to be realised, the bold, self-assertive attitude of Adjoa Moji obviously set the example and the stage for her daughter's achievements. With the symbolism, in Pan African history, of the specific date[8] of the election, Aidoo links the progressive political evolution towards a united Africa to the progressive social evolution of equality of opportunity effected through the eradication of gender-role barriers.

As a partner-complement to Sembène's "Tribal Scars," Aidoo's "She-Who-Would-Be-King" might be viewed as the other end of the historical continuum. Sembène gives us a slavery-era narrative, in which a girl-child, enduring a violent physical inscribing of her African culture is the progenitrix of an Africa rescued from foreign and domestic bondage. Aidoo's Afi Yaa is the daughter who has overcome the gender bondage of her African heritage to become the leader of an Africa finally united after assaults to its integrity from every quarter: from God, from foreigners, and from fellow Africans. Further, both stories are consciously Pan African in their scope. Aidoo's adaptation of Nkrumah's vision of a Confederation of African States, complete with capital city, is the ultimate in continental Pan Africanist political aspirations. On the other hand the complementary Pan Africanist perspective that extends beyond the continent to embrace the Diaspora is reflected in Sembène's story. The discussion among the fellows sitting around their pot of Moorish mint tea includes Africans who ended up in the Diaspora. In their inquiry into the mystery behind the tribal scars they pursue many possible theories, some of which lead them to the fact of the absence of the phenomenon in the Diaspora:

> Someone else said: 'I went to IFAN[9] and hunted around in books, but found nothing. However, I learned that the wives of the gentlemen in high places are having these marks removed from their faces; they go to Europe to consult beauticians. For the new rules for African beauty disdain the old standards of the country;

the women are becoming Americanised. It's the spreading influence of the [Sapphires][10] of Fifth Avenue, New York. And as the
trend develops, tribal scars lose their meaning and importance and
are bound to disappear.'

... If these tribal scars were signs of nobility, or of high or low
caste, why aren't they ever seen in the Americas?

Now, none of the authoritative writers on slavery and the slave
trade has ever mentioned tribal scars, so far as I know. In South
America, where fetishism and witchcraft as practiced by slaves still
survive to this day, no tribal scars have ever been seen. Neither do
Negroes living in the Caribbean have them, nor in Haiti, Cuba,
the Dominican Republic nor anywhere else. (*TS*, 103)

A comparative analysis of "Tribal Scars" and "She-Who-Would-Be-King" on the
basis of the details examined here justifies our viewing them as two points on a
historical continuum, the slavery era from Sembène and the mid-21st-century
from Aidoo; and as geographically complementary Pan African spaces.

In all three of the short-story anthologies of these two writers there are a few
stories that play out the full "Voltaïque" metaphor of social or cultural self-
redemption more dramatically than others. Those stories stand out particularly
for the valiant confrontation or revolt against "exploitative systems" that are
upheld through "entrenched attitudes and behaviours."

Aidoo's story "Two Sisters" adroitly links the issue of young women's willing
sexual involvement with "big men" for material gain, to the historical event, less
than a decade after independence, of the 1966 *coup d'état* that removed
Nkrumah's government. In this case a young, low-paid secretary enters a relationship with a 50-something, married, playboy government minister, for the
shoes, handbags, and other gifts he gives her. Typical of the profligate corruption among such men in his position, he is also able to set her up in a house
provided by state funds as well as bring valuable gifts to her family from his
travels to Europe. But all this is destroyed when the *coup* sends those politicians
to jail. However, even though Aidoo's focus is on the young woman, the author
(in the background) acknowledges the military overthrow of the government as
an effort to rid the nation of government corruption. Ironically, the loss of her
politico "sugar daddy" doesn't prevent the young woman from finding another
by the end of the story: an officer from the victorious military, i.e. the *new
government*.

Sembène also injects an event of post-independence Senegalese history into
a story of abuse of political power. In "A Matter of Conscience" we see labour
union boss Ibra, who had, during the colonial period, been considered the

"great hope of the working class." However, now, as an elected official, bene-fitting from all the associated material "perks," he betrays the labour union that he once led and which had, after independence, helped him get elected to the National Assembly:

> Then things had changed completely; those who previously slammed the door in his face now welcomed him, and the big bosses were delighted to see him at every reception. He acquired a villa and a car without paying out a penny; and he had a bank account ... He spent his holidays in France. He had an office at the Trades Union Council. (*TS*, 29)

In fact, Ibra completely abdicates his responsibility to the workers. Now, with massive lay-offs imminent, Malic, the shop steward of the railroad workers confronts Ibra with their desperate situation, only to be rebuffed by Ibra's defence of the company bosses and the complicit government. Citing the polit-ical disruption caused by the recent breakdown of the Mali Federation, disengaging Senegal from Mali, a now authoritarian Ibra uses this situation as the excuse for being too busy to attend to the workers' concerns and as the justification for the railroad company's laying off of workers. In a climactic confrontation with Ibra, who is now backed by the Labour Minister and the company director, Malic is accused of subversion and threatened with impris-onment; the other workers get pacified with a promise from the Minister. Sembène's most poignant moment of this story comes, however, *after* the confrontation. It is a moment that articulates the message of the Voltaïque, even though Malic's attempted revolt fails: It is the confession to Malic by their spokesman, the oldest factory worker. "You were quite right just now, Malic." "But you see, you must see, we hadn't the courage to back you up. Yes, it was courage that was lacking. Those types have nothing in common with us! They're black outside – but inside they're just like the colonialists."(*TS*, 33)[11] The Senegalese politicians and factory bosses have replaced the slave-hunters who had taken over the business from the Europeans.

While the struggle and revolt depicted in the two previous stories are played out at the level of national politics, the fights in the two following stories are on the domestic level of the marriage relationship. In both stories, the wife braves the family and community scandal of seeking a divorce and, in both cases, with the custody of her child at the centre of the matter. In the title story of Aidoo's first volume, "No Sweetness Here" Maami Ama, after years of mari-tal oppression and unhappiness, makes the bold decision to seek a divorce from the "selfish and bullying man, whom no decent woman ought to have married" (*NSH*, 74) and from his family, even risking the loss, through customary law, of custody of her beautiful son, the sunshine of her life. But not willing to surrender her child without a fight, she is prepared to endure the custody battle, if necessary. When asked by her young schoolteacher friend, who, by virtue of her Western education is ignorant of the customary law: "And would you succeed in keeping him if his father insisted?" Maami Ama answers: "Well, I would struggle, for my son is his father's child but he belongs to my family." Even though Maami Ama loses the custody battle, a cruelly ironic turn of fate results in the death of the child from a snake-bite, thus "depriving" even the father's family of their (literal and figurative) "prize." As for Maami Ama, she has carried out her act of revolt against both the oppressive marriage and the customary law which awards the child to his father.

Sembène's story of a beleaguered wife's revolt against an unfulfilling marriage and an oppressive customary legal system is "The Bilal's Fourth Wife." The tyrannical, lecherous holy man Suliman chooses a young fourth wife, Yacine, who was known to be "not like the other girls .... And what a tongue she had! ... a tomboy, a hard worker and joined in the young men's games and competitions, challenging them." (TS, 11). Her father eagerly gives her to the old man in marriage because of the two bulls he gave her family. However, when, after a short time and siring one baby, the aged Suliman's sexual performance proves woefully inadequate for the young wife, Yacine not only takes a younger lover, Suliman's own nephew, and bears his child, but, out of total absence of any benefit from the marriage, she eventually leaves the old man to return to her parents' home. Although Suliman would like to divorce Yacine for leaving him, he hesitates, reluctant to lose the dowry from her family. Yacine, on the other hand, knows that if she pursued a divorce on grounds that, "he [wasn't] a man anymore" or, as she states it in the divorce proceedings, "He was my husband, but later he was no longer capable of being my husband" – she would have to give back everything her husband had given her. Of greater importance, though, is custody of her second child, whose father's identity, i.e. Yacine's young lover, is public knowledge in the community. Exploiting this fact, the feisty young wife makes her case before the court with the logic of taking a lover upon the husband's failure to execute his duty. She wins custody over the contested child in the divorce (making the case also for the salience of maternity over paternity). In the final analysis the comparison of these two stories of wives who revolt against exploitative customary systems that are supported by entrenched cultural behaviours in marriage yields, for Sembène's protagonist Yacine, a true social victory that could revolutionise civil law, while Aidoo's character Maami Ama ultimately is not even accorded a bittersweet resolution; nothing changes. For her there can be "no sweetness here."

One further pair of stories from these authors provides cases of personal revolt against entrenched cultural behaviours, which result in a form of catharsis for the individuals' identity group. In Sembène's "Her Three Days" we have again a Muslim polygamous marriage. The feeling of always having to "win" her husband Mustapha's attention for her allotted three conjugal days compels Noumbe to deprive her children, who must wait until their father has eaten before and if they are to get meat to eat; it compels her to jeopardise her health by diluting with wood-ash the medicine she takes for a heart condition rather than buying more, in order to spend the money on things her husband likes to eat; "indeed, hadn't she got herself into debt so that he would be more comfortable and have better meals at her place [than at her co-wives']?" (TS, 45). Noumbe anticipates, prepares, waits, and suffers emotionally and physically, while her husband disregards any and all obligation to give her the attention prescribed by custom. But ultimately the mentally abused and physically deprived Noumbe finds a way to strike back at her negligent husband and make him feel her resentment. When he does finally drop in on the evening of her third day, accompanied by three friends, the offended wife mocks him. Not only does she speak to him with sarcastic (ir)reverence, but she emphasises it with calculated, violent, though petty, action. The husband, seeing three plates of food in different stages of decay on the table, says, with annoyance:

> "And just what are these three plates for?"
> "These three plates? She looked at him, a malicious smile on her lips. "Nothing. Or rather, my three days. Nothing that would interest you. Is there anything here that interests you ... uncle?"
> ...
> Noumbe deliberately knocked over one of the plates. "Oh, uncle, forgive me ..." Then she broke the other two plates. Her eyes had gone red; suddenly a pain stabbed at her heart, she bent double, and as she fell to the floor gave a loud groan which roused the whole compound (TS, 52).

Throughout this narrative expressions of empathy and support from other women in the compound, who have all experienced similar abusive treatement, punctuate Noumbe's story. Some had lent her a little money to buy things to make her husband's meal. Others had consoled her during her days of unfulfilled waiting. In the afternoon of the third day: "I've come to keep you company," declared Aida as she entered the room… "You mustn't get worked up about it,' went on Aida. "Every woman goes through it. Of course it's not nice! But I don't think he'll be long now" (TS, 50–51). And in the scene with her husband, the women, hearing her moans when she falls to the floor, come running. The story closes as follows: "Aida and some of the women lifted Noumbe on to the bed. She was groaning. They got her to take some of her mixture of ash and water…" Noumbe's plate-smashing revolt, while giving her only a fleeting release of frustration, was nevertheless a blow struck on behalf of her sisters who endure the same polygamous injustice.

In Aidoo's story "Payments" the fishmonger first-person narrator strikes a blow for the sorority of market-women who endure abusive treatment from arrogant middle-class customers. Without question, making a move to strike back at the symbol of the inequities in the socio-economic system is one of the most liberating forms of resistance. In this instance the striking back provides admittedly only psychological, temporary power for the fishmonger-narrator, but it undoubtedly leaves a lasting impression on the recipient of the "blow" and provides vicarious satisfaction for the other market-women who savour the story. Narrating the whole story to her sister fishmongers, she expresses (with characteristic Aidoo mischievousness) her only regret about having spat in the face of an arrogant, *arriviste* customer:

> Yes, I am glad. Even though I know my life is not going to change for the better now just because I spat into the eyes of a whore. What pains me a little is that I had chewed a stick[12] at all in the morning. Because for her type, the best is to splash them all over with something from a mouth that is stale from a whole night's sleeping. But who knows, there may be a next time yet. (*GWC*, 105)

We learn from her narrative that, for one thing, the customer is the wife of one of the despised post-independence corruption profiteers. On a more personal plane, though, the object of her hatred had, in the past, as a nurse in a pediatric ward, treated the narrator very callously and condescendingly, when her baby was a patient. So, the spitting in the customer's face, as a refusal to sell her any fish, is a strike at the disillusioning post-independence corruption, the arrogance and condescension of the so-called elites toward the lower classes, with special attention to the treatment by hospital nurses of lower-class clients (a topic that Aidoo takes up in another story "The Message"). So, the opportunity for aggressive retaliation, even though short-lived, is nevertheless sweet, especially for the fishmonger who recognises that the social and economic inequities that she catalogues simply are a fact of their lives, with no likelihood for redress. So, her act is a memorable strike in the direction of redressing those inequities. As such, her audience of fellow market-women can bask in the bravado of their sister.

The "tribal scars" on the bodies and psyches of these women and men in the stories discussed are the many acts of intrepid resistance to the various "exploitative systems" that are supported by "entrenched traditional attitudes and behaviours.". The system might be the corrupt national government that supports unscrupulous officials; the system might be common-law marriage entrenched in patriarchy; or the system might be the institutionalised maltreatment of the disadvantaged by the "elite." In some cases, even, there is not an actual institutionalised *system* buttressing the "entrenched cultural attitudes and behaviours" – especially behaviours rooted in patriarchal attitudes, such as the gender obstructions facing a would-be African Confederation president, or, even the performance expectations of a girl's physique. An appreciation of this imperative for African social and cultural self-redemption, which connects Sembène and Aidoo through their short stories, enhances our appreciation of these writers' individual force.

# Mfantse Meets English: Interpretations of Ama Ata Aidoo's Multilingual Idiom

## Esi Sutherland-Addy

Ama Ata Aidoo follows in a tradition of writers of Mfantse origin who, as part of their craft and philosophy, have chosen to explore the Mfantse language as it interfaces with the English language in their creative works. These include early 20th century anti-colonial nationalists like Kobina Sekyi and J.E. Casely Hayford as well as post-independence cultural nationalists such as Kwesi Brew and Efua Sutherland. Code-switching between Mfantse and English, for example, has certainly been the source of endless mirth among Ghanaians from all over the country, as it is seen as symbolising the height of the colonial mentality among 'anglomaniacs.' Indeed, for Kobina Sekyi, it represents a disturbing societal malaise, which he parodies mercilessly in his play *The Blinkards*.

All the writers cited above have found it necessary, as part of their craft and their discourse around their works to address the issues of their heritage and particularly their language in the colonial/postcolonial environment in which they work(ed). The question of the medium in which writers from among once-colonised peoples write is not a new one by any means.[1] What this article seeks to do is to undertake an appreciation of the body of texts offered particularly by Kobina Sekyi and Ama Ata Aidoo in which there is a conscious interplay between their mother-tongue, Mfantse, and their second language, English.

Our interest as a mother-tongue speaker of Mfantse ourselves is to engage in a reading of the works which may reveal both elements of the discourse and literary culture of the Mfantse-speaking people, as well as to seek to unearth a semiotic layer that is specific to the interface between Mfantse and English in the writing of Sekyi and Aidoo. In this regard, we shall seek to demonstrate that there is a subtext which resides within this interface which has been deliberately situated there as part of the authors' ideology of writing.

We shall dwell primarily on Ama Ata Aidoo, who, writing decades after Sekyi, goes farther than Sekyi in her craft by embedding an Mfantse idiom and prosody in her writing. She has developed a narrative style and a multi-generic body of work which 'speak' the tensions of her postcolonial subjectivity. This essay explores what happens once Mfantse meets English in the process of literary creation in the hands of a storyteller for whom these two languages cannot be brought together without raising deep historical, social, and political matters.

There would have had to be a significant historical imperative to have made the writers of Mfantse origin mentioned above so focused on the idea of language as the vehicle for both subjugation and liberation. The Mfantse-speaking people, also known more generally as Fantes, have had a long and sustained contact with Europeans since the Portuguese first came to the West Coast of Africa in 1471. Much of the drama of the interaction between Europeans and the peoples of the territory that was to host the first capital of the Gold Coast Colony was played out with the Mfantse-speaking people (Mfantsefo). This was a drama replete with alliances and betrayal, resistance and conquest. This drama was built upon relationships between the indigenous polities and merchants, mercenaries, soldiers, missionaries and government emissaries representing a wide variety of European polities, namely the Portuguese, Dutch, English and French. In their quest for dominance over the resources held in the territories of the *Mfantsefo* (Fantes), massive European-built forts and trading posts dotting the coastline are stark reminders of centuries of trade, including the infamous slave trade and deep incursions into the fabric of the lives of these peoples which mark them to this day.[2]

Formal Western education and conversion to Christianity are adjudged to have complemented trade in preparing the way for eventual colonial subjugation. By the 18th century, trading companies organised for some education to be provided for a few African children, particularly the sons of Europeans. A few of them were sent to Europe and brought back as agents of European interests. By the close of the 19th century, the adoption of Western education as well as military and economic domination is among the significant processes out of which emerged passionate tensions between tendencies of capitulation and defiance among members of Mfantse society who had exposure to Western influences:[3]

> One only needs to look at the family background of Kobina Sekyi to read traces of this history. His maternal grandfather was known as Pietersen, while his uncle was Henry Van Hein, both of them merchants. Sekyi was also a grandson of Chief Kofi Sekyi. There were enough resources in the family to send Sekyi to the University of London, after he had matriculated at the Cape Coast Collegiate School. Clearly Sekyi was set on a path to becoming an "Anglo-African" in a society whose educated members were brought up to believe that all things African were retrograde and were to be despised, and that through

Anglicisation (and Christianisation was the passport to civilisation and progress. (Langley, 1979:17)

In large measure, Onyimdzi ("Mr.Cultured"), the protagonist of *The Blinkards*, is built on the personality of the author himself. Unsurprisingly, Lawyer Onyimdzi finds himself among young ladies at a garden party, who are puzzled at the fact that he is wearing traditional cloth instead of a suit to befit his status. He obliges them with an explanation, making a comprehensive statement which encapsulates Kobina Sekyi's own trajectory. In answer to a question as to whether his education is not English, he says:

> It is mixed. I believe at school here, I was more Anglicised than I became after I had lived six months in England. By the time I finished my course, I found I had become a Fantiman who had studied and thought in England, rather than an Anglicised Fanti or a bleached Negro. (63)

Indeed it is worth noting that the seeds of nationalism were sown alongside those of colonial indoctrination, for Sekyi grew up when Cape Coast was developing into a crucible of nationalism in the Gold Coast. The resultant persona was a strong anti-colonial activist who sought to complement the activities of his nationalist uncle Henry Van Hein and others such as James Hutton Brew and J.E. Casely Hayford.

Mfantse-speaking people were indeed not a unitary state but more like a loosely aligned mosaic of small states, some coastal and others found in the hinterland. Thus unlike Kobina Sekyi, even though Ama Ata Aidoo attended the most renowned girls' secondary school in the Gold Coast – Wesley Girls' High School which was situated in Cape Coast – and spent a considerable amount of time in the cosmopolitan coastal town of Sekondi, she was deeply immersed in the culture of her ancestral community. Abeadze Kyeakor is situated in the hinterland of the Mfantse. Her people would have been known by the people of Cape Coast as *babanasefo* [rustic people].

Ama Ata Aidoo is the daughter of a chief and was exposed to the oratorical language of the court where Mfantse spoken would be deemed as pure (*krogyee*). Aidoo's command of the densely symbolic court language and the nuances of Mfantse is well known to those of us who have had the privilege of hearing her speak in different registers of Mfantse for over forty years. Indeed those who have heard Aidoo do readings of her works will realise that she makes no attempt to adopt a British or American intonation. Thus, the prosody of her reading and the phonetic pattern are revealing of the new English that she is creating in which she is very much present as an Mfantse-born-English-speaking-writer (to take a leaf from her penchant for multi-component nominals).

She herself says "...I haven't tried to speak the Queen's English. I've always tried to let the flavour of my African background come through in terms of the idioms and so on" (James 1990: 23). Further on in this essay, we suggest that this is also a part of her ideological stance. More importantly, her elders and her mother transmitted to her historical narratives, some of which were to form the basis of her own narrative corpus:

> I come from a people who told stories. When I was growing up in
> the village, we had a man who was a good story-teller. And my
> mother "talks" stories and sings songs. *Anowa*, for instance, grew
> out of a story she told ... My mother is definitely a direct
> antecedent (James 1990: 19).

Thus, as her writing demonstrates from the very beginning, her schooling did not deflect her from the culture as much as it did Kobina Sekyi. He more or less went through an epiphany and an awakening, whereas she incrementally grew in her appreciation of her culture.

While Sekyi plunged into the activist anti-colonial politics and engaged in writing largely as an avenue for polemics, it may be argued that Aidoo cut her teeth on the wave of cultural nationalism and artistic experimentation championed by the immediate post-independence generation such as Efua Sutherland, Kwabena Nketia and Wole Soyinka. It is worthy of note that Aidoo had the privilege, at age 20, of attending a writers' workshop organised by the Mbari Club in Ibadan, Nigeria, attended by writers such as Wole Soyinka, Christopher Okigbo and Chinua Achebe. She also became a mentee of Efua Sutherland and formed a life-long mother-daughter relationship which enveloped their passion for the arts and for African people. Her early works appeared in *Okyeame*, the leading literary journal, of which Sutherland was a founding editor while involved in the theatrical experimentation which took place at the Drama Studio established by Sutherland – where the modern Ghanaian Theatre was developed.

Like their counterparts who received a Western education but became convinced that the colonial enterprise was one of subjugation, taking responsibility for writing the story of the people of Africa became a sacred duty and with it came the issue of the idiom through which it was to be presented. J.E. Casely Hayford, for example, was impatient with those members of the Mfantse and indeed West African elite who did not perceive, as he did, that freedom from colonial rule meant the elaboration of deliberate policies to institutionalise the use of African languages and cultures. Using the vehicle of a dream sequence in his novel *Ethiopia Unbound*, Casely Hayford projects us into a world where there is an Mfantsipim National University. Taking over teacher training and translation work from the missionaries and colonial government, instruction is being conducted in Fante, Yoruba and Hausa, while education materials are being produced in these same languages.

Later Mfantse writers such as the playwright Efua Sutherland and the poet Kwesi Brew were also literary forebears of Aidoo and took the issue of language up in their works. In his early poetry, Kwesi Brew used language in a less experimental manner but the power of his imagery founded on African reality and often structured on forms such as proverbial language was no less palpable. His play, "The Trial of Old Kweku," for example, refracts the formality of the language of the elders (*Mpanyin Kasa*) which is found in many an African literary work placed in a setting where the community meets to discuss issues.

Efua Sutherland, in her turn, certainly experimented with the conjunction at which Mfantse meets English, writing full scripts in both English and Mfantse and exploring the dramatic potential of blending the two languages. But she is best known for her infectious fascination with oral literature and the performance traditions of the Mfantse speaking people. Thus several rites have found their way into her plays and other writing. These include the dirge tradition (*Edufa*), the militaristic music and rites of the traditional military forces (*Foriwa*, "New Life in Kyerefaso") and the story-telling tradition which pervaded her life's work (*Wo Hyee Me Bo*, *The Marriage of Anansewa*, *Ananse and the Dwarf Brigade*). These latter writers were of the generation which was translating the ideals of the anti-colonial struggle into a postcolonial reality and who inspired Ama Ata Aidoo's generation. Aidoo, being a child prodigy, started writing very early in her life, getting her Christmas story "To Us a Child Is Born" published in the *Daily Graphic* in 1958. As the Akan adage goes, "When a child becomes adept at washing his/her hands, s/he eats with the elders." Thus, Aidoo's play *The Dilemma of a Ghost*, written while she was a student at the University of Ghana, already demonstrates her awareness of the vast potentials and challenges of being a "postcolonial writer" of Mfantse origin.

This essay will concentrate on comparing the writing of Kobina Sekyi with that of Ama Ata Aidoo, to put into perspective how far Aidoo has taken an emergent writing idiom nourished by Mfantse origins. The question arises as to how exactly the texts and discourses of these writers are developed to carry, in addition to their immediate message, the burden of the dynamics of the languages and contexts in which they were created. Indeed, Mikhail Bakhtin is of the opinion that language is shot through with intentions and that each word tastes of the context and contexts in which it has lived its socially charged life. All words and forms are therefore populated with intentions (Bakhtin, 293).[4] Given the very historical conjunction out of which our writers have emerged, and their commitment to creating a new self-willed reality, this line of theory is useful in a number of ways: it makes room for an active authorial voice engaging as would a narrator in the oral culture with the substance of the narrative. The fact that this approach makes room for the legitimate presence of the author's intent as well as his/her literary antecedents and culture of speaking in the text provides an analytical framework that would not seem to require the authors to prove the legitimacy of their subversion of the notion of the omniscient but disengaged author's voice.

Secondly, the idea of language living a socially charged life, and words carrying the contexts of this life, is an attractive one for analysing an approach to writing in which the choice of language (s) means so much to the authors. At another level, the question of ideology being reflected through language in the voice of both the author and his/her characters appears to be an important one, because both Sekyi and Aidoo make very strong statements about issues such as social class and responsibility, by the clever manipulation of bilingualism as well as multiple registers. Perhaps this is the point at which to bring in two useful Bakhtinian notions being heteroglossia and polyphony which respectively refer to a single author's voice using many different registers to create a hybrid text which refract the author's intentions, on the one hand, and polyphony, where the voice of a narrator carries other voices and perspectives, even though these voices may not necessarily be represented as speaking for themselves. Thus, for example, the language of parody in Sekyi's *The Blinkards* is more a reflection of the author's attitude towards the society in which he lives, whereas Aidoo has become very much known for putting her writing at the service of the voices of women, for instance.

Bakhtin thus insists that speech or writing is a literary-verbal performance that requires the author to take a position, if only by choosing the dialect in which he or she speaks. This is naturally a supremely important observation, as far as this essay is concerned. Certainly, the notion that meaning occurs at a meeting point between speaker/writer and listener/reader championed by Bakhtin has gained currency in literary and communications studies. In the context of this study we argue that writers of Mfantse origin, Sekyi and Aidoo, in particular, imbue their texts with a texture and layers of meaning which become apparent to readers/listeners who understand both English and Mfantse. Our hypothesis arising from this assumption is that such a listener/reader can experience an enhanced appreciation of the craft and message of these two writers.

Oluwole Adejare, in discussing translation as a distinctive feature of African literature in English, argues convincingly that translation is inevitably used by African writers writing in adopted colonial languages for transferring messages and the socio-aesthetics of the source language. In this sense, translation, far from being a mere attempt to achieve some kind of authenticity, can have significant aesthetic value. He cites satire and humour as literary modes which are greatly enhanced by translation. He also makes the point that "[n]ew idioms derived from translation bring along with them a vivid perspective of the world which enriches the source language" (1998: 36). He makes a further point that African literature in English is also enriched by the new idioms, which are clearly derived from an African experience. This, it might be argued, is a process of creativity which is leading to the establishment of a postcolonial literary idiom (Omole, 1998: 57).

The following exchange between Ama Ata Aidoo and Adeola James provides a telling indication of the consciousness of the writers in question about the potentials of working in two languages:

James:     Critics have praised your handling of language. It is natural, sensitive, and gives depth to your explorations. You yourself said in "To Be a Woman" that no one else handles the English language the way you do. How do you achieve this uniqueness?

Aidoo:     Well, I think I was being frank and boasting a bit. But what I meant, all modesty aside, is that I like the way I handle English. It has to do with my background. I haven't tried to speak the Queen's English; I've tried to always let the flavour of my African background come through in terms of idioms and so on.

The rest of the essay is dedicated to a stylistic analysis of sample texts by Sekyi and Aidoo, in which there are significant indications of how they turn the literary resources of Mfantse and English to their artistic and ideological ends. There are various options available to writers working implicitly in two or more languages to ensure that their text aesthetically carries the various language idioms. As this essay is mostly about Aidoo, who indeed has produced a much larger body of texts than Sekyi, comparisons can be taken but so far. They will, however, be made from time to time to give an idea of the range of possibilities in language use. Both writers clearly have superb mastery over both languages, but one would argue that Aidoo exhibits in her writing a more daring range of registers, borrowing at the lexical and stylistic level as well as the symbolic use of Mfantse expressions. The speech culture of Mfantse women, for example, in the form of dirges and conversational styles, is one area. Just as has been mentioned above, among the array of stylistic devices at their disposal, translation and code switching play an important role.

Translation is a fascinating tool in the hands of both Sekyi and Aidoo. While writers today (almost 100 years after *The Blinkards* was written) continue to struggle with the question of the languages they write in, it is instructive that, although the language of *The Blinkards* is primarily English, it is written as a bilingual text, with large portions of the dialogue in Mfantse and then translated by the author himself. This must be seen as a revolutionary act, because, in spite of the amount of discussion that has taken place about the fundamental nature of the linguistic realities of African writers and their mission, the solution of giving visibility to their mother tongues by producing bilingual texts has not been taken up with any consistency. The provision of the translations by the author removes the hurdle for the reader of trying to interpret what the author is seeking to say. These translations by Sekyi are rendered in Standard English, signifying that the characters are competent speakers of Mfantse.

Kobina Sekyi also uses language as a marker of social status and aspiration or pretentions. Characters like Nna Sumpa, an old non-literate woman, speak in "pure" Mfanste all the time. They do not engage in code switching between English and Mfantse and are spared parody by the author. On the other hand, Sekyi's play revolves around Mr. and Mrs. Brofusem, a semi-literate couple. The wife has recently visited England and is intent on being the grand dame of the social elite back in Cape Coast. The language in which Mr. and Mrs. Brofusem speak symbolises their affectation and desperate desire to be "Anglo-Fantes."[5] Mrs. Brofusem sounds like this:

> Do behave Erminitrude. A cake is more genteel ... than *buredzi*
> *tutui*. Or else take a chocolate ... All young ladies in England chop
> creamy chocolates (31).

Here we observe that Mrs. Brofusem does not know how to translate *buredzi tutui* (roasted plantain). This would be rendered in a false British accent for comic effect. Again, the word 'chop' is a Pidgin English word for 'eat' and certainly would have no place in Mrs. Brofusem's diction if she could help it.

On the other hand, as will be demonstrated below, while Aidoo does not have long passages in Mfantse, phrases from her mother tongue are placed for various effects. Characters located in contexts where they might mispronounce an English word are allowed to do so for the purposes of linguistic realism, and her body of text is shot through with syntactic and verbal dislocations which render them as virtual transliteration. Indeed, we will seek to demonstrate later in the essay that Aidoo is one of Africa's writers who has been building 'African literary English.'

Further reflection on the diction of Aidoo and Sekyi reveals that code switching is pervasive and deployed for different purposes. For Sekyi, code switching is a tool for exposing unfounded pretentiousness among uneducated or semi-educated colonial subjects. For example, English words and phrases are assimilated through Mfantse grammatical processes both syntactic and phonetic. From the Blinkards, hybrid words like *skur-girl* ('school girl') or Mfanticised English words like *ankrr* ('uncle') are found in the speech of several characters (81). Because /r/ and /l/ are in free variation with each other in Mfantse, /r/ often replaces the less frequently used /l/ when certain words are assimilated into Mfantse: "Girl: *Me pun skur na minfeel yie*" ('I have not been feeling well since school was over').[6]

The above sentence is typical of the kind of code switching for which Mfantse speakers have been mercilessly parodied over the years by their compatriots. Sekyi counter-poses Lawyer Oyimdzi to the leaders of the emerging "Anglicised elite." Several times in the course of the play he is asked why he is wearing the cloth in the traditional way and more pertinently, why he speaks Mfantse. Indeed, speaking impeccable Mfantse by choice instead of necessity, Oyimdzi challenges the prevailing social paradigms and reverses the correlation between language and high social rank.

In making a dig at a father who does not look after his child but is proud to announce to all who care to listen that his son is in *"unifartisy,"* it is clear that Aidoo is also inclined to use code switching in satire. Beyond satire, however, Ama Ata Aidoo often turns the assimilation of English to a variety of uses. Firstly, the lyrical appropriation of the English language by rural people, far from being made to sound clumsy, is rendered as a dignified and natural use of the given assimilated word, fitting it into the texture of their own discourse. These words often represent new institutions, professions, and systems: *chicha* – the new educator; *draba*, the ubiquitous lorry driver. On the other hand, the conflict between Eulalie Rush and her husband Ato Yawson's family, is represented by their inability to pronounce her name. They call her *Hurare* and the land she comes from, *Amrika*.

The issue of translation has been raised. Firstly our authors have made choices about what to translate and what not to. To assist readers, Aidoo sometimes offers a glossary as in the 1993 edition of *Changes*. Ama Ata Aidoo differs significantly from Sekyi in particular as far as her approach to translation is concerned. For example, in the short sentence "Adjoa, you say what?"[7] [which we translate as "Adjoa, what did you say?"], translation has taken place at the primary level where the syntax and tense of the Mfantse subtext are retained. By choosing to create a new language rather than render the idea in an equivalent English idiom, Aidoo appears to be asserting a pre-existing socio-linguistic reality and culture upheld by persons living in the rustic environment. She provides an opportunity for the voices from this environment to speak for themselves. One such voice is that of the grandmother, Nana, in "The Girl Who Can" (Aidoo, 1997), who makes this statement.

Spoken Mfantse, as with most African languages, is full of evocative expressions which, while not lexical items, are essential elements of the art of speaking and carry significant meaning. At the risk of tautology it may be noted that vocalisation is an inherent characteristic of orality. This accounts for a range of non-lexical evocative particles which, when vocalised, enhance the meaning of the message that a speaker may wish to convey. For example, the fisherman, Srako in " Male-ing in the Sun (Toli Number Two)" (Aidoo, 1997) expresses his regret at having to concede that his wife had first had the good idea of sending their son to school: "Now he would forever have to give the woman the credit of being the first in bringing up the matter. Ah, ah, ah!" (1997: 114). Indeed in Mfantse a triple iteration of the particle 'ah' is an expression of regret particularly for being thwarted at something.

Aidoo might also retain Mfantse words to stay faithful to a genre. She uses the dirge form quite frequently and little wonder, since being acquainted with the traditions of royal funerals, the tones and idioms' of *kwadwom* dirge were likely to have rung in her ears. Furthermore, women in Mfantse communities are the primary composers and performers of keening and dirge-singing which constitute a powerful art form:

> we remember you so sharply – striding and gliding
> your way to sundry sites of creative construction:
>
> All in your effort to build and have 'something built.'
>
> Me na Oye-Adee-Yie,
> you knew us
> didn't you? (Aidoo, 2007: 232)

"Kwadwom from a Stillborn Creole Kingdom" is the name of a section of *Someone Talking to Sometime* which contains suitably dirge–like pieces. In this particular extract from "An Interrogation of an Academic Kind: An Essay," the epithet in Mfantse which we translate as "My-Mother-The-Builder" is placed almost at the end of the piece as a culmination of the attributes set out in the dirge.

As can be seen from the above analysis, the crafting of text taking into account more than one language in an intimate dialogue provides the author with immense possibilities. However, in addition to exploring the stylistic potential of the languages, Kobina Sekyi and Ama Ata Aidoo do take positions on a number of situations arising in the aftermath of colonialism, not least among which is 'the colonial mentality' and the self-defeating lack of commitment exhibited by the postcolonial elite. They indeed share an aversion to capitulation exhibited before the force of colonialism. Their ideological position seeps through their stylistic choices.

Aidoo takes other approaches to addressing the consequences of colonialism. For example, in a series of loosely linked short stories under the general title "Male-ing in the Sun," Aidoo also discusses quite directly the attitudes of her people to the colonials. She first refers to their passive resistance discernable through aphorisms such as the two quoted in "Toli Number One" as follows:

> *"Kobwinyi na ose ne dasefo wo Aborokyir."*
> It is a liar who claims his only witness is in Europe. (Who wants
> to go that far to bring such a witness?) (Aidoo, 1997: 108)

It may be noted that in the above extract, Aidoo chooses to state the aphorism in Mfantse followed by a translation, and in the second case she provides a comment which guides the reader/listener towards understanding the import of the phrase. Firstly, proverbs imply some form of coded language and the use of indirection which excludes the colonisers, who belong to a different culture, from detecting the underlying resentment of the colonised. However, any tendency to see Mfantsefo as the great resistors to the colonial influence is quickly dispelled in Toli Number 2 and Toli Number 3. Here, Aidoo relies on the comic elaboration of a process by which many families surrender their sacred right to name their children after their ancestors.

The cost of seeking a Western education is to have a name imposed, based on nothing but the whims of the priest – an agent of cultural imperialism. Srako ('One Shilling') the fisherman, had acquired his odd name because his family wanted to save him from the cycle of dying and being re-born only to die again. In order for his son Kojo Kuma to be admitted into school he has to have a Christian name. The Reverend is in a conflicted state marked by hesitant speech as he recalls naming in the tradition on which he has turned his back:

> He knew that his people's naming system defined each individual
> clearly, without ambiguities. However … but then … yes, he had
> to admit to himself, it was based on some … eh … unfortunately
> primitive combination of both patrilineal and matrilineal notions
> (Aidoo, 1997:116).

He proceeds to first impose a surname and a European name. Kojo Kuma tentatively becomes George K. Srako. However, upon further inspiration he translates the name Srako into the English Shilling and, for good measure and full Anglicisation he adds the suffix 'son' to Shilling since Kojo Kuma is the son of Srako. Thus, the ontologically rooted names are replaced by G.K. Shillingson, plucked in a few moments from the shallow acquaintance of the priest with an imposed foreign culture.

Aidoo's concern with the state of African womanhood is passionate. According to Maria Frias, she challenges, deconstructs, and subverts the traditional "voicelessness of the black woman" (Frias, 2003: 8). Women protagonists and key characters are the norm in Aidoo's work. As she has privileged dialogue, conversational settings and modes of speech frequently associated with women, the polyphony of women's voices is all-pervasive. The First Woman and Second Woman in The Dilemma of a Ghost amplify societal attitudes towards issues like the centrality of childbirth to the existence of women, using a register which is associated with Mfantse women in conversation. One of these is the consistent use of the interpolation "My Sister." Another feature is the way in which one speaker initiates an allegorical or proverbial statement which is completed or extended by another. Again "The Message" published in *No Sweetness Here* is often quoted as a prime example of Aidoo's use of polyphony to demonstrate, among other things, the extent to which the rural world is cut off from a menacing modernity. She, as author, intervenes very little and the force of innuendo mixed with ignorance and the suffocating empathy of a small community are fully felt by the reader:

> 'Have you heard it?'
> "What?"
> "This and this and that..."
> "A-a-ah! That is it..."
> "*Meewuo!*"
> "They don't say *meewuo*" (Aidoo, 1995: 38)

Certain expressions used here and in several other texts form part of a lexicon associated with women. Some of these words and expressions are:

- Phrases which highlight a portion of conversation such as "I say" and "They don't say."
- *Meewuo!* ('I am dead'); *Poo !* ('pity'); *Whopei* (an expression of dismay or disgust).
- "Watery male of all watery males" – a gross insult reserved by women for men who fall far below their expectations.
- "My mother silk" and "My lady silk" are variations on the same epithet of endearment where 'lady' and 'silk' reinforce each other in symbolising that which is beautiful, refined and of high quality.

Dialogue also helps the reader to understand what is being said, especially where the writer, like Aidoo, has decided to retain the expressive force of her mother-tongue by writing a text that is powerfully inlaid with Mfantse. Indeed, Aidoo's forte in her narrative is the layering of voices within one voice. She does not choose to blend these too finely, though. As a result the different voices are palpable and overt, privileging the oral.

Says Aidoo: "I totally disagree with people who feel that oral literature is one stage in the development of man's artistic genius. To me it's an end in itself....if I had my way what I would be interested in is a form of theatre where you don't only have to produce a play – where you can just sit down and relate a story... If I had any strong conception of what else could be done in literature, it is this. We don't always have to write for readers, we can write for listeners."[8]

Another area of interest is a review of ways in which meaning is achieved at an interface between two languages in a process of communication. It could be argued that the more of a linguistic culture one shares with the author, the richer the experience one would have as a reader/listener. In the following section, we give examples of a few texts and how they have impacted on us personally, based on our own facility with Mfantse and English. 'The Tailless Animal' is the name of a lorry in "Other Versions," one of the stories in *No Sweetness Here*. This seemingly inauspicious name foreshadows the climax of the story in which Kofi, the protagonist, from a home struggling with poverty and suffering the neglect of a father, works his way into university in the United States of America. He suddenly realises that, while he may be enjoying a priviledged existence, African American women just like his mother are toiling away in the kitchens of the well-meaning white persons with whom he is fraternising. He tries to give one of these women whom he meets on the subway some money because she reminds him so much of his mother and, just like her, she asks him to keep it for himself. This is the story of the proverbial animal without a tail who also manages to keep off the flies because God brushes them off it. The truck with slogans written across the back is an iconic feature on Ghana's roads. These slogans may in fact be proverbial sayings and it is quite common for only the first half of the proverb to be spoken. The second half is either understood or taken up by the second speaker or even in chorus by several participants in the conversation. Thus the full rendition "The Tailless Animal-It is God Who Acts as Its Fly Swatter," takes on a symbolism representing the trajectory of Kofi's life with his mother by his side through thick and thin.

With regards to *Our Sister Killjoy*, the subtitle "Or Reflections of a Black-eyed Squint" evokes the discourse around the eyes and how they are an effective part of the Mfantse speaking culture. Indeed the eyes can be defined as surrogates of speech because they are used to convey messages. The eyes can be used in situations of belligerence and one of them is the scrunching up of the eyes sometime described in African Diaspora culture as 'cutting one's eyes,' (*bu enyikye*, "break eye crooked" in literal Mfantse) which symbolises insolence, annoyance or envy. Aidoo could be seen as employing a technique used by persons seasoned in the "art of quarrelling." This technique involves first stating all one's defects, particularly the physical, before turning one's ire upon one's opponent. This defiant attitude shows an awareness that, although society might find her main character Sissie too aggressive, she is going to go ahead with speaking her mind nevertheless.

Finally, in *Anowa*, Anowa's mother Badua launches into a tirade over Anowa's choice of Kofi Ako as a husband, including the epithet "watery male of watery males" (*benyin nsu-nsu mu nsu-nsu*), a devastating expression in the Mfantse women's arsenal of insults aimed at the total deflation of the male ego. In the Akan culture thickness of soup, sap, etc. is a critical indication of its substance and its effectiveness. The notion of dilution, therefore, has the concomitant sense that the solution would be bleached of all substance. This metaphor under reference would therefore connote an effete, neer-do-well, irresponsible, non-achiever among other choice inadequacies. All of these are communicated to an Mfantse-speaking reader.

Indeed, the power to name gives the author the supreme capacity to hold up the character to scrutiny. Sekyi can hardly restrain himself in pouring blistering derision on some of his characters who represent the execrable traits of the Anglo-Fanti. The name *Tsiba*, for example, connotes a less-than brilliant intellect and might be rendered as 'pea brain' or 'simpleton' in English. Tsiba's full name inscribed on the invitation card for his daughter's wedding, is Mr Aldiborontiphoscophornio Chrononhontonhontonthologos Tsiba. It is, however, obvious that the length of the first names is in inverse proportion to his intellectual capacity represented by his cruelly blunt last name.

Ama Ata Aidoo also deploys the device of giving characters names in Mfantse which have a bearing on the message of the narrative in question. These names, therefore, are not merely appropriate to the cultural setting of her work, they often connote the persona of a particular character. Monka, Ato Yawson's embittered sister in *The Dilemma of a Ghost*, is a case in point. Monka means 'let it be,' and, considering that this character is the one who is consistently the most cynical and prickly, this paradoxical name simply reinforces her role in the play.

Ama Ata Aidoo has developed a style all her own that goes beyond linguistic realism (Omole, 1998: 58) or a reflection of borrowing and code switching or even translation deployed for explaining cultural concepts, aiding in characterisation, inducing humour, and so on. It would appear that she is creating in both Mfantse and English at the same time. The texture of her own writing as author is inlaid with Mfantse and not necessarily deflected onto her characters. She picks from her mother-tongue linguistic features such as lexical items, syntactic structure, particular registers, literary devices and generic forms. Below is a summary of the key elements of her style.

The conversational style is one which Aidoo has cultivated. It takes a leaf from orality in which the author can be more intimately connected with the reader. Even her essays such as "The African Woman Today" (1991) reflect this:

> To a certain extent, African women are some sort of riddle …To some West African men, the way West African women struggle to be independent is "really quite bad." They think that "these women are all over the place."

Direct speech and dialogue permeate her work and yet the author's own voice is a part of the discourse. Aidoo uses polyphony as per the Bakhtinian sense in many ways. For example, in Anowa's relating of her grandmother's desperate attempt to get her to shut up about slavery (Aidoo, 1993: 104–107) there are hints of her own (Anowa's) impending mental derangement as well as her grandmother's discomfiture overlaid with Aidoo's own horror in structuring the rising crisis in the play.

The long speech carries within it a carefully poised conflict between the childlike insistence of Anowa as a little girl importuning her grandmother for answers to questions on slavery from which the old lady is desperately trying to escape. At the same time the discourse is driven by the child, who expands on the cryptic answers of her grandmother, effectively being the one to open the lid on the dreaded truth. The Old Lady can only take refuge in throwing the accusation of witchcraft at the child. Indeed Aidoo reduces the grandmother, who should be the fount of wisdom, knowledge and eloquence, to a stammerer, lost for words to meet the demands of her precocious grandchild:

> "Like...like...but it is not good
> That a child, a child should ask questions (Aidoo, 1993: 105)

Anowa, in true story-telling form, sometimes speaks in her grandmother's voice. In this extract Anowa's questions are implied by her grandmother's answers indicating the presence of the child Anowa as a character in a story of which Anowa as an adult is the narrator:

> I do not know, child.
> You are frightening me, child.
> I was not there!
> It is too long ago!
> No one talks of these things anymore!
> All good men and women try to forget;
> They have forgotten!
> What happened to those who were taken away?
> Do people hear from them?
> How are they?... (Aidoo, 1993: 105)

The semantic density of these lines comes from many angles. The role reversal with the child in control and the grandmother attacked with a swelling panic comes across quite palpably as she resorts to the one power bestowed on her by society, which is the indisputable power of the elderly. The repetition of the word 'child' demonstrates her desperation to convince Anowa, and certainly, herself, that her granddaughter is a CHILD and not her equal.

In the story "Something to Talk about on the Way to the Funeral," another example of Mfantse discourse pattern can be discerned. As part of the foregrounding technique Mfantse allows for the creation of emphasis and the heightening of emotion by the rapid repetition of the single-word question:

"Lord, there is no type of dough of flour they say she has not mixed or fried or baked. Epitsi? Tatare? Atwemo? Bofrot? Boodo? Boodoo-ngo? Sweetbad? Hei, she went there and dashed here but they say somehow, she was not getting much from these efforts." (Aidoo,1995: 17)

To demonstrate how much of a deviation this is from a narrative structure that might qualify as Standard English a possible translation is provided below. It may be noted that the actual proper names of the foods have been left in the original Mfantse, as the passage would have been too clumsy with explanations for those foods, which have no English equivalent. This way some of the lyricism of the original passage remains:

"Lord, there is no type of dough of flour they say she has not mixed or fried or baked. Was it *epitsi, Tatare, atwemo or bofrot?* Was it *boodo, Boodoo-ngo or sweetbad?...*"

Clearly the original passage by the author is not an attempt at a translation from idiomatic Mfantse to idiomatic Standard English but a text all its own which speaks in the cadences of Aidoo's linguistic experiences.

Ama Ata Aidoo has taken to using evocative multi-component nominals[9] often found in praise poetry and dirge. These names confer attributes upon the persons to which they are addressed. They may be adulatory when used in dirges as in "Gold-Nuggets-Giver," where the subject is being praised for her immense nurturing capacity (Aidoo, 1972: 54). They may, however, also be critical or even derogatory as in the epithets heaped upon Jessy Treeson, the rude nurse in "The Message": "Scrappy-nurse-under-training, Jessy Treeson, Second-generation Cape Coaster-her grandmother still remembered at Egyaa No 7" (Aidoo, 1972: 54). As can be seen from the example above, epithets may be largely descriptive but reflect the attitude of the attributer towards his/her subject. They may be metaphorical and formed as full sentences such as The-Mouth-That-Eats-Salt-and-Pepper being the Old Man and Woman in *Anowa,* who provide two sides of the social attitudes to the happenings in the play.

The epithet is a ubiquitous literary device that is found in Aidoo's fiction and non-fiction prose, poetry and drama. Her short story,"*Choosing − A Moral from the World of Work,*" is special in this respect because the dilemma at the core of the story revolves around the protagonist seeking ways to cope with the heavy demands of making ends meet while striving to find her soul's fulfillment in her vocation. This is symbolised by lengthening or reducing the attributive nominal. She is first *The-Writer* then *The-Writer-Turned-Teacher.* She becomes *The-Writer-Turned-Teacher−and-at−the −Crossroads,* then *The-Writer−Turned-Teacher-Now Considering−Trading.* She ventures into becoming *The-Writer-Turned-Teacher-Turning-*

*into-a–Trader* and finally becomes *The-Writer-Turned-Trader*. After experiencing crushing failure, the persona of *The-Writer* starts insinuating itself into her reality until she finally reverts to that original persona but still filled with angst.

*Our Sister Killjoy* is a full work in which writing takes on the qualities of long inter-generic narratives found in the oral tradition. This book is difficult to place under any literary rubric from European literary culture. The way the book is set out graphologically also serves its vivid oral quality. Some columns have only a single word or a single sentence on them sending the reader/listener wondering and wandering with Sissie across the spectrum of her growing awareness of the situation of African people in a "global world." In addition to this, like the poems "For Kinna" and "Gynae One" published in the collection *Someone Talking to Sometime*, the manner in which words are arranged on the page forces the reader to 'hear' the words and the weight of the thoughts that they carry. Vincent Odamtten's description of Aidoo's poem "Crisis" applies in large measure to these poems as well: "The use of variable repetition, elaboration and improvisation on words, phrases and lines produces a musical effect akin to the traditional ritualistic verse. Such variable repetitions, used extensively in these poems, add a resonance to the poems..." (Odamtten, 2000: 213).[10] It may be noted that *Someone Talking to Sometime* opens with a libation which in itself is a framework for classic oration and a tribute to the word. Odamtten makes the point that "this libation...signals the increasing use of Fante as an integral part of Aidoo's new 'language' for communication of something relevant."[11]

## Conclusion

We have sought to demonstrate that as writers whose mother tongue is Mfantse, but who received formal education in English, a number of writers including Kobina Sekyi, J.E. Casely Hayford, Efua Sutherland, Kwesi Brew and Ama Ata Aidoo, have rightly seen language as an arena for examining the effects of colonisation and the struggle involved in reversing its debilitating consequences in an anticipated or actual postcolonial reality. These authors have undertaken a journey of rediscovering and repossessing the right to name and to create the idiom in which this reality will be discussed. They are perfectly comfortable with their bilingualism and seek to explore the two languages together as a resource. Each language is a resource on its own but taken together, they speak to both tensions and synergies generated by the circumstances of their meeting. The politics of anti-colonial nationalism and those of postcolonial nation-building are vividly depicted in the works of Kobina Sekyi and Ama Ata Aidoo, not simply as themes but in the very fabric of their work and in the texture of their writing.

Looking at the spectrum of work that Ama Ata Aidoo has produced, we draw the conclusion that she stretches the boundaries and joins in the process of creating a new reality at a very basic level. Standard English in the hands of this writer is not as simple at it appears, because she does not allow herself to be bound by the standard idioms of the English language. There is no equivocation about whose story she is telling and in whose voice she tells it. Her style and diction are compelling and aimed at all who live in the contemporary world for, as Yaa-Yaa observes in conversation with her friend Kate in "Some Global News:" "...girl, if it is a global village, then everybody lives in it, an-eh-h-h?" (1997:76)

# Disobedient Subversions: *Anowa*'s Unending Quest[1]

## Omofolabo Ajayi-Soyinka

Ama Ata Aidoo's *Anowa* has been chosen as the Convocation play to celebrate the 25th anniversary[2] of the founding of Obafemi Awolowo University (OAU), Ile-Ife, Nigeria. The choice of the play has not been without controversy, but that pales almost into irrelevance compared with what follows the actual production. Although, looked at from another angle, the post-production 'war' is on the same continuum as the selection process debate: a war of ideas and principles, a question of academic integrity and the sanctity of the artistic work. The production itself has gone well, and none of the political embarrassment the university administrators have feared would emanate from the so-called "campus hot-heads and radicals" does not materialise. The rather politically uneventful Convocation is the calm before the storm. No sooner had the festivities ended, than a firestorm of controversy exploded over the Convocation play. Theatre critics of different ideological hues converge at the university for an immediate post-production seminar; as the academic unit ultimately responsible for the Convocation play, the Department of Dramatic Arts is at the centre of it all. Ideological discourse extends into the politics of cultural aesthetics and flows into copyright issues and is carried on in the pages of national dailies for weeks.

Broadly, the questions to which everybody seeks answers can be summed up in the following: Which, and whose *Anowa* has been produced? Why, and what does it matter?[3] Below, I revisit the 1987 debate of *Anowa*, and issues raised. I contextualise briefly the production of *Anowa* within the general power politics of the time especially as it unfolds at OAU. In the following critical analysis of *Anowa* the play, I explore the intersection of gender ideology with the cultural aesthetics of power politics.

## Convocation Plays at Obafemi Awolowo University (OAU)

As an event highlighting the awards of relevant degrees for successfully completing three or more years of hard work in the academic community,

Convocations are hallowed rituals. Efforts are made to make the event memorable to the graduates, families and friends. At OAU, also saluted as "Great Ife," Convocation plays have become part of these rituals since Wole Soyinka's *Death and the King's Horseman* premiered to launch the newly established Department of Dramatic Arts during the 1976 Convocation ceremonies.[4] These Convocation plays especially complement and fulfill the university's unique motto: "For Learning and Culture." The Department of Dramatic Arts is ultimately responsible for choosing and producing the play, although the university Convocation Committee is informed of the play for the overall planning process, and there has never been any problem.

For its 25th anniversary, however, the Convocation Committee wants an original play, written preferably by an alumnus of the university. This is meant to be a powerful statement acknowledging and celebrating the core essence of the university– spirit of defiance, innovation, and determination – as well as the successful blend of learning with culture. In particular, because of the political context of how the university came into existence,[5] reaching this milestone is not enough; its success needs to be concretely demonstrated by showcasing the work of its product at none other place than the ceremony symbolising scholarly achievements. Unfortunately, an obvious choice for this task makes the university authorities nervous. A lecturer in the Dramatic Arts department, I also got my first degree, and recently completed my Ph.D. at Great Ife. According to the authorities, my union activities, especially as the Secretary of the Academic Staff Union of Universities (ASUU), OAU Branch, have brought me into confrontation with the Federal government, and called "unwanted attention" to the university.[6]

Indeed, the past year has been a year of discontent, not only at OAU, but also nationwide. After seventeen years of military regime in twenty–seven years of independence, and each year more repressive than the last, the nation has become military-rule-weary, and is growing restless. Universities have seen steady erosion of resource allocation, academic freedom, scholarly integrity, job satisfaction, and quality education: there seems to be no end to the distabilising interference from successive military governments. In less that two years of seizing power, the current ruler, General Ibrahim Babangida, has only further aggravated the situation, and attempts to dialogue with his administration often result in harassment and detentions; OAU campus has become a favourite hunting ground for the State Secret Service (SSS) agents. Meanwhile, the university administration desires the presence of Babangida, who in his capacity as Nigerian Head of State is the Visitor of the Federal Government universities and is expected at convocation ceremonies. As the General keeps dangling the possibility of gracing the 25th anniversary ceremonies with the might of his presence, it becomes politically expedient for OAU administrators to do all they can to assure the visitor that OAU is a 'friendly' university. If he came, it would prove that the radicals have been effectively neutralised, and the University could fall into the good graces of the President. There is a request that my play must be submitted to the Committee for approval.

Not surprisingly, the Convocation Committee rejects the submitted draft of my play as too political for the 25th anniversary celebration, and especially unsuitable for the delicate palate of the Visitor. In actual fact, the play, "*Festival of Renewal*" (*Festival*)[7] has little to do with the Babangida regime, or the on-going ASUU skirmishes with the SSS and their campus collaborators. If there were any association at all, the closest would be an indirect indictment of the failure of successive Federal governments since colonial times to take decisive action over the politically volatile co-existence of Ife and Modakeke communities. Modakeke people have been settled in Ile-Ife since the 19th century, but bitter differences still flare up at regular intervals with great devastation and loss of lives.[8] *Festival* is based on a poem inspired by another of such in 1984, and the insidious manipulation of political parties. As the title suggests, the emphasis is on *renewal* rather than despair and frustration, and the play ends on a positive note with reconciliation coming from the initiatives of women from the warring communities. In the meantime, General Babangida's regime currently in power is the second military coup since the 1984 Ife/Modakeke crisis.

An original and untested play having proved too risky and unpredictable for such delicate national considerations, a well-tested, 'politically neutral' play becomes the preference for the Convocation play. Aidoo's *Anowa* rises to the top of the various plays considered. Initially, some objections are raised within the Department that a non-Nigerian play is the choice to celebrate a uniquely Nigerian phenomenon; those quickly become irrelevant. The fundamental concept of the play encapsulates the spirit of Great Ife being celebrated. Moreover, it is a play from neighbouring Ghana with similar educational, political and cultural experiences. Even though my play has been supplanted by a non-Nigerian, non-Ife alumnus-authored play, I am excited that the work of a female playwright will be produced for the first time for an Ife Convocation. I have recently started infusing female-centred perspectives in my teaching and publication,[9] and have also begun to pay closer attention to the marginalisation of women not only in academe, but also in activist movements that purportedly seek social justice for all. I have also resolved to include *Anowa* as part of the reading list for my next course, and am actually looking forward to the production to give me a clearer perspective. I find the subversive spin that Aidoo gives the classic folkloric theme of the disobedient daughter extremely illuminating and prescient for the political turn that the 1987 Convocation has taken.

## Aidoo's *Anowa*: Gender, Patriarchy and Historical Conscience-ness

In *Anowa*, Aidoo is unequivocal about the controversial, almost 'taboo' issues she intends to explore. Within the first few lines of the Prologue in the play she lays bare the tenour of the rest of the play, when the Old Man says:

> Bring your ears nearer, my friends, so I can whisper you a secret.
> Our armies, well–organised though they may be,
> Are more skilled in squelching fires than in the art of war.
> …
>
> And yet there is a bigger crime
> We have inherited from the clans incorporate
> …
>
> Those forts standing at the door
> Of the great ocean shall remind our children
> And the sea bear witness.
> …
>
> If there be some among us that have found a common sauce-bowl,
> In which they play a game of dipping with the stranger,
> Who shall complain?
> Out of one womb can always go
> Where the rumbling hunger in their bowels be stilled,
> ….
>
> …let it not surprise us then,
> That This-One and That-One
> Depend for their well being on the presence of
> The pale stranger in our midst.
>
> (*Anowa*, 142)[10]

There is no pulling punches: it is clear the play has set out to exhume some shameful secrets that have been buried deep by the "lords of the House," the Fanti elders of Abura state. Aidoo teases out the secrets in degrees, beginning with the least damaging–the weakness of the elders in military strategies. While this is shameful, it does not imply automatic failures in other leadership areas and, so, is forgivable. However, it leads to an error of judgment causing unin-tended consequences – "dipping with the stranger." Against the Ashanti, their more powerful neighbours, Fanti elders seek protective alliance with the pale strangers who are so different they resemble " a lobster that is boiled or roasted" (185). Such an alliance pact not only compromises their own people, but also the whole region. Perhaps this could still be excused, as the Old Man points out even if with a hint of sarcasm, "We only wanted a little peace" (142. The most unforgivable crime, however, is when the elders, who should know better, allow greed to dictate their dealings with the stranger over the welfare of their people. The stranger has nothing to lose and everything to gain as "those forts standing at the door" testify.

## Slavery

The "game of dipping with the stranger" is none other than the European Trans-Atlantic Slave Trade that renames the coastline of West Africa as the 'slave-coast' and consumes its people. Slavery is the big taboo subject no one in the land wants to confront. Yet the codes of the crime of greed and its consequences are prominently visible and not hard to break: all along the West African coast are sights of children chanting "pale stranger" in their various local languages at the appearance of a European; the forts by the sea, through whose tiny doors countless of Abura people and their neighbours far and wide, pass to the land of no-return. Standing majestic, and out of place by the sea, the slave castles are testimonies to the enormous gains – political and economic powers – of the "pale stranger" while signifying the culpability of the elders, and untold losses to the land. Between the vast sea and the land, the castles are there, accusatory, screaming in silence, "Remember!" Slavery is the big elephant in the room that even now, African political, literary, or cultural leaders do not readily acknowledge, except a few like Kwame Nkrumah, Sembène Ousmane, and of course, Ama Ata Aidoo.[11] In the meantime, Africans continue to wage a ferocious battle against colonialism and its lingering effects.

The hunger fuelled by greed is never sated, and its consequences snowball from generation to generation. Slavery paves the way to colonisation, and today, Africans continue to wage various battles against colonialism and its lingering effects, but nobody makes the connection with the slave-raids that fuelled the European slave trade. To make the linkage, Aidoo situates the play in definite historical reference, as the Old man resumes his monologue:

> It is now a little less than thirty years
> When the lords of our Houses
> Signed that piece of paper
> The Bond of 1844 they call it.
>
> (*Anowa*, 144)

Without doubt what happened in 1844 in Fantiland is pivotal to events now unfolding in the play in 1874. That 1844 'piece of paper' is a series of treaties whereby Fanti elders signed (sign?) away their autonomy for British protection against the Ashanti. They get the peace, but they also get the greed, and, so, join in the lucrative slave trade as middlemen. Thirty years later, the Ashanti are defeated, and the victorious British incorporate them in the Crown Colony of the Gold Coast, throwing in the Fanti as bonus. 1874, the year that the events in *Anowa* begin, signals the onset of British colonial imperialism on the Gold Coast, the colonial name for Ghana. Colonisation and slavery are two sides of the same coin, even if one side is shinier than the other.

Innocuously, the main play takes as its point of departure the ancient tale of the disobedient daughter common in West African prescriptive morals of gender and marriage:

> *Old Woman.* That Anowa is something else! Like all the beautiful
> maidens in the tales, she has refused to marry any of the sturdy
> men who have asked for her hand in marriage. (*Anowa*, 143)

In the folktale, the girl (or boy), after rejecting all eligible partners, chooses to marry a dashing stranger who turns out to be a non-human monster. Once outside the community it subjects the girl to a terrible ordeal, until she is rescued, near death, by one of her rejected suitors. She returns home, disgraced and humiliated. By contrast, the boy, with the help of his dead mother who suddenly materialises, defeats his tormentors and returns home triumphant, and a hero.[12] In broad strokes, Aidoo follows the tale until Anowa's ordeal begins with Kofi Ako, her 'monster husband.' But here the similarities end. Indubitably, Anowa is beautiful and strong-headed, but she is also intelligent, perceptive and compassionate; her stubbornness is not mere willfulness. As everybody in the play remarks at one point or the other, Anowa is uniquely gifted. Even her mother, Badua, despite their acrimonious relationship, recognises the intelligence of her daughter, remarking that "... a captainship in the army, should not be beyond her when the time is ripe" (*Anowa*, 148). Herein lies the problem, Anowa should defer her dreams, and conform first to the cultural precepts of womanhood:

> Marry a man,
> ...
> A woman like her
> Should bear children
> Many children.
>
> (*Anowa*, 148)

Common sense tells Anowa it is best to wait until she meets a man with whom she is compatible intellectually and ideologically, or at least sufficiently different from the rest so they can grow together. As the Old Woman states candidly, "the dumbest man is always better than a woman. Or *he* thinks he is!" (*Anowa*, 182). It is a gender-role game that sustains the matrilineal patriarchy of the

Fanti social structure,[13] and Anowa refuses to participate. Her personality is too strong to pretend otherwise.

As a woman, Anowa is not only disobedient, she is subversive; she has a mind which she dares to exercise. She flouts conventions, challenges established authorities and asks uncomfortable questions whose answers indict the elders of the land. She forces them to remember. Little wonder, she is branded a wild woman whose active mind can only be accommodated in the shrines; there she can be herself by performing a subverted version of her true identity as a mimicry of the deities. However, Badua rejects priesshood on behalf of her daughter; she wants Anowa to be a 'normal' conformist woman. In any case, with the treaties of 1874, the new gods on the coast are already supplanting the deities of the land. So Anowa leaves the town that rejects her as disobedient, and is determined to subvert her identity. Equally determined to subvert their intentions, Anowa herself embarks on a subversive mission – a woman in search of freedom, her dreams and herself. Her chosen partner is Kofi Ako.

Incidentally, Kofi too could be regarded as a 'disobedient son.' He violates local marriage customs, marries an obviously head-strong girl and departs from his community with her. However, unlike Anowa, Kofi Ako is a follower. Badua sums him up perfectly "...this fool, this good-for-nothing cassava-man, this watery male of all watery males?" (151). The point is, he is still a man. Although he loves Anowa, that drive to be a man as culturally prescribed brings out the conformist, and latent greed in him. Midway through her quest, Kofi, Anowa's seemingly ideological accomplice veers off in a different direction, and so begins her ordeal. Anowa's ordeal is not physical; in fact Kofi cannot as much as lay a hand on Anowa which makes him question his identity as a man:

> Kofi Ako. ... (to himself) And what is wrong with me? Any man married to her would have by now beaten her to a pulp, a dough. But I can never lay hands on her.
>
> (Anowa, 168)

The 'ordeal' of Anowa and the ensuing breakdown of the marriage is a complex mix of the personal and the political, where gender performance intersects with collective ideology and ethical concepts. Trudging through the forest in inclement weather that threatens to destroy their animal skin business, and their health, Kofi becomes dispirited. He feels he is not being man enough putting his wife through so much hardship, and despite Anowa's assurances, he resolves to "be the new husband," and make Anowa "the new wife" (Anowa, 165). His resolve leads him down the slippery slope far away from Anowa:

> Kofi Ako: I think the time has come for us to think of looking for one or two men to help us.

*Anowa.* What men?

*Kofi Ako.* I hear they are not expensive ... and if...

*Anowa.* (*getting up so slowly that every movement of her body corresponds to syllables or words in her next speech*) MY hus-band! Am I hearing you right? (*Corking her ears*) Kofi Ako, do not let me hear these words again.

*Kofi Ako* (*mimicking her*) 'Do not let me hear these words again.' Anowa, do you think I am your son?

*Anowa.* I do not care. We shall not buy men. (*Anowa*, 167)

Kofi Ako ultimately succumbs to the temptation of buying slaves to help them in their trade of animal skins. When his wife upbraids him, and says pointedly, "Kofi, no man made a slave of his friend and came to much himself. It is wrong. It is evil" (*Anowa*, 168), she becomes the monster tormenting him. He abjures their equal partnership, stating: "I know I could not have started without you, but after all, we all know you are *a* woman and I am *the* man" (*Anowa*, 168) [emphasis mine]. Although no dead mother materialises to save him, the white man surfaces from the sea to instruct him on new ways of being a man: material accumulation at the expense of others. Kofi moves closer to the source of his new wealth by the slave castles in Oguaa (Fanti for Cape Coast) and leads an opulent life, raking in wealth on the tears and blood of others:

> *Old Man* ... money-making is like a god possessing a priest. He will never leave you until he has occupied you, wholly changed the order of your being, and seared you through up and down. Then only would he eventually leave you, but nothing of you except an exhausted wreck, lying prone and wondering who you are. (*Anowa*, 179).

By now, Anowa appears resigned to her fate. Although she has no dead mother to rush to her aid, she has her principles, and remains faithful to them. She stays poor, refusing to partake of her husband's newfound, ill-gotten wealth. She prefers to keep her mental acuity and retain her humanity in how she relates to the slaves administering to Kofi Ako. Although Kofi has re-invented himself in accordance with the emerging concept of manliness along the Europeanised Coast, Anowa makes a last ditch attempt to revive some Fantiness in him. Their childless state provides an opening. Like the rest of the community, Anowa assumes she is at fault:

> *Anowa* ... Perhaps I am the barren one. But you deserve a son; so Kofi, I shall get you a wife. One of these plump mulatto women of Oguaa ...

*Kofi Ako*. Anowa, stop that!

*Anowa*. Besides such women are much more civilised than I, who only come from Yebi. They, like you have learnt the ways of the white people.

*Kofi Ako*. Anowa, stop that! Stop it, stop it! (*Anowa*, 195)

Kofi is too far gone to retrace his steps. Anowa's discerning mind makes him nervous; he fears she will expose the lie he has been living these many years. To pre-empt the truth from coming out, he decides to send her back to Yebi–to a place she has sworn never to return, and worse, childless. Anowa rejects this double humiliation and fights back. When she starts calling for witnesses and demands that the divorce process be duly followed, Kofi becomes desperate. He plays his last male card by threatening to brand her a witch, thus stripping her of her last shred of dignity. Already isolated because of her childlessness, and strange, unwomanly behaviour, her husband's branding will be the ultimate repudiation. The old insightful, fearless Anowa resurges, questioning Kofi Ako until he admits his secret; he is the impotent one. Unbeknown to them, the whole household has gathered, and heard everything. That he commits suicide in the end is Aidoo's moral spin on the evil of greed; unconscionable accumulation of wealth emasculates:

> *Old Man* ... Besides, there must be something unwholesome about making slaves of other men, something that is against the natural state of man and the purity of his worship of the gods. Those who have observed have remarked that every house is ruined where they take slaves. (*Anowa*, 179)

Anowa's visceral reaction to slave-trading, and owning another human being is part of her ethical make-up. Spirited, fiercely independent, she abhors the subjugation of any person either because of their gender or socio-economic status. Even as an inquisitive and innocent child, Anowa desperately attempts to grasp the idea of owning another person as revealed in this difficult dialogue with her grandmother who has travelled to the coast and seen the slave castles:

> *Anowa* ... What is a slave, Nana?
> *Grandmother* ... Shut up! It is not good that a child should ask big questions.
> A slave is one who is bought and sold.
> *Anowa* ... Where did the men get the slaves?
> I asked.
> *Grandmother* ... You frighten me child
> You must be a witch, child.

They got them from the land.
*Anowa*...Did the men of the land sell the men of the land, and women and children to pale men from beyond the horizon who look like you or me peeled, like lobsters boiled or roasted?

Her grandmother's halting responses notwithstanding, they create such vivid, if incomplete images in her young mind to give her nightmares:

That night, I woke up screaming hot; my body sweating from a horrible dream. I dreamt that I was a big, big woman. And from my insides were huge holes out of which poured men, women and children. And the sea was boiling hot and steaming. And as it boiled, it threw out many, many giant lobsters, each of whom as it fell, turned into a man or woman but keeping its lobster head and claws. ... and seized the men and women as they poured out of me. (*Anowa*, 186)

Anowa is ill for weeks, such is the depth of her antipathy to this odious phenomenon of humanity; ever since, as unformed as it is, she develops a strong aversion to slavery.

A compassionate visionary, Anowa is a woman too early for her time. She is the truth that reveals the secrets hidden deep in recesses of the mind, of a people's conscience. She stands poised between the past and the future, but unable to fit into the present. As she describes herself, "Mm, I am only a wayfarer with no belongings either here or there" (175). Her fellow travellers through time, like Kofi Ako, are stuck in the present living like there is no tomorrow; others would rather forget the past than learn from it. Memories are painful as Grandmother ends her interrogation session with young inquisitive Anowa:

You are frightening me child.
I was not there!
It is too long ago!
No one talks of these things anymore!
All good men and women try to forget;
They have forgotten. (*Anowa*, 186)

Yet the past looms large in the forts along the coast, blocking the view to the future with intrusion, and waiting like spider to lure the next victim into its web. This is a past too powerful, too traumatic to forget; forgetting means a compromised future. Anowa, because of her sharp mind, has glimpses of the future, a hybrid culture which perhaps resembles the mulattos who populate the coast, and feature often in her various attempts to ground Kofi. However, nobody is ready to listen to her, not even Kofi, the man of her choice; he is blindsided by the glitters of the present, and the appearance of the power it gives him as a man. He cannot see the truth that Anowa represents and promotes rather, to him:

> It is an illness, Anowa. An illness that turns to bile all the good things of here-under-the sun. Shamelessly, you rake up the dirt of life. You bare our wounds. You are too fond of looking for the common pain and the general wrong. (*Anowa*, 178)

Aidoo's *Anowa* is a sustained indictment of cowardice in the face of tyranny, of silence before oppression, and of greed profiting from the sufferings and misfortunes of fellow human beings. Anowa is who she is because she seeks to know the truth, she knows the truth because her grandmother breaks the silence, even as she remains fearful of the powers that be; and Anowa remembers. It is a surprising development for a story modelled on the simple tale of 'why a child should obey her/his elders.' If Aidoo's Anowa disobeys, it is because the establishment logic is wrong, and unjust; she disobeys so she can effect positive changes that will benefit the majority, even if she has to go through an ordeal. Aidoo's rewriting of the ancient folktale not only transcends the story of an arrogant disobedient girl, but it also subverts prescriptive gender roles and interrogates the ethics of collective silence.

## Subverting the Subversive: The Convocation Production of *Anowa [Anowa's baby]*

Throughout my reading of *Anowa* in readiness for the production, one puzzle that stays with me is how *Anowa* merits the new criterion of "politically neutral" for the Convocation play. In what sense does it fall into this category? If the emphasis of the 25th anniversary has shifted from showcasing the university's motto and history to celebrating a 'see, hear, and speak no evil' concept, how does Aidoo's *Anowa* qualify? In what ways does the play, or the author qualify as a conformist and power-pleaser? A more disturbing question is how much critical attention is paid to Aidoo as a female playwright? Since her first play, *The Dilemma of a Ghost* (1965), she has been writing steadily by then for over twenty years. In her insightful, "Unwelcome Pals and Decorative Slaves," Aidoo refers to Femi Ojo-Ade's candid revelation that:

> African literature is a male-created, male-oriented chauvinistic art. The male writer, like the male social animal, is more fortunate

than the female. His presence is taken for granted. The publisher seeks him out. Unlike the woman whose silence is taken for granted.[14]

It would appear that by selecting her play, the OAU Convocation Committee has taken for granted Aidoo's silence on critical issues of justice and freedom central to *Anowa*. Indeed, as a colleague once admonishes her, "leave politics and such to those best qualified to handle them, and concentrate on ... writing plays and short stories" (Ojo-Ade, 15). Clearly, according to establishment logic, Aidoo's *Anowa* cannot be political. Perhaps also with the simplicity of the title, a single word, and the name of a girl, Anowa, who is also the play's heroine, there cannot be anything controversial or even profoundly relevant. After all, it is only about a disobedient girl.

Too hasty to heed the dangers of judging a book by its covers, the Convocation Committee is totally unprepared for the double suicide of Anowa and Kofi Ako; it will ruin the celebrative spirit of the 25th anniversary, in particular in the presence of His Eminence, IBB.[15] Time is running out to begin a new selection process, so the brave decision is taken to 'make over' the play to suit the political palate of the 'lords of the House.' For the grand re-writing scheme, an aspiring playwright and fresh graduate of not just the university but also of the department, and currently enrolled in the Master's programme is co-opted. Difficult situation, no doubt, but it is also an opportunity that can yield great dividends. The theme of the disobedient girl has been reworked by both Aidoo and Efua Sutherland,[16] another one would be following the tradition and by a man, too; it is the era of gender equity. So the young playwright goes to work, efficiently translating into dramatic dialogue the ideas of his Head of Department and the director of the play. In time, a new play emerges to start rehearsals, but more rewrites are needed to resolve the series of contradictions in the complexity of gender ideology and colonial imperialism that pervades the original *Anowa*.

To the credit of the production team, the theme of joyful happiness is maintained throughout. After Kofi cries out his pain in anguish and implores his wife:

> Have joy in our overflowing wealth. Enhance this beauty nature gave you with the best craftsmanship in cloth and stone. Be happy with what countless women would give their lives to enjoy for a day. Be happy in being my wife and maybe we shall have our own children. Be my glorious wife, Anowa, and the contented mother of my children. (*Anowa*, 178).

The newly minted Anowa silently listens and obeys. She repents her erring ways, jettisons such foolish ideas as unearthing uncomfortable truths, desists from being so critical and disrespectful of her husband, and becomes the subservient model wife. On his part, Kofi Ako also settles down as a real man to enjoy the sweat of his slaves, free of any guilty conscience, to the full adoration of his wife who basks in his glory. At the end of the play, Anowa is the proud mother of a bouncing baby boy! It is celebration time with music, dance and display of wealth. And Anowa lives happily ever after in the comfort of elevated bourgeoisie-ness. After all, what more could a woman ask for?

## Theatre, Politics and Ideology: An Intersecting Overview

The *Anowa* controversy is not the first in the department. The premiere of *Death and the King's Horseman* at the university also immediately got embroiled in a polemical post-production seminar. The play about the tragic confluence of colonial arrogance, abuse of power, and tradition is found ideologically reactionary under the microscopic lens of a Marxist critical ethos.[17] However, the controversy engendered by *Anowa* is different. Unlike Soyinka's *Death and the King's Horseman*, *Anowa's* is not about the play that Aidoo wrote, but rather, about the play she did *not* write that has her name attached to it.

The theatre is the most communal of all the arts; that is why it is usually in the plural: Theatre Arts, Dramatic Arts and Performing Arts. One person cannot stage a play, not even in a one-person show. By the time a play is staged, it has undergone numerous artistic enhancements from its team of performers, scene, light and costume designers, choreographers, and the director, among others. Each approaches the play from different artistic perspectives, but it is the director who must weave everything together into a fluent conversation on stage. A director enriches the envisioned world of the playwright and transforms it into a palpable multi-dimensional spectacle. Seldom involved in this process, is the playwright whose idea in all these other artists strive to realise, rather it is the director who stands as surrogate for the playwright. There is no denying that the director is also an artist. However, the director's artistic rights should not violate the playwright's. It is the trust that binds: the director's professional trust and artistic integrity are important criteria in a play production.

Of importance is what draws a director to a play: Is it the style or the concept of the play? Is it the historical significance or its timeliness, or economic viability? Or is it the playwright's reputation? Artistic impulse transcends all of these, for it enables the director to successfully harness the creativity of the production team, and to fully pursue his or her own creative impetus and blend it seamlessly with the playwright's. As the only person on the scene, it is double credit for the director. The artistic need to change the playwright's vision and philosophical concept becomes an adaptation. An adapted work operates within the *idea* of an original work but gives it a different spin, either locating it in a different time or space, giving it a new philosophical or ideological focus;

the end product is a new work with the name of the adapter appended to it. Ola Rotimi's *The Gods Are Not To Blame* is a highly acclaimed adaptation of Sophocles's *King Oedipus*. Beside the common theme of incest, Ola Rotimi's play is, to all intents and purposes, an excellent original work linguistically, historically, culturally, and theatrically which cannot, by any stretch of imagination, be said of the re-created production of *Anowa*, nor does it qualify as Aidoo's *Anowa*. It is neither here nor there, thematically, structurally or aesthetically.

It is gratifying to know that the tradition of staging socially conscious plays has continued at OAU. In her article "Ife Convocation Plays as Politics," Ogunleye provides a chronological list of OAU Convocation plays from its inception in 1976 to 1998 and comments, "Many of the plays listed above have provided sturdy political comments on the Nigerian situation" (19), although there is no indication of the tumultuous politics of the 1987 choice. Significantly, the list shows that the since 1987, Convocation plays have featured works by two alumni – Uko Atai (*Dance of Patriots*, 1989; and *Saprites*, 1995) and Ahmed Yerimah (*An Inspector Calls*, 1996), but there is no further reference to them in the rest of the article. Interestingly, both men have just come on board of the academic staff of the department, and are witnesses to, if not active participants in, the 1987 *Anowa* debate. In an ironic twist, the Convocation play Ogunleye chose to analyse closely, Rasaki Bakare's *Drums of War* (1998), is also inspired by the Ife/Modakeke perennial crisis. She notes that:

> In successive years, the Convocation plays at what is now Obafemi Awolowo University have endeavoured to conscientise people in the university environment about their political destiny.

But then she concludes that:

> Bakare's efforts to take *Drums of War* [sic] were thwarted by the relevance of the play and the extent to which he had become an interpreter of popular will: he was frustrated by those who feared that performing the play in Ife/Modakeke might endanger the performers.

Be that as it may, the safety of performers cannot be taken for granted. And since students are often involved in Convocation plays, it would be helpful to know some of the deliberations that informed the final decision. Definitely, not all plays have to be political, or even necessarily explore profound issues, entertainment is after all, an important factor in theatre. However, most plays that survive the test of time give serious considerations to various aspects of our human condition. Political plays especially are a means of expressing dissent, making politics available to ordinary folks; this becomes even more significant under repressive political powers. Just as there are those who use the power of their conviction to confront injustice, so exist those whose power of conviction is self-preservation. Invariably, any play that takes a position is bound to be challenged; diversity is the spice of our human condition. As the Yoruba say, *ona kan ko wo oja* 'one road does not lead to the market,' there are bound to be passionate differences of opinions. It is the trust that binds, and the conviction that sustains the truth.

Thankfully, Ama Ata Aidoo 's *Anowa* still survives beyond the ideologically reworked production, and many more productions stay faithful to the original work, its conceptual theme and profound philosophical explorations. Directors continue to respect the fundamental artistic vision of playwrights, even as they exercise their creative ideas in bringing plays alive on stage. Aidoo's complex, thought-provoking *Anowa* trumps the facile, flash-in-the-pan "Anowa" of the 1987 OAU Convocation play to satisfy another flash-in-the-pan phenomenon in the annals of repressive power.

# African Theatre and the Menace of Transition: Radical Transformations in Popular Entertainment[1]

## Femi Osofisan

My aim in this essay is simply to share with you a few ideas about the present evolution of popular forms of entertainment in Africa today, particularly as it concerns the practice of theatre and the home video explosion. But before I begin, perhaps I need to stress to you, right from the outset, that my perspective is going to be that of a Nigerian playwright and theatre director, one who has been active in the field for some four decades now, whose works are frequently produced in a number of countries both inside and outside Africa, and who is acknowledged to be one of the continent's leading practitioners.

This focus on Nigeria is not merely chauvinistic. Nigeria, as everybody knows, has always been central to any discussion of Africa, not least because of its vast population, widely dispersed across the globe, and its enormous human and natural resources. With particular reference to the discipline of theatre, however, and to the phenomenon that has come to be called the "home video industry" – the industry which now goes by various names such as "Nollywood," "Gollywood," "Riverwood," and so on, depending on which country one is focusing on – Nigeria's position becomes even more glaringly significant.

It was, afterall the Nigerian dramatist, Wole Soyinka, who became the first black man in history to win the much-coveted Nobel Prize for Literature, thereby attracting unprecedented world attention to African theatre. And it was also in Nigeria that the whole business of video films commenced and developed into the huge continental and Diaspora industry that it has now become; not to forget, besides, that it is Nigeria that still provides the largest market as well as the largest number of actors and producers for these films. Therefore, if for these reasons alone, it seems logical that developments in Nigeria, in these areas of cultural activity at least, can be taken to be representative of the continent as a whole. And for similar reasons, I believe that my own personal

experience, as wide and extensive as it is, could be taken as being fairly para-
digmatic, with a few variations here and there of course, of the broad
experience of theatre workers on the continent generally.

In this respect then, the first reaction I as a dramatist wish to share with you
is that of bewilderment, if not, in fact, of shock. For theatrical activity –
defined, that is, as live performances before live audiences – is in a state of crisis
on our continent. It has lost its popular appeal, and is rapidly on the wane. In
its place, bubbling and noisy like a newly sprung waterfall, is this new stock of
video films, which has completely overwhelmed the culture market.

Only the other day, one of our younger newspaper columnists, although
speaking generally of literary creativity as a whole, described the situation as
follows: "Today, while the Nollywood assumes the sky as starting point,
Nigerian literature is in the emergency ward, very close to the mortuary, and
not too far from the cemetery." I do not unfortunately have the precise reference of this quotation with me now, but those who live in Africa will agree at
once that the writer could not have put the matter more graphically.

However, in order for you to properly apprehend the dimension of this abrupt
transformation, and the reasons why it translates into a crisis for us practitioners of the traditional modes of entertainment, it would be necessary to pause
briefly at this point and set out the context against which the novel phenomenon of local videography has risen and established itself.

Again, I am obliged to be specific and personal here. As some of you already
know, perhaps, I not only come from Nigeria, but from the south-western part
of the country, an area which was until quite recently perhaps the liveliest and
most ebullient in terms of theatrical activity on the whole continent, and was
one of the most written about by scholars.

On three levels of the socio-economic divide – that is, among the rural peas-
antry, the suburban proletariat and lower middle class, and the educated elite –
the industry of drama was conspicuously busy and crowded, at least since the
1940s decade in Nigeria.

Among the first category of the population, village festivals and ritual ceremonies proliferated; while among the second group, professional troupes, and
in particular the Yoruba travelling theatre companies, led by Hubert Ogunde,
plied their trade in the urban areas, sometimes traversing the whole of the West
African coast. As for the third category, the educational establishments and
higher institutions bubbled with the activities of the Soyinkas and Sofolas, the
Clarks and the Rotimis.

These activities naturally spawned a parallel work of academic study, and
scholars like Biodun Jeyifo, Karin Barber, Joel Adedeji, and others, wrote about
them with fervour and eloquence. On the campus where I teach, as in surrounding allied institutions, numerous dissertations blossomed on the subject of

theatre and drama. But the shock is that, today, almost overnight, the bulk of all that scholarly production has turned ludicrously otiose, if not even nonsensical. Implausible as it may sound, the most recent books on the subject of Nigerian theatre have become suddenly irrelevant and embarrassingly dated, like archaeological relics.

In a manner that no one could have even dared to speculate some few years back, all these dramatic activities in south-western Nigeria seem to have simply vaporised: the traditional theatres have virtually ceased, owing mainly to the relentless exodus of rural manpower to the cities; on the campuses, economic factors and a corroding surge of "globalisation" have led to an implicit erasure of theatrical productions; and the once-flourishing travelling theatres of the cities have changed form and strategy, and dissolved into the world of the "home video" market.

If the situation is so dire in Nigeria, you may well imagine what it is like in other parts of the continent. That is why the concern nowadays, among the troubled practitioners, about the actual, or imminent, *death* of the theatre has grown into a palpable fear; and why it is a subject that haunts me, for reasons which I am certain you understand.

The irony is even more striking when you consider this development against the progress in our political history. It cannot but look strange, you will agree, that the years of creative ebullience in the theatre that we spoke about above, were the years coincident with vicious tyrannical regimes, both civilian and military, which proliferated on the continent in the latter half of the last century, along with the Apartheid government in the south.

Those were, you all recollect, the decades of the harsh suppression of human rights everywhere, when to dare to speak out at all was more or less to put your neck in the noose in the face of horrendous laws and decrees. Our rulers, with few exceptions, were corrupt and brooked no opposition to their misrule. Aided and encouraged by Western powers who had their own concealed neocolonial agendas, and by the avaricious multinational companies, our leaders looted the continent's wealth in a most extravagant manner, plunged our people into misery, and lengthened our night of underdevelopment. Naturally, they did not tolerate anyone speaking out about their corruption or profligacy, or reminding them of the people's anguish and simmering anger. So they were very sensitive to any voice of criticism and punished severely those who dared to oppose them or to attempt to unmask their evil doings. And in the racist American south, as we all remember, the story was no less brutal to the men and women unfortunate to be black and vocal.

But it is a tribute to our people that, during all those decades of tyranny and terror, many still refused to be silenced, and found various ways to sustain an unrelenting opposition to the wrongs. In the theatre, particularly, plays continued to be written and performed, which made the thieving rulers the target of attack, either by direct denunciation, or through indirect, surreptitious tactics. In the plays of Fugard, Soyinka, Ngũgĩ wa Thiong'o, and a number of others, the stage was defiantly turned into a channel of resistance, an active space of struggle, with the dramatists contributing their own talents to the grim fight for freedom, and for the ousting of the oppressors.

Naturally, therefore, the expectation was that, come the ousting of these treacherous governments, at last, and the transition to a democratic dispensation, the theatre, like the other arts, would experience a corresponding bloom, such that the repertory, hitherto circumscribed by the climate of fear, would explode like "a hundred flowers."

But surprisingly, however, that anticipated harvest has turned into a hollow illusion. Now, when the tyrants have been mostly driven from power, and the concept of democratic governance and of freedom of speech has been virtually reinstated in the constitution – it is precisely at this very moment that the creative energy on the stage seems to have drained out. Productions are sparse, the audiences thin; the scripts are, in terms of quality, neither here nor there. Worst of all, nowhere is anyone looking up any longer to the playwright for illumination or insight.

What is the reason for this paradox? Is it, as some speculate, because creativity is better stimulated by pain and distress, rather than by pleasure and satiety? There is, of course, as I have argued elsewhere, sufficient evidence in the history of art to support this line of thought – that the Muse, bruised and scandalised by anomie, grows loquaciously sensitive; whereas paradoxically, she tends to be tongue-tied in the absence of friction, to become complacently mute in the warm cocoon of success and fulfillment.

That line of speculation, therefore, has its own validity, we must concede. But if so, why is it then only in the field of the theatre that this drought is manifest? I think that before we lose ourselves in this philosophical and psychological whirlpool, it might perhaps be wiser to first concentrate on some of the more mundane factors on the socio-economic and political plane.

One area of direct pertinence, as many observers have noted, for instance, is the parlous economic situation, which has continued to worsen since the advent of flag independence and the imposition of the IMF-inspired Structural Adjustment Programmes [SAPs] on our countries. From a period of relative prosperity, of oil boom, which lasted for probably a decade in the 70s, Nigeria went burst, and plunged into what has been described as an "oil doom," a period, that is, of high inflation, massive devaluation of the national currency, and of a dubious debt peonage. Unfortunately, no regime since the early 80s has been able to repair the damage and put the economy back on a healthy course. The policies of the new democracies have not translated yet into any visible relief for the common man and woman. The redolent statistics announced in every budget seem to have gone only to further enrich the wealthy, while the poor keep falling into greater and greater desperation.

The consequences of this ruined economy on the theatre profession should not, therefore, be surprising. First of all, it meant that production costs went up, just at the same time that individual incomes were dwindling, and when more people were being retrenched from their jobs. That meant that, while on the one hand theatre companies found themselves obliged to raise the price of their tickets in order to survive, on the other hand, the bulk of the audience which came to these plays were themselves, even more than before, burdened with the problem of getting their daily bread, to the extent that the theatre soon became a luxury they could no longer afford.

To make matters worse still, the problem of social insecurity became an untamable demon, as a consequence of the spreading hunger and misery in the land, and of rising unemployment, particularly among school leavers. Violent crimes soon became commonplace; nowadays armies of social miscreants have virtually taken over the streets and the schools in the urban areas, while the forces of law and order have grown even more compromised and more inept.

This has meant that, in recent years, the majority of the population has abandoned the habit of going out for recreation after nightfall, with the exception, of course, of places such as night clubs or churches, where they can spend the whole night and stay sheltered until daybreak. Neither the theatre nor the cinema house is such a place as we know, at least not yet, and it is a further reason why they lost their audience.

Along with these reasons, we must also consider the death, in a rather strange and rapid sequence, of the giant, entrepreneurial trailblazers of the popular stage. After Duro Ladipo in Nigeria, the profession lost the pioneering Hubert Ogunde, then Ade Love, Oyin Adejobi, Ola Rotimi, Wale Ogunyemi, and several others, all within the same decade! This alarming depletion of the practitioners could not but bring a major disruption to the life of the stage, especially to the travelling theatres, given the fact that most of them were organised like traditional family enterprises, in which the lead actors were not only the producers, but also the central industrious *paterfamilias*. These giant figures were the ones who organised both the business of the companies as well as the creative products, and their audiences assembled more or less in loyalty to their particular talents, drawn to their fierce but fragile personality cults. As soon as they left the scene, therefore, the companies they led lost their followers, and eventually vanished from the scene.

But all the same, the most important of the factors leading to the decline of live theatre are undoubtedly the twin phenomena of the local video industry and the growth of Pentecostal churches, both of which have witnessed a spectacular blossoming in the last decade, and both of which are evidently products of the same severe economic slump. Both have brought astonishing transformations to the nature and practice of popular entertainment. Let us look at both in some detail.

First, it is perhaps not a surprise that the Pentecostal Christian movement should become such a huge phenomenon. After all, similar occurrences have been universally recorded throughout history at periods of economic recession and of social disequilibrium. At such dire moments, religious adoration becomes the answer to the desperation of the suffering populace. In the search for solace or escapism, for miracles and healing, for a powerful opiate against their daily anguish of living their lives, the masses of our people troop in ever increasing numbers to these churches, which have multiplied on an exponential scale in the last decade.

Whether fake or genuine, the fact is that these churches attract huge populations and, so, have been a major force in draining away both the creative agents as well as the audience of our theatres. Most of what we do on stage – the drama, the singing and dancing, the lighting and the costuming, etc. – have now been appropriated by these churches, and incorporated into their liturgical processes. The pastors have come to realise the power of drama and music as tools in the process of evangelisation, and of strengthening the illusion of wonder and supernatural presence for their besotted followers. Hence the despairing dramatists are obliged to run to these churches for the needed patronage and for what the failing secular theatres can no longer supply – such as financial remuneration, production equipment, publicity material, and so on.

So it is not surprising that some of the best actors and musicians and singers nowadays are to be found in the church "orchestras;" or that some of the most impressive musical compositions are in the church repertory. Indeed, just like in their early days at the beginning of the last century, these "Africanist churches" may be said to be the most fertile contemporary nursery for the discovery and mellowing of artistic creativity, whereas the theatre seats are now for the most part unoccupied. (I am informed, although I have not personally investigated this, that a parallel movement has begun in the mosques, as a strategic programme of countering the growing wave of Christian evangelism. If true, this will only further compound our problems in the theatre!) These religious congregations are the source of a substantial proportion of the next phenomenon we are going to discuss, that is the video market which, in Nigeria, has grown into a $250 million industry, employing thousands of school leavers.

The video industry has proved to be a marvellous expedient both for the erstwhile theatre practitioners and the suffering public. Given all the problems that the travelling theatres and their audiences have to face nowadays in the age of severe economic recession, as I briefly summarised above, recent advances in digital technology came at a most fitting time, and provided a fortuitous lifeline. Unlike celluloid films, the production of videos is relatively cheap and affordable: and as far as the popular theatres are concerned, it is a process that also helps to eliminate travelling costs, road hazards, extensive wage-bills, hall charges, and so on. At the same time it also brings in a higher revenue for much less labour.

Most crucially, besides, has been the audience's wild enthusiasm. To everyone's surprise, the public's hunger for home entertainment, given the hazards of the streets and of night life, proved to be so rabid and so insatiable, that a vast and lucrative market was soon created for these video films. "...Thank God for home video," exclaimed Larry Williams, one of our veteran actors. "If there was no home video, entertainment would have been dead in Nigeria."

This success of the home video is even the more astonishing, given the fact that it is completely homegrown and developed entirely on private initiative, through the sheer ingenuity of half-literate Nigerian entrepreneurs. Even they could not have foreseen the tremendous followership that it has won, or that this would spread beyond the borders of Nigeria, and eventually become the model for other, similar endeavours across the continent. And now the video film industry has absorbed not only the actors and producers of the travelling theatres, but virtually the entire bulk of our creative population.

Perhaps I should dwell a bit longer on this, and explain why it has won such a vast popularity not only on the continent, but in all the black Disapora, and become such a lucrative business. With some 30–40 new titles from over 300 producers flooding the shops of Idumota, Onitsha, and Kano every week, and with each film selling about 50, 000 on the average, the home video has virtually driven its Hollywood and Bollywood predecessors out of the African market. This feat has been made possible undoubtedly by the economic aspects of production. Home videos are cheap to make. Unlike the efforts of early Nigerian filmmakers like Ola Balogun and Hubert Ogunde in the 1960s, which were frustrated by the high costs of production, Nollywood movies use the new and accessible digital video technology, especially as the old bulky video cameras have given way to their digital descendants and the new High Definition cameras. Then editing, music, and other post-production work is all done with common computer-based systems, thus reducing the total cost of production by almost 80 per cent! Afterwards the films go straight to DVD and VCD disks, which are also cheap to reproduce and distribute, selling for the equivalent of about two dollars each. This, therefore, makes them quite affordable for most Nigerian families and provides as well astounding returns for the producers; although, on the negative side, it makes the films cheap for pirates!

Thirdly, because of the absence of such organisations as Actors' Equity, the producers do not usually have to pay high wages, except, of course, for the actors who have become super-stars. Indeed two years ago, in an astonishing protest against the fees charged by these actors, the producers decided on a one-year ban on using them, and resorted instead to amateur actors. They could do this because, in the main, their methods have not changed substantially from those they used in the travelling theatre days. This means that, rather than using written scripts with fixed dialogues and movements, directors for the most part rely instead on just the broad scenarios, with the action and dialogue improvised by the actors as the story unfolds. Thus actors are recruited on the basis of their looks, or of their peculiar talents – such as the ability to recite Ifa divinatory verses, or do acrobatic displays and clownish acts – which are then employed again and again in film after film. This is why amateur actors who are able to demonstrate these skills, and are sometimes just too desperate to appear in film to care about payment, are preferred to trained actors, and so bring down even further still the costs of production.

The next factor favouring these films is the use of aggressive publicity, such as posters, trailers, and especially radio and television advertising. In Nigeria, radio and television broadcasting began as long ago as the 1960s and has since expanded considerably, with both private stations and government stations in every state of the Federation. These media have also boosted the production of the home video, because government regulations soon limited the percentage of foreign films that could be broadcast any month. Hence, producers in Lagos began televising local popular theatre productions, many of which were circulated on video as well. Thus began the trade in this film genre. One important boost too, in Lagos, has been the National Theatre, whose management decided to give out its halls at heavily subsidised rates for the premieres of these films, and so ensured for many years that throngs of enthusiasts flooded the place every weekend to watch the films.

Finally, however, the strong appeal of these films to the audience must be attributed to the fact that the audience finds much in them that is a true reflection of their lives. Most of the films make use of local languages (with subtitles in translation for wider audiences), and of familiar, recognisable locations and characters with whom the audience can easily identify.

The films deal with familiar problems, problems that the audience share in their daily lives. Thus domestic stories, involving magic and the occult in the pursuit of wealth, have been very popular with producers, especially after the film, *Living in Bondage*, became the industry's first blockbuster in 1992. Failed marriages, usually shown to be a consequence of the above, are also a common theme.

But there have also been other films, such as those dealing with religious evangelism, or with the moral dilemmas facing modern Africans, and with such things as AIDS, corruption, women's rights, and other contemporary topics. Finally, we must also take into account that almost all the films try to end with some advice or moral lesson, in the tradition of folktales. This is a feature unlikely to be appreciated by Western audiences, but which is important to African spectators.

From all these, I believe it is now obvious why these films have grown spectacularly successful – it is, to summarise, because of the fact that, in the face of rampant economic deprivation and sociopolitical anomy, the filmmakers provide psychological relief for their consumers, in an inexpensive and intimate way the theatre has not been able to match.

Naturally, then, this home video phenomenon could not but lead to a number of transformations in the practice and even the definition of popular culture. African film, for instance, used to be defined exclusively by the rules set up by the West, and illustrated by the films of such legendary figures as Ousmane Sembène and his disciples. Financed largely by France through the Ministry of Cooperation and African Affairs, the films and filmmakers were mainly Francophone intellectuals, and so were inaccessible in the mainstream to most of the African public. But Nollywood has changed all that; and the home video industry is fast becoming a continental affair, with each country rushing to produce its own local version.

In addition, the industry has also brought a transformation to the audience, which has become wildly enthusiastic, almost to the point of fanaticism. Parents in particular are more approving of the profession now for their children, especially for girls eager to make acting a career. But there is a paradox, however, in this in that the public that knew and loved the experience of the live stage – both as actors and spectators – has decreased significantly with the gradual ageing of my generation; with most now sucked into religion, or business, or politics, and no longer having the time or the taste for leisure activities such as theatre.

But the transformation, in particular, that I want to talk about is the one brought to the actor and the performer.

Here there are crucial generational problems. The present youth, having been shaped by factors different from those by which we were raised and nurtured, are naturally different from us in their values, tastes and habits. No society, after all, is ever static; and we, too, are not our parents. But what is worrisome, however, is that the influences which have determined, and are determining, the character of our youth seem not to be the kind that we their parents would describe as positive. We were bred and seasoned in an environment where our culture mattered, and where our traditional customs held deep meaning. But sadly for our offspring of the "Age of Globalisation," the pivotal cultural items in their daily life are now those imbibed from American pop and media culture, dominated by such influences as the CNN, Channel O, The Face of Africa pageant, designer clothes and jewelry from abroad, lurid celebrity magazines like *Ovation* and *Encomium*, and so on.

Whereas we grew up in the age of liberation movements, of the communist struggle with capitalist power, of the fight against Apartheid, and so on; and whereas our heroes and models were iconic figures such as Mandela, Kwame

Nkrumah, Amilcar Cabral, Che Guevara, Angela Davis, Brecht, Fanon, Mother Theresa, Mahatma Ghandi and other such names, the generations which have succeeded us are those of the morning after – that is, of the age of capitalist triumphalism and the dominance of the American superpower, with its awesome control of the global media, and of the internet with its uncontrolled freedom.

Our children have grown up in the age of Structural Adjustment Policies and IMF-dictated economic policies, and of irresponsible, so-called democratic parties in power. In their time, the celebrated heroes are not the commanders of lofty dreams but rather, of what the Americans call megabucks, the ostentatious stars of the sports field or the musical charts, the barons of commerce and industry, the amoral, thieving politicians of this age of cynicism.

Hence, for the majority of the students, the greatest ambition they nurse is to emulate these figures they see daily in the media headlines and, like them, accumulate wealth by any means, however brutal, and in the shortest time possible, too. That is why, for them, the grand, humanistic themes which fill our plays have become like a grandiose hoax, bearing no relevance whatsoever to the reality they observe all around them. Their favourite entertainment is, therefore, something like the American fast food, supplying only instant and transient pleasure, rather than a more profound and more meaningful nourishment. This is the opium of the home video market.

But still, what disturbs me more about the younger generation is something I find difficult to describe, and which I will just paraphrase as "the death of the body." Because of the way most of them are now brought up, with hardly any exposure to our traditional ways and customs – some of them are not even allowed to speak our indigenous languages in their homes – the bulk of the youth that we are now bringing up on the continent are virtual aliens to our indigenous culture, with the alien's mentality and ignorance, and far different from the kind of Africans that we assumed ourselves to be!

Perhaps only the theatre people present here will understand me, but I am saddened to say that our young men and women seem to have lost – or perhaps, never developed – the kind of movements and gestures that we thought were necessary to become *African actors*. All they have, that is, are bodies, but not the bodies of *performers*.

The basic talents which we used to take for granted among our people are, sadly, no longer in the physical make-up of those following us. Senghor, for instance, was the one who boasted that anybody who was black, and who was born in Africa, would automatically know how to sing, and dance, and play a basic percussive rhythm. But no more; not with the present generation. Now we know that it was not the factor of our skin that made us so sensuous to rhythm and passion as Senghor erroneously claimed, but rather, the nature of our old societies. And unfortunately – or fortunately, depending on how you choose to look at it – those old societies are gone.

In my Yoruba society, for instance, nobody wakes the young people up with *oriki* any more, as the grandmothers used to do; nobody sings them to sleep with a folktale. Our youth no longer participate in the old festivals and ceremonies, which used to revive knowledge and rejuvenate the spirit. The young brides are no longer familiar with *ekun iyawo*, those dramatic chants and dances that accompanied them in procession to their husband's home. They know nothing of ancestral masks, other than to interpret them as the embodiment of Satan. The only songs they sing are taken from Channel O and the Euro-American Top Ten list, or from the church choirs. The costumes our children wear are jeans trousers, no longer those fascinating wrappers and headties that we older ones proudly associate with our culture; for fashion and body adornment, they take their models from CNN and the glossy American magazines.

All these factors have naturally altered not only the mentality, but also – a point crucial to the art of drama – the very *body language* of our youth. This is why it has become difficult to produce our plays, we older playwrights, since we wrote in the main precisely to flaunt and defend our culture against the incursing manners of the West. But now, all the semiotic signs that we used to assume to be intrinsic to our culture are no longer natural to the new actors. The spontaneous gestures are no longer there, nor the fluidity of movement one expects of African actors.

Thus, for instance, the flow of referents which should provoke from the actor certain spontaneous, somatic responses when you mention Ogun or Sango, or Orunmila, does not do so with the new actors, largely because they are deaf to the underlying ontological referents behind the names. Hence the attempt nowadays to produce a work of Soyinka, or Rotimi, or Ogunyemi can be a most tedious and exhausting experience, nearly like working with foreign actors.

So, what is the future, then, of formal entertainment in Africa? Will Nollywood continue to predominate, until it eclipses, and ultimately eliminates other forms, especially the practice of theatre? My own answer is that none of this will happen, that, in fact, what will come is a new era of fruitful collaboration between the practitioners of the stage and those of the home video. Just as there will be an increasing involvement of established playwrights and writers in the business of Nollywood, so will the latter too be brought to play a role in the revival of the stage.

Already, as we all know, complaints are mounting about the deficiencies of the home video films. Foreign and local critics alike talk about the films' trite plots, the poor dialogue, the terrible sound and light effects, the lack of sychronisation, the naïve use of costume and make-up, the wooden and predictable storylines, and so many other production defects. Moral purists and culture nationalists have also warned about the overwhelming prevalence of witchcraft and violence in the movies, a factor that may have a negative influence on the minds of its watchers, as well as encourage the worst stereotypes about

Africans. These complaints are leading to a fall in sales, although this may not be in any way substantial now to have any effect. But a collaboration with playwrights will undoubtedly help to correct many of these flaws.

In time, as producers become more and more conscious of the need to improve the quality of their products, they will begin to turn more and more to established playwrights and writers for scripts, and to successful books, for quality scenarios, just as in the Hollywood tradition. This will definitely lead to a greater discipline in the industry, and curb the careless reliance now on improvisation and amateur participation. The increased costs will be re-couped in higher sales.

The example is already there in the collaboration between Tunde Kelani, probably the best of the Nollywood filmmakers, and the playwright, Akinwunmi Isola. At least three blockbusters from Opamulero stable, Kelani's company – *Ko see gbe*, *Agogo Eewo*, and *Saworoide* – have been based on the works of Isola, who also did the film adaptations. Film critics still acclaim these films as among the very best in the genre.

On the other hand, theatre practitioners will also be increasingly tempted to exploit the advantage of having Nollywood celebrities in their cast. The National Troupe of Nigeria, for instance, under the direction of playwright Ahmed Yerima, regularly employs this approach now to boost attendance at its performances. Thus, famous Nollywood stars like Bimbo Akintola, Joke Jacobs, Uche Osetule, and so on have featured in Yerima's recent productions.

Similarly some of my own recent productions have featured names like Tunde Adeyemo, Gbenga Richards, Toun Oni, Yemi Solade, Edith Jane-Azu, and Michael Goualin, all well-known faces in the Nollywood industry.

The future, in other words, can be bright indeed for dramatists, either on the screen or the stage, but only if these suggestions for collaboration are taken seriously and acted upon.

# Emerging Issues from *Big Brother Africa 5*: Reflections on Reality TV, the Celebrity Status and Gender[1]

## Mansah Prah

"If you are female, chances of being evicted are high. You are not put on an equal playing field with the men."
"I am not a domestic goddess, I never was."

(Quotes from female contestants, *Big Brother Africa 5*)

"Remember u a celebrity and u got fans...they ff you and they want to be followed back just to get in touch..."

(A fan's tweet to a *BBA* 3 contestant)

On the evening of Sunday, October 17, 2010, *Big Brother Africa 5* (BBA5), themed *Big Brother Africa All Stars* – due to the fact that it featured contestants or "stars" from previous *Big Brother Africa* (BBA) shows – came to a close after 91 days of having been beamed into the homes of people in about fifty African countries twenty four hours a day, by MNet.[2] Like other *Big Brother* shows that have run in other countries, contestants are confined to a house for about three months while the world watches them as their daily lives unfold.

The *BBA 5* housemates acted out their lives in front of fifty-three cameras and one hundred microphones. Several events occurred during the 91 days that BBA5 ran: there was a love affair between two contestants which led to an on-screen engagement, women showing off their bodies, same–sex romps, a violent physical altercation between two contestants – male and female – and a range of arguments and discussions onto the screens of Africans all over the continent. Fourteen African countries were represented by the contestants. On the final day of the show, voters from eight countries selected the winner of the $200,000 cash prize, a young Nigerian man, out of five people who had made it into the finals. The first runner-up, also male, selected by seven countries, was from Zimbabwe. The competition had been fierce and very close. The managing director of MNetAfrica, Ms. Abiola Alabi, appeared on the closing show and stated that *BBA5* had enjoyed an unprecedented success, with over one million people voting via text messages and the internet.

The news about the ending of the *Big Brother* season and the fact that a Nigerian had won again (the winner from the previous show season was also a Nigerian) was reported on the internet, radio, newspapers and television in several African countries. The Nigerian President Goodluck Jonathan commented on the Nigerian win on one of his *Facebook* pages (accessed October 19, 2010). The news about the winner became controversial, because some people thought that the runner up had been cheated. By Monday, October 18, there was news on the internet, discussed in online newspapers, chat groups, fan sites and the social networking websites such as *Twitter, Facebook* and *YouTube*, that a group of businessmen from Zimbabwe had decided to raise $300,000 to compensate the runner-up. The names of two participants became worldwide trending topics that night on *Twitter*, and on October 19, 2010, at 11 p.m. GMT, the words "Uti won" were still trending worldwide on *Twitter*. When it dawned on African tweeters that *BBA* was trending world-wide, some of their tweets expressed their excitement; obviously African issues do not often become world topics on *Twitter*. On October 18, 2010, one tweet read:

> Lerato is trending? So is big brother Africa (bba) and its (sic) worldwide. Wonders shall never end.

A tweet sent out on October 19 read:

> Ok nw #uti won is trending. # nigeria going global.

The controversy about the winner continued to rage on October 19. Commenting on the negative comments, a tweeter wrote:

> Uti won, Munya tried hard it was a close race, so please stop the nastiness and let it go! 4 e sake of progress its over! Thank u!

On October 20, the UK *Daily Telegraph* published the story under the heading "Outrage in Zimbabwe after Contestant Loses African Big Brother Final."[3] According to the story, the office of President Robert Mugabe reportedly demanded recordings of the show.

Clearly, reality shows like *Big Brother* capture the hearts of their publics, evoke emotions and engender a wide range of discussions. A guest blogger on *The Zeleza Post*, January 11, 2008, wrote:

Reality TV is now a staple of the television industry. It has become a phenomenon for our increasingly fragmented societies driven by celebrity culture, titillated by voyeurism, subject to surveillance, and hungry for the communal rituals of authentic human experience. Not surprisingly, programmes like *Big Brother* and *Idol* have become highly profitable franchises. They are extremely popular and create instant celebrities even if it is for the proverbial fifteen minutes of fame. *Big Brother Africa* draws huge audiences from across Africa, offering an unprecedented forum for continental voyeurism and conversation on money and morality, cultural decency and pollution, pornography and popular culture, gender and class relations, racial and national stereotypes, globalisation and African cosmopolitanism or what some have called Afropolitanism. [4]

The reality TV genre is a fairly new global phenomenon which gained popularity in the Western world in the 1990s (Frau-Meigs, 2006). Programmes classified as reality TV have been described as a "very mixed bag" that include what are "essentially game shows, such as *Big Brother*, 'docusoaps' such as *Airport* and 'true crime' shows such as *Crimewatch UK*" (Sparks, 2007: 1). Divina Frau-Meigs (2006) describes the *Big Brother* show as "a combination of game show, talk show, soap opera and docudrama." In Africa it is catching on fast, and tends to overlap with youth culture although its audiences include the young and old. In Ghana, reality TV shows began to be aired on private television channels such as TV 3, and examples of successful ones are *Mentor, Ghana's most Beautiful*, and *Ghana's Most Talented Kid*. The first *Big Brother Africa* show directed at the audiences in a variety of African countries ran in 2003 (Dolby, 2006). Since then *BBA* has featured regularly on African TV and saw its sixth season in 2011. Academics have described *BBA* as a show that has the potential of "bridging cultural gaps" (Cardo, 2006) and it has also been cited as an example of a nascent cultural citizenship in Africa (Dolby, 2006).

By focusing specifically on *Big Brother Africa 5 – All Stars* as an example from the emerging cultural and media form of reality TV in Ghana, I hope to demonstrate that some of the issues raised by scholars who have researched reality TV and which have recurred in *Big Brother* (*BB*) studies, such as its occurrence within the context of a "new media" in an interactive and digital economy that extends beyond national borders and gives legitimacy to surveillance and panopticism (Frau-Meigs, 2006; Andrejevich, 2002); questions related to authenticity and the performance of self may also be of relevance in the African context. I explore the phenomenon of celebrities and celebrity culture, and I seek to show how celebrity culture is fostered by the media and particularly through Multichoice and DSTV in Africa. I discuss gender in *BBA 5*, and finally briefly discuss some of the ethical dilemmas I faced as I utilised data from social networking sites such as Twitter, Facebook and the chatrooms created on the *BBA 5* websites. In discussing all of the above, I draw on questionnaires answered by thirty-three Ghanaian *BBA 5* viewers and one *BBA 5* participant. The empirical part of the study is essentially audience research following the survey research. It also utilises observation.[5]

## Methodology

Questionnaires were given out to 33 people (twenty men and thirteen women) who had viewed *BBA 5* in the Cape Coast University community. The respondents were recruited using the snowball method and were mainly students and university staff, although one of the respondents was a worker at a bank located on the university campus. I managed to have one respondent who had participated in *BBA5*. This respondent filled in the questionnaire online. The total number of respondents, including the contestant, was 34. The majority of the respondents (78 per cent or 26) were between ages twenty and thirty, nine per cent or three were in the ten to twenty range and also the thirty to forty age brackets, and three per cent or one was aged between forty and fifty. Sixty per cent or 20 respondents were single, fifteen per cent or five were married, and the remaining twenty four per cent or eight were in relationships.

I also began to follow five *BBA 5* participants (four women and one man) on social networking sites such as Twitter and Facebook, in order to get a sense of the manner in which they construct themselves as celebrities. Further, I followed six other contestants on Twitter (two men and four women) who participated in other *BBA* show seasons,[6] as well as the Moderator of the weekly *BBA 5* eviction shows. There was one other important person I followed on Twitter, this was the Managing Director of MNet Africa. Following people on Twitter purposely for research created some personal challenges which I shall discuss later on in this essay. In the section that follows I discuss some of the recurring themes in *Big Brother* research, and then attempt to relate them to the findings from my audience research and observation.

## Unpacking *Big Brother*

Reality TV has aroused the interest of scholars in sociology, anthropology, media, communication, and popular culture studies. Some of the debates on the theme have ranged from the causes of its wide popularity, its generic traits which may facilitate the transmission of culture and cultural values; the ethics involved in the camera's exposure of personal aspects of ordinary life and its implications for authenticity and the performance of self; support or criticism of its democratising ethos and the role of reality TV in creating celebrities. *Big*

*Brother* is cited fairly widely by researchers in the debates on reality TV (Binessi and Nunn, 2005; Andrejevic, 2002; Hill, 2005; Turner, 2005), and there are also a number of studies devoted specifically to it (Johnson-Woods, 2002; Sparks, 2007; Frau-Meigs, 2006; Van Zoonen and Aslama, 2006; Dolby, 2006; Castro, 2002; Mathijs and Jones, 2004) and due to this, it seems justified to identify a thematic area on *"Big Brother* studies" as a sub-set of the literature on reality TV.

## The Beginnings of Reality TV, *BB* and the Ghanaian Connection

Writers like Sparks (2007) have located the upsurge of reality TV within the context of the development of the digital economy, technological changes that created cable and satellite delivery systems that made multichannel TV possible, and shifts in government policy towards broadcasting beginning in the 1970s and 1980s in the US and later in Europe. This occurred against the backdrop of a neo-liberal ideology that fostered competition and markets. The new development created challenges to national broadcasting that were met by a combination of strategies that sought to reduce payment to writers, actors, reduce rehearsals, reduce the need to pay rights fees for music and cut down on elaborate sets. Bernissi and Nunn (2005) locate the development of the genre within the context of the post-Thatcherite/Reaganite era in which social mobility and media visibility became markers of individual achievement. They also mention an ethos of late capitalist cultures whereby a diversity of life-styles, cultural pluralism, and niche marketing act together to produce fragmentation and self-reflexive individuals. Citing Frosch (1991), they argue that older, more traditional forms of authority such as the law, democratic governance, and the judiciary are critiqued and displaced by an increasing political cynicism and a turn to the self as the only possible marker of integrity. Citing Dovey (2001), Bernissi and Nunn state that the new technological forms such as the internet, the mobile phone and the video camera present the convergence of different media and the increasing emphasis on the individual subject as the guarantor of knowledge and producer of new economies of realism. Following Richards (1994) and Elliott (1996), they argue that mass forms of popular culture may provide ways of confronting and managing the basic psychic tensions of contemporary urban life (Bernissi and Nunn, 2005: 4). To me, this description of the state of the individual and his or her relationship to everyday life in the digitised age resonates with Van Zoonen and Aslama's assertion that *Big Brother* may have addressed a "post-modern zeitgeist" that extends beyond national borders (Van Zoonen and Aslama, 2006: 89).

So what does this have to do with Ghana, an African country that one would not describe as being firmly post-capitalist? The deregulation and privatisation of public broadcasting that began in Ghana in 1995 led to the proliferation of

FM radio stations in all the country's urban areas and later, from about 1998, the establishment of major private television stations such as TV3[7] (which re-transmits summarised versions of the *BBA* show), TV Africa-which began test transmission in 2002 and was launched on May 17, 2003[8] – and MetroTV. There are a number of private television stations such as Coastal TV and Crystal TV that do not have a wide outreach.

The introduction of private television and broadcasting has also created competition with the national public broadcasting system and the "new Ghanaian media" has been quick to seek niche programming. Apart from re-transmitting foreign programmes, some of them initiated their own versions of reality TV shows, a notable one being *Mentor* by TV3. The national television station, Ghana TV, or GTV, in response to the competition introduced by liberalisation, early in 2011 announced that it would soon feature 24-hour transmission. It now telecasts local versions of reality TV shows that have been successful internationally, such as the Ghanaian version of *Who Wants to be a Millionaire?* known in Ghana as *Do You Want to Be Rich?* GTV's promotion slogan is, "Still the only station with nationwide coverage" which, under the fierce competition it faces by its rivals, could soon change. The largest and possibly most sophisticated private television network that operates in Ghana (and in thirty-nine other African countries) is the Digital Satellite Television (DSTV) operated through the South African media company Multichoice which has a presence in about fifty African countries and nearby islands (Tomaselli and Heava in Dolby, 2006) and is responsible for producing *BBA* together with *Endemol*. The reality show *BBA* as well as others adapted to suit Africa such as *Deal or No Deal* and *African Idol* are all available through DSTV, which was launched in 1995 (http://en.wikipedia.org/wiki/DStv).

The transformation of the media and television industry which began to occur in Europe and the United States in the final quarter of the twentieth century was soon to have an effect in Ghana, from the late nineties. A development similar to that described by Sparks (2007) has taken place albeit on a much smaller scale, which is to be understood within the context of a relatively young media industry (see also Dolby, 2006: 35). The participation of Ghanaians in *BBA* and other local or Pan African reality TV shows could be linked to the rise of the use of the multi-media platforms such as mobile phone technology, and the internet that reality TV relies on. Ghana has seen a phenomenal rise in the use of mobile phones in the last ten years. Tracing reliable figures on mobile phone use in Ghana is difficult, but Araba Sey (2008) documented the phenomenal rise of mobile phone use with statistics from the providers. According to her, subscriptions for all mobile phone network providers had risen sharply since 2006 with Areeba (now known as MTN) consistently in the lead, and Kasapa (now known as Expresso) trailing. Areeba subscriptions grew from 5,000 in 1997 to over 2.5 million in 2006, and TiGo from 35,000 in 2001 to over 1.5 million in 2006. One Touch had 30,000 subscriptions in 2001 and almost 880,000 in 2006 while Kasapa had 2,575 subscriptions in 1997 and just over 200,000 in 2006 (Sey, 2008: 152). According to the July 2009 Audiencescapes National Survey of Ghana, 64 per cent of a sample of 2,051 adults in Ghana had television sets at home, 86 per cent had radios at home and 72 per cent had mobile phones at home.[9] The large number of mobile users in a given country in which BBA is aired facilitates the use of text messages for participation in voting contestants out. There were about 1,297,000 internet users in Ghana as of June 2010, according to the website http://www.internetworldstats.com/africa.htm#gh.

## What Characterises *BB*? Aspects of Some of the Debates in the Literature

In an article in which she demonstrates the acculturation process[10] that takes place through *BB* in Europe, Frau-Meigs (2006) also at the same time presents a fairly clear characterisation of *BB*. Frau-Meigs sees *BB* as a cultural product created out of an Anglo-American economic system,[11] broadcast by national media for the consumption of local audiences. She argues that the show is governed by rules recorded in a set of regulations which is adopted by all the countries in which *BB* is "played." It puts forward transcultural principles, applicable to all countries, requiring a homogenous adaptation: the Spartan house and lifestyle,[12] the lengthy confinement (about a hundred days), the absence of any media, the panoptic principle of surveillance, the confessional obligation, the battery of tests, the eliminating vote and the exhibition of ordinary people's private lives. All these rules are applied regardless of local custom (Frau-Meigs, 2006: 38), and a transcultural context is thereby created.

Although the *Big Brother* franchise creates rules for a world in the game that is similar wherever it is played, it allows for flexibility to contain specific cultural traits, so that different countries have slightly adapted versions. For example, the first season of *BBA* for the Africa-wide audience aired in 2003, included a "shower hour" which allowed viewers to watch contestants as they showered. The show proved to be controversial in Africa due to issues regarding perceptions of morality and decency, and some countries such as Malawi even banned it briefly (Special Report *Big Brother Africa*: Continental Voyeurism and Conversation, 2008).[13]

The image of the all-seeing *Big Brother*, representing the mediation of television, is presented like a protective family link. Unlike the intimidating figure in George Orwell's book *1984* which provides the reference for *BB*, the show aims at producing an image of power that watches and punishes in a "sympathetic, angst-less surveillance and compassionate chastisement" (Frau-Meigs, 2006: 43). The poison is taken out of *Big Brother's* fangs, making the panoptic principle amenable to the viewers and contestants. In fact, the contestants of *BBA* of the past few seasons refer to the voice of *Big Brother* as "Biggie" in quite an affectionate manner. The panoptic principle is made clear to participants and the audience from the outset, even though they do not really know how the surveillance is organised and how it is edited. Part of the mystique of the show is its open culture and supposed lack of manipulation, but in actual fact the audience and contestants become actors in a game that involves a variety of levels of authenticity. The contestants must behave in a sincere manner, and do on the screen, under the all-seeing eye of *BB*, what they would do in their everyday lives. The audience looks for authenticity in the contestants and punishes those who do not fit into the normative codes created through the interplay of the producers, the audience and the contestants. The audience is encouraged to participate and cultivate a sense of ownership of the programme by voting on which contestants should be evicted, which means they spend money through the use of their mobile phones, through the inter-net, which has websites devoted to the show[14] and also by sending text messages which may or may not appear on the news-strap at the bottom of the television screen. All this fits into the framework of the "new media":

> With reality TV formats, television is carving out its niche in the information society. Leaving to other media the production of other riskier and long-time investments, television claims itself for the interpersonal and intranational flow, for immediate use. These programmes show the current interaction between the economic order and the information order; they test the acceptable limits of what this interaction could be: it combines the acceptance of indi-vidualism in the market and the enhanced value of profit-making, with self-performance. (Frau-Meigs, 2006:44)

Andrejevic's research (Andrejevic 2002) has focused on surveillance in reality TV shows, and he unpacks reality TV in a manner similar to that of Frau-Meigs, both following a tradition linked to Marxism and the critical school. He argues that the online economy now relies increasingly on surveillance as a form of economic exploitation. As presented through reality TV as entertainment and self-expression, surveillance is actually a means whereby viewers and partici-pants are trained for their role in the "interactive" economy. The new economy behaves as though it is creating a democratic system by allowing its consumers to produce their own products–either by customising objects they consume (as for instance adding your own design to a Nike shoe online and buying it) or by participating in reality shows either as viewers who influence them through their votes or as contestants. The new interactive economy, however, does not actually give consumers the freedom they think they get; rather it subjects them to a complex system of manipulation and monitoring which is controlled by the marketing, advertising and business executives.

There are also viewpoints in the debate that take up the democratising ethos and adopt a position that is contrary to that expressed above. As Bernissi and Nunn (2005:147) have written:

> It is argued that reality TV's popular expression of social concerns and everyday events, within a highly managed environment signal the opening up of the public sphere to ordinary concerns and ordinary people who if they are popular enough and lucky enough, can become famous.

It is important to note that the opportunities inherent in reality TV as an entrée into fame and celebrity have been viewed critically by researchers like Sparks (2007), who argues that it presents a dream of escaping capitalism and alienated labour, an escape from conformity, and flowering as an individual. Contestants become celebrities for a short period during the show, but have to struggle to maintain the celebrity status afterwards.

Everywhere it was aired, the *BB* show provoked disapproval and critique for its promotion of voyeurism and immorality, and was sometimes touted as an example of low culture (Van Zoonen and Aslama, 2006; see also the *Zeleza Post* 2008 op.cit). The disapproval came more through media coverage and in Africa even from the state than through academia, and academics have described that critique as " elite moral panic" (Van Zoonen and Aslama, 2006; Dolby, 2006). What is interesting about the initial outcry against the show is that with subsequent shows everywhere including Africa the controversies appear to have been a key element in their success. Public discussion of the show has generated attention and the creation of a "discursive spectacle." Van Zoonen and Aslama (2006) have cited an example of a controversial decision taken by the producers in the Netherlands that appeared to revitalise flagging interest in the show. Here in Ghana (and in Africa generally) the controversial election of the Nigerian winner of *BBA5* described earlier in this essay, which created waves on social networking websites, the internet and African news media is a case in point. Even though a good seventy-five per cent of the respondents for this study claimed to have watched *BBA5* for entertainment purposes, thirty-nine per cent said they watched the show out of curiosity, based on things they had heard from others about the show.

In their review of *BB*, Van Zoonen and Aslama (2006) state that a recurring theme in *BB* studies is the view that the show offers audiences, particularly the youth, the frames of reference and identification that they no longer find in their lives due to the individualisation and fragmentation that is created through post-modern life. They link this theme with another recurring observation, that *BB* produces new bonds between otherwise disconnected people, citing *Big Brother* South Africa as an example. Dolby (2006) also suggests the possibility of *BB* as a potential contributory factor to African unity. I asked the viewers who responded to my questionnaires two questions related to this issue: one was their views on *BBA*'s ability to unite Africa, and the other was on the extent to which the show could erase stereotyped ideas that Africans hold about each other. Eighty-five per cent of the respondents thought the show could be a unifying factor for Africa, and the remaining fifteen per cent did not think so. On stereotypes, over fifty per cent of the respondents thought that the show had the capacity to strengthen stereotypes; twelve per cent thought the show would not be able to strengthen them, and another twenty-four per cent thought it could correct stereotypes about Africans. The following are some examples of positive responses to the first question:

> A good extent; they are doing good; it's a good way to unite Africa; at least if youth get to unify first; and the idea of picking from different countries is a good idea. I think they are doing good.
> (female respondent, aged between 10 and 20 years)

> *BBA*, hmm, I think it gives the youth something to talk about each season. Arguments over who is the best housemate actually bring individuals together, Like football (does) (sic).
> (female respondent aged between 20 and 30 years)

Viewed together with their responses to the question on stereotypes, opinions on the unifying potential of *BBA* are inconclusive. Of interest is the fact that the selected responses above reference the youth. Both viewers had responded positively to an earlier question that asked whether they thought *BBA* was directed predominantly at the youth. These answers resonate with the theme that arises in the literature on *BB*'s appeal with the youth, and also on the theme of the show's possibilities of creating, at least temporarily, a sense of unity among Africans (Van Zoonen and Aslama, 2006; Dolby, 2006).

## *Big Brother* and *Big Brother Africa*'s Viewers[15]

In the literature, *BB* viewing audiences have been characterised as young, generally female (Van Zoonen and Aslama, 2006; Frau-Meigs, 2006). Annette Hill's research showed that *BB* watchers are not different from any other reality TV viewers, apart from the fact that the show tends to attract a younger audience as well as adults who have children (Mathijis and Jones, 2004). Frau-Meigs (2006) describes the *BB* viewers as lower-middle class, mostly women and youngsters, urban, with little education. The most loyal audience is made up of young housewives between twenty and thirty years who did not attend university and are at home. This is followed by young people between twelve and twenty-five years, who are old enough to go to school but with little employment. In this way, the panoptic principle of an "angstless" or benign kind of surveillance is extended to the larger young European public, many of whom, like the contestants, have no clear occupation and have little education. This, she says, creates a common platform through which culture can be transferred across Europe's borders through the creation of the company Endemol.

In contrast to *BB* audiences, *BBA* viewers are quite different from the European viewers described above. The viewers in Ghana and other African countries are not lower middle-class but from the elite classes. This is linked to the relatively low levels of television ownership in Ghana as compared with Europe, as well as the high cost of DSTV subscriptions[16] (see also Dolby, 2006 footnote). A local television station, TV3, generally airs short thirty-minute daily summaries of the show, making it accessible to the majority of Ghanaians who do not have the DSTV service. The internet is also another source for following the show, and my survey showed that both television and the internet had been used in viewing the show. Table 1 presents the numbers for the various media forms the respondents used to watch the *BBA* 5 show:

**Table 1**: Sources for *BBA* Viewing

|  | Frequency | Per cent |
|---|---|---|
| DSTV | 19 | 57.6 |
| TV3 | 13 | 39.4 |
| Internet | 1 | 3.0 |
| Total | 33 | 100.0 |

Source: Author's fieldwork

The table shows that the majority of the respondents had watched the show on DSTV, and a respectable number on TV3. Internet viewing was represented by only one candidate, and this may be due to the relatively high cost – for students – of using the internet for *BBA* viewing or participation. It could also be linked with low bandwidth capacity in the Cape Coast community which results in slow internet access. The level of internet usage captured in this study may not reflect the reality of levels of internet use for *BBA5* viewing in Ghana. Figures from statistics of the *Big Brother* Forum on the official fan site of *Big Brother Africa* show quite impressive usage patterns within Africa, presumably created by young viewers. Table 2 presents the statistics.

**Table 2:** *Big Brother Africa* Forum Board Statistics (*Big Brother Africa* 5 – All Stars)

| Board Statistics | | |
| --- | --- | --- |
| **Totals** | **Averages** | **General** |
| Posts: 184,023 | Posts per day: 210.06 | Replies per thread: 17.89 |
| Threads: 9,742 | Threads per day: 11.12 | Newest Member: doosewa |
| Members: 40,553 | Members per day: 46.29 | Members who have posted: 15.71% |
| | Posts per member: 4.54 | |
| | Replies per thread: 17.89 | Todays top poster: Naijaninja (7 posts) |
| | | Most popular forum: Latest news (97,092 posts, 2070 threads) |

Source:www.bigbrotherafrica.com
*Big Brother Africa* Forum/Board Statistics (accessed 9.11.2010)

Although the statistics in Table 2 do not give a breakdown of communication on the website by country, they do provide material that throws some light on the general level of internet activity on the website. The statistics were accessed four weeks after the show ended, and there had been 184,023 posts from 40,553 members on 9,742 threads. The numbers of threads indicate the topics that are discussed; it is interesting to note that the averages show about 11 threads per day, from 46 members. More nuanced, gender disaggregated statistics by country and ages are needed for more meaningful academic analysis of viewer activity on the internet.

Unlike the relatively low level of education of European *BB* contestants observed by Frau-Meigs (2006), the African contestants are generally well educated, articulate young people, many of them are university graduates (see also Jacobs, 2007) who tend to be working in the areas of advertising, business, public relations, human resources. There has also been a good representation of contestants connected with the arts and design, such as singers, actors, film-directors, musicians, radio presenters, fashion designers and dancers. Due to the fact that *BBA* plays to a Pan African audience, it is necessary for the producers to recruit relatively well-educated individuals who have a good command of the English language so that they can be easily understood across Africa. Even those candidates from Lusophone countries such as Jen and Tatiana from *BBA5* displayed a satisfactory command of the English language. So far participants from French speaking Africa have not featured in the show.

## Viewers' Perspectives on the Show

In their study on viewers' attitudes and views on *BB* Belgium, Mathijs and Hessels (2004) found that their respondents tended to focus on the textual element of *BB*. They placed the contestants at the foreground of the text, often focusing on cultural stereotypes they identified in players' behaviour – in terms of personality, attitude and actions. This resonates with my observations of online discussions on the *BBA5* show as well as the comments that appeared on the *BBA5* news strap:

> I really do not like her ... she looks demonic to me
> And she lives by others helping her[17]
>> (Comment from one of several *BBA5* fan pages on Facebook)

> Uti is a real man.
> Beautiful Lerato. You rock. Uti out.
> My Lerato is a true African woman.
> Uti has no brain. He has played the game according to what Sheila told him and yet he hurt her feelings.
> Africa instead of voting that stupid Munya who insulted you, vote Uti, Lerato or Mwisho.
>> (Comments from the news strap on television from 12.10.2010)

Describing a *BBA5* housemate she admired, one of the respondents to my survey wrote:

> ...there was one fat lady who just smoked round, minding nobody's business. I loved her. She just went about the house as though it was her home, she's so real.
>> (female respondent, aged between 20–30 yrs)

An older viewer wrote:

> I thought Tatiana was genuine, honest and spontaneous in all she did and I admired her for it. She was one who was least fake.
>> (male respondent, aged between 40 and 50).

Another respondent wrote:

> Yacob was analytical and I think that made him my favourite housemate.
> Lerato was always herself which I think also won my admiration.
>> (male respondent, aged between 20–30 yrs)

As Mathijs and Hessels (2004) observed, a broad range of comments and attitudes came from the viewers, ranging from extremely negative to nuanced to extremely positive. The viewers all had opinions, and strong ones, too, on the contestants. This was also true for the respondents in my survey. The last two quotes cited relate to the question of viewers' focus on authenticity and the performance of self that recurs in the literature as one of possible explanations for the success of reality shows like BB (for example Binessi and Nunn, 2005, 2006). In their analysis of viewers' focus on authenticity, Van Zoonen and Aslama suggest that BB succeeds in settling some of the predicaments created by post-modernity by making private lives a matter of collective discussion rather than of individual struggle, and by confirming that the self is a continuous project to work on.

> The latter seems to be the key to understanding audience investments in *Big Brother* scenes; the show evokes a pleasurable exercise in assessing its realness and the authenticity of its housemates, and more generally what it means to be "true to oneself," one of the core values of hyper individualised Western societies.
>
> (Van Zoonen and Aslama, 2006: 92)

They go on to state that the audience research referred to comes from England and Germany, both developed post-modern and individualised societies in which the preoccupation with the authenticity and the self is replicated in the other media genres and magazines. They question the likelihood of the trend of the performance of self and authenticity as an important aspect of the impact of BB in "underdeveloped societies with stronger communal structures and with institutionalised social divisions" (Van Zoonen and Aslama, 2006: 92). This is of particular interest for a country like Ghana.

I have reservations about Van Zoonen and Aslama's argument, because the viewer responses I received do not reflect a lack of engagement with authenticity and the performance of self. In fact, some of the answers directly referenced the issue. Fifty-eight per cent of the respondents admired their favourite housemates in BBA5 due to the fact that they were bold and "real." In answer to a question about what it is that makes the BBA show popular the most popular answer was "because of the intrigue and the behaviours are real" (thirty-six per cent). The impact of BBA, I would argue, is felt by the elite, who have the strongest cultural and lifestyle connections with Western societies. They are the ones who consume imported media products most, and it is from the ranks of the educated and privileged African youth that the contestants are selected. The essence of the post-modern spirit, with its focus on self-reflexivity, democratisation of the celebrity status, self-performance of the ordinary person as signs of the real and authentic is felt in a country like Ghana, not by the masses, but the leading groups of the society, to whom it filters through their consumption of trans-cultural media products like *BBA*. Filtering through to the elites of Africa, the acculturation process may herald the beginnings of a kind of African cosmopolitanism or an "afro-politanism" as the blogger in the *Zeleza Post* (1980) suggests; but it should also be seen as an aspect of globalisation.

In an article that discusses the globalisation of local media and the charges of Western domination as a result of the process, Gadzekpo (2005) debates whether Western media crowds out locally relevant media content. She points out that there are moments of resistance to the process and cites public insistence on using local languages on English-language phone-in programmes. She also, however, discusses the importation and adaptation of Valentine's Day and Mother's Day in Ghana, a process spearheaded by media and business interests. The percolation of foreign cultural values into everyday Ghanaian (and African) life is obviously complex and, as Gadzekpo says, "though global cultural flow may not signal the demise of national cultures yet, there is the risk that the poorest and the weakest nations may be further weakened in the huge global marketplace."[18] In the section that follows I shall briefly examine gender in *BB* and attempt to link it up with *BBA5*.

## Gender Issues in *Big Brother* and *Big Brother Africa*

It has been argued that the format of *BB* confines it to the private, domestic leisure space, and separates the contestants from the public, productive workplace. It also does not pay the contestants wages for their time and in so doing does not recognise their labour. In this way, *BB* "feminises" the situation of its participants (Frau-Meigs, 2006). The review by Van Zoonen and Aslama (2006: 93) bemoans the fact that research has not been able to explain why *BB* is so popular with young women, why females provoke more aggressive and negative comments on websites, chat lines and blogs than men, and whether and how *BB* ties in with a feminisation of culture. There is no research on *BBA* that can explain or corroborate these findings. My observation of communication on websites and the news strap, however, adds credence to the fact that females receive more negative comments from viewers but this would need to be confirmed with empirical data. The argument that the show "feminises" the situation of the participants is feasible but there is an alternative take to the fact that the contestants do not receive compensation for their time, with researchers like Andrejevich (2002) seeing it as a plain exploitation of labour. In *BBA5* the participant known as Yacob recognised this fact and demanded compensation from *Big Brother* for being moved to the "barn," an alternative house that evicted participants were moved to. Yacob elected to leave the game prematurely when *Big Brother* refused to pay him.

Although tasks are assigned to the contestants without gender considerations, the housemates themselves tend to perform their voluntary chores following mainstream gender role scripts. In each *BBA* season there is a female contestant or more who take on the mothering, caring role, but apart from the first season of *BBA* when a woman, Cerise, from Zambia, won the game, no woman has since won. Cerise perhaps won due to the nurturing role she played; she was praised for her conduct in the house by the Zambian President Mwanawasa who said to her,

"A Zambian woman must cook and sweep, and you did exactly that. I am not surprised that you have received many marriage proposals" (Jacobs, 2007).

In subsequent seasons playing the role of a "domestic goddess" has not clinched the prize for any female contestant, and this may be due to the fact that audiences–the media, viewers, public opinion on the text of the show, the agenda of the producers, even contestants' strategies of playing the game–are variable, changing from season to season (see also Mathijs and Hessels 2004). Some of the female contestants, particularly Lerato and Sheila in *BBA5*, who did not fit into the category of "nice women who clean, cook and sweep," appeared to be acutely aware of viewer prejudices towards women contestants and which could result in pressure to conform to mainstream notions of the "good woman:"

> If you are female, chances of being evicted are high. You are not
> put on an equal playing field with the men.
> I am not a domestic goddess, I never was.

The two contestants discussed the difficulties women contestants have in winning the show, and Sheila's contention that "it is time a woman won this show" was subsequently used by the show's producers in one of its advertisements for the *Big Brother Africa* sixth season aired from May–July 2011.

The viewers in my survey had mixed responses to a question on whether they thought men were more likely to win in *BBA* than women. Thirty per cent of the viewers agreed, saying that we live in a male-dominated world. Thirty three per cent thought that both men and women have equal chances of winning, and twenty-four per cent thought that men are craftier than women and therefore stand to win. In effect, about fifty-five per cent of the viewers thought that men are more likely to win in *BBA*.

The confinement of *Big Brother* contestants for a period of three months fosters a fair amount of sexual innuendo in its texts, leading to intimate relationships between contestants, and a lot of flirtatious heterosexual behaviour. In *BBA5* the female participants spent a lot of time dressing up and applying makeup for the Saturday night parties and the Sunday eviction shows, unwittingly exhibiting stereotypical "feminine" behaviour. In this way *BBA* confirms mainstream values and attitudes towards women. At the same time, it sometimes provides opportunities for open discussion about gender (and other) issues that may be controversial or difficult for Ghanaians (and Africans generally) to discuss. In *BBA5* a verbal altercation between two barnmates that ended up with the male barnmate striking his female colleague led to a discussion on gender violence that was taken up in the print media, websites, chat rooms and text messages. The following article that appeared in the online version of the South African newspaper *Southern Times* titled *"Big Brother Africa All Stars ...A Continent Caught between Past and Future"* clearly brings this out:

> From the small screens in our living rooms, Africa has became (sic) part of its youth strategies to come to terms with the complex issues of youth sexuality and gayism; joined the house and barn mates public awareness campaign against our burden of disease in the form of malaria; routine tendering of the two houses green gardens to avoid degradation; the barn chores including early morning cow milking; ridding us of gender-based violence (GBV) by expelling the women-insensitive Ugandan contestant Hannington from the barn; condemnation of the African education system which according to the barn mates leaves much to be desired in terms of both quality and timeliness as compared to the Western education, sharing in the joy of *BBA*'s social responsibility extended to the old people's home in the form of the grand flower bouquets delivered at the door steps of an old people's home to brighten its residents' day and its reciprocal appreciation; and the debates on how to confront the HIV and AIDS pandemic and role of marriage in modern day Africa ...

But what has crowned this *BBA5* episode this far is both the house and barn mates' views on human sexuality, marriage, faithfulness and divorce and the role of traditions and customs. Their expressed strong negative reactions to Mwisho's marriage proposal to Meryl and the subsequent engagement in the house attended by Meryl's relatives illustrated Africa's fast changing culture. Both the house and barn mates kept on reminding us that Meryl is a mother of two kids, the last one being an infant.[19]

There is another event that occurred during the *BBA5* season regarding sexuality that merits mention in this section on gender issues. Meryl and another housemate Sheila were seen in bed together, presumably being intimate under the bedclothes. This created a quick, huge backlash from the viewers, particularly on the television news strap and on social networking sites. I noted a vicious remark about one of the women involved in that episode on the news strap:

Bloody, bitter lesbo. Woman banger.

Carrie Polansky commented on the incident on her blog "Gender across Borders" under the rubric "The Power of Reality Television: Lesbianism on *Big Brother Africa*" (see http://www.genderacrossborders.com/2010/08/31/the-power-of-reality-television/#more-13891):

> Though the reactions to Sheila and Meryl's actions have been critical at best and homophobic at worst, that may not be a bad thing. As Jim Burroway writes on Box Turtle Bulletin, homosexuality needs to be acknowledged and debated as the first step toward education and eventual acceptance.

Polansky rightly argues that although

> reality television is not typically considered to be a vehicle for discussing social justice, moments like the one between Sheila and Meryl are important reminders that pop culture often is a place where education and progressive messages can occur. Whether or not it was intentional, this recent moment on *Big Brother All Stars* ignited a much-needed conversation in Africa. Homophobia has produced dangerous realities in Africa, including Uganda's Anti-Homosexuality Bill, Malawi's, imprisoning of a perceived gay couple after their wedding and, police raids in Zimbabwe targeting LGBT people.
>
> Gender issues that emanated from the BBA5 season were varied and complex, reflecting the gender landscape and discourses around it as it plays out in contemporary Africa. I reflect on the show's role in the creation of celebrities in the section that follows.

## *Big Brother Africa* and the Celebrity Status

Much has been written about the stardom and the celebrity status in social science literature (Alberoni, 1972; Marshall, 1997; Dyer, 1979; Holmes and Redmond, 2006; Kurzman et al. 2007). It is not my intention to discuss the literature in this essay, but only to point out that stars and celebrities[20] are creations of the media and I hope to show how celebrities are created through *BBA*. Marshall (1997) states that celebrity is not really a coherent concept and that it represents a voice above others, success and achievement. It is often ridiculed and derided as a false value. According to Geraghty (2006: 97) the term celebrity indicates someone whose fame rests overwhelmingly on what happens outside the sphere of their work and who is famous for having a lifestyle. The celebrity is thus constructed through gossip, press and TV reports, magazine articles and public relations.

In Ghana, it used to be that the famous were found mainly among the ranks of politicians, and traditional rulers. With the expansion of the television and the print and electronic media, as well as the growth of the entertainment industry, the celebrity status has grown to include artists, actors, writers, musicians and even pastors and leaders of the new churches. Until the middle of the nineties the national TV broadcaster GTV did not feature an "entertainment" segment in the daily news telecast. It is now a regular feature, also influenced by competition from the private television stations and the growing entertainment industry. I suggest that a similar development has occurred in several African countries. *BBA5* or *BBA All Stars*, as it was themed, clearly set out to cultivate celebrities by bringing back people who had been on *BBA* on earlier seasons. They were already known to the African public, and the fact that their comeback show was named *Big Brother Africa All Stars* shows a clever construction of celebrities. Some former *Big Brother Africa* participants have risen to celebrity status after leaving the show. A good example is the Ugandan Gaetano Kagwa, who appeared in the first season of *BBA*. During the show, he had sex in the house, causing a furore in the media. He later on became a host on *Studio 53*, a lifestyle magazine show on MNet that featured celebrities, gossip and interesting venues to visit across Africa. The first hit on a Google search on him[21] came up with an item about his marriage that appeared in the online entertainment newsletter Jamati.com. Other former *BBA* participants use their link with *BBA* (or the media does it for them). News and gossip about the former *BBA5* housemates can still be accessed on www.bigbrotherafrica.com/BBA5/. In Ghana examples are three out of four former housemates – the fourth unfortunately was evicted after having been on the show for a week and is therefore not well known – who are constantly linked to the show whenever they appear in the print media. The connection with *BBA* is also used by its participants to further their careers. A former housemate describes herself on her Twitter profile as: "an ex *Big Brother* house mate, an award winning artiste, a performer/entertainer..." The sole former contestant who responded to my survey answered a question on how participation on *BBA5* has made an impact by simply saying, "It is giving me extra mileage for my career." A former participant of *BBA4* presents himself on Twitter as:

"First Moz[22] on Big Brother Africa4/DJ/Model/Martial Artist/ Public Figure/IT"

Viewers of *BBA5* who participated in my survey were asked to choose one of three terms to describe the former participants: "popular individuals," "celebrities" and "not ordinary people." About forty-nine per cent chose "popular individuals:" forty-two per cent chose "celebrities" and nine per cent said "not ordinary people." Forty-five per cent of the respondents follow the former *BBA5* participants on Facebook, Twitter and other social networking sites, while fifteen per cent watch out for news on them on the official *BBA* website.

The *BBA* celebrity construction takes place on four fronts: through the television network; through the contestants; through the print and electronic media; and is fuelled by the curiosity of their fans. It is a system, of sorts, dependent on the entertainment industry, which has expanded onto the internet. The celebrity status acquired through participation in *BBA* (and other reality shows generally) needs to be cultivated in order for it to thrive. Basically, it represents the proverbial "fifteen minutes of fame" (Sparks, 2007; Andrejevic, 2002) which may die if it is not nurtured. The democratisation of the celebrity status as described by Andrejevic and Sparks is a feature of the digital and interactive economy.

Aleks Krotoski (2011), whose research centres on the social psychology of relationships in online communities, argues in her column in the UK *Observer* newspaper[23] that the internet has changed the way the public interacts with celebrities. She says that the web has usurped the relationship between the media and the audience, and moved the power to decide who is a celebrity into the hands of the public. The entertainment industry has lost control over the public, who have upset the balance thanks to long camera lenses and a free-to-access publication platform that reaches round the world:

> But not only has the web transformed how we interact with our idols, we the audience have also wrested the power to create celebrities from the traditional star-makers. We can now act outside the system, promoting ourselves using similar techniques as the studios, using carefully placed pieces of media and cultivating followings among specifically targeted communities. We can also thrust unwitting people into the spotlight by posting a video on Twitter or Facebook for our friends to see and pass on. Web fame is a moving target and utterly unpredictable.
>
> However, Krotoski concedes that "online fame is still only second-best." It is useful to note that the democratisation of celebrity is taking place still within the context of the economic order.

## Other Matters Arising: Researching Online

There is one final issue, not directly related to *BBA*, but which has arisen in the process of researching this essay, to be reflected on. Researching this essay drew my attention to issues related to researching internet communication. Prior to the digital and interactive age, social science research dealt with real as opposed to "virtual" data. To do proper justice to an essay such as this one, it would be more satisfactory to have performed a content analysis of the comments that appeared on the *BBA5* news strap, for example, or to mine the tweets by former *BBA* housemates as well as the threads and replies that appeared on the *BBA* official websites, using software designed for that purpose. Did such software exist? I noticed that on the news strap, viewers had begun to form fan clubs around their favourite housemates and it might be very interesting to study such groups. But how could the data be harvested systematically? This data belonged to the producers, and they would not share it with me surely?

I felt challenged about how to cite people's responses, and agonised about the ethical implications of citing their responses without seeking their permission. Would I risk being sued? But, then, why is it not possible to quote opinions that have been posted on the web anyway? What are the implications of using data from social networking sites in research, granted that the data is considered as a valid source. And how authentic is such data? People use monikers widely in chatting on Bigbrotherafrica.com; how "authentic" are their statements? I eventually sent the copyright owners at Bigbrotherafrica.com an email seeking permission to use their website for my research, which they kindly granted me. These are some of the questions that I faced, and it became clear to me that there is the need for African social scientists to come to grips with such issues. As a postscript, of sorts, to the catalogue of unanswered questions listed above, I did discover an online International Journal of Internet Research Ethics (www.ijire.net) with an editorial board that, sadly, did not have any scholars from Africa.

## Closing Remarks

This essay has been rather ambitious in its attempt to sweep together the Western discourse on *Big Brother*, which traverses a broad range of disciplines such as communication studies, media and cultural studies, sociology and anthropology and relate it to the rather sparse academic literature on *Big Brother* in Africa. In doing this there have been many pages left unturned and many issues glossed over.

I have attempted to show how the rise of reality TV in Ghana has developed, as in many other countries, within the context of the liberalisation of the airwaves and changes in the media economy. *BBA* itself is a product of a burgeoning media and entertainment industry that is based in South Africa but is linked to local African entertainment industries (the largest player is probably Nigeria) and global franchises like Endemol. *Big Brother* is a trans-cultural product of the post-modern West, which is flexible enough to adapt to local conditions. In its Pan African version, it does not lose its focus on the performance of self, or panopticism, but unlike its Western sister *BB*, its consumers and performers belong to the African elite. This demonstrates the continued role of elites as a cultural bridgehead connecting the West and Africa. Both *BB* and *BBA* present an image of a benign *Big Brother* that is essential for societal acceptance of the panoptic principle in the digital, interactive economy. In Africa this might not be immediately obvious, and in the globalised economy not all changes occur in an equal spread despite the fact that the profit motive still holds sway.

The *BB* and *BBA* shows demonstrate the democratisation of the celebrity status and in the case of *BBA*, it serves as a vehicle for airing gender and other issues that ordinarily would not be put out in public spaces in Africa. One may question the need to study a show that appears to be mainly elitist. However, as an aspect of the reality TV genre that has firmly settled within the landscape of entertainment in Sub Saharan Africa's urban world, it is well worth studying due to its complexity, as a vehicle of the essence of post-modern conditions playing against pre-modern and modern frames in the construction of social change, its capacity to politicise through its capability of stimulating a discourse on issues that are controversial and at the same time to de-politicise, through its focus on the self.

# Mac Tontoh:
# The Saga of a Broken Trumpet[1]
## Kwesi Yankah

## Song Intro

Yes, Mac Tontoh must have known it was coming, and prepared the way before the final hour struck. To any great musician, the time to bow out is when the applause of the audience has not subsided.

The first time I set eyes on Mac Tontoh was in the mid-seventies when, by happenstance, a concert promoter decided that students at the university also deserved a taste of Osibisa. They had just arrived from London, their base, after a major world tour. It was hard to believe one could see Osibisa *live!* We hurriedly finished our routine chores that day, and headed towards the forecourt of the Great Hall.

Even though the scheduled time was 8 p.m., we booked our seats at 5 p.m., ensuring for ourselves ringside opportunities. But we also wanted to see it all, including the unpacking of instruments. Two huge vans soon arrived and porters started unloading huge stuff from the vans. But there was something more stunning: the sight of a bunch of white guys in their thirties carrying Osibisa instruments from van to stage. Those Caucasians appeared to be porters doing menial jobs for African super stars, Osibisa. It was hard to believe the inversion of power. A good one there! Students whispered and chuckled.

The stage was set for a great evening, and the forecourt up the Legon Hill was oversubscribed: students, lecturers, truck-loads of music lovers from Accra and beyond. Legon at the time was a lonely island, the nearest neighbourhoods being Okponglo and Madina. West Legon was spooky and nameless. East Legon, an embryo, nestled in a mother's womb. Between Legon and 37 Hospital was a long forest stretch, intermittently broken by plush house clusters on which birds feared to perch.

But the ivory tower of learning hovered above the sprawling vegetation, embracing the elements. From here it beckoned men of fame to come hobnob with Legonites and rub on the heritage. The call had been heard; and Osibisa that day was holding court underneath, to spill fragments of what had made them great. The reception was ecstatic, and the entire event explosive!

For two good hours, the convocation group of buildings throbbed and rocked to Osibisa rhythms crisscrossing the firmament, filtered through giant loud speakers symmetrically positioned. Fingers snapped to the beat, hands swayed, feet tapped in rhythm, and heads nodded in unanimous accord with Osibisa. If the forecourt were Parliament, the speaker's gavel would have been thumped to signal a unanimous vote: no nays, and no abstentions!

But there was a reason for the consensus. Osibisa had turned us all into children. We had been lured to reach back into childhood and do what we did when we were young. The large crowd, almost under hypnosis, grabbed anything within reach, fallen tree branch, empty beer bottle, and played and danced along with the world famous musicians. If we were ashamed of our politics, at least music made it great to be Ghanaian!

## Restless Warrior

All this was possible also because the entire Osibisa group were children while on stage, and had carried everybody along. They had succeeded in igniting the kid in everyman with *chechekule, kokrokoo, mumunde*. Of all the kids in the group, the 'kiddiest' was evidently the dark handsome, restless trumpeter: Mac Tontoh!!! When he was introduced by the MC, the house almost came down. And he gleefully responded, with a piercing trumpet flurry, a signature tune of sorts. Holding his trumpet aloft, he jogged his way from one end of the stage to the other, soaked in sweat, dancing, singing, screaming, excited.

Throughout the two hours, there was no dull moment for Mac Tontoh.

Call him the nomadic trumpeter: he paces back and forth; jogs to and fro; stops and blows the trumpet. In the next minute Mac Tontoh joins the chorus, stops through, runs across the stage, picks a gong-gong, strikes it and drops it; picks a whistle, blows it, drops it, dances his way to Amarfio the drummer, signals him to raise the tempo, returns, dashes to the keyboard man, raises his hands, jumps high on his feet, and lands on the final beat, to terminate the song.

*That is the man we mourn today. Call him the restless high priest pacing back and forth, dancing, spinning and twirling his body, until healing is achieved.* World music in the 70s and 80s would have been poorer without Osibisa. With this tragedy, the performance stage has been robbed of vitality in African music. World music is today bereaved. Mac Tontoh was the bunch of slim firewood that in the fireplace kept the flame alive. You know, ferocious flames are often not stoked by the huge logs piled across the furnace; it is not the big logs sprawling atop the hearth that stoke the flames; it is rather the bunch of slim firewood, *mmabaa*, that keeps the flame alive. The bunch of slim firewood, we knew, was the trumpet of Mac Tontoh.

*He would blow it, suck it, hiss, buzz like a bee... his nimble fingers would in one minute rattle or massage the valves to send a loving bouquet to the audience. In the next minute Tontoh's trumpet snarls, howls or bellows in fury when the mood demands. Here Mac Tontoh is on the prowl... playing the aggressor. In another moment, a waterfall is unleashed and trickles down in torrents to restore life to nature. That a simple piece of instrument can be made to chuckle, tickle, wail, tease or simply flip through the vagaries of human emotions with ease; that can only be the work of a divine artist, to whom even the inanimate can be obedient.*

## Sins of the Trumpet

But such feats are not achieved overnight. History recounts Mac Tontoh's sojourn through the Comet Band, Uhuru Dance band... and then Osibisa. But Mac recounted to me how it all started, and his adventures while learning to play. Mac Tontoh told me only last year that he learned to play the trumpet early in life. In the neighbourhood where he lived in Kumasi, called the Fanti New Town, he would practice the trumpet in the afternoon, a time most elders were taking a nap. The nuisance, of course, would not be tolerated in the ward. In a matter of minutes, the royal guards or the *ahemfie* police of the Ashanti King, would trace the source of the noise, and come over to terrorise him. They would seize him by the wrist, and give him a few knocks on the head. Sometimes they would lock him up in the cell, to restore tranquility in the neighbourhood. In the process Mac Tontoh's trumpet was sometimes seized; for he was disturbing the entire neighbourhood, including the king, at a time elders were at the peak of quiet contemplation.

As a young boy, then, he went in and out of prison, learning to play the right thing at the wrong time.

This went on and on, until the news got to the King, Nana Agyeman Prempeh II. Hearing this, Nana, indeed a true patron of the arts, as all kings of Ashanti are, immediately called young Mac Tontoh, and gave him back his trumpet. Nana then gave Tontoh the authority to continue his trumpet lessons in the afternoon, giving him all immunities necessary, and warning his guards to leave the young man alone. Nana Agyeman Prempeh gave Mac Tontoh the right to practice his trumpet without interference. With royal intervention, then, came a restoration of the rights to free expression, call it freedom of the trumpet, under Ashanti rights. For while others could boast of verbal fluency, the world knew Mac Tontoh for his trumpet eloquence, the art of public speaking with the trumpet.

In the Ashanti state, where a whole ward or suburb, could be named after a traditional musical ensemble, Asokwa, Apirede, Bombaa; where babies strapped to the back of mothers rock to adowa rhythms; a place where toddlers play with drum sticks before they walk – on such terrain, any censorship of children learning to create joy, would have been tragic. The Ashanti environment inspired Mac Tontoh, discovered him, nurtured him and tolerated his noise. The noise, indeed the nuisance, later turned into melody, and sent Mac Tontoh and Osibisa on a mission to transform African rhythms, and put it on the world map.

## Echoes in the Mountains

But there was another encounter with this great man we mourn. It was in the mid 1990s, somewhere up the Aburi Mountains. It must have been Tutu or Mamfe, on a July 1st holiday when I took my family to listen to him and his newly formed Kete Ensemble at Chester's Place. The place was packed to capacity; and Mac with an ensemble of kiddie drummers and dancers from Kumasi, animated the crowd of holiday-makers, punctuating the ebb and flow of Ashanti drums with strident trumpet solos. The mountains echoed from summit to summit to the boom of kete drums; tree branches and leaves rustled and murmured in solemn praise.

It was there that I saw Mac Tontoh in a unique trumpet dialogue with his audience. The flamboyant performer took his audience a step further into a world of frivolity.

Mac Tontoh then called the women to order...*beautiful women, are you there? Yeaaaa*, was the response. And when we were all ready to listen, he kissed his trumpet to welcome them all. Indeed Mac blew a kiss with the trumpet, virtually conveying a trumpet bouquet, and leaving the men cold. *I love you all*, he implied. And when it came to the turn of us men, Mac Tontoh called us and booed at us. He indeed spat through his trumpet – displaying artistic irreverence to men who had decided to follow their beautiful women to the show!

Oh what a treat! We exploded in prolonged laughter.

## ...And in the Valley

A more extended encounter with Mac Tontoh was from 2002 to 2007, when we were both on the Advisory Board of the National Commission on Culture, along with culture luminaries like Professor George Hagan, Professor Kwabena Nketiah, Nana Ayensua Saara, Professor Kofi Aniyidoho, Dr. Esi Sutherland Addy, Kwaw Ansah, Haruna Attah, Dr. Mensah Otabil, to name a few. I felt privileged to know more of Mac Tontoh: his simplicity, his sobriety (almost soft-spoken), and his passion for the indigenous. In one of our discussions on street names in Accra, I remember Mac Tontoh recounting how he took it upon himself to name the street on which he lived in Dzowulu, as **Osibisa Close**. That sounded self-serving until you realised that Mac had lived in the neighbourhood for nearly 40 years – long before opulence arrived in the vicinity. His neighbours included a high celebrity he named, living at the corner. But naming a street after his own band, was also a major statement, call it an innuendo to us all – ditto a sad commentary on years of neglect of the African artist! In spite of all their achievement for Ghana and Africa, it occurred to no one to honour Osibisa, to honour Mac Tontoh in Ghana; and that had compelled him to indulge in self-praise, as the only alternative left to immortalise his group.

Elsewhere, it would not have been a simple Tontoh we mourn tonight. The world would have been mourning a man vested with national honours.

*But that is the world! Oh what a therapist the world has lost! And what a mark of irony, to think that our restless music warrior, the restless high priest now lies motionless, not responding to song, not causing himself to stir on rhythms tickling his feet. The legs and feet that knew no rest on stage are today frozen*

If Mac Tonto is gone, he is probably gone with his trumpet. But all is not lost. Mac Tontoh's legacy lives on because he was not selfish; he allowed children to use him to light their own candles.

## Tonto's Last Hurrah

In May 2009, I invited Mac Tontoh to come and launch a youth brass band at Agona Duakwa, a community brass band initiative we had started, as a way of reviving brass band music in the cradle of Ghana's brass band – the Agona Area. Through primary school children, we were seeking to restore the musical traditions for which the Agona area was known until the last decade or so. Mac Tontoh instantly agreed to be part, so long as it entailed passing on musical traditions to children.

We wrapped the town in posters about the inauguration, about Mac Tontoh. But who is Mac Tontoh? The children asked and I narrated the saga of his trumpet that had been echoing across the years. On May 16, 2009, Mac Tontoh made a rare appearance at Duakwa. Hearing the children (fifteen boys and ten girls, mostly from primary schools) rehearse on trumpets, trombones, and euphoniums, Mac Tontoh exploded with joy.

In a matter of hours, we were on our way to the durbar grounds which had been filled to capacity by indigenes anxious for the musical renaissance. For three hours, the entire town was agog with rich brass band music, from what I call "the little lips that play big." When Mac was introduced as the guest speaker, only the older generation knew his history. The young knew little, but had memories of Osibisa's Woyaya, used as a signature tune in local drama. Mac Tontoh walked to the middle of the arena rather haltingly, not his usual sprightly self. He narrated to the gathering, his beginnings as a juvenile musician and how the trumpet transported him from obscurity to international fame. Ending, he cautioned them against social vices and asked them to remain focused both at school and in the music they were playing. "It is the music that will bring up the best in you," he said.

Thereafter, Mac Tontoh grabbed his flugelhorn, walked to the kid players and broke into a spontaneous joint performance with the little lips. The chemistry was electrifying, and the arena was quickly covered with dancing feet of men and women, as the evening clouds slowly moved westward. Mac had played along with the kids, but appeared to be wobbling in breath and energy. The magic was there, but not the shine and the flavour of yesteryear. Something must be happening, I thought. Those glorious traits were receding; but for a trumpeter close to seventy, as he told us, it was magnificent.

"The kids have a great future," he later told me, "and I can tell from the harmony of horns, and their control over loudness…and I cannot believe they are reading musical scores. That is great!! …. and just as you heard me tell them, I will organise a big performance with them in Accra," he continued as we headed home. "Indeed I can already see a lot of show boys and girls among them, I could tell from how they each responded when they were being introduced…Prof, you have a great treasure in your hands and I will help you…"

In June 2009, Mac had promised to come and see the kids play at the Basic School speech day at the University of Ghana, but could not make it. He was on his way to Kumasi.

## Footprints

In November 2009, I met Gyedu Blay Ambolley at a ceremony in Accra, who told me my friend was down with stroke! A few weeks thereafter, he had been flown out…until the sad news of Mac Tontoh's passing was trumpeted across the world. When the tragedy was announced on radio, tears welled up in the eyes of the Little Lips, whose eyelids kept vibrating in search of a mentor.

Today marks the end of it all. The rover whose footprints are on all paths has kissed goodbye to his pet horn. The master artist whose trumpet knew no leisure has bowed out, and the wonder trumpet is broken. *The bundle of energy that once animated the world stage, where is it now? The trace of red on Mac Tontoh's lips has dimmed; the master trumpeter has lost his red lips. And that means tragedy: efie gya edum – the burning torch in the household has been snuffed out.*

But we do believe in the seeds you wisely sewed in children, the thousand Mac Tontohs to whom you bequeathed your legacy. Send a remittance of good dreams to the little lips you inspired. Send them the elephant tusk, out of which a trumpet will be carved to animate your legacy.

May the parched lips of the great musician, Mac Tontoh, rest in peace.

# Section V.

*"So as for this woman e be She-King"*[1]

# Tributes

# For the Eagle Who Taught the Chickens the Meaning of Flight

## Abena P. A. Busia

*Ama Ata Aidoo*

No Black-eyed squint of a sister killjoy,
You gave us someone talking to sometime
To banish the dilemma of a ghost
And call for changes to come:

*Sankofa; every bird must claim its own song*

You gave us someone talking to sometime
When there was no sweetness here
To be a woman, to be an African woman:

*every darkness has its light*

To banish the dilemma of a ghost,
Your mouth-that-eats-salt-and-pepper came
To pronounce an angry letter in January:

*every wrong can be made right*

You call for changes to come-
Truly you gave us love stories, African love stories,
To bless, wherever, the girl who can:

*every eagle holds the power of flight.*

# In Praise of Ama Ata Aidoo's Novel, *Changes*

## Yaba Badoe

2011 was the 20th anniversary of the publication of Ama Ata Aidoo's novel, *Changes*. I love this novel, which won the Commonwealth Prize for Literature in Africa, first and foremost, for the quirky, humourous, ironic, at times exasperated tone of the author's voice. I love it for the wily wisdom of that voice and the range of characters it throws up from along the Gulf of Guinea. But most important of all, I rate the novel highly because it was the first I read that openly embraced a contemporary African's woman's sexuality, and made it the centrepiece of the narrative.

Ama Ata Aidoo is my countrywoman, friend and mentor. I count myself privileged to be of a generation of Ghanaian writers and activists who refer to her affectionately as "Auntie" Ama. So, when she agreed to be interviewed during my last week in Accra in 2010, on a Monday in May – a day she usually dedicates to writing – I felt honoured.

I arrived an hour late for the interview, confused by the demarcation between Accra, Tema and Lashibi, off the Labadi coast road. Ama Ata Aidoo was waiting patiently on the veranda of a bungalow that houses Mbaasem. I tumbled out of my car befuddled and deeply apologetic. Never one to waste time, she was reading *Wolf Hall*, Hilary Mantel's Booker Prize-winning novel. As she closed the book, she asked: "What happened to you?"

I soon discovered that those boundaries between communities that constitute the suburbs of Accra but are, in fact, the outer reaches of the port city of Tema, are every bit as perplexing as the ground I proposed to cover: "How did the writing bug bite?" "What encouraged her to become a writer?" "Who supported her?" "Where did *Changes* come from?"

"But that's already in the public domain!"

"Yes, but what of a new generation of readers who don't know about it? The new audience that's out there waiting?" I said the words, even though I felt I'd already failed in my mission by turning up late, only to parrot well-worn questions that she was tired of answering. Therein lay my dilemma: how does one elicit a fresh response from the author of a modern African classic, in order to bring it to a new audience?

In *Changes*, Ama Ata Aidoo addresses fundamental issues in the lives of African women: love, career, betrayal and family, without offering simple solutions. So, how did *Changes* come about?

"I think the stuff that makes our books comes from two or three places," Ama Ata Aidoo replied. "One of them is the obvious world: people you meet, events you participate in consciously or unconsciously. And then there is the imagination, and I think that is really the thing. I definitely don't know how my imagination mixes the factors that make up my novels or even my poems. I put in all these ingredients and the fire and the pot do their work."

Aidoo's frequently cited epigraph to *Changes*, "an exercise in 'word-eating,'" for writing a love story, when considered against her earlier objection to "writing about lovers in Accra because . . .there are so many other problems," takes on heightened significance from an author who, in 2006, edited a sumptuous anthology of *African Love Stories*!

Seated on the veranda at Mbaasem, she explained what happened:

> Obviously I must have been intrigued, although I was reluctant about writing a *love story* at all. Clearly by the time *Changes* came along, I had calmed down and got myself to recognise that love, like war, like peace, like politics, is at the core of our lives: the glue. And you're not going to get very far without love, however you see that love. So I must have been intrigued by people loving. And then, I think I had always been fascinated by how women respond to the issue of love and marriage and children, outside of what society so busily would like you to believe. People will tell you: 'In marriage one has to be a fool.' Of course they mean the woman. So I'm interested in a woman who refuses to be a fool in marriage. And people will say things like: 'If you don't have a husband, you don't have a life.' *Who says?* Or, they'll say: 'You *have* to have children. Without children you are not a woman.' *What?* So I had been interested in these counter principles to living, because I saw some women, even in the village, manoeuvring their lives in such a way that did not coincide with these so-called conventional wisdoms.

It is the author's quest to investigate the choices that real women make, the alternative roads that some of us travel on, which I admire tremendously. For as the authorial voice depicts Esi's questioning spirit, the reader chuckles, and then gasps as a multi-layered narrative is delivered that links the old to the new.

When I confessed that I particularly relished the intervention of Esi's eloquent grandmother in the story, an old woman whose critique of tradition and romantic love is searingly incisive, Ama Ata Aidoo elaborated on the grandmother's attitude to marriage:

> She said *real* love, *romantic* love, the love that sets your heart thumping – you don't marry for that one, because marriage is about security, about survival, about children. And when you go following your heart in that kind of way, sorry, it won't end well. Because she knew people who had followed their hearts in her village; whether it's among the educated elite, in England or the village, the course of true love never runs straight

I concluded by asking the author if, two decades after its publication, *Changes* has taken on a life of its own. "It's got translated into a few world languages," she told me. "As we speak, someone is working on a Catalan version." She's very clear that I shouldn't say *Spanish*, but a *Catalan* translation of it. It's come out in French. It started out in Dutch and German and Finnish and so on. Then, with a shrug and a grin, Ama Ata Aidoo sighed: "I started publishing forty years ago, and yet I'm still so poor. But twenty years on, *Changes* has held its own."

December 2010

# Ama Ata Aidoo:
# Whose Dilemma Could It Be?

## Ivor Agyeman-Duah

The Shangri-La Hotel could as well have been situated on a country acreage as a writers' temple – the muse of creative sense prevailing. But it is a hotel located from downtown Accra at the West Airport residential area on your way to the University of Ghana at Legon. Its exterior motif of wood-carved symbols features the communicator's instrument, *Dawuro*. As you enter from the parking lot you are greeted with more wooden sculptures of folkloric personages; the roof panels are made from graceful raffia mats and the doors from thick trees of the deep forests of Western Ghana or the Asante region in the central part of the country. The match of tradition and modernity is unmistakable as you walk some few meters to a sizeable swimming pool and guest suites in the guise of traditional palm huts.

We sat, on a July day in 2000 – Kwame Anthony Appiah, his sister, Abena, their mother Peggy Appiah, author of children's books, and I – in bamboo chaises longues drinking. Suddenly, Anthony Appiah exclaimed, as he lifted himself from his chair with a glass of water nearly dropping on the glass coffee table. "Ah! Ama Ata Aidoo!" He moved towards her as I turned in the direction of near intersection. Ama Ata Aidoo steadying her gait with the aid of a cane, entered, her trademark headtie appropriate for an Akan woman past middle age.

After overcoming the surprise of a chance meeting, she asked, "Kwame, what are you doing here? ... and your mum Peggy too. This is wonderful." I got up to shake her hands, as did Abena.

"You look so well!" Abena makes known to her: "We first met in Zimbabwe fifteen years ago."

"That is a long time and it makes me feel so old." Ama Ata Aidoo responds.

"Now my leg..." indicating her limping, as she makes her way to another chair near-by to meet the people she had made appointments with.

"It will be okay, it's all part of the aging process," Abena reassures her.

Ama Ata Aidoo has known Peggy Appiah from the 1960s when the English writer settled in Kumasi and started her literary career writing for children in the Ghanaian cultural context. She was besides that collecting gold weights with their proverbial meanings, a pursuit that would make this woman of distinguished British background a literary grace. Peggy Appiah was part of the group of artists that emerged in the postcolonial period, forming unions or clubs just at the time that Ama Ata Aidoo's *The Dilemma of a Ghost* had been staged in Accra, while she was completing studies at the University of Ghana, Legon. Anthony Appiah, on the other hand, had grown up, had read Ama Ata Aidoo, and also taught her works. In addition, they had both become professors of African Studies courses in the United States.

But Ama Ata Aidoo, a popular guest at the Shangri-La, had this day come to keep appointments with people already seated at her favourite spot. As she moved towards them after these long pleasantries, I requested a literary conversation with her at home some day in the near future.

"Why not here? I love this hotel and the people know it. On top of that, I can buy you lunch instead of your coming all the way to Tema[1] and the extra burden of my having to cook for you, as I like to do for my guests." We fixed a date. I was eager for this conversation. I tend to sometimes get a venerating feeling when I meet writers whose works I have enjoyed. I read *The Dilemma of a Ghost* when I was in my early 20s, the same age that she was when she wrote it as a student.

Perhaps the nostalgia lies in childhood memories. The play-song was fascinating, especially as girls of my age gathered and dramatised the song referenced in the drama's title. For me as an adult, however, the memory of the play has been its connection to the Trans-Atlantic Slave Trade and its consequences on African and African American relationships that registers most.

A day before the conversation, I had been driving along the Cape Coast-Elmina road, about two hours away from Accra, when the images in the play again crept through; the so-called Ghost Song of the play:

> One Early Morning,
> When the moon was up
> Shining as the sun,
> I went to Elmina Junction
> And there and there,
> I saw a wretched ghost
> Going up and down
> Singing to himself
> "Shall I go
> To Cape Coast
> Or to Elmina
> I don't know

I can't tell
I don't know
I can't tell."

*The Dilemma of a Ghost* (Act III)

That piece of drama, *The Dilemma of a Ghost*, Ama Ata Aidoo's literary trade-mark is better known to Ghanaians than *Anowa, No Sweetness Here*, or her first novel, *Our Sister Killjoy*, and many of her collected poems. It is not only because it became for years a standard text-book of the West Africa Examinations Council, but for its very import of historical confrontation: independence of the colony and the Civil Rights Movement as a dimension of the slave trade. Aidoo measures up – preceded only by a few cultural avant-garde figures such as Efua Sutherland – as playwright, novelist and poet, to the collective leadership, from the feminist side, of the postcolonial African women writers of influence. She complements, in that sense, Nobel Laureate Wole Soyinka's significance as playwright and poet in the post-independence male-dominated era of the 1960s.

Five years after the Shangri-La conversation with Ama Ata Aidoo, I would sit with Soyinka in a hotel in Accra, discussing fifty years of African literature under the banner of the African Writers Series. Ama Ata Aidoo and her women writer colleagues—Flora Nwapa, Buchi Emecheta, and Mariama Bâ – came up and I asked Soyinka whether he "saw what I saw;" the transition of location of writing, of the complex style of especially cosmopolitan African women writers living in London, Paris or the United States. He said:

> I wouldn't say there has been a period of transition; I think this thing has been on a very normal developmental curve, like every-thing else. Foreign publishers recognise the fact that African literature is not just a quota system: Oh, we've spoken of this regional literature for some time; it's about time we spoke of African literature. No, they are recognising now. And this has been improved by the numerous prizes – regional, Commonwealth, etc. – being cornered by African writers. You look at the young crop of female writers, in particular, especially in the novel; it is really remarkable. And the young generation of writers also stationed outside: Ben Okri, Chris Abani, Ifi Amadiume, Sefi Atta...

When I interrupted to ask, " What accounts for this, because it wasn't the case in the 60s and 70s," he thought I was mistaken:

> I don't think it's a shift; it just shows that women constantly get marginalised, whether in politics, social development, or literature,

but they have been there all the time; that's what we are all learning. If you look at the tradition of the griot, for instance, you 'll
find that some of those countries where the griot culture is deeply
entrenched, there have been female griottes traditionally, even
though the men tended to be more aggressive. I think, and I hope
I don't exaggerate here, but according to my direct experience,
especially when I was doing my research in theatre (which also
meant, of course, the epic, music and so on), that the female in our
traditional society has always been more or less at par with male
productivity. So maybe what we're witnessing is a return to that
cycle of equilibrium. I like to think so.

When I did finally sit down with Ama Ata Aidoo, for the Shangri-La conversation, three months after the first encounter in July 2000, it was primarily a
discussion of the still-marginalised frontiers from which women operate as
writers and mothers, as well as the creation of a sublime space for discourse and
writing. The vehicle for filling that need was Ama Ata's creation of the
Mbaasem Foundation in 2001.

Our conversation takes place at the Shangri-La swimming pool. The sun is
shining, even as a few clouds also gathered, as if rains want to descend, displaying one of nature's seeming contradictions. She says:

> You know Mbaasem means 'women's world' or 'women's affairs.' I
> want to reclaim the term, because, when I was growing up, and
> even today, when people don't want to listen to women's opinions
> or perspectives to issues, they say, 'Go away. This is woman stuff.'
> This is a form of denigration, as if by being Mbaasem, there is
> something unimportant, ridiculous about it.

The Foundation, which is located in Accra Central was given seed money in
2001 by the New York based organisations Women's World for Rights,
Literature and Development and the Organisation of Women Writers of Africa.
As time went on, the Ford Foundation, the African Women's Development
Fund, the World Bank Small Grant Programme and others would step in.

A couple of obvious differences between the home of Ama Ata Aidoo's
Foundation and that of one like The Ernest Hemingway Foundation, of Oak
Park, in Illinois, is that the rented premises of Mbaasem do not bear any writer's
name and secondly, it serves female writers exclusively.

"People have asked," she explained, 'Why are you setting up a writing place
for women in Ghana?'" Her answer was simple: "There is no place anywhere in
Africa for this. But my point is, we cannot undertake to meet the continental
demand, so we are staying in a small way." Apart from the writing space for

resident writers for two to twelve weeks at a time and facilities including a library that is available also to non-residents, other objectives set in 2001 were " to have a writers' workshop, to help people with writing skills, but we are not going to edit manuscripts for publication. With time, we will be able to have consultants to help people with their manuscripts."

The Mbaasem Mission is to:

a)  Provide mentoring and editorial services to aspiring writers;
b)  Build a database on African women writers and their work;
c)  Co-ordinate an African women's network;
d)  Venture into publishing and develop an Mbaasem imprint (This enterprise should provide easier access to publishing for both resident and non-resident writers in a publishing environment that seems to be shrinking daily);
e)  Collaborate with other bodies to build a viable, sustainable, book-selling network across the African continent;
f)  Provide support for selected needy but brilliant girls;
g)  Use literature to contribute to HIV/AIDS awareness.

As she expounded on these, they would be captured later as workings of the Foundation's machinery. "Creative writing and other forms of artistic expression are the oil that keeps the wheels of any society running smoothly. What a society does in the way of the pursuit of artistic exuberance and excellence is as important as its members' need for basic nourishment, good health, shelter, and clothing. Until this is understood, accepted without equivocation and incorporated into developmental philosophies, all efforts on behalf of the poor and other groups will prove sterile, at best, and ultimately useless."

But where would creating space for writers, getting consultants for them, lead to, if the Foundation did not initially intend having its own publishing operation? "One of the problems of African writers is publishing," she explained. "In the 1950s and 60s, when Heinemann started the African Writers Series, it was less of a problem." Writers have now turned to local publishing and that, from the point of view of Ama Ata Aidoo, "is as bad as the international publishers. I am learning that publishing locally does not mean that you are going to get a better deal, because publishers are publishers."

Then the issue arose, "If African writers including (the late) Flora Nwapa and Ayi Kwei Armah published on their own and you are also doing so locally, with the international and local firms being the same, what then is the future of publishing?" She answered, "That is precisely because of these frustrations. You cannot tell me that Flora Nwapa did not go to Nigerian publishers, Ayi Kwei Armah did not go to Ghanaian publishers, but started their own, as you are saying and that is precisely because of these frustrations. For years I resisted, because, for me, it was like an article of faith: I was not going to go into publishing, because I told myself I am a writer and heaven knows it is taking me a lot of pain and time to say of myself that I am a writer. But eventually I have come to thinking of publishing."

This thinking has been precipitated by the general economic conditions which deteriorated in Africa from the 1970s. Like many human activities, writing and publishing cannot insulate themselves from public policy. In the economic sphere aid and trade failed in Africa through political leadership, migration and also the international economic machinery, with the continent still as hewers of wood and drawers of water. These forces would even impact the dynamics of language: Which one conveys most truly the authentic message of the writer writing in Yoruba, Gikuyu, Twi or Igbo? The language dynamics resulting from the economic and political situation could reach as far as threatening the loss of some languages; Mbaasem acts as a small intervention force.

"The atmosphere in which one writes has changed. As a student at the University, I had a room to myself, so I could write. Today it is different: six students occupy a room meant for one. The language problem has not gone away. Some will say, 'You are Akan, Yoruba or Igbo and so why don't you write in your first language?' There are always reasons why I should, but the practicalities of it are such a monstrosity. Joseph Conrad was a Pole who wrote in French before English; but *The Heart of Darkness* is one of the best novels ever written in English. And so, what is so special about it?"

As Ama Ata Aidoo approaches her 70th birthday in 2012, Mbaasem would be a little over a decade old. It would also be twelve years after my conversation with her at Shangari-La. Yet the evening has not fallen on her writing and activism. She might have escaped the fear (in youthful days) that haunts MacArthur Fellow Chimamanda Ngozi Adichie, celebrated author of *Purple Hibiscus* – of not being able to produce a masterpiece to equal her 2007 Orange Prize book, *Half of a Yellow Sun*. In September 2009, as Ama Ata Aidoo left for Brown University, where she was visiting professor for several years, I decided on a visit to the Foundation office in Central Accra to do an unsolicited assessment of its success in fulfilling its ideals.

A visible example of support for established as well as budding writers is Mbaasem's collaboration with Ghana's leading *Daily Graphic* newspaper. At least twice a month since 2007, the newspaper was publishing short stories, poetry, drama series, by Ama Ata Aidoo herself, by other established senior and younger writers such as Atukwei Okai, Amma Darko, Yaba Badoe, and many from the ranks of emerging writers. In the complete absence of any literary journal in Ghana since the demise in the 1970s of *Okyeame;*[2]*Voices of Ghana; Talents for Tomorrow; Obaa Sima;* and *Step;* and a few others, with *Uhuru* being published from 1984 to 1988, this creative page has been the only serious regular outlet for Ghanaian writers, critics and book reviewers. Book launches, which have been of late a major avenue for marketing and advocacy for reading, have also been associated with Mbaasem Foundation's work. *Bu Me Be: Proverbs of the Akans* under the lead editorship of the late Peggy Appiah; and Ayesha Harruna Attah's *Harmattan Rain* are recent publications that have benefited from Mbaasem's encouragement.

When the Mbaasem Foundation organised, in 2002, a two-day women writer's workshop to coincide with the Ghana International Book Fair, it was a first. The 150 women who attended, apart from some writers, included other stake-holders, such as a group of 30 women from the Book Development Department of the Kwame Nkrumah University of Science and Technology in Kumasi. Other Mbaasem programmes, e.g, dramatic presentations and readings have included "A Night of Healing through Literature," a collaboration with the African Women's Development Fund, in which drama was deployed to support the fight against domestic violence and specifically for the Domestic Violence Bill, which would subsequently be passed by Ghana's Parliament. The effects of HIV/AIDS on women and children have also been featured in dramatic presentations. On the Africa region, Mbaasem's idea of database collection and publicity among other non-Ghanaian writers has been modest. The Foundation, through its internet services, promotes recent works of writers on various levels of prominence.

The 2006 publication of *African Love Stories-An Anthology* edited by Ama Ata Aidoo and published by Ayebia Clarke Publishing featured twenty one short stories and is described as "a radical collection of short stories, most published for the first time, which aims to debunk the myth about African women as impoverished victims. With origins that span the continent, it combines budding writers with award-winning authors. The result is a melting pot of narratives from intriguing and informed perspectives."[3] And more than that, one of the writers, Monica Arac de Nyeko, from Uganda, won, for her story *Jambula Tree*, the 2007 Caine Prize for African Writing. The anthology won, as well, the African Studies Association's Aidoo-Synder Award, a prize in honour of Ama Ata Aidoo and awarded by the Women's Caucus of the Association for a book by a woman that prioritises African womens' experiences.

Because of its role in civic society, literature and historiography, Mbaasem should rightfully receive some basic support from government resources. But in "depressed" economies, as the case is in most of Africa, this is not happening. Mbaasem Foundation, like the Ghanaian economy in which it operates, is dependent on others: voluntary organisations within and without Ghana – recently including the International PEN Women Writers Committee, PEN Ghana and the Organisation of Women Writers of Africa.

Ama Ata Aidoo's legacy as a writer is assured. The Mbaasem Foundation embodies the spirit of a dilemma: sometimes to see oneself solely as a writer and leave the business of publishing to others but other times succumbing to the temptation to set up a Foundation to do the same, because "publishers, whether local or international, are the same." Whatever happens, Ama Ata Aidoo's personality is a light to the Foundation she founded. We wish Mbaasem well for a long and fruitful journey. And to Ama Ata, the good old wish: *For she's a jolly good fellow. And so say all of us.*

# Marginal Notes: The Mbaasem/ *Daily Graphic* Writers' Page

## Helen Yitah

The Writers Page began in May, 2008, as a collaborative effort between Mbaasem Foundation and the *Daily Graphic*, based on an understanding between Ama Ata Aidoo, founder and Executive Director of Mbaasem, and Ransford Tetteh, the editor of the paper. Under the agreement, *Graphic* undertook to provide free space for the project. Mbaasem was to collect, edit and submit to the *Graphic* every week enough literary material to fill a page, which would be made available for publishing this work in the Saturday issue of the paper. The Page was a welcome idea to both parties: Mbaasem had one more opportunity to fulfill its mandate to maintain a writing place for women writers, and *Graphic* would perform a laudable service to society while being assured of a regular supply of material for its literary arts page. It was *a marriage made in heaven*. The Writers Page placed no limitations on writers, except that their works should have literary merit and must not present a political agenda. For the writers who got published on the Page, particularly for the first time, it was a momentous experience. Little wonder that Aidoo was so invested in the Page that she made time to edit it from May to mid-August 2008.

I had just returned from class one afternoon when my phone rang. It was Ama Ata Aidoo. She had been looking for someone to take up the editing of the Page, she said, and Manu Herbstein had suggested me and given her my phone number. Would I be willing to do it? I said I would be glad to do so, and there was no mistaking the note of relief in her voice. On my part, I was honoured that she had asked me to work with her and besides, I have a long-standing interest in working with women writers (unknown to her, in 2003 I had put my name down to serve on Mbaasem's editorial committee). For me, it was a joy to work with Aidoo, a writer whom I had read and admired and respected from a distance for many years. So, although I had difficulty hearing part of what she was saying on the phone, I had understood enough to know that I could fill her need. Therefore, we arranged to meet at Mbaasem a few days later in order to work out the details of my assignment.

Keen to ensure that I was given enough orientation for the task ahead, Aidoo made time to walk me through the process of accessing stories and poems submitted via email, determining what to look for in selecting entries for the Page, and learning how to send edited work to the features section of the *Graphic* for publication. My first day at the Mbaasem offices afforded me the opportunity to observe Aidoo close-up as she edited poems submitted by a young new writer, and generally to learn why some submissions were published and others rejected. "There is something in this poem," she said at one point, "but the language needs some work." I was later to learn that she was trying to finish a book and yet took time off her own writing to facilitate the work of others. Thankfully, she had enough confidence in me to let me work independently and this cleared some space for her to pursue her writing. In mid-August, I assumed duty as editor for the Page and leader of the editorial team which included Kinna Likimani, an Mbaasem board member, Mr. Benjamin Dowuona, a young poet and Mr. Kwabena Opoku-Agyemang, a graduate student of literature. I maintained this job until February 2010, when the Page ceased.

Once I grasped the full import of the editing process, I discovered that there was more to be done to keep the Page going. "Have you ever done fundraising?," Aidoo had asked me during that first visit. I said yes, I had done a little fundraising sometime back, but nothing on the scale that was needed to sustain the Page. In her characteristic predilection to give the appropriate orientation for every activity, Aidoo this time directed a young man who had been involved in fundraising for the Page to go over with me what needed to be done. The following months would find me, along with the two young men on the editorial team, going from one potential sponsor to the next in an effort to raise money for the administrative services pertaining to the Page. "We need to follow up on our request at the GO-E-THE Institut," one of the men said one day during fundraising, his peculiar pronunciation of the German name drawing peals of laughter from the rest of us. After the follow-up we would proceed to drop off fresh application packages for funding. Although our fundraising efforts yielded little fruit, we kept the Page running.

The Page opened up the Ghanaian literary arena in a way that is unprecedented. Submissions poured in daily from writers of varying ages, backgrounds and fields of experience, mainly in the form of fiction, poetry and book reviews, although not drama. It is perhaps easier to understand the preponderance of poetry and fiction than to explain the complete absence of drama from the corpus, despite the achievements of Ghanaian dramatists such as Efua Sutherland, Ama Ata Aidoo, Mohammed Ben Abdallah and Joe de Graft. One can only surmise from this experience that new writers find writing drama the most challenging.

The canvas of poetry submissions for the Page did not always offer a pretty picture either. A significant part of what was submitted as poetry was little more than words strung together like beads on an abacus, their only relationship being based on the experience they depict. Sometimes, even though there would be some substance in the poem, its meaning might need to be made clearer. Here is an example called, "The Name We Don:"

> This is the ancient man's blood,
> Whose memories in a cloth we clad,
> In the joy of the freedom allowed,
> From the cunning masters for the crowd
>
> As we daily crown the ancient clan,
> And take pride in the name we don,
> Let's with the sweat of our brow, fulfill a great plan,
> For praises and blessings from the yet unborn.

Obviously, this writer has some sense of poetic expression, as can be seen in the image of memories depicted as a "cloth" to be "donned" in celebration of some "freedom." However, some information on the specific "man" being referred to in the first line, who "we" are and in what sense "freedom" is used in the first stanza would clarify the subject and the context of the poem and therefore facilitate the reader's understanding. Often, poems submitted were replete with emotional outbursts which were not justified by the general feeling created by the texts. All these made editing poetry for the Page a challenging experience. Typically I would ask the writer to explain what was intended, and when this was done I would then edit the piece for publication, keeping in mind the writer's purpose and the meaning being conveyed to the reader. Looked at this way, editing entries was as much a learning process for me as it was for the writers.

I came across a few teen poets who impressed me (and readers of the Page) with brilliant works. One of these, Dominic Arituo, became a regular weekly contributor to the Page. At 18, and having just completed his secondary school education, Arituo had the poetic maturity of a seasoned poet, although his language often needed extensive editing. Here is an example from a poem he called, "King of the Dry Season;"

> What Good news does the dry season bring
> But that cold dry wind, blowing its harsh breeze
> Lips and heels becoming hordes for frolicking flies
> Fires eating up the tall and tinted grasses
> Stomachs rumbling and grumbling and murmuring
> Skins complaining and hating the sun for his harshness
> Eyes and noses groaning and cursing the wind
> For constantly throwing dust on them in disrespect

The emotional energy and the rhythm of this poem, achieved in part through the deployment of alliteration and assonance, would delight many a reader.

Not surprisingly, Arituo caught Aidoo's keen eye, for not long after his poems appeared on the Page almost ready-made, she asked me for his contact information so that she could set up a meeting with him. This gesture clearly indicated that Mbaasem is not averse to grooming male writers, despite the impression (created in part by its name) that the Foundation is solely a women's affair. Achieving such a meeting was bound to be a daunting task, as Aidoo has a very busy schedule and Arituo works in a town that is hundreds of miles from Accra. But this situation did not deter her from trying to reach out to a "fledgling," a term Arituo once used to refer to his poetic status. On June 7, 2009, I sent an email to Arituo informing him that Aidoo and I would like to interact with him and asking him whether he would be willing to meet with us. Almost immediately, I received his reply:

> Dear Helen
> I am very grateful for given [sic] me this honour in the nation. With your help I am able to prove myself worthy when before-hand I was made to think that I am worth nothing. Thank you very much. I am interested in meeting you.

Arituo was not the only contributor to the Page who testified to its impact on his life; I mention him merely as an example of the many young writers who wrote to express how deeply their lives have been touched. Some of the new adult writers who were published on the Page were no less affected, as the following letter from Kofi Marrah, which I received on May 28 2009, indicates:

> Dear Helen
> I have since heard from many friends who said they saw the poems in the paper. Of course, not all of them had taken the time to read them. Still, it is a beginning. I also hope it is the beginning of my foray into the literary world that would draw me deeper into its confines and away from the "World" in which I presently find myself. Thanks for helping.

There is a sense of fulfillment in knowing that the Writers Page, which was set up to provide a free and readily available public space for Ghanaian literary artists, helped to launch literary careers and instill confidence in the writers it featured. Young people with creative potential who were introduced to the reading public had the implicit approval of the Mbaasem team and the *Graphic* and the attention of its literary arts readership. This vote of confidence, as well as the feeling of accomplishment new writers experience on seeing their work in print, is perhaps one of the greatest things that can be done for up-and-coming writers. It was even more refreshing to note that this exposure shaped their perception of themselves and shored up their sense of self worth.

The Page has also featured more experienced poets such as Aidoo herself, Vincent Odamtten and Mawuli Adjei, who drew particular attention from their readers, and who no doubt inspired and provided models for new and aspiring writers. Their works demonstrate Aidoo's (and my own) conception of the Page as a high quality literary medium that would set some standards for creative writing, particularly among beginning writers and their readership. For it was clear from the numerous unpublishable submissions for the Page that many aspiring writers assume that the only preparation they need is a desire to tell a story, even if there is no story to begin with. There is a lack of awareness of or attention to keen observation and critical interpretation of one's surroundings, reading widely and wisely, and generally being "creative" with language and poetic form, all of which are necessary ingredients for writing good poetry.

Although none of the new writers who submitted works for the Page has specifically mentioned being influenced by what was published, there was a conscious effort by several of them to revise their earlier entries and resubmit them for consideration. While writers usually took my editorial comments into consideration, it is plausible to assume that their regular reading of the works featured on Page would also have influenced their writing. My experience with the Page indicates that there is a lot of literary talent in Ghana, but it needs to be harnessed and provided with more avenues for its expression.

The disproportionately large numbers of entries unfit to print suggests that filling the Page every week with good material was not an easy task. But this was not the only concern; there was also the issue of editing the accepted entries. In some cases it was a matter of deciding how much editing to do without editing out the writer. In addition, Aidoo had established an editorial procedure whereby edited material would be sent back to writers for their approval before it was published on the Page. As can be expected, it was not always easy to persuade very sensitive writers to accept changes made to their manuscripts. Some of the points of disagreement by writers seemed to me like minor issues. For example, one short-story writer used the phrase, "water-free community," which I changed to "water-*less* community," and my intervention did not go down well with him. Fortunately for me, he was willing to learn. "What is the difference?" he demanded in one email. His question made me realise how much we take for granted when we use English in Ghana. In Ghanaian usage, the suffix "-free" is often used to express a lack in contexts where "-less" would be more appropriate. In many cases, I found myself explaining grammatical rules, acceptable usage and matters of style. In editing the Page, therefore, one was also running a kind of daily workshop for writers.

For Mbaasem, an establishment that works with women writers, the higher number of submissions from men writers than from women was an ironic turn of events. There is no question that this situation reflects our Ghanaian lived reality: females are still left behind in many fields of achievement and experience. Nevertheless, we must commend Aidoo and Mbaasem for opening the Page up to all writers. That said, there were times when she could not hide her disappointment with regard to the dearth of literary output from females. I remember her asking me early in August 2008: "Helen, we need submissions from women; have you written any stories that you can send for the Page?" I responded in the affirmative and proceeded to dust off a short story that I had been working on, on and off, for some years without finding enough time to finish it.

Running the Writers Page was challenging in several other ways, such as working out a format with *Graphic*. Matters that needed to be decided upon included the layout of the Page and whether it should regularly occupy the same page of the Saturday *Graphic* (in many cases it was page 10, but sometimes it was page 12); what banner to maintain (banners varied from "*poetry, poetry, poetry...*", to "Short Poems", to "*Literary Arts*"); and whether *Graphic* staff should include material on the Page which did not come from Mbaasem, or alter edited material submitted for publication. For example, on one occasion, an attempt by *Graphic* staff to further "edit" a short story I submitted to them yielded a different meaning when the utterance, "She sure eats a lot," was changed to "She is sure she eats a lot." Though these may seem like minor issues, they required time, tact and patience to resolve, and here again, Aidoo, always the diplomatic person, worked to sort things out with the *Graphic*.

Editing the Writers Page was for me a journey into the unknown, since I had no idea who or what I would be dealing with from one day to the next. The Page appears to have had the effect of making many people think they can write, even if the only preparation they have is their ardent belief that they were born to write. This is not necessarily a bad thing, if one believes that once the right environment is created, creative talent can be teased out. However, my daily battle with the avalanche of bad writing made me realise that more work needs to be done on creating the awareness that in order to write well one must read large amounts of good writing. Yet something about these eager-to-be writers touched me – I think it was their sheer enthusiasm and the raw talent waiting to be sculpted, their preparedness to travel on their unsteady feet with readers into a world other than the one we inhabit.

# Reminiscences from Exile

## Kari Dako

Ama Ata Aidoo's flowing robes and her elaborately folded headgear is what we all associate with her appearance – but it is her laughter that endears her to us.

I had met Ama Ata Aidoo on and off over the years; I was familiar with her writing; I had last bought *Our Sister Killjoy* in Eldoret, Kenya; but it was when we both lived in Harare that I got to know her–if one can ever 'know' an artist as complex as Ama Ata Aidoo. She dedicated the poem "Questions from the Expatriate Community: II – On Retirement,"[1] about the exiled Ghanaian to me and Kinna, and she later wrote the preface to my short stories. Being with Ama has enriched my life.

Ama and I lived in Harare at the same time in the 1980s. She had arrived in Zimbabwe with Kinna before I arrived in early 1986, and I left the country for Ghana after she had gone back home.

There were many Ghanaians in Zimbabwe at that time, and many of them came from the Fante-speaking part of the country. Sally Mugabe[2] was still alive and many of her compatriots and relatives had sought financial and political refuge in this newly independent nation of vast opportunities.

What was Ama doing in Zimbabwe? Ama was writing. She must have come to the conclusion that, although she had always been politically engaged and had always considered herself politically well left of centre, the role of politician did not suit her. Prime Minister Mugabe, who then became President Mugabe, was a social democrat at the time–not yet to be considered antagonistic to Ama's political philosophy. Seeking refuge there did not go against her principles or her conscience. Zimbabwe was doing well, and her doors were open to Africans who might not feel so comfortable at home, be it for economic or for other reasons. Harare had welcomed many Ugandans, Zairians, South Africans, Angolans, Mozambicans, Ethiopians, Ghanaians and Nigerians ... Harare was international in those days. But the political environment was tense; the country had a hostile neighbour to the south, and Mozambique to the east was involved in a horrendously vicious civil war. Zimbabwe also hosted ANC, PAC and SWAPO offices and safe houses. Raids from across the border on these organisations were frequent – at times we had prior warning, but often not.

When sojourn was needed for ANC refugees, Ama was always ready to receive them. Most Ghanaians were not politically committed.

A small two-bedroom flat in a block of maybe five storeys was her home in exile. The building had a lift! In addition she had a cubby-hole in some unknown location where she could retreat and submerge herself in her writing. Life is not easy with a teenager in the house. We were in the same situation there.

Ama wrote by hand! She used her dining table as desk. Her assistant sat there and typed. In the kitchen was Rosemary, who baked banana breads and apple pies. After Ama left, Rosemary came to work with me. Throughout the day, Ama drank Diet Pepsi so as not to put on weight, but she also loved the Zimbabwean wine. She did not really discuss her work much, but she had ongoing discussions with my husband David Yaw Dako—and they came back to especially one topic again and again: marital rape. What opinion these two had about this I was never privy to, but on hindsight I believe Ama had begun working on her novel *Changes*, which came out in the early 1990s. A second topic was politics. Whereas Ama was of the Nkrumah tradition and an avowed leftist, my husband, although very much a social democrat in thought (he had been an active member of the Labour Party while a student in Britain) tended towards the Danquah–Busia tradition. They had wonderful political discussions together: both of them savouring a debate for the sake of a debate. And it always ended with laughter.

On the 20th of October 1986, Ama and I went to the Sheraton Hotel in Harare for two very special reasons: it had been announced that Wole Soyinka had received the Nobel Prize for Literature, but the news had come on the fifth page of the *Herald*, so far as I remember—in other words: not of any importance. The news item had been supplied by some international news agency that told us that Soyinka got the Prize because the Swedes thought that Africa should also get one. So we celebrated that Wole Soyinka got the Nobel Prize while at the same time feeling sad that Zimbabwe did not have the journalist or the writer who could highlight the significance of this honour or who cared enough about the significance of Soyinka being awarded the Prize. Additionally we then had to mourn the death or assassination of Samora Machel which had happened the previous day. So there we sat at the Sheraton and ate strawberries served in a cloud of icy mist and felt lost; we were nearly alone in the big dining room. Zimbabwe had begun to feel alien to us. Somehow the Mugabe miracle had started to unravel; xenophobia had surfaced—and especially against Ghanaians. I remember sitting at a formal dinner with a senior Zimbabwean civil servant who, after a couple of drinks too many, turned to my husband, who was then teaching at the University of Zimbabwe, and told him to his face: "We hate you people!" Rumours swirled around the country that Sally Mugabe had sent the whole production line of Toyotas to Ghana and that was the reason why Zimbabweans could not get cars to buy; that the two countries drove on opposite sides of the road was not considered an argument at all. The rumours said also that S. Mugabe was purchasing valuable property in Harare: but was it Sally Mugabe or was it Sabina Mugabe (the president's sister) who had ventured into real estate? Zimbabweans accused Sally, but some of us who had had dealings with the president's sister thought that Sabina might be the one speculating on the property market. Zimbabwe had forgotten that it was Sally who had kept her husband's name alive in Britain and the rest of Europe, especially Scandinavia, through his years of incarceration.

I am not sure whether Ama ever felt at home in Zimbabwe. Zimbabwe was a necessary stop on her way through life. She needed a place to rest–a place with a school for her daughter – she needed to get back to writing. Did Zimbabwe enable a productive period in her career? I do not know. We were in a location where we could not sink roots; for both of us it was a transient period–we were waiting to get back to Ghana.

# AAA – The Mind Reader and the Reading Mind

## Chikwenye Okonjo Ogunyemi

Enchantingly named with triple A initials, Ama Ata Aidoo makes one mindful of excellent ratings that she has now earned through her life and her works. A killjoy in her own right, she has perfected the art of globalising the local, skillfully rooting current African dilemmas in a troubling, ghostly past. Through her courage and inventiveness, she has carved out a place for African women in black Diaspora and feminist discourses. Rereading and teaching her works, one sees how she encourages change and mind healing, demonstrable in such memorable characters as Eulalie, Sissie, Anowa, and Esi.

While Aidoo was doing a stint at Oberlin College, I invited her to give a talk at Sarah Lawrence College, that creative writing centre, graced with the zip code of wealthy Bronxville. Here, with its proximity to New York City, an American writer can get a cash advance for the promise of a book not yet in print. In a mind-boggling moment, Aidoo reminded us that her works have never been out of print, but, with the monetary exchange, where the pound or the dollar seems to bring in a lot of local (African) currency which you carry in bags, royalties are a mere pittance, an insult that ensures writers almost always live in genteel poverty. Why do royalties never enrich African women writers? Do we not all buy from the same stock market? With her rhetorical questions, one thought of the diminishing returns that make writing and reading formidable chores.

However, this turn of affairs for those whose books are not recommended texts in African high schools has not deterred Aidoo from continuing with her self-enforced duties. Her versatility as a poet, children's storyteller, short story writer, essayist, scholar, lecturer, visiting professor, novelist, playwright, with a lot of drama in her life, has been her major attraction, her boldness and wit surfacing in any talk she gives. From Oberlin to Sarah Lawrence, from Barnard to Brown and places beyond, Aidoo continues to make waves as a scholar and public lecturer in college circles. This aspect of her life is a continuation of her irrepressible spirit, manifested in her flirtation with African politics. Resigning from her position as Minister of Education under Ghana's Jerry Rawlings, she precipitously fled to Robert Mugabe's Zimbabwe, without realising that he, too, would want to reign forever and not stomach criticism.

I caught up with her again in Accra in 1996 when she had returned home, and she invited a group of us working on an NEH[1] grant at the University of Ghana to lunch in her government-assigned bungalow. She produced an awesome dish of *garri fortor*. The one-pot entrée, a reminder of the eclectic quality of *Our Sister Killjoy*, had hints of Lagosian *farofa*. If one substituted rice for the West African staple, *garri*, in the dish, memories of the African Diaspora emerge – Cajun *jambalaya*, Dakarian *wolof rice*, Bahian *Haussá rice*, and Belizean cuisine. As we ate, we were reminded of the communal, especially women's involvement in cassava production in the developing world. Astonishingly, every part of the cassava is valuable, a good thing since its hardiness enables it to survive in times of drought. Thus, for us, that dish became a representation and the essence of Aidoo's literary production. The tedium of crafting ends in satisfaction and intellectual reward as the author/cook and reader/listener/spectator/devourer serendipitously coalesce. Like the cassava with its trace of cyanide, her works kill us softly with her love.

Through the lenses and the words of the numerous women traipsing the pages of her books, Aidoo lends the English language an African cadence. Working from a past lodged in a repairable DNA, she fixes the body whilst nourishing the mind and spirit through her writing, her talking, and her acting. These facets of her life have brought about changes that have earned her our admiration; they should encourage us to change.

# Ama Ata Aidoo: A Personal Celebration

## Ngũgĩ wa Thiong'o

I have known Ama Aidoo for many years. We share many personal friends who, in their different ways, have made an impact on our lives: Ime Ikiddeh, Grant Kamenju, Parsali Likimani, and Micere Mugo. The first three have passed on, but their memory is always present. All four were an integral part of my intellectual formation. Ama Ata Aidoo too has been part of my intellectual journey. We have travelled many places together, having met in Kenya, Zimbabwe, Ghana, America, England and Germany. She has been in many more places which is another way of saying that she is first and foremost a writer of the world in the world. Her infectious laughter and warm personality easily break barriers of culture and race even when and where she is at her most critical. She never compromises on questions of African dignity and standing in the world. She is a great Pan Africanist in life and thought; she embraced and was embraced by Kenya and Zimbabwe as a daughter of the land. In that sense we can paraphrase what is said of Kofi in *Anowa*, but here in a positive way, that Ama Ata Aidoo has been, is, and will always be of us. She speaks to the human condition and the world but uncompromisingly through Africa. But her embrace and defence of Africa has not meant complacency. Her embrace of the continent is through tough love: being able to see its beauty because she is also able to see clearly her warts. Dignity like any other ideal must start from home, the domestic sphere, and the sphere of self. One can pick any of her poems, stories and fiction generally to see this: but tough love was always there even in her earliest works.

Aidoo's work, including the playful mischief, is rooted in orature as much as it is in her literary inheritance from Africa and the world. This is best illustrated in the play *Anowa*. I have taught this text in Africa and America and, like Chinua Achebe's *Things Fall Apart*, I always find something new in it with every reading and analysis. It grows on me through every reading. I have never seen it on the stage so I have had to look and see its theatre and theatricality through the text.

Some of her truly unforgettable characters like the pair Old Man and Woman, together being the Mouth that Eats Salt and Pepper, are from classical African orature and from the everyday lives in an African community. They are like the Greek Chorus, itself rooted in classical Greek orature. But firmly at the centre of the stage and action is Anowa herself. She is the prime mover whether in terms of her defying tradition and communal expectancy by choosing to marry Kofi or in her defence of productive work as what constitutes the human as opposed to the parasitic living on another person's life, as in the system of slavery.

It is difficult to sum up the play and the character of Anowa. I have met her story in classical African orature in the archetype of the beautiful maiden who refuses the hand of the young men of her neighbourhood but ends up in the hands of a stranger who turns out to be an ogre. Amos Tutuola, in *The Palm-Wine Drinkard*, put his indelible mark on the archetype, in the tale of "The Complete Gentleman of the Jungle." In Gĩkũyũ orature, there is a similar story of the village beauty who defies the expectations of her immediate community by marrying, not one of the young men of her village, but a stranger who seems to promise a horizon way beyond the local confinement to the known and the safe. Is she punished for disobeying the wishes of her father and mother? Or is she paying the price that those who venture beyond the norm and the expected in the areas of ideas, have had to pay? But the story does not rest on this archetype alone. There is also an element of the spirit child born into the human world, allowed to live on condition that she becomes a priestess, wedded to the gods. The moment she marries a human, she has defied the gods and hence the tragic end. In both she is still defying the expected, the normal and the safe.

*Anowa* can also be placed in another folk tradition, particularly the European, seen in what I have called the Faust theme in literature. The theme deals with the archetype of an upright person who sells his soul to the devil for prosperity, materialism, and power. But eventually the devil claims his own. The theme is particularly prominent in the European Christian tradition because the phenomena of the soul, salvation, sin, perdition, heaven and hell are central to Christianity. If the soul is the real and the eternal, and not the ephemeral body, can one exchange the eternal for the earthly passing away, the body and its satisfaction? The Faust theme has always attracted writers of different cultures and history. In this tradition we can place Christopher Marlowe's *Faust*, England; Goethe's *Faust* and Thomas Mann's *Doctor Faustus*, Germany, and Bulgakov's *Master and Margaretta*, Russia. I touched on it in my novel, *Devil on the Cross*. The attraction of the Faust theme then is precisely in its symbolism of the opposition between materialism and morality, between materiality of possessions and the integrity of spiritual possession. The material power is there for a time. It is associated with excess, greed and power, which we see exhibited in Kofi. The Kofi who attracts Anowa, the one for whom she defies family and tradition, is the Kofi of moral integrity, who lives by his own productive labour. But the Kofi of the trade in slavery, who ultimately depends on slave labour, is the Kofi of the excess that corrupts the soul. The new Kofi, who has made a pact with the devil of material success no matter at whose cost, is already dead long before his suicide.

But Aidoo places this in history. Lest the reader/the audience forgets, the prologue invokes the Atlantic Slave Trade, the "bigger crime," the eternal witness of that crime being the many slave castles, "those forts standing at the door of the great ocean." The Big Houses mentioned are certainly those houses whose fortune was rooted in the slave trade. We recall this connection when at the end we find Kofi living in such a big house, "the Big House at Oguaa." The Bond of 1844, the protectorate status signed by the traditional elite of the time, "the lords of our Houses," "binding us to the whitemen who came from beyond the horizon," is prominently intentionally mentioned, which would place the present of the story in the year 1874. This is during the reign of Queen Victoria. Later we find her picture prominently hanging on the wall of Kofi's Big House.

The genius of Aidoo as an artist is the way she has used the image of "the bond" to explore the theme of unequal power relationships at different moments in history and society. The image of the bond connects unequal gender relationships in whatever society to those of class in any society. Positively of course there is the bond of love like that which draws Kofi and Anowa together; this may collide with the family bond when that bond is itself bound up in uncompromising traditionalism. But it may and does collide with the bond of slavery, domestic or Atlantic, or colonial and neocolonial. One cannot view or read the mis-en-scene in the third and final part of *Anowa*, with the pictures of Queen Victoria on the wall, without of course bringing to mind the neocolonial setting of the present in the writing of the play, which is also the present of our times, of what I have described in my novel, *Wizard of the Crow*, as corpolonialism Thus written in 1965, the play talks squarely to our times.

That's Aidoo for me. Whether in her short stories, books for children, novels, plays and essays, Ama Ata Aidoo speaks to the most urgent issues of our time. She is a writer for all seasons.

# Reference Documents on the
# Life and Work of Ama Ata Aidoo

# A Bibliography of Writing
# by and on Ama Ata Aidoo:
# A Compilation in Progress

### James Gibbs

In offering this bibliography, I am acutely aware of my debts to those who have already turned their hands to this task; I have stood on many backs to reach down information. Relevant names will emerge from the pages that follow, but first and foremost I must mention Bernth Lindfors. My debts to the *Black African Literature in English* series can be traced on every page that follows, and I am aware that his invaluable lists of citations would draw attention to a further store of entries in which Ama Ata Aidoo's is considered along with that of other writers. Mention should also be made here of Brenda F. Berrian, who published a ground-breaking bibliography thirty years ago, and of Sharon Verba, who, keeping pace with technology, has uploaded a useful list of resources. Inevitably I have followed up and included references in articles, theses and monographs dedicated to the work of Ama Ata Aidoo. One thing leads to another.

Lists like those that follow are 'compilations in progress' and I am acutely aware that readers will find gaps and mistakes, errors of omission and commission. I trust, however, that there will be compensations in the form of obscure items located and of narratives pieced together from the different entries and from the occasional annotations. Part of the 'story' of the 'emergence of Ama Ata Aidoo' and of the 'critical reception of Aidoo's work' are apparent because of the layout I have adopted. Grouping entries by year of publication allows the list of primary sources to show Aidoo establishing herself as a public intellectual, seeking to place her work and making use of a variety of outlets. As can be seen, she published both critical and creative writing at home and abroad, and was then, after the production of her first play, signed up by a leading British publisher-Longman. Thereafter, as she made literary history, she balanced international exposure with an interest in publishing in Ghana.

The list of interviews and profiles that follows the primary sources is a leaky category. Some of the brief biographies that appear in reference works might have been included here, but I chose to isolate these particular entries because they allow Aidoo to speak for herself. She is a vigorous, invariably original, sometimes frank, characteristically trenchant, not infrequently contentious interviewee. In the encounters itemised here, she speaks revealingly about, for example, the genesis of particular works, and about her–sometimes fraught – relationships with publishers and critics. The interviews and profiles reveal who has been interested in recording what Ama Ata Aidoo has had to say and, in most cases, who have shared her words with readers. I write 'in most cases' because I have taken the liberty of including some interviews that have not (yet?) been published and some that can be watched on-line but not *read*.

One of the advantages of the chronological layout of the secondary sources is that readers can register the kind of attention Aidoo's work attracted as year followed year. It is apparent that interest initially found expression through book reviews, and that there was a sharp exchange with fellow Ghanaians in the pages of *The Legon Observer*. After Aidoo had published a significant body of work, the critical discussion warmed up, papers nosed their way into journals, and themes she had treated provided the focus for conference panels. While all this was happening, murmurs from classrooms, where her writing was being studied, were more and more clearly heard, and there was an increase in the number of people delivering lectures about her work on university campuses. Educational publishers responded to market forces with study aids for pupils and academic volumes for students. Particularly important milestones in the emergence of a body of serious critical work on Aidoo include the publication, in 1994, of Vincent Odamtten's monograph, and the appearance five years later of the collection of essays edited by Ada U. Azodo and Gay Wilentz. The volume of essays you hold in your hand marks a new stage in the relationship between the writer and her readers, particularly those in Ghana. It is significant that, while there are international dimensions to this volume, it has been edited in Ghana and it is being published by a Ghanaian. However, it is significant that the publisher operates a long way from her hometown of Larteh and readers will reflect on the implications of her Oxfordshire OX16 postcode.

In attempting to make these lists worthy of this volume, I have been engaged into the early hours with the tsunami of information that is available on the internet. A Google search of "Ama Ata Aidoo" has just produced twenty-six and a half thousand 'results'! The 'gold' sieved from the spur of this mountain of virtual information that I have scoped has been checked, whenever possible given restraints, against 'hard-copy.' In doing that, I have had to get out the library steps again and again and to say a silent word of thanks to my wife, Patience Addo Gibbs, who has filled shelves and bookcases with copies of publications such as *Asemka*, *Okyeame*, *The Legon Journal of the Humanities*, and *The Legon Research Review*. There has been a division of labour, but this has been a joint task, a shared interest lasting many years.

Experience of the sheer quantity of online information suggests that these are perilous times for bibliographers; 'we' have to know when to call a halt to research and how to be ruthless about what to exclude. To illustrate the new ways in which relevant material arrives, I will point to the three entries in the secondary sources for the month in which I am writing, January 2011. The first entry is a reference to a YouTube clip about Aidoo's retirement from Brown University, the second is to is latter necessary? an on-line article from a Nigerian newspaper and the third is a tribute from a Ghanaian teacher that was 'published' by My Joy online. Some of these postings have attracted comments, others have been included in blogs and at least one has been tweeted. With the thought 'that way madness lies,' I have not attempted to untangle those threads or to tie up those loose ends.

Although I have not included those kinds of 'on-line publications' (?), I have made extensive use of the resources of the web. The penultimate list below is a 'webography' in which I have listed sites I have found useful-and that seem to be relatively stable.

My contribution to this volume rolls to a halt with a list of productions of Aidoo's plays, a sort of 'playography' or 'theatre check-list'. This wholly inadequate section begins with a reference to the premiere of *The Dilemma of a Ghost* in the open-air theatre behind Commonwealth Hall, on the campus of the University of Ghana, Legon. The date was 12 March 1964, and the director was Olu Neye Ogunsanwo. Readers will notice that I have not found a single contemporary review or commentary on that production! In other words, for the text-bound bibliographer, it seems that the original production of a play that has proved widely popular was watched in stony silence, that it elicited no reactions and prompted no critical discussion. Of course that is nonsense. I know it is nonsense partly because I attended many productions in that open-air theatre during the 1960s, and on every occasion I found myself part of a noisily responsive audience, one that was quick to react and happy to comment (vociferously!) about on-stage action. This was an audience that Ola Rotimi, who presented *The Gods Are Not to Blame* at Legon in the late sixties, dubbed 'instamatic,' an audience familiar with story-listening, story-reacting conventions and totally at ease with the expression of instantiations responses. An 'instamatic audience' can be a delight to a playwright, but it may produce few, in any 'reviewers,' and, perhaps, no 'critics,' none who want to distil their responses in elegant, authoritative prose-and have access to a means of publishing their opinions. I will use this textual silence about the production to indicate the limitations of this bibliographical endeavour, and of many like it. I am sure that Aidoo's 1964 audience was loudly responsive to the production and followed moment by moment the demonstration of the storyteller's art. Moreover, I hazard that the 12 March 1964 represented an important experience for the playwright. To get a glimpse of what it might have meant to her, we only have to listen to her talking to Theo Vincent in 1981 about watching a later production of the same play. Aidoo told Vincent how, in 1995, she had taken her place, unrecognised, in the audience at the Accra Arts Centre, and had derived great pleasure from the responses of those around her. She said: '... from their reaction I didn't even know people could enjoy this play so much.' Roll back to 1964 and I can imagine that the undergraduate author of the play must have been nervous and thrilled at the same time. I suspect she savoured the 'instamatic' response of the audience of her peers, that she relished every gasp, every bellow of laughter, every shock of communal recognition, every shared intake of breath. Briefly, I think she must have delighted in knowing that, as the storyteller-playwright, she was in charge of the heaving, gasping creature that is an audience.

Evidence that *Dilemma* showed Aidoo her vocation as a playwright is provided by the fact that she then wrote *Anowa*. That second play made a ghostly appearance in 1968 as 'Anua,' published in a Ghanaian literary magazine. In a national theatre tradition in which scandalously few plays have been published, *Anowa* was published with surprising speed, perhaps because Longman wanted a 'follow-up' to *Dilemma*. At the point of publication there is another eerie silence because the text breaks convention by not including the details of the premiere. This prompts the question 'when was *Anowa* first produced?' The absence of any date in the published text suggests that, in setting aside usual practice, the text was published before it had been staged. The first record of a production of *Anowa* that I have found is for 1991! I look forward to being put right on that, but, in the meantime, it seems likely that Aidoo had to wait for some years before she watched life being breathed into her lines. I can imagine that this delay ate into her soul. Perhaps the delay explains why a writer whose talents are so clearly suited to the theatre turned to other ways of being a storyteller. Frustrated in her ambitions as a playwright-and with the pressures that drove her to travel and work outside Ghana – Aidoo's gifts found expression not on the stage but on paper. Publishers, editors and readers were 'winners' as Aidoo turned to poetry, prose and fiction. The theatre and those who loved it were the losers.

Let me conclude by saying that this bibliographical venture has a history, and I hope a future. It began life as a small selection of 'entries' extracted from a bibliography on the Ghanaian theatre—a work (still) in progress. From there, as I attempted to come to terms with Aidoo's versatility as a writer, her importance as a thinker, her burgeoning international reputation, and her contributions as an activist, it 'just grew.' In the hope that it has a future as a 'serviceable' electronic document I have included features that make it 'searchable.' In order to navigate through the primary sources of an e-version of this 'document,' please search with date plus hash, for the interviews and profiles section search with date plus 'at sign' and for the secondary sources use date plus asterisk. This feature makes it possible to bounce through the sections and down the years. It looks ahead to a time when a (constantly updated) version of this compilation might be available online. Freed from print and paper, it would then be widely accessible, easily amended, and almost effortlessly corrected.

James Gibbs, Bristol 31 01 2011

Arrangement of material and entries:

- Abbreviations used
- Primary Sources, search with: year plus #
- Interviews and Profiles, search with year plus @
- Secondary Sources, search with year plus *
- Webography
- Plays in Production ('Playography')

Within each section, entries are listed by year of publication, and where appropriate in alphabetical order within the year.

**Abbreviations used** (I am aware there are some inconsistencies in the use of abbreviations. I have tried to avoid too many servings of alphabet soup and to include occasional 'reminders' of abbreviations)

| | |
|---|---|
| ALA | African Literature Association |
| ASA | African Studies Association |
| AWP | Africa World Press |
| BALE | *Black African Literature in English*, ed. Bernth Lindfors (On occasions I have included BALE reference numbers) |
| Azodo and Wilentz | The volume of essays edited by Ada U. Azodo and Gay Wilentz, and entitled *Emerging Perspectives on Ama Ata Aidoo* (1999) is the single most significant source of articles on Aidoo. |
| HEB | Heinemann Educational Books |
| RAL | *Research in African Literatures* (initially Austin, Texas, then Bloomington: Indiana) |

**Primary Sources** publishing initially as 'Christina Ama Ata Aidoo'

Late fifties
Early writing included a Christmas story that appeared in a local paper.

1963#
Review of Moore, *Seven African Writers. Transition* (Kampala) 4, 10 (1963) 45–6.

'No Sweetness Here.' *Black Orpheus* (Ibadan), 12 (n.d. I follow Benson: 1986, 290, in using 1963 as the date for this. This was the story that won a prize offered by Mbari in 1962. Like other early 'scattered stories,' it was collected into a single volume in 1970.)

1964#

'The Last of the Proud Ones' and 'Sebonwoma.' (Poems) *Okyeame* (Accra), 2, 1 (1964), 9–11.
'Sebonwa.' *Presence Africaine* (Paris), 49 (1964) 199–200.
'The African Poet, His Critics and His Future.' *Legonite*, no number (1964), 57–9. (Note Aidoo's use of conventions about the gender of possessive, typical of the time. A Legon publication.)
[*The Dilemma of a Ghost*, produced Legon, March. See Playography]

1965#

*The Dilemma of a Ghost*. London: Longman, 1965. (The play has been re-published several times, for example, New York: Collier, 1971; Longman included it in their African Creative Writing Series, 1977. An extract appeared in *Ghanaian Writing Today 1* (Tema), 1974, 1974, 88–97.)
'The Late Bud.' *Okyeame*, 2, 2 (1965), 29–36.
'In the Cutting of a Drink.' In *Pan-African Short Stories*. Ed. Neville Denny, London: Nelson, 1965.

1966#

'The African Literary Tradition.' *New African* (London), 5, 6 (1966), 126–7.
Review of Okoye, *African Responses*, *Transition* (Kampala,) 5, 24, 55–6. (Summarised Benson: 1986, 141–2.)

1967#

'The Message.' In *African Writing Today*. Ed. Ezekiel Mphahlele, Harmondsworth: Penguin, 1967, 87–95.
Review of Odinga, *Not Yet Uhuru*, *Transition*, '64' (1967), 179–81. (NB This issue number, from Berrian, cannot be correct. See Benson.)
'Thank you, Mr. Howe.' *Transition*, 29 (1967), 5. (Contribution to debate about Nkrumah. See Benson: 1986, 299.)

1968#

'Anua.' *Okyeame* (Accra), 4, 1 (1968), 41–50. (Cf with *Anowa*.)
'Cut Me a Drink.' *Modern African Stories*. Ed. Ezekiel Mphahlele, London: Faber, 1968, 13–9.
[*Dilemma* was published in Polish in *Dialog* (Warsaw), 6 (1968), 65–90. I have only listed a few translations of Aidoo's work.]

Review of Soyinka, *Idanre and Other Poems*, *West Africa* (London), 13 January 1968, 40–1.

## 1969#

'Certain Winds from the South.' (Poem.) *Political Spider*. Ed. Ulli Beier. London: Heinemann and New York: Africana, 1969, 101–9. (A collection of material from *Black Orpheus*.)

'No Saviours.' (Criticism.) *New African*, 52 (1969), 37–9. (A major statement on Armah's *The Beautyful Ones Are Not Yet Born* that raises issues of structure, mood, attitude and imagery. Reprinted in *African Writers on African Writing*. Ed. G D Killam, London: Heinemann, 1973, 14–18. See also Aidoo's 'Introduction' to the New York: Collier Macmillan edition of Armah's book, 1969.)

'Of Love and Commitment.' *Zuka* (Nairobi), 4 (1969), 9–11.

## 1970#

*Anowa*. London: Longman, 1970. (Subsequently anthologised. See, for example, *Post-Colonial Plays: An Anthology*. Ed. Helen Gilbert, London: Routledge, 101–127. And *African Contemporary Plays*. Ed. Martin Banham and Jane Plastow, London: Methuen, 1999, 137–206. Introductory comment, xvii- xix.)

'For Kinna.' *Zuka*, 5 (1970), 15–6.

'A Gift from Somewhere.' *New African Literature and the Arts* (New York), 1 (1970), 177–88.

*No Sweetness Here: A Collection of Short Stories*. Harlow: Longman, 1970, and Garden City New York: Doubleday, 1971. (A note in this publication indicates the publications, some indicated above, in which Aidoo's work had appeared. 'Two Sisters' had been recorded by the Transcription Centre, London. Collection appeared from New York: Feminist Press, 1995, and 'No Sweetness Here.' In *Concert of Voices: An Anthology of World Writing in English*. Ed. Victor J. Ramraj, Peterborough, Ontario: Broadview Press, 1995.

Review of Sebukima, *A Son of Kabira*, *Zuka*, 5 (1970), 69–70.

## 1971#

'Commitment'. In *Burning Issues in African Literatures* (University of Cape Coast English Department Work Papers), 1, (March 1971).

*The Dilemma of a Ghost*. New York: Collier. (With an Introduction by Karen C. Chapman, 1971. See also *Sturdy Black Bridges: Visions of Black Women in Literature*. Garden City, New York: Garden Books, 1979.)

## 1972#

'Challenging Years,' 'Greetings from London.' *Zuka*, 6 (1972), 66–7.

'On "The Fires Next Time" Talking to A.N. Mensah, Talking about Jawa's Poem.' *The Legon Observer* (Legon) 30 June 1972, 313–4. (Poem. Note: Jawa Apronti's

'The Fire Next Time' had appeared in *The Legon Observer*, 7, 9 (5–18 May 1972), 220 and 222. A N Mensah's verse rejoinder appeared in the issue of the same fortnightly published on 2 June, 269.)

1973#

'Cornfields in Accra.' In *The Word Is Here: Poetry from Modern Africa*. Ed Keorapetse Kgositsile, New York: Anchor/ Doubleday, 1973, 113–16.

'Poem'. In *You'd Better Believe It: Black Verse in English from Africa the West Indies and the United States*. Ed. Paul Breman, New York: Penguin, 1973, 472–73.

'Sebonwoma.' *Poems from Africa*. Ed. Samuel Allen, New York: Crowell, 1973, 17.

1974#

'Our Sister Killjoy on Why We Die Like Flies.' *Asemka* (Cape Coast), 1, 2 (1974), 105–8.

1975#

'Everything Counts.' In *Giant Talk: An Anthology of Third World Writing*. Ed. Quincy Troupe, New York: Random House, 1975, 35–9.

1977#

*Our Sister Killjoy: or Reflections from a Black-Eyed Squint*. Harlow: Longman, 1977. (Republished New York: Nok, 1979.)

1978#

'Prelude.' In *The Penguin Book of Women Poets*. Ed. Carol Cosman, *et al.*, New York: Penguin, 1978, 309.

1980#

'Ghana: To Be a Woman'. In *Creative Women in Changing Societies*, Conference Proceedings, UNITAR Seminar, Oslo, July 1980. (See also *Sisterhood is Global: The International Women's Movement Anthology*. Ed. Robin Morgan, Garden City, New York: Anchor Press/Doubleday, 1984, 258–65. An end-note to 'Unwelcome Pals' (1981) indicates that the papers over-lap. Material may have been reworked for audiences and readers over a number of years.)

1981#

'Unwelcome Pals and Decorative Slaves.' In *Medium and Message*, Proceedings of the International Conference on African Literature and the English Language, University of Calabar, Nigeria, 1981. Also see *Ifa: Journal of Creative Writing*, 1982, 40–41; *Literature and Society: Selected Essays on African literature*. Ed. Ernest Emenyonu, University of Calabar, Dept. of English and Literary Studies, Zim Pan African Publishers, 1986, 1–19; Azodo and Wilentz, 11–24.

'Two Sisters.' In *Cowries and Kobos: The West African Oral Tale and Short Story*. Ed. Kirsten Holst Pietersen and Anna Rutherford, Aarhus: Dangaroo, 1981, 104–113. (Already published in collection of stories, 1970.)

## 1985#

'Certain Winds from the South.' In *African Short Stories*. Ed. Chinua Achebe and C.L. Innes, Oxford: Heinemann (African Writers Series), 1985, 8–15. (From the 1970 collection.)

'The Girl Who Can.' *Ms* (Arlington, Virginia), 1985, 99–101. (Included in the 1996 collection.)

'The Loneliness of the African Writer.' *South* (London), 60 (October 1985), 191.

'Sisterhood is Global.' *Essence* (New York), March 1985, 12–13, 15, 134, 137.

*Someone Talking to Sometime*. Harare: College Press, 1985. (Poems.)

## 1986#

'*The Eagle and the Chicken' and Other Stories*, Enugu: Tana. 1986. (Writing for children.)

'To Be an African Woman Writer – an overview and a detail.' Paper presented at Second African Writers' Conference, Stockholm, 1986. Published in *Criticism and Ideology*. Ed. Kirsten Holst-Petersen, Uppsala: Scandinavian Institute of African Studies, 1988, 155–172.

## 1987#

'*Birds' and Other Poems*. Harare: College Press, 1988. (Writing for children.)

['*The Dilemma of a Ghost' and 'Anowa.'* Harlow: Longman, 1987. (New Edition with both plays in a single volume.)]

## 1988#

'Women and Food Security: The Opportunity for Africa.' *Development*, 2–3 (1988), 56–62.

## 1989#

'For Kinna ... VII.' *West Africa* (London), 6–11 March 1989, 357.

## 1990#

'Nowhere Cool.' *Callaloo* (Lexington, Kentucky), 13, 1 (Winter 1990), 62–70.

## 1991#

[*Anowa* published by L'Aquila translated by Roberta Falcone, with her introduction and notes, Rome: L.U. Japadre, 1991.]

*Changes*. London: Women's Press, 1991. (Also New York: Feminist Press, 1993; Accra: Sub-Saharan, 1994, both editions with 'Afterword' by Tuzyline Jita

Allan, 171–96 and 164–95 respectively; London: Heinemann, 2003.

'Satisfaction.' (A story.) *Imaginative Writing* (University of Cape Coast, English Department), 3 (1991), pagination not available.

'Modern African Stories' and 'A Path in the Sky or 7 A.M. and Airborne.' *Literary Review*, Summer 1991, 434–36.

'That Capacious Topic: Gender Politics.' Conference presentation at the Dia Centre for the Arts. Published in *Critical Fictions: The Politics of Imaginative Writing*. Ed. Philomena Mariani, Seattle: Bay Press, 1991, 151–54.

'Whom do we thank for Women's Conferences.' *Ms*, January/February 1991, 96.

1992#

*An Angry Letter in January and Other Poems*. Coventry: Dangaroo Press, 1992.

'The African Woman Today.' *Dissent*, 39 (Summer, 1992), 319–325. See also *Sisterhood, Feminisms and Power: From Africa to Diaspora*. Ed. Obioma Nnaemeka, Trenton: AWP, 1998, 39–50.

1993#

'Male-ing names in the Sun.' In *Unbecoming Daughters of the Empire*. Eds Shirley Chew and Anna Rutherford, Sydney: Dangaroo, 1993. (See also Podis and Saak, 1997, 85–6. Included in *The Girl Who Can and Other Stories*, 1996.)

1994#

'Everything Counts' and 'In the Cutting of a Drink.' In *Global Cultures: A Transnational Short Fiction Reader*. Ed. Elizabeth Young-Bruehl, Middletown, Connecticut: Wesleyan UP, 1994. (Stories had appeared in the 1970 collection.)

1996#

*The Girl Who Can and Other Stories*, Legon: Sub-Saharan, 1996. (Some previously published stories appear in the collection. Later appeared from London: Heinemann, 2002.)

'Literature, Feminism and the African Woman Today.' In *Reconstructing Womanhood; Reconstructing Feminism: Writing of Black Women*. Ed Delia Jarrett-Macauley, London and New York: Routledge, 1996, 156–74. See also version in *Challenging Hierarchies: Issues and Themes: in Colonial and Postcolonial African Literature (Society and Politics in Africa)*. Ed Leonard A. Podis and Yakubu Saaka, New York: Peter Lang, 1998, 15–35. Sometimes abbreviated to 'Podis and Saaka'.)

1997#

'The Genesis of "Male-ing Names in the Sun".' and 'Male-ing Names in the Sun.' In Podis and Saaka, 1997, 85–6 and 87–9. (Introduction and short story.)

1999#

[*The Dilemma of a Ghost/Le Dilemme d'un revenant. Revue Noire: Contemporary African Art* (Paris), 32 (July 1999) 38–39. (A page of the text in English and French.)]


2000#

'Women's Voices in Construction...' In *Women and Activism: Women Writers' Conference*. Harare: Zimbabwe International Book Fair Trust in Association with Zimbabwe Women Writers, 2000.

'She Who Would Be King.' In Anyidoho and Gibbs, 2000, 197–202. (Also appeared in the 1996 collection. Note *FonTomFrom* was some eight years in the making and 'we' were holding Aidoo's material for that time!)

'Millenium hangovers.' *New Internationalist* (Wallingford), 324 (June 2000), 5.

'What "Hopeless Continent"?' *New Internationalist* (Wallingford), 327 (September 2000), 5.

'Diamonds: the madness and the mess.' *New Internationalist* (Wallingford), 330 (December 2000), 5.


2001#

'And all the jokes are cruel.' *New Internationalist* (Wallingford), 333 (April 2001), 5.


2002#

'Gender and African Languages.' Paper presented at Gender and Literature in Cross-Cultural Contexts Workshop I: Conceptualising Gender in Different Cultural Contexts, London (SOAS and UCL), May 2002. (Abstract on line at http://www.soas.ac.uk/literatures/Projects/Gender/gender1abstracts.pdf)


2003#

'Of Forts, Castles and Silences' and 'Sourcing Our Self Confidence.' Dubois-Padmore-Nkrumah Pan-African Lecture Series delivered in Accra, August 2003. (A blog reference suggests the lectures appeared in print. See http://yoavguttman.blogspot.)

*The Girl Who Can and Other Stories*, London: Heinemann, 2003.


2006#

Edited *African Love Stories*: An Anthology. Banbury: Ayebia, 2006.


2007#

'An Interrogation of an Academic Kind.' In *The Legacy of Efua Sutherland*. Ed. Anne V. Adams and Esi Sutherland Addy, Oxford: Ayebia, 2007, 230–3.

2011#

With Esi Sutherland-Addy and Kati Torda Dagadu, *Ghana: Where the Bead Speaks*, Accra: Foundation for Contemporary Art, 2011.

2012#

*Diplomatic Pounds and Other Stories*. Oxfordshire: Ayebia Clarke.

## Interviews and Profiles.

1967@

Lautré, Maxine. 'An Interview with Ama Ata Aidoo.' *Cultural Events in Africa* (London), 35 (October 1967) 1–4. (Rpt 1972. CEIA was a cyclostyled publication produced by Dennis Duerden's Transcription Centre.)

1972@

Duerden, Dennis and Cosmo Pieterse, eds. *African Writers Talking*, London: Heinemann, 1972, 19–27. (The 1967 interview.)

1981@

Vincent, Theo. *Seventeen Black and African Writers on Literature and Life*. Lagos; Centre for Black and African Arts and Civilisation/ Consulting Publishers, 1981, 1–8. (Aidoo on her forthcoming *Our Sister Killjoy* and writing *Dilemma* and later watching it in Accra.)

1987@

Chetin, Sara. 'Interview with Ama Ata Aidoo.' *Wasafiri* (London), 6–7 (Spring-Autumn, 1987), 23–25, 27.

1990@

James, Adeola. *In Their Own Voices: African Women Writers Talk*. Oxford: Currey, 1990, 9–28.

Maja-Pearce, Adewale. 'We were feminists in Africa first.' *Index on Censorship* (London), 19, 8 (October 1990), 17–18.

1991@

Anon. 'Ama Ata Aidoo on Africa and *Changes*.' *Spare Rib* (London) July 1991, 32–6. (Includes excerpt from the novel.)

Hemming, Sarah. 'Word of Mouth.' *Independent* (London), 3 April 1991, 14. (See this and next entry in context of the 1991 production of *Anowa* and of the promotion of 'their author' by the Women's Press.)

Jaggi, Maya. 'Changing Her Tune.' *Guardian* (London), 2 April 1991, 17. (On *Changes*.)

Modebe, Sarah. 'In Conversation with ... (Ama Ata Aidoo).' *New African* (London), 288 (September 1991), 18. (Rpt *New Nation*, 13 February 1992.

Modebe, Sarah. 'Remembering Tomorrow: A Conversation with Ama Ata Aidoo.' *African Woman*, 5 (Autumn 1991), 31–33.

## 1992@

Barton, Judy L. 'Public Affairs, Politics and the Destinies of People: An Interview with Ama Ata Aidoo.' *World Literature Written in English* (Singapore), 32 (2) – 33 (1) (1992–1993), 12–21.

Paton, Lesley. 'Sorry Teacher; This Poet Can Feed Her Family Now.' South, 2 May 1992, 15; 2 July 1992, 15.

## 1993@

Gacheru, Margaretta wa. 'Ghanaian Mother's Reflections on Her Rewarding Links with Kenyan Artists.' error in latter *Sunday Nation Lifestyles* (Nairobi), 5 December 1993, 4. (Return to Kenya to visit dying writer Jonathan Kariara.)

George, Rosemary Marangoly and Helen Scott. '"A New Tail to an Old Tale:" an Interview with Ama Ata Aidoo.' *NOVEL: A Forum on Fiction* (Brown Univ., Providence, Rhode Island), 26, 3 (Spring 1993), 297–308.

Mackay, Mary. 'Ama Ata Aidoo.' *Belles Lettres* (Arlington, Virginia), 9, 1 (1993), 32–35. *Post Express* (Lagos), 28 September 1966, 12

## 1994@

Lemly, John. Interview. (Unpublished. See footnote 21 to Lemly: 2007.)

Tonfield, Michael. 'A Chat with Ama Ata Aidoo.' *Uhuru* (Accra), 6, 1 (1994), 49–51; also *Okike* (Nsukka) 32 (1996), 101–15.

Tonfield, Michael. 'Women's Publishing Firm Will Help.' *Ghana Today*, February 1994, 9–10.

## 1995@

Abissath, Mawutodzi Kodzo. 'Africa Must Develop Its Own Democratic Structures.' *Uhuru* (Accra), 7 (1995), 20.

Karpf, Anne. 'The Arrival of Aidoo.' *Guardian* (London), 8 September 1995, T21.

Needham, Anuradha Dingwaney. 'An Interview with Ama Ata Aidoo.' *Massachusetts Review*, 36, 1 (Spring 1995) 123–33. (Aidoo reflects on her own dilemmas.)

## 1997@

Pietro Deandrea. Interviews. Unpublished, conducted on 10 June and 3 July, 1997. (See Deandrea: 2002, page 16 f.n. 64 for the issue of 'copyright' on 'No Sweetness Here' (Aidoo or Armah?), compare Fraser, 1980; Deandrea page

21 for Aidoo on the responses of European feminists to *Changes* and for her 'problem with marriage'.)

**1998@**

Koomson, George. 'Time with Ama Ata Aidoo.' *African Agenda* (Accra), 1, 16 (1998), pages not known.

**1999@**

Azodo, Ada U. 'Facing the Millennium: An Interview with Ama Ata Aidoo.' In Azodo and Wilentz, 1999, 429–41, and 'Afterword: Interviewing and Transcribing an Oral Artist, 443–455.

**2000@**

Rhonda Cobham Sander and John Lemly, 'A Conversation with Ama Ata Aidoo.' *Ink* (Five Colleges), 3, 1 (1999–2000), 15–21. (Note one of the 'five colleges' is Mount Holyoke where Aidoo taught for a number of years.)

**2002@**

Agyeman-Duah, Ivor. 'Home at last.' *West Africa* (London), 29 April – 5 May 2002, 35.

Wilson-Tagoe, Nana. 'Ama Ata Aidoo in Conversation.' *Wasafiri*, 37 (Winter 2002), 47–49.

**2003@**

Frias, Maria. 'An Interview with Ama Ata Aidoo: "I Learnt My First Feminist Lessons in Africa".' *Revista Alicantina de Estudios Ingleses* (University of Alicante), 16 (November 2003). (With an Introduction and Notes, this issue is devoted entirely to Aidoo. It represents a major source of information. Recorded January 1998. See http://rua.ua.es/dspace/bitstream/10045/1294/1/RAEl_16_23.pdf accessed 25 January 2011.

**2007@**

Walling, Michael. 'Dialogue with Ama Ata Aidoo.' See http://www.youtube.com/watch?v=VuxPvJqQp0I Accessed 13 December 2010. (The theatre director draws out the playwright on the genesis of *Dilemma*.)

**2010@**

Wood, Molara. 'I've published Less than I Would Have Wished.' NEXT 234 (Lagos), 8 June 2010. http://234next.com/csp/cms/sites/Next/ArtsandCulture/Books/5576862-147/story.csp accessed 25 January 2011

*Undated*

Interview with Eckhard Breitinger, recorded while Aidoo was at Cape Coast, on file Jahn Library for African Literatures, Mainz.

## Secondary Sources

1965*

Jones, Eldred. (Review of *Dilemma*.) *Bulletin of the Association for African Literature in English* (Fourah Bay), 2 (1965), 33–4. (*BAALE* was a cyclostyled publication.)

1966*

Dipoko, Mbella Sonne. (Review of *Dilemma*.) *Presence Africaine: Revue Culturelle du Monde Noir/Cultural Review of the Negro World* (Paris), 30, 58 (1966), 254.

Lindfors, Bernth. (Review of *Dilemma*.) *Books Abroad* (Norman, Oklahoma, 40, 2 (1966), 358–9. (This publication became *World Literature Today* in 1977.)

Pieterse, Cosmo, 'Dramatic Riches.' *Journal of Commonwealth Literature* (Leeds), 2 (1966), 168–171. (Review of *Dilemma* with other plays. Aidoo's play is described as 'a determined and at time distinguished socio-economic morality.' 170.)

1968*

Rea, C.J. 'The Culture Line: A Note on *The Dilemma*.' *African Forum* (New York), 4, 1 (1968), 41–50. (Rea regrets Aidoo did 'not have an experienced stage director to help work out a final version [of the text] before publication.')

1969*

Nagenda, John. 'Generations in Conflict: Ama Ata Aidoo, J. C. De Graft and R. Sarif Easmon.' In *Protest and Conflict in African Literature*. Ed. Cosmo Pieterse and Donald Munro, London: Heinemann, 1969, 101–108. (Volume subsequently published in New York by Africana. The essay is basically a review.)

1970*

Anon. (Review of *Anowa* and *No Sweetness Here*.) *Cultural Events in Africa* (London), 62 (1970), 6.

Armah, Ayi Kwei. *Fragments*. Oxford: Heinemann (African Writers Series), 1970. (New York: Collier, 1971. (NB Dedication reads 'for AMA ATA & ANA LIVIA'. See in context of Aidoo's early essay on Armah.)

1971*

Britwum, Ata. 'New Trends.' *Burning Issues in African Literature* (Cape Coast), 1 (1971).

De Munbrun, Bob. Review of *Anowa*. *Books Abroad*, 45 (1971), 363.

'K.W.' (Presumably Kaye Whiteman.) Review of *Anowa and No Sweetness Here*. *West Africa* (London), 4 February 1971, 113 or 133.

1972*

Condé, Maryse. 'Three Female Writers in Modern Africa: Flora Nwapa, Ama Ata Aidoo and Grace Ogot.' *Presence Africaine* (Paris), 82 (1972), 132–43. (Important recognition.)

Jahn, Janheinz, Ulla Schild and Almut Nordman. 'Ama Ata Aidoo.' *Who's Who in African Literature*. Tübingen: Horst Erdman, 1972, 25–6

Mensah, A.N. (Review of *No Sweetness Here*.) *Legon Observer*, February 1972, 61–2.

Mensah, A.N. 'Society and Poetry, a reply to Atta Britwum and Ama Ata Aidoo.' *Legon Observer* (Legon), 1972, 314–5. (Aidoo figures as a 'dour-faced *tricoteuse*' 'at the foot of the guillotine' in Mensah's imagery. He refers to her 'strictures' on his publication in the midst of a high-octane exchange. Aidoo may allude to this dispute in 'Unwelcome Pals' (end-note 7; she identified 'vulgarity and venom' in the response to her 'intellectual challenge.' The Aidoo/Mensah exchanges can fruitfully be followed through.)

1973*

Burness, Donald B. 'Womanhood in the Short Stories of Ama Ata Aidoo.' *Studies in Black Literature* (Fredericksburg, Virginia), 4, 2 (1973), 21–24.

Dorkenoo, Kodzo Tom. 'Ama Ata Aidoo, Playwright, Short Story Writer.' *Growth: Literary Magazine for Young People*, (Accra: Arts Council), 3 (1973), 72–74.

1974*

Brown, Lloyd W. 'Ama Ata Aidoo: The Art of the Short Story and Sexual Roles in Africa.' *World Literature Written in English* (Guelph), 13, 2 (1974), 172–83.

Grant, Liz. (Review of *No Sweetness Here*.) *Black World*, 23, 5 (1974), 96–7.

Ridden, Geoffrey M. 'Language and Social Status in Ama Ata Aidoo.' *Style*, 8, (1974), 452–61.

1975*

Adelugba, Dapo. 'Literature As Social Justice.' *Ba Shiru* (University of Wisconsin – Madison), 6, 1 (1975).

Brown, Lloyd W. 'The African Woman as Writer.' *Canadian Journal of African Studies* (Published by Canadian Association of African Studies), 9, 3 (1975), 493–501.

1976*

Adelugba, Dapo. 'Language and Drama: Ama Ata Aidoo.' *African Literature Today* (*ALT*, Oxford), 8 (1976), 72–84.

Banham, Martin with Clive Wake. *African Theatre Today*, London: Pitman, 1976.

Brown, Lloyd. 'Sutherland and Aidoo: The Theatre As Tradition.' Paper presented at African Literature Conference (ALA), Ibadan, 1976.

Jones, Eldred Durosimi. 'Review: Ama Ata Aidoo: *Anowa.*' *ALT* (Oxford and New York), 8 (1976), 142–4.

## 1977*

Jones, Eldred D. *et al.* 'Aidoo, Christina Ama Ata.) In *Modern Commonwealth Literature*. Ed. John H. Ferres and Martin Tucker, New York: Frederick Ungar, 1977, 13–15. See also *Modern Black Writers*, ed. Michael Popkin, same publishers, 1978, 20–23.

Ngara, J. (Review of *Our Sister Killjoy*.) *African Woman* (London), 12 (1977) 65–6.

## 1978*

Kern, Anita, (Review) 'Ama Ata Aidoo's *Our Sister Killjoy*.' *World Literature Written in English*, 17, 1 (April 1978), 56–7.

Larson, Charles. (Review of *Our Sister Killjoy*.) *World Literature Today* (Norman, Oklahoma,) 32, 2 (1978), 65–6. (Previously *Books Abroad*.)

## 1979*

Anon. 'Ama Ata Aidoo.' In *Horizonte-Magazin*. Ed. Ulrich Eckhardt, Berlin: Berliner Festspiele GmbH, 1979, 104.

Anon. (Review of *Our Sister Killjoy*.) *Ebony* (Chicago), 34 (1979), 31.

Bruner, Charlotte H. 'Child Africa as Depicted by Bessie Head and Ama Ata Aidoo.' *Studies in the Humanities* (University of Pennsylvania in Indiana), 7, 2, (1979), 5–12.

Berrian, Brenda F. 'The Afro-American West African Marriage Question: Its Literary and Historical Contexts.' Paper presented at African Studies Association Conference, Los Angeles, November 1979.

Chapman, Karen C. 'Introduction to Ama Ata Aidoo's *Dilemma of a Ghost*.' In *Sturdy Black Bridges: Visions of Black Women in Literature*. Ed. Roseann P. Bell, Bettye J. Parker, Beverly Guy-Sheftall, Garden City, New York: Doubleday, 1979, 25–38.

McCaffrey, Kathleen. 'Images of the Mother in the Stories of Ama Ata Aidoo.' *Africa Woman* (London), 23, (1979), 40–41. (Check *JCL*, 12 (1979), 40–1.)

## 1980*

Bishop, Rand. (Review of *Our Sister Killjoy*.) *Obsidian: Black Literature Review* (Raleigh, North Carolina), 6, 1–2, (1980), 251–54.

Fraser, Robert. *The Novels of Ayi Kwei Armah*. London: Heinemann, 1980. (Refers to 'the phrase borrowed by Ama Atta Aidoo for her volume of stories so similar in mood, "No Sweetness Here".' 26.)

Grant, Jane W. *Ama Ata Aidoo: The Dilemma of a Ghost. A Study Guide*, Harlow: Longman, 1980. (49 pages.)

Randall-Tsuruta, Dorothy. (Review of *Our Sister Killjoy*), *Black Scholar* (San Francisco), 11, 6 (1980), 74–5.

Vincent, Theo. 'Form in the Nigerian Novel: An Examination of Aidoo's *Our Sister Killjoy* ... and Okphewo's *The Last Duty*.' Paper presented at the African Studies Association meeting at Philadelphia, October 1980.


1981*

Anon. 'Aidoo, (Christina) Ama Ata.' *Contemporary Authors*, Gale: Detroit, 101 (1981), 12.

Bedu-Addo, (Ato). '*Our Sister Killjoy*, or *Reflections of a Black-eyed Squint*: The latest Ama Ata Aidoo.' *Sankofa* (Accra), 5, 1 (1981), 22–23, 39.

Berrian, Brenda F. 'Bibliographies of Nine Female African Writers.' *RAL*, 12, 2 (Summer 1981), 214–237. (An important document for students of Aidoo's writing.)

Brown, Lloyd W. *Women Writers in Black Africa*. Westport, Conn: Greenwood, 1981.

McCaffrey, Kathleen. *Images of the Women in the Literature of Selected Developing Countries (Ghana, Senegal, Haiti, Jamaica)*. Washington D.C.: Office of Women in Development, Agency for International Development, 1981.

Okai, Atukwei. 'Vision, Image, and Symbol in Ghanaian Literature.' *Pacific Quarterly Moana* (Hamilton, New Zealand), 6 (1981), 51–61.

Petersen, Kirsten Holst. 'Ama Ata Aidoo.' In *Cowries and Kobos: The West African Oral Tale and Short Story*. Ed. Kirsten Holst Pietersen and Anna Rutherford, Aarhus: Dangaroo, 1981, 100–103. (Begins: 'Ama Ata Aidoo is an angry and committed writer.')


1982*

Adetuyi, V. Tai. "*The Dilemma of a Ghost*," Ama Ata Aidoo: *Notes, Model Questions and Answers*. Stevelola English Literature Aids, 2. Ibadan: Stevelola Publishers, 1982.

Amankulor, J. 'Ama Ata Aidoo: *The Dilemma of a Ghost*.' *Okike Educational Supplement* (Nsukka), 3 (1982), 137–150.

Assensoh, A.B. 'Restoring Standards in Ghana.' *West Africa* (London), 20 September 1982, 2411, 2413. (On Aidoo's work as Education Secretary under Rawlings.)

Berrian, Brenda F. 'African Women as Seen in the Works of Flora Nwapa and Ama Ata Aidoo.' *College Language Association Journal* (Atlanta, Georgia), 25, 3 (1982), 331–339.

Etherton, Michael. *The Development of African Drama*. London: Hutchinson. 1982, 194–242. (And New York: Africana.)

Hill-Lubin, Mildred. 'The Relationship of African Americans and Africans: A Recurring Theme in the Work of Ama Ata Aidoo.' *Presence Africaine* (Paris), 124 (1982), 190–201. (Places Aidoo among 'the old guard'.)

Ojo-Ade, Femi. 'Still a Victim? Mariama Ba's *Une si longue letter.' African Literature Today*, 12 (1982), 71–87.


1983*

Crow, Brian. *Studying Drama*, London: Longman, 1983.

Iheakaram, P O. 'Ama Ata Aidoo's *The Dilemma of a Ghost*: An Analytical Study.' *Nka* (Owerri), 1 (1983), 47–51.

Nicholson, Mary Naana. *The Affirmation of African Womanhood in the Works of Ama Ata Aidoo*. MA Thesis, University of Florida, 1983. (See Odamtten 1994; note Nicholson and Naana Banyiwa Horne are one.)

Nyika, Oliver. 'Ama Ata Aidoo: Mother of Africa.' *Mahogany* (Harare), October-November 1983, 46–47.

Oje-Ade, Femi. 'Female Writers, Male Critics.' *African Literature Today*, 13 (1983), 158–79. (Aidoo cites a paper with this title and the sub-title 'Criticism, Chauvinism, Cynicism … and Commitment,' as 'unpublished' in her 1999 paper 'Unwelcome Pals.')

Zell, Hans M., Carol Bundy, and Virginia Coulon. *A New Reader's Guide to African Literature*. London: Heinemann, revised edition 1983 348–349. (Profile etc.)


1984*

Gunnar, Elizabeth. *A Handbook for Teaching African Literature*. London and Exeter, New Hampshire: Heinemann, 1984. (Unit 9, eight pages on *Anowa*.)

Lurdos, Michèle. 'Une situation-cliché renouvelée: L'épouse occidentale dans The Dilemma of a Ghost.' In Visages de la Féminité. Pref. A-J Bullier and J-M Racault, St Denis: Université de Réunion, 1984, 255–62.

Taiwo, Oladele *Female Novelists of Modern Africa*, London: St Martin's Press, 1984.


1985*

Angmor, Charles. 'Classical Heritage and Modern African Literary Theatre.' *African Theatre Review* (Yaounde), 1, 1 (1985), 47–58.

Anthonio, Peju. *Stevelola Notes, Questions and Answers on Ama Ata Aidoo's 'Anowa.'* Stevelola English Literature Aids 11, Ibadan: Stevelola Publishers, 1985.

Cooper, Brenda. 'Chaiba the Algerian versus *Our Sister Killjoy*: The Case for a Materialist Black Aesthetic. *English in Africa*, 12, 2 (October 1985), 21–51. (View at http://www.jstor.org/pss/40238571.)

Ogunyemi, Chikwenye Okonjo. "Womanism: The Dynamics of Black Female Writing in English." *Signs: Journal of Women in Culture and Society*, 11, 1 (1985), 63–80. (Sometimes cited as 'The Dynamics of the Contemporary Black

Female Novel in English.' The article was translated and reprinted. See Okonjo Ogunyemi, 1996, 344.)

Okafor, Chinyere G. 'Ama Ata Aidoo: *Anowa.' Okike, Educational Supplement* (Nsukka), 4 (1985), 137–146.

Onibonoje, 'Biodun. *'Anowa:' Notes, Q/A.* Ibadan: A. Onibonoje Agencies, 1985.

Owusu-Kwarteng, Yaw. *Notes on Ama Ata Aidoo's 'Anowa' for O-Level Candidates.* (Cyclostyled) Achimota, 1985, 19 pages.

1986*

Benson, Peter. *'Black Orpheus' 'Transition and Modern Cultural Awakening in Africa.* Berkley: University of California Press, 1986.

Graham-White, Anthony. 'Ghana: Drama.' In *European-Language Writing in Sub-Saharan Africa.* Ed. Albert Gérard, Budapest: Akadémiai Kiado, 1986, 810–820. (Includes analysis of plays, helpful emphasis on productions, and comments on directors.)

Heywood, Annemarie. 'The Liberation of Women: Reflections in Two West-African Works of Fiction.' *Logos* (Windhoek), 6, 2 (1986), 45–61. (On *Anowa.*)

Lyonga, Nalova. *'Anowa:* The Woman Playwright's Perspective on Africa's History.' *Annales de la Faculté de Lettres et Science Humaines de Yaoundé,* 2, 1 (1986), 89–101. Also *African Theatre Review* (Yaoundé), 1, 2 (1986), 41–51.

'M.N.N.' (Review.) *Someone Talking to Sometime. Africa Now,* January 1986, 41–2. (Recognises combination of 'unique writing style with trenchant observation.')

Nwankwo, Chimalum. 'The Feminist Impulse and Social Realism in Ama Ata Aidoo's *No Sweetness Here* and *Our Sister Killjoy.'* In *Ngambika: Studies of Women in African Literature.* Ed. Carole Boyce Davies and Anne Adams Graves. Trenton, New Jersey: AWP, 1986, 151–159.

1987*

Anyon, Nicholas. 'Ama Ata Aidoo as a Short Story Writer: An appraisal of *No Sweetness Here.' Kuka* (Zaria), 1987–88, 38–42.

Berrian, Brenda F. 'The Afro-American-West African Marriage Question: Its Literary and Historical Contexts.' *African Literature Today,* 15 (1987), 152–9. (Links *Dilemma* with *Raisin in the Sun* by Hansberry. Assumes Aidoo is 'realistic,' and possibly resentful. Quotes Leslie Lacy, *The Rise and Fall of a Proper Negro,* New York: Macmillan. Refers to African Americans in Ghana during the early 1960s. Same title as a conference paper listed above.)

Elder, Arlene. 'Ama Ata Aidoo and the Oral Tradition: A Paradox of Form and Substance.' *African Literature Today* (Oxford), 15 (1987), 109–18.

July, Robert W. *An African Voice: The Role of Humanities in Africa.* Independence, Durham: Duke University Press, 1987. (Background on theatre in Ghana.)

Shehu, Halima. *Feminism in the Writings of Ama Ata Aidoo and Mariama Ba.* MA thesis, Ahmadu Bello University, 1987.

Thies-Torkornoo, Susanne. 'Die Rolle der Frau in der afrikanischen Gesellschaft: Eine Betrachtung von Ama Ata Aidoos *Anowa* und Efua T. Sutherlands *Foriwa.*' *Matatu* (Frankfurt), 1 (1987), 53–67.

## 1988*

Adelugba, Dapo. 'Language and Drama: Ama Ata Aidoo. In Priebe ed., 1988. (See below. Article previously published 1976.)

Akpagu, Zana Itiumbe. 'Aidoo and Experimental Prose Fiction: Visual Patterning as a Foregrounding Device in *Our Sister Killjoy.*' *Liwuram: Journal of the Humanities* (Maiduguri), 4–5 (1988–89) 292–310.

Angmor Charles. 'Drama in Ghana.' In Priebe ed., 1988.

Brown, Lloyd W. 'Ama Ata Aidoo: The Art of the Short Story.' In Priebe ed. 1988.

Etherton, Michael. 'Aidoo, Ama Ata.' In *Cambridge Guide to World Theatre.* Ed. Martin Banham, Cambridge: C.U.P, 1988. (Reprinted: 1994 in *The Cambridge Guide to African and Caribbean Theatre*, 40.)

Graham-White, Anthony. 'Aidoo, Ama Ata.' In *Contemporary Dramatists*, 4th Ed. Ed. D.L. Kirkpatrick, Chicago and London: St James Press, 1988, 9–11. Revised in 5th Edition, ed. K.A. Berney, 1993.

Hill-Lubin, Mildred A. '"Tell Me, Nana": The Image of the Grandmother in the Works of Ama Ata Aidoo.' *Sage: a Scholarly Journal on Black Women* (Atlanta), 5, 1 (Summer 1988), 37–42.

Kusunose, Keiko. 'Women Writers in African Literature: Ama Ata Aidoo and Her works.' *Studies in African Literature* (Osaka), 3 (1988), 91–112. (In Japanese.)                  Odamtten, Vincent Okpoti. *The Developing Art of Ama Ata Aidoo.* PhD Dissertation, State University of New York at Stony Brook, 1988 (Abstract in *Dissertation Abstracts International*, Ann Arbor, Michigan, 50, 1303A.)

Povey, John. 'Aidoo.' In *African Literatures in the Twentieth Century: A Guide.* General Ed. Leonard Klein, Harpenden: Old Castle Books, 1988.

Priebe, Richard, ed. *Ghanaian Literatures.* New York, Westport: Greenwood, 1988. (Various references to Aidoo. See contributions listed here.)

Ufflemann, Inge. 'Our Sister Killjoy or Reflections from a Black-Eyed Squint.' In *Kindlers Neues Literatur Lexikon.* Ed. Walter Jens, Munich: Kindler, 1988–91, 1, 157–58.6

## 1989*

Adewusi, Emanuel Olufemi. *Towards an Aesthetic Valuation: Drama of Efua Sutherland and Ama Ata Aidoo.* MA thesis, University of Ibadan, 1989.

Coussy, Denise. 'Is Life Sweet? The Short Stories of Ama Ata Aidoo.' In *Short*

*Fiction in the New Literatures in English*. Ed. Jacqueline Bardolph and André Viola, Nice iii: Faculté des Lettres & Sciences Humaines, 1989, 285–90.

Dunton, Chris. '"Wheyting Be Dat?:" The Treatment of Homosexuality in African Literature.' *RAL*, 20, 3 (1989), 422–48.

Hill-Lubin, Mildred A. 'The Storyteller and the Audience in the Works of Ama Ata Aidoo.' *Neohelicon* (Amsterdam), 16, 2 (1989), 221–45. See http://www.springerlink.com/content/t742v486g1024842/

Lazarus, Neil. 'Ama Ata Aidoo.' In *Longman Anthology of World Literature by Women 1875–1975*. Ed. Marian Arkin and Barbara Sholler, New York and London: Longman, 1989, 981–2.

Sutherland-Addy, Esi. 'Narrative Technique and the Role of Commentators in Ama Ata Aidoo's Works.' *Research Review* (Legon), 5, 2 (1989), 60–70. See http://archive.lib.msu.edu/DMC/African%20Journals/pdfs/Institue%20of%2 0African%20Studies%20Research%20Review/1989v5n2/asrv005002006.pdf Accessed 24 01 2011.

Owusu, Kofi. *Fictionalising as Fiction-Analysing: A Study of Select 'Critical' Fiction by Ayi Kwei Armah, Wole Soyinka, Ama Ata Aidoo and Chinua Achebe*. Ph.D. Dissertation, University of Alberta, Edmonton, Alberta, Canada.

1990*

Agovi, J.E.K. 'A Dual Sensibility: The Short Story in Ghana, 1944–80. In *Literature and Black Aesthetics*. Ed. Ernest N. Emenyonu HEB: Ibadan, 247–271. (Agovi is particularly alert to the positive way in which Aidoo portrays rural characters.)

Appiah-Padi, Stephen Kodjo. *'The Dilemma of a Ghost': Notes and Comments*. Accra: Educational Press, 1990.

Ekpong, Monique O. 'Feminist Consciousness in Aidoo's *Our Sister Killjoy* and Hurston's *Their Eyes Were Watching God*. Calabar Journal of Liberal Studies (CAJO-LIS), 2, 1 (1990), 84–96.

Owusu, Kofi. 'Canons under Siege: Blackness, Femaleness and Ama Ata Aidoo's *Our Sister Killjoy*.' *Callaloo* (Charlottesville, Virginia), 13, 2 (Spring 1990), 341–63.

Roy, Modhumita. 'Class and Gender in the Novels of Mariamba Ba, Buchi Emecheta, and Ama Ata Aidoo.' Paper presented at the Annual Conference of the African Studies Association Conference, November 1990, Baltimore, Maryland.

1991*

Anon. 'Sharp-minded progressive.' *West Africa*, 22–28 April 1991, 593.

Banham, Martin, 'Ama Ata Aidoo.' In *International Dictionary of Theatre, Vol. 2*, Chicago: St James, 1991.

Brydon, Diana. 'Contracts with the World: Redefining, Home, Community and

Identity in Aidoo, Brodber, Garner and Rule.' In *The Commonwealth Novel since 1963*. Ed Bruce King, Basingstoke and London: Macmillan, 1991, 198–215.

Chetin, Sara. *Rereading and Rewriting African Women: Ama Ata Aidoo and Bessie Head*. Ph.D. Dissertation, University of Kent, Canterbury, 1991.

Hassell, Graham. 'Hit the Road, Jill.' *What's On?* (London), 17 April 1991. (Review of *Anowa* at the Gate Theatre, London.)

Innes, C.L. "Mothers or Sisters? Identity, Discourse and Audience in the Writing of Mariama Bâ and Ama Ata Aidoo.' In *Motherlands: Black Women's Writing from Africa, the Caribbean and South Asia*. Ed. Susheila Nasta, London: Women's Press, and New Brunswick New Jersey: Rutgers University Press, 1991, 129–51. (Rpt in Jeyifo ed. 2002.)

Makanjuola, Bola. 'A Modern Woman's Dilemma.' *West Africa* (London), 1–7 April 1991, 474. (Review of *Changes*.)

Ojo-Ade, Femi. 'Of Culture, Commitment and Construction: Reflections on African Literature.' *Transition: An International Review*, 53 (1991), 4–24. (*Transition* is published by Indiana University Press on behalf of the W.E.B. Du Bois Institute.)

Rooney, Caroline. 'Are We in the Company of Feminists? A Preface for Bessie Head and Ama Ata Aidoo.' In *Diverse Voices: Essays on Twentieth Century Women Writers in English*. Ed. Harriet Devine Jump, New York: St. Martin's Press and London: Harvester Wheatsheaf, 1991.

Rooney, Caroline. 'Dangerous Knowledge and the Poetics of Survival: A Reading of *Our Sister Killjoy* and *A Question of Power*.' In *Motherlands: Black Women's Writing from Africa, the Caribbean and South Asia*. Ed. Susheila Nasta, London: Women's Press, and New Brunswick, New Jersey: Rutgers UP, 1991. 99–126.

Saro-Wiwa, Ken, Jr. 'Symbols of Black Womanhood Today.' *Sunday Times* (London), 28 April 1991, 6. (Aidoo in London promoting *Changes*.)

Wilentz, Gay. 'The Politics of Exile: Ama Ata Aidoo's *Our Sister Killjoy*.' *Studies in Twentieth Century Literature* (Dept of Modern Languages, Kansas State Univ., Manhattan; Univ. of Nebraska-Lincoln), 15, 1 (1991), 159–73. (Republished twice during 1999.)

1992*

Asante, Samuel Y. *The Politics of the Role of the Modern African Woman: Chinua Achebe, Ngũgĩ wa Thiong'o, Mariama Ba and Ama Ata Aidoo*. M.A. Thesis: University of Guelph, Guelph, Ontario, Canada. 1992.

Buck, Claire. Ed. *Bloomsbury Guide to Women's Literature*. London: Bloomsbury, 1992. (Includes entry on Aidoo.) BALE 21282.

Chanda, Ipshita. 'In Search of Sweetness: Ideas of the Diaspora in the Works of Ama Ata Aidoo.' Paper Presented at Conference on Women in Africa and the African Diaspora, July, 1992, Nsukka, Nigeria. Conference also linked to

Indianapolis: Association of African Women Scholars (AAWS), Indiana University, Women's Studies Programme, 3, 1992.

Choto, Ray. 'Read us, writer tells African politicians.' Horizon (Harare,) July 1992, 36–7. (Aidoo speaks out in Zimbabwe.)

Hill-Lubin, Mildred A. 'Ama Ata Aidoo and the African Diaspora: Things "All Good Men and Women Try to Forget": But I Will Not Let Them.' Paper Presented at ALA Conference, April May 1992, Brock University, St. Catharine's, Ontario, Canada.

Horne, Naana Banyiwa. 'Ama Ata Aidoo.' In Dictionary of Literary Biography: Twentieth Century Caribbean and Black African, 117. Ed. Bernth Lindfors and Reinhard Sander, Detroit: Gale, 1992, 34–40.

Horne, Naana Banyiwa. 'Love and the Contemporary African Woman: Ama Ata Aidoo's Changes.' Paper presented at the ALA Conference, April-May 1992, Brock University, St. Catharine's, Ontario, Canada. ('Banyiwa-Horne' is hyphenated in relation to this paper, but not generally. Catalogued here under 'Horne'. Also see Nicholson above.)

Inyama, Nnadozie. 'The "Rebel Girl" in West African Literature: Variations on a Folklore Theme.' In Power and Powerlessness of Women in West African Orality. Ed. Raoul Granqvist and Nnadozie Inyama, Umea Papers in English 15, Umea, 1992, 109–121.

Korang, Kwaku Larbi, 'Ama Ata Aidoo's Voyage Out: Mapping the Coordinates of Modernity and African Self-hood in Our Sister Killjoy.' Kunapipi (Aarhus), 14, 3 (1992), 50–61. (Korang emphasises Aidoo's African approach to the novel form.)

Opoku-Agyemang, J(ane) N(aana). "'A Girl Marries a Monkey:" The Folktale as an Expression of Value and Change in Society.' Asemka (Cape Coast), 7 (September 1992), 5-12. (Rpt in Arms Akimbo: Africana Women in Contemporary Literature. Ed. Janice Liddel and Yakini B. Kemp, Gainesville: University Press of Florida, 1999.)

Opoku-Agyemang, Kwadwo. 'A Crisis of Balance: The (Mis)representation of Colonial History and Slave Experience as Themes in Modern African Literature.' Asemka (Cape Coast), 7 (September 1992), 63–77. (Argues that the issue of slavery is not the major theme in Anowa.)

Turci, M. A Study of the Writings of Ama Ata Aidoo. ASLIB Index to Theses (London), 41 (1992), MA University of Canterbury, Kent.

Wilentz, Gay. Binding Cultures: Black Women Writers in Africa and the Diaspora. Bloomington and Indiana: Indiana University Press, 1992.

Wilentz, Gay. 'Toward a Diaspora Literature: Black Women Writers from Africa, the Caribbean and the United States.' College English, 54, 4 (1992), 385–405. Rpt She'r (Fall 1995), 50–52. (In Persian). Wilentz, Gay. 'The Politics of Exile: Ama Ata Aidoo's Our Sister Killjoy.' Studies in Twentieth Century English Literature, 15, 1 (1991), 159–170.

1993*

Adams, Anne V. 'Pidgin/Patois/Creole as Cultural (Con)Texts: Ama Ata Aidoo, Erma Brodber, Dany Bebel-Gisler.' Paper Presented at the ALA Conference, April, 1993, Gosier, Guadeloupe; Ithaca, New York: Cornell University, Department of African Studies.

Allan, Tuzyline Jita. "Afterword." *Changes: A Love Story*. New York: Feminist Press at City University of New York, 1993.

Amankulor, J. Ndukaku. 'English Language Drama and Theatre.' In *A History of Twentieth Century African Literature*. Ed. Oyekan Owomoyela, Lincoln: University of Nebraska Press, 1993. 138–72. (Writes that Kofi can't 'communicate positively with (*Anowa*), especially about his impotence...')

Asante, Yaw. '(Re) Discovering Europe: Ama Ata Aidoo's *Our Sister Killjoy*.' *In-between:Essays & Studies in Literary Criticism* (Dept of English, Ram Lal Anand College, University of New Delhi), 2, 1 (1993), 17–28.

Barton, Judy L(ynne). *The Subversion and Redeployment of the Popular: Counter-discursive strategies in Ama Ata Aidoo's "Changes: A Love Story."* MA Thesis, University of Guelph, 1993

http://home.cc.umanitoba.ca/~brydond/brydoncv.pdf

Bryce, Jane and Kari Dako. 'Textual Deviancy and Cultural Syncretism: Romantic Fiction as a Subversive Strain in Black Women's Writing.' *Wasafiri* (London), 17 (1993), 10–14. (Originally a 1992 conference paper. A later version appeared in Anyidoho and Gibbs, 2000, 155–164.)

Booth, James. "Sexual Politics in the Fiction of Ama Ata Aidoo." *Commonwealth Essays and Studies* (Dijon), 15, 2 (1993), 80–96.

Chetin, Sara. 'Reading from a Distance: Ama Ata Aidoo's *Our Sister Killjoy*.' In *Black Women's Writing*. Ed. Gina Wisker, New York: St. Martin's, 1993, 146–59.

Cole, Catherine M. 'Ama Ata Aidoo's *Anowa* as Historical Discourse.' Paper Presented at the ALA Conference, April 1993, Gosier, Guadeloupe.

Dunton, Chris. 'Conversational Disputes.' *West Africa*, 8–14 February 1993, 216. (Review of *An Angry Letter in January*.)

Eke, Maureen N. 'Distortions and Revisions of Africa in Kennedy's and Aidoo's Drama.' Paper Presented at the ALA Conference April,1993, Gosier, Guadeloupe.

Chetin, Sara. 'Dislocation and Nation: The Writing of Ama Ata Aidoo.' In *Aspects of Commonwealth Literature*. Ed Liz Gunner, London: University of London Institute of Commonwealth Studies (Seminar Papers), 1993, vol. 3, 48–57.

Harrow, Kenneth W. 'Paths of Return across the Ocean: Aidoo and Walcott.' Paper Presented at ALA Conference, April 1993, Gosier, Guadeloupe.

Niklas-Salminen, Ritva. *Johdatus Afrikan Maiden Kirjallisuuteen*. Tampere: Tampereen yliopisto, 1993.

Opoku-Agyemang, Naana Jane. 'A Reading of Ama Ata Aidoo's *Anowa*.'*The Afro-*

*Centric Scholar: The Journal of the National Council of Black Studies*, 2 (December 1993), 70 – 83. (Rpt 1997.)

Owomoyela, Oyekan, ed. *A History of Twentieth Century African Literatures*. Lincoln, Nebraska: University of Nebraska Press, 1993.

Splawn, P. Jane. 'African and African American Rituals in Shange's *Coloured Girls* and Aidoo's *Changes.'* Paper Presented at the ALA Conference, April 1993, Gosier, Guadeloupe.

Willey, Ann Elizabeth. *Fictional Nations/National Fictions: The Search for National Literatures in Kenya, Senegal and Ghana*. PhD thesis, Northwestern University, 1993. (Abstract in *Dissertation Abstracts International*, Ann Arbor, Michigan, 54 (1993), 1799a.

1994*

Asante, Samuel Yaw. '"Good Night Africa, Good Morning Europe:" Europe's (Re) Discovery by a Black African Woman: Ama Ata Aidoo's *Our Sister Killjoy.'* *Africa Quarterly* (New Delhi), 34, 3 (1994), 64–75. Rpt in *Mightier Than the Matchet*. Ed. Harish Narang, New Delhi: Indian Council for Cultural Relations, 1995, 64–75.

Blankson, Naadu I. (Review.) *Changes: A Love Story*. *Quarterly Black Review of Books* (Hastings on Hudson, New York), 28 February 1994.

Coussey, Denise. 'L'oeuvre d'Ama Ata Aidoo.' *Notre Librairie: Revue des littératures du Sud*, (Paris: Association pour la diffusion de la pensée française – adpf), 118 (1994), 36–40.

Davies, Carol Boyce. *Black Women, Writing and Identities: Migrations of the Subject*, London: Routledge, 1994. (Chapter entitled: 'Deconstructing African Female Subjectivities: *Anowa's* Borderlands.')

Dunton, Chris. 'Aidoo, Ama Ata.' In *Encyclopaedia of Post-Colonial Literatures in English*. Ed. Eugene Benson and L.W. Connolly, London: Routledge, 1994, 27–28.

Ekpong, Monique O. 'Feminist Tendencies in West African Drama: An Analysis of Ama Ata Aidoo's *Anowa.'* In *Current Trends in Literature and Language Studies in West Africa*. Ed. Ernest N. Emenyonu and Charles E. Nnolim, Ibadan: Kraft Books, 1994, 20–33.

Gardner, Susan. 'Culture Clashes: Review of *Changes* by Aidoo and *Kehinde* by Buchi Emecheta.' *Women's Review of Books* (Philadelphia, Pennsylvania), 12 (1994), 22–3.

Gourdine, Angeletta Kim Marie. 'Bridging the Middle Passage: reading and (re)reading Diasporic Politics in Alice Walker's *Possessing the Secret of Joy* and Ama Ata Aidoo's *Changes.'* PhD thesis, Michigan State University, 1994. [Abstr. in *Dissertation Abstracts International* (Ann Arbor, MI) (55) 1995, 3841a

Gunner, Liz. 'Mothers, Daughters and Madness in Works by Four Women Writers: Bessie Head, Jean Rhys, Tsitsi Dangarembga, and Ama Ata Aidoo.'

*Alif: Journal of Comparative Poetics* (Cairo), 14 (1994), 136–51 (English section), 189 (Arabic section).

Hill-Lubin, Mildred. 'Aidoo, Ama Ata.' In *Encyclopedia of World Literature in the 20th Century, Vol. 5 Supplement.* Eds. Steven R. Serafin and Walter D. Glanze, New York: Continuum, 1994., 6–7. Rpt Third edition 1999, 1: 25–26.

Innes, C. L. 'Reversal and Return in Fiction by Bessie Head and Ama Ata Aidoo.' In *"Return" in Post-Colonial Writing.* Ed. Vera Mihailovich-Dickman, Amsterdam: Rodopi, 1994.

Nnolim, Charles. 'The House Divided: Feminism in African Literature. In *Feminism in African Literature.* Ed. Helen Chukwuma, Enugu, New Generation Books, 248–261. (Refers to Aidoo's 'Unwelcome Pals,' 1982.)

Odamtten, Vincent O. *The Art of Ama Ata Aidoo: Polylectics and Reading against Neocolonialism.* Gainesville: University of Florida Press, 1994. (A milestone!)

Ogede, Ode. 'The Defence of Culture in Ama Ata Aidoo's *No Sweetness Here*: The Use of Orality as a Textual Strategy.' *International Fiction Review* (Dept of Culture and Language Studies, University of New Brunswick, Fredericton), 21, 1 and 2 (1994), 76–84.

Ogundipe-Leslie, Omolara. *Recreating Ourselves: African Women and Critical Transformations.* Trenton, New Jersey: AWP, 1994.

Osofisan, Femi. 'Drama (West Africa).' In *Encyclopaedia of Post-Colonial Literatures in English.* Ed. Eugene Benson and L.W. Connolly, London: Routledge, 1994, 408–12.

Phillips, Maggi. 'Engaging Dreams: Alternative Perspectives on Flora Nwapa, Buchi Emecheta, Ama Ata Aidoo, Bessie Head, and Tsitsi Dangarembga's Writing.' *Research in African Literatures* (Bloomington, Indiana), 25, 4 (1994), 89–103.

Swinimer, Ciarunji Chesaina. *Perspectives on Women in African Literature.* Nairobi: Impact Associates, 1994. (Aidoo, Sutherland.)

1995*

Asante, Samuel Yaw. 'Reinventing Africa, Reimag(in)ing the African Woman: Ama Ata Aidoo's *Our Sister Killjoy* and *Changes: A Love Story*.' *Chimo* (Guelph), 30 (1995), 11–13. (May be abstract of paper that was presented at the Annual Conference of the Canadian Association of African Studies, May, 1996, McGill University, Montreal.)

Clerk, Jayana and Ruth Siegel. *Instructor's Manual to Accompany Modern Literatures of the Non-Western World: Where the Waters Are Born.* New York and London: Harper Collins, 1995.

Fister, Barbara. *Third World Women's Literatures: A Dictionary and Guide to Materials in English.* Westport Connecticut and London: Greenwood, 1995.

Innes, C.L. 'Conspicuous Consumption: Corruption and the Body Politic in the Writing of Ayi Kwei Armah and Ama Ata Aidoo.' In *Essays on African Writing*

2: *Contemporary Literature*. Ed. Abdulrazak Gurnah, Oxford: Heinemann, 1995, 1–18.

Katrak, Ketu H. 'Afterword: "Telling Stories and Transforming Post-Colonial Society"' to *No Sweetness Here and Other Stories*. New York: Feminist Press, 1995, 135–160.

MacKenzie, Clayton G. 'The Discourse of Sweetness in Ama Ata Aidoo's *No Sweetness Here.*' *Studies in Short Fiction* (Newberry College, Newberry, South Carolina), 32, 2 (1995), 161–70. See http://findarticles.com/p/articles/mi_m2455/is_n2_v32/ai_17268501/ accessed 13 12 2010.

Mamudu, Ayo. 'Ama Ata Aidoo as a Short Story Writer.' *Commonwealth Essays & Studies* (Dijon), 17, 2 (1995), 19–24.

Newson, Adele S. [Review of] '*The Art of Ama Ata Aidoo: Polylectics and Reading against Neo-colonialism.*' *World Literature Today* (Norman, Oklahoma), 69, 4 (1995), 851. (Meta-criticism!)

Opoku-Agyemang, Naana Jane. 'Lest We Forget: A Critical Survey of Ghanaian Women's Literature.' *Asemka* (Cape Coast), 8 (1995), 61–84.

Samantrai, Ranu. 'Caught at the Confluence of History: Ama Ata Aidoo's Necessary Nationalism.' *Research in African Literatures* (Indiana), 26, 2 (1995), 140–57.

Sudhakar, G. 'Struggle for Survival: A Study of Ama Ata Aidoo's "Three Poems for Chinua Achebe."' *Commonwealth Review* (New Delhi), 7, 2 (1995–6), 154–61. Rpt. 1997 see BALE 34750.


1996*

Agho, Jude Aigbe. *Towards a Literature of Socio-Political and Cultural Commitment in Africa*. Agbor: Pon, 1996.

Angmor, Charles. *Contemporary Literature in Ghana 1911–1978*. Accra: Woeli, 1996.

Bardolph, Jacqueline. 'Celebration of Life; Celebration of Language: Two short stories by Ama Ata Aidoo and Patricia Grace.' In *A Talent(ed) Digger: Creations, Cameos, and Essays in honour of Anna Rutherford*. Ed Hena Maes-Jellinek, *et al.* Amsterdam and Atlanta: Rodopi, 1996, 237–43. (Cross Current Series.)

Dzregah, Augustina E. *Feminism, Conflict and Conformity in the Works of Ama Ata Aidoo and Toni Morrison*. MPhil, University of Ghana, 1996.

Essel, S.E.K. 'Conflict, Dilemma and Feminism in *The Dilemma of a Ghost.*' *Drumspeak* (Cape Coast), 1 (1996), 62–71.

Franks, Jill. 'Aidoo, (Christina) Ama Ata.' In *Contemporary Novelists*, 6th Ed. Ed. Susan Windisch Brown, New York: St James Press, 1996.

Ghosh, Bishnupriya and Brinda Bose. *Interventions: Feminist ialogues on Third World Women's Literature and Film*. New York; London: Garland, 1996.

Gilbert, Helen and Joanna Tompkins. *Postcolonial Drama, Theory, Practice, Politics*. London: Routledge, 1996.

Gyimah, Miriam C. 'Speaking Texts Unheard: Sycorax(ing) Anowa.' Paper presented at ALA Conference. March 1999, SUNY. Published in *Crossing: A Counter-Disciplinary Journal* (Bringhamton, New York) 1, 2 (1997) 57–81. Rpt in *Migrating Words and Worlds: Pan-Africanism Updated*. Ed. Anthony Hurley, E., Rene Larrier and Joseph McLaren, Trenton, New Jersey: AWP, 1999. See for part of text only 31 January 2011, http://crossings.binghamton.edu/gyimah.htm

Jones, Eldred D. *et al*. 'Aidoo, Ama Ata.' In *Modern Women Writers*. Ed. Lillian Robinson, New York: Continuum, 1996, 39–46. (Extracts from critics.)

Jones, Myrtle J. 'Aidoo, Ama Ata, *No Sweetness Here*' In *Teaching the Short Story: A Guide to Using Stories from Around the World*. Ed. Bonnie H. Neumann and Helen M. McDonnell, Urbana II, National Council of Teachers of English, 1996, 12.

Jones, Wilma L. *Twenty Contemporary African Women Writers: A Bio-Bibliography*. ERIC Document ED 386 752, MD: ERIC 1996. (BALE 20930.)

Mensah, A.N. 'Ama Ata Aidoo's *Changes*: A Man's Reading of a Women's Liberationist Novel.' *Marang* (Gaberone), 12–13 (1996–97), 33–42.

Odamtten, Vincent O. 'Ama Ata Aidoo.' In *Benet's Reader's Encyclopedia, 4th Ed*. Ed. Bruce Murphy, New York: HarperCollins, 1996, 15–16

Ogunyemi, Chikwenye Okonjo. *Africa Wo/Man Palava: The Nigerian Novel by Women*. Chicago: The University Press, 1996. (Valuable background.)

Phillips, Maggi. (Review of) *The Art of Ama Ata Aidoo: Polylectics and Reading against Neo-colonialism. RAL*, 27 (1996), 189–93.

Opoku-Agyeman, Naana Jane. 'Sankofa or the Uses of Memory.' In *Images of African and Caribbean Women: Migration, Displacement, Diaspora*. Ed. Stephanie Newell, Stirling: Centre of Commonwealth Studies, Occasional Papers, 1996, 85–96.

Sudhakar, C. 'Conflict between Cultures: Ama Ata Aidoo's "Everything Counts".' *Commonwealth Review* (New Delhi), 8, 2 (1996–7), 84–89.

Sutherland-Addy, Esi. 'Orthodox Feminism and the African Woman Writer: A Reappraisal.' *Legon Journal of the Humanities*, 9 (1996), 81–98.

West, Carol L. 'Space and Mobility as Feminist Issues in Ama Ata Aidoo's *Changes* and Buchi Emecheta's *Kehinde*.' Paper Presented at the African Studies Association Conference, November 1996, San Francisco.

Wright, Derek. 'Returning Voyagers: The Ghanaian Novel in the Nineties.' *Journal of Modern African Studies* (London), 34, 1 (1996), 179–92.

1997*

Alexander, Jacqui and Chandra Mohanty. Eds *Feminist Genealogies: Colonial Legacies, Democratic Futures*. New York: Routledge, 1997.

Behrent, Megan. 'Aidoo's *Anowa*: Dramatising Socio-historical Allegory.' http://www.postcolonial web.org/africa/ghana/aidoo/anowa2.html Accessed 26 January 2011.

Bottcher-Wobcke, Rita. 'Perception and Depiction of Reality in Ama Ata Aidoo's Work.' In *Levels of Perception and Reproduction of Reality in Modern African Literature.* Ed. Hilke Meyer-Bahlburg, Leipzig: Institut for Afrikanistik, 1997, 21–25.

Chetin, Sara. 'Dislocation and Nation: the Writings of Ama Ata Aidoo.' *Aspects of Commonwealth Literature*, vol. 3. London: Univ. of London, Inst. of Commonwealth Studies, 1993, 48–58. (Collected seminar papers, 46.)

Chew, Shirley. 'Ama Ata Aidoo.' In *African Writers, I.* Ed. C. Brian Cox, New York: Scribners, 1997, 37–48.

Innes, Lyn and Caroline Rooney. 'African Writing and Gender.' In *Writing and Africa: Cross-Currents Series.* Ed Mpalive-Hangson Msiskia and Paul Hyland, Harlow and New York: Longman and Addison Wesley, 1997, 193–215.

Mennel, Barbara. '"Germany is Full of Germans Now:" Germanness in Ama Ata Aidoo's *Our Sister Killjoy* and Chantal Akerman's *Meetings with Anna.*' In *Gender and Germanness: Cultural Productions of Nation.* Ed. Patricia Herminghouse and Magda Mueller, Providence, Rhode Island: Berghahn Books, 1997, 235–47.

Nfah-Abbenyi, Juliana. Makuchi *Gender in African Women's Writing: Identity, Sexuality and Difference.* Bloomington: University of Indiana, 1997. (Includes Chapter on '(Re) Constructing Identity and Subjectivity: Buchi Emecheta, Ama Ata Aidoo Tsitsi Dangarembga.')

Opara, Chioma. 'Narrative Technique and the Politics of Gender: Ama Ata Aidoo's *Our Sister Killjoy* and *No Sweetness Here.*' In *Writing African Women: Gender, Popular Culture and Literature in West Africa.* Ed. Stephanie Newell, London and Atlantic Highlands, New Jersey: Zed Books, 1997, 137–46.

Opoku-Agyemang, Naana J. 'A Reading of Ama Ata Aidoo's *Anowa.*' In *Nwanyibu: Womanbeing and African Literature.* Ed. Phanuel A. Egejuru and Ketu H. Katrak, Trenton, New Jersey: AWP, 1997, 21–31. (See also 1993.)

Opoku-Agyemang, Naana J. 'Recent Literary Voices from Ghana.' In *English in Ghana.* Ed Kropp Dakubu, Accra: Ghana English Association, 1997, 225–47.

Ramirez, Victoria Ann. '"Writing is but a Different Name for Conversation:" Dialogism, Narrator, and Narratee in Sterne's *Tristram Shandy*, Aidoo's *Our Sister Killjoy*, and Pynchon's *Gravity's Rainbow.* PhD thesis, State University of New York at Binghamton, 1997. See *Dissertation Abstracts International*, Ann Arbor, Michigan, 58 (1997), 1702A.

Rooney, Caroline. 'Clandestine Antigones.' *Oxford Literary Review* (School of English and Linguistics, Univ. of Durham), 19, 1 and 2 (1997), 47–78. (On *Our Sister Killjoy*.)

Verba, Sharon. 'Feminist and Womanist Criticism of African Literature: A Bibliography.' Preamble dated 20 July 1997, fifteen entries. http://www.indiana.edu/~librcsd/bib/verba/all.html Accessed 1 February 2008 and 25 January 2010. Willey, Elizabeth. 'National Identities, Tradition, and Feminism: The Novels of Ama Ata Aidoo Read in the Context of the Works of Kwame Nkrumah.' In *Interventions: Feminist Dialogues on Third World Women's*

Literature and Film. Ed. Bishnupriya Ghosh and Brinda Bose, New York: Garland, 1997, 3–30.

Williams, Lena. 'Celebrating Writers Who Defy All the Odds.' *New York Times*, 22 October 1997, E1. (At Yari Yari conference.)

Wilson-Tagoe, Nana. 'Reading Towards a Theorisation of African Women's Writings: African Women Writers with Feminist Gynocriticism.' In *Writing African Women, Gender, Popular Culture and Literature in West Africa*. Ed. Stephanie Newell, London: Zed Books, 1997, 149–156.

Wiredu, J.F. and Danysh, I.M. 'The Ghanaian Voice, a Ghanaian's Statement: Language in Ama Ata Aidoo's *Changes*.' *Legon Journal of the Humanities*, 10 (1997), 89–111. (Close linguistic analysis of Aidoo's writing shows how she uses English to 'carry the weight' of Ghanaian experiences.)

## 1998*

Anon. 'Aidoo, (Christina) Ama Ata.' *Contemporary Authors: New Revised Series* (Detroit), 63 (1998), 5–6

Hoeller, Hildegard. 'Ama Ata Aidoo (1942– ).' In *Postcolonial African Writers: A Bio-Bibliographical Critical Source Book*. Ed. Pushpa Naidu Parekh and Siga Fatima Jagne, Greenwood: Westport, Connecticut, 1998, 32–39.

Booker, M.K. *The African Novel in English: An Introduction*. Portsmouth, New Hampshire: Heinemann, and Oxford:, James Currey, 1998. (Chapter 6, 'Ama Ata Aidoo: *Our Sister Killjoy*,' is a thoroughly researched discussion of Aidoo's novel, together with historical and biographical notes. References to Conrad, C. L. R. James and Fanon place Aidoo in a creative and intellectual context. Booker affirms that the novel 'was copyrighted in 1966' but that publication was delayed eleven years. Citation needed.)

Brillmann-Ede, Heike. 'Aidoo, Ama Ata.' In Autorinnen-Lexikon. Ed. Ute Hectfischer *et al*, Stuttgart and Weimar: Metzler, 1998, 11–12.

Obiols Llandrich, Maria Rosa. 'L'oralitat i altres aspectes de la cultura africana a partir de dos contes d'Ama Ata Aidoo.' *Studia Africana* (Barcelona), 9 (1998), 83–93.

Odamtten, Vincent O. 'Beside Every Good Woman There Was a Good Man.' Podis and Saaka, 99–107.

Ogundipe-Leslie, Omolara. 'Literature and Development: Writing and Audience in Africa.' In *Mapping Intersections: African Literature and Africa's Development*. Ed. Anne V. Adams and Janis A. Mayes, Trenton: AWP, 1998.

Onochie, Ernest B. 'A Study of Cross-Cultural Communication in Ama Ata Aidoo's *The Dilemma of a Ghost*.' *Nigerian Theatre Journal* (Benin City), 5, 1 (1999) 120–131.

Opoku-Agyemang, Naana. 'Gender Role Perceptions in the Akan Folktale.' In *Gender Perceptions and Development in Africa: A Socio-Cultural Approach*. Ed. Mary Modupe, Lagos, Nigeria:

Kolawole Arrabon Academic Publishers, 1998, 83–120. (See *RAL*, 30, 1 (Spring 1999), 116–139.)

Pujolrás, Esther. 'L'art d'Ama Ata Aidoo: L'engendrament d'una literatura africana. *Studia Africana* (Barcelona), 9 (1998), 107–28.

1999*

Aguiar, Marian. 'Aidoo, Ama Ata.' In Kwame Anthony Appiah and Henry Louis Gates Jr. *Africana: The Encyclopedia of the African and African American Experience.* New York: Basic Civitas Books, 1999 54–55.

Alumenda, Stephen. 'The Cradle of Literature.' *Moto* (Gweru, Zimbabwe), 196 (1999), 30–31. (On Aidoo's writing for children and young people.)

Azodo, Ada U. 'Afterword: Interviewing and Transcribing a Writer-Oral Artist.' In Azodo and Wilentz.

Azodo, Ada U. '*The Dilemma of a Ghost*: Literature and the Power of Myth.' In Azodo and Wilentz, 213–40.

Azodo, Ada U. 'The Multifaceted Aidoo: Ideologue, Scholar, Writer, and Woman.' In Azodo and Wilentz, 399–425.

Azodo, Ada Uzoamaka and Gay Wilentz (Eds). *Emerging Perspectives on Ama Ata Aidoo.* Trenton: AWP, 1999. (Azodo and Wilentz)

Banham, Martin and Jane Plastow. 'Introduction.' *African Contemporary Plays.* ed. Martin Banham and Jane Plastow, London: Methuen, 1999, vii-xxix.

Bryce, Jane. '"Going Home Is Another Story:": Constructions of Nation and Gender in Ama Ata Aidoo's *Changes.*' *West Africa Review*, (1999), 1–11

Daniel, Ebow. *Mr. Registrar: The Making of an Amanuensis.* Accra: Woeli, 1999. (Daniel's interest in drama is reflected throughout this book. He includes, for example, names of original cast members in *Dilemma*.)

Eke, Maureen. 'Diasporic Ruptures and (Re)membering History: Africa as Home and Exile in *Anowa* and *The Dilemma of a Ghost*.' In Azodo and Wilentz, 61–78.

Elder, Arlene A. 'Ama Ata Aidoo: The Development of a Woman's Voice.' In Azodo and Wilentz, 157–69.

Elia, Nada. '"To Be an African Working Woman:" Levels of Feminist Consciousness in Ama Ata Aidoo's *Changes.*' *RAL*, 30, 2 (1999), 136–47.

Garcia-Viunesa, Maya. 'Communal Voices and Irony in Ama Ata Aidoo's *Changes.*' In *On Writing (and) Race in Contemporary Britain*. Ed. Fernando Galván and Mercedes Bengoechea, Alcalá: Publicaciones Universidad de Alcalá, 1999.

Gourdine, Angeletta K.M. 'Slavery in the Diaspora Consciousness: Ama Ata Aidoo's Conversations.' In Azodo and Wilentz, 27–44. Gyimah, Miriam C. 'Sexual Politics and Phallocentric Gaze in Ama Ata Aidoo's *Changes: A Love Story*.' Azodo and Wilentz, 377–97.

Haiping, Yan. 'Transnationality and its Critique: Narrative Tropes of "Borderland" in *Our Sister Killjoy*.' In Azodo and Wilentz.

Harrow, Kenneth W. 'Of Those Who Went Before.' In Azodo and Wilentz, 171–86. (Aidoo's 'Other Versions' and Walcott's 'Omeros'.)

Hill-Lubin, Mildred A. 'Ama Ata Aidoo and the African Diaspora: Things "All Good Men and Women Try to Forget," But I will Not Let Them.' In Azodo and Wilentz, 45–6. See 1992.

Horne, Naana Banyiwa. 'The Politics of Mothering: Multiple Subjectivity and Gendered Discourse in Aidoo's Plays.' In Azodo and Wilentz, 303–31.

Ladele, Omolola. 'The Aesthetics of Feminism in Ama Ata Aidoo's Drama.' In *Perspectives in Linguistics and Literature*. Ed. Ojo Olorunleke and Lola Ladele, Lagos: Ilu Project Associates, 1999, 39–52.

Littleton, Jacob. *'Dilemma of a Ghost'*. In *World Literature and Its Times*. Ed. Joyce Moss and Lorraine Valestuk, Detroit: Gale, 1999, 87–95.

McWilliams, Sally. '"Strange As It May Seem": African Feminism in Two Novels by Ama Ata Aidoo.' In Azodo and Wilentz, 333–61.

Mari, Christopher. 'Aidoo, Ama Ata.' In *World Authors 1990–1995*. Ed. Clifford Thompson, New York and Dublin: H H Wilson, 1999, 6–8.

Morgan, Paula. 'The Risk of (Re)Membering My Name: Reading "Lucy" and *Our Sister Killjoy* as Travel Narratives.' In Azodo and Wilentz, 187–211.

Nfah-Abbenyi, Juliana Makuchi. 'Flabberwhelmed or Turning History on Its Head? The Postcolonial Woman-as-Subject in Aidoo's *Changes: A Love Story*.' In Azodo and Wilentz, 281–302.

Odamtten, Vincent O. 'The Bird of the Wayside: From "An Angry Letter" to "The Girl Who Can".' In Azodo and Wilentz, 241–52.

Opara, Chioma. 'Hunted, Haunted, and Handicapped: The Disabled Women in Ama Ata Aidoo's *Changes* and Ngũgĩ wa Thiong'o's *Devil on the Cross*.' Paper Presented at the Conference on Women in Africa and the African Diaspora: Health and Human Rights, Indianapolis, October, 1998.

Opoku-Agyemang, Naana J. 'Narrative Turns in Ama Ata Aidoo's *No Sweetness Here*.' In Azodo and Wilentz, 127–144.

Pichler, Susanne. '"Being an Outsider within": Analysis of (an) Exile in Ama Ata Aidoo's *Our Sister Killjoy or Reflections from a Black-Eyed Squint*.' *Moderne Sprachen* (Inst. für Anglistik, Univ. of Salzburg), 43, 1 (1999), 24–32.

Rooney, Caroline. 'The Gender Differential Again and Not Yet.' In *Literature and the Contemporary: Fictions and Theories of the Present*. Ed. Roger Luckhurst and Peter Marks, Harlow: Longman, 1999, 139–55.

Stine, Peter Wilfred. 'The Language of Endurance in the Short Stories of Ama Ata Aidoo.' In Azodo and Wilentz, 255–63.

Strong-Leek, L. 'Inverting the Institutions: Ama Ata Aidoo's *No Sweetness Here* and Deconstructive Theory.' In Azodo and Wilentz, 145–55.

Sutherland-Addy, Esi. 'Ama Ata Aidoo: une voix pour les femmes.' *Notre Librairie* (Paris), 140 (April- June 2000).

Uwakweh, P.O. 'Free but Lost: Variations in the Militant's Song.' In Azodo and Wilentz, 363–75..

Wilentz, Gay. 'African Woman's Domain: Demarcating Political Space in Nwapa, Sutherland and Aidoo.' In Azodo and Wilentz.

Wilentz, Gay A. 'Aidoo's Critical Voice: Reading the Critical Writer.' In Azodo and Wilentz.

Wilentz, Gay. 'The Politics of Exile: Ama Ata Aidoo's *Our Sister Killjoy.*' In *Arms Akimbo: Africana Women in Contemporary Literature*. Ed. Belinda Kemp Yakini and Janice Lee Liddell, Gainesville: University Press of Florida, 1999, 162–175. Also, as 'The Politics of Exile: Reflections of a Black-Eyed Squint in *Our Sister Killjoy.*' In Azodo and Wilentz, 79–92. First published 1991.

Wu, Wei-Hsiung (Kitty). '"Devouring Gods" and "Sacrificial Animals": The Male/Female Relationship in Ama Ata Aidoo's *Changes: A Love Story.*' In *Arms Akimbo: Africana Women in Contemporary Literature*. Ed. Belinda Kemp Yakini and Janice Lee Liddell, Gainesville: University Press of Florida, 1999, 92–102.

Yan, Haiping. 'Transnationality and Its Critique: Narrative Tropes of "Borderland".' In Azodo and Wilentz, 93–124.

2000*

Anyidoho, Kofi and James Gibbs, eds. *FonTomFrom: Contemporary Ghanaian Literature, Theatre and Film, Matatu* (Amsterdam), 21–22 (2000). (Includes several essays on Aidoo and background on the drama situation in Ghana.)

Asante, Samuel Y. *In My Mother's House: A Study of Selected Works by Ama Ata Aidoo and Buchi Emecheta.* Ph.D. Dissertation, University of Calgary, Calgary, Alberta, Canada, 2000.

Baneseh, Mabel Aku. 'Ama Ata Aidoo at Sixty … a Blaze of Achievements.' *Spectator* (Accra), 7 October 2000.

Danysh, Irene M. 'Ama Ata Aidoo's *Changes*: The Woman's Voice in African Literature.' Anyidoho and Gibbs, 2000, 165–172.

Djisenu, John K. 'The Art of Narrative Drama.' Anyidoho and Gibbs, 2000, 37–43.

Dunton, Chris. 'This Rape is Political: The Siteing of Women's Experiences in Novels by Aidoo, Ngugi, Farah and El Saadawi.' *English in Africa* (Inst. for the Study of English in Africa, Rhodes University, Grahamstown), 27, 1 (2000), 1–35.

Fallon, Erin, *et al. A Reader's Companion to the Short Story in English.* Westport: Greenwood, 2000.

Killam, Doug and Ruth Rowe, Eds. *The Companion to African Literature.* Oxford: Currey, Bloomington: Indiana U P, 2000, 21.

Needham, Anuradha D. *Using the Master's Tools: Resistance and the Literature of the African and South Asian Diasporas.* New York: St. Martin's Press, 2000.

Odamtten, Vincent O. '"For Her Own (Works) Quality:" The Poetry of Ama Ata Aidoo.' Anyidoho and Gibbs, 2000, 209–216.

Smith, Pamela J Olubunmi. (Review) *The Girl Who Can and Other Stories.' World Literature Today* (Norman, Oklahoma), 74, 2 (Spring 2000), 342.


## 2001*

Adams, Anne V. 'The Gender of Ambiguity: *L'Aventure ambiguë, Le Baobab fou*, and *Our Sister Killjoy.'* In *Littératures and Sociétés africaine festschrift für Janos Riesz.* Ed. Hans-Jürgen Lüsebrink and Papa Samba Diop, University of Bayreuth: Tübingen, 2002, 549–566.

Agoro, N.A. *Topics in Modern African Drama.* Eleyele, Ibadan: Caltrop, 2001.

Karavanta, Assimina. 'Rethinking the Specter: Ama Ata Aidoo's *Anowa.' Mosaic* (Winnipeg), 34, 4 (December 2001), 107–22. See Bookrags and http://www.enotes.com/contemporary-literary-criticism/aidoo-ama-ata/assimina-karavanta-essay-date-december-2001 accessed 11 01 2011.

Quartey, Rex. 'What Goes into a Play?' *Mirror* (Accra), 11 August, 2001,21.

Wehrs, Donald R. *African Feminist Fiction and Indigenous Values.* Gainesville, Florida: University of Florida Press. 2001. (See 'Ambiguous Freedom in Ama Ata Aidoo's *Changes.'*134–169.)

Wilentz, Gay. 'Demarcating Political Space: African Women's Domain in the Writings of Flora Nwapa and Ama Ata Aidoo.' Paper presented at Southeastern Regional Seminar in African Studies, October 2001, East Carolina University, on line at www.ecu.edu/african/sersas/Papers/WilentsGayFall01.htm


## 2002*

Deandrea, Pietro. *Fertile Crossings: Metamorphosis of Genre in Anglophone West African Literature.* Amsterdam: Rodopi, 2002. (Celebrates Aidoo's versatility in 'recovering oral strategy in written prose.', 16–20.)

Jeyifo, Biodun, ed. *Modern African Drama.* New York: Norton, 2002. (Volume includes *The Dilemma of a Ghost* together with critical essays by Brown (1981), Innes (1991), and Odamtten (1994).)

Ndiaye, Ibrahima. 'Space, Time and Empowerment in Ama Ata Aidoo's *Changes.' Jouvert*, 6, 3 (Spring, 2002). To see this document follow http://www.africabib.org/query_p.php?la=1&PG=572@                    to http://english.chass.ncsu.edu/jouvert/v613/aidoo.htm

Nouryeh, Andrea J. 'Concert Party Performance vs. Aidoo and Sutherland's Drama: Staging Gender in Ghana.' Presented at Conference on Gender and Literature in Cross-Cultural Contexts, May 2002, Semester in London Programme, St. Lawrence University.

Oduyoye, Amba Mercy. *Beads and Strings: Reflections of an African Woman on Christianity in Africa.* Yaoundé and Akropong: Editions Clé and Regnum Africa.

Olaogun, Modupe. 'Slavery and Etiological Discourse in the Writing of Ama Ata Aidoo, Bessie Head, and Buchi Emecheta.' *RAL*, 33, 2 (June 2002), 171–93.

Olaussen, Maria, '"About Lovers in Accra": Urban Intimacy in Ama Ata Aidoo's *Changes: A Love Story.*' *RAL*, 33, 2 (2002), 61–80.

Yan, Haiping. 'Staging Modern Vagrancy: Female Figures of Border-crossing in Ama Ata Aidoo and Caryl Churchill.' *Theatre Journal* (Baltimore), 54 (2002), 245–62. (See http://muse.jhu.edu/login?uri=/journals/theatre_journal/v054/54.2yan.html accessed 31 January 2011.

2003*

Anon. (A review) *The Girl Who Can.*' *African Business*, I June 2003.

Adams, Anne V. 'Literary Panafricanism.' *Thamyris/Intersection, Place, Time, Sex and Race,* 11(2003), 137–51.

Migraine-George, Therese. 'Ama Ata Aidoo's Orphan Ghosts: African Literature and Aesthetic Postmodernity.' *RAL*, 34, 4 (Winter 2003), 83–95.

Ezeigbo, Akachi. 'Constraints and Challenges of the Woman Glass Ceiling Crasher: The Woman Writer's Perspective.' *Vanguard* (Lagos), 28 November 2004. (The second part of the article is on http://allafrica.com/stories/200411291329.html Accessible by subscription.)

Ezenwa-Ohaeto, Review of *Emerging Perspectives on Ama Ata Aidoo*, *RAL*, 34, 3 (Fall 2003), 184–7.

Horne, Naana B. 'Female Child Agency: Political and Social Consciousness in Ama Ata Aidoo's Works. Paper Presented at ASA Meeting, October-November, 2003, Boston, Massachusetts.

Owusu, Martin Okyere and Benjamin Okyere Asante. 'Notes' to Pupils Edition of *Anowa*, Harlow: Pearson Education, 2003. (This edition, 'for BECE', has some 20 pages of Notes and Questions. The authors are under the misapprehension that the play 'achieved instant international acclaim.'(4))

2004*

Cancel, Robert. 'Gestures of Belonging and Claiming Birth Rights: Short Stories by Bessie Head and Ama Ata Aidoo.' In *Emerging Perspectives on Bessie Head.* Ed. Huma Ibrahim, Trenton, New Jersey: AWP, 2004.

Hoeller, Hildegard. 'Ama Ata Aidoo's Heart of Darkness.' *RAL*, 35, 1 (Spring 2004), 130–147.

Ojo-Ade, Femi. *Being Black, Being Human: More Essays on Black Culture.* Trenton, New Jersey: AWP, 2004. (See chapter on 'Talking and Singing for Africa: The Revolutionary Poetry of Ama Ata Aidoo and Micere Githae Mugo.')

Opoku-Agyemang, Kwadwo. 'Ama Ata Aidoo: The Literary Artist and the Creative Process.' Paper presented at the Sasakaw Conference Centre, University of Cape Coast, May 2004.

Richards, Audrey. 'What Is To Be Remembered?: Tourism to Ghana's Slave Castle-Dungeons.' *Theatre Research International* (London), 57, 4 (December 2005), 617–638. (Relevant background for Aidoo's writing.)

Uko, Iniobong. 'A Failed Sexual Rebellion: The Case of Ama Ata Aidoo's *Anowa.*' *African Literature Today* (Oxford and New Trenton) 24 (2004), 130–137.

Wilson-Tagoe, Nana 'The Semantics and Politics of Childbearing and Motherhood in Contemporary African Writing. In *National Healths: Gender, Sexuality and Health in a Cross-cultural Context.* Ed. Nana Wilson-Tagoe and Michael Worton, London: UCL Press, 2004.

2005*

Lambert, Jade Maia. *Ama Ata Aidoo's "Anowa": Performative Practice and the Post-colonial Subject.* MA Thesis, Miami University, 2005.

2006*

The following papers were presented at the ALA Conference Accra, some have moved or are moving towards publication.

- Ajayi-Soyinka, Omofolabo. (Univ. of Kansas, Lawrence): 'If We Count Slaves, Secrets Will... OUT?'
- Androne, Mary Jane (Albright College): 'Male Characters in Ama Ata Aidoo's *Changes: A Love Story*-Nervous Masculinities.'
- Azodo, Ada U. (Indiana Univ. Northwest): 'Recasting Postcolonialism: Ama Ata Aidoo's Project of Re-visioning the Past and Re-Envisioning the Present in *Anowa.*
- Eke, Maureen N (Central Michigan Univ): 'Resisting the Erasure of Slavery: Ama Ata Aidoo's Recovery of Diaspora Memory in *Anowa* and *The Dilemma of a Ghost.*'
- Lambert, Jade Maia. 'Ama Ata Aidoo's *Anowa*: Performative Practice and the Postcolonial Subject.'
- Opoku-Agyemang, Naana (Univ. of Cape Coast): 'Memory as Resistance: Ama Ata Aidoo on the Subject of the African Diaspora.'

Kapi, Catherine Afua. *Writing as a Cultural Negotiation: A Study of the Works of Mariama Ba, Marie Ndayie and Ama Ata Aidoo.* PhD Dissertation, Louisiana State University, Baton Rouge, 2006. (See http://etd.lsu.edu/docs/available/etd-04042006-140255/unrestricted/Kapi_dis.pdf Valuable bibliography.)

2007*

Adams, Anne V. and Esi Sutherland-Addy eds. *The Legacy of Efua Sutherland* Oxford: Ayebia, 2007

Asiedu, Awo Mana. 'Slavery and Folklore in the Plays of Ama Ata Aidoo.' In *Theatre and Slavery.* Ed. Michael Walling, London: Border Crossings, 2007, 99–118.

Fricker, Karen. 'The Dilemma of a Ghost.' *Guardian* (London), 21 April 2007, (Review of Dublin production,)

Lemly, John. 'Hesitant Homecomings in Hansberry's and Aidoo's First Plays.' In Adams Sutherland Addy, 122–130.

Migraine-George, Therese. 'From Exile to Dislocation: Anowa's Wandering Agency in Ama Ata Aidoo's *Anowa*.' In *African Literatures at the Millennium*. Ed. Arthur D. Drayton, Omofolabo Ajayi-Soyinka, and Peter I. Ukpokodu, Trenton, New Jersey: AWP, ALA Series, 13 (2007), 95–103.

Richards, Sandra. 'Dramatising the Diaspora's Return: Tess Onwueme's *The Missing Face* and Ama Ata Aidoo's *Dilemma of a Ghost*. In Adams, Sutherland-Addy, 113–121.

Secovnie, Kelly O. 'Cultural Translation in Ama Ata Aidoo's *The Dilemma of a Ghost* and Tess Onwueme's *The Missing Face*. In *Journal of African Literature and Culture –JACL*, 2007, 127–49.' See http://www.africaresearch.org/Jlc4_2.htm

2008*

Walling, Michael. 'Border Crossings: Setting up a Joint Accra-London Production.' In *African Theatre: Companies*. Ed James Gibbs, Oxford: James Currey, 2008, 109–122.

2009*

Note: The Harlem Book Fair, held a symposium on The Politics and Legacy of Ama Ata Aidoo, 18 July 2009. (See http://www.c-spanvideo.org/program/ 287796-7. Elizabeth Nunez chaired a panel that consisted of Tuzyline Allan, Rashidah Ismaili AbuBakr, Carol Boyce-Davies, and Naana Banyiwa Horne. One of an increasing number of Google videos on line this was accessed 25 January 2011.)

Gibbs, James. 'The Call to the Priesthood and Other Stories in Ama Ata Aidoo's *Anowa*.' *Nkyin-Kyin: Essays on the Ghanaian Theatre*. Amsterdam: Rodopi, 2009, 143–154.

Wetmore, Kevin J. 'A Rotimi in the Sun: Lorraine Hansberry, Ola Rotimi and the Connections of African Diasporean Theatre.' *Profformio* (Swansea), 1, 1 (2009), 5–14. (Refers to *Dilemma* in context of *Raisin in the Sun*.)

2010*

MacKenzie, Clayton G. 'Hope and Purification in the Writings of Ayi Kwei Armah and Ama Ata Aidoo,' *Orbis Litterarum* (a Wiley-Blackwell publication), 65, 2 (2010) 134–48. Article first published online 24 March 2010, http://onlinelibrary.wiley.com/doi/10.1111/j.1600-0730.2009.00975.x/full

Tichaona Chinyelu. 'The Resurrecting Writers Series: Ama Ata Aidoo.' http://www.inthewhirlwind.com 2010. Accessed 11 01 2011. See also http://EzineArticles.com/?expert=Tichaona_Chinyelu

2011*

'Brown Bids farewell to Playwright Ama Ata Aidoo.' 21 January 2011. http://www.youtube.com/watch?v=JW5V1GH7F6E accessed 28 January 2011.

Adichie, Chimamanda Ngozi. 'On Ama Ata Aidoo.' 20 January 2011. (http://www.theafricareport.com/archives2/society-a-culture/5135644-chimamanda-ngozi-adichie-on-ama-ata-aidoo.html (This warm tribute from a younger author was tweeted and blogged about. Accessed on date of posting.)

Haffar, Anis 'Ama Ata Aidoo makes Ghana Proud.' 4 January 2011. Seehttp://news.myjoyonline.com/features/201101/58624.asp Accessed 20 January 2011.

**Webography sites accessed 13 December 2010**

In addition to links indicated in specific entries, the following are among the sites that have biographical and/or bibliographical material.

http://www.answers.com/topic/ama-ata-aidoo

http://www.africabib.org/query_w.php?PG=274@ African Women Bibliographic Database. Includes links to texts of articles.

http://www.bbc.co.uk/worldservice/arts/features/womenwriters/aidoo_life.shtml
http://www.bookrags.com/Ama_Ata_Aidoo
http://www.britannica.com/EBchecked/topic/10410/Ama-Ata-Aidoo

http://www.complete-review.com/reviews/ghana/aidooaa1.htm (of *Our Sister Killjoy*.)

http://www.enotes.com/anowa

http://www.essortment.com/all/amaataaidoob_rwpz.htm

http://kirjasto.sci.fi/aidoo.htm

http://www.postcolonialweb.org/africa/ghana/aidoo/aidoov.html

http://www.postcolonialweb.org/africa/ghana/aidoo/bibliography.html Megan Behrent's work is particularly important.

http://www.questia.com/library/literature/literature-of-specific-countries/african-literature/ama-ata-aidoo.jsp The Questia site has links to on-liner copies of papers.

http://en.wikipedia.org/wiki/Ama_Ata_Aidoo

Ama Ata Aidoo – the following homepage at the National University of Singapore was not available 27 January 2011.

http://www.thecore.nus.edu.sg/post/aidoo/aidoov.html

Mbaasem, NGO founded by Ama Ata Aidoo: http://mbaasemghana.org/wp/

Kinna Reads, literary blog from Ghana with links to Aidoo: http://kinnareads.wordpress.com/

**Productions of Aidoo's plays include the following:**
(Please note: This 'playography' is a foray into a neglected area). The inadequacy of the list is an argument for the desirability of review writing and archiving by those involved in the Ghanaian theatre. The silences – as in all bibliographies – are very eloquent.

1964

March 12, 13, 14 première of *Dilemma* at Commonwealth Hall Amphitheatre Open-Air Theatre, Legon, directed by Olu Neye Ogunsanwo with a University of Ghana student group and others including Akosua Nketia (now 'Perbi') and her late brother, Kwabena. Sources on this include: Daniel: 1999.

1975

December production of *Dilemma* at the Arts Centre, Accra. In a 1981 interview described watching a 1975 production, Vincent: Interview, 1981, 5. At the time of writing, I have no other written reference to the production.

1991

*Anowa* at The Gate Theatre, Notting Hill, London, as part of the Women in World Theatre season. Directed by Dele Charley. (See interviews from this period and Secondary Sources 1991 for reviews.)
*Anowa* put on at Exeter University, dir. (or 'The story is directed by') Leslie Read. See www.ex.ac.uk/drama/projects/anowa/anowa.html. (Six photographs on Google images. Accessed 11 January 2011.)
Production of *Dilemma* at the Centre for National Culture, Eastern Region, Koforidua. (See Stephen Sedofu, 'Aids.' *The Horn*, April–June 1995, 18–22.)

2002/3 Season
*Anowa* directed by Jade Maia Lambert, School of Fine Arts, University of Miami. For reference and photographs, see http://arts.muohio.edu/category/ photo-gallery-departments/theatre/2002-2003

2003

In October, AfriCan Theatre Ensemble (ATE) mounted the Canadian première of *Anowa* in Toronto. It was directed by Rhoma Spencer with choreography by Albert Otto. Spencer apparently used a 'Greek-style chorus, the movement of the Ashantis and music to inform her directorial approach.' Aidoo attended the performance. See http://www.africantheatre.org/testimonials.php accessed 11 01 2011. Site carries comments by Kofi Mensah (*Pride News*) and Jon Kaplan (*NOW magazine.*)
*Anowa*, directed by Mohammed Ben-Abdallah, was presented (in October 2003) at the National Theatre, Accra. It followed the celebration, in the Living

Legends Series, of Aidoo, Awoonor, Armah (not present) and Brew.

2007
There were the following productions of *Dilemma* during the year
- April put on in Dublin Arena, directed by Bisi Adigun.
- August 23–26 put on in Accra as part of the programme of Classic Ghanaian Plays to celebrate Ghana @ 50.
- Month unknown, a production at the University of Cape Coast, directed by Elolo Gharbin.
- Autumn, put on by Border Crossings in Leeds, London, etc. Directed by Michael Walling; cast included Dzifa Glikpo, Agnes Dapaah, Adeline Ama Buabeng, see Walling: 2008. See http://www.bbc.co.uk/africabeyond/africa-narts/17676.shtml Walling's of audience response includes quotations from feedback questionnaires.

James Gibbs
Senior Visiting Research Fellow,
University of the West of England, Bristol

# Chronology of the First Seventy Years in the Life of Ama Ata Aidoo

## Kinna Nana Adjoa Kwesiwa Likimani

| | |
|---|---|
| 1940, March 2 | Born (Christina) Ama Ata Ejinma Aidoo in Abeadze Dominase to Nana Manu III (aka Nana Yaw Fama) and Elizabeth Aba Abasema Bosu. Grows up in her father's household in Abeadze Kyeakor, in the Central Region of Ghana. |
| 1946 | Enrols at Abeadze Kyeakor Local Council Primary, the first school in the village, which her father built. |
| 1950, January | Is shipped out to Takoradi, to live with her cousin Mr. James Bonsu Abban (aka Teacher Abban), a teacher and later a pharmacist, and his wife Mrs. Doris Abban. |
| 1950 | Enrols in Apowine Methodist Primary, Takoradi. |
| 1954 | Wins a scholarship to Wesley Girls High School in Cape Coast. Publishes poems and drama skits in the school's magazine during her time there. |
| 1958 | Completes Form 4 and the Cambridge 'O' Level examination. |
| 1958, Christmas | Wins *The Daily Graphic*'s Christmas short story competition with "*To Us a Child Is Born.*" |
| 1960 | Completes Cambridge 'A' Level examination. Is part of the first batch of students to complete their entire secondary school, education, through Upper Six, at Wesley Girls. |
| 1960/1 | Teaches Literature and History at Wesley Girls while waiting to attend university. |
| 1961, September | Attends University of Ghana, Legon, to study for a B.A. degree in English. |

| 1961–1964 | Attends public lectures by Prof. Kofi Abrefa Busia, Dr. R. P. Baffour (Vice Chancellor of KNUST) and Malcolm X. |
|---|---|
| 1962 | Wins the 3rd All Africa Short Story Competition, given by Mbari Club, University of Ibadan, Ibadan, Nigeria. |
| 1963 | Completes writing *The Dilemma of a Ghost*<br>Wins The Gurrey Prize for Poetry, given by University of Ghana, Legon. |
| 1964 | Graduates with BA degree from University of Ghana, Legon<br>First production of *The Dilemma of a Ghost* by the Students' Theatre, Legon, at the Open-Air Theatre, Commonwealth Hall, University of Ghana, Legon<br>Edits *Firaw*, the journal of Volta Hall, University of Ghana, Legon |
| 1964–1966 | Joins Institute of African Studies at the University of Ghana, Legon, as Junior Research Fellow and as an assistant to Dr. Efua Sutherland. |
| 1965 | Publishes *The Dilemma of a Ghost* |
| 1966 | Represents Ghana at the 1966 Harvard International Seminar |
| 1967 | Wins a fellowship for the Advanced Creative Writing Course, Stanford University, California. Presented a paper on "Contemporary Theatre in Ghana" at the African Studies Centre, UCLA. |
| 1967–1968 | Lives in London and Oxford writing, broadcasting and freelancing for The Transcription Centre, BBC (African Service), The New African, New Society, West Africa, etc. Visits the Irish Republic, France and the Republic of Sudan. |
| 1968–1969 | Travels to East Africa to give seminars at the School of Drama, University of Dar es Salaam, Tanzania and at the Department of Literature, University of Nairobi, Kenya; Reader for Oxford University Press, Nairobi. |
| 1969 | Birth of daughter, Kinna, in Nairobi |
| 1970 | Publishes *Anowa*<br>Publishes *No Sweetness Here* |
| 1970–1982, Jan | Joins and teaches in the Department of English at the University of Cape Coast as a Lecturer and Co-ordinator of the African Literature Programme. |

Serves as Director on a number of national statutory boards including those of: The Ghana Broadcasting Corporation, The Ghana Medical Council, and The Arts Council of Ghana.

1973      Member, Ghana delegation to the World Youth Festival, Berlin.

1974–1975      Consulting Professor to the Washington Bureau of Phelps-Stokes Fund's Ethnic Studies Programme. Based at Dillard and Xavier universities, New Orleans, Louisiana. Presents papers and conducts seminars to over 18 Black American Colleges including Savannah State University (Georgia), Lincoln University (Pennsylvania) and Illinois State University (Normal, Illinois).

1976      Attends Congress of Young Writers From Asia and Africa, Tashkent, USSR.

1977      Publishes *Our Sister Killjoy*

1979, Jan–May      Joins the Department of African Studies, University of Florida, as Visiting Professor of African Literature

1982, Jan–
1983, June      PNDC Secretary (Minister) for Education, Government of Ghana. As both political and administrative head, authors of the 1982/1983 draft proposal for restructuring the educational system.

1983, July-1999      Leaves Ghana. Lives and writes in Harare, Zimbabwe

1985      Publishes *Someone Talking to Sometime*

1986      Publishes *The Eagle and the Chickens*
Wins URTNA 2nd African Prize for Radio Drama with *Changes: The Radio Play*

1987      Wins the Nelson Mandela Prize for Poetry with *Someone Talking to Sometime*

1988      Publishes *Birds and Other Poems*
Joins the Great Lakes Colleges Association as a Fulbright Scholar-in-Residence; works on modern African literature, creative writing and women's studies.

1989, Spring      Is appointed Writer-in-Residence at the University of Richmond, Virginia

1989 – 1990      Chairperson, Africa Regional Panel of Judges, Commonwealth Writer's Prize, The Commonwealth Foundation, London.

| 1991 | Publishes *Changes: A Love Story*<br>First Chairperson, Zimbabwe Women Writers, Harare, Zimbabwe<br>Production of *Anowa* by the Gate Theatre, London. |
|------|---|
| 1992 | Publishes *An Angry Letter in January*<br>Wins the Commonwealth Writers' Prize for Africa with *Changes* |
| 1993–1999 | Teaches at various universities and institutions, including:<br>Visiting Professor, Department of English, Hamilton College<br>Distinguished Visiting Professor, Department of English, Oberlin College<br>The Madeleine Haas Russell Visiting Professor of Non-Western and Comparative Studies, Brandeis University<br>Visiting Professor, English & Theatre Departments, Smith College<br>Visiting Professor, English Department, Mount Holyoke College |
| 1997 | Publishes *The Girl Who Can and Other Stories* |
| 1999 | Receives Honourary Doctoral Degree in Humane letters from Mount Holyoke College<br>Receives *Member of the Volta* (civilian honours) from the State and Peoples of Ghana<br>Returns to live in Ghana |
| 2000 | Founds Mbaasem Foundation to support African women writers |
| 2000–2001 | Writes columns for *The New Internationalist* |
| 2002 | *Anowa* is included in Africa's 100 Best Books of the 20th Century. |
| 2003 | Celebrated, with Kofi Nyidevu Awoonor and Kwesi Brew, in the 'Living Legends Series' by the National Theatre as part of its 10th Anniversary celebrations. |
| 2004 – 2010 | Teaches at Brown University, where she is appointed Visiting Professor in Africana Studies |
| 2005 | Wins Women of Substance Award, given by the African Women's Development Fund (AWDF)<br>Wins Millennium Award for Literary Excellence, given by Millennium Excellence Awards Foundation, Accra |
| 2006 | Edits *African Love Stories Anthology* |
| 2007 | *The Dilemma of a Ghost* is selected by Ghana @ 50 Secretariat as one of 10 theatre classics for production to commemorate Ghana's independence jubilee. |

The Women's Caucus of the African Studies Association inaugurates the *Aidoo-Snyder Book Prize*
Production of *Anowa* at the Rites & Reason Theatre, Brown University

2008        Wins the Aidoo-Snyder Book Prize with *African Love Stories*
Receives the highest honour, the Flagstar, from The Arts Critics and Reviewers Association of Ghana (ACRAG)

2011        Receives a Ghana Women of Excellence Award for her contributions to Culture and Literature, given by the Ministry of Women and Children's Affairs, Ghana

# Notes on Contributors

1.  **Anne Adams** is Professor Emerita in Africana Studies and Comparative Literature from Cornell University. After retirement she served for five years as Director of the W.E.B. Du Bois Memorial Centre for Pan-African Culture, in Accra, during which time she came to appreciate Ama Ata Aidoo's Ghana and its appreciation of her. Recent publications include *The Legacy of Efua Sutherland: Pan-African Cultural Activism*, co-edited with Esie Sutherland-Addy (2007).
2.  **Akosua Adomako Ampofo** is Professor of African and Gender Studies and Director, Institute of African Studies, University of Ghana. Her research, teaching and civil interests address African knowledge systems; race & identity politics; gender-based expressions of violence; constructions of masculinities; and representations of women in popular music. She won the 2010 Sociologists for Women in Society Feminist Activism Award, and incorporates many of the texts of foremost Ghanaian feminist, Ama Ata Aidoo, in her courses.
3.  **Omofolabo Ajayi-Soyinka** is Professor of Theatre, and Women, Gender and Sexuality Studies at the University of Kansas, Lawrence, Kansas. Her teaching and research focus is on critical analysis of gender aesthetics in the literary and performing arts, and cultural paradigms in Africa and the Diaspora. Author of numerous publications, she is a dancer/choreographer, and currently working on the plays of Efua Sutherland, a book of poems, and co-editing a collection of essays on "Trading Women, Traded Women."
4.  **Emmanuel Akyeampong** is Professor of History and of African and African American Studies at Harvard University. He is a Fellow of the Ghana Academy of Arts and Sciences, and a Corresponding Fellow of the Royal Historical Society (UK). He is the author of several books and articles including *Drink, Power, and Cultural Change: A Social History of Alcohol in Ghana, c.1800 to Recent Times* (1996); and is co-editor-in-chief, with Henry Louis Gates, Jr., of the *Dictionary of African Biography* (2011).
5.  **Mary Jane Androne** is Professor of English and Co-Director of Africana Studies at Albright College in Reading, Pennsylvania, where she teaches courses on African Literature and Gender Studies. She has published articles on various African and African American women writers including Tsitsi Dangarembga, Mariama Bâ, Nawal El Saadawi and Julie Dash.
6.  **Kofi Anyidoho** is Professor of Literature, Director of the CODESRIA African Humanities Institute Programme & former Head of the English Department,

University of Ghana. Well-known for his poetry in English and Ewe (including CD & Cassette recordings), he has also published widely on African and African Diaspora literatures, histories and cultures. He is a Fellow of the Ghana Academy of Arts and Sciences and 1st occupant of the Kwame Nkrumah Chair in African Studies, University of Ghana, Legon.

7.  **Susan Arndt** is Professor of English and African Literatures at the University of Bayreuth, Germany. The writings of Ama Ata Aidoo led her to study African literature in the early 1990s. After reading novels such as *Changes* she developed a keen interest in feminism in Africa and in questioning her own history as a white feminist. *Anowa* taught her to look at literature meeting orature, as did *Our Sister Killjoy*, to revisit the entangled histories of Africa → Europe. As a result, she pursued Critical Whiteness Studies, subsequently writing about racism in Germany.

8.  **Kofi Asare Opoku** was at the Institute of African Studies, University of Ghana, Legon 1967–1994 as a Research Fellow in Religion and Ethics. After retiring from Legon, he taught at North Carolina State University and Lafayette College, Easton PA, until 2006. He has been Vice President, Institutional Vision and Advancement at the African University College of Communications in Accra since 2008 and writes on African Religion and Culture. He is also a farmer in the Akuapem Hills, growing local foodstuffs and tending a 30-acre tropical forest as his gift to the world.

9.  **Awo Mana Asiedu** is currently the Acting Director of the School of Performing Arts, University of Ghana. She has published essays on a number of African playwrights including Ama Ata Aidoo, Efo Kodjo Mawugbe, Tess Onwueme and Tracie Chima Utoh-Ezeajugh. She has known Ama Ata Aidoo since the 1970s. She is currently working on a book project on Ghanaian theatre makers.

10. **Yaba Badoe** is a Ghanaian-British documentary filmmaker and writer, who worked as a civil servant in Ghana before becoming a General Trainee with the BBC. She has taught in Spain and Jamaica, and her short stories have been published in *Critical Quarterly* and in *African Love Stories: An Anthology* edited by Ama Ata Aidoo (Ayebia: 2006). In 2009, her first novel, *True Murder* was published by Jonathan Cape.

11. **Abena P.A. Busia** is Chair, Department of Women's & Gender Studies, Rutgers University, is author of two volumes of poems, *Testimonies of Exile* (1990) and *Traces of a Life* (2008). A critic in the fields of colonial discourse and black women's culture she co-edited the four-volume Women Writing Africa project of the Feminist Press. Her poem is a heartfelt thank-you to Ama Ata Aidoo for the encouragement and kindness she has shown her over the years.

12. **Jane Bryce** is Professor of African Literature and Cinema at the University of the West Indies, Cave Hill. Born in Tanzania, she was educated there, the UK, and Nigeria. She has been a freelance journalist and fiction editor and has published in a range of academic journals and essay collections. She is also a creative writer and teacher, curator of a film festival and editor of *Poui: Cave Hill Journal of Creative Writing*.

13. **Margaret Busby OBE** (Nana Akua Ackon I) was born in Ghana and educated in Britain, is a writer, editor, critic and consultant. Co-founder of the London-based publishing house Allison & Busby, she also compiled the pioneering anthology *Daughters of Africa* (1992), has contributed to many publications and judged several literary prizes. Her writing for the stage includes *Yaa Asantewaa: Warrior Queen* (2001–02) and *African Cargo* (2007). She is currently chair of the board of *Wasafiri* magazine: *http://www.wasafiri.org*

14. **Maryse Condé** is a Guadeloupean novelist and scholar, has written over ten novels, including *Heremakahonon, I, Tituba, Black Witch of Salem, Segu, The Children of Segu, Last of the African Kings,* and *Tree of Life.* A retired professor of literature from Columbia University, she is one of the pioneers in scholarship on African and Diaspora women's writing and on Caribbean identity.

15. **Kari Dako** teaches Language in the Department of English, University of Ghana. However, she dabbles in literature – translating fiction, writing fiction and writing on Ghanaian fiction. She has lived in Ghana on and off for several decades, as she was married to a Ghanaian and raised her two sons there. She came to know Ama Ata Aidoo in Harare when they both lived there in the 1980s.

16. **Carole Boyce Davies** is an African Diaspora Studies scholar and Professor of Africana Studies and English at Cornell University with over a hundred published articles and book chapters, nine edited collections of literary theory and cultural criticism and the prize winning: *Left of Karl Marx. The Political Life of Black Communist Claudia Jones* (2008). *Black Women, Writing and Identity: Migrations of the Subject* (1994) is considered a theoretical base for related studies in this area. The general editor of the *Encyclopedia of the African Diaspora* (2008), *Claudia Jones: Beyond Containment* (2011), her forthcoming book is "Caribbean Spaces: Escape Routes from Twilight Zones."

17. **Ivor Agyeman-Duah** is founder of the Centre for Intellectual Renewal, a public policy organisation that looks into the role of arts, culture, and communication, and their bearing on economic growth. He is author or editor of ten books, including the anthology, *Some African Voices of Our Time* (1997); *Bu Me Be: Akan Proverbs* with Peggy Appiah and Kwame Anthony Appiah, which was launched in Accra by Ama Ata Aidoo in 2001. Also a documentary filmmaker, Agyeman-Duah was part of the BBC and PBS documentaries, *Into Africa* and *Wonders of the African World* presented by Henry Louis Gates, Jr.

18. **Femi Osofisan** is a Nigerian writer and wears many caps as journalist, social activist, poet, novelist, essayist, scholar and most especially playwright, actor, songwriter and theatre director. Widely produced and widely studied in and outside the continent, and winner of many awards, he retired recently from the University of Ibadan after 38 years in service.

19. **James Gibbs** is a retired university lecturer, taught at the University of Ghana at the end of the sixties. Since then he has taken an interest in Ghanaian writing, and, in 2000, he and Kofi Anyidoho were delighted to be able to include a short story by Ama Ata Aidoo in a double volume of *Matatu* they had put together. The volume, entitled *FonTomFrom*, was devoted to contemporary Ghanaian literature, theatre and film.

20. **Naana Banyiwa Horne** is a Professor of English and African and African Diaspora literature at Santa Fe College, Gainesville, Florida, is an alumna of Cape Coast University who has known Ama Ata Aidoo since the early 1970s. Horne has published various articles and given many presentations on Aidoo. Her MA thesis (1983) was one of the early full-length manuscripts on the author. Horne is currently working on gender in Ghanaian literature.

21. **Sue E. Houchins** is an Associate Professor at Bates College (Maine, USA) in the Programmes of Women and Gender and African American Studies, where she teaches courses in the literatures of the Diaspora – Africa, African America, and Caribbean. She has translated and written the historical-critical introduction with

Baltasar Fra-Molinaro of the eighteenth-century hagiography of Sor Teresa Chicaba, an Ewe woman who was captured, enslaved in Spain and then freed to become a Dominican nun. This work, soon to be published by Vanderbilt University Press, is a rare European example of a slave narrative.

22. **Biodun Jeyifo** is Emeritus Professor of English at Cornell University and Professor of Comparative Literature and African and African American Studies at Harvard University. He has published many books, monographs and essays on Anglophone African and Caribbean writings, drama, Marxist and postcolonial literary and cultural studies. His *Wole Soyinka: Politics, Poetics and Postcolonialism* (Cambridge University Press, 2004), won one of the American Library Association's Outstanding Academic Texts (OATS) awards for 2005. The two-volume *Oxford Encyclopedia of African Thought* which he co-edited with Abiola Irele was published in March 2010.

23. **Ketu H. Katrak** was born in Bombay, India, is Professor in the Department of Drama at the University of California, Irvine (UCI). Author of *Contemporary Indian Dance: New Creative Choreography in India and the Diaspora* (2011); *Politics of the Female Body: Postcolonial Women Writers* (2006), *Wole Soyinka and Modern Tragedy* (1986), co-editor, *Anti-feminism in the Academy* (2006), and published essays in postcolonial and Diaspora Literature and Third World Women Writers.

24. **Helen Lauer** is Associate Professor and head of the Department of Philosophy and Classics, University of Ghana, Legon, has taught there full-time since 1988. She edits interdisciplinary anthologies of African scholars, e.g. with Kofi Anyidoho, *Reclaiming the Human Sciences and Humanities through African Perspectives* (2012); and an earlier three-volume anthology, *History and Philosophy of Science for African Undergraduates* (2003).

25. **Kinna Likimani** works with Mbaasem, a foundation that supports Ghanaian and African women writers and their creative output. Following studies in the U.S, she worked at Columbia University before emigrating back to Ghana. She has consulted for the Ministries of Health and Communications. She is also active in rural development and is a founding member of the Abeadze Women's Development Organisation. An avid reader, she promotes books and reading through her blog, Kinna Reads.

26. **Mĩcere Gĩthae Mũgo** is Meredith Professor for Teaching Excellence; past chair, Department of African American Studies (AAS); past director, Africa Initiative and past director, Graduate Studies in AAS at Syracuse University. She is a poet, play-wright and literary critic who has published six books, eight co-edited supplementary school readers, three monographs and edited *Third World in Perspective* (journal). Mĩcere has been an activist most of her life. She embraces her daughters, Mũmbi and Njeri, as fellow-activists and best friends.

27. **Ngũgĩ wa Thiong'o** is currently a Distinguished Professor of English and Comparative Literature at the University of California, Irvine. Ngũgĩ is a novelist, essayist, playwright, journalist, editor, academic and social activist from Kenya. His most recent publications are *Wizard of the Crow* (2006), *Something Torn and New: An African Renaissance* (2009), and *Dreams in a Time of War: A Childhood Memoir* (2010). He is currently working on book 2 of his memoirs, *In the House of the Intrepreter.*

28. **Vincent O. Odamtten** is a Professor in English at Hamilton College, Clinton, New York. He has written and lectured on African, Caribbean and African American

literature and culture. He has also contributed articles to critical anthologies including *Encyclopedia of African Literature, Emerging Perspectives on Ama Ata Aidoo, Of Dreams Deferred, Dead Or Alive: African Perspectives on African-American Writers*, edited *Broadening the Horizon: Critical Introductions to Amma Darko*, and the acclaimed *The Art of Ama Ata Aidoo*.

29. **Atukwei Okai** is a Ghanaian a poet and graduate of the Gorky Literary Institute, Moscow (1967) and the University of London (1971), Okai taught at the University of Ghana, Legon and the University of Education, Winneba, for four decades. Elected a Fellow of the Royal Society of Arts (UK) in 1968, Okai is the Secretary General of the Pan African Writers' Association (PAWA). He has seven volumes of poetry in print.

30. **Naana Jane Opoku-Agyemang** is Vice-Chancellor of the University of Cape Coast, after having served previously as Head of the English Department, Dean of the Faculty of Arts, and Dean of the Graduate School. She is Ghana's representative to the executive committee of UNESCO. Her scholarly publications include numerous articles on African and Diaspora literatures.

31. **Akosua Perbi** is a Senior Lecturer in the History Department, University of Ghana, Legon, specialising in indigenous slavery. Her book *A History of Indigenous Slavery in Ghana from the 15th to the 19th Century* (2004) was well received and awarded Honourable Mention at the Noma Awards Ceremony in South Africa, 2006. She has over 20 articles in journals and chapters in books. In 1964 Akosua and her brother acted as "Boy and Girl" in Ama Ata Aidoo's play *The Dilemma of a Ghost*.

32. **Mansah Prah** is an Associate Professor of Sociology at the Department of Sociology and Anthropology, University of Cape Coast. Her research interests are in popular culture, gender and development, and rural sociology. She is the author of *Ghana's Feminist Movement: Aspirations, Challenges, Achievements*. Ama Ata Aidoo is a mentor and a big sister to her entire family.

33. **Ram Prasansak** is currently a faculty member in the Department of English and Communications at Ubon Ratchathani University, Thailand. He received his doctoral degree from the University of Washington, 2011. His dissertation, "Giving Ghana at the Edge of the Salt Water," examines the dialectic of "work" and "gift" through the complexity of Ghana's political economy in a selection of postcolonial Ghanaian novels that include Ama Ata Aidoo's *Our Sister Killjoy* and *Changes: A Love Story*.

34. **Esi Sutherland-Addy** is Professor at the Institute of African Studies, University of Ghana. Publications include (ed) with Aminata Diaw, *Women Writing Africa, West Africa and the Sahel* (2005); with Anne Adams *The Legacy of Efua Sutherland, Pan-African Cultural Activism* (2007). *Ghana: Where the Bead Speaks* (2011) is a coffee-table photo/poetry/essay book designed by Kati Torda Dagadu, whose authorship she proudly shares with Ama Ata Aidoo.

35. **Nana Wilson-Tagoe** is a Visiting Professor of Black Studies at the University of Missouri, Kansas City, US. She has taught African and African Diaspora literature at SOAS, University of London and at universities in Ghana, Nigeria and Kenya. She has published *Historical Thought and Literary Representation in West Indian Literature* and *A Readers' Guide to West Indian and Black British Literature*. She has co-edited *Gender, Sexuality and Health in Cross-cultural Perspectives* and has forthcoming books on Ama Ata Aidoo and Yvonne Vera. She is a friend and former colleague of Ama Ata Aidoo.

36. **Cheryl Toman** is an Associate Professor of French and Women's Studies and Director of the Ethnic Studies Programme at Case Western Reserve University. She is the author of *Contemporary Matriarchies in Cameroonian Francophone Literature* (2008) and the translator and volume editor for Thérèse Kuoh-Moukoury's *Rencontres essentielles/ Essential Encounters* (MLA Texts and Translations Series, 2002). She is a 2011 recipient of a Dora Maar Fellowship for her forthcoming book on women writers of Gabon.

37. **Toyin Falola** is a Distinguished Teaching Professor and the Frances Higginbotham Nalle Centennial Professor in History at the University of Texas at Austin. He is the author of numerous books, and the 2011 recipient of the Distinguished Africanist Award by the African Studies Association. His memoir, *A Mouth Sweeter Than Salt*, captures his childhood and received various awards. He has an Honourary Doctorate from Monmouth University, USA. He is the current Chair of the Herskovits Prize for the African Studies Association, a member of the M. Klein Book prize committee for the American Historical Association, and the Joel Gregory Prize committee for the Canadian Association of African Studies.

38. **Kwesi Yankah** is Professor of Linguistics and former Pro-Vice Chancellor of the University of Ghana, after serving as Head of Linguistics Department and Dean of the Faculty of Arts. He is currently visiting professor at the University of California at Berkeley. Professor Yankah's area of specialisation is ethnography of communication. He has published extensively in several local and international journals. His widely quoted works include *Speaking for the Chief* and *The Proverb in the Context of Akan Rhetoric*, which are used in universities across the world. He is a warm admirer of Ama Ata Aidoo, and appreciates particularly her close observation and description of the African cultural experience. Ama Ata Aidoo, to Yankah, is a quintessential Griot of the African experience, having brought to the literary production, pristine imprints of indigenous oral traditions.

39. **Helen Yitah** is a Senior Lecturer and Head of the Department of English, University of Ghana. She was editor for the Writers Page, a weekly literary arts page that was a collaborative effort between Ama Ata Aidoo's organisation for writers, the Mbaasem Foundation and the *Daily Graphic* newspaper. She teaches African, African American and postcolonial literature, and her research interests are in gender identity in literature.

# Notes

**Notes to Introduction "Someone should lend me a tongue"**

1   Ama Ata Aidoo, *The Dilemma of a Ghost* (New York: Macmillan, 1971), p. 50.

2   Kathleen M. Fallon and Anna-Liisa Aunio, "The Domestic Terrain within Transnational Activism: Ghana and the 'Marital Rape' Clause," *Conference Papers – American Sociological Association*, 2006 Annual Meeting, Montreal, p1, 20p. Although the paper focuses specifically on the "marital rape" clause, which was a part of the original bill, the bill that passed did not include the clause.

3   *New African*, Nov. 2010, p. 96

4   Ama Ata Aidoo, *Our Sister Killjoy*, (Harlow: Longman, 1988), p. 112.

5   Ama Ata Aidoo, "To Be an African Woman Writer – an Overview and a Detail," in Kirsten Holsten Petersen and Per Wästberg, eds., *Criticism and Ideology: Second African Writers' Conference, Stockholm 1986* (Uppsala: Scandinavian Institute of African Studies, 1988), pp 155–172.

6   Ama Ata Aidoo, "Literature, Feminism, and the African Woman Today," in Leonard Podis and Yakubu Saaka, eds. *Challenging Hierarchies: Issues and Themes in Colonial and Postcolonial African Literature* (New York: Peter Lang, 1998) pp. 15–35. The caption was triggered by a 1995 article in *West Africa*, in which a discussion on the state of African literature yielded no mention of any women writers.

7   In the interview with Femi Ojo-Ade mentioned later in this paragraph, Aidoo says: "I have had over the last nearly twenty years since it's been out so many approaches from European publishers proposing to translate the books into European languages and then nothing has happened, and then when I go back to inquire people say: 'Oh, we never said that we were interested.' It's not a matter of people saying: 'Oh, actually, we can't translate it,' but people pretending they had not made the offer which, after a time, convinced me that they are just uncomfortable with the books." Femi Ojo-Ade, "Conversation with Ama Ata Aidoo, and Memo to My Sister Killjoy," 1996, p. 25.

8   Ibid.

9   Ivor Agyeman-Duah interviews Kwame Anthony Appiah, *West Africa* 9:16 (January 1995).

10  Daughters of Africa: an international anthology of words and writings by women of African descent from the ancient Egyptian to the present (New York: Pantheon, 1992)

11  Lloyd W. Brown, *Women Writers in Black Africa* (Westport: Greenwood, 1981); Eldred Durosimi Jones, ed. *Women in African Literature Today* (Trenton: Africa World Press, 1987).

12  M.J. Daymond, Dorothy Driver, Sheila Meintjes, eds., Women Writing Africa: Volume 1: The Southern Region (New York: Feminist Press of CUNY, 2003).

13  Esi Sutherland-Addy and Aminata Diaw, eds. Women Writing Africa: Volume 2: West Africa and the Sahel (New York: Feminist Press of CUNY, 2005).

14  Amandina Lihamba, Fulata L. Moyo, Mugaybuso M. Mulokozi and Naomi L. Shitemi, eds. Women Writing Africa: The Eastern Region (v. 3) (New York: Feminist Press of CUNY, 2007).

15  Fatima Sadiqi, Amira Nowaira, Azza El Kholy and Moha Ennaji, eds., Women Writing Africa: The Northern Region (v. 4) (New York: Feminist Press of CUNY, 2009).

16  E.g., C.L. Innes' The Cambridge Introduction to Postcolonial Literatures in English (Cambridge: Cambridge UP, 2007); or Tejumola Olaniyan and Ato Quayson's African Literature: An Anthology of Criticsm and Theory (Oxford: Blackwell, 2007); more genre-specific volumes such as Biodun Jeyifo's Modern African Drama: Backgrounds and Criticism (New York: Norton, 2002); or F. Odun Balogun's. Tradition and Modernity in the African Short Story: An Introduction to a Literature in Search of Critics (New York: Greenwood, 1991).

17  Gainesville: UP Florida.

18  Trenton: Africa World Press, 1999.

19  H.K. Wright, "Cultural Studies as Praxis: (Making) an Autobiographical Case." Cultural Studies 17(6) 2003, 805–822.

20  Ama Ata Aidoo, ed., African Love Stories (Oxfordshire: Ayebia Clarke, 2006).

21  Aidoo, 1998, p. 25.

## Notes to Section I Introduction

1  Ama Ata Aidoo, "Something to Talk About on the Way to the Funeral' No Sweetness Here (New York: Anchor,, 1972), 146.

2  Micere Githae Mugo, Writing and Speaking from the Heart of My Mind, (Trenton: Africa World Press, 2012).

3  Published in Anne V. Adams and Janis A. Mayes, eds., Mapping Intersections: African Literature and Africa's Development (Trenton: Africa World Press, 1988).

## Condé: Notes to "Three Female Writers in Modern Africa: Flora Nwapa, Ama Ata Aidoo and Grace Ogot"

1  Présence Africaine 81 (1972), 132–143.

2  Chinua Achebe in Things Fall Apart

3  Germaine Gree

## Notes to "A Conversation: Micere Mugo and Ama Ata Aidoo"

1  Dr. Kwegyir Aggrey (1875–1927) was Gold Coast's most respected early educator. On the subject of admitting girls to the all-male Achimota College, he said: "The surest way to keep people down is to educate the men and neglect the women. If you educate a man you simply educate an individual, but if you educate a woman, you educate a family."

2  Convention People's Party

3  Angelou

4   University of Ghana, Legon
5   Efua Sutherland
6   University of California at Los Angeles

**Note to Section II Introduction**
1   Ama Ata Aidoo,"To the reader, a confession ..." *Changes*.(London: Women's Press, 1991) unnumbered page.

**Falola: Notes to "The *Amistad*'s Legacy: Reflections on the Spaces of Colonisation"**
1   For various accounts of the Amistad in published works, among others, see Mary Cable, *Black Odyssey: The Case of the Slave Ship Amistad* (Viking Press, 1971); Howard Jones, *The Mutiny on the Amistad: The Saga of a Slave Revolt and its Impact on American Abolition, Law, and Diplomacy* (Oxford Univ. Press, 1987); William Owens, *Slave Mutiny: The Revolt on the Schooner Amistad* (J. Day Co., 1953); David Pesci, *Amistad* (1997); and Karen Zeinert, *The Amistad Slave Revolt and American Abolition* (1997).
2   W. E. B. Du Bois, *The Souls of Black Folk*, 1903 (New York: Norton, 1999), 11.
3   Carter G. Woodson, *The Mis-education of the Negro*, 1933 (Trenton, NJ: Africa World Press, 1990), xii-xiii.
4   Alexander Falconbridge, *An Account of the Slave Trade on the Coast of Africa* (London, 1788).
5   Rudyard Kipling, "The White Man's Burden," in *Collected Verse* (New York: Doubleday, 1907), 215–217.
6   For two accessible books on the subject, see Toyin Falola, ed., *Africa*, vols 3 and 4 (Durham: Carolina Academic Press, 2002–04).
7   Among others, see Chinua Achebe, *Things Fall Apart* (London: Heinemann, 1958).
8   Walter Rodney, *How Europe Underdeveloped Africa* (Washington D.C.: Howard UP, 1972).
9   Toyin Falola, *Nationalism and African Intellectuals* (Rochester, NY: University of Rochester Press, 2001).
10  Molefi Asante, *The Afrocentric Idea* (Philadelphia: Temple UP, 1998).
11  Martin Bernal, *Black Athena: The Afroasiatic Roots of Classical Civilisation, Vol. 1, The Fabrication of Ancient Greece 1785–1985* (New Jersey: Rutgers UP, 1987); *Vol. 2, The Archaeological and Documentary Evidence* (New Jersey: Rutgers UP, 1991); Mary Lefkowitz, *Not Out of Africa: How Afrocentrism Became An Excuse to Teach Myth as History* (New York: Basic Books, 1996); and Martin Bernal, *Black Athena Writes Back: Martin Bernal Responds to his Critics* (Durham, NC: Duke UP, 2001)
12  The literature on this successful cultural tradition has become extensive. Among others, see Cary D. Wintz, *Black Culture and the Harlem Renaissance* (Houston: Rice UP, 1988); James De Jongh, *Vicious Modernism: Black Harlem and the Literary Imagination* (New York: Cambridge UP, 1990); David Levering Lewis, *When Harlem Was in Vogue* (New York: Random House, 1981); and J. Martin Favour, *Authentic Blackness: The Folk in the New Negro Renaissance* (Durham: Duke UP, 1999).
13  United Nations, 1992 Charter of Courmayeur adopted at the International Workshop of the Protection of Artistic and Cultural Patrimony.
14  Toyin Falola, *The Power of African Cultures* (Rochester, NY: University of Rochester Press, 2003).

15  Paul Gilroy, *The Black Atlantic: Modernity and Double Consciousness* (Cambridge: Harvard UP, 1993).

16  On these various back-to-Africa projects see, among others, Robert Johnson, Jr., *Retuning Home: A Century of African-American Repatriation* (Trenton, NJ: Africa World Press, 2005); and James T. Campbell, *African American Journeys to Africa, 1787–2005* (New York: Penguin Press, 2006).

17  Notable examples include the *Amistad* (1997) directed by Steven Spielberg, with a writing credit to David Franzoni.

### Jeyifo: Note to "Radical, Comparative Postcolonialism"...

1  This is a slightly revised text of a lecture given in June 22, 2004 at Cornell University, Ithaca, NY, USA. It was given in my capacity as one of the faculty of the summer institute of the School of Criticism and Theory (SCT) for that year. I am greatly indebted to all who participated, colleagues and students, in the very lively debate that ensued after the delivery of the lecture.

### Jeyifo: Works Cited

Bessie Head, *A Question of Power*, London: Heinemann Educational Books, 1974.

Theresa Hak Kyung Cha, *Dictée*, Berkeley: Third Woman Press, 1995.

Norbert Elias, *The Civilising Process*, New York: Urizen Books, 1978.

Stanley Fish, *Is There a Text in this Class? – The Authority of Interpretive Communities*, Cambridge, MA: Harvard UP, 1982.

Michel Foucault, *The Birth of the Clinic: An Archeology of Medical Perception*, New York: Pantheon Books, 1973.

_____, *Discipline and Punish: the Birth of the Prison*, New York: Vintage Books, 1995.

_____, *The History of Sexuality*, New York: Pantheon Books, 1978.

_____, *Madness and Civilisation: A History of Insanity in the Age of Reason*, New York: Vintage Books, 1973.

Jurgen Habermas, *Autonomy and Solidarity: Interviews with Jurgen Habermas*, New York and London: Verso, 1992.

_____, *The Future of Human Nature*, Malden, MA: Polity Press, 2003.

_____, *The Philosophical Discourse of Humanity: Twelve Lectures*, Cambridge, MA: MIT Press, 1987.

Mary Jacobus, "Is There a Woman in this Text?," in *Reading Woman: Essays in Feminist Criticism*, New York: Columbia UP, 1986.

Thomas Pynchon, *Gravity's Rainbow*, New York: Bantam Books, 1973.

Edward Said, *Culture and Imperialism*, New York: Knopf, 1994.

_____, *Orientalism*, New York: Pantheon Books, 1978.

Jean Paul Sartre, *Critique of Dialectical Reason*, London, New York: Verso, 1990.

Raymond Williams, *Culture and Society, 1780–1950*, London: Chatto and Windus, 1958.

_____, *The Long Revolution*, London: Chatto and Windus, 1961.

### Anyidoho: Notes to "Literary Visions of a 21st Century Africa"

1  An extract from a longer paper titled "Writing the Future: Literary Visions of a 21st Century Africa." Addison Locke Roach Memorial Lecture, Indiana University-Bloomington. April 21, 2004.

2  Ama Ata Aidoo, *An Angry Letter in January & Other Poems* (Coventry: Dangaroo Press,

1992). pp. 15–17.

3    Casely Hayford, *Ethiopia Unbound* (London: Frank Cass & Co. Ltd, 1911).

4    Kwame Nkrumah, "The African Genius: "Speech Delivered at the Opening of the Institute of African Studies on 25th October 1963. In *African Studies: The Vision and the Reality*. (Institute of African Studies, University of Ghana, Legon. March 1992). p. 14.

5    Ama Ata Aidoo, "She Who Would Be King," in *The Girl Who Can and Other Stories*, and also in *FonTomFrom: Contemporary Ghanaian Literature, Theatre & Film*. Eds. Kofi Anyidoho & James Gibbs (Matatu 21–22; Amsterdam-Atlanta, GA: Editions Rodopi, 2000:197–207).

6    Ama Ata Aidoo, ibid., 199.

7    Two segments of Armah's lectures "Re-Membering the Dismembered Continent" and a follow-up interview, were subsequently telecast as part of Ghana Television's *African Heritage Series*.

## Opoku-Agyemang: Note to "Writing for the Child in a Fractured World"

1    Paper originally delivered on the occasion of the 2009 International African Writers' Day on November 7.

## Lauer: Notes to "Who's African?"

1    Prince Kwame Adika (2011) observes in contemporary Ghanaian poetry (e.g. by Kofi Anyidoho, Kobina Eyi Acquah, Kofi Awoonor, Abena Busia) an ascendant view of postcolonial nationalism as a limitation upon individual emancipation, whereby transnational references deliberately cast a wider horizon for self recognition and fulfilment, one that unites the search for "social liberation" in "the Diaspora and the Homeland together." He notes that other literary critics who have elaborated this theme include: Gloria Anzaldua, Arjun Appadurai, Saskia Sassen, Biodun Jeyifo, and Benedict Anderson. However the interpretation of Ama Ata Aidoo's "In Memoriam: The Ghana Drama Studio" that I broach here differs from the one Adika provides at the end of his paper, "The Transnational Logic of Contemporary Ghanaian Poetry," delivered to the Ninth Faculty of Arts Colloquium, University of Ghana, April 15, 2011. I am grateful to Dr. Adika for discussions during and since that presentation.

2    More generally, in the political philosophy literature, 'cosmopolitanism' covers a broad range of perspectives that minimise to varying degrees the significance of national boundaries in determining principles of legal authority and moral obliga-tion, basic human rights and civic entitlements, dignified treatment, distributive justice, humanitarian conventions, natural disaster and environmental ethics, retri-bution and criminal law, war crime. See the anthology edited by Gillian Brock and Harry Brighouse (2005).

3    Kwame Gyekye (1997: 92–95, 113) advocates a notion of "meta-nationality" as an elaboration of Connors' proposal (1972) to reinforce a nation-state's prospects for stability by ensuring that through language unification and other measures, the entire population shares a univocal mindset (Connor, 1972: 353). Together with a mistaken view of the role that language plays in sustaining people's beliefs about themselves and the world, Connor's caveat inspired Gyekye to suggest that "good nation-building" entails a government's enforcing a uniform national language policy in order to build "a cohesive cultural identity."

4   According to Kwame Gyekye (1997, 163) a "meta-nationality" is something that can only be "consciously and purposively pursued" to transform African communitarian loyalties into broader, more ecumenical images of belonging.

5   The theme of African identity is central as well to her fiction, plays, poetry and novellas earlier in her corpus and since, *No Sweetness Here* (1970), *Changes: A Love Story* (1991), *The Dilemma of a Ghost* (1965), *Anowa* (1970) and the short poem "In Memoriam: The Ghana Drama Studio" (2004) all reflect views anticipating the modern critique of cosmopolitanism which are pursued and developed in the present commemorative essay.

6   Analyses of 'racial histories' on scientific grounds in Appiah's *In My Father's House* (1992: 31–32) suggest a liberating positivist foundation for universalism whereby *every* event of world history comprises an episode in each of our own people's histories – in that all of it has happened remotely, in a positivist sense, to all of us. A fuller and more faithful treatment of Appiah's early cosmopolitan claims (1992) would reveal that it is quite incorrect to level the critical points made in this essay against his views in particular; but there is insufficient space here to elaborate his cosmopolitanism accurately; see Appiah (2004).

7   Jeffrey Sachs, author of the UN MDGs ratified in 2000, proposed the somewhat ill-phrased "develop global partnership for development" as the last goal. .

8   Quoting from 2007 speech of Minister J.O. Obetsebi-Lamptey, Ministry of Tourism and Modernisation of The Capital City, Accra, Ghana http://www.africa-ata.org/gh9.htm, accessed May 2011.

9   One such pretence is the ready tendency of Europeans to embrace Africans by compartmentalising all of them together or sub-regionally or ethnically at every opportunity ("Into A Bad Dream," *OSK*, 10).

10  Chris Stringer, (1987) "The Genetic Evidence for Human Evolution," *The Natural History Museum*. www.fathom.com/feature/190159/index.html

11  Kwame Appiah (2006) makes the point with beguiling simplicity: "This is a genuine problem, one that afflicts people in many communities: they're too poor to live the life they want to lead."

12  I use the term here following Olúfémi Táíwo (2010) who states explicitly in his concluding remarks the message of Aidoo in *Our Sister Killjoy*: ". . . So even if an African wishes to be 'Western' she must do so in *her own way* or, failing that, suffer the stigma of inauthenticity," p. 274).

13  Mokgatle (1971: 216–224) vividly describes his regimen for cultivating Black Consciousness which inspired his powerful contribution to the success of the anti-apartheid struggle. He writes that he intentionally provoked abuse, contriving to routinely expose himself to the worst excesses of physical brutality and psychological humiliation by breaking pass laws conspicuously so that he would be caught by authorities and dealt with in the degrading way apportioned to his identity under apartheid law. He says this discipline taught him to lose his fear of police and prison.

14  This was spelled out to me in conversation by one of the founders of the Black Consciousness Movement, the ANC activist and colleague of the late Steven Biko, Dr. Mamphela Ramphele, New York City, August 1984. This approach of renouncement has served both Dr. Ramphele's nation and her global recognition very well; among many other accomplishments including honourary doctorates and

various influential World Bank posts, in 2004 she was voted 55th of the Top 100 Great South Africans.

15  "As for the African Miss . . . How charming. And they gaped at her, pointing at her smile. Her nose. Her lips. Their own eyes shining. Not expecting her to feel embarrassed . . ." ("The Plums," *OSK*, 43).

16  Standard scientific rigour is absent from assessments of hypotheses about the pathogenesis of epidemiological patterns observed in African populations that are not replicated on other continents. Standard methods of testing, reporting, and theorising about chronic contagions and high mortality are replaced with theories based on generalisations about African sexual depravity (Eileen Stillwaggon 2004).

17  In her prose poems throughout *Our Sister Killjoy*, Aidoo is explicit in her disapproval of those lies (e.g. "From Our Sister Killjoy" 90).

18  Ama Mazama (2003: 9).

19  Most recently in his contribution to the Opening Plenary Session of the African Literature Association 32nd Annual Conference: *Pan-Africanism In The 21st Century: Generations In Creative Dialogue*. Accra, Ghana, May 17–21, 2006.

20  *BBC Worldservice* November 14–16, 2006.

21  A vast literature has accumulated since the 1960s theorising about the impact of literature, media images and the social construction of knowledge on the self perceptions and motivating anti-social behaviour of African American (see "Notes" in D'Souza, 1995: 557–700). In particular, the prejudicial response of teachers to students of distinct ethnic groups has a statistically significant depreciation on the scholastic aptitude of African American children (Bowles, 1975: 263–269).

22  Aidoo's strongest moral protagonists disparage the advice of Western pundits and their development theories about Africa as invasive and inadequate (*OSK*, 86, 114).

23  ". . . Second rate experts giving first-class dangerous advice. . . expressing uselessly fifth-rate opinions" ("Everything Counts," *No Sweetness Here* 1).

**Lauer: Works Cited**

Aidoo, Ama Ata. *Two Plays: The Dilemma of a Ghost. Anowa.* (1965). London: Longman, 1985.

_____. *No Sweetness Here.* (1969) Garden City, NY: Doubleday, 1972.

_____. *Our Sister Killjoy.* London: Longman, 1970.

_____. *Changes: A Love Story.* London: Women's Press, 1991.

_____. *The Girl Who Can and Other Stories.* Accra: Sub-Saharan Press, 1997.

_____. "In Memoriam: The Ghana Dance Studio." In Woeli A. Dekutsey and John Sackey. Eds. *An Anthology of Contemporary Ghanaian Poems.* Accra: Woeli Publishing, 2004,pp. 26–28.

Ake, Claude. *Social Science as Imperialism. The Theory of Political Development.* University of Ibadan Press, 1982.

Amin, Samir. *Delinking: Towards a Polycentric World.* London: Zed, 1990.

Appiah, Kwame Anthony. *In My Father's House.* Oxford: Oxford UP, 1992.,

_____. *Ethics of Identity.* Princeton UP, 2004.

_____. "The Case for Contamination," *The New York Times Sunday Magazine.* January 1. Excerpted from *Cosmopolitanism: Ethics in a World of Strangers.* New York: W.W. Norton, 2006..

Arnold, Millard. Ed. *Steve Biko: Black Consciousness in South Africa.* NY: Random House, 1978.

Bowles, Samuel. "Unequal Education and the Reproduction of the Social Division of Labour," in A.P. Coxon and C.L. Jones (eds.) *Social Mobility*, Middlesex: Penguin, 1975..

Connor, Walker. "Nation-Building or Nation-Destroying?" *World Politics* 24.3 (1972) 319–355.

D'Souza, Dinesh. *The End of Racism*, NY: Free Press, 1995.

Gyekye, Kwame. *Tradition and Modernity*. New York: Oxford UP, 1997.

Honneth, Alex. "Integrity and Disrespect: Principles of a Conception of Morality Based on the Theory of Recognition," *Political Theory* 20.2 (1992)187–202.

_____. "Recognition: The Epistemology of Recognition," *Proceedings of the Aristotelian Society* 75.1 (2001.) 111–126.

Jaggar, Alison. *Feminist Politics and Human Nature*. New Jersey: Rowman and Allanhead, 1980.

Lauer, Helen. "Realities of 'Social Construct': A comment upon K.A. Appiah's 'Illusions of Race,', *Quest* VII.2 (1993.) 106–113.

_____. "Treating Race as a Social Construction," *Journal of Value Inquiry* 30.3 (1996.) 445–451.

_____. "Worldviews and Identities: How Not to Explain Collectively Intentional Actions," *Legon Journal of International Affairs* (LEJIA) 4.1 May (2007) 43–65.

Mazama, Ama. Ed. "Introduction," *The Afrocentric Paradigm*. Trenton, New Jersey: Africa World Press, 2003.

Stillwaggon, Eileen. *AIDS and the Ecology of Poverty*. New York: Oxford UP, 2006.

Táíwo, Olúfémi. *How Colonialism Preempted Modernity in Africa*. Bloomington: Indiana UP, 2010.

## Arndt: Notes to "The Longevity of *Whiteness* and Ama Ata Aidoo's *Our Sister Killjoy*"

1   Ama Ata Aidoo, *Our Sister Killjoy*. New York, London, Lagos: NOK Publishers International, 1979 (1977).

2   Toni Morrison, *Playing in the Dark: Whiteness and the Literary Imagination*. Cambridge, Mass.: Harvard UP, 1992; hooks, bell. "Representations of *Whiteness*." in: Id. *Black Looks. Race and Representation*. Boston, MA 1992: 165–178.

3   Aristotle. *Politics*, I.5., cited under http://classics.mit.edu/Aristotle/politics.1.one.html.

4   Aristotele. *Politics*, I.5, cited under http://classics.mit.edu/Aristotle/politics.1.one.html.

5   Thomas Poiss. „Die Farbe des Philosophen. Zum Motiv des 'weißen Menschen' bei Aristoteles." in: Wolfgang Ulrich and Juliana Vogel, eds. *Weiß*. Frankfurt am Main: S. Fischer Verlag 2003: 144–154, here: 152.

6   Cf.: Jackson, Henry. "Aristotle's Lecture Room and Lectures." in: *Journal of Philology* 35 (1920): 191–200.

7   Eschenbach, Wolfram von. *Parzival*. Translated by A.T. Hatto. London 2004 (1984): 30.

8   Eschenbach, Wolfram von. *Parzival*. I. 1–8. Stuttgart: Reclam, 2004: I.2 91 5, S. 158.

9   Cf.: Eschenbach, Wolfram von. *Parzival*. I. 1–8. Stuttgart: Reclam, 2004: I.1 55 25: 96–97; I.2 94 11–15, S. 162/163.

10  Cf.: Eschenbach, *Parzival*, 34; Cf.: Dôpflac diu küneginne/ Einer werden süezer

minne,/ und Gamuret ir herzen trût./ ungelîch war doch ir zweier hût."
(Eschenbach, Wolfram von. *Parzival*, I.1 44 27–30: 78/79).

11  Eschenbach, *Parzival*, I.1 57, 16: 100–101.
12  Eschenbach, *Parzival*, 25.10–16: 40; Cf.: wîz und swarzer varwe er schein .../Als ein
    agelster wart gevar/sîn hâr und ouch sîn vel vil gar." (Eschenbach, Wolfram von.
    *Parzival*. Band I. Buch 1–8. Stuttgart, Reclam, 2004: I.1 57 17, 27–28, S. 100/101).
13  Cf.: "diu küngîn juste in sunder twâl/ vildicke an sînbu blanken mâl" (Eschenbach,
    *Parzival*, I.1 57 19–20, S. 100–101).
14  Eschenbach, *Parzival*, I.1 1 1–14: 6–7.
15  Loomba, Ania. "Religion, Colour, and Racial Difference." in: Ania Loomba.
    *Shakespeare, Race, and Colonialism*. Oxford: Oxford UP, 2002: 45–74, here: 47–48.
16  Duncan-Jones, Katherine, ed. *Shakespeare's Sonnets*. London: Thompson Learning:
    The Arden Shakespeare 1997: 130 (1–4); p. 369.
17  Duncan-Jones, *Shakespeare's Sonnets*, 127 (1–4); p. 375.
18  Arndt Susan. Myths and Masks of 'Travelling': Colonial Migration and Slavery in
    Shakespeare's *Othello*, *The Sonnets* and *The Tempest*." in: Lars Eckstein, Christoph
    Reinfandt (Hrsg.): *Anglistentag 2008 Tübingen: Proceedings*. Trier: WVT 2009: 213–226.
19  This allegory is continued by the fact that Othello kills himself with his "sword of
    Spain" (5.2.254).
20  Still off-stage, Caliban is characterised by Prospero as "a freckled whelp, hag-born
    ... not honoured with A human shape" (1.2.282–283). Thus, the (*white*
    Elizabethean) audience is taught to see what all the other *white* characters continu-
    ously declare: that Caliban was a monster (2.2.31, 155, 159; 3.2.3, 4, 7, 24, 28;
    5.1.258, passim), devil (1.2.321; 2.2.58, 99, passim), fish or other kind of animal
    (1.2.283–4, 318; 2.2.25–6, 85, 107; 3.2.20, 28; 5.1.266, passim), or "a thing most
    brutish" (1.2.359), "a bastard" and a "thing of darkness" (5.1.268, 272–5).
21  Caliban assures Trinculo and Stephano that he is willing to make them the masters
    of the island and to be their servant, making them believe that the 'New World' was
    indeed to be conquered by "fire water." In fact, however, he merely pretends to be
    submissive and drunk, in order to lure them into supporting his plan to gain free-
    dom and independence (2.2. 180–7).
22  Thus, for example, Prospero knows that Caliban "never/Yields us kind answer" and
    insults him by employing racist vocabulary – such as calling him a "tortoise,"
    "poisonous slave," "devil" and "wicked dam" (1.2.318, 321–2) – at the precise
    moment that Caliban counters his confession that "We cannot miss him: he does
    make our fire,/Fetch in our wood and serves in offices/That profit us" with: "There's
    wood enough within" (1.2.316).
23  Lentin, Alana: "Europe and the Silence about Race." in: *European Journal of Social
    Theory* 10 (4) 2008, S. 487–503.
24  Cf.: Aanerud, Rebecca. "Fiction of *Whiteness*: Speaking the Names of *Whiteness* in US
    Literature." In: *Displacing Whiteness: Essays in Social and Cultural Criticism*, ed. by Ruth
    Frankenberg. Durham, London: Duke UP, 1997: 35; David Roediger R. *Towards the
    Abolition of Whiteness: Essays on Race, Politics, and Working Class History*. London, New
    York: Verso, 1994: 12.
25  Shankar Raman, *The Racial Turn: Race,' Postkolonialität, Literaturwissenschaft*, in: *Einführung
    in die Literaturwissenschaft* hg. von Miltos Pechlivanos, Stefan Rieger, Wolfgang Struck
    und Michael Weitz, Stuttgart 1995, S. 241–255, here 255, cf. also: Arndt, Susan.

Weißsein – zur Genese eines Konzepts. Von der griechischen Antike zum postkolonialen 'racial turn.'" in: Jan Standke, Thomas Düllo (Hrsg.): *Theorie und Praxis der Kulturwissenschaften*. Culture Discourse History. Band 1. Berlin: Logos Verlag, 2008: 95–129.

26  Guillaumin, Colette. *Racism, Sexism, Power and Ideology*. London: Routledge Chapman & Hall, 1995: 107.

27  Attitudes and behaviours of *white* people and cultures have already been analysed by earlier theorists of racism such as Frantz Fanon, Albert Memmi and Edward Said (Cf.: Fanon, Frantz. *Les damnés de la terre*. Paris, F. Maspero 1961; Memmi, Albert. *Portrait du colonisé précédé du Portrait colonisateur*. Paris: Gallimard, 1966; Memmi, Albert. *Le racisme: description, définition, traitement*. Paris: Gallimard, 1984 [1982]); Said, Edward. *Orientalism*. New York: Vintage Books 1978. Yet it was only in the early 1990s that the field of research known as 'Critical *Whiteness* Studies' emerged which takes *whiteness* into account in addition to Blackness and in its complex relationship to Blackness, thus resituating 'race'/*race* as a relational category of knowledge and criticism. For an introduction to this field see Toni Morrison, *Playing in the Dark*; Frankenberg, Ruth. *Displacing Whiteness: Essays in Social and Cultural Criticism*. Durham, London: Duke UP, 1997; Eggers, Kilomba, Piesche & Arndt, *Mythen, Masken und Subjekte*.

28  Cf.: Arndt, Susan. "The Racial Turn.' Kolonialismus, Weiße Mythen und Critical *Whiteness* Studies." in: Marianne Bechhaus-Gerst, Sunna Gieseke & Reinhard Klein-Arendt. *Koloniale und postkoloniale Konstruktionen von Afrika und Menschen afrikanischer Herkunft in der deutschen Alltagskultur*. Frankfurt a.M., Peter Lang 2007: 11–26.

29  Cf.: Frankenberg, Ruth. "Introduction. Local *Whitenesses*, Localising *Whiteness*." in Ruth Frankenberg, ed., *Displacing Whiteness. Essays in Social and Cultural Criticism*. Durham: Duke UP, 1997: 1–33, here 15.

30  Cf.: Yancy, George. "Introduction." In: Ibid, ed. *What White Looks Like: African-American Philosophers on the Whiteness Question*. New York: Routledge, 2004: 8–9, 14.

**Wilson-Tagoe: Works Cited**

Aidoo, Ama Ata. *The Dilemma of a Ghost and Anowa*. London: Longman, 1970/1983.
_____. *Our Sister Killjoy or Reflections from a Black-eyed Squint*. London: Longman, 1977.
_____. *Changes. A Love Story*. London: The Women's Press, 1991.
Dunton, Chris. "Wheyting be Dat?" The Treatment of Homosexuality in African Literature." *Research in African Literature*. 20. 3 (1989): 422–48.
Ivory, James M. "Self-colonization, Loneliness and Racial Identity" in Ama Ata Aidoo's *Our Sister Killjoy or Reflections From a Black-eyed Squint. Postcolonial Perspectives on Women Writers From Africa, the Caribbean and the US*. Ed. Martin Japtok. Trenton, NJ: Africa World Press, 2003.
Korang. Kweku Larbi. "Ama Ata Aidoo's Voyage Out: Mapping the Coordinates of Modernity and African Selfhood" in *Our Sister Killjoy, Kunapipi*. 14. 3 (1992): 50–61
Owusu, Kofi. "Canons Under Seige. Blackness and Femaleness" in Ama Ata Aidoo's *Our Sister Killjoy*. Research in African Literature. 13. 2 (1990): 341–63.
Samantrai, Ranu. "Caught at the Confluence of History: Ama Ata Aidoo's Necessary Nationalism." *Research in African Literatures*. 26. 2 (1995): 140–157.
Tate, Claudia. *Psychoanalysis and Black Novels. Desire and the Protocols of Race*. New York: Oxford University Press, 1998.

Todorov, Tzvestan. *Mikhail Bakhtin The Dialogical Principle*. Trans. Wlad Godzich Minneapolis: University of Minnesota Press, 1984.

**Katrak: Notes to "Teaching Aidoo: Theorising via Creative Writing"**

1   Ama Ata Aidoo, Interview in Cosmo Pieterse and Dennis Duerden, *African Writers Talking* (New York: Africana Publishing, 1972).

2   Ama Ata Aidoo, "The African Woman Today," *Dissent* 39 (1992), 319–325.

3   Ama Ata Aidoo, *The Dilemma of a Ghost and Anowa* (New York: Longman Publishing Group, 2005, first published, *Dilemma*, 1965, *Anowa*, 1970).

4   Tuzyline Jita Allan, Afterword, *Changes: A Love Story* (New York: The Feminist Press, 1993), 171–196.

5   Essays by Ama Ata Aidoo: "Ghana: To Be a Woman," in Robin Morgan, ed. *Sisterhood is Global* (New York: Anchor Press, 1985); "To be an African Woman – An Overview and a Detail," *Criticism and Ideology: Second African Writers' Conference, Stockholm, 1986*. Ed. Kirsten Holst Petersen (Uppsala, Sweden: Scandinavian Institute of African Studies, 1988); Untitled, in *Critical Fictions: The Politics of Imaginative Writing*. Ed. Philomena Mariani (Seattle: Bay Press, 1991), 149–153. Interviews with Aidoo: in Adeola James ed. *In Their Own Voices: African Women Writers Talk* (London: Heinemann, 1990); Sara Modebe, "Ama Ata Aidoo – In Conversation," *New African* 288 September 1991, 40.Ngũgĩ wa Thiong'o, *Penpoints, Gunpoints and Dreams: Towards a Critical Theory of the Arts and the State in Africa* (Oxford: Clarendon Press, 1998); Wole Soyinka, *Myth, Literature and the African World* (Cambridge: Cambridge UP, 1976); Soyinka, *Art, Dialogue and Outrage: Essays on Literature and Culture* (Ibadan: Horn Press).

6   Barbara Harlow, Guest-editor and Introduction, *Critical Exchange* 22 (Spring 1987), i-iv, 85–86.

7   Ketu H. Katrak, *Politics of the Female Body: Postcolonial Women Writers of the Third World* (New Brunswick and London: Rutgers UP, 2006).

8   Ama Ata Aidoo, *No Sweetness Here and Other Stories* (New York: The Feminist Press, 1995, first published, 1970) Afterword By Ketu H. Katrak.

9   Carole Boyce Davies, and Anne Adams Graves, eds. *Ngambika: Studies of Women in African Literature* (Trenton, N.J Africa World Press, 1986); Ada Uzoamaka Azodo and Gay Wilentz, eds. *Emerging Perspectives on Ama Ata Aidoo* (Trenton, New Jersey, and Asmara, Eritrea: Africa World Press, 1999); Vincent O. Odamtten, *The Art of Ama Ata Aidoo: Polylectics and Reading Against Neocolonialism* (Gainesville, Florida: University of Press of Florida, 1994); Chandra Talpade Mohanty, *Feminism Without Borders: Decolonising Theory, Practicing Solidarity* (Durham and London: Duke UP, 2003); Hazel Carby, "White Woman Listen! Black Feminism and the Boundaries of Sisterhood," *The Empire Strikes Back: Race and Racism in 70s Britain* (London: Hutchinson, 1982), 212–235; Lucille Mathurin Mair, *The Rebel Woman in the British West Indies During Slavery* (Kingston: The Institute of Jamaica, 1975),

10  Chandra Talpade Mohanty, Ann Russo, Lourdes Torres, eds., *Third World Women and the Politics of Feminism* (Bloomington and Indianapolis: Indiana UP, 1991), 7. Introduction by Mohanty: 1–47.

11  Frantz Fanon, *The Wretched of the Earth*. Trans. Constance Farrington (New York: Grove Press, 1961, repr. 1977).

12  Neil Lazarus, *Resistance in Postcolonial African Fiction* (New Haven, CT: Yale UP, 1990).

13  Christine Obbo, *African Women: Their Struggle for Economic Independence* (London: Zed

Press, 1980); Edna Bay and Nancy Hafkin, eds., *Women in Africa: Studies in Social and Economic Change* (Stanford: Stanford UP, 1976); Ifi Amadiume, *Male Daughters, Female Husbands: Gender and Sex in an African Society* (London: Zed Press, 1987); Claire Robertson and Iris Berger, eds., *Women and Class in Africa* (New York and London: Africana Publishing Company, 1986); Patricia Hill Collins, *Black Feminist Through: Knowledge, Consciousness, and the Politics of Empowerment* (New York: Routledge, 1991); Cheryl Johnson-Odim, "Common Themes, Different Contexts: Third World Women and Feminism" in Mohanty et al, eds. *Third World Women and the Politics of Feminism;* Johnson-Odim and Nina Emma Mea, *For Women and the Nation: Funmilayo Ransome-Kuti of Nigeria* (Urbana and Chicago: University of Illinois Press, 1997), Karen Sacks, *Sisters and Wives: The Past and Future of Sexual Equality* (1982); Ella Shohat, "Area Studies, Transnationalism, and the Feminist Production of Knowledge," *Signs* 26, no. 4 (Summer 2001), 1269–1272; Shohat and Robert Stam, *Unthinking Eurocentrism: Multiculturalism and the Media.*

14  Walter Rodney, *How Europe Underdeveloped Africa* (Washington D.C: Howard UP, 1974, repr. 1982); Joy James, ed., *The Angela Davis Reader* (Oxford: Blackwell, 1998).

15  Waler Ong, *Orality and Literacy: The Technologizing of the Word* (New York: Routledge, 2002, first published 1982); Isidore Okpewho, *African Oral Literature: Backgrounds, Character, and Continuity* (Bloomington and Indianapolis: Indiana UP, 1992); Tedlock, D. "On the Translation of Style in Oral Literature," *Journal of American Folklore* 84 (1971), 114–133.

## Note to Section III Introduction

1  Ama Ata Aidoo, "Literature, Feminism, and the African Woman Today," in Leonard Podis and Yakubu Saaka, eds. *Challenging Hierarchies: Issues and Themes in Colonial and Postcolonial African Literature* (New York: Peter Lang, 1998), 25.

## Androne: Notes to "Nervous Masculinities: Male Characters in Ama Ata Aidoo's *Changes*"

1  In *Making Men in Ghana*, Stephan Miescher writes that while he was researching for his book in Ghana, he "noticed a truck with an inscription 'To be a man is hard,'" and "the ideas and anxieties that seemed to underlie that slogan traveled with me up to Kwanu. What does it mean to be a man in Ghana?" (Miescher 1). The back cover of his book includes a picture of the truck with its slogan.

2  In Nana Banyiwa Horne's analysis of Aidoo's male protagonist Kofi-Ako in *Anowa*, she records the same dilemma, since he too "replaces the communal ethos of reciprocity at the heart of the Big Man model with a western, individualistic, feudalistic/capitalistic ethos based on exploitation" (Horne, 197).

## Androne: Works Cited

Aidoo, Ama Ata. *Changes: A Love Story*. New York: Feminist Press, 1991.

Akyeampong, Emmanuel. "*Wo pe tam pe ba*" ('*You like cloth but you don't want children*') Urbanisation, Individualism & Gender Relations in Colonial Ghana c. 1900–1939." In *Africa's Urban Past*. Ed. David Anderson and Richard Rathbone. Oxford: James Curry, 2000. 222–234.

Allan, Tuzyline Jita. Afterword. In *Changes: A Love Story*. By Ama Ata Aidoo. New York: Feminist Press, 1991.

Barber, Karin. "How Man Makes God in West Africa: Yoruba Attitudes Toward the

Orisa." *Africa: The Journal of the International African Institute* 51: 3 (1981) 724–745.

Bhabha, Homi. "Of mimicry and man: The ambivalence of colonial discourse." In *The Location of Culture*. London and New York: Routledge, 1994.

Gikandi, Simon. Afterword. In *Masculinities in African Literary and Cultural Texts*. Ed. Helen N. Mugambi and Tuzyline J. Allan. Oxfordshire, Ayebia Clarke Publishing, 2010. 295–297.

Gyimah, Miriam. "Sexual Politics and the Phallocentric Gaze in Ama Ata Aidoo's *Changes: A Love Story*" in *Emerging Perspectives on Ama Ata Aidoo*. Ed. Ada Azodo and Gay Wilentz. Trenton, New Jersey: Africa World Press, 1991. 377–397.

Horne, Naana Banyiwa. "Sexual Impotence as Metonymy for Political Failure: Interrogating Hegemonic Masculinities in Ama Ata Aidoo's *Anowa*." In *Masculinities in African Literary and Cultural Texts*. Ed. Helen N. Mugambi and Tuzyline J. Allan. Oxfordshire: Ayebia Clarke Publishing, 2010. 178–199.

Lindsay, Lisa and Stephan Miescher. Introduction. *Men and Masculinities in Modern Africa*. Portsmouth, New Hampshire: Heinemann, 2003. 1–29.

McWilliams, Sally. "Strange As It May Seem: African Feminism in Two Novels byAma Ata Aidoo." In *Emerging Perspectives on Ama Ata Aidoo*. Ed. Ada Azodo and Gay Wilentz. Trenton, New Jersey: Africa World Press, 1991. 333–361.

Miescher, Stephan. *Making Men In Ghana*. Bloomington and Indianapolis: U. of Indiana Press, 2005.

Odamtten, Vincent. *The Art of Ama Ata Aidoo: Polylectics and Reading Against Neo-colonialism*. Gainesville: U. of Florida Press, 1994.

## Prasansak: Notes to "Gendering Commodity Relations in Ama Ata Aidoo's *Changes*"

1 I would like to thank Professor Laura Chrisman at the University of Washington for her comments on multiple drafts of this article. Any flaws are of course my own.

2 See, for example, Miriam C. Gyimah, "Sexual Politics and Phallocentric Gaze in Ama Ata Aidoo's *Changes: A Love Story*," *Emerging Perspectives on Ama Ata Aidoo*, eds. Ada Uzoamaka Azodo and Gay Alden Wilentz (Trenton, NJ: Africa World Press, 1999); Maria Olaussen, "'About Lovers in Accra': Urban Intimacy in Ama Ata Aidoo's *Changes: A Love Story*," *Research in African Literatures* 33.2 (2002); and Wei-hsiung (Kitty) Wu, "'Devouring Gods' and 'Sacrificial Animals:' The Male-Female Relationships in Ama Ata Aidoo's *Changes: A Love Story*," *Arms Akimbo: Africana Women in Contemporary Literature*, eds. Janice Liddell and Yakini Belinda Kemp (Gainesville: UP of Florida, 1999). All references to the novel cited parenthetically are to Ama Ata Aidoo, *Changes: A Love Story* (New York: Feminist Press, 1993).

3 Aidoo's critical attention to and sympathetic treatment of market women also manifest in others of her works such as *The Girl Who Can and Other Stories*.

4 Donald R. Wehrs, *African Feminist Fiction and Indigenous Values* (Gainesville: UP of Florida, 2001), 166. I am greatly indebted to Wehrs's scholarship that draws my attention to the spare parts business on which my historical research is built.

5 Jonathan Dawson, "Development of Small-Scale Industry in Ghana: A Case Study of Kumasi," *Small-Scale Production: Strategies for Industrial Restructuring*, eds. Henk Thomas, Francisco Uribe-Echevarría and Henny Romijn (London: Intermediate Technology Publications, 1991), 186.

6 Emmanuel Kwaku Akyeampong, *Drink, Power, and Cultural Change: A Social History of*

*Alcohol in Ghana, C. 1800 to Recent Times* (Portsmouth, NH; Oxford: Heinemann; James Currey, 1996).

7   Ibid., 103.

8   All references to this work are to Ama Ata Aidoo, *No Sweetness Here and Other Stories* (New York: Feminist Press at the City University of New York, 1995).

9   Akyeampong, *Drink, Power, and Cultural Change: A Social History of Alcohol in Ghana, C. 1800 to Recent Times*, 49.

10  Ibid., 115.

11  Fredric Jameson, *The Political Unconscious: Narrative as a Socially Symbolic Act* (Ithaca, N.Y.: Cornell UP, 1981), 49.

12  See Michel Foucault, "Governmentality," *The Foucault Effec : Studies in Governmentality: With Two Lectures by and an Interview with Michel Foucault*, eds. Michel Foucault, Graham Burchell, Colin Gordon and Peter Miller (Chicago: University of Chicago Press, 1991).

13  Waleska Saltori Simpson, "'What Fashion of Loving Was She Going to Consider Adequate?' Subverting the 'Love Story' in Ama Ata Aidoo's *Changes*," *English in Africa* 34.1 (2007): 159.

14  According to her empirical data, "[w]hile it [the trade in prepared foods] accounted for only 30.5% of the chief occupations of the 1971–72 small sample, 63.8% of the women had participated in it at some time in their lives. In 1978 it was the most popular trade among the women aged 39 to 50" (106). Claire C. Robertson, *Sharing the Same Bowl?: A Socioeconomic History of Women and Class in Accra, Ghana* (Bloomington: Indiana UP, 1984).

15  Kwame A. Ninsin, *The Informal Sector in Ghana's Political Economy* (Accra: Freedom Publications, 1991), 7.

16  Aidoo's short story "Choosing" gives a good account of what small traders face in their everyday life. The protagonist, who is a poor writer, finds it difficult for her to prosper as a hawker in the city market where she experiences the hierarchal order between settled traders and newbies, the bargaining power of buyers, the harassment from market wardens, and the theft by market tsotsis. See Ama Ata Aidoo, *The Girl Who Can and Other Stories* (Oxford: Heinemann, 2000).

17  See Gracia Clark, "Gender and Profiteering: Ghana's Market Women as Devoted Mothers and 'Human Vampire Bats,'" *"Wicked" Women and the Reconfiguration of Gender in Africa*, eds. Dorothy Louise Hodgson and Sheryl McCurdy (Portsmouth, NH: Heinemann, 2001)

18  Brodie Cruickshank, *Eighteen Years on the Gold Coast of Africa: Including an Account of the Native Tribes, and Their Intercourse with Europeans*, vol. 2 (London: Cass, 1966), 36.

19  Ibid., 36.

20  See Mike Oquaye, *Politics in Ghana, 1972–1979* (Christiansborg, Accra: Tornado Publications, 1980).

21  Robertson, *Sharing the Same Bowl? : A Socioeconomic History of Women and Class in Accra, Ghana*, 111.

22  See Nada Elia, "'To Be an African Working Woman': Levels of Feminist Consciousness in Ama Ata Aidoo's *Changes*," *Research in African Literatures* 30.2 (1999).

23  Juliana Makuchi Nfah-Abbenyi, "Flabberwhelmed or Turning History on Its Head?: The Postcolonial Woman-as-Subject in Aidoo's *Changes: A Love Story*," *Emerging Perspectives on Ama Ata Aidoo*, eds. Ada Uzoamaka Azodo and Gay Alden Wilentz

(Trenton, NJ: Africa World Press, 1999), 287.

24 Ernest Kweku Dumor, "Commodity Queens and the Distributive Trade in Ghana: A Sociohistorical Analysis," *African Urban Studies*.12 (1982): 34.

25 Claire C. Robertson, "The Death of Makola and Other Tragedies," *Canadian Journal of African Studies* 17.3 (1983): 472.

26 Emmanuel Hansen, *Ghana under Rawlings: Early Years* (Lagos: Malthouse Press, 1991), 68–69.

27 See Robertson, "The Death of Makola and Other Tragedies," 478.

28 Oquaye recounts a relevant story concerning the corrupt network and operation between influential traders and state officers: "Two famous kiosks labeled "Lomnava" and "Sly Corner" had such a variety of food items that they must have become the envy of even Kingsway Stores, UTC and GNTC Supermarkets. Situated conspicuously by the Continental Hotel and en route Burma Camp, they sold at prohibitive prices with impunity and when finally a hue and cry was raised against these "Government-designated kiosk-supermarkets" by the public, a mock arrest was staged, the shops were closed and their owners let loose to operate elsewhere whether by open or underground *Kalabule*" (22). Oquaye, *Politics in Ghana, 1972–1979*, 22.

29 Nana Wilson-Tagoe, "Ama Ata Aidoo with Nana Wilson-Tagoe," *Writing across Worlds: Contemporary Writers Talk*, ed. Susheila Nasta (London; New York: Routledge, 2004), 299.

## Prasansak: Works Cited

Aidoo, Ama Ata. *Changes : A Love Story*. New York: Feminist Press, 1993. Print.

Aidoo, Ama Ata. *The Girl Who Can and Other Stories*. Oxford: Heinemann, 2000. Print.

Aidoo, Ama Ata. *No Sweetness Here and Other Stories*. New York: Feminist Press at the City University of New York, 1995. Print.

Akyeampong, Emmanuel Kwaku. *Drink, Power, and Cultural Change:: A Social History of Alcohol in Ghana, c. 1800 to Recent Times*. Portsmouth, NH; Oxford: Heinemann; James Currey, 1996. Print.

Clark, Gracia. "Gender and Profiteering: Ghana's Market Women as Devoted Mothers and 'Human Vampire Bats.'" *"Wicked" Women and the Reconfiguration of Gender in Africa*. Eds. Dorothy Louise Hodgson and Sheryl McCurdy. Portsmouth, NH: Heinemann, 2001. 293–311. Print.

Cruickshank, Brodie. *Eighteen Years on the Gold Coast of Africa: Including an Account of the Native Tribes, and Their Intercourse with Europeans*. Vol. 2. London: Cass, 1966. Print.

Dawson, Jonathan. "Development of Small-Scale Industry in Ghana: A Case Study of Kumasi." *Small-Scale Production: Strategies for Industrial Restructuring*. Eds. Henk Thomas, Francisco Uribe-Echevarría and Henny Romijn. London: Intermediate Technology Publications, 1991. 173–207. Print.

Dumor, Ernest Kweku. "Commodity Queens and the Distributive Trade in Ghana: A Sociohistorical Analysis." *African Urban Studies*.12 (1982): 27–45. Print.

Elia, Nada. "'To Be an African Working Woman:' Levels of Feminist Consciousness in Ama Ata Aidoo's *Changes*." *Research in African Literatures* 30.2 (1999): 136–47. Print.

Foucault, Michel. "Governmentality." *The Foucault Effect: Studies in Governmentality: With Two Lectures by and an Interview with Michel Foucault*. Eds. Michel Foucault, et al. Chicago: University of Chicago Press, 1991. 87–104. Print.

Gyimah, Miriam C. "Sexual Politics and Phallocentric Gaze in Ama Ata Aidoo's *Changes: A Love Story.*" *Emerging Perspectives on Ama Ata Aidoo.* Eds. Ada Uzoamaka Azodo and Gay Alden Wilentz. Trenton, NJ: Africa World Press, 1999. 377–97. Print.

Hansen, Emmanuel. *Ghana under Rawlings: Early Years.* Lagos: Malthouse Press, 1991. Print.

Jameson, Fredric. *The Political Unconscious: Narrative as a Socially Symbolic Act.* Ithaca, N.Y.: Cornell UP, 1981. Print.

Nfah-Abbenyi, Juliana Makuchi. "Flabberwhelmed or Turning History on Its Head?: The Post-colonial Woman-as-Subject in Aidoo's *Changes: A Love Story.*" *Emerging Perspectives on Ama Ata Aidoo.* Eds. Ada Uzoamaka Azodo and Gay Alden Wilentz. Trenton, NJ: Africa World Press, 1999. 281–302. Print.

Ninsin, Kwame A. *The Informal Sector in Ghana's Political Economy.* Accra: Freedom Publications, 1991. Print.

Olaussen, Maria. "'About Lovers in Accra:' Urban Intimacy in Ama Ata Aidoo's *Changes: A Love Story.*" *Research in African Literatures* 33.2 (2002): 61–80. Print.

Oquaye, Mike. *Politics in Ghana, 1972–1979.* Christiansborg, Accra: Tornado Publications, 1980. Print.

Robertson, Claire C. "The Death of Makola and Other Tragedies." *Canadian Journal of African Studies* 17.3 (1983): 469–95. Print.

———. *Sharing the Same Bowl? : A Socio-economic History of Women and Class in Accra, Ghana.* Bloomington: Indiana UP, 1984. Print.

Simpson, Waleska Saltori. "'What Fashion of Loving Was She Going to Consider Adequate?' Subverting the 'Love Story' in Ama Ata Aidoo's *Changes.*" *English in Africa* 34.1 (2007): 155–71. Print.

Wehrs, Donald R. *African Feminist Fiction and Indigenous Values.* Gainesville: UP of Florida, 2001. Print.

Wilson-Tagoe, Nana. "Ama Ata Aidoo with Nana Wilson-Tagoe." *Writing across Worlds : Contemporary Writers Talk.* Ed. Susheila Nasta. London; New York: Routledge, 2004. 11–28. Print.

Wu, Wei-hsiung (Kitty). "'Devouring Gods' and 'Sacrificial Animals:' The Male-Female Relationships in Ama Ata Aidoo's *Changes: A Love Story.*" *Arms Akimbo: Africana Women in Contemporary Literature.* Eds. Janice Liddell and Yakini Belinda Kemp. Gainesville: UP of Florida, 1999. 92–102. Print.

**Toman: Notes to "African Women and Power: Ama Ata Aidoo's Essays …"**

1  "To Be a Woman" in *Sisterhood is Global,* ed. Robin Morgan (New York: Doubleday) 258–265.

2  Published in 1986, *Speak Out, Black Sisters* is the English translation of Thiam's book.

3  Amadiume revolutionised the term 'matriarchy' which had been virtually dismissed in Western anthropology throughout most of the 20th century since it was only understood as the antithesis of patriarchy. (See *Contemporary Matriarchies* by Toman, 1–15)

4  A reprint of Ama Ata Aidoo's "The African Woman Today" follows the introduction to *Sisterhood, Feminisms and Power* (see pages 39–50).

5  Chikwenye Okonjo-Ogunyemi cites Cheryl Johnson-Odim's 1991 quote in her essay, "Ectomies." However she does not provide any further information about the origin of the citation.

6   Emecheta maintained that polygamous marriage often freed women from some of their obligations, allowing time for travel or furthering education or career (178–179).

7   These are Aidoo's words transcribed as part of the notes included in the section "From the discussion" (181–185) which follows Emecheta's published talk, 173–181.

8   'Live Aid' was comprised of four concerts held simultaneously in four countries (United Kingdom, United States, Germany, and Australia) on July 13, 1985.

9   There is currently no published English translation of Tanella Boni's text. Thus, all translations here from the French are my own.

10  Boni's original citation in French: "Elles apprennent en situation les nouveaux codes et savent que les circuits mondiaux par où passent toutes sortes de marchandises ne sont pas faciles à pénétrer. Douaniers, transitaires, police des frontières ne sont pas, pour elles, des mots abstraits. Elles se familiarisent avec un nouveau vocabulaire et de nouvelles manières de gérer leurs entreprises."

11  Boni writes "les rues et les marchés font partie des territoires des femmes d'Afrique."

12  Boni describes the market as "un lieu d'échange d'informations, de connaissances, mais aussi un espace de survie et de respiration."

13  Indeed, numerous studies on rituals such as the 'anlu' in Cameroon in complement with case studies of recent takeovers and shutdowns of Shell by Nigerian women due to unacceptable operating conditions attest to the power of women which men are forced to accept.

14  Boni's citation in French is as follows: "Le corps de la femme africaine n'est jamais nu mais habillé et paré de cultures de la tête aux pieds. Ainsi un corps n'est pas seulement vêtu de tissus mais aussi habillé de signes. Les Africaines en sont conscientes."

15  On page 23, Boni points out that "[l]es Africaines vivent à la croisière de plusieurs cultures" and that "les dépliants touristiques, les photos, et les cartes postales" all suggest "une recherche d'une Afrique 'authentique'."

16  Boni states in French: "Aujourd'hui, de nombreuses Africaines, instruites ou non, ne se contentent pas de prodiguer des conseils aux hommes dans l'ombre ou sur l'oreiller, elles se donnent le droit de penser par elles-mêmes, de concevoir, d'imaginer des solutions, de prendre des initiatives, d'agir, même quand elles sont analphabètes."

## Toman: Works Cited

Aidoo, Ama Ata. "Choosing – A Moral from the World of Work." in *The Girl Who Can and Other Stories*, Oxford: Heinemann 2002, pp, 3–26.

_____. *The Girl Who Can and Other Stories*. Oxford: Heinemann, 2002.

_____. *Changes: A Love Story*. New York: The Feminist Press, 1993.

_____. "The African Woman Today." *Dissent*. 39: 3 (July 1992), 319–325.

_____. "To Be a Woman." In *Sisterhood is Global*, Ed. Robin Morgan. New York: Doubleday, 1984, pp. 255–265.

_____. *Our Sister Killjoy*. New York, Longman, 1977.

Allan, Tuzyline Jita. "Afterword" to Ama Ata Aidoo's *Changes: A Love Story*. New York: The Feminist Press, 1993, pp. 171–196.

Amadiume, Ifi. Personal interview. 30 March 2011.

_____. *Reinventing Africa: Matriarchy, Religion, and Culture*. New York: St. Martin's Press, 1997.

_____. *Afrikan Matriarchal Foundations: The Igbo Case*. Surrey: Karnak House, 1987.

Azodo, Ada Uzoamaka and Gay Wilentz, eds. *Emerging Perspectives on Ama Ata Aidoo*. Trenton: Africa World Press, 1999.

Boni, Tanella. *Que Vivent les Femmes d'Afrique?* Paris: Panama, 2008.

Diop, Cheikh Anta. *The Cultural Unity of Black Africa: The Domains of Patriarchy and of Matriarchy in Classical Antiquity*. Chicago: Third World Press, 1978.

_____. *L'Unité Culturelle de l'Afrique Noire*. Paris: Présence Africaine, 1959.

Emecheta, Buchi. "Feminism with a Small 'f.'" *Criticism and Ideology*. Ed. Kirsten Holst Petersen. Uppsala: Scandinavian Institute of African Studies, 1988. 173–185.

Frank, Katherine. "Women without Men: The Feminist Novel in Africa." *Women in African Literature Today*. Eds. Eldred Durosimi Jones and Eustace Palmer. Trenton: Africa World Press, 1987. 14–34.

French, Marilyn. *From Eve to Dawn: A History of Women. Volume IV: Revolutions and the Struggles for Justice in the 20th Century*. New York: The Feminist Press, 2008.

Hafkin, Nancy J. and Edna J. Bay, eds. *Women in Africa: Studies in Social and Economic Change*. Stanford, CA: Stanford UP, 1976.

Jones, Eldred Durosimi and Eustace Palmer, eds. *Women in African Literature Today*. Trenton: Africa World Press, 1987.

Mama, Amina. *Beyond the Masks: Race, Gender, and Subjectivity*. New York: Routledge, 1995.

Millet, Kate. Message to the Organisers. Dix Heures Contre le Viol (event). Paris. 26 June 1976.

Mohanty, Chandra. "Under Western Eyes: Feminist Scholarship and Colonial Discourses." *boundary 2: On Humanism and the University I: The Discourse of Humanism*. 12:3 (Spring – Autumn) 1984, 333–358.

Morgan, Robin, ed. *Sisterhood is Global: The International Women's Movement Anthology*. New York: Doubleday, 1984.

Nfah-Abbenyi, Juliana Makuchi. *Gender in African Women's Writing: Identity, Sexuality, and Difference*. Bloomington: Indiana UP, 1997.

Nicol, Davidson, Mallica Vajrathon and Torill Stokland, eds. *Creative Women in Changing Societies: A Quest for Alternatives*. Dobbs Ferry, N.Y.: Transnational Publishers, Inc., 1982.

Nnaemeka, Obioma, ed. *Sisterhood, Feminisms, and Power: From Africa to the Diaspora*. Trenton: Africa World Press, 1998.

Okonjo, Kamene. "The Dual-Sex Political System in Operation: Igbo Women and Community Politics in Midwestern Nigeria." *Women in Africa: Studies in Social and Economic Change*. Eds. Nancy J. Hafkin and Edna J. Bay. Stanford, CA: Stanford University Press, 1976. 45–58.

Okonjo-Ogunyemi, Chikwenye. "Ectomies: A Treasury of Fiction by Africa's Daughters." *African Women and Feminism*. Ed. Oyèrónké Oyěwùmí. Trenton: Africa World Press, 2003. 231–256.

Oyěwùmí, Oyèrónké ed. *African Women and Feminism: Reflecting on the Politics of Sisterhood*. Trenton: Africa World Press, 2003.

_____. "Introduction: Feminism, Sisterhood, and Other Foreign Relations." *African Women and Feminism*. Ed. Oyèrónké Oyěwùmí. Trenton: Africa World Press, 2003. 1–24.

_____. "The White Woman's Burden: African Women in Western Feminist Discourse." *African Women and Feminism*. Ed. Oyèrónké Oyěwùmí. Trenton: Africa World Press, 2003. 25–43.

Petersen, Kirsten Holst, ed. *Criticism and Ideology*. Uppsala: Scandinavian Institute of African Studies, 1988.

Seager, Joni. *The Penguin Atlas of Women in the World*. New York: Penguin Books, 2009.

Steady, Filomina. *The Black Woman Cross-Culturally*. Cambridge: Schenkman, 1981.

Sutherland-Addy, Esi and Aminata Diaw, eds. *Women Writing Africa. Volume 2: West Africa and the Sahel*. New York: The Feminist Press, 2005.

Thiam, Awa. *Speak Out, Black Sisters: Feminism and Oppression in Black Africa*. Dorothy S. Blair, trans. London, Pluto Press, 1986.

_____. *La Parole aux Négresses*. Paris: DeNoël, 1978.

Toman, Cheryl. *Contemporary Matriarchies in Cameroonian Francophone Literature*. Birmingham: Summa, 2008.

Troare, Aminata. "Africa Is Not Poor: An Interview with Debra S. Boyd." *Women Writing Africa.Volume 2: West Africa and the Sahel*. Eds. Esi Sutherland-Addy and Aminata Diaw. New York: The Feminist Press, 2005. 448–453.

## Horne: Notes to "She-Kings in the Trinity of Being"

1   Titles such as Francoise Lionnet's "Geographies of Pain" and Liz Gunner's "Mothers, Daughters and Madness in Works by Four Women Writers" attest to the grossly oppressive material and psychological contexts of women's lives. While these works do more than just delineate the dehumanising factors that push women to extreme states, they also, of necessity give considerable attention to the oppressive situations that decentre these female protagonists.

2   Lindsay Pentolfe Aegerter, in "A Dialectic of Autonomy and Community: Tsitsi Dangarembga's *"Nervous Conditions"* (1996), explores female personhood in Dangarembga's novel. Her women characters "engage in the interplay of traditional preservation and progress, dancing a dialectic of autonomy and community . . . that synthesises traditional notions of African community from a womanist perspective with women's autonomy defined from an 'African' perspective" (231).

3   Thus far, I have identified only three rather short references to Aidoo's girl-child protagonists. In *The Art of Ama Ata Aidoo* (107–108) Vincent Okpoti Odamtten devotes a little over a page to discussing "The Late Bud" and in "The Bird of the Wayside: From An Angry Letter . . . to The Girl Who Can" he discusses both "She-Who-Would-Be-King" and "The Girl Who Can" from 246–248. In Naana Opoku Agyemang's "Narrative Turns in Ama Ata Aidoo's *No Sweetness Here*," "The Late Bud" appears on 138–139.

4   "The Late Bud." *No Sweetness Here* (New York: The Feminist Press, 1995), pp. 103–113; "The Girl Who Can" and "She-Who-Would-Be-King." *The Girl Who Can and Other Stories* (Portsmouth, NH: Heinemann, 2002), pp. 27–33, and 55–62. Subsequent references to these works will be made parenthetically.

5   In "The Politics of Mothering: Multiple Subjectivity and Gendered Discourse in Aidoo's Plays," Horne explores matrilineality, a female-centred system of human organisation and its efficacious connection of the womb's organic rootedness to human conservation to the multiple subject positions of females.

6   The process of redefining creates room for females to maintain control of gender roles by determining the value assigned to roles gendered female. Homemaking, which is the most elemental role ascribed to females, is essential to ensuring quality of life for humankind. In that context, no role is more definitive than that.

7   The appeal of "The Late Bud" rests on the manner in which a serious problem at the heart of socialisation is explored in this story to expose the vulnerabilities of both mothers and their children and, at the same time, reinforce the enduring values such as tenacity, courage, compassion, etc. that uphold the womanist epistemology needed to cultivate worthy human beings. It takes mothers not giving up on their children, good or bad, to bring about the necessary transformation that generates a dynamic citizenry. Opoku-Agyeman's portrayal of Yaaba's mother underplays her effectiveness in relating to her difficult child by overstressing the unrealistic dreams of mothers for naturally "good" children.

8   Vincent Okpoti Odamtten extensively defines the dilemma tale in *The Art of Ama Ata Aidoo* (1994, 18–25).

9   Even though it is stated that "at least, four generations of the family [are gathered] in the room" (56), only three generations – the Old Queen, Adjoa Moji, and Afi-Yaa – participate in the actual story.

## Horne: Works Cited

Aegerter, Lindsay Pentolfe. "A Dialectic of Autonomy and Community: Tsitsi Dangarembga's *Nervous Conditions*. *Tulsa Studies in Women's Literature* Vol. 15, No. 2 (Fall 1996), 231–40.

Aidoo, Ama Ata. "The Late Bud," in *No Sweetness Here* (1970) New York: The Feminist Press, 1995), 103–113.

_____. "The Girl Who Can," in *The Girl Who Can and Other* Stories. (1997) Oxford and Portsmouth, NH: Heinemann, 2002, pp. 27–33.

_____. "She-Who-Would-Be-King," in *The Girl Who Can and Other Stories* (1997) Oxford and Portsmouth, NH: Heinemann, 2002, pp. 55–62.

Gunner, Liz. "Mothers, Daughters and Madness in Works by Four Women Writers: Bessie Head, Jean Rhys, Tsitsi Dangarembga and Ama Ata Aidoo," in *Alif: Journal of Comparative Poetics*, No. 14 (1994), 136–151.

Henderson, Mae Gwendolyn. "Speaking in Tongues: Dialogics, Dialectics, and the Black Woman Writer's Literary Tradition." Gates, H.L. (ed.) *Reading Black, Reading Feminist: A Critical Anthology* New York: Penguin, 1990, pp.116–142.

Horne, Naana Banyiwa. "The Politics of Mothering: Multiple Subjectivity and Gendered Discourse." Azoda, Ada Uzoamaka Azoda and Gay Wilentz (eds). *Emerging Perspectives on Ama Ata Aidoo*. Trenton, NJ: Africa World Press, 1999, pp. 303–331.

Lionnet, Francoise. "Geographies of Pain: Captive Bodies and Violent Acts in the Fictions of Myriam Warner-Vieyra, Gayl Jones, and Bessie Head." *Callaloo*, Vol. 16, No. 1 (Winter, 1993), pp. 132–152.

Odamtten, Vincent Okpoti. *The Art of Ama Ata Aidoo: Polylectics and Reading Against Neocolonialism*. Gainesville, FL: U Florida Press, 1994.

_____. "The Bird of the Wayside: From *An Angry Letter* to *The Girl Who Can*." Azoda, Ada Uzoamaka Azoda and Gay Wilentz (eds). *Emerging Perspectives on Ama Ata Aidoo*. Tremton: NJ: Africa World Press, 1999, pp. 241–252.

Opoku-Agyemang, Naana Jane. "Narrative Turns in Ama Ata Aidoo's *No Sweetness Here*." Azoda, Ada Uzoamaka Azoda and Gay Wilentz (eds). *Emerging Perspectives on Ama Ata Aidoo* Trenton, NJ: Africa World Press, 1999, pp. 127–144.

Davies: Notes to "Black Women of a Certain Age, Power and Presence"

1    A version of this paper was presented at the panel honouring Ama Ata Aidoo at the Harlem Book Fair, July 18, 2009, carried on CSPAN. The Toni Morrison portion was written for the conference in her honour in Paris, 2010 for the panel, "Visualising Toni Morrison."

2    (CNN International, "African Voices," broadcast date 7/11/09)

3    New York: Anchor Books, 2010.

4    New York: Feminist Press, 1993.

5    Robin Morgan, ed. *Sisterhood is Global*. (New York: Anchor Press/Doubleday, 1984).

6    Covering the entire continent by geographical regions, oral and written literary tradition, these edited collections were published by Feminist Press in which the West Africa and the Sahel and the South African editions are available (New York: Feminist Press, 2003). Abena Busia and Tuzyline Jita Allan have been the primary organisers and general editors of this project.

7    Carole Boyce Davies and Anne Adams Graves, eds. *Ngambika. Studies of Women in African Literature*. Africa World Press, 1986.

8    *Sunkwa Revisited*. (Poems) (Trenton, New Jersey: Africa World Press, 2007.)

9    Editor of: *Emerging Perspectives on Buchi Emecheta* (Africa World Press, 1995) and *Emerging Perspectives on Florence Nwapa: Critical and Theoretical Essays* (Africa World Press, 1998).

10   *Francophone African women Writers. Destroying the Emptiness of Silence* (UP of Florida, 1994) and *A Rain of Words. A Bilingual Anthology of Poetry by Women in Francophone Africa* (University of Virginia Press, 2009). (Translated by Janis Mayes).

11   *Male Daughters, Female Husbands. Gender and Sex in an African Society* (Zed Press, 1987).

12   *The Politics of (M)Othering: Womanhood, Identity and Resistance in African Literature* (Routledge, 1997).

13   *The Invention of Women. Making an African Sense of Western Gender Discourses* (University of Minnesota Press, 1997).

14   Longmans edition, 1997. Published initially by NOK Publishers International with the subtitle. *Reflections from a Black-Eyed Squint* (1979).

15   UP of Florida, 1994.

16   Edited by Ada Azodo and Gay Willentz (Africa World Press, 1999).

17   Mary Naana Nicholson, M.A. thesis, "The Affirmation of African Womanhood in the Works of Ama Ata Aidoo."(University of Florida, Gainesville).

18   *Black Women Writing and Identity. Migrations of the Subject*. See chapter on "Deconstructing African Female Subjectivites: Anowa's Borderlands," pp. 59–79)

19   (New York: Anchor Press, Doubleday): 258–265

20   *Left of Karl Marx. The Political Life of Black Communist Claudia Jones* (Duke, 2008).

21   *Dissent* (Summer, 1992): 319–325.

22   Seattle Washington: Bay Press, 1991.

23   http: www.african-union.org/root/au/documents/treaties/documents/test/protocol (Accessed February 14, 2011).

24   Isidore Okpewho, ed. *The New African Diaspora* (Indiana UP, 2009). See for example Paul Zeleza's essay in this collection.

25   New York: The Feminist Press, 1995 (First published 1971).

26   Portsmouth: Heinemann, 2002.

27   Ayebia Publishing, 2006.

28 See my "Secrets of My Mother's Sweetness," in *Caribbean Erotic*, ed. Opal Palmer Adisa and Donna Weir Soley (Leeds: Peepal Tree Press, 2010).

29 *Black Looks: Race and Representation* (South End Press, 1999).

30 "We Were not Mated" in Tony Martin. *Amy Ashwood Garvey: Pan-Africanist, Feminist, and Wife No. 1 or A Tale of Two Amies.* (Boston: The Majority Press, 2007), 364.

31 in Veronica Gregg, ed., *Caribbean Women: An Anthology of Non-Fiction Writing 1890–1980.* (University of Notre Dame Press, 2005).

32 This is how the panel titled "Visualising Toni Morrison" for the October 2010 Toni Morrison Society Conference in Paris was described.

33 Stokely Carmichael (Kwame Ture) with Michael Thelwell, *Ready for Revolution. The Life and Struggles of Stokely* Carmichael (Kwame Ture). (Scribner, 2005).

34 (Norton, 2009).

35 Sylvia Wynter, "Jonkonnu in Jamaica: Towards the Interpretation of Folk Dance as a Cultural Process," *Jamaica Journal* 4:2(1970), 34–48.

36 Michael Barnett, "Rastafari" in *Encyclopedia of the African Diaspora*, ABC-CLIO: 2008: 792–795.

## Asiedu and Adomako Ampofo: Notes to "Towards Alternative Representations of Women ..."

1 The authors are grateful to the editor of this volume, and to the anonymous reviewers for their careful comments on earlier versions of the paper. They also acknowledge grants from the University of Ghana Office for Research, Innovation and Development, and the UK Department for International Development, Dfid, which supported the research under the Women's Empowerment Research Project Consortium.

2 A music competition, organised as part of our research project, aimed at encouraging the creation of empowering songs about women, produced three winners who were all male. Additionally, a few African male writers are noted for their positive and empowering representations of women. See for example, Femi Osofisan's *Moremi, Altine's Wrath*, and *Tegoni*, to mention but a few of his plays, and Sembene Ousmane's short stories and films.

3 Some researchers in Egypt have also recently embarked on a project of rewriting the Arabian Nights, which is extremely negative in its representation of women, to [re]present more empowering images of women.

4 These representations seem to cut across the various genres of music, though the older highlife genre tended to be a bit more subtle and less "in your face" as compared to the more recent genres of hip-life, rap and hip hop.

5 See Samuel Adu-Poku (2001) for a discussion of the need for a conscious reorientation of men born and brought up in male-dominated societies such as ours, towards true feminist consciousness. See, for example, a discussion of Kodjo Mawugbe's play *In The Chest of a Woman* (Asiedu, 2010)

6 Such distinctions, obvious in European contexts, have often been assumed as true in the African context, but as Stephanie Newell has shown, such distinctions between the literary and the popular are not so simplistic in the African context (see Newell, 2000:158–160).

7 CEGENSA was set up in 2004 with a mandate to conduct research, develop curricula, provide documentation, design policies, and carry out advocacy and outreach

on gender issues. The Centre was also mandated to establish services for sex assault crisis counseling and the mentoring of junior faculty.

8   This translates as 'I am a Woman.'

9   'I am aware' is a term for jeans and skirts with low cuts which expose parts of one's underwear and skin at the back.

10  This section of the Ghana police service has now been renamed Domestic Violence Support Unit (DOVSU).

## Asiedu/Ampofo: Works Cited

Adams, Anne. "'No Sweetness Here' for 'Our Sister,' 'La Noire'? Lauer, Helen, Nana Aba Appiah Amfo, Jemima Asabea Anderson, eds. *Identity Meets Nationality: Voices from the Humanities*. Legon, Accra: Sub-Saharan 2011, pp. 202–224.

Adinkrah, Mensah. "Witchcraft Themes in Popular Ghanaian Music." *Popular Music and Society*, Vol. 31, No. 3, 2008: 299–311.

Adu-Poku, Samuel. "Envisioning (Black) Male Feminism: A Cross-cultural Perspective" in *Journal of Gender Studies*, 2001.

Asiedu, Awo Mana. "West African Theatre Audiences: A Study of Ghanaian and Nigerian Audiences of Literary Theatre in English." Unpublished PhD Dissertation, University of Birmingham, UK, 2003.

_____. "Making Use of the Stage in West Africa: The Role of Audiences in the Production of Efficacious Theatre." *Studies in Theatre and Performance*, 2008, Vol.28, 3 pp. 223–36.

_____. 'Masculine Women Feminist Men: Assertions and Contradictions in Mawugbe's 'In the Chest of a woman'. *Theatre Histories*, 2010, Vol. 30

Barber, Karin. *The Generation of Plays: Yoruba Popular Life in Theatre*, Bloomington, Indianapolis: Indiana UP, 2000.

Cole, Catherine M. "'Give Her a Slap to Warm Her Up:' Post-Gender Theory and Ghana's Popular Culture" in *Africa After Gender?* Ed. C. M. Cole, T. Manuh and S.F. Miescher. Indiana: Indiana UP, 2007.

Collins, John. "Nkrumah and Highlife." In *The New Legon Observer: Special Issue on Highlife* Vol.2.No.7, April 2008, pp. 5–7

Collins, E.J. "The Generational Factor in Ghanaian Music: Past, Present and Future." Plenary Paper read at the Playing with Identities in African Music Conference of the Nordic African Institute at Turku/Abo. Finland, 19–22, October 2000.

Danysh, Irene, M. "'ma Ata Aidoo's *Changes*: The Woman's Voice in African Literature" in Kofi Anyidoho and James Gibbs (eds.) *Fon Tom From: Contemporary Ghanaian Literature, Theatre and Film*. Amsterdam, Atlanta: Rodopi, 2000, pp. 165–172.

Editorial *The New Legon Observer: Special Issue on Highlife* Vol.2.No.7, April 2008, pp. 1–4.

Frederiksen, Bodil Folke. "Popular Culture, Gender Relations and the Democratisation of Everyday Life in Kenya." *Journal of African Studies*, Vol. 26, No. 2 (June 2000), pp. 209–222. (http://jstor.org/stable/2637490; accessed July 7, 2008).

Gecau, Kimani. "Popular song and social change in Kenya." *Media, Culture & Society*, Vol. 17 (1995), pp. 557–575.

Gilbert, Shirli. "Singing Against Apartheid: ANC Cultural Groups and the International Anti-Apartheid Struggle." *Journal of Southern African Studies*, Volume 33, Number 2 (June 2007), pp. 421 – 441.

*Graphic Showbiz*, Thursday, May 1, 2008

*Mirror*, Wednesday, 2 November 2005.

Ntangaare, Mercy Mirembe. "Portraits of Women in Contemporary Ugandan Theatre" in Jane Plastow (ed.) *African Theatre: Women* Oxford: James Curry, 2002, pp. 58–65.

Osofisan, F. *Insidious Treasons: Drama in a Postcolonial State*, Ibadan: Opon Ifa Readers, 2001.

Vambe, Maurice Taonezvi. "Popular Songs and Social Realities in Post-Independence Zimbabwe." *African Studies Review*, Volume 43, Number 2, (September 2000), pp. 73–86.

## Akyeampong: Notes to "Ties that Bound: Slave Concubines/Wives and the End of Slavery in the Gold Coast, c.1874–1900

1   Anowa in the historical play *Anowa* (Essex: Pearson Education Limited, 2003 [1969]); and Esi in *Changes* (Essex: Heinemann, 1991).

2   Claire Robertson and Martin A. Klein, eds., *Women and Slavery in Africa* (Madison: University of Wisconsin Press, 1983).

3   Claude Meillassoux, *The Anthropology of Slavery: Womb of Iron and Gold* (Chicago: University of Chicago Press, 1991).

4   See Suzanne Miers and Igor Kopytoff, "Introduction," in Miers and Kopytoff, eds., *Slavery in Africa: Historical and Anthropological Perspectives* (Madison: University of Wisconsin Press, 1977), 3–81; and Jane I. Guyer and Samuel M. Eno Belinga, "Wealth in People as Wealth in Knowledge: Accumulation and Composition in Equatorial Africa," *Journal of African History*, 36: 1 (1995), 91–120.

5   Paul E. Lovejoy and Jan Hogendorn, *Slow Death for Slavery: the Course of Abolition in Northern Nigeria, 1897–1936* (Cambridge: Cambridge UP, 1993); and Richard L. Roberts, "Ideology, Slavery and State Formation: The Evolution of Maraka Slavery in the Middle Niger Valley," in Paul Lovejoy, ed., *The Ideology of Slavery in Africa* (Beverly Hills: Sage, 1981), 170–99.

6   On the assimilation of slaves in Africa using the ideology and discourse of "kinship," see Miers and Kopytoff, "Introduction."

7   Sandra E. Greene, *Gender, Ethnicity, and Social Change on the Upper Slave Coast: A History of the Anlo-Ewe* (Portsmouth: Heinemann, 1996), 38–9.

8   Suzanne Miers and Richard Roberts, eds., *The End of Slavery in Africa* (Madison: University of Wisconsin Press, 1988). The court cases in this chapter are drawn from the Public Records and Archives Administration Department (PRAAD), Accra, Ghana.

9   Raymond Dumett and Marion Johnson, "Britain and the Suppression of Slavery in the Gold Coast, Ashanti and the Northern Territories," in Miers and Roberts, *End of Slavery*, 79–80. Two ordinances were gazetted in March 1875: Ordinance No. 1 of 1874 ("To Provide for the Abolition of Slave Dealing") and Ordinance No. 2 of 1874 ("To Provide for the Emancipation of Persons Holden in Slavery").

10   Suzanne Miers, "Slavery to Freedom in Sub-Saharan Africa: Expectations and Reality," *Slavery and Abolition*, 21:2 (2000), 239.

11   Roberts, "Maraka Slavery in the Middle Niger Valley:" Miers, "Slavery to Freedom," 253.

12   Akosua Adoma Perbi. *A History of Indigenous Slavery in Ghana* (Accra: Sub-Saharan Publishers, 2004), 172.

13   Dumett and Johnson, "Suppression of Slavery," 83; Perbi, *Indigenous Slavery*, 182–3.

14   Miers, "Slavery to Freedom," 255–6.

15 PRAAD, Accra, ADM 41/4/2. Civil Record Book 1885–1890. Buafo vs Quaccoe Duah, October 29, 1889.

16 Miers, "Slavery to Freedom," 258.

17 PRAAD, Accra, ADM 41/4/21. Criminal Record Book. Regina per K. Moshi versus Chief Amagashi of Aferingba and Quitta. DC's Court, Quittah, February 4, 1886.

18 PRAAD, Accra, ADM 41/4/21. Criminal Record Book. DC's Court, Quittah, January 11, 12, and 14, 1886.

19 Dumett and Johnson, "Suppression of Slavery," 94. On pawnage in Africa, see Toyin Falola and Paul Lovejoy, eds., *Pawnship in Africa: Debt Bondage in Historical Perspective* (Boulder: Westview Press, 1994).

20 Gareth Austin, "Human Pawning in Asante, 1800–1950: Markets and Coercion, Gender and Cocoa," in Falola and Lovejoy, *Pawnship in Africa*, 119–59.

21 This conforms to the distinction Miers and Kopytoff make between slaves "belonging to" the kin group, while free born kin members "belong in" the kin group. Miers and Kopytoff, "Introduction."

22 PRAAD, Accra, ADM 41/4/21. Adedie versus Fiato. DC's Court Quittah, December 12, 1886.

23 PRAAD, Accra, ADM 41/4/24. Keta Criminal Record Book, 1891–92. Regina per Husunuyo vs Begyie, and Husunuyor vs Milebah.

24 Jean Allman and Victoria Tashjian, *"I will not eat stone." A Women's History of Colonial Asante* (Portsmouth: Heinemann, 2000).

25 T. C. McCaskie, *State and Society in Pre-Colonial Asante* (Cambridge: Cambridge UP, 1995), 182.

26 Penelope Roberts, "The State and the Regulation of Marriage: Sefwi Wiawso (Ghana), 1900–1940," in Helh Afshah, ed., *Women, State and Ideology: Studies form Africa and Asia* (London: Macmillan, 1987), 48–69; and Jean Allman, "Rounding up Spinsters: Gender Chaos and Unmarried Women in Colonial Asante," *Journal of African History*, 37:2 (1996), 195–214.

27 See, for example, Roger Gocking, "Competing Systems of Inheritance before the British Courts of the Gold Coast," *International Journal of African Historical Studies*, 23:4 (1990), 601–18.

## Note to Section IV Introduction

1 Ama Ata Aidoo, *Our Sister Killjoy*. Harlow: Longman 1973) 133.

## Perbi: Notes to "A Historical Case Study of a Slave Girl in Asante Mampong"

1 I deem it an honour and a privilege to be invited to contribute to this Festschrift for Professor Ama Ata Aidoo. As someone who has followed her distinguished career as a writer, it is certainly a great pleasure to do so, for my first association with her was in 1964 when as an eleven-year-old girl, my younger brother and I played the roles of girl and boy in her first play entitled *The Dilemma of a Ghost*. This was staged at the amphitheatre of Commonwealth Hall, University of Ghana, Legon.

2 See for example A.A. Perbi, "The Acquisition of Female Slaves in Pre-Colonial Ghana: Labour or Love?, *Legon Journal of Humanities*, University of Ghana, Legon, Volume 13, 2002 p.1–18.

3 Oral Tradition collected at Asante Mampong during Fieldwork in 1990. Report of the Judicial Committee of the Asante Regional House of Chiefs July 1991 reported

on the front page of the Pioneer Newspaper No. 11086 July 17 1991. Twenty Page Judgement of the Chieftaincy Tribunal of the National House of Chiefs delivered on July 28 1992. The Ghana Law Reports 1995–96 Vol. I, published by the Council for Law Reporting, Accra, Ghana, 2004 (hereafter quoted as 1 GLR 1995–96).

4   R.S. Rattray, *Tribes of the Ashanti Hinterland Vol. I*, London 1932, p. 232.

5   A. Adu Boahen, *Ghana: Evolution and Change in the Nineteenth and Twentieth Centuries*, London 1975, reprinted by Sankofa Educational Publishers, Accra, Ghana 2000, p.2.

6   A.K. Awedoba, "Modes of Succession in the Upper East Region of Ghana," paper presented at the International Conference on Chieftaincy in Africa: Culture, Governance and Development, University of Ghana, Legon 6–10 January 2003, p.1.

7   Awedoba, ibid.

8   A.W. Cardinall, *Ashanti and Beyond*, London 1927.

9   J.A. Braimah & J.P Goody, *Salaga the Struggle for Power*, London 1967. For more information on what happened in Northern Ghana see also B. Der, *The Slave Trade in Northern Ghana*, Accra, Ghana 1998.

10  Fieldwork I conducted in the Upper East and Upper West Regions of Ghana from 22nd to 27th July 2009.

11  M. Johnson, *Salaga Papers Vol. 1*, Institute of African Studies, University of Ghana, Legon 1965, SAL/8/6.

12  M. Johnson, *Salaga Papers Vol I*, Institute of African Studies, University of Ghana, Legon 1965, SAL/39/2.

13  R.S. Rattray, *Ashanti Law and Constitution*, London 1929, p. 36.

14  See for example C.C. Robertson & M.A. Klein (Eds.), *Women and Slavery in Africa*, Wisconsin, USA. 1983; P. Manning, *Slavery and African Life*, Cambridge 1990.

15  Adu Boahen, *Ghana Evolution and Change*, p.15–16; Osei Kwadwo, *An Outline of Asante History Part 2 Volume 1*, Kumase, Ghana 2000, p.49.

16  For more information on the Silver Stool see for example A.A. Nketia, "The Significance of the Silver Stool in the History of Mampong Ashanti", B.A. Dissertation, History Department, University of Ghana, Legon 1974.

17  See for example A.A. Perbi, *A History of Indigenous Slavery in Ghana from the 15th to the 19th Century*, Accra, Ghana 2007, p.114–115.

18  K. Nkansa-Kyeremateng, *Akan Heritage*, Accra, Ghana 1999, p.77–78.

19  Asare Konadu Yamoah, *The People Today-The Kingdom of Ashanti*, Accra, Ghana 1997, p.5, 20–21.

20  Interview with Obaapanin Akosua Kufuor on 24th January 1992.

21  Interview with Obaapanin Akosua Kufour on 24th January 1992.

22  1 GLR 1995–96, p. 132.

23  For more information on slaves and strangers membership to kinship and family, their rights, privileges and disabilities see for example, Perbi, *Indigenous Slavery*, p.111–132.

24  See Perbi, Indigenous Slavery, p.123–130.

25  K. Nkansa-Kyeremateng, *Akan Heritage*, p.66.

26  1 GLR 1995–96, p. 140.

27  1 GLR 1995–96, p. 132.

28  Osei Kwadwo, *An Outline of Asante History*, p. 53.

29   Osei Kwadwo, *An Outline of Asante History*, p .4.

**Houchins: Notes to "Anowa, Paradoxical Queenmother of the Diaspora"**

1   This essay is taken from a larger work-in-progress which I began and developed during two residences as Research Associate at the Women's Studies in Religion Programme (WSRP) at Harvard Divinity School. I am grateful for the funding from WSRP during my first appointment and from Woodrow Wilson Career Enhancement Fellowship during my second stay.

2   Ama Ata Aidoo, *Anowa* (London: Longman, 1970). All references to this play will be cited parenthetically in the text.

3   Vincent O. Odamtten, *The Art of Ama Ata Aidoo: Polylectics and Reading Against Neocolonialism* (Gainesville: University of FL P, 1994), 56. Subsequent references to this work will be cited parenthetically within the text.

4   Jonathan Loesberg, "Deconstruction, Historicism, and Overdetermination: Dislocations of the Marriage Plots in *Robert Elsmere* and *Dombey and Son*," *Victorian Studies: A Journal of Humanities, Arts and Sciences* 33 (1990): 441–2.

5   "The value of. . .a *fefewo* or total narrative performance does not end with the telling of one particular episode or story but goes on to involve the audience-reader in the total aesthetic and ideological critical experience" (82). Earlier in his text, Odamtten defines the "dilemma tale" as a genre that facilitates, indeed, requires, this kind of audience participation: "Essentially, the dilemma tale is a narrative whose primary function is to stimulate serious, deep-probing discussion of social, political, and moral issues that confront human beings in their everyday lives" (18). Thus he observes that the both the dilemma tale and the *fefewo* "facilitate 'interminable palavers'" that are the result of "their (ir)resolution" (82). In *Anowa*, Aidoo deploys the convention of the dilemma tale . . . (45).

6   I am fully aware that many think of the term "barren" as solely a referent for biological/physical infertility; however, when researching the topic in bibliographic resources, the results fall into two categories: those covering matters with biological/physical etiologies and those with metaphysical or spiritual causes. It is my contention, that the childlessness depicted in *Anowa* is of this second type – *metaphysical or trop(e)ic barrenness*. This article will posit a number of reasons for the couple's "infertility," or "barrenness" – among them, their relationship to slavery; Anowa's wandering or her refusal of the vocation to be a priestess; and/or Kofi Ako's having recourse to witchcraft, the "selling of his seeds." Kinship is more than a structure of relationship and power among African peoples; it is also an epistemology – a structure of knowledge, a means to understand. In this regard, offspring are of primary importance in the matrilineal society depicted in this play; thus, children or the lack of them represents even more than social and economic consequences in material lives; questions of fertility take on meanings that are greater than their objective reality. I contend that is how "barrenness" operates in *Anowa* (and in novels by other African women authors: i.e. Flora Nwapa, Buchi Emecheta, Rebeka Njau, and Yvonne Vera). Further, some theorists contend that the absence of reproduction impacts the structure of narratives. Later in this article I will argue that the presence of *barrenness* in the "marriage plot" has a particular *narrative* function and that Anowa's childlessness is requisite for her ability to act as a National Symbolic, the Mother of the Diaspora.

7   The traditional "marriage plot" represents courtship from the meeting of the two

members of a heterosexual couple through social, economic or physical obstacles, to a conclusion in marriage. The typical example of this kind of story finds closure in replicating the ideology of the society that produces the text – i.e. marriage or the forming of a new heterosexual pair thereby assuming biological reproduction and the reproduction of the relations of production. That is, the plot concludes by endorsing prevailing social and economic values. (Judith Roof, *Come As You Are: Sexuality and Narrative* [New York: Columbia UP, 1996], xii-xiv.) *Anowa* is a variation on this configuration, in part, because it foreshortens the period of courtship and moves quickly to marriage, by-passing or ignoring the obstacles (i.e. parental disapproval), and because, despite all attempts to reproduce (a child) and to replicate the relations of production (an economy based on slavery), the plot appears to end in failure – the deaths of both members of the couple. This essay examines and interrogates that apparent failure.

8   Claire C. Robertson and Martin A. Klein, "Woman's Importance in African Slave Systems," in *Women and Slavery in Africa*, eds. Robertson and Klein (Portsmouth, NH: Heinemann, 1997), 3. Subsequent citations of this article will be indicated parenthetically in the text.

9   Saidya Hartman, *Lose Your Mother: A Journey along the Atlantic Slave Route* (New York: Farrar, Straus and Giroux, 2007), 5. All other citations for this work are in the text parenthetically.

10  Because fig trees do not seem to bloom, yet they produce luscious womb-like fruit filled with flesh and seeds, folklore maintains that the tree is parthenogenetic. Among many ethnic groups across Africa, this tree has religious significance – for example, among the Akan and the Kikuyu.

11  Eva Lewin Richter Meyerowitz, *The Akan of Ghana: Their Ancient Beliefs* (London: Faber and Faber, 1958), 24–29. Emphasis added. Subsequent references are made parenthetically in the main text and in the explanatory endnotes.

12  Orlando Patterson, *Slavery and Social Death: A Comparative Study* (Cambridge, MA: Harvard UP, 1982).

13  In addition to Robertson and Klein cited in the text, Claude Meillassoux writes on the subject in, "Female Slavery," in *Women and Slavery in Africa*, eds. Claire C Robertson and Martin A. Klein (Porstmouth, NH: Heinemann, 1997), 50, 64. Subsequent references are in the text.

14  Carole Boyce Davies in *Black Women, Writing and Identity: Migrations of the Subject* (New York: Roultedge, 1994) devotes a chapter to *Anowa*, which she entitled "Deconstructing African Female Subjectivities: Anowa's Borderlands" 59–79. Professor Davies and I reach many of the same conclusions albeit usually via different routes. Her treatise is likewise concerned with liminal subject positions and the open-endedness and intertextuality of this play. She examines "homosociality in the construction of masculinity" as it pertains to Kofi Ako and his attempt to assert male dominance and power, and she draws a compelling comparison between Anowa's husband and Jody in Hurston's *Their Eyes Were Watching God*. Further, she argues: "[M]ale homosexuality can be seen as essentially different from female homosexuality in that men have recourse to power and a certain exclusivity which is constitutive of maleness. In other words, the tendency is often to equate gay and lesbian identity, but these are not symmetrical. For Kofi Ako can become, in spite of his questionable "masculinity" by the society's standards, a man of significance,

while Anowa is not allowed to occupy the sexually transgressive (same-sex, queer) position (read as "lesbian" in the West), i.e. constructed outside of heterosexuality and wifehood (72). However, I would argue this point even more forcefully: Kofi Ako becomes "a man of significance" despite his inability to procreate – to reproduce biologically – precisely because he pursues so ruthlessly and single-mindedly capitalistic economic reproduction. Had he been a failure at both trade and fathering, his reputation would have suffered more severely as the topic of vitriolic gossip. As it is, his suicide at the play's end is narrative retribution. On the other hand, Anowa is doubly transgressive – sexually and economically – refusing, as she does, to approve and replicate the dominant ideology and failing to reproduce an offspring; thus, she bears a greater brunt of social disapprobation. Also, as a woman, she is less powerful than Kofi Ako to deflect social criticism. But my essay is even more concerned with objects of desire and desiring subjects; and so the triangulation of Kofi's and Anowa's desires onto the Oguaa woman becomes significant in this regard. Therefore, Anowa's transgression may be more sexually freighted in my readings.

15  Martin Klein, "Women in Slavery in the Western Sudan" in *Women and Slavery in Africa*, eds. Claire C. Robertson and Martin A Klein (Portsmouth, NH: Heinemann, 1997), 87. Subsequent references are parenthetical.

16  Edward A. Alpers, "The Story of Swema: Female Vulnerability in Nineteenth-Century East Africa" in *Women and Slavery in Africa*, eds. Claire C.Robertson and Martin A. Klein (Portsmouth, NH: Heinemann, 1997), 199.

17  Margaret Strobel, "Slavery and Reproduction of Labour in Mombasa" in *Women and Slavery in Africa*, eds. Claire C. Robertson and Martin A. Klein (Portsmouth, NH: Heinemann, 1997), 119.

18  In coastal communities near slave forts – i.e. Oguaa/Cape Coast – there developed a class of concubine slave women who either served as prostitutes or who were acquired for more sustained liaisons outside wedlock. It became common for European men and wealthy African traders habitually to seek the female offspring of these mixed unions as concubines, thereby creating a "class" of women valued as consorts. Robert J. C. Young in *Colonial Desire: Hybridity in Theory, Culture, and Race* (New York: Routledge, 1995) reminds us that miscegenation and its products, the mulatto and the quadroon, are sites of erotic fantasy for the European, Euro-American bourgeoisie (115, 144–9). "[H]omosexuality became associated with the degenerate products of miscegenation" (26).

19  If one extends interpretation of the trope of reincarnation beyond that of a "spirit child" identified by Vincent Odamtten (54–55; 183 n. 21) to what Meyerowitz calls the reincarnation/recirculation of the queenmother's 'kra, then Anowa's drowning, her claiming of a watery habitat, becomes not the end of the plot trajectory – a sign of failure – but signals the birth of another cycle, a revivification of the people, the kin. As Meyerowitz in *The Akan of Ghana* explains the concept, the 'kra is that force, energy, or soul which animates individuals and which is transmitted in the process of life continuation or regeneration. A woman possessed by the 'kra or the spirit of the Mother Goddess might "give birth to an *obosom*," in other words, to a "visible manifestation of the 'kra. . . [p]ersonified as a goddess" (25). And that woman, by following the dictates of her *obosom*, founds a clan (*nton*) or a larger community composed of several clans – that is, "a nation" – is a queenmother. To the 'kra of the

founding queenmother, who is a daughter or incarnation of the Mother Goddess, adhere the 'kras of her successors, thus forming the collective ancestral 'kra of that clan or state. Each person born into that lineage both partakes of that lifeforce and is duty bound to add to it, to fill it "to the brim with goodness" (96). The Ghanaian philosopher J. B. Danquah, in the *Akan Doctrine of God* (London: Cass, 1968) explained reincarnation through the analogy of the cocoa pod – a simile reminiscent of Anowa's nightmare in which her body is imaged as a pod expelling its offspring into the rending claws of lobsters. "Cultivators know that the seed ejected from the dried fruit of the cocoa plant must appear to have died in order to reproduce a new tree. So, too, those individuals who are secure in their sense of belonging to a community are conscious that death is nothing but a stage in the consciousness of the race [people], the experience of [their] kind. The primary fact with [them] is that within [them] is an inheritance, the blood of [their] race and from [them] must go that heritable treasure to other descendants, the blood of their own bodies. For such, death, *owu*, is only an aspect of birth, *awo*, an instrument of the total destiny, the continuity of the kind, the permanence and the persistence of the organic whole which is the greatest good" (157).

20 Mercy Amba Oduyoye. *Daughters of Anowa: African Women and Patriarchy* (New York: Orbis, 1995), 10. Subsequent references are in the text

21 Adeola James, "Ama Ata Aidoo – An Interview" in *In Their Own Voices: African Women Writers Talk* (Portsmouth, New Hampshire, 1990), 9–29.

22 Ayi Kwei Armah, *Two Thousand Seasons* (Chicago: Third World Press, 1984), 7. Subsequent references are in parentheses in the text.

23 Ama Ata Aidoo, *Our Sister Killjoy or Reflections from a Black-Eyed Squint* (New York: NOK Publishers International, 1979), 32. This is a reference to Aidoo's first novel; and, in a sense, this work continues where *Anowa* leaves off by interrogating, analysing, and resisting: "the ideological and economical operations of the neocolonial state," which are the inevitable outcome of an oppressive past complicity between European interests and an emerging African indigenous class of politicians, scholars, and traders/entrepreneurs (Odamtten, 114–117).

24 I made a series of inquiries of scholars of Akan, particularly Fante, folklore to find out the sources of the Anowa tale but to no avail. Then I decided to derive a reconstructed sketch from the few clues I had at my disposal, to speculate about Anowa's background/provenance. I began by tracing the literary relationship between Aidoo and Armah which some sources said was particularly close in the 1960s. She wrote an introduction to the American edition of Armah's first novel. Armah dedicated *Fragments* to Aidoo. So, I decided to read her play against his novel, assuming that they probably influenced each other's works, that, though each work develops the character differently, Anowa/Anoa was undoubtedly a topic in their conversations. I also relied on Mercy Oduyoye's hints about this question. Further, even though Oduyoye did not specifically connect the source of the character common in the Saltpond area with those queenmothers who founded lineages and discovered new lands and sources of water and whom she analogized to Anowa, I assumed that her intimate knowledge of her people's culture triggered this intuitive link. I, therefore, speculate that Anowa may have been a historical figure to whom has accreted the folkloric/mythic motifs of queenmotherhood, reincarnation, and she may be a variation on an autochthonous female deity – an earth goddess, an archaic mother.

These traits identify her as a kinswoman to the mermaid figure in *The Autobiography of My Mother*, to the archaic, "oceanic" mother or phantasmagoric mother – the first Xuela – of that Kincaid novel and to the Xuela who narrates the text and who envisions her body as exploding forth her dead offspring in an inversion of the Anowa image in Aidoo's play. These female sexually ambiguous figures are subjects in one of my related essays on Rebekah Njau's *Ripples in the Pool*. In other words, the queen-mother and, by extension, Anowa/Anoa, though an incarnation of the great earth mother, is often associated with bodies of water – springs and pools; it, therefore, seemed possible that Anowa's disappearance into the ocean, like Anoa's escape overboard into the sea in *Two Thousand Seasons*, gestures toward a thematic connection or trop(e)ic linkage with the female water spirits revered by barren women, Mama Wata. Further, according to Kofi Asare Opoku and Kathleen Wicker who worked together on Mami Wata, some Fante consider Mami Wata to be the daughter of Bosompo, the chief water deity who is invoked in the libational scene at *Anowa's* beginning. In addition, they cite an example of a priestess who metaphorises her relationship to Mami Wata in consonance with the Fante "commitment to matrilineages in which [the divinity] is her mother" not her spouse, as is more common in relationships between priests and the gods they mediate. This strong woman-to-woman bond between votary and divinity reflects that aspect of matriliny where the strongest ties of kinship between generations is through the mother, and within a given generation is between female siblings, a sisterhood. Kofi Asare Opoku and Kathleen O'Brien Wicker, "Abidjan Mamiwater and Aba Yaba: Two Profiles of Mami/Maame Water Priesthood in Ghana" in *Sacred Waters: Arts for Mami Wata and Other Divinities in Africa and the Diaspora*, ed. Henry John Drewal (Bloomington: Indiana UP, 2008) 170 – 189. See also the discussion of Mammywata in the Caribbean in an article by Rhonda Cobham entitled "MWEN NA RIEN, MSIEU" Jamaica Kincaid and the Problem of Creole Gnosis," *Callaloo*, Vol. 25, No. 3 (Summer, 2002), pp. 868–884. I make the case that Sissie Killjoy and Anowa, members of matrilineages, figure the race trans-national relationship through their affective kinship to both men and women as their sisters. Thus, suturing Mami Wata motifs to Anowa/Anoa seems consistent with the syncretic nature, the characteristic of assemblage that is the customary aspect of this mermaid who grafts herself to existing folk beliefs, local deities, and narratives.

25   Douglas H. Johnson and David Anderson. "Revealing Prophets" in *Revealing Prophets: Prophecy in Eastern African History*, eds. David Anderson and Douglas Johnson (Athens, OH: Ohio UP, 1995), 7. Subsequent references are in the text.

26   Nancy Jay. *Throughout Your Generations Forever: Sacrifice, Religions, and Paternity*. (Chicago: U of Chicago P, 1992), 67–8. Subsequent references are in the text.

27   In *Writing Beyond the Ending: Narrative Strategies of Twentieth Century Women Writers*, Rachel Blau Du Plessis (Bloomington: Indiana UP, 1985), explores the ways feminist novels escape the strictures of heterosexual ideology which govern plot trajectories. Marilyn R. Farwell, *Heterosexual Plots and Lesbian Narratives* (New York: New York UP, 1996), 60–1. Farwell explains that some deformation in the traditional plot trajectory which usually ends in marriage creates a medium felicitous to the representation of a queer subjectivity. Judith Roof, *Come as You Are: Sexuality and Narrative* (New York: Columbia UP, 1996), 35–7. Roof and Farwell explore ideological reasons (gendered/sexual and economic) that inhibit plot closure or

"unification." Carole Boyce Davies (cited above) also makes use of Du Plessis's model of narrative open-endedness to explore intertextual relations between black women's works. This open-endedness is the hallmark of textual ambiguity and is well suited to the riddle tale.

28  Patricia Berry. *Echo's Subtle Body: Contributions to an Archetypal Psychology*. (Dallas: Spring Publications, 1982), 148. Subsequent references are in the text.

29  Mami Wata, Mami Watas are ubiquitous throughout Africa and the black Diaspora – see, for example, *Texaco* by Patrick Chamoiseau (New York: Pantheon, 1997) and *Blessed is the Fruit* by Robert Antoni (New York: New York: Henry Holt and Co., 1997); or the figure of La Sirene in Haitian vodun. Henry John Drewal, who has produced several studies on Mami Wata, maintains that she was dispersed through-out the black world by sailors going from port to port. ["Mama Wata: Arts for Water Spirits in Africa and its Diasporas," an exhibition preview, *African Arts* Summer (2008): 60 – 4]. Kathleen O'Brien Wicker, "Mami Water in African Religion and Spirituality" in *African Spirituality: Forms, Meanings, and Expressions*, ed. Jacob K. Olupona (New York: The Crossroad Publishing Co., 2000), 198–222. Wicker discusses the spirit's dispersal throughout the black world, her migration and assemblage/syncretism among African and African Diasporic peoples."Water divinities and spirits are arguably the most adaptable, flexible, and innovative of all African divinities, since fluidity is the essence of their being . . . One result of the creolisation of African water divinities can be seen in the production of Mami Water. Mami Water is the name applied by Africans to a class of female and male divinities or spirits that have accreted elements from several European, New World, and Indian cultural traditions" She also explains that "the ambiguous nature of water divinities is reflected . . . in their gender identities and representations. Originally hermaphroditic, they are now more commonly portrayed as male-female pairs" (198–9). Opoku and Wicker find that Mami Wata, as a water divinity, is not foreign to the Ewe and the Fante. However, the representation of Mami Wata as a mermaid/man, a spirit that is half woman and half fish, is not traditional. Acceptance of this representation is the devotees' way of expressing the unknow-able immensity and the infinite unfathomableness of the divine, and helps them to a greater and more profound appreciation of divinity. For the devotees, the door is always open for new revelations of the divine (179 – 187). I would argue further that the figure of Anowa, as deployed first by Aidoo and then by Armah, is a simi-larly flexible image, a technology of the Racial Symbolic, which serves black feminists in representing their sex, race, and sexual social locations.

30  Flora Nwapa. *Efuru* (London: Heinemann, 1966), 183. This novel portrays a barren Igbo woman who finds solace in devotion to Mami Wata. Professor Helen Nabasuta Mugambi reminded me in the course of a conversation of the resem-blance between Mami Wata's minnow-kindling and spermatozoa. In *Yoruba Ritual: Performers, Play, Agency* (Bloomington: Indiana UP, 1992), Margaret Drewal discusses the iconography and symbolic representations in Mami Wata rituals where a bowl and a fish figure act as representations of sex roles in reproduction: womb-like bowl and fish-like sperm (172–190). Her depiction as a mermaid, part woman and part fish, is a relatively new but logical syncretism to her representation, given her close association with fish.

31  Toni Morrison. *Beloved* (New York: Knopf, 1987), 267.

32  Nancy Jay, *Throughout Your Generations Forever: Sacrifice, Religion, and Paternity* (Chicago: U of Chicago P, 1992) 5. Subsequent citations in the text.

33  Professor Canaan Banana, former scholar of religious studies in Harare, Zimbabwe, suggested the term "living timeless" to Professor Kathleen Wicker and me at a conference convened by the Religion Department, Scripps College, Claremont California, as the appropriate designation for the ancestors who bear witness to one's kinship and belonging to (a) community(ies).

34  Lauren Berlant, *The Anatomy of National Fantasy: Hawthorne, Utopia, and Everyday Life.* (Chicago: U of Chicago P, 1991), 20.

35  In *Lose Your Mother*, Sadiya Hartman tells of a small community of AfricanAmericans living near the old El Mina slave castle, who called themselves *"The tribe of the Middle Passage"* (102). Emphasis in the original. A few lines later, she observes the following: "The Middle Passage was the birth canal that spawned the tribe. The Middle Passage was the death canal . . ." (103).

36  Jeffrey W. Bolster, *Black Jacks: AfricanAmerican Seamen in the Age of Sail.* (Cambridge: Harvard UP, 1997), 62–3.

37  Paul Gilroy, *The Black Atlantic: Modernity and Double Consciousness.* (Cambridge: Harvard UP, 1993). Subsequent references are in the text.

38  Michelle Cliff, *Free Enterprise.* (New York: Dutton, 1993).

39  Fred D'Aguiar, *Feeding the Ghosts.* (Hopewell, NJ,: The Ecco Press, 1999).

40  M. NourBese Philip, *The Zong!* (Middletown, CT: Wesleyan UP, 2008).

41  Ama Ata Aidoo. "Literature, Feminism, and the African Woman Today" in *Reconstructing Womanhood, Reconstructing Feminism: Writings on Black Women*, ed. Delia Jarrett-Macauley. (London: Rooutledge, 1996), 156 –174.

42  Paule Marshall, *Praisesong for the Widow* (New York: Putnam, 1983)

43  Julie Dash (dir.), *Daughters of the Dust.* (New York: Kino Video, 1992)

44  Rosemarie Robotham. "Spirit" in *Spirits of the Passage: The Transatlantic Slave Trade in the Seventeenth Century*, eds. Madeline Burnside and Rosemarie Robotham (New York: Simon and Schuster, 1997) 11–15.

45  Eric Lott, "Routes" (a review of *The Black Atlantic* by Paul Gilroy), *The Nation* 2 May 1994, 602–4.

## Gibbs: Notes to "The Call to the Priesthood and Other Stories"

1  Sara Chetin, "Interview with Ama Ata Aidoo." *Wasafiri* (London), 6–7 (Spring-Autumn, 1987), 23–25, 27.

2  Bridgid M. Sackey, "The Call to Traditional Priesthood Among the Akan of Ghana and the Consequences of its Renunciation, A Research Note." Unpublished.

3  *African Contemporary Plays*, Martin Banham and Jane Plastow, eds London: Methuen, 1999, 137–206. All subsequent quotations from *Anowa* are from this edition.

## Asare Opoku: Works Cited

Achebe, C. *Thngs Fall Apart.* New York: Anchor Books, 1994.

Adekunle, Olunade. *Proverbs and Maxims As Mechanisms For Conflict Resolution in Ibadan.* M.A. Thesis, University of Ibadan. January, 2008.

Albert, Isaac O. Et. al. *Informal Channels For Conflict Resolution in Ibadan, Nigeria.* Ibadan: IFRA, 1995.

Areje, Raphael A. *Yoruba Proverbs.* Ibadan: Daystar Press, 1985.

Chakanza, J. C. *Wisdom of the People: 2000 Chinyanja Proverbs.* Blantyre:Christian Literature Association of Malawi, 2000.

Cotter, George. *Ethiopian Wisdom: Proverbs and Sayings of the Oromo People.* Ibadan: Sefer/Daystar, 1996.

Dzobo, Noah. *African Proverbs: A Guide to Conduct. Vol. III: The Moral Values of Ewe Proverbs.* Accra: Woeli Publishing Services, 2006.

Gleason, Norma. *Macmillan Book of Proverbs From Around The World.* London: Macmillan, 1992.

Hamutyinei, Mordikai A & Plangger, Albert B. *Tsumo Shumo: Shona Proverbial Lore and Wisdom.* Harare: Mambo Press, 1987.

Khan, Bamba & Khan, Mariama. *Proverbs of the Senegambia.* Birkama New Town: Sandeng Publishers, 2004.

Kleinewillinghofer, Ulrich. *Bogon Aduuna na Binde Atawisa: A Collection of Proverbs and Wise Sayings of the Chala People.* Legon: Institute of African Studies, 2007.

Korem, Albin & Abissath, M. K. *Traditional Wisdom in African Proverbs: 1915 Proverbs from 40 African Countries.* Accra: Publishing Trends Ltd. 2004.

Kuusi, Matti. *Ovambo Proverbs with African Parallels.* Helsinki, 1970.

Lule, Joseph. *The Hidden Wisdom of the Baganda.* Arlington, Va.: Humbolt and Hartmann, 2006.

Madumulla, J. S. *Proverbs and Sayings: Theory and Practice.* Dar es Salaam: Institute of Kiswahili Research, 2005.

Massek, A. Ol'Oloisolo & Sidai, J. O. *Wisdom of Maasai.* Nairobi: Transafrica Publishers, 1974.

Njururi, Ngumbu. *Gikuyu Proverbs.* London: Macmillan, 1969.

Nyembezi, C. L. S. *Zulu Proverbs.* (New Edition). Pietermaritzburg: Shuter and Shooter, 1990

Olaoba, A. O. *Yoruba Legal Culture.* Ibadan: John Archers (Publishers) Ltd., 1999.

Opoku, Kofi Asare. *Hearing and Keeping: Akan Proverbs.* Pretoria: UNISA Press, 1997.

Owomoyela, O. Oyekan. *Yoruba Proverbs.* Lincoln and London: University of Nebraska Press, 2005.

Plaatje, Solomon. T. *Sechuana Proverbs* (with literal translations and their European equivalents). London: Kegan Paul, Trench, Trubner & Co., Ltd. 1916.

Wanjohi, Joseph Gerard. *Under One Roof: Gikuyu Proverbs Consolidated.* Nairobi: Paulines Publications Africa, 2001.

Whitting, C. E. J.*Hausa Fulani Proverbs.* Lagos: Gov't. Printer,

**Odamtten: Work Cited**
Aidoo, Ama Ata. *The Eagle and the Chickens and Other Stories.* Accra, Ghana: Afram Publications, 1989.

**Bryce: Notes to "Someone Talking to Sometime: A Dialogue Across Time and Space"**

1   Editor's note: The "outspoken contribution" that Aidoo made at the 1985 Zimbabwe International Book Fair was published as "To Be an African Woman Writer – an Overview and a Detail," in Kirsten Holst Petersen and Per Wästberg, eds. *Criticism and Ideology: Second African Writers' Conference, Stockholm 1986* (Upsala: Scandinavian Institute of African Studies, 1988) pp. 155–172.

2   See Jane Bryce, "Half and Half Children: Third Generation Women Writers and the

New Nigerian novel." *Research in African Literatures*, 39, 2, 2008. 49–67.

## Bryce: Works Cited

Achebe, Chinua. "The Novelist as Teacher" in *Hopes & Impediments*. London: Heinemann Educational, 1975, 40–46.

_____. "The African Writer and the English Language," in *Transition* 18 (1965).: 27–30.

Aidoo, Ama Ata. "For Whom Things Did Not Change," in *No Sweetness Here*, Harlow: Longman, 1970.

_____. *Our Sister Killjoy: Or, Reflections from a Black-Eyed Squint*. UK: Longman, 1977; New York: NOK, 1979

_____. *Someone Talking to Sometime*. Harare: College Pre, 1985.

_____. *Changes – A Love Story*. London: Women"s Press, 1991.

Bryce, Jane. "Going Home Is Another Story: Constructions of Nation and Gender in Ama Ata Aidoo's *Changes*." Online in *West Africa Review*: 1999. http//:www.west-africareview.com/vol1.1/jane/html (9/10/10)

_____. "Women and Books Dominate Zimbabwe Book Fair", in *The Guardian* (Lagos), Sunday, August 18, 1985: 9.

_____. "Literacy and Literature: Whose Concern?" in *New African*, October, 1985: 53.

_____. 1985. Interview with Ama Ata Aidoo, Harare (unpublished).

_____. "Ama Ata Aidoo: a Further Departure," in *New African*, November, 1985: 46.

_____. "Two exile African women relate experience," in *The Guardian* (Lagos), Monday, January 10, 1986. (no page number).

Eliot, T.S. *The Wasteland*. London: Faber, 1922.

Marechera, Dambudzo. *Pictures, Poems, Prose, Tributes*. Compiled and edited by Flora Veit-Wild and Ernest Schade. Harare: Baobab Books, 1988.

McNee, Lisa. "Translation and the African Novel/Reading as Re/Membering," in *Teaching the African Novel*, ed. Gaurav Desai. New York: The Modern Language Association of America, 2009:102–117.

Odamtten, V. *The Art of Ama Ata Aidoo: Polylectics and Reading Against Neo- colonialism*. UP of Florida, 1994.

Ogunyemi, Chikwenye. *African Wo/man Palava: The Nigerian Novel by Women*. University of Chicago Press, 1996.

Ngũgĩ wa Thiong'o. *Decolonising the Mind: The Politics of Language in African Literature*. Oxford: Heinemann, 1986.

## Adams: Notes to "Tribal Scars" on the Body of "The Girl Who Can"

1   A few of the ideas of this paper were published as "'No Sweetness Here' for 'Our Sister,' 'La Noire'?" Helen Lauer, Nana Aba Appiah Amfo, Jemima Asabea Anderson, eds. *Identity Meets Nationality: Voices from the Humanities*. Legon, Accra: Sub-Saharan 2011, pp. 202–224.

2   Edris Makward." Ousmane Sembène: Griot of Modern Times & Advocate of a Casteless African Society. In Kofi Anyidoho, Abena P.A. Busia and Anne V. Adams (eds.) *Beyond Survival: African Literature and the Search for New Life*. Kofi Anyidoho, Abena P.A. Busia and Anne V. Adams (eds.) Trenton, NJ, 1999.

3   Of the seventeen writers of Africa whose short-story collections Balogun inventories in his study, none of the three women – Bessie Head and Nadine Gordimer being the other two – made it into his list of "great masters."

4    "[C]'est la critique de la société africaine, critique où l'auteur assigne aux Africains eux-mêmes une grande part de la responsabilité de leur sort, des vices et des fautes qu'on trouve en Afrique. Et voilà ce qui donne, à a dernière nouvelle, sa valeur représentante." (S.K. Boafo, "'Voltaïque' d'Ousmane Sembène: Commentaires et observations." *Présence Francophone* Automne 1977, No. 15: 11–30).

5    *Saa*: "whaddya know!" or "well, I'll be damned!"

6    Of course, the need to recognise the idea that females as bodies and as whole persons are good for other things besides childbirth is not unique to Africans. And, along with other societies in the world, African societies are evolving in the sphere of gender equality. As Aidoo, a self-acknowledged feminist, has said repeatedly, not only have there been forms of feminism in Africa for ages, quite apart from any Western influence, but that it must be through African feminism that the struggle for gender equality among Africans can be satisfactorily waged.

7    This development is a fictional fulfillment, sixty years later, of the vision of Kwame Nkrumah in the early 1960s, about whom it was said that he was trying to move too fast for the continent.

8    25th May 1963 was the date of the founding of the OAU, which, in Nkrumah's vision, was a first step to a united continent. Since then it is celebrated as a public holiday, in some nations, at least, as Africa Unity Day.

9    IFAN: French Institute on Black Africa at the University of Dakar

10   I have substituted this translation of Sembène's term "blackesses," which I believe he used to avoid using the problematic "négresses." The translator's term "darkies" is, of course, entirely unacceptable.

11   In its setting and conflict this story is a revision of one sub-plot in Sembène's novel *God's Bits of Wood*.

12   The chewing stick used to clean teeth and breath.

## Adams: Works Cited

Aidoo, Ama Ata. *No Sweetness Here*. (1970). New York: Anchor Books, 1972.

_____. *The Girl Who Can and Other Stories*. (1997) Portsmouth: Heinemann, 2002.

Balogun, F. Odun. *Tradition and Modernity in the African Short Story: An Introduction to a Literature in Search of Critics*. New York: Greenwood, 1991

Boafo, S.K. "'Voltaïque' d'Ousmane Sembène: Commentaires et Observations." *Présence Francophone* Automne 1977, No. 15: 11–30

Makward, Edris. "Ousmane Sembène: Griot of Modern Times & Advocate of a Casteless African Society." In Kofi Anyidoho, Abena P.A. Busia and Anne V. Adams (eds.) *Beyond Survival: African Literature and the Search for New Life*. Trenton, NJ, 1999.

Odamtten, Vincent O. *The Art of Ama Ata Aidoo: Polylectics and Reading against Neo-colonialism*. Gainesville. University of Florida Press, 1994.

Sembène Ousmane. *Voltaïque*. Présence Africaine, 1962; *Tribal Scars and Other Stories* (transl. Len Ortzen). London: Heinemann, 1974.

## Sutherland-Addy: Notes to "Mfantse Meets English"

1    See Obiajunwa Wali's famous piece: "The Dead End of African Literature?" first published in *Transition* 10 (1963)13–15. Indeed in the 2007 anthology edited by literary critics Tejumola Olaniyan and Ato Quayson under title *African Literature: an Anthology of Criticism and Theory*, the editors have done a yeoman's task of assembling

the arguments giving a perspective on the issues which have exercised critics and writers over time and how the issues have evolved in time. The issue of the medium of writing is certainly one of them. While aspects of essays in each section touch on this question, part II on orality and literacy and part IV on the language of African Literature are particularly helpful.

2    A succinct summary on Christianity and education on the Gold Coast can be found at     http://education.stateuniversity.com/pages/529/Ghana-HISTORY-BACK-GROUND.html">Ghana. For an interesting angle on the evolution of a colonial elite on the Gold Coast also see Stephanie Newell (2002). *The Literary Culture in Colonial Ghana: 'How to Play the Game of Life'* Stephanie Newell (2002).

3    Chapter 2 of Vincent Odamtten's *The Art of Ama Ata Aidoo: Polylectics and Reading Against Neo-colonialism* (1994) is meant to provide a historical context for her play *Anowa*, but it is also a very helpful concise history of the Mfantse people, especially dwelling on the age of state formation among them and their neighbours, and the encounter with Europe.

4    This précis of Bakhtin's key ideas was taken from the following articles: Linda M. Parker-Fullers "Voices: Bakhtin's Heteroglossia and Polyphony and the Performance of Narrative Literature." Published in *Literature in Performance* 7 1986:1–12, and James P. Zappers' contribution to Michael G. Moan and Michel Ballif (Eds) *Twentieth Century Rhetoric and Rhetoricians: A Critical Study"* (2005) entitled "Mikhail Bakhtin 1895–1975"

5    This is a slight variation on the term "Anglo-African" coined by Sekyi for colonial subjects who attempt to turn themselves into black Englishmen and women. It is the subject of several of his works including "The Anglo-African."

6    This appears on page 87 of *The Blinkards.* The translation is also the author's own translation.

7    Aidoo 1997:10

8    (note 6) from María Frías 2003 "An Interview with Ama Ata Aidoo: 'I Learnt My First Feminist Lessons in Africa'" *Revista Estudios Inglesis* 16 (p.8)

9    Akosua Anyidoho in her article "Linguistic Parallels in Traditional Akan Appellation Poetry" discusses this stylistic device which is often found in praise poetry.

10   "The Poetry of Ama Ata Aidoo" by Vincent Odamtten in Anyidoho, K. and J. Gibbs, J. *Fontomfrom: Contemporary Ghanaian Literature, Theatre and Film*, Matatu 21–22, 2000 Amsterdam-Atlanta Ga.: Rodopi. (209–216)

11   (Odamtten) " The Poetry of Ama Ata Aidoo in K.Anyidoho and J.Gibbs (Eds) Fontomfrom: Contemporary Ghanaian Literature Theatre and Film Matatu 21 (2000): 211

## Sutherland-Addy: Works Cited

Acquah, L. "A Repertoire of Tropes: A Study of Fante-Akan Asafo Song Text from the Cape Coast Area of the Central Region of Ghana." University of Cape Coast (Unpublished Thesis), 2002.

Adams A. and E. Sutherland-Addy. *The Legacy of Efua Sutherland*. Oxfordshire: Ayebia Clarke Publishing Ltd, 2008.

Adejare, O. "Translation: A Distinctive Feature of African Literature in English" in Epstein, E.L. and R. Kole. (Eds). *The Language of African Literature*. Trenton NJ: Africa World Press, 1996.

Aidoo, A, A. *Our Sister Killjoy*. Essex: Longman Publishers, 1977.

_____. *Someone Talking to Sometime*. Harare: Zimbabwe: College Press

_____. *The Dilemma of A Ghost and Anowa*. Essex: Longman 1987.

_____. *Changes: A Love Story*. New York: The Feminist Press, 1991.

_____. *An Angry Letter in January*. Coventry, UK: Dangaroo Press, 1992.

_____. *The Girl Who Can and Other Stories*. Legon, Ghana: Sub-Saharan Publishers, 1997.

Anyidoho, A. "Linguistic Parallels in Traditional Akan Appellation Poetry." *Research in African Literatures*, Spring 1991 Vol.22 No.1.

Anyidoho, K. and J. Gibbs. *Fontomfrom: Contemporary Ghanaian Literature, Theatre and Film. Matatu* 21–22, 2000.

Casely-Hayford, J. *Ethiopian Unbound: Studies in Race Emancipation*. London: Frank Cass and Co. Ltd., 1969.

Epstein, E.L. and R. Kole (Eds). *The Language of African Literature*. Trenton NJ: Africa World Press, 1996.

Frias M. "An Interview with Ama Ata Aidoo: "I Learnt My First Feminist Lessons" in *Africain Revista Estudios Inglesis 16*. 2003.

James, A. (Ed). *In Their Own Voices: African Women Talk*. London: James Currey.

Jones, E. et al .*Women in Africa Literature Today*. Trenton NJ: Africa World Press, 1987.

Parker-Fullers, L. "Voices: Bakhtin's Heteroglossia and Polyphony and the Performance of Narrative Literature" in *Literature in Performance 7*. 1986.

Odamtten, V.O. *The Art of Ama Ata Aidoo: A Polylectics and Reading Against Neo-colonialism*. Gainesville: UP of Florida, 1994.

Olaniyan, T. and A. Quayson (Eds). *African Literature: An Anthology of Criticsim and Theory*. Oxford: Blackwell Publishing, 2007.

Omole, J. "Code-Switching in Soyinka's *The Interpreters*." in Epstein, E.L. and R. Kole. (Eds). *The Language of African Literature*. Trenton NJ: Africa World Press, 1996.

Page, N. (Ed). *The Language of Literature*. London: The Macmillan Press Ltd., 1984

Sekyi, K. *The Blinkards*. London: Heinemann Educational Books, (1974) 1994.

Sutherland, E. *Edufa*. London: Longmans. 1967.

_____. *Foriwa*.Tema: Tema Publishing Corporation. 1971.

_____. "New Life in Kyerefaso" in Charlotte Brunner (Ed) *Unwinding Threads* Cambridge: Heinemann, 1994.

_____. *Ananse and the Dwarf Brigade* (DVD) Accra: Film Africa. 2006

_____. "Wo Hyee Me Bo" (Unpublished Manuscript)

_____. Odasani" (Unpublished Manuscript)

Sutherland, E. et al (Eds). *Okyeame* Vol.2, No. 1: 1964.

_____. *Okyeame* Vol.2, No. 2, 1965.

_____. *Okyeame* Vol.5. 1972.

Zappen, J. "Mikhail Bakhtin 1895–1975" in Moran, M and M. Ballif (Eds). *Twentieth Century Rhetoric and Rhetoricians: A Critical Study*. West Port: Greenwood Press, 2000.

**Ajayi-Soyinka: Notes to "Disobedient Subversions: *Anowa*'s Unending Quest"**

1   I want to thank Anne Adams who remembers, and encourages me to revisit this incident that I have tried to suppress.

2   The year was 1987.

3   I acknowledge Toyin Bifarin Ogundipe (Nigeria) and Jolade Kilanko Pratt "JK" (USA), my general reference consultants who readily refresh my memory where it

has gone a bit hazy. Both were students at OAU, and JK played Anowa.

4  Instituted formally in 1977, the Department of Dramatic Arts was one of the departments that was created when the Institute of African Studies was dissolved. In previous years, Ori-Olokun Theatre, as part of the Institute was responsible for theatre performances and other artistic activities at the university. See also: Foluke Ogunleye. "Ife Convocation plays as Politics: An Examination of Some Past Productions." 18–25. In *African Theatre Playwrights & Politics*. Eds. Banham, Martin, James Gibbs and Femi Osofisan. Oxford: James Currey, 2001.

5  OAU was founded in 1962 as The University of Ife, in protest of the Ashby Commission Report of 1960 which did not recommend an additional university to the existing University College of Ibadan (UCI) in the then Western Region of Nigeria. Western Region felt the decision had been politically motivated as it ignored the projected statistics that showed UCI would not be able to accommodate the tertiary educational demands in the region in the next few years. Furthermore, UCI, founded by the colonial Government in 1948 was too elitist and not grounded in the people's culture. See A. I. Asiwaju, Ashby Revisited: A Review of Nigeria's Educational Growth, 1961–1971 *African Studies Review*, Vol. 15, No. 1 (Apr., 1972), pp. 1–16.

6  My stint as Secretary ASUU, Unife Branch, (1985–86, with G. G. Darah as President) was one of the more volatile periods of ASUU in the 1980s. Along with ASUU national, we were in constant running battle with the Babangida regime over the dwindling resources to and quality of university education, loss of university autonomy and salary remuneration. Often beholden to the Federal government, and not only financially, many university administrative officials cast vocal ASUU members as the enemy and actively collaborated with the Secret Service to haul us into detention.

7  *Festival of Renewal* premiered at the University of Kansas in 1992.

8  For further discussions on the Ife / Modakeke crisis see:
Akinjogbin, I. A. 1992. "Ife: The years of Travail 1793–1893" in I. A. Akinjogbin (ed.) *TheCcradle of Race: Ife from Beginning to 1980*. Port Harcourt: Sunray Publications. Oladoyin Anthony Mayowa 2001. "State and Ethno-Communal Violence in Nigeria: The case of Ife-Modakeke." *Africa Development*, Vol. XXVI, Nos. 1 & 2 pp. 195–223. Toriola Olu Joseph 2001. The Ife – Modakeke crisis: An insider view. *Ife Psychologia* 9 (3), pp. 21–29.

9  See my "Women in Transition: Zulu Sofola's Plays." *Nigerian Theatre Journal*, 1, 1, 1983.

10  Ama Ata Aidoo. *Anowa* in *Contemporary African Plays*. Editors Martin Banham and Jane Plastow. London: Methuen, 1999. Subsequent quotations from the play shall be from this edition.

11  See Sembene Ousmane. *Voltaïque*, (Paris: Présence Africaine, 1962) / *Tribal Scars and Other Stories* trans. by Len Ortzen, (London: Heinemann, 1974)

12  I have drawn from the Nigerian Yoruba version of the tale here.

13  The Fanti, and other matrilineal cultures trace descent through the female line, but power and authority reside in the males. That is why Anowa is the responsibility of her mother's brothers, but not her father.

14  Ama Ata Aidoo, "Unwelcome Pals and Decorative Slaves," in A.U. Azodo and G. Wilentz, eds., *Emerging Perspectives on Ama Ata Aidoo* (Trenton: Africa World Press, 1999) p. 19.

15  President Babangida.

16  Efua Sutherland's *Foriwa* (1961) is also based on the same tale of the disobedient daughter, but with the progressive idea of ethnic tolerance and embracing difference.

17  see Jeyifo. *The Truthful Lie*. London: New beacon Books, 1985, & Soyinka, W. in *Art, Dialogue and Outrage* "Who's Afraid of Elesin Oba?" 110–131. Ibadan: New Horn Press Limited, 1988.

### Ajayi-Soyinka: Works Cited

Aidoo, Ama Ata. Anowa in *Contemporary African Plays*. Editors Martin Banham and Jane Plastow. London: Methuen, 1999.

_____. "Unwelcome Pals and Decorative Slaves." (1981) Reprinted in Emerging Perspectives on Ama Ata Aidoo. Editors Azodo, Ada and Gay Wilentz. Eritrea: Africa World Press, 1999. 11–24.

Akinjogbin, I. A., ed. *The Cradle of Race: Ife from Beginning to 1980*. Port Harcourt: Sunray Publications. 1992.

Ashby, Eric. *Investment in Education: The Report of the Commission on Post-School Certificate and Higher Education in Nigeria*. London: St. Clement Press, 1960.

Asiwaju, A. I. 'Ashby Revisited: A Review of Nigeria's Educational Growth, 1961–1971.' PDF – African Studies Review Vol. 15, No. 1 (Apr., 1972), pp. 1–16.

Azodo, Ada and Gay Wilentz, eds. *Emerging Perspectives on Ama Ata Aidoo*. Eriteria: Africa World Press, 1999.

Fafunwa, A.B. *A History of Higher Education in Nigeria Lagos*: Macmillan & Co. (Nig.) Ltd. 1971.

Jeyifo, Biodun. *The Truthful Lie*. London: New Beacon Books, 1985.

Ogunleye, Foluke. "Ife Convocation plays as Politics: An Examination of Some Past Productions." 18–25. In *African Theatre Playwrights & Politics*. Eds. Martin Banham, James Gibbs and Femi Osofisan. Oxford: James Curry, 2001.

Ojo-Ade, Femi. "Female Writers, Male Critics: Criticism, Chauvinism, Cynicism and Commitment." Unpublished paper quoted in Aidoo (1999).

Oladoyin Anthony Mayowa. "State and Ethno-Communal Violence in Nigeria: The Case of Ife-Modakeke" Africa Development, Vol. XXVI, Nos. 1 & 2 (2001) 195–223.

Soyinka, W. *Art, Dialogue and Outrage*. Ibadan: New Horn Press Limited, 1988.

Toriola Olu Joseph "The Ife – Modakeke Crisis: An Insider View." Ife Psychologia 9, 3, (2001) 21–29.

### Osofisan: Note to "African Theatre and the Menace of Transition"

1  This paper was first presented, in a slightly different form, at the York University, Toronto, Canada during my visit to the African Theatre Ensemble, led by Prof Modupe Olaogun, for the production of my play, *Esu and the Vagabond Minstrels* in the autumn of 2006.

### Prah: Notes to "Emerging Issues from Big Brother Africa 5: Reflections on Reality TV, the Celebrity Status, and Gender"

1  I am completely indebted to my research assistant, Ms. Gladys Nketiah, who tirelessly supported me in the collection of data for this study. I am also grateful to all

those who willingly responded to the questionnaires.

2   MNet is a television channel which is part of the South African digital satellite.

3   http://www.telegraph.co.uk/news/worldnews/africaandindianocean/zimbabwe/8073804/Outrage-in-Zimbabwe-after-contestant-loses-African-Big-Brother-final.html, accessed October 20, 2010.

4   http://zeleza.com/blogging/african-affairs/sepcial-report-big-brother-africa-conti-nental-voyeurism-and-conversation, accessed August 16, 2010.

5   I watched the show from the beginning to the end and noted down viewers' comments on the television, as well as the *BBA All Stars* web site created by DSTV. I also observed tweets and other social networking communication of the contestants.

6   I found it useful to follow participants from other *BBA* seasons, because some of them are friends and communicate with each other on Twitter.

7   www.tv3.comgh/aboutus.asp

8   (http://www.tvafricaonline.com/AboutTVAfrica.aspx?ID=9ac4dc02-98b4-4878-8872-29541c39aabc) accessed 9/5/2011

9   http://www.audiencescapes.org/country-profiles-ghana-media-communication-overview-television-radio-internet-mobile%20phones-newspapers-word-of-mouth-opinion accessed 30th March 2011

10  I am here more interested in presenting her characterisation of the *Big Brother* show than in her arguments on the show and the process of acculturation.

11  Although BB originated from a Dutch company, Endemol, owned by John de Mol, Frau-Meigs (2006) argues that it was inspired by the tradition of American game shows.

12  Actually the *BBA* houses are quite well furnished and cannot fully be designated as 'Spartan;' however aspects of life on the show, such as sleeping in a dormitory, sharing bathroom facilities, occasional rationing of food and alcohol, being subjected to regular early morning exercise could justify that description. In *BBA5*, competitors who were voted out were sent to a 'barn' which could be described as 'Spartan' generally and in comparison with the main *BBA* house.

13  http://www.zeleza.com/blogging/african-affairs/sepcial-report-big-brother-africa-continental-voyeurism-and-conversation

14  See, for example, www.bigbrotherafrica.dstv.com which is linked to *Facebook*, *Twitter* and to RSS feeds; www.bigbrotherafrica.com; outside Africa – www.channel4.com/bigbrother/; bigbrothernetwork.com; bigbrotheronline.co.uk.

15  By "viewer" or "audience" I am referring to those who actually viewed the show. Ernest Mathijs and Wouter Hessels have (2004) argued that there are different notions of the audience, depending on the perspective taken towards the viewer. Audiences are not unchanging, but shifting, and rather fluid groupings. The media, the producers, public opinion, within the context of particular *BB* seasons are all audiences.

16  Depending on the number of channels or "bouquets" (packages) available, DSTV subscriptions in Ghana currently in 2011, range from about $19 to US$50 per month, which is quite high for most salaried workers. The current minimum wage is Ghana Cedis 3.73 or about $2.45 daily.

17  http://www.facebook.com/group.php?gid=141615172543414&v=wall  accessed 9.5.2011

18  We might not be weakened, but perhaps we live by performance of roles drawn from a mosaic of cultural scripts and roles underpinned by several different ideolo-

gies and philosophies which we take up and perform according to what we do. There appear to be a variety of differentiated and nuanced 'cultural scripts' that colour the lives of people in Ghana and several African countries and come into play in different contexts in the various roles people encumber and perform in everyday life. For example, a university professor of science may have been a highly trained scientist but could at the same time be strongly influenced in his or her personal life by a belief in magic. My colleague Professor Nancy Lundgren has described this as a co-existence of pre-modern, modern and post-modern frames of thought. We have not fully studied this phenomenon. Globalisation may have made the process of living out our everyday lives even more complicated.

19   http://www.southerntimesafrica.com/article.php?title=Big%20Brother%20Africa %20All%20Stars...%20A%20continent%20caught%20between%20past%20and %20future%C2%A0&id=4946

20   What is the difference between stars and celebrities? This is a question that has baffled me for a while, since both concepts are very close. And yet, it appears that in the popular imagination, stars are those who have earned their fame through talent and their accomplishments while celebrities are simply famous people. In this paper I refer to celebrities.

21   Performed on 10.5.2011

22   "Moz" means Mozambican

23   See Aleks Krotoski, What effect has the internet had on celebrity? In "Untangling the Web." UK Observer, 23 January 2011. http://www.guardian.co.uk/technology/2011/jan/23/effect-of-internet-on-celebrity/print. Accessed 23.1.2011

## Prah: Works Cited

Andrejevich, Mark. . "The Kinder, Gentler Gaze of *Big Brother*: Reality TV in the Era of Digital Capitalism." New Media and Society. 2002 Vol. 4(2) 251–270.

Biressi, Anita and Heather Nunn. *Reality TV: Realism and Revelation*. London and New York: Wallflower Press. 2005.

Cardo, Valentina. "Towards a New Citizenship? The Politics of Reality TV." *University of East Anglia Papers on European and International Studies*. 2006. Working Paper 1.

Cashmore, Ernest. *Celebrity/Culture*. London: Routledge. 2006.

Castro, Cosette. "The *Big Brother* Phenomenon in the Multicultural Societies and the Intercultural Question". IAMCR/AIECS/AIERI Barcelona, 21–26 of July 2002. http://www.portalcomunicacion.com/bcn2002/n_eng/program/prog_ind/papers/c/pdf/c005_castr.pdf accessed 18.10.2010.

Dolby, Nadine. "Popular Culture and Public Space in Africa: The Possibilities of Cultural Citezenship." *African Studies Review*, 2006. Vol. 49. No. 3:31–47.

Dyer, Richard. *Stars*. London: British Film Institute. 1998.

Gadzekpo, Audrey. *The Chief is Dead: Long Live the BBC: Globalisation, Culture and Democratisation in Ghana*. 2005. http://www.ghanacommunity.com/forums/index.php?showtopic=3597 accessed 28.10.2010.

Geraghty, Christine. "Re-examining Stardom: Questions of Texts, Bodies and Performance." Redmond, Sean and Su Holmes. *Stardom and Celebrity. A Reader*. London: Sage. 2007.

Hill, Annette. *Reality TV. Audiences and Popular Factual Television*. Abingdon/New York: Routledge. 2005.

Jacobs, Sean. "*Big Brother*, Africa is Watching." *Media, Culture and Society*. 2007 Vol. 29 (6) 851–868.

Johnson-Woods, Toni. *Big Bother: Why Did That Reality Show Become Such a Phenomenon?* Brisbane: University of Queensland Press. 2002.

Kurzman, Charles, Chelsie Anderson, Clinton Key, Youn Ok Lee, Mairead Moloney, Alexis Silver, and Maria W. Van Ryn. "Celebrity Status." *Sociological Theory* 25: 4. 347–367. 2007.

Marshall, David. *Celebrity and Power: Fame and Contemporary Culture*. Minneapolis: University of Minnesota Press. 1997.

Mathijs, Ernest and Wouter Hessels. "What Viewer? Notions of "the Audience" in the Perception of *Big Brother* Belgium." Mathijs, Ernest and Janet Jones. Eds. *Big Brother International: Format, Critics and Publics*. London and New York: Wallflower Press. 2004.

Mathijs, Ernest and Janet Jones. Eds. *Big Brother International: Format, Critics and Publics*. London and New York: Wallflower Press. 2004.

Redmond, Sean and Su Holmes. *Framing Celebrity: New Directions in Celebrity Culture*. London: Routledge. 2006.

Redmond, Sean and Su Holmes. *Stardom and Celebrity. A Reader*. London: Sage. 2007.

Sey, Araba. "Mobile Communication and Development: A Study of Mobile Phone Appropriation in Ghana." Unpublished PhD thesis in Communication, presented to the Graduate School of the University of Southern California. 2008. http://digital-library.usc.edu/assetserver/controller/item/usctheses-m1318/etd-Sey-20080707.pdf accessed 28.10.2010.

Sparks, Colin. 2007. "Reality TV: The *Big Brother* Phenomenon." *International Socialism, a Quarterly Journal of Socialist Thought*. Issue 2007:114. http://www.isj.org.uk/index.php4?id=314&issue=114 accessed 20.10.2010.

Turner, Graeme. "Cultural Identity, Soap Narrative and Reality TV." *Television and New Media* 2005. 6:415. http://tvn.sagepub.com/content/6/4/415.refs.html accessed 9.12.2010.

Van Zoonen, Liesbet and Minna Aslama. "Understanding *Big Brother*: An Analysis of Current Research." *Javnost-The Public. Journal of the European Institute for Communication and Culture*. 2006. Vol.13, No.2: 85–96.

**Yankah: Note to "Mac Tontoh: The Saga of a Broken Trumpet"**
1    Eulogy delivered August, 2010

**Note to Section V Introduction**
1    Ama Ata Aidoo, "She-Who-Would-Be-King." *The Girl Who Can and Other Stories.* (Oxford: Heinemann 2007) 62.

**Agyemang-Duah: Notes to "Ama Ata Aidoo: Whose Dilemma Could It Be?"**
1    The industrial town built in the period following Independence as the country opted for industrialisation under Kwame Nkrumah.
2    Established in 1961 by The Writers Workshop under the inspiration of Kwame Nkrumah with Kofi Awoonor as founding editor, *Okyeame* was to give a "new African Identity" even if to some critics it lost its literary neutrality by so doing and stood accused of being "Nkrumah's foot-soldiers in the cultural field."

3    Publisher's description on back cover.

### Dako: Notes to "Reminiscences from Exile"
1    Editor's note: The poem was later published in Aidoo's collection *An Angry Letter in January*.
2    Editor's note: The late Mrs. Sally Mugabe was a Ghanaian.

### Ogunyemi: Note to "The Mind Reader and the Reading Mind"
1    National Endowment for the Humanities

# Index